Communications
in Computer and Information Science   2141

Rationale

The CCIS series is devoted to the publication of proceedings of computer science conferences. Its aim is to efficiently disseminate original research results in informatics in printed and electronic form. While the focus is on publication of peer-reviewed full papers presenting mature work, inclusion of reviewed short papers reporting on work in progress is welcome, too. Besides globally relevant meetings with internationally representative program committees guaranteeing a strict peer-reviewing and paper selection process, conferences run by societies or of high regional or national relevance are also considered for publication.

Topics

The topical scope of CCIS spans the entire spectrum of informatics ranging from foundational topics in the theory of computing to information and communications science and technology and a broad variety of interdisciplinary application fields.

Information for Volume Editors and Authors

Publication in CCIS is free of charge. No royalties are paid, however, we offer registered conference participants temporary free access to the online version of the conference proceedings on SpringerLink (http://link.springer.com) by means of an http referrer from the conference website and/or a number of complimentary printed copies, as specified in the official acceptance email of the event.

CCIS proceedings can be published in time for distribution at conferences or as postproceedings, and delivered in the form of printed books and/or electronically as USBs and/or e-content licenses for accessing proceedings at SpringerLink. Furthermore, CCIS proceedings are included in the CCIS electronic book series hosted in the SpringerLink digital library at http://link.springer.com/bookseries/7899. Conferences publishing in CCIS are allowed to use Online Conference Service (OCS) for managing the whole proceedings lifecycle (from submission and reviewing to preparing for publication) free of charge.

Publication process

The language of publication is exclusively English. Authors publishing in CCIS have to sign the Springer CCIS copyright transfer form, however, they are free to use their material published in CCIS for substantially changed, more elaborate subsequent publications elsewhere. For the preparation of the camera-ready papers/files, authors have to strictly adhere to the Springer CCIS Authors' Instructions and are strongly encouraged to use the CCIS LaTeX style files or templates.

Abstracting/Indexing

CCIS is abstracted/indexed in DBLP, Google Scholar, EI-Compendex, Mathematical Reviews, SCImago, Scopus. CCIS volumes are also submitted for the inclusion in ISI Proceedings.

How to start

To start the evaluation of your proposal for inclusion in the CCIS series, please send an e-mail to ccis@springer.com.

Lazaros Iliadis · Ilias Maglogiannis ·
Antonios Papaleonidas · Elias Pimenidis ·
Chrisina Jayne
Editors

Engineering Applications of Neural Networks

25th International Conference, EANN 2024
Corfu, Greece, June 27–30, 2024
Proceedings

 Springer

Editors
Lazaros Iliadis ⓘ
Democritus University of Thrace
Xanthi, Greece

Ilias Maglogiannis ⓘ
University of Piraeus
Piraeus, Greece

Antonios Papaleonidas ⓘ
Democritus University of Thrace
Xanthi, Greece

Elias Pimenidis ⓘ
University of the West of England
Bristol, UK

Chrisina Jayne ⓘ
Teesside University
Middlesbrough, UK

ISSN 1865-0929 ISSN 1865-0937 (electronic)
Communications in Computer and Information Science
ISBN 978-3-031-62494-0 ISBN 978-3-031-62495-7 (eBook)
https://doi.org/10.1007/978-3-031-62495-7

EANN 2024 Preface

The Engineering Applications of Neural Networks conference is 29 years old. It has been alive and continuously present in the literature for a *quarter of a century*. Artificial Intelligence, Machine Learning, Deep Learning and Neural Networks are like Russian Dolls, each one contained within the former, having a superset-subset relationship. In the early twenty-first century, Artificial Neural Network (NN) algorithms constitute the real core of Deep Learning, and they are still considered as robust real-world modeling approaches employed in various domains (e.g., Image and Speech Recognition, Natural Language Processing and many more). ChatGPT stands as an exciting advancement of Deep Learning Generative AI. Recent advances such as Generative Adversarial Neural Networks try to fuse "imagination" to Artificial Intelligence (AI), and Convolutional Neural Networks significantly contribute to the enhancement of pattern recognition, machine translation, anomaly detection and machine vision. Generative AI is capable of generating videos, image datasets, realistic photographs of human faces, cartoon characters, Image to Image Translation, Face Aging, Photos to Emojis, Photo Blending and Super Resolution.

EANN is gradually changing its name to EAAAI (Engineering Applications and Advances in Artificial Intelligence/ex-EANN). It is a historical, robust and well-established conference, having a life of more than 2 decades in the literature. Following the cataclysmic technological revolution, it is gradually evolving and becoming broader, in order to embrace all AI aspects and achievements. This transition aims to bring together scientists from all AI domains and to give them the chance to exchange ideas and to announce their achievements.

Since the first conference in 1995, EANN (now EAAAI) has provided a great discussion forum on engineering applications of all Artificial Intelligence technologies, focusing on Artificial Neural Networks. More specifically, it promotes the use of modeling techniques from all subdomains of AI in diverse application areas where significant benefits can be derived. The conference also reports advances in theoretical AI aspects. Thus, both innovative applications and methods are particularly appreciated. EAAAI/EANN is a mature and well-established international scientific conference held in Europe. Its history is long and very successful, following and spreading the evolution of Intelligent Systems. The first EANN event was organized in Otaniemi, Finland, in 1995. Since then, it has had a continuous and dynamic presence as a major global, but mainly European, scientific event. More specifically, it has been organized in Finland, the UK, Sweden, Gibraltar, Poland, Italy, Spain, France, Bulgaria, Greece and Spain. It has been technically supported by the International Neural Networks Society (INNS) and more specifically by the EANN/EAAAI Special Interest Group.

This is the Proceedings volume, and it belongs to Springer's CCIS (*Communications in Computer and Information Science*) Series. It contains the papers that were accepted to be presented orally at the 25th EANN conference in Corfu, Greece under the auspices of the Ionian University, Department of Informatics.

The diverse nature of the papers presented demonstrates the vitality of Artificial Intelligence algorithms and approaches. The conference is not limited only to Neural Networks, but it certainly provides a very wide forum for AI applications as well. The event was held in a hybrid mode (both physically and remotely attended via Webex) from the 27th to the 30th of June 2024. In total, 85 papers were initially submitted. All papers were peer reviewed by at least two independent academic referees in a single-blind process. Where needed, a third referee was consulted to resolve any potential conflicts. A total of 47% of the submitted manuscripts (41 papers) were accepted to be published in the Springer proceedings as full papers while at the same time 2 short papers were accepted due to their significant academic strength.

The 4th Workshop on AI and Ethics (AIETH 2024) was organized and coordinated by Professor John Macintyre under the auspices of EANN 2024. It included short presentations from the panel members and an open Q&A session where the audience members were able to ask, and answer, important questions about the current and future development of Generative AI models. It aimed to emphasize the need for responsible global AI. The respective scientific community must be preparing to act preemptively and ensure that our societies will avoid negative effects of AI and of the 4th Industrial Revolution in general.

The authors of submitted papers came from 20 different countries from all over the globe (from 4 continents: Europe, Asia and both Americas) namely: Bangladesh, Brazil, Canada, China, Germany, Greece, Denmark, Hungary, India, Italy, Japan, Kuwait, Lebanon, Morocco, Tunisia, Norway, Poland, Spain, the UK and the USA.

June 2024

Lazaros Iliadis
Ilias Maglogiannis
Antonios Papaleonidas
Elias Pimenidis
Chrisina Jayne

Organization

General Co-chairs

John Macintyre   DUTh, Greece and University of Dundee, UK
Lazaros Iliadis   Democritus University of Thrace, Greece
Chrisina Jayne   Teesside University, UK
Ilias Maglogiannis   University of Piraeus, Greece

Program Co-chairs

Elias Pimenidis   University of the West of England, UK
Antonios Papaleonidas   Democritus University of Thrace, Greece
Ioannis Karydis   Ionian University, Greece
Serafin Alonso   Universidad de León, Spain

Steering Committee

Lazaros Iliadis   Democritus University of Thrace, Greece
Elias Pimenidis   University of the West of England, UK
Chrisina Jayne   Teesside University, UK

Honorary Chairs

Plamen Angelov   Lancaster University, UK
Vera Kurkova   Czech Academy of Sciences, Czech Republic

Organizing Co-chairs

Markos Avlonitis   Ionian University, Greece
Antonios Papaleonidas   Democritus University of Thrace, Greece
Anastasios Panagiotis Psathas   Democritus University of Thrace, Greece
Manuel Domínguez   Universidad de León, Spain

Advisory Co-chairs

Barbara Hammer   Bielefeld University, Germany
George Magoulas   Birkbeck, University of London, UK
Anastasios Tefas   Aristotle University of Thessaloniki, Greece

Doctoral Consortium Chair

Antonio Morán   University of León, Spain

Publication and Publicity Co-chairs

Ioannis Karydis   Ionian University, Greece
Antonios Papaleonidas   Democritus University of Thrace, Greece
Anastasios Panagiotis Psathas   Democritus University of Thrace, Greece
Athanasios Kallipolitis   Hellenic Air Force/University of Piraeus, Greece

Workshops Co-chairs

Katia Linda Kermanidis   Ionian University, Greece
Spyros Sioutas   University of Patras, Greece
Peter Hajek   University of Pardubice, Czech Republic
Christos Makris   University of Patras, Greece

Special Sessions and Tutorials Co-chairs

Andreas S. Andreou   Cyprus University of Technology, Cyprus
Harris Papadopoulos   Frederick University, Cyprus

Program Committee

Achilleas Andronikos   Centre for Research and Technology Hellas,
                              Greece
Adrien Durand-Petiteville   Federal University of Pernambuco, Brazil
Alaa Mohasseb   University of Portsmouth, UK
Alexander Ryjov   Lomonosov Moscow State University, Russia

Alexios Papaioannou	Centre for Research and Technology Hellas, Greece
Aliki Stefanopoulou	Centre for Research and Technology Hellas, Greece
Anastasios Panagiotis Psathas	Democritus University of Thrace, Greece
Andreas Kanavos	Ionian University, Greece
Antonio Morán	University of León, Spain
Antonios Kalampakas	AUM, Kuwait
Antonios Papaleonidas	Democritus University of Thrace, Greece
Aristidis Likas	University of Ioannina, Greece
Asimina Dimara	Centre for Research and Technology Hellas, Greece
Athanasios Kallipolitis	University of Piraeus, Greece
Athanasios Koutras	University of the Peloponnese, Greece
Athanasios Tsadiras	Aristotle University of Thessaloniki, Greece
Banafsheh Rekabdar	Portland State University, USA
Binyu Zhao	Harbin Institute of Technology, China
Bo Mei	Texas Christian University, USA
Boudjelal Meftah	University Mustapha Stambouli of Mascara, Algeria
Cen Wan	Birkbeck, University of London, UK
Charalampos Lazaridis	Centre for Research and Technology Hellas, Greece
Chengqiang Huang	Huawei Technologies Co. Ltd., China
Christos Diou	Harokopio University of Athens, Greece
Christos Makris	University of Patras, Greece
Claudio Giorgio Giancaterino	Intesa Sanpaolo Vita, Italy
Cunjian Chen	Monash University, Australia
Cyril de Bodt	UCLouvain, Belgium
Daniel Pérez	University of León, Spain
Daniel Stamate	Goldsmiths, University of London, UK
Daniel Vašata	Czech Technical University in Prague, Czech Republic
David Dembinsky	German Research Center for Artificial Intelligence, Germany
Davide Zambrano	CWI, Netherlands
Dehao Yuan	University of Maryland, USA
Denise Gorse	University College London, UK
Diana Laura Borza	Babeş-Bolyai University, Romania
Diego García	University of Oviedo, Spain
Dimitrios Michail	Harokopio University of Athens, Greece
Doina Logofatu	Frankfurt University of Applied Sciences, Germany

Douglas McLelland	BrainChip, France
Douglas Nyabuga	Mount Kenya University, Rwanda
Dulani Meedeniya	University of Moratuwa, Sri Lanka
Eleni Vlachou	Ionian University, Greece
Elias Dritsas	University of Patras, Greece
Elias Pimenidis	University of the West of England, UK
Evangelos Alvanitopoulos	Ionian University, Greece
Federico Corradi	Eindhoven University of Technology, Netherlands
Federico Vozzi	CNR, Italy
Flora Ferreira	University of Minho, Portugal
Florin Leon	Technical University of Iasi, Romania
Fotios Kounelis	Imperial College London, UK
Gaetano Di Caterina	University of Strathclyde, UK
George Magoulas	Birkbeck, University of London, UK
Georgios Alexandridis	University of the Aegean, Greece
Georgios Drakopoulos	Ionian University, Greece
Georgios Karatzinis	Centre for Research and Technology Hellas, Greece
Gerasimos Vonitsanos	Hellenic Open University, Greece
Gregory Gasteratos	Ionian university, Greece
Habib Khan	Sejong University, South Korea
Haopeng Chen	Shanghai Jiao Tong University, China
Hina Afridi	NTNU, Norway
Hiroyasu Ando	Tohoku University, Japan
Honggang Zhang	University of Massachusetts Boston, USA
Hongye Cao	Northwestern Polytechnical University, China
Hugo Carneiro	University of Hamburg, Germany
Iakovos Michailidis	Centre for Research and Technology Hellas, Greece
Ignacio Díaz-Blanco	University of Oviedo, Spain
Ilias Maglogiannis	University of Piraeus, Greece
Ioannis Hatzilygeroudis	University of Patras, Greece
Ioannis Karamitsos	RIT, United Arab Emirates
Ioannis Livieris	University of Pireaus, Greece
Ioannis Papaioannou	Centre for Research and Technology Hellas, Greece
Ioannis Pierros	Aristotle University of Thessaloniki, Greece
Ioannis Karydis	Ionian University, Greece
Iraklis Varlamis	Harokopio University of Athens, Greece
Jan-Gerrit Habekost	University of Hamburg, Germany
Jérémie Sublime	ISEP, France
Jianhua Xu	Nanjing Normal University, China

Joost Vennekens	KU Leuven, Belgium
Juan J. Fuertes	University of León, Spain
Kamil Dedecius	Czech Academy of Sciences, Czech Republic
Katia Lida Kermanidis	Ionian University, Greece
Khoa Phung	University of the West of England, UK
Kohulan Rajan	Friedrich Schiller University, Germany
Konstantinos Moutselos	University of Piraeus, Greece
Kostadin Cvejoski	Fraunhofer IAIS, Germany
Kun Zhang	Inria and École Polytechnique, France
Kyriakoula Fanaridou	Centre for Research and Technology Hellas, Greece
Laurent Mertens	KU Leuven, Belgium
Laurent Perrinet	AMU CNRS, France
Lazaros Iliadis	Democritus University of Thrace, Greece
Leon Bobrowski	Bialystok University of Technology, Poland
Lia Morra	Politecnico di Torino, Italy
Ling Guo	Northwest University, China
Madalina Erascu	West University of Timisoara, Romania
Magda Friedjungová	Czech Technical University in Prague, Czech Republic
Marcello Trovati	Edge Hill University, UK
Matthew Evanusa	University of Maryland, USA
Matthias Möller	Örebro University, Sweden
Matus Tomko	Comenius University in Bratislava, Slovakia
Md Delwar Hossain	Nara Institute of Science and Technology, Japan
Michail-Antisthenis Tsompanas	University of the West of England, UK
Michel Salomon	Université de Franche-Comté, France
Miguel Ángel Prada	Universidad de León, Spain
Minal Suresh Patil	Umeå Universitet, Sweden
Mirjana Ivanovic	University of Novi Sad, Serbia
Mohamed Elleuch	ENSI, Tunisia
Narendhar Gugulothu	TCS Research, India
Nathan Duran	University of the West of England, UK
Nikolaos Avgoustis	Ionian University, Greece
Nikolaos Marios Polymenakos	Ionian University, Greece
Nikolaos Passalis	Aristotle University of Thessaloniki, Greece
Nikolaos Polatidis	University of Brighton, UK
Nikos Kanakaris	University of Patras, Greece
Nikos Karacapilidis	University of Patras, Greece
Odysseas Bouzos	Centre for Research and Technology Hellas, Greece
Olivier Teste	Université de Toulouse, France

Oscar Fontenla-Romero	University of A Coruña, Spain
Panagiotis Pintelas	University of Patras, Greece
Panayotis Gratsanis	Ionian University, Greece
Paulo Cortez	University of Minho, Portugal
Petia Koprinkova-Hristova	Bulgarian Academy of Sciences, Bulgaria
Petr Hajek	University of Pardubice, Czech Republic
Petra Vidnerová	Czech Academy of Sciences, Czech Republic
Petros Kefalas	University of Sheffield International Faculty, Greece
Petros Tzallas	Centre for Research and Technology Hellas, Greece
Ricardo Marcacini	University of São Paulo, Brazil
Riccardo Renzulli	University of Turin, Italy
Rodrigo Clemente Thom de Souza	Federal University of Paraná, Brazil
Roman Mouček	University of West Bohemia, Czech Republic
Salvatore Aiello	Politecnico di Torino, Italy
Seiya Satoh	Tokyo Denki University, Japan
Serafin Alonso	University of León, Spain
Shu Eguchi	Aomori University, Japan
Simon Hakenes	Ruhr University Bochum, Germany
Song Guo	Xi'an University of Architecture and Technology, China
Sotiris Kotsiantis	University of Patras, Greece
Stefanos Nikiforos	Ionian University, Greece
Stylianos Papargyris	Aristotle University of Thessaloniki, Greece
Thanasis Moustakas	Centre for Research and Technology Hellas, Greece
Theodor Panagiotakopoulos	Hellenic Open University, Greece
Tiyu Fang	Shandong University, China
Tomasz Kapuscinski	Rzeszow University of Technology, Poland
Toshiharu Sugawara	Waseda University, Japan
Umer Mushtaq	Université Paris-Panthéon-Assas, France
V. Ramasubramanian	International Institute of Information Technology Bangalore, India
Vaios Papaioannou	University of Patras, Greece
Vandana Ladwani	International Institute of Information Technology Bangalore, India
Vilson Luiz Dalle Mole	UTFPR, Brazil
Xia Feng	Civil Aviation University of China, China
Xingpeng Zhang	Southwest Petroleum University, China
Xuewen Wang	China University of Geosciences, China
Yang Shao	Hitachi Ltd., Japan

Keynote Lectures

Developmental Robotics for Language Learning, Trust and Theory of Mind

Angelo Cangelosi

University of Manchester and Alan Turing Institute, UK

Abstract: Growing theoretical and experimental research on action and language processing and on number learning and gestures clearly demonstrates the role of embodiment in cognition and language processing. In psychology and neuroscience, this evidence constitutes the basis of embodied cognition, also known as grounded cognition (Pezzulo et al. 2012). In robotics and AI, these studies have important implications for the design of linguistic capabilities in cognitive agents and robots for human-robot collaboration and have led to the new interdisciplinary approach of Developmental Robotics, as part of the wider Cognitive Robotics field (Cangelosi & Schlesinger 2015; Cangelosi & Asada 2022). During the talk we will present examples of developmental robotics models and experimental results from iCub experiments on the embodiment biases in early word acquisition and grammar learning (Morse et al. 2015; Morse & Cangelosi 2017) and experiments on pointing gestures and finger counting for number learning (De La Cruz et al. 2014). We will then present a novel developmental robotics model, and experiments, on Theory of Mind and its use for autonomous trust behavior in robots (Vinanzi et al. 2019, 2021). The implications for the use of such embodied approaches for embodied cognition in AI and cognitive sciences and for robot companion applications will also be discussed.

AI and Cybersecurity: Friend or Foe?

Haris Mouratidis

University of Essex, UK

Abstract: We live in an era of unprecedented technological advancement that has an impact on every aspect of human life. Within that environment, artificial intelligence and cybersecurity are two areas where innovation and challenges intersect with profound implications. On one hand, AI, with its transformative capabilities, is revolutionising how we process information, make decisions and interact with technology, while on the other hand, cybersecurity provides essential tools to safeguard the digital infrastructures that we depend on. In this talk I will discuss the interplay between the two, exploring both the benefits of using AI for cybersecurity and cybersecurity for AI, but also the challenges that such co-existence introduces. Drawing on real-world case studies and insights, I will discuss how machine learning, threat detection and analytics can empower organisations and individuals to improve their cybersecurity but also how AI-driven tactics give rise to sophisticated cyber threats. I will then emphasize the necessity for collaborative initiatives spanning both AI and cybersecurity domains. I will stress the importance of continuous shared research and education to foster an environment where the coexistence of AI and cybersecurity not only enhances our digital landscape but also minimizes associated risks.

An Evolutionary Approach to the Autonomous Design and Fabrication of Robots for Operation in Unknown Environments

Emma Hart

Edinburgh Napier University, UK

Abstract: Robot design is traditionally the domain of humans – engineers, physicists, and increasingly AI experts. However, if the robot in intended to operate in a completely unknown environment (for example clean up inside a nuclear reactor) then it is very difficult for human designers to predict what kind of robot might be required. Evolutionary computing is a well-known technology that has been applied in various aspects of robotics for many years, for example to design controllers or body-plans. When coupled with advances in materials and printing technologies that allow rapid prototyping in hardware, it offers a potential solution to the issue raised above, for example enabling colonies of robots to evolve and adapt over long periods of time while situated in the environment they have to work in. However, it also brings new challenges, from both an algorithmic and engineering perspective. The additional constraints introduced by the need for example to manufacture robots autonomously, to explore rich morphological search spaces and develop novel forms of control require some re-thinking of "standard' approaches in evolutionary computing, particularly on the interaction between evolution and individual learning. I will discuss some of these challenges and propose and showcase some methods to address them that have been developed during a recent project.

Contents

Reinforcement/Natural Language

Biomedical/Classification

Deep Learning/Convolutional

Reinforcement/Natural Language

Active Learning with Aggregated Uncertainties from Image Augmentations

Tamás Janusko[1]([⊠]), Colin Simon[1], Kevin Kirsten[1], Serhiy Bolkun[1],
Eric Weinzierl[1], Julius Gonsior[2][iD], and Maik Thiele[1][iD]

[1] Hochschule für Technik und Wirtschaft Dresden, Dresden, Germany
{tamas.janusko,colin.simon,kevin.kirsten,serhiy.bolkun,
eric.weinzierl,maik.thiele}@htw-dresden.de
[2] Technische Universität Dresden, Dresden, Germany
julius.gonsior@tu-dresden.de

Abstract. Active learning and data augmentation are both standard techniques for dealing with a lack of annotated data in the field of machine learning. While active learning aims to select the most informative data sample for annotation from a pool of unlabeled data, data augmentation enhances the data set's volume and variety, introducing modified versions of existing data. We propose a method that combines both approaches and exploits their benefits beyond mere data quantity by taking into account the relationship of original image and augmentation tuples from the perspective of the underlying machine learning model. Namely, we explore the distribution of uncertainties within these tuples and their effect on model performance. Our research shows that with equal annotation effort aggregated uncertainties across image augmentations yield improved results compared to a baseline without augmentations, however certain configurations can be detrimental for the performance of the resulting model.

Keywords: Active Learning · Machine Learning · Image
Classification · Image Augmentation

1 Introduction

Active learning (AL) has gained significant attention in machine learning (ML) as a means to overcome the limitations of traditional supervised learning, which relies heavily on large labeled data sets. The main idea behind active learning is to actively select the most informative samples from a large pool of unlabeled data for (human) annotation with the goal of training accurate models using minimal labeled data. The basis for quantifying informativeness is the models uncertainty regarding its own classification decisions.

Another standard ML technique to overcome the limited availability of a large labeled data set is data augmentation. It addresses the issue by artificially increasing the size and diversity of the data set by introducing variations in its

L. Iliadis et al. (Eds.): EANN 2024, CCIS 2141, pp. 3–16, 2024.
https://doi.org/10.1007/978-3-031-62495-7_1

characteristics. In this work we examine image data and augment its spatial characteristics, color distributions, and noise levels, thus enhancing a trained model's ability to handle diverse real-world scenarios at virtually no additional cost.

Combining AL with data augmentation presents a straightforward approach, yielding n additional labeled samples with each annotation cycle. However, our goal extends beyond merely expanding the data set size. We propose to analyze the relationship between original images and their augmentations within the context of the ML model employed in the AL framework. Our focus narrows down to assessing the mean and standard deviation of uncertainties associated with an original image and its augmentations. A high mean uncertainty indicates a robust invariance across all augmented instances, whereas a significant standard deviation points to a beneficial heterogeneity among samples, potentially enhancing the model's generalization capabilities. This analysis aims to elucidate the balance between exploration (seeking new information) and exploitation (leveraging existing knowledge), a well-documented conundrum in the field of AL [2,18].

Contributions. We present a method to combine two proven ML techniques to address two crucial weaknesses of AL, that of sparse data and the balancing of the exploitation/exploration dilemma. To this end we examine the effect of image augmentations in the context of active learning and strategies to incorporate augmentations into the sampling process. Our findings contribute to a deeper understanding of how active learning and data augmentation can be integrated more effectively, presenting a novel perspective on optimizing model training processes.

Outline. Section 2 introduces the main concepts and techniques relevant for this paper, namely active learning and augmentations. The details on combining both approaches are given in Sect. 3. In Sect. 4 resources and implementation details are laid out as well as the overall experimental architecture. The results are presented in Sect. 5, followed by the discussion of our findings in Sect. 6 and a presentation of related work and concluding words in Sect. 7 and Sect. 8.

2   Foundations

2.1   Active Learning 101

AL Cycle. AL implies the existence of some notion of good or bad candidate samples that yield a better performing model compared to randomly labelling the same amount of data. The whole AL process can be visualized as a cycle (see Fig. 1, right) that identifies and utilizes suitable data points in an iterative manner. A subset of the unlabeled set of data points U is transformed into a labeled set L.

First the acquisition model is used to quantify the uncertainty of each data point in regard to the model. Using these uncertainties a query strategy now determines the m data points that will make up the query U_q. This query is directed to the oracle, which typically is a human annotator. There the query is labeled and the resulting set L_q is added to the set of all labelled samples L. On this labelled set the acquisition model is (re)trained and thus the current AL cycle iteration completed.

Entering the next iteration the updated model is used to compute uncertainties for the remaining samples in U. The AL cycle proceeds until a *stopping criterion* is met or until U is out of queries, meaning the whole data set is labelled. Stopping criteria can be performance thresholds of various metrics, such as classification accuracy, or simply the exhaustion of the labeling budget.

Query Types. Based on the data set at hand and the particular conditions of deployment, the approach to directing queries to an oracle can vary significantly. This variability encompasses techniques like stream-based selective sampling, where individual data points are evaluated in real-time; membership-query synthesis, which involves creating new, synthetic examples that resemble the original data set for evaluation; and pool-based sampling, a method that selects multiple samples from a pre-existing pool based on specific criteria [15]. In this paper, we utilize pool-based sampling which is advantageous when multiple samples need to be queried simultaneously based on a specific query strategy.

Query Strategies. The selection of annotation candidates can be categorized into three strategies: heterogeneity-based, performance-based and representativeness-based. Though performance-based strategies, which consider the model's predictive performance, and representativeness-based strategies, which aim for a balanced representation of the data distribution, are also noteworthy, the heterogeneity-based approach is most commonly emphasized in the literature for its direct impact on improving model accuracy and efficiency through strategically selecting the most uncertain data points [15].

2.2 Augmentations

Data augmentation in deep learning offers numerous benefits, including increased data set size, improved model generalization and reduced over-fitting [20,24]. However, the exact nature of "good" augmentations is not always clear. Given the computationally intensive nature of AL, it is desirable not to have to allocate too much computing power on the augmentations. Fortunately, Trivial Augment [17] promises state-of-the-art results with very little expenses.

Opposed to more complex augmentation policies such as AutoAugment [5], where the optimal combination of augmentation hyper-parameters is searched for in a vast space, Trivial Augment randomly selects one augmentation type per image and applies it with a random strength (0–30). This yields state-of-the-art results while being up to 800 times faster than methods with comparable performance, since there is no search overhead [17].

The number of augmentations is also important for the aggregation strategies, since more augmentations give more room for metrics like mean and standard deviation to unfold, even more so in regard to the random augmentation method of Trivial Augment.

3 Active Learning and Image Annotations

Our research aims to investigate the incorporation of augmented images along-side their associated uncertainties into the AL framework to enhance the selection process of the most informative queries from the AL pool. To this end each original image in U is augmented n times, and these augmented images are considered alongside the original ones in the selection process. In our methodology, when we refer to a query size of m, it denotes the selection of $\frac{m}{n+1}$ original samples, and for each original sample, n augmented versions are implicitly included in the query. This augmentation is achieved through applying diverse transformations to each original image, generating n augmented images per original. These sets of original and augmented images are treated collectively as a single unit within the selection strategy delineated in Sect. 3.1.

The AL process is iterative, with the cycle concluding once every data point in the pool has been labeled. This approach ensures that both the original and the augmented images, along with the uncertainties they encapsulate, are integral to optimizing the query selection from the AL pool, thereby enhancing the learning efficiency and model performance.

3.1 Incorporating Augmentations into Active Learning

Image augmentation gives us distinct but semantically equivalent images that are the basis for our aggregation strategies. Therefore, each data point in U is subject to augmentation, generating n augmented versions per original data point. This expanded consideration creates an augmented unlabeled set U_{aug}, where each member is a tuple consisting of an original data point and its n augmentations. Thus, the query strategy not only selects the most informative original data points but also their associated augmented versions, forming an augmented query set $U_{q,aug}$.

Within the AL cycle for each original image and its corresponding augmentations the uncertainties are computed, forming a tuple of uncertainties associated with the original image and its augmented versions.

In order to take advantage of the affiliation within tuples we revisit the notion of exploration/exploitation and devise aggregation strategies accordingly. Aggregates are defined as the mean and standard deviation of the uncertainty tuples, denoted as *mean* and *std*. This resembles a minimalist implementation of exploration/exploitation regarding data heterogeneity. High-uncertainty data benefits model fine-calibration but might not take into account all relevant areas of the feature space. Conversely, incorporating data points with lower uncertainty could

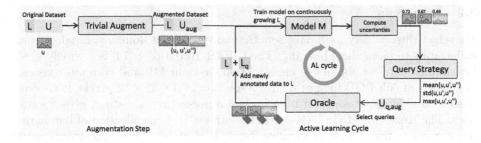

Fig. 1. The Active Learning Cycle enhanced with Augmentations

help cover more of the feature space, providing a more comprehensive under-standing and ensuring a balanced approach between exploring new, potentially informative areas and exploiting known areas for model refinement. The *mean* of uncertainties offers insight into the general informativeness of the data set, whereas the *std* reflects the diversity within the data points selected for labeling. Additionally, we devise a strategy *max* that selects for the tuples containing an image (augmented or original) with the highest uncertainty while disregarding the remaining uncertainties within the tuple. This combines a radical exploita-tion approach (maximizing uncertainty) with the benefits of "free" annotations provided through augmentation.

Using these aggregates we can select an optimal AL query to present to the oracle. Note, that original and augmented images are selected as a unit to be included into the query and no single image is ever labelled when using this mean or standard deviation strategy (except in the baseline setup with no augmentations). An overview of the process is given in Fig. 1.

4 Experimental Setup

4.1 Active Learning Loop

For the implementation of the AL loop we employ the Baal framework [1] which enables simple uncertainty estimation with the Monte Carlo Dropout method [8]. Here, the acquisition model is used to infer predictions on the unlabeled images in U with dropout-layers randomly activated. Repeating this step yields an ensem-ble of slightly altered models from whose prediction's distribution the uncertainty for each image is computed. Ensemble size is set to 15 as well as the learning epochs for the underlying acquisition models. Initial pool size and subsequent query sizes are set to 1,000. The rather large query size is chosen due to com-putational constraints. A minimum ensemble size is required to account for the stochasticity introduced by randomly activating dropout. Each of the ensem-ble members infer predictions on the whole unlabelled data set which in turn is expanded n-fold through augmentations. The loop terminates after 40 iterations.

Note, that we do not consider random annotation as a base since we focus on the impact of augmentations and possibilities of further leveraging them.

4.2 Data Sets

We select three widely used data sets that cover distinct domains, ranging from calligraphy to biomedical imaging: The CIFAR-10 data set [14] is a widely-used benchmark data set for image classification tasks in ML and computer vision. It consists of 60k RGB images with a resolution of $3 \times 32 \times 32$ pixels. It encompasses 10 different classes, with each class representing a distinct object category. The Kuzushiji MNIST (K-MNIST) data set [4] is a collection of handwritten characters from classical Japanese texts. It contains 70k grayscale images of 28×28 pixels. The Fashion-MNIST data set [22] consists of 70k grayscale images. Each image is a 28×28 pixel square, representing various types of clothing and fashion items covering 10 different classes. The PathMNIST data set [13] consists of 98k $3 \times 28 \times 28$ pixels (RGB) image patches extracted from histological images related to colorectal cancer cover nine tissue types/classes.

4.3 Neural Network Models

We apply a diverse selection of model architectures with distinctive architectural details yet representative for the field of neural networks for computer vision. Implementations from the public torchvision models package are used without pre-training[1] in order to prevent biases introduced by the pretraining data. This is apparent if one considers the everyday motives depicted in CIFAR-10 in contrast to the highly domain-specific content of PathMNIST.

VGG16. The VGG16 is a convolutional neural network (CNN) architecture in the VGG-family [21] that is characterized by its deep structure. VGG16's architecture has served as inspiration for many subsequent CNN models. We include it into our experiments as it is a proven and robust model as well as a representative of a medium sized and relatively simple CNN architecture.

DenseNet121. As the name suggests, DenseNet [11] is characterized by having connections between all layers within the network. DenseNet is inspired by ResNet [9] but as an improvement each layer is inputted with the concatenation of feature-maps from *all* proceeding layers which effectively combats the vanishing-gradient problem. For our experiments we use the DenseNet121 variant.

MobileNetV3. MobileNetV3 [10] is an improved version of the MobileNet architecture and as such aimed at running in environments with hardware constraints. The main innovations are enhanced efficiency by replacing traditional convolutional layers with depthwise-separable convolution that allow for the use of smaller filters. For our experiments we use the MobileNetV3-Small variant.

---

[1] https://pytorch.org/vision/0.17/models.html.

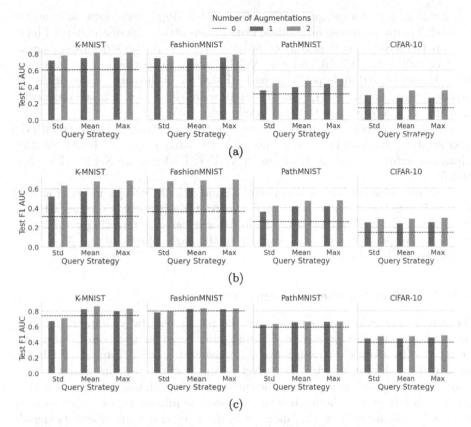

Fig. 2. AUC results of VGG16 (a), MobileNetV3-Small (b) and DenseNet121 (c) per Data Set

5 Results

This section presents the findings from our comprehensive analysis, which scrutinizes the different aggregation strategies, the influence of augmentations, data set complexities, and the performance across different CNN models. We report macro F1 test scores recorded after each AL step as well as the AUC. As a baseline we provide macro F1 test scores for AL-runs without augmentations.

5.1 Aggregation Strategies

In many cases all three strategies yield comparable results (Figs. 4(a), 4(b), 4(e), 4(f), 5(e) and 5(f)). However, mean and max-strategies appear to be closely connected and performing best in most cases with std legging behind (Figs. 3(c) to 3(e), 4(c), 4(d), 4(g), 4(h), 5(c), 5(d), 5(g) and 5(h)) but also taking the lead in certain scenarios (Figs. 3(e) and 3(f)).

Standard deviation stands out as often performing poorly, especially on the K-MNIST data set across all models, even undercutting the unaugmented baseline on DenseNet (see Figs. 5(a) to 5(d)). Furthermore the std-strategy seems to work well on CIFAR-10, and with VGG16 evens yields the best performance. With DenseNet, std underperforms on PathMNIST in the early stages of the AL process (Figs. 5(g) and 5(h)). On CIFAR-10 with MobileNet and one augmentation the *std-strategy* takes the lead briefly (Fig. 4(e)).

Our *mean-strategy* is generally the best performing strategy together with the max-strategy, succumbing to max mostly in the early stages of the AL process. Mean outperforms all other strategies on K-MNIST with DenseNet (see Figs. 5(c) and 5(d)).

The *max-strategy* yields consistently good results except in see Fig. 3(h) where we observe irregular drops in F1 score. Otherwise it is on par with the other strategies and outperforms them in some cases. Interestingly this strategy seems to provide a slight advantage in the early phases of the AL-process (Figs. 4(c), 4(d), 5(f) and 5(g)).

5.2   Impact of Number of Augmentations

As intended, augmentations jump-start the AL process by yielding n-fold data set sizes and we observe steeper learning curves across the board, most pronounced with MobileNet taking the unaugmented baseline around 15 labeling steps to take off (Fig. 4) while DenseNet performs above random from the start (Fig. 5). Correspondingly, performance milestones and plateaus are reached more quickly and differences between strategies become miniscule. Nevertheless some models benefit more from this increase in data set size than others. Generally augmentations benefit the AL process but to a varying degree. While two augmentations roughly double the F1-AUC (Fig. 2(b)), the benefits of augmentations on DenseNet are much smaller and even erased when using std-strategy on the K-MNIST (Fig. 2(c)).

5.3   Impact of Data Sets

Since data sets differ in complexity of the classification problem and objects as well as class imbalances among others, it is necessary to compare results across data sets. For K-MNIST we observe the clearest distinctions between strategy performances (Figs. 4(c), 4(d), 5(c) and 5(d)) and a consistent underperformance of std (Figs. 3(c), 3(d), 4(c), 4(d), 5(c) and 5(d)), even undercutting the baseline by a large margin with DenseNet (Figs. 5(c) and 5(d)). The std-strategy is detrimental for AL on K-MNIST data with all considered models. Further, training on CIFAR-10 stands to gain most from the std-strategy. Interestingly, MobileNet trained on FashionMNIST shows similar results for all strategies.

5.4 Impact of Underlying Models

Although all the models considered belong to the class of CNNs, there are significant differences between them. The formation of the decision boundary by which we determine the uncertainties can differ, which makes a comparative analysis of the model results necessary. The most apparent observation is that models require different amounts of training data to outperform random guessing. MobileNet needs a few AL-steps/few thousand data samples (Fig. 4) whereas DenseNet surpasses that threshold from the first AL-step (Fig. 5). It appears that VGG16 is, in our setting, the most capable model in terms of overall performance. It is also the model where the standard deviation strategy works best, first in absolute terms on CIFAR-10 (Figs. 3(e) and 3(f)), and second by having comparable performance on PathMNIST (Figs. 3(g) and 3(h)) as well as showing a much smaller performance gap on K-MNIST than other models (Figs. 3(c) and 3(d)).

6 Discussion

Our results are encouraging, highlighting that image augmentation distinctly boosts the AL process. By leveraging both mean and max aggregation methods, we can harness these advantages efficiently, without the need for extra annotation efforts. When comparing aggregation strategies we find that selecting for standard deviation generally results in poorer performance. One explanation for this is that the model fails to learn proper generalizations when exposed to overly diverse data sets. Or taking a more data-centric position, selecting for diversity favors outliers which confuse the models. VGG16 and MobileNet yield contradicting results regarding their CIFAR-10 performance when using the std-strategy compared to the others. Thus one explanation might be, that models with a certain minimum capability are needed to take advantage of the introduced variability.

In any case the sometimes negative results of the std-strategy uncover a critical weakness: it overlooks the real uncertainties present within the image tuples. A solution would be to introduce an upper limit for uncertainties of candidate samples or combine them with the mean-strategy. One could argue that this is the opposite of the max-strategy where in a selected tuple one item was maximally uncertain yet there was no constraint on the remaining images. Thus ensuring model fine-calibration and simultaneously permitting diversity.

We also find that in certain stages of the AL process one strategy yields superior results but is overtaken by another. This observation lends the idea to identify these events in the AL process and dynamically shift to a more promising strategy.

While the trends in the resulting F1-scores are evident, they exhibit volatility, particularly with PathMNIST. This is due to the fact that the query size of $1,000$ is rather large for this setup to mitigate the resource consumption of our AL experiments, requiring to iteratively train CNN models of nontrivial size.

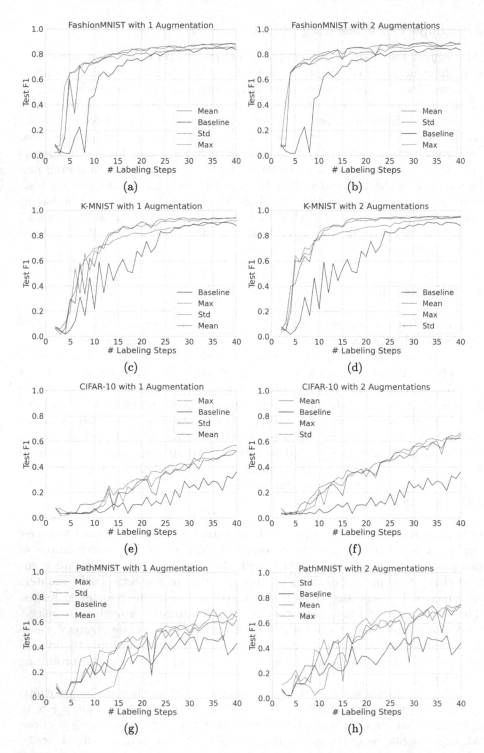

Fig. 3. Test F1 Scores for VGG16 using Std, Mean and Max Query Strategies on different Data Sets with one, two and no Augmentations

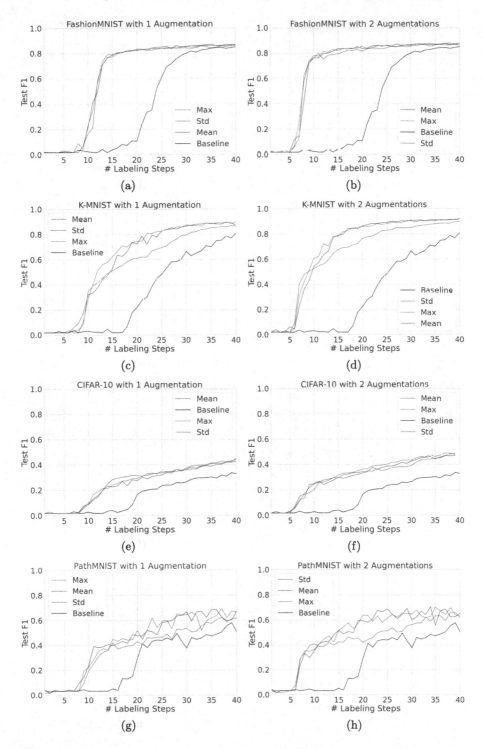

Fig. 4. Test F1 Scores for MobileNetV3-Small using Std, Mean and Max Query Strategies on different Data Sets with one, two and no Augmentations

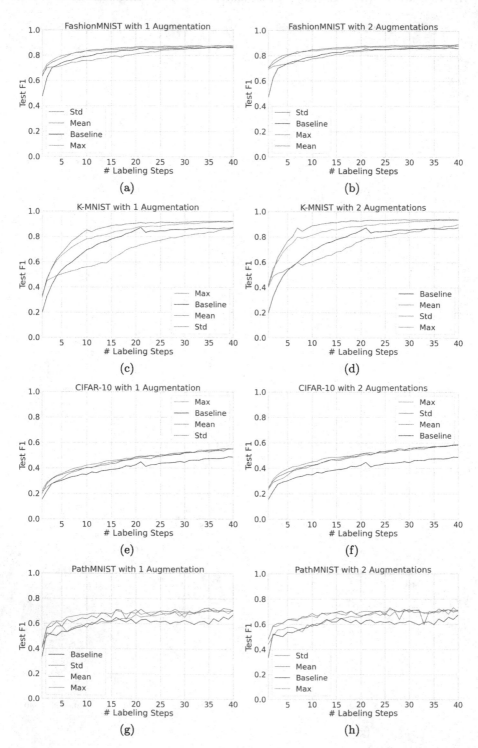

Fig. 5. Test F1 Scores for DenseNet121 using Std, Mean and Max Query Strategies on different Data Sets with one, two and no Augmentations

Jelenić et al. [12] found that the sequence order of query selection plays a fundamental role in assessing the transferability of actively learned data sets. Their devised *acquisition sequence mismatch* metric presents a way to qualitatively examine the correlations between our aggregation strategies.

According to Roth et al. [19] different learning configurations gain non-overlapping knowledge. This might explain in parts the different preferences of the examined models regarding the best performing uncertainty aggregation strategy.

7 Related Work

Although both AL and data augmentation are well known techniques, we are not aware of prior work combining them in a similar fashion to ours, namely affiliating original and augmentations before query selection. However, there is recent work that brings together both approaches in a variety of domains and modalities: Duong et al. [6] use AL to distill point cloud data sets for autonomous driving with targeted augmentations modelling vehicle ego-motion. The design of adequate augmentation policies specifically for AL setting is focus of works of Yang et al. [23]. Fonseca et al. [7] use augmentation purposefully to oversample underrepresented classes as part of their AL pipeline. The concept of augmented queues in the work of Malialis et al. [16] is in effect similar to our max-strategy. However, only the original images are taken into account upon query selection and augmentations are performed afterwards. Chen et al. [3] focus on expected model change and asses query members in terms of their potential for diverse augmentation results before actually selecting and augmenting them.

8 Conclusion

In this paper, we explored the integration of AL and image augmentations, aiming to leverage the relationship between original and augmented images. This approach emphasizes minimizing the need for annotations while maximizing the utility of the data available. Our findings reveal that leveraging aggregated uncertainties leads to performance improvements without incurring additional annotation costs. We observed that a strategy favoring exploitation over pure exploration is generally more effective, although allowing for variability within pairs of images often provides a critical advantage. This underscores the importance of adopting a hybrid strategy for aggregating data. Nonetheless, the effects of employing more than two types of augmentations remain an area for future investigation.

References

1. Atighehchian, P., Branchaud-Charron, F., Lacoste, A.: Bayesian active learning for production, a systematic study and a reusable library (2020)
2. Bondu, A., Lemaire, V., Boullé, M.: Exploration vs. exploitation in active learning: a Bayesian approach. In: IJCNN, pp. 1–7 (2010)

3. Chen, Z., Zhang, J., Wang, P., Chen, J., Li, J.: When active learning meets implicit semantic data augmentation. In: Avidan, S., Brostow, G., Cissé, M., Farinella, G.M., Hassner, T. (eds.) ECCV 2022. LNCS, vol. 13685, pp. 56–72. Springer, Cham (2022). https://doi.org/10.1007/978-3-031-19806-9_4

4. Clanuwat, T., Bober-Irizar, M., Kitamoto, A., Lamb, A., Yamamoto, K., Ha, D.: Deep learning for classical Japanese literature. CoRR abs/1812.01718 (2018)

5. Cubuk, E.D., Zoph, B., Mane, D., Vasudevan, V., Le, Q.V.: AutoAugment: learning augmentation policies from data (2019)

6. Duong, N.P.A., Almin, A., Lemarié, L., Kiran, B.R.: Active learning with data augmentation under small vs large dataset regimes for semantic-KITTI dataset. In: de Sousa, A.A., et al. (eds.) VISIGRAPP 2022. CCIS, vol. 1815, pp. 268–280. Springer, Cham (2023). https://doi.org/10.1007/978-3-031-45725-8_13

7. Fonseca, J., Bacao, F.: Improving active learning performance through the use of data augmentation (2023). https://doi.org/10.1155/2023/7941878

8. Gal, Y., Ghahramani, Z.: Dropout as a Bayesian approximation: representing model uncertainty in deep learning (2016)

9. He, K., Zhang, X., Ren, S., Sun, J.: Deep residual learning for image recognition (2015)

10. Howard, A., et al.: Searching for MobileNetV3 (2019)

11. Huang, G., Liu, Z., van der Maaten, L., Weinberger, K.Q.: Densely connected convolutional networks (2018)

12. Jelenić, F., Jukić, J., Drobac, N., Šnajder, J.: On dataset transferability in active learning for transformers (2023)

13. Kather, J.N., Krisam, J., et al.: Predicting survival from colorectal cancer histology slides using deep learning: a retrospective multicenter study. PLoS Med. **16**(1), 1–22 (2019)

14. Krizhevsky, A.: Learning multiple layers of features from tiny images. Technical report (2009)

15. Kumar, P., Gupta, A.: Active learning query strategies for classification, regression, and clustering: a survey (2020). https://doi.org/10.1007/s11390-020-9487-4

16. Malialis, K., Papatheodoulou, D., Filippou, S., Panayiotou, C.G., Polycarpou, M.M.: Data augmentation on-the-fly and active learning in data stream classification (2022)

17. Müller, S.G., Hutter, F.: TrivialAugment: tuning-free yet state-of-the-art data augmentation (2021)

18. Osugi, T., Kim, D., Scott, S.: Balancing exploration and exploitation: a new algorithm for active machine learning. In: ICDM (2005)

19. Roth, K., Thede, L., Koepke, A.S., Vinyals, O., Hénaff, O., Akata, Z.: Fantastic gains and where to find them: on the existence and prospect of general knowledge transfer between any pretrained model (2023)

20. Shorten, C., Khoshgoftaar, T.M.: A survey on image data augmentation for deep learning (2019)

21. Simonyan, K., Zisserman, A.: Very deep convolutional networks for large-scale image recognition (2015)

22. Xiao, H., Rasul, K., Vollgraf, R.: Fashion-MNIST: a novel image dataset for benchmarking machine learning algorithms. CoRR abs/1708.07747 (2017)

23. Yang, J., Wang, H., Wu, S., Chen, G., Zhao, J.: Towards controlled data augmentations for active learning. In: Proceedings of the 40th International Conference on Machine Learning, vol. 202, pp. 39524–39542. PMLR (2023)

24. Yang, S., Xiao, W., Zhang, M., Guo, S., Zhao, J., Shen, F.: Image data augmentation for deep learning: a survey (2023)

An Approach to Predict Optimal Configurations for LDA-Based Topic Modeling

Mou Saha and Doina Logofătu[✉]

Department of Computer Science and Engineering, Frankfurt University of Applied
Sciences, 60318 Frankfurt am Main, Germany
logofatu@fb2.fra-uas.de

Abstract. This paper describes an approach toward the efficient optimization of hyperparameters in Latent Dirichlet Allocation (LDA) topic modeling under stringent computational constraints. The main aim is to improve performance and outcomes by fine-tuning the LDA model's alpha, beta, and topic parameters in the Mallet implementation. The difficulty comes from the time-consuming task of manually adjusting hyperparameters and the high computational expense of experimenting with different parameter combinations. To get around this, we suggest an automated hyperparameter tuning approach based on the recursive binary search algorithm, aiming to reduce the model's complexity and hence improve performance. Our process, which was created for the competition Predicting Good Configurations for Topic Models at the Genetic and Evolutionary Computation Conference, offers a quick way to optimize the hyperparameters while avoiding the use of heuristics and manual labor. The study provides an extensive description of our technique, findings, and an in-depth evaluation, making a significant contribution to the field of topic modeling's automated hyperparameter optimization.

Keywords: topic modeling · hyperparameter · optimization · mallet

1 Introduction

Technology has made it possible for humans to produce an unprecedented amount of text, and the efficient and effective use of that information is now essential to productivity in a variety of fields. From news articles and academic literature to social media feeds and business reports, text data is everywhere, making the field of text analysis essential across numerous domains. Topic modeling is a powerful technique that helps us find underlying thematic structures in a huge set of documents, which also gives an efficient way to find the topic from the data. In order to use topic modeling, some parameters have to be configured [1]. The Latent Dirichlet Allocation (LDA) method is widely used in topic modeling, which is a generative statistical approach that explains why certain parts of data have similarities. LDA models are efficient, but tuning them

© The Author(s), under exclusive license to Springer Nature Switzerland AG 2024
L. Iliadis et al. (Eds.): EANN 2024, CCIS 2141, pp. 17–27, 2024.
https://doi.org/10.1007/978-3-031-62495-7_2

to optimize performance remains a challenge, mostly because multiple hyperparameters are involved, such as alpha (α), beta (β), and the number of topics (N). A model's results are influenced significantly by these parameters, so it is crucial that there is a correct configuration of these parameters so that the model will work properly [2–4]. The need for automated methods to optimize these parameters and classify the various topics present within a particular text corpus becomes increasingly vital. The Genetic and Evolutionary Computation Conference (GECCO)[1] has created the *Predicting Good Configurations for Topic Models Competition* to address this issue. The purpose of this paper is to present our approach to dealing with this problem in the context of the competition in which designing a solution that optimizes the alpha (α), and beta (β), and number of topic parameters for the LDA implementation in Mallet while meeting stringent computational constraints at the same time. We detail our methodology, present the results, and provide a comprehensive discussion, ultimately contributing to the broader field of automated hyperparameter optimization in topic modeling.

2   Problem Description

Before we commence our discussion on the existing and potential solution methodologies, we will describe the problem along with the dependencies.

The adjustment of hyperparameters, specifically alpha (α), beta (β), and the number of topics (N), is a crucial step in the use of LDA-based topic modeling. Finding the ideal values for these hyperparameters is a common challenge when using LDA for a particular text corpus. Researchers from several fields concur that there is no single method that is optimal for all datasets [12,17]. The number of topics (N) reflects the thematic granularity of the corpus. While the alpha (α) parameter regulates the mixture of topics for any given document, the beta parameter regulates the mixture of words for each topic [9]. The selection of these hyperparameters has a significant impact on the LDA model's performance and interpretability; hence, it is essential that they are configured correctly for the model to function as intended.

Despite the fact that these hyperparameters are crucial, their tuning is difficult and frequently depends on heuristics or exhaustive searches, both of which take a lot of time, demand manual intervention, and don't always generate the best result. Additionally, finding the ideal configurations can be difficult due to the high computing cost of testing the LDA model for different combinations of hyperparameters.

The challenge of machine learning model hyperparameter optimization is not completely solved. The goal is to implement a method that can predict good configurations of hyperparameters with limited time on a single core instance while measuring the perplexity, a metric that represents the model's performance. Perplexity is a function of the likelihood of what was observed in the given model, and it is directly related to these probabilities. The framework is

---

[1] https://gecco-2023.sigevo.org/HomePage.

more certain about its predictions when the perplexity is lower. The fit of statistical topic models is evaluated in-depth using a variety of different techniques in this research [4]. The researchers have presented extensively the challenges of evaluating topic models using perplexity. Our approach will make topic modeling more effective, practical, and accessible overall by removing the need for manual intervention and heuristics while simultaneously improving LDA-based topic modeling's performance.

Previously, many researchers worked on optimizing hyperparameters for machine learning models where they use random search and grid search algorithms [9,10]. Random search is a very common method for hyperparameter tuning. Within a predetermined range, it samples hyperparameter combinations at random, which is not a good solution for finding optimal configurations. When the hyperparameter space is big, it can be quicker than grid search since it examines new combinations quickly, but it may overlook significant areas of the hyperparameter space and be less efficient when particular hyperparameters interact with one another. On the other hand, grid search is computationally expensive as more hyperparameters and their values are added, and it may not be appropriate for continuous hyperparameter space because it thoroughly examines every possible combination of the specified hyperparameter values in the grid. The ideal hyperparameter values could be missed if the grid resolution is set too broadly. The search space and processing needs, however, are dramatically increased if the grid resolution is too fine.

Therefore, the main goal of this research is to approach the problem of hyperparameter optimization in a way that can produce high-quality outcomes while still being computationally feasible.

3   Related Work

Some researchers have explored the field of automatic hyperparameter tuning in machine learning and topic modeling, further validating the significance and necessity of this work. Over the years [13–17], researchers have suggested many methods to automate the LDA hyperparameter tuning procedure. Early work by Griffiths and Steyvers set the foundation for knowledge of the alpha (α), and beta (β) LDA parameters [3]. They analyzed the hidden themes of scientific writings using a probabilistic technique, exposing the underlying thematic structure.

Prior to model training, hyperparameters were typically fixed as a best practice. This research questioned this strategy and proposed an alternative online learning technique for hyperparameters in LDA models [11]. Their approach makes use of stochastic variational inference, allowing for small-step modifications to the hyperparameters for each new document viewed. The model's performance in terms of the held-out likelihood of unseen documents may be improved by using this method, which offers a more flexible, data-dependent model.

Bergstra and Bengio compared random and grid search methods for hyperparameter optimization [8]. They highlighted the efficiency and effectiveness of random search over traditional grid search, mainly when the search space includes irrelevant dimensions.

Bardenet et al. proposed a novel approach to hyperparameter optimization that uses a bandit-based configuration, providing computational efficiency [5]. Although this method offers promising results, it was not explicitly set as a target for text data and LDA model optimization.

In addition to random search, Bayesian optimization techniques have also been applied to hyperparameter tuning. Snoek et al. introduced a practical Bayesian optimization approach for a hyperparameter configuration that outperforms random search [6]. They demonstrated the efficiency of their method in several machine learning and neural network scenarios.

Regarding topic modeling specifically, Yao et al. proposed a novel approach to tune hyperparameters in online variational Bayes for LDA, which adapts the parameters during the learning process based on past gradients [7]. However, their work is limited to online settings.

This paper [1] investigates the customization of topic modeling parameters for optimal information retrieval from software development forums like Stack Overflow and GitHub. It reveals that standard parameters sometimes provide the best results, with each platform needing unique configurations. The study also introduces a method to predict optimal settings for unseen corpora, offering improved text data comprehension efficiency for developers and researchers.

In light of these works, our paper extends this line of research by targeting the efficient prediction of hyperparameters for LDA topic modeling under strict computational constraints while ensuring high-quality results.

4 Methodology

The main objective of the implemented method is to optimize the hyperparameters (namely, the number of topics N, alpha (α), beta (β)) LDA model, used to derive topics from the dataset. The optimization criterion is to minimize the perplexity of the model, which is a common measure of performance for probabilistic models. Perplexity is a measure of how well a probability model predicts a sample. Mallet[2], version 2.0.8's LDA implementation, was used for all of our work. Figure 1 shows a flowchart of the implementation of our work process. The detailed implementation is as follows:

4.1 Data Pre-processing

The dataset that is used is a textual corpus consisting of the entire text of the play "King Richard II" and "Romeo and Juliet" written by William Shakespeare. The dataset comes from the Project Gutenberg collection, an extensive collection of free eBooks, and these are text files. The text file of "King Richard II" consists of 22,972 words, and "Romeo and Juliet" consists of 24,843 words. The data is in an unstructured textual format, featuring both prose and dialogue. It contains the entire play, including act and scene indicators, a list of characters, and the dialogue associated with each character.

---

[2] http://mallet.cs.umass.edu/download.php, last accessed on 28 July 2023.

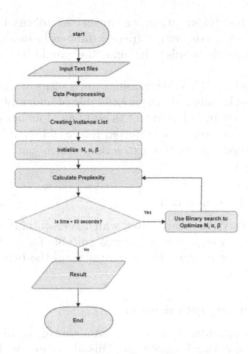

Fig. 1. Workflow of predicting Configurations

We collect the text documents as a data set and pass them through several pre-processing steps to make them suitable for topic modeling. We have done several steps for pre-processing that transform raw text data into a format that can be efficiently used:

- **Tokenization:** Tokenization is the initial stage in our preprocessing data workflow. Here, we split the text into its component words or tokens. Punctuation marks are also eliminated as part of the procedure because they frequently do not aid in understanding the topics within the text. For example, the sentence "She could have run and waddled all about." would be tokenized into ["She", "could", "have", "run", "and", "waddled", "all", "about"].
- **Stopwords Removal:** In our data preprocessing strategy, We included the important stopwords removal step. These typically include words like 'the', 'is', 'in', and 'and', which frequently appear in almost all text, but generally do not carry significant meaning on their own. These words can increase the dataset's noise and cover the more significant, content-rich terms that may provide useful modeling information. So the removal of these stopwords accomplishes two goals: (1) it reduces the noise in the data, improving the computational efficiency of the model; and (2) it enhances the topic allocation process of the LDA model by concentrating on content-rich words, making the discovered topics more interpretable.

- **Lowercasing:** After tokenization, we convert all tokens to lowercase. This process ensures that words are not treated differently based on their capitalization. For instance, the words "The" and "the" would be treated as the same token after lower casing.
- **Feature Extraction:** After lowercasing, we transform our tokens into features that machine learning models are capable of understanding. Tokens are converted to numbers by searching for them in an alphabet rather than being stored as strings. Each token is converted into a unique integer id using this procedure, also known as feature extraction, which can then be utilized as input to our model.

4.2   Creating an Instance List

Using the Mallet library, we create a list, which is essentially a list of instances where each instance is a sequence of features suitable for feeding into machine learning algorithms. The instance list is created from the text documents using a set of Pipes from Mallet.

4.3   Hyperparameter Optimization

Our methodology for optimizing the hyperparameters of the LDA model is based on the recursive Binary Search algorithm. This algorithm, which helps you discover a specific item in a sorted list, is essentially a divide-and-conquer strategy. Additionally, it demonstrates its skill in optimization issues when the goal is to maximize or minimize a specific function. In our case, we are trying to minimize the perplexity of an LDA model over a range of hyperparameters. Moreover, as a result of the algorithm's large reduction of the search space and computational overheads, optimization becomes effective and efficient. This entire process is carried out independently for each hyperparameter—the number of topics (N), alpha (α), and beta (β). While this assumes that the optimal value of each hyperparameter is independent of the others, it greatly simplifies the problem and, in most cases, results in good hyperparameters for the LDA model. The specific application of the Binary Search algorithm in our methodology is as follows:

- **Defining Initial Boundaries:** The initiation phase involves setting the boundaries for our search space in the first step. For each hyperparameter - the number of topics (N), alpha (α), and beta (β), we define a range of possible values. We might define the range of N as 10 to 1000. This is our initial search space, and it will get progressively smaller as the algorithm proceeds. The initial range for alpha (α) is set between 0.01 and 0.1. Alpha (α) corresponds to the document-topic density - with a higher alpha (α), documents are made up of a mixture of most of the topics, and with a lower alpha (α), documents will likely consist predominantly of a single topic. Lastly, for beta, the initial range is derived from the optimized alpha value, ranging from optimized alpha $(\alpha)/100$ to optimized alpha $(\alpha)/10$. Beta pertains to the topic word density - with a high value, topics are assumed to consist of most of the words, and with a low value, they are considered to consist of few words.

- **Computing Perplexity:** The second step involves computing the perplexity of the LDA model for the lower and upper boundary values of each hyperparameter. The perplexity is an effective metric for the optimization of the hyperparameters. This computed perplexity forms the base for further calculations.
- **Binary Partitioning of the Search Space:** The fundamental 'divide-and-conquer' strategy of the Binary Search algorithm is represented by this stage. The algorithm divides the search space for each hyperparameter in half based on the estimated perplexities for the lower and upper boundary values. The algorithm discards the lower half of the search area if the perplexity is lower at the top end of the search space. On the other hand, the method ignores the upper half if the perplexity is higher towards the bottom end of the space. As a result, the search area is effectively reduced, improving process efficiency.
- **Iterative Process:** Steps 2 and 3 are repeated for the updated search space. At each iteration, the search space is halved, which gradually gets us closer to the optimal hyperparameter values that offer the minimum perplexity.
- **Defining Termination:** The iterative process of the algorithm continues until the minimum possible perplexity is located or when the maximum allowable computation time is reached. The latter prevents the algorithm from running indefinitely, particularly in cases where it is not possible to further minimize the perplexity. Thus, the time constraint ensures a feasible solution within a reasonable time frame. For each hyperparameter optimization, 15 s limit is set. The elapsed time since the start of the method exceeds the maximum duration, which is 15 s in this case. This means the search is taking too long, and the best value found so far is returned.
  If an optimal value is found in less than 15 s, the method simply returns this value, and the remaining time is not used. The time limit is just an upper bound to ensure that the optimization doesn't run indefinitely, but it does not have to be fully utilized if the optimization finishes early. A total of 1 min is set to find all optimal hyperparameters.

5   Experiment Result and Discussion

The experimental results demonstrate the impact of varying the hyperparameter on the model's Perplexity (P) and aid in defining the initial boundary of the hyperparameter. We conducted thorough evaluations by experimenting with different ranges of topics (N), ranging from N = 10 to higher values. The test results are shown in Table 1 and 2, showing the corresponding perplexity values and the optimized number of topics based on the initial range of N.

As expected, we observed a general trend of decreasing Perplexity with increasing N up to a certain threshold. However, beyond this point, the Perplexity tended to plateau or even increase, suggesting potential over-fitting and diminishing returns. To create a balance between model complexity and performance, we chose to begin with a smaller range of N (N = 10 to N = 100) and progressively expanded it to assess the model's behavior.

Notably, when we increased the upper limit of N, the Perplexity initially decreased until N = 1000. After this point of N, the Perplexity started to increase again, with no significant changes in its value. We set the upper limit of N = 1000 to achieve a reasonable performance from the model.

Furthermore, we explored the impact of increasing the lower limit of N. We observed that the Perplexity decreased up to N = 700, after which it started to increase. This observation suggested that a lower range of N might be better for the performance of the model. We decided to take the field of N from 700 to 1000 as it gives the lowest Perplexity of the model. Overall, these results show the need to choose the N range for LDA topic modeling effectively. We can establish a balance between model interpretability and performance by optimizing the number of topics within the required range, producing informative and insightful topic representations in sizable text corpora.

Table 1. Adjustments with Upper Limit for initial N

N Range	Optimized N	Perplexity (P)
[10, 100]	32	−45.40
[10, 300]	82	−45.73
[10, 500]	157	−46.32
[10, 800]	207	−46.42
[10, 1000]	257	−47.12
[10, 1200]	307	−47.05

Table 2. Adjustments with Lower Limit for initial N

N Range	Optimized N	Perplexity (P)
[100, 1000]	325	−46.95
[200, 1000]	400	−47.24
[300, 1000]	475	−47.34
[500, 1000]	625	−47.68
[700, 1000]	775	−48.00
[800, 1000]	950	−47.88

In order to determine the initial value of the alpha (α) hyperparameter, significant experimentation was needed as well. We tested the lower limit of alpha from alpha (α) = 0.007 to alpha(α) = 0.8 throughout a range of values close to zero. The findings, shown in Tables 3 and 4, clearly show that alpha (α) values between alpha (α) = 0.01 and alpha (α) = 0.1 result in the lowest value of perplexity when compared to other values. These results led us to choose an alpha

(α) value of 0.1 as the starting point for the future optimization procedure. Our goal is to increase the efficiency and effectiveness of the hyperparameter optimization by starting with this carefully selected initial alpha (α) value, ensuring that the model captures the underlying theme structures of the text corpus more precisely and persistently.

For the initial beta value, the range was set from optimized alpha (α)/100 to optimized alpha (α)/10, where the value of alpha was determined earlier as alpha (α) = 0.03 based on our alpha (α) hyperparameter range.

Table 3. Adjustments with Lower Limit for initial alpha (α)

Alpha range	Optimized alpha (α)	Perplexity (P)
[0.001, 0.1]	0.03	−47.94
[0.007, 0.1]	0.03	−47.97
[0.03, 0.1]	0.05	−47.74
[0.01, 0.1]	0.03	−48.00
[0.06, 0.1]	0.07	−47.80
[0.09, 0.1]	0.09	−47.94

Table 4. Adjustments with Upper Limit for initial alpha (α)

Alpha Range	Optimized alpha (α)	Perplexity (P)
[0.01, 0.2]	0.15	−47.65
[0.01, 0.4]	0.11	−47.80
[0.01, 0.6]	0.16	−47.57
[0.01, 0.8]	0.21	−47.49
[0.01, 0.9]	0.03	−47.88

6   Conclusion and Future Work

In this paper, with the goal of automating the fine-tuning of hyperparameters for LDA topic modeling, we introduced a novel method. The optimized number of topics (N), alpha (α) and beta (β) values, which have an important effect on the performance and understanding of the LDA model, were efficiently searched for using a binary search technique. Our tests showed that we could find the configurations that produce the least confusion and, hence, the most powerful topic models by iteratively reducing the hyperparameter ranges. Our study's findings showed how important it is to determine the right number of topics, starting with alpha (α) and beta (β) values. We discovered that the quality and interpretability of the generated topics are greatly influenced by the choice of hyperparameters. We discovered through a process of systematic testing that particular ranges of hyperparameter values resulted in lower perplexity, indicating an improved fit between the model and the data.

To further evaluate and improve the quality of the discovered optimal configurations, we can also consider including additional evaluation metrics, including topic coherence and topic distinctiveness. Additionally, we may explore how our method can be used generally to handle larger and more varied text corpora, as well as explore its potential use in practical scenarios like text classification and sentiment analysis.

In conclusion, our work proposes a reliable and effective strategy for automating the fine-tuning of hyperparameters in LDA topic modeling, with promising results in identifying configurations that maximize the performance of the model depending on the perplexity value. Our study contributes to the creation of automated and scalable methods for obtaining valuable insights from large text corpora as the area of natural language processing continues to advance.

References

1. Treude,C., Wagner, M.: Predicting good configurations for github and stack overflow topic models. In: 2019 IEEE/ACM 16th International Conference on Mining Software Repositories (MSR), Montreal, QC, Canada, pp. 84–87 (2019). https://doi.org/10.1109/MSR.2019.00022
2. Blei, M., Ng, A.Y., Jordan, M.I.: Latent Dirichlet allocation. J. Mach. Learn. Res. **3**(Jan), 993–1022 (2003)
3. Griffiths, T.L., Steyvers, M.: Finding scientific topics. Proc. Natl. Acad. Sci. **101**(suppl 1), 5228–5235 (2004)
4. Wallach, H.M., Murray, I., Salakhutdinov, R., Mimno, D.: Evaluation methods for topic models. In: Proceedings of the 26th Annual International Conference on Machine Learning, pp. 1105–1112 (2009)
5. Bardenet, R., Brendel, M., Kégl, B., Sebag, M.: Collaborative hyperparameter tuning. In: Proceedings of the 30th International Conference on Machine Learning (ICML-13), pp. 199–207 (2013)
6. Snoek, J., Larochelle, H., Adams, R.P.: Practical Bayesian optimization of machine learning algorithms. In: Advances in Neural Information Processing Systems, pp. 2951–2959 (2012)
7. Yao, L., Mimno, D., McCallum, A.: Efficient methods for topic model inference on streaming document collections. In: Proceedings of the 15th ACM SIGKDD International Conference on Knowledge Discovery and Data Mining, pp. 937–946 (2009)
8. Bergstra, J., Bengio, Y.: Random search for hyper-parameter optimization. J. Mach. Learn. Res. **13**(Feb), 281–305 (2012)
9. Jelodar, H., et al.: Latent Dirichlet allocation (LDA) and topic modeling: models, applications, a survey. Multimed. Tools Appl. **78**(11), 15169–15211 (2018). https://doi.org/10.1007/s11042-018-6894-4

10. Sasi, S., Lilywala, T.Y., Bhattacharya, B.S.: Optimising hyperparameter search in a visual thalamocortical pathway model. In: 2022 International Joint Conference on Neural Networks (IJCNN), Padua, Italy, pp. 1–8 (2022). https://doi.org/10.1109/IJCNN55064.2022.9892380
11. Asuncion, A., Welling, M., Smyth, P., Teh, Y.W.: On smoothing and inference for topic models. arXiv (2012). https://doi.org/10.48550/ARXIV.1205.2662
12. Hughes, M.: Reliable and scalable variational inference for the hierarchical Dirichlet process. In: Artificial Intelligence and Statistics. PMLR (2015). proceedings.mlr.press/v38/hughes15.html
13. Panichella, A.: A systematic comparison of search-based approaches for LDA hyperparameter tuning. Inf. Softw. Technol. **130**, 106411 (2021). https://doi.org/10.1016/j.infsof.2020.106411
14. Panichella, A., Dit, B., Oliveto, R., Di Penta, M., Poshynanyk, D., De Lucia, A.: How to effectively use topic models for software engineering tasks? An approach based on genetic algorithms. In: 2013 35th International Conference on Software Engineering (ICSE), San Francisco, CA, pp. 522–531 (2013). https://doi.org/10.1109/ICSE.2013.6606598
15. Teh, Y.W., Jordan, M.I., Beal, M.J., Blei, D.M.: Hierarchical Dirichlet Processes. J. Am. Stat. Assoc. **101**(476), 1566–1581 (2006). https://doi.org/10.1198/016214506000000302
16. Arun, R., Suresh, V., Veni Madhavan, C.E., Narasimha Murthy, M.N.: On finding the natural number of topics with latent Dirichlet allocation: some observations. In: Zaki, M.J., Yu, J.X., Ravindran, B., Pudi, V. (eds.) PAKDD 2010. LNCS (LNAI), vol. 6118, pp. 391–402. Springer, Heidelberg (2010). https://doi.org/10.1007/978-3-642-13657-3_43
17. Binkley, D., Heinz, D., Lawrie, D., Overfelt, J.: Source code analysis with LDA. J. Softw.: Evol. Process **28**(10), 893–920 (2016). https://doi.org/10.1002/smr.1802

An Autoencoder-Based Approach for Anomaly Detection of Machining Processes Using Acoustic Emission Signals

Antonio Nappa[1]([✉]) [iD], Juan Luis Ferrando Chacón[1] [iD], Izar Azpiroz[1] [iD],
and Pedro José Arrazola[2] [iD]

[1] Vicomtech Foundation, Basque Research and Technology Alliance (BRTA),
Mikeletegi 57, 20009 Donostia-San Sebastián, Spain
{anappa,jlferrando,iazpiroz}@vicomtech.org
[2] Faculty of Engineering, Mondragon University, 20500 Mondragon, Spain
pjarrazola@mondragon.edu

Abstract. In recent years the growing amount of data generated in industrial processes has enabled the development of data-driven decision-making systems, placing strong interest on artificial intelligence, particularly when the world of Internet-of-Things is considered. Managing and monitoring this data flow is crucial in machining processes, where the health of the system is assessed through the analysis of different sources, such as vibration, temperature, electric and acoustic signals. Currently, the main theme in tackling this task is anomaly detection: identifying an anomalous state is equivalent to having adequate control of the process and being able to make decisions accordingly, which, if achieved in the early stages, gives an incredible return, avoiding failures and production interruptions. In this paper an approach combining Wavelet Packet Decomposition and Autoencoders for anomaly detection of CNC machining processes is presented. To this end, acoustic emission signals of a real-world use case are considered. To prove the effectiveness of the proposed system, a comparison with an Isolation Forest algorithm, a well-known benchmark in this field, is made. The results show an improvement of nearly 10% in terms of F1-score and accuracy, as well as the advantages of the encoding procedure.

Keywords: Machining Process · Acoustic Emission · Anomaly detection · Wavelet Packet Decomposition · Multi-Resolution Analysis · Autoencoder

1 Introduction

Nowadays, data-driven decision making has become an integral part of industrial processes. The large volume of data that can be collected and processed with modern tools allows for significant insights, while introducing new challenges in process management: although in such environments total control of each workflow is expected, real-world scenarios can face changes in the data (such as new classes, clusters, and features) resulting into a change in the domain in which the models are employed. Traditional models can be easily fooled in such situations, suffering performance degradation over time, which is why topics such as process management and automation, fault detection and diagnosis, are becoming increasingly important. Keeping track of and validating the quality of data is crucial, particularly in the area of anomaly detection. Here the joint effort of application-domain experts and data science is leading to the development of continuously more complex and comprehensive models, achieving remarkable results [6].

Most studies on artificial intelligence for anomaly detection are in the cybersecurity context, while, in comparison, there are very few use cases in industry [5,11]; this is mainly due to the difficulties related to Internet-of-Things (IoT) ecosystems in industrial machinery and, above all, to the lack of challenging public datasets [5]. In this regard, a further split seems to be given by the type of signals analyzed: one of the most preferred ways to monitor tools and processes conditions is the use of vibration signals, followed by temperature and electrical signals [5,15]. Acoustic emissions, although commonly considered interesting, still struggle to find sufficient applications.

Traditionally, signal analysis has always relied on statistical methods, then integrated with the study of the frequency domain, making use of Fast-Fourier Transform (FFT) or Discrete Wavelet Transform (DWT). With the advancement of machine learning, these techniques were first relegated to the preprocessing phase only and then totally supplanted by deep learning, which is known to be able to obtain excellent results starting from raw data [4,13]. The disadvantage of deep learning is that it requires considerable computing power and, therefore, needs further optimization to effectively implement edge processing, which is a crucial aspect in IoT systems [15]. In fact, the most widespread neural networks in this field are Convolutional Neural Network (CNN) and Long Short-Term Memory (LSTM), characterized by a considerable number of parameters and therefore computationally expensive to train and deploy.

In this paper an approach combining discrete Wavelet Packet Decomposition (WPD) and autoencoders for anomaly detection of machining processes using acoustic emission signals is proposed, supported by the fact that in several stud ies it has been shown how FFT and autoencoders together can be an effective way to improve the performance of anomaly detection [5]. On the one hand, WPD, compared to DWT, gives better resolution in applications where the signal contains relevant high-frequency information; the autoencoder, on the other hand, is another well-known neural network in anomaly detection tasks, thanks to its ability to compress data and provide accurate low-dimensional representations. To the best of our knowledge, this is the first implementation of such an approach in machining process anomaly detection.

The remainder of the paper is organized as follows. The Materials and Methods section describes the dataset, explains the pre-processing steps performed, and gives the theoretical fundamentals of the proposed approach. The Results section presents the outcome of this strategy, evaluating its performance and comparing it with a state-of-the-art benchmark, Isolation Forest. Conclusions and future work are reported in the last section.

2   Materials and Methods

This section describes the dataset details and presents the approach followed to process the acoustic emission signals and address the anomaly detection task. The methodology is depicted in Fig. 1 and summarised as follows:

1. Signal pre-processing: the interesting part of the signal is extracted by detecting its change points with a dynamic programming algorithm, a high-pass Butterworth filter is applied, the signal is finally split into one second-lasting segments.
2. Time-frequency domain signal analysis: the signal is processed with a Wavelet Packet Transform, after which a Multi-Resolution analysis is applied to extract the main features of the signal at different frequency scales.
3. Dimensionality reduction: since the features extracted with the Multi-Resolution analysis are multiple and contain redundant information, a dimensionality reduction phase is performed; to this end, an autoencoder is trained, whose latent-space representation constitutes the reduced feature space.
4. Anomaly detection: two algorithms, Autoencoder (specifically, the decoder of the previously trained autoencoder) and Isolation Forest, are fed with the data processed in the previous steps.

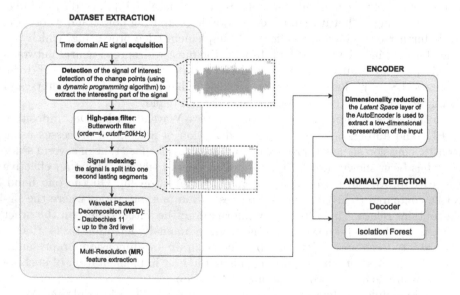

Fig. 1. Graphical representation of the proposed workflow.

The key concepts of this workflow are further discussed in the next sections.

2.1 Pre-processing

One of the main challenges in signal analysis lies in effectively managing the continuous streams of data produced by different sensors, processing them in a way that makes them suitable for the models to which they will be supplied. The choice of the possible steps to take and the order in which to carry them out strongly depends on the application of interest and the characteristics of the data. In general, the main steps include segmentation and filtering.

Robust condition monitoring systems require methods of selecting representative segments of sensor signals that are reliable and repeatable. For this reason, an automatic selection criterion should be an essential part of any monitoring system, as manual actions are difficult to replicate and, above all, extremely prone to human error. Moreover, the criterion must inevitably be adapted to the application field, taking into account the timing and frequency of data acquisition. The most commonly used method consists of exceeding the signal value by a preset threshold; although simple and intuitive, it can be affected by signal disturbances, which occur very often in industrial applications [3,10]. To this end, in this paper a dynamic programming algorithm was implemented: using the signal standard deviation, it works by systematically examining all possible segmentations of the given signal with a dynamic programming approach; its goal is to find the exact minimum of the sum of costs associated with each segmentation. On average, a segment lasting thirty seconds was extracted from each signal.

As regards filtering, to reduce the mechanical noise of the process, the signal was filtered with a fourth-order Butterworth high-pass filter, whose cut-off frequency was set at 20 kHz [16].

Finally, the representative signal obtained with the segmentation was further split into N segments of one second duration [7]. This is to cope with the high sampling frequency of the signals and to avoid that with a full-scale analysis the features could get mixed.

2.2 Wavelet Packet Decomposition

The wavelet transform is a powerful tool for analyzing and processing signals and is extremely efficient in various fields of application, such as compression and denoising, and in general when dealing with non-stationary signals [14]. It is in fact capable of characterizing both long-term trends at low frequencies and short-term trends at high frequencies while keeping track of their temporal dependency.

The disadvantage of the Fourier expansion is that it only has frequency resolution and not time resolution. This means that although it is possible to determine all the frequencies that compose the signal, it is not possible to receive any temporal information that somehow indicates "when" a specific frequency component appeared. To overcome this problem, throughout the history of mathematics, various solutions have been developed to represent a signal simultaneously in the time and frequency domain, of which the wavelet transform is currently the most successful example.

The analysis at various resolution scales, typical of the wavelet transform, is obtained by constructing a set of basis functions by translating and modifying the scale of a single function, $\psi(t)$, called *mother wavelet*:

$$\psi_{ab}(t) = \frac{1}{\sqrt{a}} \, \psi \left(\frac{t-b}{a} \right) \tag{1}$$

where a and b are, respectively, the scale and translation parameters.

With the Continuous Wavelet Tranform (CWT) a signal is analyzed continuously by means of basic functions which are continuously translated and scaled versions of themselves. This means that this transform has a certain degree of redundancy, i.e. that many values are not really useful for reconstructing the signal. Furthermore, it often requires a considerable computational cost, due to the calculation of the integral, which is not acceptable in the field of signal processing where efficiency and speed are required. For these reasons the CWT is often replaced with the Discrete Wavelet Transform (DWT), which returns a less redundant transform, and with a sufficient amount of information to still allow the perfect reconstruction of the signal, through an accurate choice of the values of the parameters a and b.

The common method of implementing the DWT is through a filter bank: a sequence of low-pass and high-pass filters whose coefficients, when convolved with the input signal, respectively return the so-called *approximation* (node a) and *detail* (node d) of the signal itself. In DWT, subsequent applications of the filters are made only on the approximation, thus limiting the amount of information extracted. In the case of Wavelet Packet Decomposition (WPD), instead, the filters are applied to both branches of the decomposition, leading to a more detailed frequency resolution.

In this paper, a Wavelet Packet Decomposition with the *Daubechies_11* wavelet up to third order was performed [8], resulting in 15 decomposition nodes. A Multi-Resolution (MR) feature extraction step was then applied: it consists of extracting features at different resolution scales, i.e. at each decomposition node. The following features were extracted: maximum, median, mean, standard deviation, peak-to-peak, root mean square, and kurtosis, thus, resulting in a total of 105 extracted features.

2.3   Autoencoder

Autoencoders are a particular class of deep learning algorithms used for creating compact representations (or "encodings") of complex data in an unsupervised manner. Using input as output, they are able to learn from unlabeled data (in this sense, they are usually referred to as self-supervised models because they generate their own labels from the training data) and can be employed in various domains, of which anomaly detection is one of the main ones [4,13]. In the literature, this type of network has been shown to be very efficient in learning complex encodings; in this regard, the number of parameters plays a crucial role because, if improperly increased, it leads the network to simply learn to copy its input into the output, mimicking the identity function. Techniques to overcome this problem consist of implementing a stacked architecture and regularization methods, such as the *sparsity constraint* [12].

The main components of an autoencoder are three, encoder, latent-space representation and decoder, where the decoder's layer structure is commonly symmetric to the encoder's one. The encoder compresses the information contained in the input and produces the latent-space representation, also known as code; this code is then used by the decoder to reconstruct the input. The peculiarities of autoencoders are linked precisely to the compression aspect; in fact, they are: data-specific, in the sense that they are only able to significantly compress data similar to that on which they have been trained (since they learn specific characteristics for the training data, they are different from a standard data compression algorithm); lossy, i.e. there will always be a minimum reconstruction error that will not make the output exactly equal to the input, the representation will be similar to a certain degree.

Given what has just been said, the advantages in the field of anomalies analysis are evident. During training, the model's attention is focused on learning the behaviour of normal data, so anomalies are not included in the training set. Consequently, during the prediction phase, the deviations that the anomalies are expected to have compared to the normal data increase the reconstruction error (RE). Therefore, it is immediately clear that monitoring the RE allows the definition of data classification criteria, for example by setting a threshold. Moreover, by investigating data with time dependence, it is possible to identify the degradation, the timestamp after which the RE starts to increase [1,5].

Figure 2 shows the architecture of the autoencoder: the input nodes are 105, equal to the number of decomposition nodes (15) multiplied by the number of features calculated in each decomposition node (7) with the Multi-Resolution analysis. The encoder is implemented by stacking two more layers, reaching then the latent-space, composed of 16 nodes. The decoder is symmetrical to the encoder. Stochastic Gradient Descent (SGD) was chosen as optimizer, with learning rate 0.1 and momentum 0.9, Mean Absolute Error (MAE) as loss function. The training process was monitored with an early-stopping criterion, having patience of 10 epochs and a minimum delta of $1 \cdot 10^{-4}$.

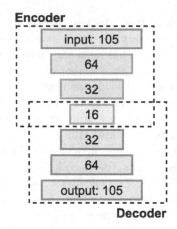

Fig. 2. Architecture of the autoencoder implemented in this paper.

2.4 Isolation Forest

Isolation Forest (IF) is a widespread algorithm for anomaly detection tasks. It makes use of binary trees to classify data through a path-length-based anomaly score, relying upon the characteristics of anomalies, i.e., being few and different, and therefore easily separable from normal data [9].

Even though the IF algorithm is known to have some issues, such as *swamping* (the difficulty in identifying a separation criterion between normal instances and anomalies) and *masking* (the detection of anomalous data is hindered by the clustering of a large number of anomalies), when exposed to an excessive amount of data, it has considerable success in detecting anomalies [2,5] and is therefore an excellent benchmark for the autoencoder performance.

The comparison with the autoencoder was performed considering three different IF models: 1) an IF trained on the encoding of the autoencoder, 2) an IF trained without encoding, i.e., with all the features extracted by MR analysis, 3) an IF trained without WPD, i.e., using the features extracted from the original signal only. These three models will be referred to as 'IF w/ encoding', 'IF w/o encoding' and 'IF w/o WPD' respectively in the Results section. Moreover, in order to properly compare the algorithms, the concept of contamination factor of the IF (i.e. the expected proportion of outliers in the dataset) was used as a reference to define the decoder threshold on the reconstruction errors. Since this contamination factor was set to 0.1, the 90th percentile of the reconstruction errors of the training set was chosen as threshold.

2.5 Performance Metrics

In classification problems, the most common metric is accuracy, because it is easy to calculate and interpret. However, when dealing with imbalanced data, of which anomaly detection is the best known case, accuracy turns out to be misleading. A more suitable metric is the F1-score. The main criticisms leveled at the F1-score concern its lack of symmetry, which makes it particularly sensitive to variations in labeling. For these very reasons, the test set was defined so to have a balanced representation of both classes (50% normal data, 50% anomalies). In this paper, the calculated metrics are F1-score and accuracy; however, F1-score was considered the reference metric.

2.6   Dataset

The data was collected from a conventional 3D turning operation, which is the most common machining procedure for wear testing, performed in a Sinumerik Computer Numerical Control (CNC) lathe. CNC machines are automated, computer-driven machines that execute pre-programmed sequences of controlled commands; to this end, various sensors are installed on the machine for process monitoring. In the context of this paper, acoustic emission signals, recorded with a sampling frequency set at 1 MHz, were taken into account. Further details on the experimental procedure and data capture can be found in [8].

The total number of records extracted with the procedure described in the previous sections is 2315, each having 105 features.

Regarding the definition of anomalies, the following criterion was adopted: having observed the final wear state of a given tool, the acoustic emission signals extracted through the segmentation process (see Sect. 2.1) are assigned, via interpolation, a wear value. Signals that correspond to a wear state greater than 250 μm [8] are considered anomalies.

The definition just provided established that approximately 7% of the available dataset consisted of anomalies. Given that the proposed approach involves the training of an autoencoder, an 85-15 training-test sets splitting was used, including anomalies in the test set only. Thus, in the training set there were no anomalies, while the test set consisted of half normal data and half anomalies, which implied a two-class balanced test set. The training set was further split by 25% to form the validation set, which was then used to monitor the training process. In order to validate the results, this splitting procedure, as well as the training of the autoencoder and Isolation Forest, was repeated 1000 times.

3   Results

Figure 3 shows the WPD decomposition of one of the anomalous signals in the dataset, at the third level of decomposition with the *Daubechies_ 11* wavelet [8]. When looking at the time domain, a given event is not always evident in all bands, which is why Multi-Resolution analysis is useful. High-amplitude acoustic emission shots, associated with discrete acoustic emission events, stand out above the continuous acoustic emission level across the entire signal. They exhibit distinct characteristic frequencies, and while some events are detectable within specific frequency bands, others may not be as noticeable in other bands. These shots are linked to tool wear, where several acoustic emission sources could be active, such as increased frictional contact between the workpiece and the tool or plastic deformation [8]. On the other hand, as explained previously, tool wearing is associated with the definition of anomaly; therefore, being able to identify and analyze these events is fundamental for the purposes of anomaly detection tasks. The spectrum of each node confirms the correct bandwidth selection by the WPD.

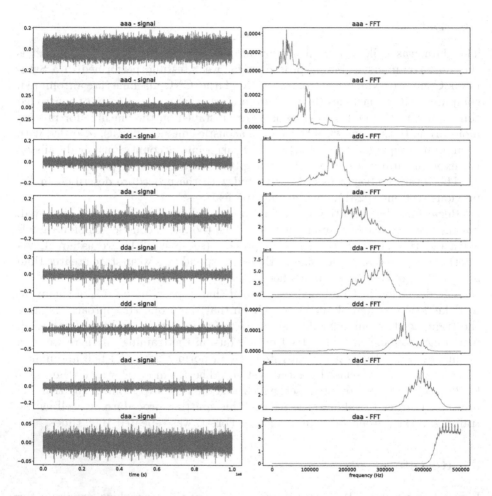

Fig. 3. Wavelet Packet Decomposition of a sample anomalous signal. The third level of decomposition using *Daubechies_11* wavelet is shown, having the time-domain on the left and the frequency-domain on the right.

Figure 4 shows the reconstruction error of one of the 1000 considered iterations. The ideal scenario would have the two classes, normal data and anomalies, perfectly distinguishable from each other, with the anomalies having reconstruction errors much higher than the normal data on which the network was trained.

In this case, a real-world use case, it is quite evident how the difficulty in defining an anomaly reflects in the struggle for the network to separate, using the reconstruction errors, the samples of the balanced test set. Nonetheless, the decoder threshold, defined using the idea of the contamination factor, seems to work well.

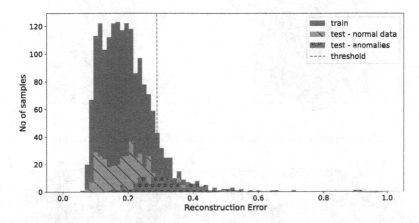

Fig. 4. Considering one of the 1000 iterations, the reconstruction error of both training and (balanced) test sets is shown.

The results obtained by repeating the experiment 1000 times are shown in Fig. 5. Considering the F1-score, i.e. the reference metric, the performance of the decoder and the Isolation Forest making use of the encoding are quite similar. Lower results, of nearly 10%, are obtained by the Isolation Forest when no Wavelet Packet Decomposition is used, i.c. having the features extracted from the original signal only. In the case of the Isolation Forest without encoding phase, the result worsens significantly: compared to the autoencoder, the F1-score value is lowered by almost 20%. This proves that the Multi-Resolution analysis must necessarily be combined with a dimensionality reduction technique, and that the autoencoder seems to be able to capture the essential information contained in the signals. The accuracy follows the same behavior.

The analysis made for the models and F1-score is also verified with the confusion matrices, shown in Fig. 6. By labeling anomalies as the negative class, i.e. 1, removing the encoding step reduces the ability to detect anomalies, resulting in an increase in false positives. It is useful to observe that the percentage of false negatives seems to be equal and low for all the models. The models, therefore, are quite confident in handling normal data while they face problems in detecting an anomalous event when it is present. This outcome is inevitably related to the anomaly definition procedure. Anyway, the results prove that the autoencoder is the best model to handle anomalies, as it has the lowest rate of false positives and the highest rate of true negatives.

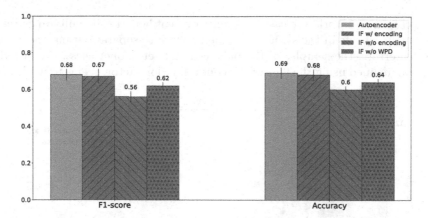

Fig. 5. Comparison of the metrics of the different models considered.

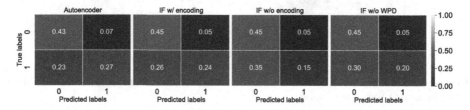

Fig. 6. Comparison of the confusion matrices of the different models considered.

4   Conclusions and Future Work

In addressing the problem of anomaly detection in machining processes, an approach combining Wavelet Packet Decomposition (WPD) and autoencoders is presented. By processing the acoustic emission signals of a real-world use case, segmentation was performed with a dynamic programming algorithm and features were extracted with a Multi-Resolution (MR) analysis.

The proposed approach was compared with an Isolation Forest (IF) algorithm. The comparison was actually made in three different ways: 1) with an IF trained on the encoding of the autoencoder, 2) with an IF trained without encoding, i.e., without reducing the high dimensionality linked to the MR extracted features, 3) with an IF trained without WPD, i.e., trained using the features extracted from the original signal only. The results showed an improvement of nearly 10% in terms of F1-score and accuracy when comparing autoencoder and IF without WPD, as well as the effectiveness of the encoding which indeed led to similar performance of the decoder and IF. Furthermore, labeling anomalies as the negative class, the analysis of the confusion matrices highlighted that the models differ mainly on the false positive rate, i.e. in classifying anomalies as normal data. From this point of view, the autoencoder proved to be the best model in handling anomalies, as it had the highest values of true negatives and the lowest values of false positives. In general, the difficulty in appropriately identifying an anomaly can also be attributed to the particular use case addressed, which is characterized by signals of considerable time duration and high sampling frequency.

Current anomaly detection techniques are mostly tested on synthetic dataset or not particularly challenging use cases. It is important to point out that real-world data substantially differ from simulated data, especially in terms of quality and variability; these are relevant aspects that should be the main focus of future research. Complex real-world use cases are a must when theoretical approaches need to be validated.

In future work, the presented case study will continue to be deepened, improving the proposed approach and integrating further analysis. Other real-world scenarios will be evaluated, attempting to extract general behaviors to support the line of research. In addition, this approach will be studied in the context of Federated Learning, a very important topic in industry. Different aggregation strategies will be tested and a new one based on neural network alignment will be implemented.

Acknowledgements. This research was partially funded by the department of Industry of the Basque Government within Elkartek programme KK-2022/00119.

Data Availibility Statement. Data sharing not applicable.

Disclosure of Interests. The authors have no competing interests to declare.

References

1. Ahmad, S., Styp-Rekowski, K., Nedelkoski, S., Kao, O.: Autoencoder-based condition monitoring and anomaly detection method for rotating machines. In: 2020 IEEE International Conference on Big Data (Big Data), pp. 4093–4102. IEEE (2020)
2. Barbariol, T., Chiara, F.D., Marcato, D., Susto, G.A.: A review of tree-based approaches for anomaly detection. In: Tran, K.P. (ed.) Control Charts and Machine Learning for Anomaly Detection in Manufacturing. SSRE, pp. 149–185. Springer, Cham (2022). https://doi.org/10.1007/978-3-030-83819-5_7
3. Bombiński, S., Błażejak, K., Nejman, M., Jemielniak, K.: Sensor signal segmentation for tool condition monitoring. Procedia CIRP **46**, 155–160 (2016)
4. Chalapathy, R., Chawla, S.: Deep learning for anomaly detection: a survey. arXiv preprint arXiv:1901.03407 (2019)
5. Chevtchenko, S.F., et al.: Anomaly detection in industrial machinery using IoT devices and machine learning: a systematic mapping. IEEE Access **11**, 128288–128305 (2023)
6. Cook, A.A., Mısırlı, G., Fan, Z.: Anomaly detection for IoT time-series data: a survey. IEEE Internet Things J. **7**(7), 6481–6494 (2019)
7. De Barrena, T.F., Ferrando, J.L., García, A., Badiola, X., de Buruaga, M.S., Vicente, J.: Tool remaining useful life prediction using bidirectional recurrent neural networks (BRNN). Int. J. Adv. Manuf. Technol. **125**(9–10), 4027–4045 (2023)

8. Ferrando Chacón, J.L., Fernández de Barrena, T., García, A., Sáez de Buruaga, M., Badiola, X., Vicente, J.: A novel machine learning-based methodology for tool wear prediction using acoustic emission signals. Sensors **21**(17), 5984 (2021)
9. Liu, F.T., Ting, K.M., Zhou, Z.H.: Isolation forest. In: 2008 Eighth IEEE International Conference on Data Mining, pp. 413–422. IEEE (2008)
10. Mohamed, A., Hassan, M., M'Saoubi, R., Attia, H.: Tool condition monitoring for high-performance machining systems-a review. Sensors **22**(6), 2206 (2022)
11. Nassif, A.B., Talib, M.A., Nasir, Q., Dakalbab, F.M.: Machine learning for anomaly detection: a systematic review. IEEE Access **9**, 78658–78700 (2021)
12. Ng, A., et al.: Sparse autoencoder. CS294A Lect. Notes **72**(2011), 1–19 (2011)
13. Pang, G., Shen, C., Cao, L., Hengel, A.V.D.: Deep learning for anomaly detection: a review. ACM Comput. Surv. (CSUR) **54**(2), 1–38 (2021)
14. Rhif, M., Ben Abbes, A., Farah, I.R., Martínez, B., Sang, Y.: Wavelet transform application for/in non-stationary time-series analysis: a review. Appl. Sci. **9**(7), 1345 (2019)
15. Serin, G., Sener, B., Ozbayoglu, A.M., Unver, H.O.: Review of tool condition monitoring in machining and opportunities for deep learning. Int. J. Adv. Manuf. Technol. **109**, 953–974 (2020)
16. Sikorska, J., Mba, D.: Challenges and obstacles in the application of acoustic emission to process machinery. Proc. Inst. Mech. Eng. Part E: J. Process Mech. Eng. **222**(1), 1–19 (2008)

An EANN-Based Recommender System for Drug Recommendation

Hadi Al Mubasher$^{(\boxtimes)}$ and Mariette Awad

Maroun Semaan Faculty of Engineering and Architecture,
American University of Beirut, Beirut, Lebanon
hma154@mail.aub.edu, ma162@aub.edu.lb

Abstract. Recommender systems aim to improve the user experience in a world where data and available alternatives are expanding at an unprecedented rate. Integrating Natural Language Processing and Artificial Neural Networks have resulted in better performance when compared to other recommender systems. This paper showcases the optimization of an artificial neural network-based recommender system that is used for drug recommendation, where the optimization process involves adopting ResNet-50 and a Multiple Criteria Decision Making-based recommender system to tune the learning rate of the neural network models on which the system is based. Results show that our proposed approach leads to a system that outperforms the existing similar systems.

Keywords: Machine Learning · Multiple Criteria Decision Making · Hyperparameter Tuning · Recommender Systems · Natural Language Processing · Deep Learning · Artificial Neural Networks · Drug Recommendation

1 Introduction

Recommender systems, a subset of Machine Learning, leverage data to predict and narrow down user preferences among a growing number of alternatives [28].

There are generally few types of recommender systems among which we mention Demographic Recommendation Systems (DRSs), Collaborative Filtering Recommender Systems (CFRSs), Content-Based Recommender Systems (CBRSs), and hybrid recommender systems. DRSs leverage user demographic features such as age, gender, location, education, etc. CFRSs suggest items by analyzing the preferences and interactions of similar users; they operate under the assumption that users with shared preferences in the past will likely have similar tastes in the future. CBRSs focus on the attributes of the items themselves; they recommend items similar to those a user has previously selected, based on those items' features. Hybrid recommender systems combine the strategies of collaborative filtering and content-based methods used in CFRSs and CBRSs to enhance the accuracy of predictions.

A hybrid recommender system that is based on different Artificial Neural Network (ANN) architectures and uses different features was proposed in [2].

L. Iliadis et al. (Eds.): EANN 2024, CCIS 2141, pp. 41–55, 2024.
https://doi.org/10.1007/978-3-031-62495-7_4

AlexNet was applied to high-dimensional feature sets and it enhanced data processing efficiency. Despite achieving marginal improvements in precision, recall, and F1-score over the *XGBOOST* model [18], the use of *AlexNet* has been critiqued for prolonged inference times due to its deep structure [10,19]. Replacing *AlexNet* with a more contemporary, optimized model could further boost performance while reducing inference delays.

Multiple Criteria Decision Making (MCDM) is a discipline focused on addressing decision-making problems that involve multiple criteria [24]. It offers a systematic and structured approach, employing various mathematical and computational techniques to aid decision-makers in evaluating and comparing alternatives based on their performance across several criteria [25]. These techniques are designed to enhance understanding of the trade-offs involved between different criteria and to support decision-makers in choosing the optimal alternative(s) that align with their objectives [25].

A recommender system that aims to tune the learning rate of a certain ANN model was proposed in [9]. The system is based on very well known MCDM methods which are Weighted Sum Method (WSM), Weighted Product Method (WPM), Technique for Order Performance by Similarity to Ideal Solution (TOPSIS), and Preference Ranking Organization Method for Enrichment Evaluation (PROMETHEE). The system was proven to be efficient and effective in tuning different ANN architectures for various applications.

To motivate to further improve on the ANN-based recommender system for drug recommendation [2], this paper adopts the *ResNet-50* model with the MCDM-based recommender system. Results confirm that the improvements are significant and motivate follow on research. The following is a breakdown of the paper's structure. A survey about related work is presented in Sect. 2. Sections 3 and 4 provide overviews about the ANN-based system and MCDM-based system, respectively. Section 5 details the optimization process of the existing ANN-based recommender system and the obtained results. The work is concluded and research opportunities are highlighted in Sect. 6.

2   Related Work

In the literature, there were several existing recommender systems that have been extensively designed and implemented across various domains. The work presented in [20] aimed for developing a collaborative filtering cloud-based recommender system for book recommendation. The system was developed using three distinct methods within the matrix factorization framework: Singular Value Decomposition, Alternating Least Squares, and a Deep Neural Network. But the system had some issues, where it did not effectively address the cold-start problem, which refers to challenges in making recommendations for new users or items with limited data. The system also had limited exploration of Natural Language Processing (NLP) techniques, which could impact its ability to provide highly accurate and personalized book recommendations. Moreover, the system relied on Singular Value Decomposition which is somehow computationally expensive [11].

An ensemble-based hotel recommender system was proposed in [22]. The system was based on sentiment analysis and aspect-based categorization, where it aimed to provide users with personalized hotel recommendations tailored to their preferences and requirements. Unconventionally, there were no preprocessing applied to the data used to build the system, resulting in lack of checking for misspells and typographical errors. Furthermore, the system failed to leverage a range of NLP techniques that can extract deeper insights from reviews and therefore improve the quality of its recommendation.

The authors in [14] proposed *CapsMF*, a novel product recommender system that is based on combining Capsule Networks and Matrix Factorization. The system is computationally expensive and had high inference time due to the use of Capsule Networks [14].

The work presented in [3] showcases developing a restaurant recommender system that utilizes natural language processing techniques, sentiment analysis, and semantic similarity methods to extract user preferences from online comments about restaurants. The system was based on features resulting from applying NLP methods on the user reviews only, disregarding their demographic information, which limited the system's ability to provided customized recommendations.

The authors in [2] worked on a hybrid recommender system that is based on ANNs. The system used features resulting from applying several NLP methods, and different feature combinations were made. Some feature combinations had a huge number of features, so a Convolutional Neural Network (CNN) architecture was adopted, namely *AlexNet*. With a huge number of features, CNNs have the ability to streamline the process and efficiently manage the extensive data load. But *AlexNet* has a long inference time due to its deeper structure and absence of optimized architectural features [10,19]. Also, the system had slight improvements over similar existing systems, with a training accuracy of 97.22% and a testing accuracy of 93.42%.

To that end, this paper presents an Enhanced Artificial Neural Network (EANN)-based recommender system that is used for drug recommendation. The system is formed by optimizing the existing ANN-based recommender system proposed in [2].

3   A Neural Network-Based Recommender System for Drug Recommendation

Proposed in [2], the recommender system aims to recommend a drug based a certain condition. The system is built using the UCI Drug Review dataset [23]. The dataset contains 215,063 records and 7 features, the features are as follows:

1. UniqueID: The ID of the drug.
2. drugName: The name of the drug.
3. condition: The condition.
4. review: The patient review.

5. rating: A 10-point patient rating.
6. date: The date of review entry.
7. usefulCount: The number of users who found the review useful.

Bulding the framework required preprocessing and cleaning the data, generating features through applying different NLP methods, forming different feature combinations, and adopting different ANN architectures for each feature combination. A roadmap is presented in Fig. 1.

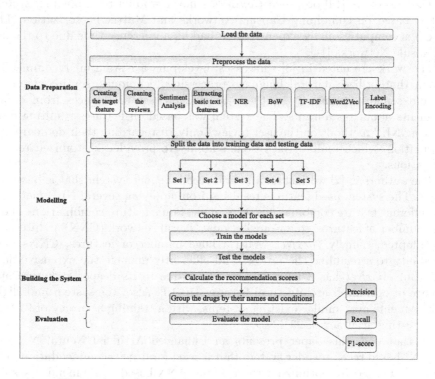

Fig. 1. A roadmap of the neural network-based system [2].

3.1 Preprocessing

Creating the Target Feature. The target feature was created using the *rating*. For each record, if the *rating* is above 5, then the value of the target feature is 1, which means that the rating is positive, or it's 0 otherwise, indicating that the rating is negative.

Cleaning the Reviews. The *reviews* were cleaned by eliminating digits, extra spaces, and stopwords, stemming the words, and lower-casing the letters.

Feature Generation. Different features were generated by applying various NLP methods. The applied methods are Sentiment Analysis, basic text feature extraction, Named Entity Recognition (NER), Topic Modeling, Bag of Words (BoW), Term Frequency-Inverse Document Frequency (TF-IDF), Word2Vec, and Label Encoding. A summary of the aim of each applied NLP method, in addition to the features at which the NLP method was applied on is shown in Table 1.

Table 1. Adopted NLP methods with their aims and their usages.

NLP Method	Aim	Applied On
Sentiment Analysis	Determining the emotional tone of a certain text [5]	*reviews, cleaned reviews*
Basic Text Feature Extraction	Transforming raw text data into a structured format [26]	*cleaned reviews*
NER	Identifying and classifying entities within a given text such as location, person, organization, etc. [17]	*cleaned reviews*
Topic Modeling	Discovering the topics that occur in a corpus of documents [7]	*cleaned reviews*
BoW (*unigram* and *n-gram*)	Simplifying the representation of a certain text by turning it into fixed-length vectors by counting how many times each word appears (unigram), or how many times n words appear (n-gram) [4]	*cleaned reviews*
TF-IDF (*unigram* and *n-gram*)	Reflecting the importance of a word (*unigram*), or *n* words (*n-gram*) in a corpus of documents [21]	*cleaned reviews*
Word2Vec	Extracting semantic relatedness, synonym detection, concept categorization, sectional preferences, and analogy across words or products [8]	*cleaned reviews*
Label Encoding	Converting labels to numbers [27]	*condition, year*

Forming Different Feature Combinations. Different dataset feature combinations were made. Important features resulting from basic text feature extraction, NER, and topic modeling, were chosen by a Random Forest Classifier. After that, five different feature combinations were made. The five sets commonly include important features, and sentiment scores. The first and second sets incorporate features derived from applying the unigram BoW model and TF-IDF model, respectively, resulting in 7,340 features. On the other hand, the third and fourth sets include features resulting from applying the n-gram BoW model and TF-IDF model, respectively, resulting in 2,314 features. As for the fifth set, it comprises features generated by applying Word2Vec, resulting in 331 features.

3.2 Building the System

Chosen Models. For the initial two sets, characterized by a large number of features, *AlexNet* [15] was employed. *AlexNet* is a CNN composed of eight layers. The architecture includes five convolutional layers followed by three fully connected layers. The ReLU activation function is used throughout, with the exception of the output layer, which utilizes a Sigmoid function to address the classification problem. *AlexNet* has demonstrated superior performance compared to existing models [15].

As for sets 3 and 4, a feed–forward Deep Neural Network (DNN) with 13 hidden layers was used. On the other hand, a feed–forward DNN with 7 hidden layers was used for set 5. For both models, the neurons of the hidden layers are activated with the ReLU, while that of the output layer is with Sigmoid.

Determination of the Recommendation Score. To determine the recommendation score for each drug, the labels generated by the models are summed up, and the sum is then multiplied by the normalized *usefulCount* for each drug. The equations of the normalized *usefulcount* and that of the recommendation score for drug d are shown in Eqs. 1 and 2, respectively.

$$u_d = \frac{U_d - m}{a - m} \tag{1}$$

where U_d is the *usefulCount* of d, m is the minimum *usefulCount*, and a is the maximum *usefulCount*.

$$Rscore_d = \sum_{i=1}^{5} p_i \times u_d \tag{2}$$

where p_i is the value predicted by model i.

The testing set was used to build the system, where the models were used to predict whether the review of each drug is positive or negative. Then the normalized *usefulcount* and recommendation score of each drug were determined using Eqs. 1 and 2, respectively. The drugs are later grouped by condition, recommendation scores of drugs with similar name and *condition* were summed up.

3.3 Limitations of the Neural Network-Based Recommender System

There are some issues in the recommender system. First, the system adopted *AlexNet*, which showed an excellent performance upon dealing with the large number of features, but as mentioned before, *AlexNet* tends to have longer inference times compared to more modern architectures. Second, the models of sets 3, 4, and 5 achieved a performance that is worse than that of the CNN models of sets 1 and 2 [2]. So these models can be tuned so that their performance improves.

4   MCDM-Based Recommender System for Learning Rate Tuning

The learning rate is a pivotal hyperparameter in neural network training and it dictates the step size the network takes when updating its parameters [9]. A small learning rate can decelerate the learning process, potentially leading to prolonged training times, while a high learning rate risks overshooting the optimum and causes divergence [9]. Therefore, selecting an appropriate learning rate for a specific neural network architecture is essential, as it significantly influences the model's performance and necessitates meticulous consideration [9]. A system that recommends the learning rate that can be used by a certain ANN model to achieve the best performance was proposed in [9]. The system is based on simple but powerful MCDM methods which are WSM, WPM, TOPSIS, and PROMETHEE.

4.1   Used MCDM Methods

The WSM combines multiple criteria by assigning weights to each criterion and summing up their normalized values [24]. WPM is similar to WSM but it multiplies the normalized values instead of adding them up [24]. As for TOPSIS, it determines the best alternative by measuring the geometric distance between each alternative and the ideal and non-ideal solutions [16]. On the other hand, PROMETHEE assesses alternatives based on pairwise comparisons and assigns preference values. It then computes net outranking flows to rank the alternatives [1].

4.2   Learning Rate Recommendation Process

In order for the recommendation process to happen, the system inputs the ANN model, dataset, batch size, and a pool of learning rates. After that, the dataset is divided into subsets and the model is trained and tested for each subset with different learning rates. For each learning rate, the averages for certain performance metrics are determined, performance metrics can include accuracy, precision, recall, Mean Absolute Error (MAE), and Mean Squared Error (MSE). Then the MCDM methods are applied, where the alternatives are the different learning rates and the criteria are the determined performance metrics. The recommendation score of each learning rate is calculated, where it is the geometric mean of the scores of the MCDM methods. The system finally recommends the learning rate having the highest recommendation score.

The system is proven to be light as it is based on simple MCDM methods. Also, the system was validated using different ANN architectures with various applications.

4.3   Adopting the MCDM-Based System

The MCDM-based system is adopted to tune the learning rates of the models of the existing neural network-based system, upon adopting the MCDM-based system, the chosen performance evaluation metrics are the accuracy, F1-score, and Area Under the Curve (AUC). The accuracy is a measure of how well a machine learning model is able to make predictions based on data. The F1-score the harmonic mean of precision and recall. Precision measures the accuracy of positive predictions, while recall measures the coverage of actual positive instances [13]. The AUC is a metric used to evaluate the performance of a certain binary classification model. It represents the degree of separability; how well the model is able to distinguish between the two classes [6]. A roadmap of the adopted system is shown in Fig. 2.

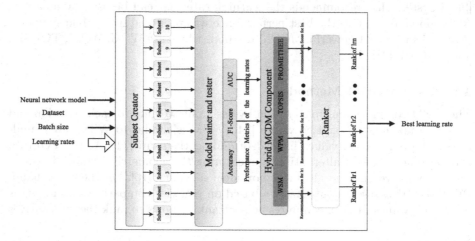

Fig. 2. A roadmap of the adopted MCDM-based system.

5   Enhancing the Existing Neural Network-Based System

The issues discussed in Sect. 3.3 can be addressed by reducing the system's inference time through adopting a better CNN model for sets 1 and 2, and improving the performance of the models of sets 3, 4, and 5 through tuning their hyperparameters.

The CNN model of sets 1 and 2, namely *AlexNet* had a large inference time, where it took almost 8 h for the model to train on each set. To reduce the inference time, we replaced it with *ResNet-50* [12]. *ResNet-50* employs residual connections, allows for smoother gradient flow, and enables training of very deep networks [12]. Also, *ResNet-50* addresses the vanishing gradient problem, resulting in more stable training, faster convergence, and therefore, a less inference time compared to other CNNs.

The MCDM-based recommender system is adopted to tune these models. Upon tuning, the models of sets 3, 4, and 5 were trained with the subsets using different learning rates and the evaluation metrics were determined. The results are presented in Tables 2, 3 and 4. After that, the MCDM methods were applied and the recommendation score was determined for each learning rate, the scores are shown in Tables 5, 6 and 7. As the results show, for sets 3, 4, and 5, the learning rates with the highest recommendation scores are 0.00055, 0.000325, and 0.0001, respectively. Therefore, using these learning rates will lead to the best model performance.

Table 2. Evaluation metrics for the neural network model of set 3.

Learning Rate	Accuracy	Val. Accuracy	F1-score	Val. F1-score	AUC	Val. AUC
0.000100	0.707895	0.707825	0.819531	0.824721	0.571309	0.576310
0.000325	0.725576	0.719992	0.828115	0.825536	0.639296	0.630384
0.000550	0.712787	0.712097	0.824718	0.825621	0.653152	0.647808
0.000775	0.705113	0.704523	0.824041	0.823714	0.524718	0.525378
0.001000	0.705339	0.704696	0.823329	0.824097	0.527495	0.529525
0.003250	0.700968	0.700974	0.822873	0.822830	0.498420	0.500000
0.005500	0.700968	0.700974	0.822856	0.822830	0.498719	0.500000
0.007750	0.700968	0.700974	0.822863	0.822830	0.498494	0.500000
0.010000	0.700968	0.700974	0.822896	0.822830	0.496953	0.500000
0.032500	0.700968	0.700974	0.822824	0.822830	0.499075	0.500000
0.055000	0.700968	0.700974	0.822824	0.822830	0.498005	0.500000
0.077500	0.700968	0.700974	0.822891	0.822830	0.497585	0.500000
0.100000	0.700968	0.700974	0.822880	0.822830	0.500659	0.500000
0.325000	0.700968	0.700974	0.822803	0.822830	0.498799	0.500000
0.550000	0.579345	0.580390	0.000000	0.000000	0.500176	0.500000
0.775000	0.419074	0.419610	0.000000	0.000000	0.499978	0.500000
1.000000	0.338548	0.339221	0.000000	0.000000	0.500333	0.500000

The adopted *ResNet-50* model was trained with sets 1 and 2, it took 3.5 h to be trained. Also, the tuned models of set 3, 4, and 5 were trained using the learning rates recommended by the MCDM-based system. The training and testing accuracies for each model are presented in Table 8.

The EANN-based drug recommendation system was built with the same approach used for building the existing ANN-based system, where the testing set was used and the enhanced models were used to predict whether the review of each drug is positive or negative. After that, the drug recommendation scores were determined using Eqs. 1 and 2. Upon using the enhanced models of sets 1 and 2, the number of correctly predicted drug reviews increased by 0.015% and 6.93%, respectively. As for using the tuned models of sets 3, 4, and 5, the number of correctly predicted drug reviews increased by 1.62%, 2.19%, and 5.68%,

Table 3. Evaluation metrics for the neural network model of set 4.

Learning Rate	Accuracy	Val. Accuracy	F1-score	Val. F1-score	AUC	Val. AUC
0.000100	0.707895	0.707825	0.819531	0.824721	0.571309	0.576310
0.000325	0.725576	0.719992	0.828115	0.825536	0.639296	0.630384
0.000550	0.712787	0.712097	0.824718	0.825621	0.653152	0.647808
0.000775	0.705113	0.704523	0.824041	0.823714	0.524718	0.525378
0.001000	0.705339	0.704696	0.823329	0.824097	0.527495	0.529525
0.003250	0.700968	0.700974	0.822873	0.822830	0.498420	0.500000
0.005500	0.700968	0.700974	0.822856	0.822830	0.498719	0.500000
0.007750	0.700968	0.700974	0.822863	0.822830	0.498494	0.500000
0.010000	0.700968	0.700974	0.822896	0.822830	0.496953	0.500000
0.032500	0.700968	0.700974	0.822824	0.822830	0.499075	0.500000
0.055000	0.700968	0.700974	0.822824	0.822830	0.498005	0.500000
0.077500	0.700968	0.700974	0.822891	0.822830	0.497585	0.500000
0.100000	0.700968	0.700974	0.822880	0.822830	0.500659	0.500000
0.325000	0.700968	0.700974	0.822803	0.822830	0.498799	0.500000
0.550000	0.579345	0.580390	0.000000	0.000000	0.500176	0.500000
0.775000	0.419074	0.419610	0.000000	0.000000	0.499978	0.500000
1.000000	0.338548	0.339221	0.000000	0.000000	0.500333	0.500000

Table 4. Evaluation metrics for neural network model of set 5.

Learning Rate	Accuracy	Val. Accuracy	F1-score	Val. F1-score	AUC	Val. AUC
0.000100	0.838508	0.807534	0.888753	0.867121	0.873301	0.831562
0.000325	0.807120	0.782502	0.873845	0.856822	0.781992	0.749700
0.000550	0.793004	0.767415	0.867733	0.850222	0.743144	0.714610
0.000775	0.828083	0.798694	0.883275	0.861546	0.847824	0.810741
0.001000	0.804593	0.779943	0.872278	0.856313	0.785532	0.754708
0.003250	0.772187	0.757371	0.855967	0.845534	0.700156	0.683673
0.005500	0.738165	0.734215	0.839589	0.837350	0.610726	0.608927
0.007750	0.746303	0.742966	0.836790	0.838957	0.659419	0.641353
0.010000	0.700968	0.700974	0.822843	0.822830	0.500176	0.500000
0.032500	0.700968	0.700974	0.822898	0.822830	0.497776	0.500000
0.055000	0.700968	0.700974	0.822896	0.822830	0.501283	0.500000
0.077500	0.700968	0.700974	0.822881	0.822830	0.498832	0.500000
0.100000	0.700968	0.700974	0.822835	0.822830	0.500879	0.500000
0.325000	0.700968	0.700974	0.822899	0.822830	0.498846	0.500000
0.550000	0.700968	0.700974	0.822896	0.822830	0.499606	0.500000
0.775000	0.700619	0.700974	0.822075	0.822830	0.500727	0.500000
1.000000	0.700167	0.700974	0.820900	0.822830	0.498300	0.500000

Table 5. MCDM scores of the neural network model of set 3.

Learning Rate	WSM	WPM	TOPSIS	PROMETHEE	Recommendation Score
0.000100	1.831601	1.817282	0.899139	0.752418	1.224996
0.000325	1.968995	1.968401	0.978641	1.000000	1.395550
0.000550	1.988629	1.988584	0.984502	0.992263	**1.401959**
0.000775	1.732634	1.687937	0.845835	0.748549	1.166520
0.001000	1.739657	1.697879	0.849401	0.802708	1.191270
0.003250	1.677247	1.606979	0.819071	0.297872	0.900512
0.005500	1.677531	1.607434	0.819216	0.297872	0.900654
0.007750	1.677316	1.607091	0.819107	0.297872	0.900547
0.010000	1.675842	1.604732	0.818354	0.297872	0.899812
0.032500	1.677867	1.607973	0.819388	0.309478	0.909471
0.055000	1.676840	1.606338	0.818865	0.239845	0.852841
0.077500	1.676448	1.605703	0.818663	0.297872	0.900114
0.100000	1.679398	1.610383	0.820166	0.402321	0.971940
0.325000	1.677598	1.607548	0.819252	0.274662	0.882006
0.550000	1.254203	1.218896	0.290087	0.050290	0.386444
0.775000	1.086742	1.082194	0.110528	0.007737	0.178081
1.000000	1.003246	1.003216	0.003290	0.000000	0.000000

Table 6. MCDM scores of the neural network model of set 4.

Learning Rate	WSM	WPM	TOPSIS	PROMETHEE	Recommendation Score
0.000100	1.917935	1.914635	0.929648	0.932710	1.335815
0.000325	1.999192	1.999192	0.997519	1.000000	**1.413050**
0.000550	1.929519	1.927100	0.938934	0.842991	1.309793
0.000775	1.819872	1.811023	0.868955	0.435514	1.056796
0.001000	1.786407	1.764130	0.836908	0.671028	1.153406
0.003250	1.659935	1.592076	0.759743	0.325234	0.898937
0.005500	1.659192	1.590895	0.759289	0.314019	0.890687
0.007750	1.659254	1.590992	0.759327	0.358879	0.920957
0.010000	1.661639	1.594748	0.760784	0.437383	0.969032
0.032500	1.662532	1.596156	0.761330	0.448598	0.975706
0.055000	1.662695	1.596412	0.761429	0.437383	0.969644
0.077500	1.660121	1.592371	0.759857	0.325234	0.899037
0.100000	1.662622	1.596298	0.761384	0.437383	0.969602
0.325000	1.661430	1.594439	0.760657	0.325234	0.899743
0.550000	1.242446	1.209742	0.208719	0.037383	0.329080
0.775000	1.124400	1.115315	0.114091	0.074766	0.321602
1.000000	1.003095	1.003068	0.004322	0.000000	0.000000

respectively. Therefore, the recommendation scores generated by the drug recommendation system are 3.29% more accurate. A sample of the recommendation
scores of the optimized system in addition to a sample of those of the existing

Table 7. MCDM scores of the neural network model of set 5.

Learning Rate	WSM	WPM	TOPSIS	PROMETHEE	Recommendation Score
0.000100	2.000000	2.000000	1.000000	1.000000	**1.414214**
0.000325	1.766296	1.766273	0.757344	0.833935	1.184777
0.000550	1.650317	1.650128	0.651121	0.711191	1.059701
0.000775	1.917751	1.917650	0.932127	0.927798	1.335434
0.001000	1.756333	1.756310	0.764644	0.805054	1.173878
0.003250	1.528314	1.528254	0.542418	0.638989	0.948547
0.005500	1.302209	1.302024	0.310013	0.505415	0.717930
0.007750	1.363771	1.362205	0.417493	0.555957	0.810342
0.010000	1.006413	1.006366	0.005384	0.148014	0.168551
0.032500	1.005577	1.005525	0.003197	0.137184	0.145111
0.055000	1.006972	1.006923	0.007147	0.212996	0.198214
0.077500	1.005960	1.005911	0.003716	0.126354	0.147642
0.100000	1.006677	1.006630	0.006464	0.158845	0.179601
0.325000	1.006005	1.005955	0.003747	0.180505	0.161750
0.550000	1.006302	1.006253	0.004622	0.158845	0.165120
0.775000	1.004432	1.004413	0.005696	0.079422	0.146164
1.000000	1.000209	1.000209	0.000957	0.000000	0.000000

system are presented in Table 9. It can be noticed that the difference between the scores is slight. On average, the recommendation scores changed by 0.18%.

With the tuned models, the EANN-based recommender system has an average training accuracy of 98.28%, and an average testing accuracy of 98.09%. The values of the system's precision, recall, and F1-score, in addition to their percentages of improvement over the existing systems are summarized in Table 10. The results show that optimizing the system proposed in [2] is effective.

Table 8. Training and testing accuracies of the enhanced models.

Set No.	No. of Epochs	Training Accuracy	Testing Accuracy
1	50	0.9980	0.9983
2	46	0.9981	0.9988
3	457	0.9608	0.9639
4	423	0.9692	0.9549
5	500	0.9879	0.9886

Table 9. Samples of the recommender system results.

Condition	Drug Name	Recommendation Score (EANN System)	Recommendation Score (Existing System [2])
Anemia	Epoetin Alfa	0.003098373	0.003098373
	Procrit	0.00929512	0.0116189
	Oxymetholone	0.0116189	0.00929512
Anxiety	Alprazolam	26.43377227	26.21688613
	Atarax	2.597986057	2.430673896
	Bupropion	3.309837335	3.206041828
	Clorazepate	1.45236251	1.402788536
Asthma	Decadron	0.0580945	0.0464756
	Triamcinolone	0.00929512	0.0116189

Table 10. Evaluation metrics of the EANN-based system and their percentage of improvement over those of existing systems.

Evaluation Metric	EANN-Based Model	Percentage of Improvement Over the XGBOOST-Based Model [18] (%)	Percentage of Improvement Over the Neural Network-Based Model [2] (%)
Precision	98.39%	4.08%	3.95%
Recall	98.89%	3.94%	3.48%
F1-score	98.64%	4.017%	3.72%

6 Conclusion

This paper details the optimization of a neural network-based recommender system for drug recommendations. The optimization involved replacing *AlexNet* with *ResNet-50*, which offers improved performance, and fine-tuning the feedforward neural network models. This tuning process utilized a MCDM-based approach. Results from this study confirm that the optimized system surpasses the performance of similar existing systems. Future directions for this research include extracting additional features using various NLP techniques, such as intent analysis and emotion detection, and implementing more efficient deep learning models.

References

1. Abdullah, L., Chan, W.: Application of PROMETHEE method for green supplier selection: a comparative result based on preference functions. J. Ind. Eng. Int. **15** (2018). https://doi.org/10.1007/s40092-018-0289-z
2. AlMubasher, H., Doughan, Z., Sliman, L., Haidar, A.M.: A novel neural network-based recommender system for drug recommendation. In: Iliadis, L., Maglogiannis, I., Alonso, S., Jayne, C., Pimenidis, E. (eds.) EANN 2023. CCIS, vol. 1826, pp. 573–584. Springer, Cham (2023). https://doi.org/10.1007/978-3-031-34204-2_46
3. Asani, E., Vahdat-Nejad, H., Sadri, J.: Restaurant recommender system based on sentiment analysis. Mach. Learn. Appl. **6**, 100114 (2021)
4. Benamara, F., Taboada, M., Mathieu, Y.: Evaluative language beyond bags of words: linguistic insights and computational applications. Comput. Linguist. **43**(1), 201–264 (2017). https://doi.org/10.1162/COLI_a_00278
5. Birjali, M., Kasri, M., Beni-Hssane, A.: A comprehensive survey on sentiment analysis: approaches, challenges and trends. Knowl.-Based Syst. **226**, 107134 (2021). https://doi.org/10.1016/j.knosys.2021.107134
6. Carrington, A.M., et al.: Deep roc analysis and AUC as balanced average accuracy to improve model selection, understanding and interpretation. arXiv preprint arXiv:2103.11357 (2021)
7. Churchill, R., Singh, L.: The evolution of topic modeling. ACM Comput. Surv. **54**(10s) (2022). https://doi.org/10.1145/3507900
8. Di Gennaro, G., Buonanno, A., Palmieri, F.A.: Considerations about learning word2vec. J. Supercomput. 1–16 (2021)
9. Doughan, Z., Al Mubasher, H., Sliman, L., Haidar, A.: A multiple criteria decision making-based recommender system for neural network learning rate initialization [unpublished]. SSRN (2023). https://doi.org/10.2139/ssrn.4500557
10. Grm, K., Štruc, V., Artiges, A., Caron, M., Ekenel, H.K.: Strengths and weaknesses of deep learning models for face recognition against image degradations. IET Biomet. **7**(1), 81–89 (2017) https://doi.org/10.1049/iet-bmt.2017.0083, http://dx.doi.org/10.1049/iet-bmt.2017.0083
11. Guo, Q., Zhang, C., Zhang, Y., Liu, H.: An efficient SVD-based method for image denoising. IEEE Trans. Circuits Syst. Video Technol. **26**(5), 868–880 (2015)
12. He, K., Zhang, X., Ren, S., Sun, J.: Deep residual learning for image recognition (2015)
13. Isinkaye, F., Folajimi, Y., Ojokoh, B.: Recommendation systems: principles, methods and evaluation. Egypt. Inform. J. **16**(3), 261–273 (2015). https://doi.org/10.1016/j.eij.2015.06.005
14. Katarya, R., Arora, Y.: Capsmf: a novel product recommender system using deep learning based text analysis model. Multimed. Tools Appl. **79**(47), 35927–35948 (2020)
15. Krizhevsky, A., Sutskever, I., Hinton, G.E.: ImageNet classification with deep convolutional neural networks. In: Pereira, F., Burges, C., Bottou, L., Weinberger, K. (eds.) Advances in Neural Information Processing Systems, vol. 25. Curran Associates, Inc. (2012). https://proceedings.neurips.cc/paper/2012/file/c399862d3b9d6b76c8436e924a68c45b-Paper.pdf
16. Krohling, R., Pacheco, A.: Information technology and quantitative management (ITQM 2015) a-TOPSIS - an approach based on TOPSIS for ranking evolutionary algorithms. In: ITQM, vol. 55, pp. 308–317 (2015).https://doi.org/10.1016/j.procs.2015.07.054

17. Li, J., Sun, A., Han, J., Li, C.: A survey on deep learning for named entity recognition. IEEE Trans. Knowl. Data Eng. **34**(1), 50–70 (2022). https://doi.org/10.1109/TKDE.2020.2981314
18. Marshetty, R.: Drug recommendation system (2022). https://medium.com/@marshettyruthvik/drug-recommendation-system-1b32d1cda680
19. Mohiuddin, M., Islam, M.S., Islam, S., Miah, M.S., Niu, M.B.: Intelligent fault diagnosis of rolling element bearings based on modified AlexNet. Sensors **23**(18) (2023). https://doi.org/10.3390/s23187764, https://www.mdpi.com/1424-8220/23/18/7764
20. Omar, H.K., Frikha, M., Jumaa, A.K.: Big data cloud-based recommendation system using NLP techniques with machine and deep learning. TELKOMNIKA (Telecommun. Comput. Electron. Control) **21**(5), 1076–1083 (2023)
21. Rahman, S.S.M.M., Biplob, K.B.M.B., Rahman, M.H., Sarker, K., Islam, T.: An investigation and evaluation of N-gram, TF-IDF and ensemble methods in sentiment classification. In: Bhuiyan, T., Rahman, M.M., Ali, M.A. (eds.) ICONCS 2020. LNICST, vol. 325, pp. 391–402. Springer, Cham (2020). https://doi.org/10.1007/978-3-030-52856-0_31
22. Ray, B., Garain, A., Sarkar, R.: An ensemble-based hotel recommender system using sentiment analysis and aspect categorization of hotel reviews. Appl. Soft Comput. **98**, 106935 (2021)
23. Repository, U.I.M.L.: UCI machine learning repository: drug review dataset (drugs.com) data set. https://archive.ics.uci.edu/ml/datasets/Drug+Review+Dataset+%28Drugs.com%29
24. Shao, M., Han, Z., Sun, J., Xiao, C., Zhang, S., Zhao, Y.: A review of multi-criteria decision making applications for renewable energy site selection. Renew. Energy **157**, 377–403 (2020). https://doi.org/10.1016/j.renene.2020.04.137, https://www.sciencedirect.com/science/article/pii/S0960148120306753
25. Shimray, B.: A survey of multi-criteria decision making technique used in renewable energy planning. Int. J. Comput. (IJC) **25**, 124–140 (2017)
26. Tabassum, A., Patil, R.R.: A survey on text pre-processing & feature extraction techniques in natural language processing. Int. Res. J. Eng. Technol. (IRJET) **7**(06), 4864–4867 (2020)
27. Xie, Y.: Improve text classification accuracy with intent information (2022). https://doi.org/10.48550/ARXIV.2212.07649
28. Zhang, S., Yao, L., Sun, A., Tay, Y.: Deep learning based recommender system: a survey and new perspectives. ACM Comput. Surv. **52**(1) (2019). https://doi.org/10.1145/3285029

Automation of the Error-Prone Pam-4 Sequence Discovery for the Purpose of High-Speed Serial Receiver Testing Using Reinforcement Learning Methods

Manav Madan[1]($\boxtimes$)(iD), Christoph Reich[1](iD), Anton Unakafov[2],
Valentina Unakafova[2], and Alexander Schmitt[2]

[1] Institute for Data Science, Cloud Computing, and IT Security, Furtwangen
University, Furtwangen, Germany
{manav.madan,christoph.reich}@hs-furtwangen.de
[2] BitifEye Digital Test Solutions GmbH, Herrenberger Str. 130, 71034 Böblingen,
Germany

Abstract. In modern high-speed serial communications (PCIe 6.0, Terabit Ethernet, etc.), pam-4 (pulse amplitude modulation 4-level) signaling is frequently used. pam-4 encodes two bits of data using four different voltage levels. Compared to conventional NRZ (non-return-to-zero) encoding, which employs two voltage levels to represent one bit of information, pam-4 is a more effective technique to convey data. However, not every pam-4 sequence is equally easy to reconstruct at the receiver, and some sequences are more error-prone than others. Traditionally, worst-case sequences are identified analytically or numerically in terms of susceptibility to certain impairments, like jitter or intersymbol interference, but such methods do not provide reliable prediction of the errors at the receiver. An alternative is the data-driven identification of the error-prone sequences, and in this paper, we utilize RL (reinforcement learning) for this task. In total, we compare six different RL algorithms. The utilized algorithms are Q-Learning, MAB (Multi-Armed Bandit), MCTS (Monte Carlo Tree Search), DQN (Deep Q Learning), A2C (Advantage Actor Critic), and PPO (Proximal Policy Optimization). Almost all algorithms have their limits to the length of the sequences they can learn. However, our experiments show that higher scalability leads to high memory requirements, especially in the case of MCTS and MAB.

Keywords: SerDes · Reinforcement Learning · Sequence Discovery · Receiver Test Automation · ML · High-speed serial · pam-4

1 Introduction

High-speed serial (HSS) communications are essential for many modern applications, such as artificial intelligence, streaming video, and cloud computing [8].

Supported by the Ministry of Economic Affairs, Labor and Tourism Baden-Württemberg.

The pam-4 (pulse amplitude modulation 4-level) is used today in many HSS systems to boost the data rate beyond 30 Gb/s per lane [20,27]. A pam-4 signal has four different levels, where each level corresponds to the transmission of two bits [21]. Data transferred by means of pam-4 is represented by symbols 0, 1, 2 and 3. To achieve an efficient HSS receiver design these systems undergo testing to ensure reliable operation at high data rates. Apart from simple counting of the erroneously received symbols, receiver testing may involve analysis of symbol sequence triggering errors [25]. The test sequences that are used are quite long as they cover various aspects, including jitter tolerance, eye diagram analysis, and error rate measurements but the length usually varies with specific requirements and standards. One example is the PRBS13Q which is 8191 symbols long [1].

The test sequences contain sub-sequences having a high probability of causing an error called as problematic sub-sequences (PSSs). These subsequences can be found in compliant problematic sequences (CPS) or test sequences that are used for compliance testing to stress the receiver and expose potential weaknesses. Analysis of PSSs can increase the reliability of the receiver testing and identify receiver design problems. PSS's depend on the specific parameters of the receiver that is tested and the environment in which the receiver will be used. Due to many factors influencing the different PSS's, their identification is a complex problem. Recently, rather than the traditional manual methods, different RL (reinforcement learning) and ML (machine learning) algorithms have been used for HSS modeling and system design optimization [12,13].

However, different RL methods for pam-4 sequence generation and identification of sub-sequences haven't been studied extensively. Therefore, the motivation behind this work was to check if the signal used for testing which is generally a pseudorandom binary sequence (PRBS) can be replaced with a RL generated signal. For this, a comparison of different RL algorithms has been made for the purpose of pam-4 sequence discovery which can then be used as a test signal.

2   Related Works

Existing works on identification of the data sequences that are problematic for a HSS receiver focus on the sequences that are worst-case in terms of susceptibility to a single clearly defined signal impairment, like intersymbol interference [6] or data dependent jitter [5]. In contrast to these tasks, identification of the sequences that are likely to cause a receiver error, cannot be done analytically and requires extensive analysis of error distribution, for example, by ML or RL methods. As a starting point for identifying PSS's we considered the standard sequences such as PRBSQ (Pseudo-Random Binary Sequence) or SSPRQ (short stress pattern random quaternary), commonly used for testing and development pam-4 HSS receivers [2,4,14].

2.1   Challenges and Applications of HSS Receiver Testing

While reliable communication requires data transmission with low error rate, the challenges associated with introduction of multi-level signaling schemes like pam-4 made errors in received data unavoidable. Consequently, modern HSS Physical layer specifications (PCIe 6.0, Terabit Ethernet, etc.), allow compliant receivers to perform with Symbol Error Ratios (SERs) as high as 1E−4. This high error ratio should be reduced by the Forward Error Correction.

With SER of 1E−4 and baud rates above 20 GBd, thousands of errors can take place in just one second, which allows identification of the subsequences that most frequently cause errors at Receiver Under Test (Problematic Symbol Subsequences, PSS's). Idea of such identification through statistical analysis was first formulated in [24,25], here we consider possible implementation of this concept.

2.2 RL and ML Based Solutions

This work focuses on solving this problem with RL. Past attempts in this direction can be summarized as follows. The authors in [20] discuss the challenges and opportunities in developing ML-assisted design frameworks for HSS links. Authors in [12] use generative adversarial networks (GANs) to model high-speed receivers. They assessed the performance of the suggested technique in a real-world scenario where it resulted in a precise and optimized receiver. Additionally, in the study by [17], ML methods are examined for their potential to produce the best signals possible for quasi-coherent optical communication systems employing low-cost hardware. The authors provide a reinforcement learning workflow that can be trained to produce sequences that increase system bit-rate by 20% while lowering the error rate. Towards the general use case of RL for sequence discovery the authors [19] propose a new method for sequence discovery using deep reinforcement learning (DRL). In the proposed method, a DRL agent is trained to generate sequences that optimize a given objective function. The authors evaluated the proposed method on a variety of sequence discovery tasks, including machine translation, protein design, and music composition but not related to HSS communications. The development of intelligent systems can be revolutionized by the use of DRL. The authors in [3] provide a thorough survey on RL and DRL.

3   Background Material and Environment Design

The setup of a test environment for a HSS receiver consists of many sequential processes. Some of the blocks involved in the test are the generator, encoder, channel, and device under test (DUT). The generator produces a sequence of symbol, which is then sent to the DUT via the channel [21] as shown in Fig. 1. Ultimately, at the DUT the SER is calculated and it is evaluated whether the sequence was received correctly [2]. Our work does not emphasize on the other processes involved in the test environment but rather focuses on how to use the RL for the generation process. The design of other components of receiver testing is a separate domain more on which can be found in the work by [26].

Fig. 1. A simple block diagram illustrating the test environment of a HSS receiver.

PAM4 sample error sequences
303010130100221101113010333002011232201
211212103112133320131002323112301221313
030013001111333000031212233233311101200
022332100302311130232231312310200310203
321211111102021120330302022002223230021
223212023213102301010031112113310303020
200213232012221201302232321213333320313
301210030200203302213213232311110303101
303021113212211130300013133110130122302
211210200133323132220301302322011221221

PSS	Index
130	18
3131	36
1111	8
3210	4
12033030	15
0303	32
01302	21
01313	21

Fig. 2. Defining error sequences in a lookup table with corresponding shorter PSS's, the position is also recorded in the table.

3.1 Sequences for HSS Receiver Testing

In general, a variety of test sequences should be used to get a more complete picture of the HSS receiver's performance [2]. Error sequences can be independent in their entirety or they can contain dependencies in themselves as small patterns. These smaller error patterns are called problematic sub-sequences (PSS's). An error sequence would thus be atomic if it cannot be divided into further individual PSS's. An example of a test PRBS sequence of length 64 generated by MATLAB PRBS generator [16] is as follows:

– Sequence s1: 3, 3, 3, 0, 0, 2, 0, 0, 3, 0, 2, 2, 0, 3, 3, 2, 0, 2, 3, 0, 1, 2, 2, 1, 3, 1, 3, 0, 3, 2, 2, 2, 3, 3, 1, 0, 0, 1, 0, 2, 1, 0, 1, 1, 2, 3, 1, 1, 0, 3, 1, 2, 0, 1, 3, 2, 3, 2, 1, 2, 1, 1, 1, 0

In the sample sequence s1, the PSS's could be sequences that are smaller than the actual sequence but are contained in the original sequence. An example might be the sub-sequence (3, 3, 3) starting at the starting position that might cause an error resulting in higher error rate. The goal of this work is to use RL for finding either as many PSS's as possible in a given sequence or finding specific individual sequences of pam-4 Symbols.

For solving this task with RL a list of predefined sequences could be used as shown in Fig. 2. If one assumes a maximum error sequence of 40 symbols, one obtains $4^{40} = 1.2089258196146E{+}24$ possible combinations. This shows that not all sequences can be tested and the knowledge about error causing behavior of some sequences such as PSS's allows the simplification of the definition of an environment as it is shown in Fig. 2.

The goal of this work is to evaluate whether different PSS's can be learned and joined together to form a sequence using RL. The learned PSS's can later be used to create test sequences where more PSS's are present in order to quickly find design errors in HSS receivers through the use of such adapted sequences.

Tested PSS's Sequences. In order to evaluate whether sub-patterns i.e., the PSS's can be learned, two different types of definitions for PSS's were created. These are shown in the Table 1.

Table 1. Example for the types of PSS's searched in sequences.

Example	Explanation
.....0000...	A single PSS of length four is designated at a certain position in the whole sequence and index is noted. But there is only one PSS in the whole sequence
...0000, 1111, 2222 and etc.	Multiple PSS's of length four were designated in one sequence and their index were noted. This was done in order to check whether different PSS's can be recognized in the same sequence

3.2 Basics of Reinforcement Learning (RL)

Reinforcement learning (RL) is a sub-category of machine learning (ML) that enables systems (agents) to learn how to carry out tasks by interacting with their surroundings through earning rewards [22]. As shown in Fig. 3, the agent chooses actions (a_t) and monitors the states (s_t) and rewards (r_t) that ensue. The agent's objective is to maximize reward through optimal action selection and environments provide the feedback in terms of the next state and reward. RL agents are frequently trained in a simulated setting. After training, the agent can be used in a real-world setting.

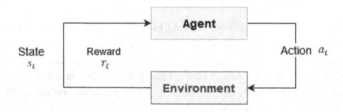

Fig. 3. RL framework consisting of an agent and an environment.

RL problems can usually be solved in different ways. In general, one of these three solution approaches can be chosen and learned first, Value Function ($V^\pi(s)$), Strategy (Policy, π) and lastly learning the internal environment model. Furthermore, the RL algorithms can be classified as value-based, policy-based, or model-based algorithms [22]. Other than the individual categories there also exists overlap between the categories, e.g. value-based and policy-based methods that can be combined to exploit the strengths of both methods [10].

3.3   RL Environment and Simulated Sequences

As mentioned before, the individual sequences independent of each other and error sequences with position-dependent PSS's were used for the investigation of different RL algorithms. The types of PSS's were described in Table 1, however to be able to better distinguish them with the whole sequences, the following identifications are introduced for sequences and their related environments:

- Complete Independent Fault Sequence Environment (CIF): From a list of sequences find some specific sequence or sequences. These are independent or individual sequences that cannot be further split.
- Index-based PSS Feedback (IPF) environment: An environment that searches for index-dependent single PSS from a list of sequences and returns a single reward as an acknowledgment to the agent. The count of PSS's is not considered.
- Index-based PSS counter environment (IPC): In a given test sequence, the contained position-fixed PSS's are counted. The reward level depends on the number of PSS's. This is for checking if we can find multiple PSS's at the same time.

In finding a solution to the sequence discovery or sequence generation problem, the so-called sparse reward and stochastic nature of HSS receiver testing represents a particular challenge. Sparse rewards are a much-noticed and important problem of RL which is described as in scenarios where rewards are very rarely generated during the learning process. In other words, the environment gives very little positive feedback back to the agent. This behavior makes it difficult for the agent to make optimal decisions initially. Stochastic environment setting represents challenges of HSS receiver testing where the execution of an error sequence does not always lead to an error. The errors observed are probabilistic in nature. These two points are taken into consideration for designing the test environments for different RL algorithms.

4   Algorithms and Experiments

4.1   Algorithms Overview

Reinforcement learning (RL) algorithms enable agents to learn from experience and make optimal decisions in complex environments. These algorithms can be categorized based on their learning approach (model-free or model-based), policy updates (on-policy or off-policy), and the focus on policy or value function optimization. The algorithms used in this work are as following:

Q-Learning: Q-learning is a model-free reinforcement learning algorithm that learns an action-value function (Q-function) to evaluate the expected reward for taking a given action in a given state, and updates the Q-table iteratively to estimate the expected reward for performing an action in a specific state [23]. The agent learns to make decisions that result in larger rewards by making updates to the Q-table.

Deep Q Learning (DQN): DQN is also a model-free algorithm, can be seen as an improvement in Q-learning, as it makes use of a neural network to approximate the Q-function. DQN is an approximation of dynamic programming (ADP) [7]. The primary distinction between DQN and Q-learning is that the latter is unable to handle the much bigger and more intricate state spaces than the former. This is so that DQN can capture more intricate links between states as it can learn a distributed representation of the state space.

Multi Armed Bandit (MAB): The MAB algorithm is a classic model-free algorithm in which an agent must choose from K actions with unknown reward distributions to maximize reward over time. It is a single-state algorithm where the agent makes one decision per time step, similar to slot machines. Each action (test sequence) is represented by a slot machine, and the agent must determine which lever to pull to maximize its reward [18]. Under the MAB, the ϵ-Greedy procedure is used for this work [22].

Monte Carlo Tree Search (MCTS): MCTS is a model-based RL algorithm that chooses actions by combining Monte Carlo simulation and tree search. MCTS is a powerful algorithm because it is able to explore a large number of possible actions and select the action that is most likely to lead to a high reward [15]. The RL agent in MCTS learns the value of different actions in a given state of the environment and these values can be described as a policy.

Advantage Actor Critic (A2C): A2C is a policy gradient algorithm commonly used in RL. It is an actor-critic method, which means that it learns both a policy and a value function [9]. Policies are used to select actions, and value functions are used to estimate the expected reward of performing a particular action. The policy is explicitly represented by a neural network that takes the current state of the environment as input and outputs a probability distribution over possible actions. This policy network is trained to maximize the expected cumulative reward of the agent's actions over time.

Proximal Policy Optimization (PPO): PPO is another policy gradient algorithm that is similar to A2C [9]. However, PPO uses a different update rule designed to improve the stability of the learning process. The policy is represented by a neural network that takes the current state as input and outputs a probability distribution over actions. PPO addresses challenges of policy gradient methods, such as high variance and large destabilizing policy updates. It uses the trust region optimization technique to constrain policy updates within a limit, preventing excessive changes at each update.

A detailed overview on all these algorithms can be found in the following work [9,15,18].

4.2   Experiment Design

To combine and compare such different algorithms for the use case, adaptations were made in the experiment setup. Another thing to note is that in this work the RL environments did not model the behavior of the receiver. The only goal was to check if sequences with certain properties could be generated or not. In this section, it is explained what different adaptations were made for faster experimentation.

Firstly, the problem of sequence discovery dictates that the algorithms for continuous state and action spaces can be neglected. The selection of symbols for a test sequence has only a discrete set of values i.e., 0, 1, 2, and 3 which can be selected. For further simplification, binary values 0 and 1 can be used for designing the experiments which later could be adapted for symbols (0,1,2, and 3). In some cases, the binary values were used for experimentation to reduce computation time. Wherever this is the case it will mentioned with the algorithm.

Secondly, the sparse reward [11] condition poses an additional challenge, as the environment provides little positive feedback to the agent until the end sequence is reached. This makes it difficult for the agent to make optimal decisions, as the reward tends towards zero during evaluation, requiring long learning times to generate any rewards. To address this, a solution is to combine individual actions into partial sequence groups for evaluation, rather than relying on single-action assessments which can be time-consuming and yield low rewards. Combination creates artificial state chains in which states based on the positions of the partial sequences can be then further combined and jointly evaluated. This procedure is illustrated in Fig. 4. Starting from the starting state S0, in which no sequence group has yet been selected, the next following subsequences are selected as actions. Wherever such joint partial sequences are used this information will also be mentioned. Even with such adaptations, the developed sequences adhere to the environments defined in Sect. 3.3 i.e., the RL algorithms were tested with position-dependent partial sequences (IPF and IPC) and independently atomic error sequences (CIF).

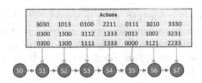

Fig. 4. Division of sequences into partial sequence groups for the construction of error sequences.

Now, the individual setup for each algorithm is described (Table 2).

Table 2. Summary of algorithms

Algorithm	Sequences Generation summary	Remarks
Q-Learning	Bit sequences of length 7 were generated. The environment used was CIF as described in Sect. 3.3 where whole sequences are evaluated to check whether interesting sequences can be learnt by comparing them from a list of predefined sequence database. In the database, sequences were saved with labels 0 and 1 indicating whether there are any PSS's present or not. Example of sequences are shown in following Table. | Example sequence	label
---	---
...00..00	0
...00..01	0
...00..10	1		The RL agent has to learn how to generate sequences by choosing bits from a set of 0, 1. Once the Q-table is learned the best actions are fixed and are deterministic.
MAB	Symbol sequences tested were of length 16. The action space for MAB was defined of length 8 which means that total 4^8 levers (individual test sequences). Two actions were joined to generate a single sequence of length 16. All three environment described in Sect. 3.3 [CIF, IPF and IPC] were used for testing the algorithm (MAB with ϵ-Greedy)	The RL agent does both generation (combining two actions, where action represent chosen lever) and discovery as two actions (length 8) are joined to form a single sequence which is then evaluated.
MCTS	Symbol sequences of length 40 were tested. The root state represents the start state. Subsequent states are reached by selecting an action. The environment used was IPF and IPC as described in Sect. 3.3 within which the position of PSS's and the count is noted.	The RL agent has to learn which path to follow (policy) and learn the Q-values for each node. A single node of the tree represents a sub-sequence of length 4 (0011, 0010, 0000, and etc.) which is selected from an empty root node to reach the next state until the 10th node to give a final sequence of 40.
DQN	Symbol sequences tested were of length 40. The environment used was IPF and IPC as described in Sect. 3.3. In environment IPC the found PSS's are counted and returned as a reward and in IPF case it is checked whether the generated sequence contains at least one PSS and then returns a confirmation in the form of a reward with the value 1. Example of sequences are shown in following Table. | Example Sequences	Reward
---	---
...02220000333311112222333	5
...30211100001113232112222	10		The RL agent has to learn how to generate sequences by choosing symbols as actions from a set of 0, 1, 2, 3. But the actions have probabilities rather than the deterministic values in Q-learning.

(continued)

Table 2. (*continued*)

Algorithm	Sequences Generation summary	Remarks
A2C	Symbol sequences of length 40 were tested. A total of ten PSS's with a length of four symbols were pre-defined and provided to the agent. The environment used was IPF and IPC as described in Sect. 3.3 within which the position of PSS's and the count is noted. The agent learns the Probability distribution for the next symbols or symbol groups in a way that most of the pre-defined PSS's are covered. Based on a sequence index, each possible action i.e. a symbol has a probability for its selection.	The RL agent will learn a policy to select the best action (symbol) at each time step. A positive reward of 1 for each occurrence of a PSS out of the pre-defined 10 is provided while giving a small negative reward for every non-important sub-sequence generated in the final sequence of 40.
PPO	Symbol sequences of length 40 were tested. A total of ten PSS's with a length of four symbols were pre-defined and provided to the agent. In contrast to A2C, PPO uses a single agent (a single NN) and with a surrogate objective function to update the policy, which helps to reduce the policy's variance. The environment used for testing the algorithm was IPF and IPC as described in Sect. 3.3 within which the position of PSS's and the count is noted.	The agent in PPO learns a stochastic policy that maps states to a probability distribution over actions. The optimization of the policy is performed by the policy gradient. A positive reward of 1 is provided every time the agent generates a sub-sequence that matches one of the important sub-sequences.

One thing to note is the different sequence lengths that have been tested with the algorithms. This variable was updated throughout the work as the aim was to generate sequences of length greater than thousands of symbols. Each algorithm was tested with a smaller number first to whether sub-sequences (PSS's) can be learned and also to evaluate the resources required for a larger sequence length.

5 Results

All the experiments were performed on a machine with 11th Gen Intel i7-1165G7 @ 2.80 GHz with 32 GB RAM. The approaches discussed in this work can be divided into classical approaches and Deep learning-based approaches. Classical approaches are those that learn the action-state interaction based on a fixed set of learnable values and these are Q-learning, MCTS, and MAB. These are particularly suitable for environments with manageable state and action spaces as it is evident from the results depicted in Table 3. Other than the A2C and Q-learning algorithm, generating a length of 40 sequences took a minimum of 1.15 h for PPO and 15 h for MCTS. On further evaluation with all the algorithms other than A2C, it was found that to generate a sequence of length 8191 (length of a PRBS13Q sequence) would take more than 15 h approximately which is not ideal when multiple sequences are required for testing a single receiver.

Experiments show that for classical approaches q-tables can become very large with the increase of sequence length, which means that for some states no Q-values can be further calculated implying that suitable actions for individual states will remain unknown. On the other hand, in deep learning based RL approaches the Value functions and policies are approximated by the neural network (NN), which allows one to learn how to act in complex environments. These approaches are Deep Q-learning, A2C, and PPO. NN employed in these algorithms can determine probabilities for actions in order to control the sequence construction through which multiple sequences can be generated. Furthermore, to check how PPO, A2C and DQN behave with increasing number of iterations, the IPC environment was selected. This is the environment that counts the PSS's. The results are depicted in Fig. 5 which show that A2C learns to recognize more PSS's quickly than the others.

Table 3. Overview of the results for RL algorithms used in symbol sequence generation problem.

Algorithm	Sequence Length	Learning duration
Q-Learning	7	15 min
MAB	16	3:10 h
MCTS	40	15 h
Deep Q-Learning	40	2:30 h
A2C	40	10 min
PPO	40	1:15 h

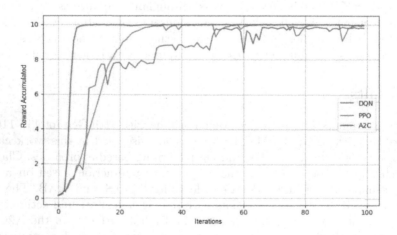

Fig. 5. Comparison of rewards accumulated over multiple iterations of the different Deep RL algorithms in the IPC counter environment.

6   Conclusion

Classical Solutions i.e., Q-learning, MAB, and MCTS, that have been presented in this work, do not use neural networks to make decisions about their actions in the RL paradigm. These approaches often only determine one solution path. This means that after training, only the same actions for specific states are used to generate the output sequences. Multiple sequences are required generally for specific testing of standards in HSS (High-speed serial) receivers beyond basic compliance for tasks such as stress and interoperability testing. Under stress testing, the receiver behavior is analyzed under worst-case scenarios with challenging patterns like high jitter content or extreme data transitions. Therefore a high degree of variation and stochasticity is needed in the sequence generation process. With classical approaches, it is often not possible to generate alternative sequences with variations that are needed for the actual testing of HSS receivers. On the other hand, the Neural network-based approaches can determine probabilities for actions to control the sequence construction due to which multiple sequences can be generated rather than just one. This behavior is desirable in the solution to obtain a higher variance and thus different sequences of interest.

To make sure that receivers used in HSS can accurately understand the data sent over the channel, conformance testing is an essential step. Variety in the symbol sequences employed in conformance testing is crucial. To find any vulnerabilities in the receiver's design, such as its sensitivity to particular data patterns or its susceptibility to noise and interference, it is helpful to test the receiver's ability to handle a range of data patterns, including those with a high degree of variation. As shown by our results, Neural network-based RL agents can be used to generate such sequences, which have the properties of variation, and statistical significance. However, the length of sequences offers a major challenge for RL-based solutions and this requires further research in this direction as described in related works the sequences required for testing are long (length = 8191 for PRBS13Q). It is clear from our experiments that RL might not be able to generate longer sequences in a reasonable time when the solution is built under real-time conditions.

Acknowledgements. The contents of this publication are taken from the research project "START - Self-Adapting Tool for Automated Receiver Test based on Artificial Intelligence". The major part of the experiments were done by Mr. Alexander Wagner in his master thesis at Hochschule Furtwangen (Summer Semster 2023). The project START is funded as a part of the Invest BW program by the Ministry of Economic Affairs, Labor and Tourism Baden-Württemberg.

References

1. PAM4 transmitter test challenges. https://harrisburg.psu.edu/files/pdf/16861/2019/05/06/tektronix_penn_state_si_april_12_2019.pdf. Accessed 26 Feb 2024
2. Arora, S., Aflaki, A., Biswas, S., Shimanouchi, M.: SERDES external loopback test using production parametric-test hardware. In: 2016 IEEE International Test Conference (ITC), pp. 1–7. IEEE (2016)

3. Arulkumaran, K., Deisenroth, M.P., Brundage, M., Bharath, A.A.: Deep reinforcement learning: a brief survey. IEEE Signal Process. Mag. **34**(6), 26–38 (2017)
4. Chang, F.: PAM4 signaling and its applications. In: Datacenter Connectivity Technologies: Principles and Practice, p. 279 (2018)
5. Dmitriev-Zdorov, V.: Determining worst-case bit patterns based upon data-dependent jitter (2016)
6. Dolatsara, M.A., Hejase, J.A., Becker, W.D., Kim, J., Lim, S.K., Swaminathan, M.: Worst-case eye analysis of high-speed channels based on Bayesian optimization. IEEE Trans. Electromagn. Compat. **63**(1), 246–258 (2020)
7. Fan, J., Wang, Z., Xie, Y., Yang, Z.: A theoretical analysis of deep Q-learning. In: Learning for Dynamics and Control, pp. 486–489. PMLR (2020)
8. Foley, D., Danskin, J.: Ultra-performance pascal GPU and NVLink interconnect. IEEE Micro **37**(2), 7–17 (2017)
9. Graesser, L., Keng, W.L.: Foundations of Deep Reinforcement Learning. Addison-Wesley Professional (2019)
10. Grondman, I., Busoniu, L., Lopes, G.A., Babuska, R.: A survey of actor-critic reinforcement learning: standard and natural policy gradients. IEEE Trans. Syst. Man Cybern. Part C (Appl. Rev.) **42**(6), 1291–1307 (2012)
11. Hare, J.: Dealing with sparse rewards in reinforcement learning. arXiv preprint arXiv:1910.09281 (2019)
12. Kashyap, P., et a.: RxGAN: modeling high-speed receiver through generative adversarial networks. In: Proceedings of the 2022 ACM/IEEE Workshop on Machine Learning for CAD, pp. 167–172 (2022)
13. Kim, J., et al.: Bayesian exploration imitation learning-based contextual via design optimization method of PAM-4-based high-speed serial link. IEEE Trans. Electromagn. Compatib. (2023)
14. Li, L.: Application of general map detection theory for pam signals to the analysis of TDECQ and SSPRQ. J. Lightwave Technol. **41**, 5942–5950 (2023)
15. Luo, F.M., Xu, T., Lai, H., Chen, X.H., Zhang, W., Yu, Y.: A survey on model-based reinforcement learning. arXiv preprint arXiv:2206.09328 (2022)
16. Matlab-PRBS: Pseudorandom binary sequence - MATLAB prbs - MathWorks Deutschland—de.mathworks.com. https://de.mathworks.com/help/serdes/ref/prbs.html. Accessed 18 Oct 2023
17. Ortiz Parra, C.: Machine Learning algorithms for optimal signal generation in a Quasi-Coherent system with cost-effective devices. Master's thesis, Universitat Politècnica de Catalunya (2021)
18. Plaat, A.: Deep reinforcement learning, a textbook. arXiv preprint arXiv:2201.02135 (2022)
19. Shao, Y., Liew, S.C., Wang, T.: AlphaSeq: sequence discovery with deep reinforcement learning. IEEE Trans. Neural Netw. Learn. Syst. **31**(9), 3319–3333 (2019)
20. Song, S., Sui, Y.: System level optimization for high-speed SERDES: background and the road towards machine learning assisted design frameworks. Electronics **8**(11), 1233 (2019)
21. Stauffer, D.R., et al.: High Speed SERDES Devices and Applications. Springer, Heidelberg (2008). https://doi.org/10.1007/978-0-387-79834-9
22. Sutton, R.S., Barto, A.G.: Reinforcement Learning: An Introduction. MIT Press, Cambridge (2018)
23. Tan, F., Yan, P., Guan, X.: Deep reinforcement learning: from Q-learning to deep Q-learning. In: Liu, D., Xie, S., Li, Y., Zhao, D., El-Alfy, E.S. (eds.) ICONIP 2017, Part IV. LNCS, vol. 10637, pp. 475–483. Springer, Cham (2017). https://doi.org/10.1007/978-3-319-70093-9_50

24. Unakafov, A., Koebele, W., Unakafova, V., Sanchez-Guerra, V.R., Stephens, R., Stehling, H.: Method, computer program product, test signal and test device for testing a data-transferring arrangement including a transmitter, channel and receiver (2022)
25. Unakafov, A., Unakafova, V., Deuchler, F., Raju, P., Stephens, R., Schmitt, A.: START: self-adapting tool for automated receiver testing - error analysis helps find failures in transmission link design. In: DesignCon (2024)
26. Xie, W., Cao, G., Ji, W.: Research on high-speed SERDES interface testing technology. In: 2021 22nd International Conference on Electronic Packaging Technology (ICEPT), pp. 1–5. IEEE (2021)
27. Zou, D., Song, K., Chen, Z., Zhu, C., Wu, T., Xu, Y.: FPGA-based configurable and highly flexible PAM4 SERDES simulation system. IEEE Trans. Very Large Scale Integr. (VLSI) Syst. **31**(9), 1294–1307 (2023). https://doi.org/10.1109/TVLSI.2023.3286803

Binary Black Hole Parameter Estimation from Gravitational Waves with Deep Learning Methods

Panagiotis N. Sakellariou$^{(\boxtimes)}$ and Spiros V. Georgakopoulos

Department of Mathematics, University of Thessaly, 3rd km. Old National Road,
Lamia-Athens, 35100 Lamia, Greece
{psakellariou,spirosgeorg}@uth.gr

Abstract. A new era in observational astrophysics has been inaugurated by the discovery of gravitational waves, offering a unique lens into celestial phenomena that are elusive to conventional electromagnetic detection. The potential of extracting vital parameters from gravitational waves emitted by Binary Black Hole systems is explored, leveraging the capabilities of Deep Learning Methods. A Convolutional Neural Network architecture is introduced in this work, specifically designed for the precise estimation of the masses and distances of Binary Black Hole systems. The effectiveness and robustness of the proposed architecture in accurately estimating these parameters is demonstrated. This research signifies a significant stride towards enhancing our understanding of Binary Black Hole phenomena and underscores the transformative role of Artificial Intelligence in observational astrophysics.

Keywords: Deep Learning · Neural Networks · Gravitational Waves · Black Holes · Parameter Estimation · Convolutional Neural Networks

1 Introduction

According to Einstein's general theory of relativity, "matter tells spacetime how to curve, and curved spacetime tells matter how to move". Events occurring between highly massive objects can distort spacetime, creating ripples known as gravitational waves. Despite being theorized in 1916, concrete evidence of gravitational waves emerged in 2015 when the Laser Interferometer Gravitational-Wave Observatory (LIGO) detected waves generated by colliding black holes 1.3 billion light-years away, marking the inception of Multimessenger Astrophysics. This field enables the identification of celestial objects without relying on electromagnetic radiation emissions.

Until now, the primary means of studying black holes involved theoretical mathematical models and computational simulations or observations of their impact on surrounding matter. Gravitational waves offer a novel avenue for black hole research, emanating from these cosmic entities during their formation and merger. Subsequently, computational techniques can be employed to derive crucial information about the originating black holes, encompassing their masses, spins, inclination, and the distance of the gravitational wave event. In recent years, the progress in Machine Learning, particularly Deep Learning methods, has facilitated the development of models capable of extracting this information from gravitational wave signals in real-time with remarkable accuracy [19]. This advancement holds significant importance, enabling the integration of gravitational wave detection with other electromagnetic signals emitted during the same cosmic events.

While any accelerating object theoretically produces gravitational waves, current detection capabilities are limited to events involving immensely massive objects undergoing rapid accelerations [1]. Notable sources include binary black hole systems, binary neutron star systems, neutron star-black hole pairs, and exploding massive stars. Presently, our focus lies on Compact Binary Inspiral Gravitational Waves, specifically those from binary black hole systems.

Currently, LIGO, Virgo, and KAGRA (Kamioka Gravitational Wave Detector) serve as the primary detectors observing gravitational wave events. To achieve this, these detectors employ a device similar to a Michelson interferometer [1], which is a device that splits a beam of light into two beams that travel different paths and subsequently recombines them. The detector's interferometer is designed to detect minute changes in the lengths of the two arms of the interferometer, which are caused by the passage of gravitational waves. However, a significant challenge arises from the extreme sensitivity of these detectors, making them susceptible to various sources of noise [20]. Consequently, the detection of gravitational waves and the extraction of vital parameters about the systems that generated them are challenging tasks because of the presence of noise and the low Signal-to-Noise Ratio (SNR) of the observed signals. The SNR is defined as the ratio of the signal power to the noise power and is a measure of the strength of the signal relative to the noise. In order to solve problems of this nature, various signal-processing techniques, such as matched filtering, have been employed. Machine Learning techniques have also been utilized to address these issues, with promising results.

Advantages of Machine learning, and specifically Deep learning methods, compared to traditional matched filtering are:

- Flexibility: Machine learning methods, particularly deep learning, offer greater flexibility in modeling complex relationships within data compared to traditional matched filtering techniques.
- Adaptability: Deep learning models can adapt to different types of signals and noise characteristics without requiring explicit parameter tuning for each specific scenario, unlike matched filtering which relies on predefined waveform templates.

- Feature Extraction: Deep learning methods automatically learn hierarchical representations of features from raw data, potentially capturing subtle features that may be overlooked by manual waveform template matching.
- Robustness to Noise: Deep learning models can learn to distinguish between true signals and noise more effectively, leading to improved performance in noisy environments compared to traditional methods.
- Scalability: Deep learning models can handle large datasets and scale well to high-dimensional data, making them suitable for analyzing the vast amount of gravitational wave data generated by detectors like LIGO and Virgo.
- Generalization: Once trained on a diverse set of data, deep learning models can generalize well to unseen data, allowing for more robust and reliable parameter estimation across a range of astrophysical scenarios.
- Potential for Discovery: Deep learning methods may uncover new insights or patterns in the data that traditional methods might miss, potentially leading to new discoveries or breakthroughs in astrophysics.

In this work, the potential of Deep Learning methods to detect gravitational waves and estimate the parameters of the systems that generated them is explored. The objective of our study is to develop distinct Deep Neural Network architectures for the estimation of parameters such as distance, mass, and spin (M, J) for Binary Black Hole (BBH) systems. This estimation is based on the gravitational wave data generated by these BBH systems. In the scope of this work, our emphasis lies on the development of Convolutional Neural Networks (CNNs) with the primary objective of estimating the masses of the two black holes and determining the spatial distance at which the gravitational wave event has transpired, as deduced from the emitted gravitational wave signals.

The outline of this work is as follows: Sect. 2 provides a brief overview of related work. Section 3 describes the methodology employed in this study, how the data were generated, and the architecture of our model. Finally, Sect. 4 presents the results of our experiments and a discussion of our findings.

2   Related Work

In recent years, Deep Learning has been applied to several gravitational-wave physics problems. Research in BBH merger detection and parameter estimation with Deep Learning has been conducted by several scientists. In the study conducted by [7], "Deep Filtering" which presents two CNN models, hereinafter referred to as Shallow-CNN (S-CNN) and Deep-CNN (D-CNN), was introduced for the detection of gravitational waves and the estimation of the masses of the systems producing them. Notably, D-CNN outperformed S-CNN in terms of loss. Building on this work, [8] applied these models to detect real gravitational waves from Advanced LIGO.

Until now, Gravitational-wave detection strategies were based on a signal analysis technique known as matched filtering. However, [5, 6] used CNN to show the potential of Deep Learning in the detection of gravitational waves. In addition, for the same purpose, [3] implemented auto-encoder models, while [10] used Bayesian Neural Networks and Long Short-Term Memory (LSTM) networks to not only detect gravitational waves but also identify the full-length of the event duration including the inspiral stage. Another notable study is that of [11] in which CNN models were used to identify all the reported gravitational wave events in the first and second observation runs by LIGO-VIRGO Scientific Collaboration, and that of [21] that identified all the BBH mergers reported during the second and third observing runs of Advanced LIGO with a false rate of 1 misclassification for every 2.7 days of searched data.

In the context of BBH parameter estimation, [19] focused on real-time parameter reconstruction models based on the BBH catalog presented by the LIGO and Virgo Scientific Collaborations. Furthermore, [18] quantified the efficacy of deep learning in estimating BBH merger parameters, including the final spin (a_f) and quasinormal modes. Another study by [12] utilized deep learning to estimate the chirp mass and mass ratio of a BBH signal in detector noise. Additionally, [17] employed matched-filtering convolutional neural networks to identify Massive BBH mergers in data from Lisa. Moreover, [14] developed a CNN model to estimate the total mass of BBH systems using 2D images representing time-frequency evolution.

Shifting focus to gravitational waves from Neutron Stars, [4] applied "Deep Filtering" by George and Huerta to effectively recognize the presence of gravitational wave signals and the estimation of luminosity distance, right ascension, and declination of the compact binary star mergers. [9] centered their research on parameter estimation from Binary Neutron Star (BNS) systems. A related study by [16] extended this exploration to parameter estimation from Binary Neutron Star-Black Hole (BNS-BH) systems. Additionally, [13] conducted research on parameter estimation from BNS gravitational waves in the Einstein Telescope.

This study places emphasis on the estimation of masses and distances for Binary Black Hole (BBH) systems using CNN models. The objective is to enhance the accuracy of the parameter estimation process and to facilitate a more comprehensive understanding of BBH systems

3 Methodology

Inspired by [7], a CNN architecture is proposed, that is capable of predicting not only the masses of the BBH systems but also their spatial distance. It is imperative to underscore that the training of CNN models necessitates a substantial volume of training data.

3.1   Data Generation

To attain our research objectives, our initial approach was to leverage the recorded gravitational wave strains from actual events cataloged within the Gravitational Wave Open Science Center (GWOSC) as training data for our models. However, it became evident that the dataset available in GWOSC was insufficient to adequately train our computational systems. Consequently, we embarked on the generation of synthetic time-domain waveforms representing gravitational waves. These synthetic waveforms were generated by applying Effective-one-body (EOB) numerical-relativity (NR) waveform models specifically designed for spin-aligned binary black hole systems, known as the SEOBNR [2] models. In our study, we employ the SEOBNRv4 algorithm, which yields both the cross and plus polarization components of gravitational waves as seen in Fig. 1. The polarizations of a gravitational wave are 45°C apart, and are dimensionless. These components are subsequently transformed to match the characteristics of the H1, V1, and L1 detectors through the utilization of the PyCBC library [15]. Figure 2 illustrates a representative time-domain gravitational wave waveform as received by H1, for every distance.

For this work, it is assumed that the signals are optimally oriented with respect to the detectors, and that the individual spins and orbital eccentricities are zero. The dataset employed for training our models comprises time-domain gravitational wave strains sampled at a rate of 8192 Hz with a low-frequency cutoff ($f_{low} = 10$ Hz). These waveforms originate from binary black hole systems with individual masses ranging from 5 times the mass of the Sun ($5M\odot$) to 100 times the mass of the Sun ($100M\odot$). To ensure the exclusion of duplicate events, a constraint is imposed where the mass (M1) of one black hole is consistently equal to or greater than the mass (M2) of the other, as illustrated in Fig. 3.

Moreover, for the generated gravitational wave strains, the distance parameter is systematically varied from $50Mpc$ to $1000Mpc$ in increments of $50Mpc$. This adjustment is implemented to enable our models to accurately estimate the distance of the observed events. Recognizing that diverse combinations of masses yield gravitational waves with distinct durations, a temporal window capturing the final second of each strain is employed. Consequently, all strains are standardized to a length of 8192 values. In instances where the duration of the strain is less than a second, zero values are appended to the termination of the oscillation, ensuring a consistent total length of 8192 values. The resultant dataset is then randomly partitioned, with 60% allocated for training, 10% for validation, and 30% for testing purposes.

3.2   Neural Networks Architecture

As previously delineated, our investigation involves the estimation of masses and distances for BBH systems utilizing CNN models. For that purpose, motivated by the Deep-CNN (D-CNN) from [7], we proposed a CNN architecture which is capable to estimate these parameters.

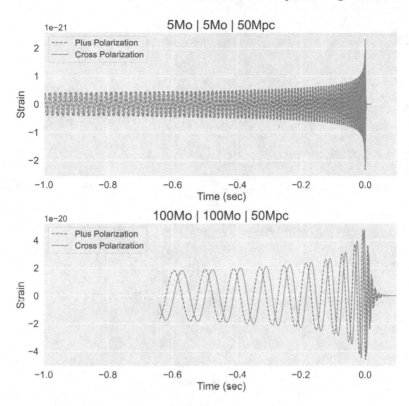

Fig. 1. The cross and plus polarization components of a Gravitational-Wave produced by two Black Holes with mass $5M\odot$ and $5M\odot$ in distance $50Mpc$ and two Black Holes with mass $100M\odot$ and $100M\odot$ in distance $50Mpc$.

The architecture of the proposed CNN model closely resembles that of D-CNN, except for the removal of the final 1-dimensional Convolutional layer with a depth of 512. Additionally, since the proposed CNN is tasked with estimation not only the masses but also the distances of a BBH system, the proposed architecture incorporates a final layer comprising three neurons. The first two neurons are designated for the estimation of masses, while the third neuron is dedicated to distance estimation.

Giving the details of the proposed CNN. precisely, the first layer entails a 1-dimensional Convolutional (Conv1d) layer with a depth of 64, kernel size of 16, strides of 1, dilation rate of 1, and a Rectified Linear Unit (ReLU) activation function. Subsequently, a 1-dimensional MaxPooling (Maxpooling1d) layer with a kernel size of 4 and strides of 4 is employed, given an input shape of (8192). The second layer comprises a Conv1d layer with a depth of 128, kernel size of 16, strides of 1, dilation rate of 2, and a ReLU activation function. This is succeeded by a MaxPooling1d layer with a kernel size of 4 and strides of 4. In the third layer, a Conv1d layer with a depth of 256, kernel size of 16, strides of 1,

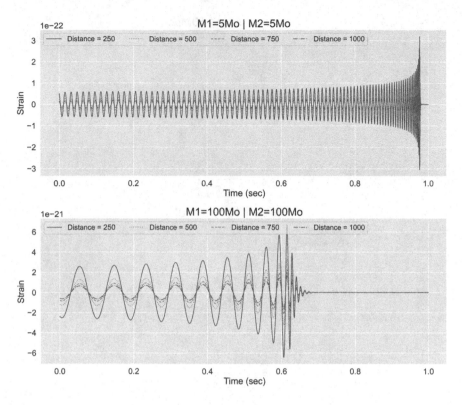

Fig. 2. Typical Strain of a Gravitational-Wave produced by two Black Holes with mass $5M\odot$ and $5M\odot$ and $100M\odot$ and $100M\odot$ respectively, in every distance, as received by H1. The pick of the strain shows that the Black Holes merged.

dilation rate of 2, and a ReLU activation function is utilized. This is followed by a MaxPooling1d layer with a kernel size of 4 and strides of 4. Subsequent to these convolutional and pooling layers, the data is flattened to facilitate the use of a linear layer with a depth of 128 and a ReLU activation function. This is further succeeded by another linear layer with a depth of 64 and a ReLU activation function. The final layer is a linear layer with a depth of 3, representing the number of parameters predicted by our model. The architecture is explicitly outlined in Table 1.

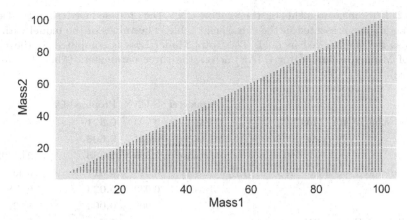

Fig. 3. The distribution of component masses in BBH systems is illustrated in this figure. Notably, Mass1 consistently equals or exceeds Mass2, precluding the occurrence of events with identical pairs of masses.

Table 1. The architecture and the number of parameters of the proposed CNN Model.

Proposed CNN Model		
Layer (type)	Output Shape	Param
Conv1d	(8177, 64)	1088
MaxPooling1d	(2044, 64)	0
Conv1d	(2014, 128)	131200
MaxPooling1d	(503, 128)	0
Conv1d	(473, 256)	524544
MaxPooling1d	(118, 256)	0
Flatten	(30208)	0
Dense	(128)	3866752
Dense	(64)	8256
Dense	(3)	195
Total params: 4532035		

4   Experimental Evaluation

In this section, we evaluate the proposed CNN architecture against the Shallow-CNN (S-CNN) and Deep-CNN (D-CNN) of [7] for the estimation of masses and distance of BBH system. Since the S-CNN and D-CNN have originate proposed for masses only estimation their architecture, at the final output layer, is modified accordingly in order to estimate both masses and distances.

All models were trained utilizing gravitational wave strains as input, employing a batch size of 128 samples over 300 epochs. The mean absolute error loss function was employed to quantify the loss of the models. Figure 4 illustrates

Table 2. Error measurements for the Shallow-CNN, the proposed CNN, and the Deep-CNN models are presented in the subsequent table. The values of the model with the least loss are emphasized in bold. The Total Model Loss is computed as the mean value of Mean Absolute Error (MAE) across the three parameters (Mass 1, Mass 2, Distance).

Error	Parameter	S-CNN	Proposed-CNN	D-CNN
Mean Absolute Error (MAE)	Mass 1	0.963	**0.821**	18.838
	Mass 2	0.831	**0.606**	18.752
	Distance	2.380	**1.686**	249.202
Mean Absolute Percentage Error (MAPE)	Mass 1	0.018	**0.017**	0.458
	Mass 2	0.032	**0.024**	0.888
	Distance	0.006	**0.004**	1.227
Mean Relative Error (MRE)	Mass 1	0.020	**0.018**	0.453
	Mass 2	0.044	**0.032**	0.863
	Distance	0.006	**0.005**	1.226
Mean Percentage Error (MPE)	Mass 1	2.034	**1.882**	45.337
	Mass 2	4.450	**3.251**	86.336
	Distance	0.657	**0.557**	122.674
Root Mean Squared Error (RMSE)	Mass 1	1.315	**1.143**	23.013
	Mass 2	1.655	**0.892**	22.936
	Distance	3.720	**2.629**	288.581
Mean Squared Error (MSE)	Mass 1	1.730	**1.307**	529.626
	Mass 2	1.358	**0.797**	526.100
	Distance	13.840	**6.915**	83279.255
R2 Score	Mass 1	0.996	**0.997**	−0.023
	Mass 2	0.997	**0.998**	−0.027
	Distance	0.999	**0.999**	−0.006
Total Model Loss (TML):		1.392	**1.038**	95.597

the loss per epoch for the S-CNN, the D-CNN and the proposed CNN model respectively. Various error metrics are provided for each model based on our test data in Table 2, with *Total Model Loss (TML)* indicates the mean value of Mean Absolute Error (MAE) over the three parameter estimation. A lower loss value signifies superior model performance for this specific problem.

$$MAE = \frac{1}{n} \sum_{i=1}^{n} |x_i - x|$$

Upon comparing the figures and the table provided, it is evident that the S-CNN exhibited proficiency in predicting the masses and distances of Binary Black Hole (BBH) systems. However, our proposed CNN model, featuring a deeper architecture, managed to minimize the TML, showcasing improved performance. In addition, the D-CNN, despite its increased depth compared to our

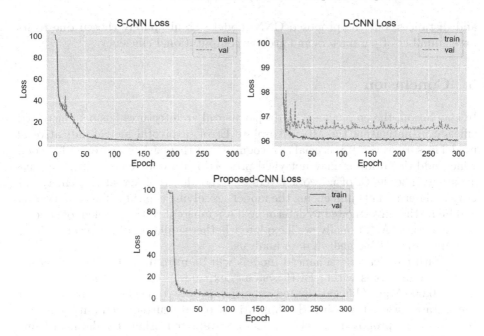

Fig. 4. Loss per epoch for the Shallow-CNN and Deep-CNN Model and the Proposed-CNN. Mean Absolute Error serves as our chosen loss metric.

proposed CNN model, encountered challenges during training and failed to converge. Notably, in the study [7], where the sole objective was the estimation of BBH system masses, the D-CNN exhibited lower loss than the S-CNN. As highlighted in the same study, the employment of deeper networks is anticipated to enhance accuracy at the expense of evaluation speed. Nonetheless, our findings underscore the nuanced nature of model performance in relation to depth.

Comparing the three models considering only the estimation of masses at a distance of $1000Mpc$, the S-CNN model achieved a TML (over the masses only) of 1.084, the D-CNN model achieved a TML of 0.539, while the proposed CNN model achieved a TML of 0.851. This indicates that the D-CNN may be more effective for the estimation of masses only. However, the proposed CNN model is more adaptive and achieves better performance when the task involves the estimation of both masses and distances.

It is suggested that the impediment faced by the D-CNN in our scenario may stem from the final 1-dimensional Convolutional layer with a depth of 512 and kernel size of 32. This layer seemingly struggled to discern informative patterns within the gravitational waveforms. After conducting extensive experimentation, it is conjectured that replacing this layer with a 1-dimensional Convolutional layer featuring a depth of 256 and a kernel size of 8 could potentially enhance the model's ability to train effectively. The model with this change exhibited a comparable performance to the proposed CNN model in the estimation of masses and distances, but the proposed CNN model was ultimately chosen due to its lower number of parameters and greater computational efficiency.

5   Conclusion

In conclusion, the employment of deeper neural architectures has demonstrated efficacy in mitigating the Mean Absolute Error, a pivotal metric indicative of model loss. However, it is crucial to recognize that there exists a threshold beyond which additional layers may not yield proportional improvements in predictive accuracy. The depth of network layers and the choice of kernel size emerge as critical determinants influencing the model's resolving capacity. This observation will be further investigated to determine if it's inherent to the problem or specific to the dataset. Additionally, we'll explore whether similar findings occur in other domains, such as biomedical data analysis.

In future endeavors, enhanced models will be introduced for the estimation of masses and spins within BBH systems, expanding the analysis to distances up to 10,000 Mpc. This anticipated extension is poised to substantially augment the dataset size, surpassing the limitations of our current computing infrastructure. The proposed model will also be evaluated using real data, utilizing transfer learning techniques for training. Consequently, alternative data handling methodologies will be imperative to facilitate the training of these models.

References

1. Bailes, M., et al.: Gravitational-wave physics and astronomy in the 2020s and 2030s. Nat. Rev. Phys. **3**(5), 344–366 (2021)
2. Bohé, A., et al.: Improved effective-one-body model of spinning, nonprecessing binary black holes for the era of gravitational-wave astrophysics with advanced detectors. Phys. Rev. D **95**, 044028 (2017). https://doi.org/10.1103/PhysRevD. 95.044028
3. Corizzo, R., Ceci, M., Zdravevski, E., Japkowicz, N.: Scalable auto-encoders for gravitational waves detection from time series data. Expert Syst. Appl. **151**, 113378 (2020). https://doi.org/10.1016/j.eswa.2020.113378
4. Fan, X., Li, J., Li, X., Zhong, Y., Cao, J.: Applying deep neural networks to the detection and space parameter estimation of compact binary coalescence with a network of gravitational wave detectors. Sci. China Phys. Mech. Astron. **62**(6) (2019). https://doi.org/10.1007/s11433-018-9321-7
5. Gabbard, H., Williams, M., Hayes, F., Messenger, C.: Matching matched filtering with deep networks for gravitational-wave astronomy. Phys. Rev. Lett. **120**, 141103 (2018). https://doi.org/10.1103/PhysRevLett.120.141103
6. Gebhard, T.D., Kilbertus, N., Harry, I., Schölkopf, B.: Convolutional neural networks: a magic bullet for gravitational-wave detection? Phys. Rev. D **100**, 063015 (2019). https://doi.org/10.1103/PhysRevD.100.063015
7. George, D., Huerta, E.A.: Deep neural networks to enable real-time multimessenger astrophysics. Phys. Rev. D **97**, 044039 (2018). https://doi.org/10.1103/PhysRevD. 97.044039

8. George, D., Huerta, E.: Deep learning for real-time gravitational wave detection and parameter estimation: results with advanced LIGO data. Phys. Lett. B **778**, 64–70 (2018). https://doi.org/10.1016/j.physletb.2017.12.053

9. Krastev, P.G., Gill, K., Villar, V.A., Berger, E.: Detection and parameter estimation of gravitational waves from binary neutron-star mergers in real LIGO data using deep learning. Phys. Lett. B **815**, 136161 (2021). https://doi.org/10.1016/j.physletb.2021.136161

10. Lin, Y.C., Wu, J.H.P.: Detection of gravitational waves using Bayesian neural networks. Phys. Rev. D **103**, 063034 (2021). https://doi.org/10.1103/PhysRevD.103.063034

11. Ma, C., Wang, W., Wang, H., Cao, Z.: Ensemble of deep convolutional neural networks for real-time gravitational wave signal recognition. Phys. Rev. D **105**, 083013 (2022). https://doi.org/10.1103/PhysRevD.105.083013

12. McLeod, A., Jacobs, D., Chatterjee, C., Wen, L., Panther, F.: Rapid mass parameter estimation of binary black hole coalescences using deep learning (2022)

13. Miller, A.L., Singh, N., Palomba, C.: Enabling multi-messenger astronomy with continuous gravitational waves: early warning and sky localization of binary neutron stars in Einstein Telescope (2023)

14. Moreno, A.B.A., Moreno, C.: Convolutional neural network regression to estimate the mass parameter of astrophysical binary black hole systems. In: LatinX in AI Workshop at ICML 2023 (Regular Deadline) (2023)

15. Nitz, A., et al.: GWastro/PyCBC: v2.3.2 release of PyCBC (2023). https://doi.org/10.5281/zenodo.10137381

16. Qiu, R., Krastev, P.G., Gill, K., Berger, E.: Deep learning detection and classification of gravitational waves from neutron star-black hole mergers. Phys. Lett. B **840**, 137850 (2023). https://doi.org/10.1016/j.physletb.2023.137850

17. Ruan, W.H., Wang, H., Liu, C., Guo, Z.K.: Rapid search for massive black hole binary coalescences using deep learning. Phys. Lett. B **841**, 137904 (2023). https://doi.org/10.1016/j.physletb.2023.137904

18. Shen, H., Huerta, E.A., O'Shea, E., Kumar, P., Zhao, Z.: Statistically-informed deep learning for gravitational wave parameter estimation. Mach. Learn. Sci. Technol. **3**(1), 015007 (2021). https://doi.org/10.1088/2632-2153/ac3843

19. Shen, H., Huerta, E.A., Zhao, Z.: Deep learning at scale for gravitational wave parameter estimation of binary black hole mergers. arXiv abs/1903.01998 (2019)

20. Trozzo, L., Badaracco, F.: Seismic and Newtonian noise in the GW detectors. Galaxies **10**(1) (2022). https://doi.org/10.3390/galaxies10010020

21. Wei, W., Khan, A., Huerta, E., Huang, X., Tian, M.: Deep learning ensemble for real-time gravitational wave detection of spinning binary black hole mergers. Phys. Lett. B **812**, 136029 (2021). https://doi.org/10.1016/j.physletb.2020.136029

Comparative Analysis of Large Language Models in Structured Information Extraction from Job Postings

Kyriaki Sioziou[1]([✉]), Panagiotis Zervas[1], Kostas Giotopoulos[2], and Giannis Tzimas[1]

[1] Data and Media Laboratory, Department of Electrical and Computer Engineering, University of Peloponnese, 22131 Tripolis, Greece
`ksioziou@gmail.com`, `{pzervas,tzimas}@uop.gr`
[2] Department of Management Science and Technology, University of Patras, 26334 Patras, Greece
`kgiotop@upatras.gr`

Abstract. The recent progress in Large Language Models has opened up new possibilities for their application in different domains. This study focuses on exploring the potential of LLMs in structured information extraction, specifically in the context of job postings. We compare commercial and open-source LLMs to see how well they can extract key information from job postings in Greece's tourism sector. Our goal is to understand the performance differences between these models and assess their general applicability in real-world information extraction tasks. We aim to evaluate and compare the capability of these models in accurately identifying and extracting specific data points such as Job Title, Company, Industry, Location, Soft Skills, and Hard Skills. This research contributes to our understanding of how practical LLMs are in real-world information extraction tasks and highlights the differences in performance among various state-of-the-art models.

Keywords: Large Language Models · Natural Language Processing · Labor Market Analysis · Information Extraction · Online data

1 Introduction

Within the context of the modern digital landscape, the management and utilization of data from multiple sources, particularly in relation to the labor market, present a noteworthy challenge. Job postings, an important yet often underutilized data source, provide valuable information about market dynamics. Conventional techniques used for labor market analysis, which are mostly manual or semi-automated, have certain limitations in terms of scalability, speed and depth of analysis. The shift to modern data processing methods, particularly in the organization and categorization of job listings, is of utmost importance in order to uncover valuable insights, such as the emergence of skill trends and shifts in the economy. The development in data analysis signifies a broader movement towards more advanced tools, shifting from manual resume analysis to software-based methods in corporate sectors, emphasizing a transformation in comprehending job market trends [2].

© The Author(s), under exclusive license to Springer Nature Switzerland AG 2024
L. Iliadis et al. (Eds.): EANN 2024, CCIS 2141, pp. 82–92, 2024.
https://doi.org/10.1007/978-3-031-62495-7_7

The shift from conventional labor market analysis methods to natural language processing (NLP) represents a significant development. The traditional methods have been fundamental in the field, yet their effectiveness was restricted by their operational capacity and the limits in their analytical scope. However, the rising of NLP, especially ever since the introduction of the transformer architecture [1] and Large Language Models (LLMs), has led to increased efficiency and improved comprehension. Areas, such as summarization, translation and contextual interpretation, that had proved challenging for conventional approaches, have witnessed advancement by the capabilities of LLMs, particularly of those designed for analytical tasks [4]. The introduction of models like GPT-3 (Generative Pre-trained Transformer) marks a major breakthrough in applying AI to language processing in labor market analysis [5].

The objective of this study is to explore how the use of LLMs impacts the extraction of information from job postings. We seek to identify how LLMs can be valuable for analyzing the labor market by examining a dataset of job advertisements from various online platforms, specifically in Greece's tourism industry. This approach enables a more in-depth and analytical examination of labor market dynamics that were less accessible previously.

A significant advancement in this area of study is the integration of LLMs in the analysis of labor market data. The scope of market analysis is expanded and the accuracy of AI models in predicting outcomes is improved. This research aims to contribute to the evolving field by evaluating how different LLMs perform in processing job posting data. Thus, providing a more thorough understanding of labor market trends and enabling decision-making based on data.

The following is the paper's outline: We begin with a detailed review of related work that offers an overview of the historical evolution and contemporary advancements of NLP applications regarding labor market data analysis. This is followed by a detailed description of our methodology, including the methods and computational approaches we employed in our study. The dataset of job postings we used is introduced in the Data Description section, where the emphasis on the Greek tourism industry is noted and its selection and applicability are explained. We report our results from using NLP approaches on this dataset in the Results section, providing insights into their intricacies and effectiveness. The Discussion and Conclusion section concludes the paper. Here, we critically evaluate the implications of our study, integrate our findings with existing academic discussions and suggest possible directions for future research in the labor market analytics. This structured approach aims to methodically explore the intersection of traditional data analysis and the evolving field of natural language processing, providing valuable insights to the field.

2 Related Work

Information extraction (IE) techniques have advanced significantly over time, moving from simple rule-based frameworks to complex machine learning models. In the beginning, IE mainly used statistical techniques combined with manually created rules to extract structured data from collections of unstructured text. Nevertheless, these initial approaches displayed integral limitation regarding their scalability and adaptability to diverse datasets and domain-specific situations.

Technological developments in Natural Language Processing (NLP) have been essential in overcoming the previously described constraints. A significant transformation in NLP has been brought by the application of machine learning techniques, especially deep learning approaches. As a result, it is now possible to directly learn from data [24]. A decisive step in this evolution has been the introduction of the transformer architecture [1], which signified the start of a new era in NLP. It has rendered training models on vast data sets more efficient. Based on the transformer architecture, the subsequent innovations, such as Bidirectional Encoder Representations from Transformers (BERT) [16] and the GPT series [4, 25], have significantly improved text comprehension, generation, and inference capabilities.

LLMs can be applied to a number of different fields, showing thus, their capabilities and flexibility. For instance, LLMs have been utilized in the healthcare to extract vital patient information from clinical notes, in order to improve the factor of efficiency and accuracy in the medical record-keeping. [26]. Likewise, in the financial sector LLMs have been used to analyze sentiment in the news about economy, providing valuable insights for predicting market trends and shaping investment strategies [27]. However, and despite the above-mentioned successful examples, the adaptation of LLMs to sector-specific requirements is not without challenges, such as addressing biases included in the training datasets that can, potentially, influence model outputs and decision-making processes [19, 28].

With respect to the domain of interest in this study, the labor market, the utilization of LLMs in its analysis indicates a significant shift towards advanced NLP techniques for extracting insights from job postings and resumes. Research has highlighted the profound capabilities of LLMs to enrich our comprehension of labor market trends and skill demands [3, 21]. The field, though still in its embryonic stages, is offering vast opportunities for future studies to evaluate the effectiveness of various LLMs in discerning detailed information across heterogeneous job markets [32].

An important source of insights in the labor market is the study of job postings. A range of information extraction (IE) methodologies, from simple keyword extraction to sophisticated deep semantic analysis, has been employed mining essential data from them, such as requisite skills, qualifications, and job descriptions [17]. These methodological studies establish a solid foundation for our subsequent analysis, aiming to assess how LLMs can enhance the detail and accuracy of information derived from job postings, in that way offering a richer understanding of labor market dynamics [18].

Comparative analyses between commercial and open-source LLMs have outlined distinct variations in terms of performance and accessibility [14]. Commercial LLMs are typically characterized by their sophisticated features and comprehensive support services, catering to a wide array of complex applications. Conversely, open-source LLMs are prized for their transparency and adaptability, allowing for extensive customization and facilitating research transparency [29, 30]. This contrast serves as the foundation for our comparative study, which seeks to illustrate how different LLMs perform in labor market analysis, thus providing insights into the optimal choice of models based on specific analytical needs [15].

Despite the extensive applications of LLMs across various domains, notable research gaps persist, especially concerning sector-specific analyses and the investigation of emerging labor markets, such as Greece's tourism sector. In this study we aim to address these omissions, by utilizing LLMs to gather insights from job postings in this underexplored sector. The intention is to illuminate the unique labor dynamics and skill requirements of Greece's tourism industry, contributing this way to the scant literature in this area and enhancing the understanding of sector-specific labor market trends.

The selection of the tourism domain was realized as the specific domain is crucial for the economy of Greece [31]. Because of its significant economic impact and the diversity of job categories available, the economy of Greece presents a special case for exploring labor market trends. Given this context, we can surmise how valuable LLMs can be at extracting additional details from job postings, thus improving our comprehension of the dynamics of employment in a given industry.

3 Database Description

In [23], the authors describe the use of web crawling techniques, specifically tools like BeautifulSoup and Scrapy, to collect job postings from various online platforms in an automated manner. The dataset underwent thorough processes to ensure its accuracy and reliability, including error correction, duplicate removal, special character elimination, and exclusion of irrelevant content. Additionally, discrepancies in location and educational credentials were systematically resolved through manual verification in conjunction with the implementation of Python scripts for data cleansing. Consequently, the comprehensive Real Job Posting (RJP) dataset, comprising more than 10,000 job postings collected from 5 reputable online sources, proves to be an invaluable asset in comprehending the dynamics of the labor market. The carefully selected assortment of job listings, described in [23], gives a complete overview of the job market during that specific time frame. It provides valuable information for conducting in-depth research on labor market trends and patterns.

The study utilized a random selection of 3000 postings from this dataset to ensure diversity in the subset. Based on the dataset, hotels and similar accommodations make up the majority of the listings, followed by a comparatively smaller number of listings associated with restaurants and catering services. These industries emerge as the primary focal points of economic interest, suggesting the tourism sector's expansion despite the pandemic. Additionally, the dataset includes listings related to travel agency activities and jobs in real estate agencies and management, though to a lesser extent.

Through careful examination of the occupation codes, we have discovered a total of 159 distinct codes. In line with previous observations, the majority of job postings are focused on the service industry, which reflects the economic structure of Greece, where tourism and related services play a crucial role [31]. Notably, a significant number of job openings are for occupations such as waiters, cooks, hotel receptionists, bartenders, cleaners, chefs, sales assistants, and kitchen helpers. The prevalence of these jobs indicates that these sectors are experiencing resilience or rebounding, possibly due to an increase in domestic tourism or the implementation of measures like offering takeout services in the food industry. The presence of real estate agents in the list of common job listings was also significant and could be attributed to ongoing activity in the property market, potentially fueled by changes in housing preferences or investments during the pandemic.

The diversity of the dataset, its depth and its careful preparation increase the credibility of our analysis, laying a robust foundation for assessing LLMs' efficiency in extracting structured information from complex job postings. This way we can gain a deeper understanding of the current situation of the labor market and also establish a standard for future studies and research by highlighting the potential of automated data collection and sophisticated analytical techniques to further develop our comprehension of labor market dynamics.

4 Methodology

In the current work, we conducted an empirical evaluation to assess the effectiveness of state-of-the-art LLMs in identifying and parsing semantically relevant information from an unedited dataset of job descriptions. This collection, consisting of data from 2020, was assembled from well-known job advertisement platforms and was intentionally preserved in its original format. The aim of this approach was to simulate the real-world data environment that LLMs would encounter in end-user situations.

The study involved a selected suite of LLMs chosen for their linguistic processing abilities and computational efficiency on consumer-grade hardware. To complete this task, we decided to use the OpenAI model GPT-3.5-Turbo and the LLaMA-2-7B-Chat.ggmlv3.q4_0.bin, Mistral-7B-Instruct-v0.1.Q4_0.gguf, Orca-Mini-3B-gguf2-q4_0.gguf open LLMs. We selected the open models based on their capacity to efficiently run on a GTX 3060 12 GB and their rankings on platforms like Hugging Face's Open LLM Leaderboard [33] (Fig. 1).

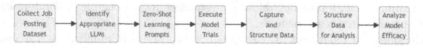

Fig. 1. Overview of the Job Posting Analysis Workflow

Through this process we certified that the models were suitable for standard personal computers, by assessing linguistic accuracy, their efficiency in operation, and how they responded within typical computational resource constraints.

- GPT-3.5-turbo (OpenAI): Optimized for chat applications, this model is cost-effective and supports up to 4,096 tokens, demonstrating high efficiency [5, 6].
- Llama-2-chat-7b (Meta): Known for generating relevant responses with 7 billion parameters and a 4,096-token context window, it advances conversation generation [7].
- Mistral 7b (Mistral AI): Balances efficiency and computational costs with 7 billion parameters and employs Grouped-query Attention (GQA) and Sliding Window Attention (SWA) for enhanced text processing [8–11].
- Orca-mini-3b: Builds on OpenLLaMa-3B, trained on datasets for explanatory responses, showcasing innovative dataset construction methods [12, 13].

The OpenAI API provided operational access for gpt-3.5-turbo, whereas GPT4All enabled offline access to the other models, utilizing OpenAI API compatibility feature and preserving privacy [22].

In this exploratory study, a zero-shot learning methodology was preferred to pre-training [20]. The methodology is based on extracting information form job descriptions, without prior specific training, by creating suitable prompts. This approach allows for the evaluation of the built-in ability of the LLMs to parse and semantically interpret unknown textual data. Prompts were meticulously crafted to direct LLMs in analyzing textual content and structuring the extracted information into a specific JSON format. This evaluation assists in assessing how effectively the models organize and manage data for practical real-world applications.

In the execution phase, LLMs were tasked with identifying and extracting specific information from the job descriptions, including job titles, employers, industry classifications, locations and required professional skills. This phase evaluated the models' capability to identify and organize the various components within the natural language text systematically.

After the extraction process, the raw outputs were converted into a structured CSV format. This transformation was necessary, as it ensured the data from different LLMs were unified in a format suitable for comparative analysis.

The methodological framework concluded with a detailed analysis of the data extracted by each LLM, evaluating the accuracy and structure of the information extracted by each model, as well as their performance on standard consumer-grade computing devices. The accuracy was assessed by comparing it to the information manually extracted from the original dataset. The analysis provided vital insights into each model's functionality and limitations, underscoring their applicability and effectiveness for users with average computational resources.

To illustrate, consider a job posting as input:

"Elivi skiathos situated in Skiathos island and its aim is to create truly memorable 5-star hide away experiences. Inspired from the unique nature and heritage of the region, the renowned greek hospitality, our main aim is to deliver a more personalized and intuitive service, and to form tailored guest experiences. If the provision of discrete quality services in a luxury environment energizes, you, we will be glad to receive your resume. Front office receptionist we are looking to recruit an experienced FO receptionist responsible to provide customer focused service to the guests, ensuring their stay will become an unforgettable experience.

Key responsibilities: responsible for day-to-day operations of the front office, such as handling guest arrivals and departures, dealing in all FO related tasks and procedures. Operate relevant switchboard, call center and pms software as per all front office related activities identifies and ensures the highest standards of guest care is maintained, deals with any special request, complaints etc. Works closely with the housekeeping department for room turn around in order to allo-cate arriving guest in accommodation with a minimum of lost time. Must have a pleasant personality with excellent communication and interpersonal skills that promotes a helpful and professional image to the client and gives full cooperation to any customer requiring assistance. Requirements: 3–5 years working experience in a relevant position in 5 hotel hospitality degree written and verbal communication skills (english, greek, italian) proficiency in computer skills (windows, hotel pms and several industry platforms) team spirit and customers-oriented approach benefits: competitive remuneration package exciting and dynamic working environment food & accommodation (if not a local resident)."

A prompt designed for an LLM to extract the specified information might read:

"""Your task is to parse an unstructured job posting and turn it into a JSON containing the most important information.
The job posting can describe one or more jobs at the same company. The JSON should consist of the following information:
- id (field name: "id", field type: num)
- The company name (field name: "companyName", field type: string)
- The job title (field name: "jobTitle", field type: string),
- the industry of the job(field:"industry:, field type:string)
- the location of the job (field name: "location", field type: string
- any specific soft skills that might be stated (field name: "softskills", field type: string).
- any specific hard skills that might be stated (field name: "hardskills", field type: string).
In general, if certain information is not stated, set the respective field to null.
If the company seeks more than one person for the same role, include the role only once.
This is the job posting:
%s
The structured JSON representation is:
```json
{"job": [
*   {*
*   "id": %s,*
*   "companyName":string,*
*   "jobTitle", string,*
*   "industry": string,*
*   "location": string,*
*   "softskills": string,*
*   "hardskills": string }]*

}"""

The resulting JSON output from the LLM could look like this:

{"Job Title": " front office receptionist",
* "Company": " elivi skiathos",*
* "Industry": " hospitality",*
* "Location": " skiathos island",*
* "Soft Skills": ['pleasant personality', 'excellent communication and interpersonal skills']",*
* "Hard Skills": ['computer skills (windows, hotel pms and several industry platforms)',}*

This example underscores the LLMs' ability in dissecting and organizing job postings into structured data, highlighting their potential to streamline information extraction tasks for end-users across various computing environments.

5 Results

The analysis of the performance of the four LLMs used resulted in varied outcomes, showing differences in the accuracy of the outputs produced by each model. The examination began by assessing the validity of the outputs across the models, as depicted in Fig. 2, below. Analysis showed that GPT 3.5 Turbo and Llama2 demonstrated a high rate of valid outputs across nearly all entries. Conversely, the Orca and Mistral models manifested valid outputs in merely half of the evaluated entries. Notably, in instances where Orca and Mistral failed to generate valid outputs, their responses defaulted to a template outlining the expected JSON structure, without populating it with extracted data. This response pattern suggests a fallback mechanism employed by these models, when they struggle to accurately extract required information, indicated by their use of a structural template instead of specific data.

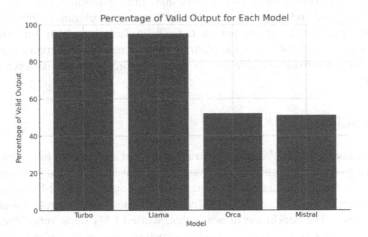

Fig. 2. Valid Outputs per model

Subsequent to the initial output evaluation, the study employed BERT embeddings to analyze the extracted data for "Job Title", "Company", "Location", and "Industry".

Cosine similarity was used to assess the alignment of model outputs with the original dataset, enabling a quantitative accuracy evaluation. As shown in Fig. 3. Similarity Scores below, the analysis revealed no significant variations in similarity scores among the models, with GPT-3.5-Turbo and Mistral showing slightly better performance.

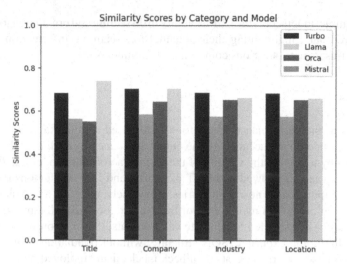

Fig. 3. Similarity Scores

GPT-3.5-Turbo consistently yielded medium to high similarity scores, indicating its relative efficacy in understanding the task and generating relevant outputs. Llama2's performance was moderately comparable to GPT-3.5-Turbo's, in both similarity scores and the proportion of valid outputs. Mistral, while demonstrating competency in the instances where it provided valid responses, paralleled Orca in its inconsistency in output generation.

6   Conclusion

The study examined LLMs' ability to extract structured information from unstructured text, showing varying performances. Although LLMs have the potential for wide-ranging use, the results suggest that their effectiveness in extracting structured information varies. More specifically, the models GPT-3.5-Turbo and Llama2 demonstrate a higher level of performance. The conclusion drawn is that, while LLMs show versatility, there is potential for increased efficiency in extracting structured information within the specified conditions.

The observed differences in performance and error-handling strategies among the models provide crucial insights into how they operate. This emphasizes the need for additional optimization to meet the practical demands of end-users. Due to the rapid advancements in the field, it is worth considering that these limitations could be overcome by exploring innovative approaches or advancements in model technology.

Future research should take into consideration the exploration of emerging models and innovative training methodologies in order to enhance the capabilities of structured information extraction. A comprehensive analysis of error categories and the influence of input data complexity on model performance could offer specific approaches for enhancing accuracy. Furthermore, by integrating observations from cognitive science and the linguistics studies, via interdisciplinary research, could lead to the emergence of more sophisticated and efficient LLMs. As natural language processing and machine learning continue to evolve, there are constant opportunities for innovation. This suggests that with more research and technological advancements, the current challenges in structured information extraction by LLMs can be overcome, allowing for their expanded use in various applications.

Building on the insightful conclusions of this study, it is imperative to recognize the broader socio-economic implications of employing LLMs for structured information extraction from job postings. The potential to refine recruitment processes, tailor educational programs to market needs and enhance policy-making with data-driven insights opens new avenues for societal advancement. This underscores the importance of ethical considerations, data privacy, and the mitigation of algorithmic biases in future LLM development and application, ensuring that the benefits of AI in labor market analysis are equitably distributed across all sectors of society.

Acknowledgments. The work presented here is funded under the ERASMUS-EDU-2023-PI-FORWARD project titled "MICRO-credentials: Identifying, DEveloping, testing and Assessing innovative approaches", acronym "MICROIDEA" and project number 101132889. The content of this document reflects the views only of the authors, and the programme authorities are not liable for any use that may be made of the information contained therein.

References

1. Vaswani, A., et al.: Attention is all you need. In: Advances in Neural Information Processing Systems 30: Annual Conference on Neural Information Processing Systems 2017, Long Beach, CA, USA, 4–9 December 2017, pp. 5998–6008 (2017). https://doi.org/10.48550/arXiv.1706.03762
2. Vukadin, D., Kurdija, A.S., Delač, G., Šilić, M.: Information extraction from free-form CV documents in multiple languages. IEEE Access **9**, 84559–84575 (2021). https://doi.org/10.1109/ACCESS.2021.3087913
3. Wei, J., et al.: Emergent abilities of large language models (2022). https://doi.org/10.48550/arXiv.2206.07682
4. Brown, T., et al.: Language models are few-shot learners. In: Advances in NeurIPS, vol. 33, pp. 1877–1901. Curran Associates, Inc., (2020). https://doi.org/10.48550/arXiv.2005.14165
5. Ye, J., et al.: A comprehensive capability analysis of GPT-3 and GPT-3.5 series models (2023). https://doi.org/10.48550/arXiv.2303.10420
6. OpenAI developer platform. https://platform.openai.com/docs/models/gpt-3-5
7. Touvron, H., et al.: Llama 2: open foundation and fine-tuned chat models (2023). https://doi.org/10.48550/arXiv.2307.09288
8. Jiang, A.Q., et al.: Mistral 7B (2023). https://doi.org/10.48550/arXiv.2310.06825
9. Ainslie, J., Lee-Thorp, J., de Jong, M., Zemlyanskiy, Y., Lebrón, F., Sanghai, S.: GQA: training generalized multi-query transformer models from multi-head checkpoints (2023). https://doi.org/10.48550/arXiv.2305.13245
10. Child, R., Gray, S., Radford, A., Sutskever, I.: Generating long sequences with sparse transformers (2019). https://doi.org/10.48550/arXiv.1904.10509
11. Beltagy, I., Peters, M.E., Cohan, A.: Longformer: the long-document transformer (2020). https://doi.org/10.48550/arXiv.2004.05150

12. pankajmathur/orca_mini_3b – Hugging Face. https://huggingface.co/pankajmathur/orca_m ini_3b
13. Mukherjee, S., Mitra, A., Jawahar, G., Agarwal, S., Palangi, H., Awadallah, A.: Orca: progressive learning from complex explanation traces of GPT-4 (2023). https://doi.org/10.48550/arXiv.2306.02707
14. Mohammed. Types of open source & closed source LLMs (Large language Models). Medium (2023). https://medium.com/@techlatest.net/types-of-open-source-llms-large-language-mod els-3b7d8b8d1af2
15. Yu, H., et al.: Open, Closed, or Small Language Models for Text Classification? (2023). https://doi.org/10.48550/arXiv.2308.10092
16. Devlin, J., et al.: BERT: pre-training of deep bidirectional transformers for language understanding (2018). https://doi.org/10.48550/arXiv.1810.04805
17. Singh, S.: Natural language processing for information extraction (2018). https://doi.org/10.48550/arXiv.1807.02383
18. Li, N., Kang, B., De Bie, T.: LLM4Jobs: unsupervised occupation extraction and standardization leveraging Large Language Models (2023). https://doi.org/10.48550/arXiv.2309.09708
19. Jeong, C.: Fine-tuning and Utilization Methods of Domain-specific LLMs (2024). https://doi.org/10.48550/arXiv.2401.02981
20. Wei, J., et al.: Finetuned Language Models are Zero-Shot Learners (2021). https://doi.org/10.48550/arXiv.2109.01652
21. Ghosh, P., Sadaphal, V.: JobRecoGPT–explainable job recommendations using LLMs (2023). https://doi.org/10.48550/arXiv.2309.11805
22. GPT4All. https://gpt4all.io
23. Skondras, P.: Panagiotis-Skondras/Informatics: MDPI Information Paper. GitHub. https://git hub.com/Panagiotis-Skondras/informatics
24. LeCun, Y., Bengio, Y., Hinton, G.: Deep learning. Nature **521**(7553), 436–444 (2015). https://doi.org/10.1038/nature14539
25. Radford, A., Narasimhan, K., Salimans, T., Sutskever, I.: Improving language understanding by generative pre-training (2018). https://openai.com/research/language-unsupervised
26. Esteva, A., et al.: A guide to deep learning in healthcare. Nat. Med. **25**(1), 24–29 (2019). https://doi.org/10.1038/s41591-018-0316-z
27. Hu, Z., Liu, W., Bian, J., Liu, X., Liu, T.Y.: Listening to chaotic whispers: a deep learning framework for news-oriented stock trend prediction. In: Proceedings of the Eleventh ACM International Conference on Web Search and Data Mining, pp. 261–269 (2018). https://doi.org/10.48550/arXiv.1712.02136
28. Bender, E.M., Gebru, T., McMillan-Major, A., Shmitchell, S.: On the dangers of stochastic parrots: can language models be too big? In: Proceedings of the 2021 ACM Conference on Fairness, Accountability, and Transparency, pp. 610–623 (2021). https://doi.org/10.1145/344 2188.3445922
29. Howard, J., Ruder, S.: Universal language model fine-tuning for text classification (2018). https://doi.org/10.48550/arXiv.1801.06146
30. Rajkomar, A., Oren, E., Chen, K., et al.: Scalable and accurate deep learning with electronic health records. NPJ Digi. Med. **1**, 18 (2018). https://doi.org/10.1038/s41746-018-0029-1
31. Kalantzi, O., Tsiotas, D., Polyzos, S.: The contribution of tourism in national economies: evidence of Greece (2023). https://doi.org/10.48550/arXiv.2302.13121
32. Eloundou, T., et al.: GPTs are GPTs: an early look at the labor market impact potential of large language models (2023). https://doi.org/10.48550/arXiv.2303.10130
33. Open-LLM-leaderboard (open LLM leaderboard). https://huggingface.co/open-llm-leader board

Comparative Study Between Q-NAS and Traditional CNNs for Brain Tumor Classification

Fabio Cardoso[1][(✉)], Marley Vellasco[1], and Karla Figueiredo[2]

[1] Pontifical Catholic University of Rio de Janeiro, Rio de Janeiro, Brazil
slynrick@gmail.com, marley@ele.puc-rio.br
[2] Rio de Janeiro State University, Rio de Janeiro, Brazil
karlafigueiredo@ime.uerj.br

Abstract. Brain tumours caused approximately 251,329 deaths worldwide in 2020, with the primary diagnostic method for these tumours involving medical imaging. In recent years, many works and applications have observed the use of Artificial Intelligence-based models using Convolution Neural Networks (CNNs) to identify health problems using images. In our study, we searched for new architectures based on CNN using the Q-NAS algorithm. We compared its performance and number of parameters with traditional architectures such as VGG, ResNet, and MobileNet to classify types of brain tumors in MRI images. The best architecture found by Q-NAS achieved an accuracy of 92% on the test data set, with a model with less than one million parameters, which is much smaller than that found in the selected traditional architectures for this study. It shows the potential of the Q-NAS algorithm and highlights the importance of efficient model design in the context of accurate and feature-aware medical image analysis.

Keywords: Quantum Inspired Evolutionary Algorithm · Neural Architecture Search · Classification · Brain Tumor

1 Introduction

Brain Tumours (BT) are abnormal growths of brain cells, which include those associated with cancer. A benign tumour is composed of inactive cells, while a malignant is composed of cancerous cells that can potentially spread. Brain Tumours can be separated into two main types: primary and metastatic. The first originates inside the brain, while the other has been spread to the brain from another part of the body [16].

There are many types of BTs, being the three most common Glioma, Meningioma and Pituitary tumours [1,17]:

- Gliomas occur in specific parts of the brain, such as cerebral peduncles and spinal cord, and are one of the most aggressive types of brain tumours, as it is responsible for one-third of all BTs and also 80% of primary malignant BTS;

L. Iliadis et al. (Eds.): EANN 2024, CCIS 2141, pp. 93–105, 2024.
https://doi.org/10.1007/978-3-031-62495-7_8

- Meningiomas originate within the meninges, the protective layers that envelop the brain and spinal cord;
- Pituitaries develop in the pituitary gland, which is responsible for the hormone production

Brain Tumors have approximately 308,102 new cases and 251,329 deaths globally per year, according to the Global Cancer Statistics 2020 by the International Agency for Research on Cancer (IARC) [2].

Deep Learning (DL) [5] models are rapidly transforming the landscape of medical diagnosis, empowering medical experts to provide better and faster diagnoses. These models use patient imaging data, such as X-Ray, Computerized Tomography (CT) and Magnetic Resonance Imaging (MRI), to perform tasks such as classification and segmentation, paving the way for improved patient care [11, 12].

Traditional architecture design is recognized to be time-consuming, with intensive manual work [10]. In order to improve and create architectures custom-designed for a specific task in an automated way, the Neural Architecture Search (NAS) technique can be used. NAS algorithms aim to find an optimal neural network architecture that improves performance and computational efficiency [4].

In this work, we propose a new convolutional architecture found by the Quantum Inspired Neural Architecture Search (Q-NAS) algorithm to classify brain tumours as glioma, meningioma, pituitary and healthy. The contributions are:

- Provide a smaller and more accurate architecture for brain tumour classification;
- Compare the performance with traditional convolutional architectures like VGG, ResNet and MobileNet.

The paper is organized as follows: Sect. 2 presents the literature review of DL classification techniques used in medical applications. Section 3 presents the Q-NAS background. Then, in Sect. 4, we present the experimental details of the problem, with results and discussions presented in Sect. 5. In Sect. 6, we summarize our findings and present the future directions of this work.

2 Related Works

A recent study by Özkaraca et al. [23] combined three publicly available datasets (figshare, SARTAJ dataset, and Br35H) to create a new dataset of 7,021 MRI images categorized into four classes: Glioma, Meningioma, Pituitary, and Healthy. Four different Convolutional Neural Network (CNN) architectures were trained on this new dataset: a Basic CNN, VGG16, DenseNet, and a Modified CNN. The Modified CNN achieved the highest precision of 96%, outperforming the other models for this task.

Gómez-Guzmán et al. [6] also combined three publicly available datasets (figshare, SARTAJ dataset, and Br35H) to create a new dataset of 7,023

MRI images categorized into four classes: Glioma, Meningioma, Pituitary, and Healthy. This work compared the performance of seven models: Generic CNN, ResNet50, InceptionV3, InceptionResNetV2, Xception, MobileNetV2 and EfficientNetB0. The best model, archiving 97% of accuracy, is InceptionV3.

The work of Zulfiqar et al. [22] use the figshare dataset with 3064 MRI images of brain tumours. They evaluated the performance of EfficientNet to classify the three types of brain tumours presented on a dataset: Glioma, Meningioma, and Pituitary. They compared the performance of five variants of EfficientNet pre-trained on the figshare dataset and a fine-tuning on an EfficientNet using imagenet weights. The fine-tuned model achieved 98% of accuracy in this task.

HAQ et al. [7] proposed a new architecture, named DCNNBT, and compared its performance with six pre-trained architectures such as Efficient-Net, ResNet, SENet, and SE-ResNe to classify brain tumours on MRI images between four classes: Glioma, Meningioma, Pituitary and Healthy. The authors used two datasets to compare the MICCAI-RSNA dataset with around 400,000 images and the CE-MRI dataset with 3,064 images. The best model proposed in this work achieved 99% accuracy in the first dataset and 90% accuracy in the second dataset.

The work of Pilla and colleagues [14] proposed a classification of brain tumour types on a dataset of 251 MRI images using transfer learning on three models, VGG16, InceptionV3, and ResNet50, with a fine-tuned adding dropout, flatten, and dense layers. The VGG16 model was the best in this comparison, with 91% of accuracy.

Our research aims to develop a more efficient and computationally economical architecture for classifying brain tumours using the Q-NAS algorithm [13,19]. The search algorithm prioritizes accuracy, and while it does not guarantee smaller architectures, it consistently identifies a better solution and generally has fewer parameters than traditional convolutional architectures.

3 Quantum Inspired Neural Architecture Search (Q-NAS)

This section explains the Quantum-inspired Neural Architecture Search (Q-NAS): an algorithm proposed by Szwarcman et al. [19]. Q-NAS constitutes a quantum-inspired evolutionary algorithm designed to construct a deep neural network for a predefined task.

The Q-NAS algorithm encodes the network architectures in quantum individuals, that is inspired by quantum physics, which a singular quantum individual can generate multiple classical individuals. The classical individual represents the discrete architecture space and the quantum individual represents the distribution of it from where the classical individual are generated based on observations. It is important to notice that Q-NAS algorithm does not evolve the weights of the networks.

The architecture search space is represented as a *chain-like* structure that comprises building blocks (layers functions) and one of those blocks is a no-operation layer that is responsible for passing the input data to the output and shrink the number of parameters and layers of the architecture found. The user can define the search space by selecting the maximum number of building blocks (maximum number of layers in the CNN) that will be stacked during the search phase. When the network generated by a classical individual is being created, a fully connected (FC) classifier layer is included at the end of the structure found.

Considering that the blocks generated by the classical individuals can reduce the feature map size, Szwarcman et al. [19] decided to penalize invalid architecture. This works evaluating the network that is being built, and when it reaches the allowed number of reducing layers, which is a parameter of the algorithm, the fitness of that architecture is penalized.

The Q-NAS algorithm has three main operations: generate the population, evaluate classical individuals, and update quantum individuals. Algorithm 1 provides a summary of the Q-NAS evolutionary process. At the beginning, the user defines the probability distribution among the available function blocks. After the first generation, the classical individuals' evaluations update the quantum individual probabilities.

Algorithm 1. Q-NAS evolving algorithm

1: **Input:** Training data D
2: **Input:** Architecture search space $\mathcal{A}$
3: **Input:** Number of epochs E
4: **Initialize:** $t \leftarrow 0$, $Q(0) \leftarrow$ uniform random distribution
5: **while** $t < E$ **do**
6:     **Sample:** Generate classical population $C(t)$ according to $Q(t)$
7:     **Evaluate:** $F(C(t)) = \text{evaluate}(C(t), D)$
8:     **Update Q-values:** $Q(t+1) \leftarrow \text{UpdateQNAS}(Q(t), C(t), F(C(t)))$
9:     $t \leftarrow t + 1$
10: **end while**

Algorithm 2 describes how the quantum individuals are updated based on the classical individuals at each generation.

Algorithm 2. Q-NAS Network Quantum Update

1: **Initialize:** Generate random mask based on *update_quantum_rate* , Chosen nodes positions $\leftarrow$ idx
2: **for** $i \in idx$ **do**
3:     $p_i \leftarrow f(i)$ { Probability of node i }
4:     $\Delta p_i \leftarrow \text{random}() \times 0.05$
5:     $p_i \leftarrow p_i + \Delta p_i$
6:     Subtract Δp_i from the probabilities other than $f(i)$ proportionally to their current size
7: **end for**

For this work the Fig. 1 shows the Q-NAS processing diagram, from the pre-processing stage to the retrain and evaluation stage of the best architecture. The initial phase involves pre-processing, which is responsible for applying data augmentation utilizing random cropping and left or right inversion and normalizing the image by the average data value.

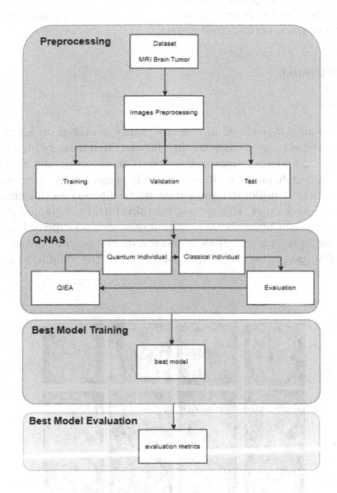

Fig. 1. Q-NAS Diagram

After preprocessing, the dataset was divided to ensure a fair basis for model comparison. The dataset is separated into three sets: training, validation, and test; training and validation are used for the architecture search phase, and training the best model. The test set is used for model evaluation.

During the search phase, the algorithm trains the architectures found in the classic individuals with the limited training and validation set to reduce the search time. After evaluating the classical individuals, the quantum individual is updated to improve the classical individuals it generates.

After the search algorithm find the best architecture, this architecture will pass through the training phase, which consists in train the model with the complete training and validation set to solve the image classification problem.

The final phase is responsible for evaluating the best model, which involves presenting the test set to the model trained in the previous phase and calculating its accuracy, the main performance metric.

4 Experiments

4.1 Dataset

The brain tumour dataset used in this case study is hosted on kaggle [20]. Significant improvements were made in this dataset: removing redundant data for sample consistency, image normalization based on the grayscale histogram, and resizing to 256×256 pixels with aspect ratio preservation. The standardized dimensions ensure a uniform representation, facilitating better model results using brain tumour images. This dataset contains images of glioma, meningioma, and pituitary types of brain tumour, and images with no type of tumour, called healthy. Figure 2 presents examples of those four classes. The dataset was separated into 1800 images for the training set, 200 for the validation set, and 351 for the test set.

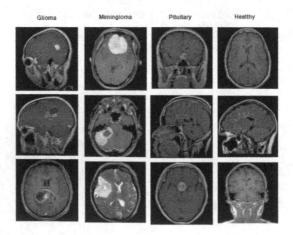

Fig. 2. Examples of each class inside the dataset

4.2 Q-NAS

In order to determine the most effective architecture, the Q-NAS algorithm explored the search space using a data set limited to 800 images for training and validation. The evolutionary process unfolded over a maximum of 300 generations, with six quantum individuals in each generation. Subsequently, these quantum individuals give rise to classical individuals, each made up of a stack of a maximum of 10 building blocks. A protocol of 50 epochs, using a batch size of 32 and the Root Mean Square Propagation (RMSProp) [3] optimizer, was applied throughout the training phase to calculate the fitness of each classical individual.

Table 1 shows the set of possible building blocks available for the Q-NAS algorithm in this study. It includes two polling blocks, ten different convolutional blocks characterized by various kernels, strides, and filters, and a block with no operation. The no-operation block has the task of reducing the number of active layers in the network to a value below the selected maximum since it simply produces the output without making any changes to the input.

Table 1. Archtecture search space

Building Blocks	Kernel	Strides	Filters
AvgPooling	2	2	–
MaxPooling	2	2	–
ConvBlock	1	1	32
ConvBlock	1	1	64
ConvBlock	3	1	32
ConvBlock	3	1	64
ConvBlock	3	1	128
ConvBlock	3	1	256
ConvBlock	5	1	32
ConvBlock	5	1	64
ConvBlock	5	1	128
ConvBlock	5	1	256
NoOp	–	–	–

After identifying the best model through the search process, this best architecture goes through a retraining phase using all the data in training and validation data set, instead of the limited data used in evolution phase. Retraining is carried out for 300 epochs, using a batch size 32, also the Momentum optimizer was applied with a momentum value of 0.9, and the initial learning rate set to 0.1, those are the same parameters used in Noce et al. work [13]. In addition, a learning rate scheduler following a cosine function is incorporated into the training regime.

4.3   Traditional Convolutional Neural Network (CNN) Architectures

The Residual neural network (ResNet) family [8] of architectures are known for being very deep networks with the characteristic of shortcuts between their blocks. It is possible to identify the depth of the model by its name; for example, ResNet-101 is made up of 101 layers. For this work, the models ResNet-50 and ResNet-101 were selected.

The Visual Geometry Group (VGG) Family [18] is known for its simplicity and uniform architecture; it consists of several convolutional layers with small filter sizes (3×3) and max-polling layers between those convolutional layers. This kind of network usually has a large number of parameters, which can make it computationally expensive. Popular variants of this architecture family, VGG16 and VGG19 models, were included in this work.

The last architecture family used in this work was the MobileNet Family [9], designed to be lightweight and efficient for devices with less resources, such as mobiles and edge devices. In this kind of network, the standard convolution is split into depthwise and pointwise, considerably reducing the computational cost. We used the MobileNet version 2(V2) [15] because it is built upon the first version, introducing inverted residuals, linear bottlenecks, variable expansion factor, and improvements in efficiency and performance.

Table 2 shows a resumed comparison between those architecture families. It is possible to notice that those three families have different characteristics in terms of computational efficiency.

Table 2. Comparison of VGG, ResNet, and MobileNet families

Feature	VGG	ResNet	MobileNet
Architecture	Sequential stacking	Residual connections	separable convolutions
Depth	Deeper networks	Very deep networks	Lighter networks
Parameter Size	Larger	Moderate	Small
Strengths	Good for transfer learning	Easy to implement	Efficient and lightweight

The proposed training and evaluation methodology for the selected architectures is illustrated in Fig. 3. The initial phase involves preprocessing, exactly the same as Q-NAS, which is responsible for resizing images to the model's input dimensions ($224 \times 224 \times 3$) and applying data augmentation through random crops and left or right flips.

After the preprocessing, the dataset was split to ensure an equitable basis for model comparison. The dataset was separated into three sets: training, validation, and test; the training and validation were used for the training phase, and the test set was used for performance evaluation.

During the training phase, all the models had a transfer learning [21] utilizing the ImageNet dataset. Each model was trained using two configuration of the classification network after the convolutional layers, the first configuration is

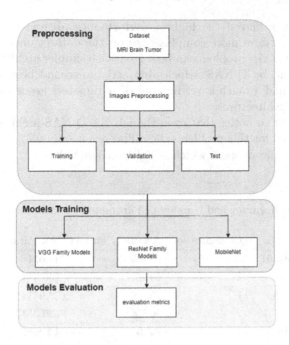

Fig. 3. Training and evaluation diagram for traditional architectures

composed of a flattened layer followed by a output layer with softmax activation function and the second configuration is composed if a flattened layer, a dense layer with 1024 neurons and dropout of 0.5 followed by a output layer with softmax activation function. The training process continues for 50 epochs or until early stopping is invoked based on validation loss, with a patience parameter set to 3.

The final phase is responsible for the models evaluation, which involves submitting the test set to all models and calculating the primary performance metrics accuracy.

The models were trained for a maximum of 50 epochs or until the early stop mechanism was triggered. The early stop was configured with a patience parameter set to 3, monitoring the validation loss data to stop the training process when there was no improvement. The training was performed by freezing the convolutional layers with the weights from transfer learning, and the fine-tuning was done by training the classification part of the network.

5   Discussion and Results

As shown in Table 3, the ResNet-101 model performed worse on test data than the others and the reason is that this architecture is a more complex than the others and simpler models perform better for this brain tumour classification problem.

The VGG-16 achieved the highest performance, demonstrating that simpler models outperform more complex ones on the dataset under investigation. Another proof that the problem can be solved with simpler architectures was the architecture found by Q-NAS, which obtained the second best accuracy of all the models and had a much lower number of parameters needed in the network than the other architectures.

It is important to notice that even though the Q-NAS architecture is in the second best model for this problem, the difference is only 0.3% of accuracy and has 0.05 millions parameters, which is lighter than VGG-16, wich was the best model.

Table 3. Accuracy and Number of Parameters of each architecture

Model	Configuration	Accuracy on test	No. Parameters
ResNet-101	1	38.4%	43.0M
	2	64.9%	145.4M
ResNet-50	1	75.2%	23.9M
	2	56.7%	126.3M
VGG-16	**1**	**92.3%**	**14.8M**
	2	88.9%	40.4M
VGG-19	1	74.4%	20.1M
	2	87.2%	45.7M
MobileNetV2	1	80.1%	2.5M
	2	82.6%	66.4M
Q-NAS	–	**92.0%**	**0.05M**

Table 4 shows the best architecture found by the Q-NAS algorithm. It is possible to notice that there is a prevalence of polling layers, which means less information is required for the brain tumour classification task. Furthermore, with six building blocks out of the maximum ten, the required trainable parameters are considerably minimized. Also, compared with the MobileNet model, it has less than a million parameters, while the MobileNetV2 on second configuration has more than 2 million in the experiment.

It is important to notice that the top network applied to the last convolutional layer of each architecture increase the number of trainable parameters because is used a dense layer between the flatten and output layer as described in the last section.

Table 4. Best architecture found by Q-NAS

Building Blocks	Kernel	Strides	Filters
MaxPooling	2	2	–
ConvBlock	3	1	128
AvgPooling	2	2	–
MaxPooling	2	2	–
ConvBlock	1	1	64
AvgPooling	2	2	–
MaxPooling	2	2	–
ConvBlock	3	1	64
AvgPooling	2	2	–
NoOp	–	–	–

6   Conclusion and Future Work

This research aimed to compare the performance and number of parameters of different models used to classify tumour types through the analysis of MRI images. This comparative evaluation involves the architecture developed by the Q-NAS algorithm, as well as the selected traditional CNN architectures. Transfer learning was employed, leveraging pre-trained weights from the ImageNet dataset.

The results of this investigation revealed that the best overall architecture was found by the Q-NAS algorithm exhibited an accuracy of 92% on the test set with 0.05 million parameters, even though the VGG-16 model in the first configuration is 0.3% higher on accuracy it also has much more parameters with a total of 14.8 millions parameters. Among the traditional CNN architectures used in this study VGG-16, in both configurations, was the one with the best performance in classifying brain tumours.

Furthermore, it was observed that the architecture found by the Q-NAS algorithm had numerous pooling layers. This observation suggests that for the problem of brain tumour classification, images with large amounts of information (high-quality images) or detailed images may not be essential. The substantial presence of pooling layers played a key role in reducing the number of architecture parameters encountered.

As part of future works, we propose an exploration of the applicability of the Q-NAS technique in domains beyond medical imaging. This comparative analysis could show the versatility of this approach in different contexts. Furthermore, an interesting investigation path involves using datasets with a large volume of images. This allows full comparisons between the Q-NAS technique and models employing transfer learning, as well as those with weights initialized randomly.

To increase the depth of the analysis, it would be beneficial to incorporate a broader range of model families. This approach would contribute to a more comprehensive understanding of the strengths and weaknesses between the architectures and those found by the Q-NAS algorithm.

References

1. Badža, M.M., Barjaktarović, M.Č: Classification of brain tumors from MRI images using a convolutional neural network. Appl. Sci. **10**(6), 1999 (2020)
2. WHOIA for Research on Cancer (IARC) (2020). https://www.iarc.who.int/. Accessed 05 Dec 2023
3. De, S., Mukherjee, A., Ullah, E.: Convergence guarantees for RMSProp and ADAM in non-convex optimization and an empirical comparison to nesterov acceleration (2018). https://doi.org/10.48550/ARXIV.1807.06766
4. Gong, X., Chang, S., Jiang, Y., Wang, Z.: AutoGAN: neural architecture search for generative adversarial networks. In: 2019 IEEE/CVF International Conference on Computer Vision (ICCV). IEEE (2019). https://doi.org/10.1109/iccv.2019.00332
5. Goodfellow, I., Bengio, Y., Courville, A.: Deep Learning. Adaptive Computation and Machine Learning. MIT Press (2016). https://books.google.co.in/books?id=Np9SDQAAQBAJ
6. Gómez-Guzmán, M.A., et al.: Classifying brain tumors on magnetic resonance imaging by using convolutional neural networks. Electronics **12**(4) (2023). https://doi.org/10.3390/electronics12040955. https://www.mdpi.com/2079-9292/12/4/955
7. Haq, M.A., Khan, I., Ahmed, A., Eldin, S.M., Alshehri, A., Ghamry, N.A.: DCNNBT: a novel deep convolution neural network-based brain tumor classification model. Fractals **31**(06), 2340102 (2023). https://doi.org/10.1142/S0218348X23401023
8. He, K., Zhang, X., Ren, S., Sun, J.: Deep residual learning for image recognition. CoRR abs/1512.03385 (2015). http://arxiv.org/abs/1512.03385
9. Howard, A.G., et al.: MobileNets: efficient convolutional neural networks for mobile vision applications (2017)
10. Liu, C., et al.: Auto-deeplab: hierarchical neural architecture search for semantic image segmentation. In: 2019 IEEE/CVF Conference on Computer Vision and Pattern Recognition (CVPR). IEEE (2019). https://doi.org/10.1109/cvpr.2019.00017
11. Lundervold, A.S., Lundervold, A.: An overview of deep learning in medical imaging focusing on MRI. Zeitschrift für Medizinische Physik **29**(2), 102–127 (2019). https://doi.org/10.1016/j.zemedi.2018.11.002. https://www.sciencedirect.com/science/article/pii/S0939388918301181. Special Issue: Deep Learning in Medical Physics
12. Montagnon, E., et al.: Deep learning workflow in radiology: a primer. Insights Imaging **11**(1), 22 (2020). https://doi.org/10.1186/s13244-019-0832-5
13. Noce, J., et al.: Applied enhanced Q-NAS for COVID-19 detection in CT images. In: Mahmud, M., Ieracitano, C., Kaiser, M.S., Mammone, N., Morabito, F.C. (eds.) AII 2022. CCIS, vol. 1724, pp. 419–433. Springer, Cham (2022). https://doi.org/10.1007/978-3-031-24801-6_30
14. Pillai, R., Sharma, A., Sharma, N., Gupta, R.: Brain tumor classification using VGG 16, ResNet50, and InceptionV3 transfer learning models. In: 2023 2nd International Conference for Innovation in Technology (INOCON), pp. 1–5 (2023). https://doi.org/10.1109/INOCON57975.2023.10101252

15. Sandler, M., Howard, A., Zhu, M., Zhmoginov, A., Chen, L.C.: MobileNetv2: inverted residuals and linear bottlenecks (2019)
16. Saranya, C., Priya, J.G., Jayalakshmi, P., Pavithra, E.H.: Withdrawn: brain tumor identification using deep learning (2021)
17. Sharif, M.I., Li, J.P., Khan, M.A., Saleem, M.A.: Active deep neural network features selection for segmentation and recognition of brain tumors using MRI images. Pattern Recogn. Lett. **129**, 181–189 (2020)
18. Simonyan, K., Zisserman, A.: Very deep convolutional networks for large-scale image recognition (2015)
19. Szwarcman, D., Civitarese, D., Velasco, M.: Quantum-inspired neural architecture search. In: 2019 International Joint Conference on Neural Networks (IJCNN), pp. 1–8. IEEE (2019)
20. Thomas: Brain tumors 256 × 256 (2023). https://www.kaggle.com/datasets/thomasdubail/brain-tumors-256x256
21. Zhuang, F., et al.: A comprehensive survey on transfer learning (2020)
22. Zulfiqar, F., Ijaz Bajwa, U., Mehmood, Y.: Multi-class classification of brain tumor types from MR images using efficientnets. Biomed. Signal Process. Control **84**, 104777 (2023). https://doi.org/10.1016/j.bspc.2023.104777. https://www.sciencedirect.com/science/article/pii/S1746809423002100
23. Özkaraca, O., et al.: Multiple brain tumor classification with dense CNN architecture using brain MRI images. Life **13**(2) (2023). https://doi.org/10.3390/life13020349. https://www.mdpi.com/2075-1729/13/2/349

Deep Echo State Networks for Modelling of Industrial Systems

José Ramón Rodríguez-Ossorio[1]([✉]) [iD], Claudio Gallicchio[2] [iD],
Antonio Morán[1] [iD], Ignacio Díaz[3] [iD], Juan J. Fuertes[1] [iD],
and Manuel Domínguez[1] [iD]

[1] SUPPRESS Research Group, Escuela de Ingenierías, Universidad de León,
Campus de Vegazana, 24007 León, Spain
{jrodro,a.moran,jjfuem,mdomg}@unileon.es

[2] Department of Computer Science, University of Pisa, Largo Bruno Pontecorvo 3,
56127 Pisa, Italy
gallicch@di.unipi.it

[3] Electrical Engineering Department, University of Oviedo,
Edif. Departamental Oeste 2, Campus de Viesques s/n, 33204 Gijón, Spain
idiaz@uniovi.es

Abstract. In the industrial field, the modelling of complex systems is a relevant task to understand their evolution, to infer their most representative characteristics, or to detect anomalous situations. Nevertheless, this modelling is notably challenging within the industrial environment, with large amounts of data to be processed but several difficulties in extracting knowledge from these data.

In this paper, we work with an industrial plant with four water tanks, focusing on estimating the levels of two sequentially connected tanks. For this purpose, Deep Echo State Networks (Deep ESNs), within the framework of Reservoir Computing (RC), are used, representing an increasingly popular methodology for efficient learning to modelling systems with diverse time-scale dynamics.

Specifically, we have designed a learning system that makes use of a dedicated Deep ESN module for the prediction of the level of each tank. We conducted numerical experiments to examine how the performance of the predictions is affected by the number of layers. Our findings indicate that increasing the number of recurrent layers leads to better predictions, and also highlight noteworthy differences in the dynamics of the upper and lower tanks.

Keywords: Reservoir Computing · Echo State Networks · Deep Echo State Networks · Dynamics · Data-based modelling

1 Introduction

Modelling and representing the behaviour of complex systems over time is a task of great relevance in the field of industrial engineering: it can be used to

L. Iliadis et al. (Eds.): EANN 2024, CCIS 2141, pp. 106–119, 2024.
https://doi.org/10.1007/978-3-031-62495-7_9

better understand how the modelled physical system works and how it evolves, to know which are its most representative characteristics or to detect anomalous or faulty situations. All of this information leads to an enhancement of efficiency and an improvement of the performance of the whole process, in the context of an industry that continuously focuses on increasing production and reducing costs [1].

This system representation is particularly challenging when working within the industrial environment, where large amounts of data are acquired from the process, but extracting knowledge of the dynamic behaviour of the process is not that straightforward [17]. Taking into account the need for industrial processes to be increasingly more efficient, better optimised and with more and better functionalities, it is of the utmost importance to achieve a faithful modelling of these processes, by obtaining and representing the aforementioned dynamics.

Machine learning tools are typically used to solve modelling tasks based on this data. More specifically, deep learning models have progressively gained more relevance, mainly due to the possibility they offer to simplify complex machine learning tasks by dividing them into several levels of abstraction [14]. However, the use of these complex architectures implies a higher computational load and a greater time demand for training the models [9].

This drawback is solved by improvements in the hardware with the use of Graphics Processing Units (GPUs) and the distribution of the workload, leading to less time-consuming procedures [18]. However, not in all scenarios is it possible to have the necessary hardware resources to run these models, and algorithms with more efficient training are needed.

In this regard, *Reservoir Computing* (RC) [16] is presented as an interesting alternative approach for the design of *Recurrent Neural Networks* (RNNs) through fast and efficient training, with a lower demand on hardware resources [5]. Within RC, one of the most popular models are Echo State Networks (ESNs) [10,11], in which the reservoir weights are randomly initialised and the only trained layer is a linear readout [20].

With the recently introduced Deep ESNs [6], RC is brought into the world of deep learning, with the development of hierarchical architectures that concatenate several layered reservoirs. These architectures surpass the performance of standard Shallow ESNs by including the representation of multiple time scales from the input data stream [8].

In this paper, we propose the application of Deep ESNs for the modelling of an industrial plant composed of four water tanks, to analyse the improvements in the performance of the models used with the introduction of hierarchical deep RC architectures. Previous work has already tested the performance of Shallow ESNs in the modelling of this four-tank plant [19], and it is of interest to quantify the improvements introduced in the same industrial process with Deep ESNs.

This paper is structured as follows. First, Sect. 2 introduces reservoir computing and the ESN architectures applied in this paper. Section 3 describes the experimental setup on which the ESN models previously described are applied. Section 4 presents the experiments and the results obtained. Finally, Sect. 5 brings the conclusions.

2   Reservoir Computing

This section provides an insight into the Reservoir Computing recurrent neural networks applied in this paper. More specifically, Echo State Networks are described as a particular class of RC, with the standard shallow variant in Sect. 2.1 and its deep RC approach in Sect. 2.2.

2.1   Shallow Echo State Networks

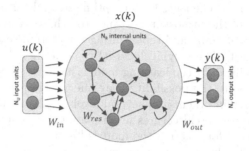

Fig. 1. Architecture of a Shallow ESN.

Echo State Networks (ESN) [10], as a particular implementation within the Reservoir Computing paradigm, are an efficient approach for modelling *Recurrent Neural Networks* (RNN) [6]. ESNs consist of a static, randomly generated *reservoir* and a trainable *readout*. The reservoir operates based on a random nonlinear recurrent model, which processes an N_U-dimensional vector of input signals $\mathbf{u}(k) \in \mathbb{R}^{N_U}$ into a high-dimensional vector with N_R reservoir states $\mathbf{x}(k) \in \mathbb{R}^{N_R}$. An interesting and frequently used variation includes a leaky integrator to regulate the recall of the previous states of the ESN [12]. This variant is commonly known as LI-ESN (Leaky Integrator ESN), and it is the architecture used in this work for Shallow ESNs. In a LI-ESN, the state equation of the leaky integrator reservoir units is defined as:

$$\mathbf{x}(k) = (1 - \mathrm{lr})\,\mathbf{x}(k-1) + \mathrm{lr}\,\mathbf{tanh}(\mathbf{W}_{res}\mathbf{x}(k-1) + \mathbf{W}_{in}\mathbf{u}(k) + \theta) \qquad (1)$$

where $\mathbf{x}(k) \in \mathbb{R}^{N_R}$ and $\mathbf{u}(k) \in \mathbb{R}^{N_U}$ respectively represent the reservoir and input state vectors at time k, $\mathbf{W}_{res} \in \mathbb{R}^{N_R \times N_R}$ is the reservoir weight matrix, $\mathbf{W}_{in} \in \mathbb{R}^{N_R \times N_U}$ is the input-to-reservoir weight matrix, $\theta \in \mathbb{R}^{N_R}$ is the input bias vector, $\mathrm{lr} \in [0, 1]$ denotes the leaking rate parameter of the leaky integrator, and **tanh** is the element-wise application of the activation function (hyperbolic tangent).

The readout function then maps the reservoir states to an N_Y-dimensional vector of outputs $\mathbf{y}(k) \in \mathbb{R}^{N_Y}$ via a linear model with trainable weights, which are typically determined using standard least squares methods. The ESN output function is shown in the equation:

$$\mathbf{y}(k) = \mathbf{W}_{\text{out}}\mathbf{x}(k) + \theta_{\text{out}} \tag{2}$$

where $\mathbf{y}(k) \in \mathbb{R}^{N_Y}$ is the output at time k, $\mathbf{W}_{\text{out}} \in \mathbb{R}^{N_Y \times N_R}$ is the reservoir-to-readout weight matrix and $\theta_{\text{out}} \in \mathbb{R}^{N_R}$ is the reservoir-to-output bias vector.

The architecture of a Shallow ESN is represented in Fig. 1, where bias terms are omitted for simplicity. Architecturally speaking, the echo state network is structured into three layers: the *input* layer, the reservoir itself, and the *readout* or output layer. First, the *input* layer, which is characterized by the matrix $\mathbf{W}_{\text{in}}$, connects the N_U inputs in the input vector $\mathbf{u}(k)$ to the reservoir. Then, the reservoir layer is made up of a substantial number N_R of internal units or *nodes*, with activations or states $x_1(k), \ldots, x_{N_R}(k)$, forming the state vector $\mathbf{x}(k)$ at time k. The nodes within the reservoir have feedback and mutual connections, both weighted by the reservoir weight matrix $\mathbf{W}_{\text{res}}$. Finally, the *readout* or output layer, which links the N_R reservoir states in $\mathbf{x}(k)$ to the N_Y outputs in $\mathbf{y}(k)$, based on the weights in the matrix $\mathbf{W}_{\text{out}}$.

The matrices $\mathbf{W}_{\text{res}}$ and $\mathbf{W}_{\text{in}}$ are constructed using random values, with some adjustments made to promote chaotic dynamics within the reservoir. These random weights are typically sparsified by retaining only a small percentage of random non-zero elements and setting the remaining weights to zero. The reservoir matrix $\mathbf{W}_{\text{res}}$ is generally scaled to have its largest eigenvalue ρ_{max} or spectral radius close to 1 (or even slightly above) to maintain the dynamic modes near the edge of stability and satisfy what is called Echo State Property (ESP) [3, 22]. The input matrix $\mathbf{W}_{\text{in}}$ is scaled by a given factor *is* in a range $[-is, is]$.

If the reservoir is applied recursively to an input sequence $\{\mathbf{u}(k)\}_{k=1}^{N_k}$, it produces a sequence of high-dimensional state vectors $\{\mathbf{x}(k)\}_{k=1}^{N_k}$. Then, these states are combined in the readout with trainable weights to produce the output sequence $\{\mathbf{y}(k)\}_{k=1}^{N_K}$. If we arrange the sequences of state vectors and outputs into matrix forms, the output can be obtained as $\mathbf{Y} = \mathbf{W}_{out}\mathbf{X}$. The readout matrix $\mathbf{W}_{out}$ is usually trained with *ridge regression* method, and it is the approach used in this work.

While there are other configurations and variations of this Shallow ESN model, such as incorporating an output feedback connection by including $\mathbf{y}(k)$ in the reservoir state function (see Eq. 1), or direct connections from the input to the readout, these will not be discussed here. A more comprehensive and extended insight can be found in [15].

2.2 Deep Echo State Networks

The *Deep ESN* model enables the introduction of ESNs and their advantages in the world of deep learning algorithms. This architecture, which was presented in [6], involves the concatenation of different reservoir layers organised hierarchically so that the first reservoir is fed directly by the input vector, while the rest of the reservoirs receive as input the output of the previous reservoir (the generated state vector). A representation of the *Deep ESN* architecture is shown in Fig. 2.

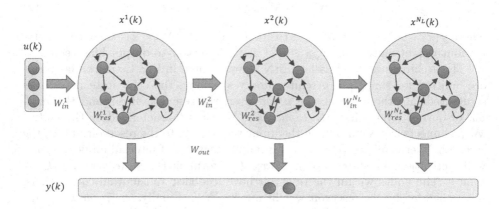

Fig. 2. Architecture of a Deep ESN.

Generally speaking, a set of reservoirs with the same number of units N_R in each one is considered. Thus, for a setup defined with N_L layers, the total amount of units in the hierarchical reservoir architecture is computed as $N_T = N_R \times N_L$. The state function of the first layer ($l = 1$) is defined as follows:

$$\mathbf{x}^1(k) = (1 - lr^1)\,\mathbf{x}^1(k-1) + lr^1\,\mathbf{tanh}(\mathbf{W}_{res}^1\mathbf{x}^1(k-1) + \mathbf{W}_{in}^1\mathbf{u}(k) + \theta^1)\ (3)$$

while for other layers ($l > 1$) the state equation is given by:

$$\mathbf{x}^l(k) = (1 - lr^l)\,\mathbf{x}^l(k-1) + lr^l\,\mathbf{tanh}(\mathbf{W}_{res}^l\mathbf{x}^l(k-1) + \mathbf{W}_{in}^l\mathbf{x}^{l-1}(k) + \theta^l)\,(4)$$

In these equations, $\mathbf{u}(k) \in \mathbb{R}^{N_U}$ represents the input state vector at time k, $\mathbf{x}^l(k) \in \mathbb{R}^{N_R}$ is the state vector for reservoir at layer l and time k, $lr^l \in [0,1]$ represents the leaking rate parameter at layer l; $\mathbf{tanh}$ is the hyperbolic tangent activation function; $\mathbf{W}_{res}^l \in \mathbb{R}^{N_R \times N_R}$ is the reservoir matrix for layer l; and $\mathbf{W}_{in}^l$ denotes the input weight matrix for layer l, having $\mathbf{W}_{in}^1 \in \mathbb{R}^{N_R \times N_U}$ for first layer and $\mathbf{W}_{in}^l \in \mathbb{R}^{N_R \times N_R}$ for successive layers.

The principle of operation of Deep ESNs is quite similar to that of Shallow ESNs: the reservoirs are initialised following a random uniform distribution, such as $[0, 1]$ and scaled to guarantee certain conditions that keep the system on the edge of stability, and then left untrained. The conditions sought in this case are given by the Echo State Property of Deep ESNs, which is detailed in [4]. It works similarly to the property for Shallow ESNs, likewise looking for the largest eigenvalue ρ_{max}^l to be less than 1 for each reservoir. Similarly, the input matrix

$\mathbf{W}_{in}$ and the connection matrices between reservoirs $\{\mathbf{W}_{in}^l\}_{l=2}^{l=N_L}$ are generated from a uniform random distribution and scaled in a range $[-is, is]$.

For the calculation of the model output, the most standardised approach is to connect the outputs of all reservoirs to the readout, as can be seen in the schematic in Fig. 2. Hence, the network output is obtained according to the following equation, as a weighted sum of the states from the different layers:

$$\mathbf{y}(k) = \mathbf{W}_{out}\mathbf{x}(k) + \theta_{out} = \mathbf{W}_{out}\begin{bmatrix} \mathbf{x}^1(k) \\ \mathbf{x}^2(k) \\ \cdots \\ \mathbf{x}^{N_L}(k) \end{bmatrix} + \theta_{out} \tag{5}$$

Here, $\mathbf{W}_{out} \in \mathbb{R}^{N_Y \times N_L N_R}$ represents the output weight matrix, the concatenation of the states from all the reservoir layers is $\mathbf{x}(t) \in \mathbb{R}^{N_L N_R}$, and $\theta_{out} \in \mathbb{R}^{N_R}$ denotes the output bias vector.

Deep ESNs have some advantages over Shallow ESNs. To begin with, Deep ESNs are able to generate a representation of multiple time-scale dynamics between the different layers, hierarchically structured so that higher layers have slower dynamics. Furthermore, for the same total number of reservoir units, Deep ESNs have a larger memory capacity than Shallow ESNs, allowing the effect of changes that have occurred earlier in the inputs to be taken into account. In addition, distributing the total number of units among several reservoirs reduces the total number of non-zero recurrent connections, allowing for more efficient operation. Therefore, with the use of Deep ESNs, using the same total number of reservoir units, the overall model performance is considerably improved over Shallow ESNs. Further analysis and details about Deep ESN advantages can be found in [7].

3   Experimentation System

This section describes the environment in which the experiments of the present work have been carried out. In this paper, an experimental setup at the Remote Laboratory of Automatic Control of the University of León is used [2]. This setup is an implementation with real industrial equipment of the four-tank system proposed by Karl Henrik Johansson [13], and it consists of four water tanks arranged vertically in pairs so that the water drained out of the upper tanks ends up in the lower ones. Twin pumps regulated by variable speed drives generate water flow from a lower supply tank to these four tanks.

Water distribution among the tanks is managed by two three-way valves that cross the supplied flows between the tanks. With this system, each pump supplies water to specific tanks, creating a complex control system where the water levels in each tank are influenced not only by pumps and valves but also by the level of other tanks with different dynamics.

Pressure sensors at the base of each tank measure water levels, enabling experiments to control these levels using the aforementioned pumps and valves.

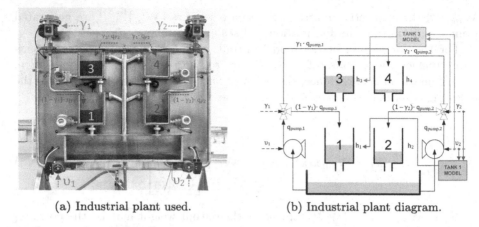

(a) Industrial plant used.   (b) Industrial plant diagram.

Fig. 3. Industrial plant and its diagram.

Solenoid valves introduce disturbances to the water flow. The implemented industrial plant is illustrated in Fig. 3. In addition, the relevant variables that define this plant, such as pump and valve ratios, total pump flow, and tank water levels, are represented in Table 1.

Table 1. Variables of the quadruple-tank process.

Variable	Units	Description
h_i	$0-100\%$	water level in tank i
v_j	$0-100\%$	ratio of pump j
$q_{\text{pump},j}$	cm^3/s	total flows of pump j
γ_j	$0-100\%$	ratio of valve j

The plant operates as a Multiple Input, Multiple Output (MIMO) system, where pump and valve settings are input variables and desired tank levels are output variables. Alternatively, other scenarios can be explored by treating the plant as Multiple Input, Single Output (MISO) subsystems, focusing on controlling the level of a single tank.

The mathematical model of the four-tank process is derived from Bernoulli's and mass balance laws, resulting in differential equations for each tank's level. A state-space model, commonly used in control engineering, is employed to describe the system. However, implementing theoretical models in real industrial systems like this pilot plant presents challenges due to nonlinearities introduced by industrial equipment, such as sensors noise, nonlinear pump characteristics, and asymmetrical valve responses. These real-world complexities necessitate advanced techniques like machine learning for accurate modelling and control, as linear approaches may lack precision.

4   Experiments and Results

This section describes the experiments conducted in this work, the process for hyperparameter selection and the results obtained.

The main objective of this paper is to compare the performance of Shallow ESNs and Deep ESNs in their application to the industrial pilot plant. For this purpose, it is decided to work with two ESN models, which are represented in Fig. 3b and are the following ones:

- **Tank 3 MISO model**
  - **Inputs:** Pump 2 rate + Valve 2 position
  - **Outputs:** Tank 3 level
- **Tank 1 MISO model**
  - **Inputs:** Pump 2 rate + Valve 2 position
  - **Outputs:** Tank 1 level

The aim is, for these two defined models, to evaluate their performance depending on the number of reservoir layers used, starting with a single layer, in what would be a standard Shallow ESN, and progressively increasing the number of layers to observe the improvements in network performance and select the number of layers that yields the best results.

This approach is interesting because different time-scale dynamics take place in these two models: as the tanks are connected in series, setpoint changes in pump 2 and/or valve 2 will take longer to be reflected in the lower tank (level 1 modelled by tank 1 MISO model) than in the upper tank (level 3 modelled by tank 3 MISO model). Similarly, more memory capacity will be needed for the lower tank than for the upper tank, and the lower tank will have slower dynamics than the upper tank.

The data used for the model development were obtained from closed-loop experiments with a proportional controller to adjust the tank level with the pump power setpoint. It was decided to work in a closed loop as it is a more faithful recreation of a real industrial plant automation. These experiments had several stages of 60 s each, where the controller setpoint, the valve opening percentage, or even both variables simultaneously, were changed. More specifically, these experiments were run for 24 h, to generate enough random scenarios and obtain enough data to model the industrial plant.

A Python application was used to acquire the data from the plant controller, with a sampling rate of 100 milliseconds, and then the data was resampled to 5 s, filtered and split into 60% for training, 20% for validation, and 20% for testing.

The ESN models were programmed, set up and trained using Python and the *ReservoirPy* library [21], a modular library that lets different ESN components as reservoir or readout be parameterized and connected independently. The *hyperopt* library, which is also included in *ReservoirPy*, was used to search and optimize the hyperparameters for the ESN model. It performs a random search within a specified range of values and picks the ones that minimize the model output error.

To evaluate the performance of the Deep ESN models depending on the number of layers, as described above, we proceeded as follows: first, for each number of layers tested, and using the training and validation data, 100 possible combinations of hyperparameters are evaluated using the *hyperopt* library, with several random initialisations for each combination; then, with the hyperparameters that have produced the best results, a new model is generated, trained and tested with the test data. For each number of layers, the errors obtained in validation and test are stored, to later compare the performance of the models according to the architecture design used.

To quantify and compare the accuracy obtained with the different models, the *Root Mean Squared Error* (RMSE) and the R^2 coefficient are used. It should be noted that, for the experiments conducted, both outputs of tank levels 3 and 1 are scaled from 0% to 100%.

Table 2. Tested ranges of hyperparameters.

Hyperparameter	Tested values
Total internal units (N_T)	1200
Spectral radius (sr)	0.1, 0.5, 0.9, 1.3
Leaking rate (lr)	10^{-6}, 10^{-4}, 10^{-2}, 10^{-0}
Input scaling (iss)	1
Inter-layer scaling (ils)	0.1, 0.5, 1, 1.5
Input bias scaling (bs)	0.2, 0.4, 0.8, 1
$\mathbf{W}_{res}^l$ connectivity (rc)	0.15
$\mathbf{W}_{in}^l$ connectivity (ic)	0.15
Ridge regularizer (α)	10^{-9}, 10^{-6}, 10^{-3}, 10^{-1}

Following the proposed methodology, and with the data from the dataset described above, the best hyperparameters for each number of layers are sought, according to the values shown in Table 2. Specifically, the best hyperparameters are searched for each number of layers N_L between 1 and 10.

For each combination of hyperparameters tested, the reservoirs in the different layers of the Deep ESN model are initialised with the same hyperparameters, each generated independently and with different random seeds, as usual in experiments with such hierarchical architectures.

To start with, different values for the input bias scaling are tested in the range between 0.2 and 1. In addition, as far as the scaling of the input weight matrices is concerned, there will be a difference depending on the layer: the scaling of the first input weight matrix $\mathbf{W}_{in}^1$ is set to 1, a value that has worked adequately in previous experiments with Shallow ESNs, while for the scaling of the inter-reservoir matrices $\{\mathbf{W}_{in}^l\}_{l=2}^{l=N_L}$, different values are tested between 0.1 and 1.5, to evaluate which one produces better results in the model.

Conversely, the connectivity of the reservoir input weight matrices $\mathbf{W}_{in}^l$, as well as of the reservoir weight matrices $\mathbf{W}_{res}^l$, are set to 0.15, since this is a value that also tends to yield good results in previous experiments.

Table 3. RMSE and R^2 on test dataset, and best hyperparameters obtained: number of layers (N_L), input bias scaling (**bs**), inter layer scaling (**ils**), leaking rate (**lr**), spectral radius of reservoir weight matrix (**sr**) and readout regularizer (α).

Model	N_L	bs	ils	lr	sr	α	RMSE	R^2
Tank 3	1	0.4	–	1.0	0.9	10^{-1}	0.0510	0.9710
	2	0.4	0.1	1.0	0.9	10^{-3}	0.0519	0.9703
	3	0.4	0.1	1.0	0.9	10^{-3}	0.0504	0.9709
	4	0.4	0.1	1.0	0.9	10^{-3}	0.0478	0.9743
	5	0.4	0.1	1.0	0.9	10^{-3}	0.0467	0.9760
	6	1.0	0.1	1.0	0.9	10^{-6}	0.0459	0.9764
	7	1.0	0.1	1.0	0.9	10^{-6}	**0.0456**	**0.9768**
	8	1.0	0.1	1.0	0.9	10^{-6}	0.0470	0.9754
	9	1.0	0.1	1.0	0.9	10^{-6}	0.0470	0.9753
	10	1.0	0.1	1.0	0.9	10^{-6}	0.0490	0.9733
Tank 1	1	1.0	-	1.0	1.3	10^{-6}	0.1070	0.8704
	2	1.0	0.1	1.0	0.9	10^{-6}	0.1205	0.8388
	3	1.0	0.1	1.0	0.9	10^{-6}	0.1160	0.8506
	4	1.0	0.1	1.0	0.9	10^{-6}	0.1012	0.8859
	5	1.0	0.1	1.0	0.9	10^{-6}	0.0978	0.8936
	6	1.0	0.1	1.0	0.9	10^{-6}	0.0907	0.9085
	7	1.0	0.1	1.0	0.9	10^{-6}	0.0827	0.9238
	8	1.0	0.1	1.0	0.9	10^{-6}	0.0824	0.9242
	9	1.0	0.1	1.0	0.9	10^{-6}	**0.0823**	**0.9244**
	10	1.0	0.1	1.0	0.9	10^{-6}	0.0837	0.9223

Finally, as previous work has shown that the performance of the model is better the higher the number of units in the reservoir, this parameter is left fixed at 1200 at the model level regardless of the number of layers. Thus, the total number of units N_T is divided among all the reservoirs and, if the division is not exact, the remaining units are assigned to the reservoir in the first layer.

After applying the proposed methodology to evaluate the performance of Deep ESN models according to the number of layers, the results obtained are shown in Fig. 4. This figure presents the evolution of the RMSE as a function of the number of layers, between 1 and 10, for validation and test data. The RMSE displayed is the average between the executed guesses initialised with different random seeds. The standard deviation of these guesses is also shown. On the other hand, the obtained test RMSE and R^2 values, as well as the best hyperparameters selected for each number of layers and model, are displayed in Table 3. The best RMSE and R^2 results for each model are highlighted in bold.

Analysing the results it can be seen that, with the same total number of units in the reservoirs N_T, the performance of the models improves significantly as the

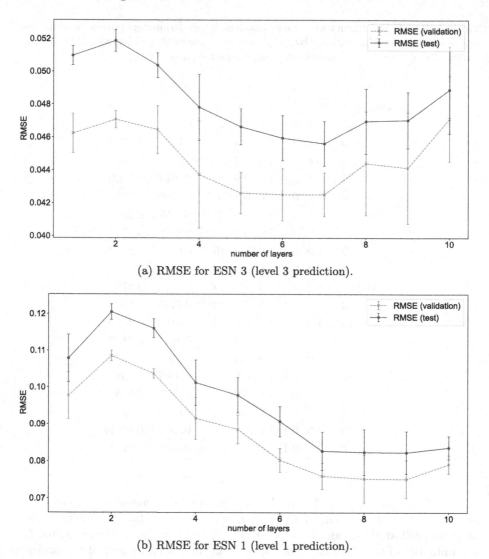

(a) RMSE for ESN 3 (level 3 prediction).

(b) RMSE for ESN 1 (level 1 prediction).

Fig. 4. RMSE obtained in validation and test with different number of layers.

number of layers increases, reducing the RMSE compared to the Shallow ESN model (where the number of layers N_L is equal to 1). More specifically, Deep ESN is able to improve the predictive performance of Shallow ESN reducing the RMSE by up to approximately 11% in the tank 3 setup and up to approximately 23% in the tank 1 setup. The difference is even greater when considering the R^2 coefficient, since it improves by 0.6% for tank 3 and by 6% for tank 1, a percentage 10 times greater for tank 3 than for tank 1. The improvement by Deep ESN is more substantial with the tank 1 problem, as this corresponds to the case in which the system can benefit more from the presence of slower dynamics in the reservoir systems.

Furthermore, it can be observed that the best average RMSE is reached with 7 layers for the tank 3 model, while for the tank 3 model it is reached with 9 layers. This confirms that there are different time-scale dynamics in the upper and lower tank levels, as initially deduced. Thus, changes in the pump and/or valve take longer to be reflected in the lower tank than in the upper tank, and more layers with more global memory are needed to obtain a better level prediction in the case of the lower tank.

Finally, as far as the best hyperparameters are concerned (see Table 3), it should be noted that the values obtained are quite similar irrespective of the model applied and the number of layers tested. Therefore, the improvements in the performance of the models are essentially associated with the increase in the number of layers.

5   Conclusions

This work presents an experimental implementation of Deep ESNs in an industrial pilot plant. The industrial plant is composed of four water tanks interconnected with a main water supply regulated by pumps and valves. The purpose of the industrial application is to model the level of the tanks depending on the ratio of pumps and valves. More specifically, two tanks connected sequentially are modelled, knowing that the water flow is delivered with a pump and a valve to the upper tank, and the drainage of this tank ends up in the lower tank.

One model is designed to estimate the level of the upper tank and another one is to predict the level of the lower tank. Deep ESN architectures with different numbers of layers are tested to assess the model performance with hierarchical layouts, looking for the best hyperparameters for each model and a number of layers between 1 and 10.

Based on the results, it can be observed that, with the same total number of reservoir units, increasing the number of layers in the model leads to a significant reduction of the errors given by the predictions. Furthermore, the best performance for the upper tank is obtained with fewer layers than for the lower tank. These results confirm the expected circumstance of the lower tank having slower dynamics than the upper one, thus requiring more model memory to better estimate the tank level.

Future work will focus on the modelling of the four tanks of the plant as a whole MIMO system, exploring different reservoir layouts and multi-layer hierarchical architectures. Moreover, further analysis of the dynamics that are developed within the different layers of the Deep ESN architectures will be addressed.

Acknowledgements. This work was supported by the Spanish State Research Agency, MCIN/ AEI/ 10.13039/ 501100011033 under Grant PID2020-117890RB-I00 and Grant PID2020-115401GB-I00; and by EU-EIC EMERGE (Grant No. 101070918) and NEURONE, a project funded by the Italian Ministry of University and Research

(PRIN 20229JRTZA). The work of José Ramón Rodríguez-Ossorio was supported by a grant from the *2020 Edition of Research Programme of the University of León*.

References

1. Diez-Olivan, A., Del Ser, J., Galar, D., Sierra, B.: Data fusion and machine learning for industrial prognosis: trends and perspectives towards industry 4.0. Inf. Fusion **50**, 92–111 (2019). https://doi.org/10.1016/j.inffus.2018.10.005
2. Domínguez, M., Reguera, P., Fuertes, J.J.: Laboratorio remoto para la enseñanza de la automática en la universidad de león (españa). Revista Iberoamericana de Automática e Informática industrial **2**(2), 36–45 (2010)
3. Gallicchio, C., Micheli, A.: Architectural and Markovian factors of echo state networks. Neural Netw. **24**(5), 440–456 (2011). https://doi.org/10.1016/J.NEUNET.2011.02.002
4. Gallicchio, C., Micheli, A.: Echo state property of deep reservoir computing networks. Cogn. Comput. **9** (2017). https://doi.org/10.1007/s12559-017-9461-9
5. Gallicchio, C., Micheli, A.: Deep Echo State Network (DeepESN): A Brief Survey (2020). arXiv:1712.04323 [cs, stat]
6. Gallicchio, C., Micheli, A., Pedrelli, L.: Deep reservoir computing: a critical experimental analysis. Neurocomputing **268**, 87–99 (2017). https://doi.org/10.1016/j.neucom.2016.12.089
7. Gallicchio, C., Micheli, A., Pedrelli, L.: Design of deep echo state networks. Neural Netw. **108**, 33–47 (2018). https://doi.org/10.1016/J.NEUNET.2018.08.002
8. Gallicchio, C., Micheli, A., Pedrelli, L.: Hierarchical temporal representation in linear reservoir computing. In: Esposito, A., Faundez-Zanuy, M., Morabito, F.C., Pasero, E. (eds.) WIRN 2017 2017. SIST, vol. 102, pp. 119–129. Springer, Cham (2019). https://doi.org/10.1007/978-3-319-95098-3_11
9. Gao, W., et al.: Deep learning workload scheduling in gpu datacenters: taxonomy, challenges and vision (2022). https://doi.org/10.48550/arXiv.2205.11913, [cs]
10. Jaeger, H.: The "echo state" approach to analysing and training recurrent neural networks-with an erratum note. In: German National Research Center for Information Technology GMD Technical Report, Bonn, Germany, vol. 148, no. 34, p. 13 (2001)
11. Jaeger, H., Haas, H.: Harnessing nonlinearity: predicting chaotic systems and saving energy in wireless communication. Science **304**(5667), 78–80 (2004)
12. Jaeger, H., Lukoševišius, M., Popovici, D., Siewert, U.: Optimization and applications of echo state networks with leaky-integrator neurons. Neural Netw. **20**(3), 335–352 (2007). https://doi.org/10.1016/j.neunet.2007.04.016
13. Johansson, K.H.: The quadruple-tank process: a multivariable laboratory process with an adjustable zero. IEEE Trans. Control Syst. Technol. **8** (2000). https://doi.org/10.1109/87.845876
14. LeCun, Y., Bengio, Y., Hinton, G.: Deep learning. Nature **521**(7553), 436–444 (2015). https://doi.org/10.1038/nature14539
15. Lukoševičius, M.: A practical guide to applying echo state networks. In: Montavon, G., Orr, G.B., Müller, K.-R. (eds.) Neural Networks: Tricks of the Trade. LNCS, vol. 7700, pp. 659–686. Springer, Heidelberg (2012). https://doi.org/10.1007/978-3-642-35289-8_36
16. Lukoševičius, M., Jaeger, H.: Reservoir computing approaches to recurrent neural network training. Comput. Sci. Rev. **3**(3), 127–149 (2009)

17. MacGregor, J., Cinar, A.: Monitoring, fault diagnosis, fault-tolerant control and optimization: data driven methods. Comput. Chem. Eng. **47**, 111–120 (2012). https://doi.org/10.1016/j.compchemeng.2012.06.017, fOCAPO 2012
18. Pandey, M., et al.: The transformational role of GPU computing and deep learning in drug discovery. Nat. Mach. Intell. **4**(3), 211–221 (2022). https://doi.org/10.1038/s42256-022-00463-x
19. Rodríguez-Ossorio, J.R., Morán, A., Alonso, S., Pérez, D., Díaz, I., Domínguez, M.: Echo state networks for anomaly detection in industrial systems. IFAC-PapersOnLine **56**(2), 1472–1477 (2023). https://doi.org/10.1016/j.ifacol.2023.10.1836, 22nd IFAC World Congress
20. Tortorella, D., Gallicchio, C., Micheli, A.: Hierarchical dynamics in deep echo state networks. In: Pimenidis, E., Angelov, P., Jayne, C., Papaleonidas, A., Aydin, M. (eds.) ICANN 2022. LNCS, pp. 668–679. Springer, Cham (2022). https://doi.org/10.1007/978-3-031-15934-3_55
21. Trouvain, N., Pedrelli, L., Dinh, T.T., Hinaut, X.: *ReservoirPy*: an efficient and user-friendly library to design echo state networks. In: Farkaš, I., Masulli, P., Wermter, S. (eds.) ICANN 2020. LNCS, vol. 12397, pp. 494–505. Springer, Cham (2020). https://doi.org/10.1007/978-3-030-61616-8_40
22. Yildiz, I.B., Jaeger, H., Kiebel, S.J.: Re-visiting the echo state property. Neural Netw. **35**, 1–9 (2012). https://doi.org/10.1016/j.neunet.2012.07.005

Empirical Insights into Deep Learning Models for Misinformation Classification Within Constrained Data Environment

Jayendra Ganesh Devisetti(✉)(iD), S. Sanjana(iD), Shubhankar Kuranagatti(iD), Abhishek Hiremath(iD), and Arti Arya(iD)

Department of Computer Science, PES University, Bengaluru, India
`jayendraganesh21@gmail.com`

Abstract. Misinformation stands as a significant threat to society posed by technology advancements. Its gruesome consequences has made misinformation detection a widely researched area in the recent past. While many studies have focused on creating datasets and effective machine learning models to combat them, detecting misinformation using deep learning in a nuanced setting where there is a lack of data remains a challenge. This study aims to identify deep learning techniques that assist in classifying misinformation for small datasets. It compares the effectiveness of transfer learning on past, related data initially, followed by few-shot and zero-shot learning on the smaller dataset, against directly training the language models on the small dataset. It also aims to uncover the driving factors that affect model performance while detecting misinformation in a small dataset using deep learning. Our findings suggest that training language models on smaller datasets while considering key indicators of performance like model architecture and learned representation transfer is more beneficial than pre-training the models with past, related data.

Keywords: Misinformation classification · Transfer Learning · BERT · Transformers · Zero-shot learning · Few-shot learning

1 Introduction

In the recent times, the influence of technology has reshaped the daily lives of individuals, owing to the evolution of digital tools and the widespread access to internet. This transformation has interconnected people from across the world, fostering rapidity in accessing information. However, this advancement has introduced numerous challenges, with misinformation dissemination being a prominent concern.

Misinformation stands as a pressing concern in today's digital age, due to its immense reach on social media. Its consequences extend to daily lives, political and economical affairs and even global events, largely impacting societal discourse. The proliferation of misinformation has led to tangible consequences in the last decade. The false claims advocating the consumption of high doses of Vitamin C as a cure for COVID-19 resulted in people losing lives. Political misinformation campaigns during the 2020 American election cycle stirred significant controversy and confusion. Sensational claims such as Russians intercepting adrenochrome shipments bound for America further fueled misinformation narratives, sowing distrust and animosity among nations.

Due to its impact on society, misinformation has recently gained significant research attention. Since the boom of Machine Learning, many transformers and Large Language Models (LLMs) [6] such as BERT (Bidirectional Encoder Representations from Transformers) [8], GPT (Generative Pre-Trained Transformer) [2], RoBERTa [9] etc. have evolved, facilitating effective and accurate detection. Technologies like TinEye, Whois and Google Fact Check Tools [19] have also been developed to detect misinformation across various formats including video, audio or text.

In this study, we have explored various techniques that can be employed to curb the spread of misinformation. This study assists in examining the steps to take in order to make the best use of the restricted resources in terms of data. Misinformation must be detected quickly in order to minimize its impact on public perception and prevent the spread of misleading narratives. Navigating this complex landscape emphasizes the necessity of staying ahead of the curve in detecting and combating misinformation, eventually contributing to the preservation of a well-informed and healthy digital society.

Key contributions of this work include:

- A comprehensive evaluation of the effectiveness of transfer learning in misinformation classification tasks.
- A comparative analysis between zero-shot and few-shot learning techniques within the transfer learning paradigm.
- Empirical analysis for assessing and comparing the performance of modified transformer architectures for misinformation classification.
- Identification of the optimal knowledge representation method for maximizing information capture from small datasets.

2   Motivation for the Study

Detecting misinformation is a difficult endeavour due to its multifaceted nature and dynamic characteristics. When dealing with a new event gaining popularity on social media, the data around such incidents are initially sparse, posing a significant challenge to distinguish between accurate information and misinformation quickly. Despite the significant challenge, it is crucial to detect misinformation at the earliest phase to mitigate its consequences and hinder its exponential outreach.

Various studies have focused on misinformation detection, advancing from conventional machine learning algorithms to complex neural networks. The dominance of Large Language Models (LLMs) in today's linguistic landscape is attributed to their ability to comprehend both syntactic and semantic features of text, facilitated by neural networks. However, leveraging deep learning models effectively in contexts marked by data scarcity has remained a challenge. This challenge impedes the realization of their full potential, particularly in combating misinformation, where the need for nuanced understanding and contextual analysis is paramount.

Emphasizing the importance of deep learning in misinformation classification is crucial. Deep learning models excel at extracting intricate patterns and understanding the complex relationships present in textual data, enabling them to discern subtle cues indicative of misinformation. In contexts where misinformation is pervasive and rapidly evolving, the agility and adaptability of deep learning architectures become indispensable. By harnessing the power of deep learning, researchers can develop models that not only detect misinformation with high accuracy but also adapt to new forms of deceptive content in real-time.

Highlighting the necessity of a study focusing on enabling the classification of misinformation using a limited dataset is cardinal. It holds pivotal significance in addressing real-world scenarios where misinformation detection is imperative, yet comprehensive labeled datasets are scarce. By honing techniques that allow deep learning models to operate effectively in data-constrained environments, this study not only contributes to the advancement of misinformation detection methodologies but also facilitates their practical deployment in settings characterized by limited data availability.

3   Related Work

Misinformation has become a widely researched topic in the last decade. Numerous studies suggest novel approaches to curb its impact through effective methodologies for sentence representation and classification.

Vlad-Iulian Ilie et al. [7] evaluated deep learning architectures for context-aware misinformation detection using a unique approach. When CNN (Convolutional Neural Network) and LSTM (Long Short-Term Memory) with Attention were compared, LSTM performed better than the recurrent models, and CNN successfully included global word context. The work emphasised the value of word embeddings and text pre-processing in raising model accuracy.

A. Dhankar et al. [4] investigated the use of transfer learning in the identification of COVID-19 disinformation on social media. By combining general and context-specific embeddings, they improved the performance metrics of classification models and produced statistically significant gains in weighted F1 scores. Comparisons between models trained with Augmented Transfer Learning and Concatenated Transfer Learning revealed significant increases over baseline models through f-statistic and p-value analysis, demonstrating the effectiveness of transfer learning approaches in enhancing classification model performance for misinformation detection.

Valeriya Slovikovskaya et al. [16] focused on using BERT, RoBERTa, and XLNet transformers to improve the stance identification in the Fake News Challenge Stage 1 (FNC-1). Their model design included LSTM layers to encode word embeddings from headlines and articles, followed by a neural network for classification. Fine-tuning BERT resulted in remarkable performance improvements. The results showed a noteworthy increase in F1 scores, with BERT outperforming other models in several tasks by a large margin.

For the purpose of detecting misinformation, Nasir et al. [13] presented a hybrid deep learning model that combines CNN and RNN (Recurrent Neural Network). This combination improved textual data processing by utilising CNN's capacity to recognise spatial features and RNN's comprehension of sequential language. With nearly 100% accuracy on the ISOT dataset and approximately 60% accuracy on the FA-KES dataset, the model's performance highlighted the value addition of combining recurrent and convolutional neural networks. Additionally, the model's strong generalisation across a variety of datasets suggested its ability to be scalable and reused to counteract the spread of false information in the current digital era.

Shushkevich et al. [15] investigated using machine learning to detect COVID-19 misinformation, highlighting the challenge of small datasets. They used regularisation techniques and ensemble learning to combat overfitting. They trained and assessed 15 machine learning setups using a small amount of data, making sure that the settings were reliable by employing techniques including dataset splitting, hyperparameter tuning, and cross-validation.

Ciprian-Octavian Truică et al. [18] offered a new deep learning architecture, MisRoBERTa, for detection of misinformation. The study examined several transformer models and transfer learning approaches, focusing on the effect of dataset size, vocabulary dimension, and learning methods on accuracy. Their custom model achieved an accuracy of 92.50% surpassing other transformer models and transfer learning approaches.

Waad Alhoshan et al. [1] explored zero-shot learning for classification of software requirements into either functional or non-functional in a data-constrained environment. Using contextual word embeddings and transformer-based language models, their approach achieved notable F1 scores: 0.66 for Functional Requirements(FR)/Non-Functional Requirements(NFR) classification, 0.72–0.80 for NFR identification, and 0.66 for security classification, all without any training data. Their study demonstrated that zero-shot learning can effectively mitigate data scarcity in requirements engineering.

Tianyu Gao et al. [5] introduced a method designed for fine-tuning large language models using few-shot learning. By guiding the model with prompts and incorporating task examples, it enhanced the model performance across various natural language processing tasks. The evaluations demonstrate that the model outperformed standard fine-tuning by up to 30%, with an average improvement of 11%. However, it exhibited high result variance, and its automatic prompt generation may not generalize well with limited training data.

Xu Luo et al. [12] explored few-shot classification, investigating factors like dataset scale, adaptation algorithms, and shot numbers. It found that increasing classes in the training dataset was more effective than augmenting samples per class for supervised models. Vanilla Finetune was observed to have outperformed newer algorithms.

While multiple research studies have focused on developing methodologies to detect misinformation, suppressing its proliferation instantly remains a challenge due to the difficulty associated with training models on limited data. In this work, we aim to answer three research questions:

- Can past, available and related data be used to generalize to new situations that lack enough data through transfer learning?
- Can customized model architectures enhance the accuracy of misinformation detection on small datasets compared to using only pre-trained models?
- Which knowledge representation from pre-trained models is best suited for small datasets?

4   Proposed Approach

4.1   Dataset Construction and Pre-processing

Two publicly available misinformation datasets were used for this study.

Russia-Ukraine War dataset [17]: A pre-existing, annotated dataset of tweets relevant to the Russia-Ukraine war was utilized. This dataset provided Tweet IDs along with their corresponding label indicating whether the tweet was misinformation. Leveraging Apify, a web scraping tool, these tweets were extracted, retrieving various fields, including tweet content, author information such as username and verification status, the timestamp of the tweet, and engagement metrics like likes and retweets.

To prepare this data for misinformation classification, a multi-step pre-processing pipeline was implemented. First, the URLs, hyperlinks and punctuations were removed from the dataset with the help of regular expressions. Next, the stop words were eliminated to retain only the relevant information using the NLTK library [11]. Only the fields - tweet text and label were retained. Finally, stemming was applied using Porter Stemmer to reduce words to their root forms and reduce the complexity of the text.

The dataset was split into training, testing and validation sets using the Scikitlearn library in the ratio of 75:20:5 respectively, maintaining the equilibrium between training and validating the models. Following pre-processing, the dataset consisted of 1954 text entries, each classified as either "misinformation" or "not misinformation". 1324 instances with label "not misinformation" instances and 630 'misinformation' instances were present in the dataset. The training set comprised 1465 instances and the testing and validation set consisted of 391 and 98 instances respectively. Notably, the number of misinformation and not misinformation samples were balanced in each of the three sets to facilitate unbiased learning and evaluation. For zero-shot learning, the models were directly tested on the Russia-Ukraine war test set without any prior training. In few-shot learning, a support set comprising 15 not misinformation and 15 misinformation instances from Russia-Ukraine war dataset was chosen to evaluate the model's ability to generalize and accurately predict with minimal labeled data. This setup simulates real-world scenarios with limited data availability, assessing the model's performance under practical constraints. Subsequently, the model's classification performance was evaluated on the same test set of 391 instances.

General Misinformation dataset [14]: In order to evaluate the impact of transfer learning on past, relevant data in classifying misinformation in newer scenarios, a publicly available dataset of general misinformation was obtained. This dataset comprised 102661 instances, each labeled as either 'misinformation' or 'not misinformation'. The dataset included a variety of subjects like taxes, hurricanes, Russia, Trump, and government. This dataset was chosen because it offers extensive coverage of modern themes, facilitating transfer learning across a wide range of commonly occurring misinformation subjects. The dataset underwent cleaning and pre-processing by its creators, resulting in predefined train and test sets with 92,394 and 10,267 instances, respectively. Therefore, this study did not involve additional pre-processing of the general misinformation dataset. Creation of validation set was deemed unnecessary for training the models on general misinformation as the primary objective of its utilization was weight initialization for the downstream task of classification on the smaller dataset.

4.2 Training

Multiple deep learning methodologies were used in order to understand the driving factors of misinformation classification for small datasets. The first strategy involved employing transfer learning for training on past, related and already available data to comprehend the models' ability to be relevant while classifying misinformation in a new setting. Models were pre-trained on the larger general misinformation data, following which zero-shot and few-shot learning was performed on the smaller Russia-Ukraine war data. Zero-shot learning, referring to the act of classifying instances with no prior training, was performed by directly testing on the Russia-Ukraine war test set. Few-shot learning involved training on 15 instances of each label on the Russia-Ukraine war training data and subsequently evaluating its classification abilities on its test set. In order to discover the importance of neural network architecture in classification of misinformation, the vanilla transformer models, BERT, AlBERT [10] and RoBERTa and custom, modified transformer models were trained on the Russia-Ukraine war data and compared. The selection of BERT, RoBERTa, and ALBERT variants for modified architectures was rooted in their advanced technical characteristics. BERT's bidirectional transformer architecture excels in capturing bidirectional context dependencies through self-attention mechanisms, crucial for comprehensive contextual understanding in text classification. RoBERTa further enhances this by refining pre-training with modifications like the removal of next sentence prediction and training on larger datasets, resulting in nuanced linguistic understanding and improved performance. ALBERT's parameter reduction techniques, including factorized embedding parameterization and cross-layer parameter sharing, offer superior computational efficiency and scalability, making it well-suited for resource-constrained environments. These models collectively provided strong foundations for training, enabling fine-tuning for specific classification tasks while maintaining robust performance across diverse domains. The modified architectures had an additional layer of LSTM or CNN framework stacked on top of the mentioned transformer architecture. LSTM and CNN layers were added to BERT variations because of their unique ability to handle textual, sequential and spatial information. Long-range relationships and sequential patterns are excellently modelled by LSTMs, which improves the model's comprehension of context throughout lengthy sequences. CNNs, on the other hand, are skilled in identifying hierarchical structures and local characteristics in the text, adding a variety of spatial relationships to the model's representation. Through the integration of CNN and LSTM layers, the updated architectures take advantage of each other's strengths to capture contextual information that is both local and global, improving classification accuracy in a synergistic manner. The subsequent points detail the modified architectures:

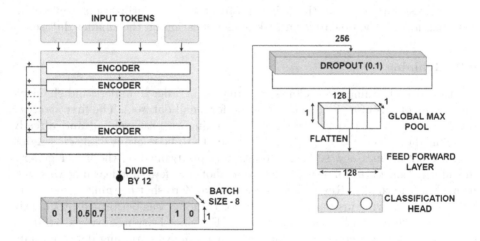

Fig. 1. Data Flow in CNN Variant models

- CNN: In order to enhance the ability to capture information more effectively, a Convolutional Neural Network (CNN) layer was incorporated. The data flow in CNN variant models is shown in Fig. 1. The output embedding from the BERT variants underwent a reshaping and permutation process to match the expected input shape of dimensions (8, 12, 768) to the CNN layer. The reshaped embeddings were then passed into the Conv1d layer, where features were extracted from the data. This layer consisted of 256 output channels with a kernel of size 3. The output of the convolutional operation was processed by the Rectified Linear Unit (ReLU) activation function; this introduced non-linearity to efficiently capture complex patterns and to make sure the convoluted values did not become negative in the data. To extract the

Table 1. CNN Model Configuration

Parameter	Value
Number of Convolution Layers	2
Number of Max Pooling Layers	2
Number of Dense Layers	1
Number of Fully Connected Layers	1
Loss Function	Binary Cross Entropy
Activation Function	ReLU
Learning Rate	5e−5
Optimizer	AdamW
Number of Epochs	15
Batch Size	8

most significant features from the convolutional output across all dimensions and reduce dimensionality, Global Max Pooling was applied. A dropout layer with value 0.1 was added after the pooling operation to prevent overfitting, which randomly set a certain number of random input units to zero during training. The output vector of size 256 was fed into a fully connected layer (Linear layer) from the dropout layer. This layer applied a linear transformation to the input features in order to generate the final logits, representing the raw predictions for each class and returned an output vector of size two.

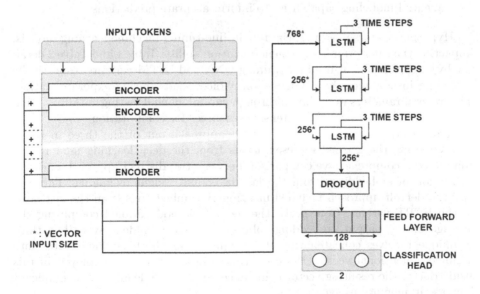

Fig. 2. Data Flow in LSTM Variant models

Table 2. LSTM Model Configuration

Parameter	Value
Number of LSTM Cells	3
Number of Dropout Layers	1
Number of Fully Connected Layers	1
Loss Function	Binary Cross Entropy
Activation Function	TanH, Sigmoid
Learning Rate	5e−5
Optimizer	AdamW
Number of Epochs	15
Batch Size	8

– LSTM: The embeddings from the BERT variants were processed through three LSTM layers, which is specialized for learning long-term dependencies in sequential data. The data flow in LSTM variant models is depicted in Fig. 2. Following the LSTM layers, each with a hidden dimension of 256, the final hidden state was extracted and passed through a dropout layer with a drop out factor of 0.1 to prevent overfitting. This output underwent transformation through a fully connected layer to yield logits, representing raw predictions. During training, binary cross-entropy loss was computed between the logits and ground truth labels. The architecture facilitated a better understanding of input sequences, leveraging ALBERT's contextual embeddings and LSTM's sequential modeling capabilities to inform accurate predictions.

Hyperparameters play a crucial role in fine-tuning machine learning models, impacting their performance and generalization ability. Table 1 and Table 2 detail the hyperparameters utilized for training CNN and LSTM variants respectively, providing insight into the configuration choices made during experimentation. The hyperparameters were chosen through careful manual testing, as automating the process would necessitate extensive resources for computation.

This study also explored the optimal approach out of the three methods for extracting the learned representations from the deep learning models. We conducted a comprehensive comparison between two distinct approaches: direct extraction of embeddings from the last layer and weight averaging. The first and the default approach included utilizing the embeddings from the last layer of the BERT variant. Conversely, the second method entailed computing the average of the output embeddings obtained at each hidden layer. The third technique involves concatenating the weights from all the hidden states into a single-dimensional vector. However, this approach was not employed in this study due to the resulting vector being excessively large, leading to a significant increase in memory usage.

5   Results and Discussion

A compendium of transformer models were trained employing different techniques for misinformation classification and the outcomes on the testing data are discussed in this section. Table 3c shows zero-shot learning results after pre-training on general misinformation. All the models exhibited comparable levels of accuracy with AlBERT+LSTM showing the highest accuracy of 0.36. Table 3a shows the results obtained for misinformation classification when the models were not pre-trained on general misinformation and were subjected to few shot learning with Russia-Ukraine war data. The highest accuracy was reported by BERT+CNN at 0.50. Table 3b depicts the few-shot learning results after pre-training on general misinformation with improved accuracies. BERT+CNN outperformed the other models with an accuracy of 0.70 with few-shot learning. The models trained directly on Russia-Ukraine war data without pre-training on general misinformation data, shown in Table 4, reported the best results for classification with RoBERTa+CNN achieving an accuracy of 0.90 followed by BERT+CNN yielding an accuracy of 0.87.

The outcome of zero-shot learning on models trained on general misinformation illustrate the models' incapacity to accurately classify misinformation in novel contexts. Misinformation, distinguished by its nuanced structures and varied linguistic patterns, necessitates consideration of context and writing style for effective identification. Through zero-shot learning, the model was evaluated on new data pertaining to a novel event, which hindered the generalization of its learning to the Russia-Ukraine war context. In contrast to zero-shot learning, a significant increase in accuracy was observed when the models were subjected to few-shot learning. Furthermore, the accuracy within the few-shot learning paradigm improved when the models were pre-trained on general misinformation, highlighting the significance of learning related data during transfer learning. The improved performance can be attributed to the models' initially learning the intricacies of performing binary classification on general misinformation data, followed by exposure to a limited number of instances related to the Russia-Ukraine war conflict, thereby enhancing contextual understanding. The models trained only on Russia-Ukraine war dataset outperformed the models pre-trained with general misinformation, across both zero-shot and few-shot learning scenarios. These findings suggest that training on smaller, contextually relevant datasets while considering additional performance metrics mentioned in the following paragraphs, is advantageous. However, if the data is scanty or unavailable, few-shot learning with pre-training on past and related data can be employed and the accuracy can be improved by increasing the number of samples in the support set [3]. Our experimental results, shown in Table 3a, also indicate that increasing the number of samples from 30 to 60 in the support set increases the accuracy of the models for the classification task.

Upon examination of Table 4, which displays the accuracies of the modified transformer architecture models alongside their corresponding vanilla models, it is evident that all the hybrid models exhibit superior accuracy in comparison to their respective vanilla models. Notably, the RoBERTa + CNN hybrid

Table 3. Classification results for Zero-Shot and Few-Shot learning

(a) Few-Shot without Transfer-Learning

Model	30 samples				60 samples
	Accuracy	F1 Score	Recall	Precision	Accuracy
RoBERTa + CNN	0.33	0.37	0.40	0.35	0.42
BERT + CNN	0.50	0.48	0.54	0.44	0.51
AlBERT + CNN	0.33	0.33	0.33	0.33	0.40
AlBERT + LSTM	0.47	0.43	0.40	0.46	0.50
BERT + LSTM	0.43	0.45	0.50	0.41	0.47
RoBERTa + LSTM	0.47	0.43	0.40	0.46	0.47
RoBERTa	0.33	0.37	0.40	0.35	0.40
BERT	0.33	0.37	0.40	0.35	0.37
AlBERT	0.33	0.37	0.40	0.35	0.37

(b) Few-Shot with Transfer-Learning

Model	30 samples				60 samples
	Accuracy	F1 Score	Recall	Precision	Accuracy
RoBERTa + CNN	0.67	0.69	0.73	0.64	0.71
BERT + CNN	0.70	0.71	0.73	0.69	0.73
AlBERT + CNN	0.60	0.57	0.61	0.53	0.67
AlBERT + LSTM	0.67	0.71	0.75	0.67	0.71
BERT + LSTM	0.63	0.64	0.67	0.62	0.69
RoBERTa + LSTM	0.67	0.71	0.75	0.67	0.71
RoBERTa	0.50	0.48	0.54	0.44	0.57
BERT	0.57	0.60	0.62	0.59	0.60
AlBERT	0.53	0.53	0.57	0.50	0.57

(c) Zero-Shot with Transfer-Learning

Model	Accuracy	F1 Score	Recall	Precision
RoBERTa + CNN	0.37	0.39	0.46	0.33
BERT + CNN	0.30	0.28	0.29	0.27
AlBERT + CNN	0.33	0.37	0.55	0.29
AlBERT+LSTM	0.37	0.39	0.43	0.35
BERT + LSTM	0.33	0.37	0.55	0.29
RoBERTa + LSTM	0.37	0.39	0.46	0.33
RoBERTa	0.33	0.37	0.40	0.35
BERT	0.30	0.28	0.29	0.27
AlBERT	0.33	0.37	0.40	0.35

Table 4. Classification results with training directly on Russia Ukraine dataset without pre-training on general misinformation

Model	Accuracy	F1 Score	Recall	Precision
RoBERTa + CNN	0.90	0.92	0.92	0.92
BERT + CNN	0.87	0.90	0.90	0.90
AlBERT + CNN	0.86	0.90	0.89	0.90
AlBERT+LSTM	0.85	0.89	0.89	0.88
RoBERTa + LSTM	0.87	0.90	0.91	0.89
BERT + LSTM	0.86	0.90	0.91	0.88
RoBERTa	0.87	0.91	0.87	0.96
BERT	0.84	0.88	0.89	0.87
AlBERT	0.82	0.87	0.85	0.89

model emerges as the most exceptional classifier, with an accuracy rate of 0.90 while the highest accuracy obtained by a vanilla transformer, RoBERTa, is 0.87. AlBERT+LSTM reported the lowest accuracy of 0.85 among the modified transformer models while AlBERT had the lowest accuracy of 0.82 among the vanilla models. This indicates that model architecture plays a vital role in capturing linguistic features for small datasets.

Table 5. Classification results for different learned representations

Model	Average	Last
RoBERTa + CNN	0.90	0.86
BERT + CNN	0.87	0.85
AlBERT + CNN	0.86	0.83
RoBERTa + LSTM	0.87	0.84
BERT + LSTM	0.86	0.82
AlBERT + LSTM	0.85	0.83

Table 5 shows that the results obtained from models employing the weights from the last layer of BERT variants as input compared to those utilizing the average of all hidden states differ significantly. The models trained using the average of hidden states' weights exhibit superior performance compared to those relying solely on the embeddings from the last layer. The best performing model, RoBERTa + CNN, achieves a remarkable result of 0.90 when employing layer averaging, whereas the same model using only the last layer yields a lower accuracy of 0.86. The difference in the accuracy between the two approaches highlights the significance of capturing information from multiple layers. Averaging the weights from each hidden state enhances the models' ability to extract meaningful features from each layer, thereby contributing to more effective classification, especially in settings with small datasets.

6   Conclusion and Future Work

Misinformation on social media has become increasingly sophisticated and hence detecting it immediately is essential to ensure the integrity of information that is being widespread across nations. In this work, we have aimed to combat misinformation, addressing situations characterized by sparse data, and achieved an accuracy of 90%.

This study can be extended by reproducing the analysis across various other small datasets to test the generalisability of the proposed techniques. Furthermore, exploring the role of additional features like user engagement, temporal data and geographic details in complementing textual information can aid in comprehensive misinformation detection capabilities.

References

1. Alhoshan, W., Ferrari, A., Zhao, L.: Zero-shot learning for requirements classification: an exploratory study. Inf. Softw. Technol. **159**, 107202 (2023)
2. Buchholz, M.G.: Assessing the effectiveness of GPT-3 in detecting false political statements: a case study on the liar dataset (2023)
3. Cao, T., Law, M., Fidler, S.: A theoretical analysis of the number of shots in few-shot learning (2020)
4. Dhankar, A., Samuel, H., Hassan, F., Farruque, N., Bolduc, F., Zaïane, O.: Analysis of Covid-19 misinformation in social media using transfer learning. In: 2021 IEEE 33rd International Conference on Tools with Artificial Intelligence (ICTAI), pp. 880–885 (2021). https://doi.org/10.1109/ICTAI52525.2021.00141
5. Gao, T., Fisch, A., Chen, D.: Making pre-trained language models better few-shot learners (2021)
6. Hu, B., et al.: Bad actor, good advisor: exploring the role of large language models in fake news detection (2024)
7. Ilie, V.I., Truică, C.O., Apostol, E.S., Paschke, A.: Context-aware misinformation detection: a benchmark of deep learning architectures using word embeddings. IEEE Access **9**, 162122–162146 (2021). https://doi.org/10.1109/ACCESS.2021.3132502
8. Kaliyar, R.K., Goswami, A., Narang, P.: FakeBERT: fake news detection in social media with a BERT-based deep learning approach. Multimed. Tools Appl. **80**(8), 11765–11788 (2021)
9. Kitanovski, A., Toshevska, M., Mirceva, G.: DistilBERT and RoBERTa models for identification of fake news. In: 2023 46th MIPRO ICT and Electronics Convention (MIPRO), pp. 1102–1106 (2023). https://doi.org/10.23919/MIPRO57284.2023.10159740
10. Lan, Z., Chen, M., Goodman, S., Gimpel, K., Sharma, P., Soricut, R.: ALBERT: a lite BERT for self-supervised learning of language representations. CoRR abs/1909.11942 (2019). http://arxiv.org/abs/1909.11942

11. Loper, E., Bird, S.: NLTK: the natural language toolkit. CoRR cs.CL/0205028 (2002). https://doi.org/10.3115/1118108.1118117
12. Luo, X., Wu, H., Zhang, J., Gao, L., Xu, J., Song, J.: A closer look at few-shot classification again (2023)
13. Nasir, J., Khan, O., Varlamis, I.: Fake news detection: a hybrid CNN-RNN based deep learning approach. Int. J. Inf. Manag. Data Insights 1, 100007 (2021). https://doi.org/10.1016/j.jjimei.2020.100007
14. roupenminassian: roupenminassian/twitter-misinformation. https://huggingface.co/datasets/roupenminassian/twitter-misinformation
15. Shushkevich, E., Cardiff, J.: Detecting fake news about Covid-19 on small datasets with machine learning algorithms. In: 2021 30th Conference of Open Innovations Association FRUCT, pp. 253–258 (2021). https://doi.org/10.23919/FRUCT53335.2021.9599970
16. Slovikovskaya, V.: Transfer learning from transformers to fake news challenge stance detection (FNC-1) task (2019)
17. Toraman, C., Ozcelik, O., Şahinuç, F., Can, F.: Not good times for lies: misinformation detection on the Russia-Ukraine war, Covid-19, and refugees (2022)
18. Truică, C.O., Apostol, E.S.: MisroBERTa: transformers versus misinformation. arXiv abs/2304.07759 (2022). https://api.semanticscholar.org/CorpusID:246847976
19. Yang, Q., Christensen, T., Gilda, S., Fernandes, J., Oliveira, D.: Are fact-checking tools reliable? An evaluation of Google fact check. arXiv preprint arXiv:2402.13244 (2024)

Enhancing Bandwidth Efficiency for Video Motion Transfer Applications Using Deep Learning Based Keypoint Prediction

Xue Bai[1], Tasmiah Haque[1], Sumit Mohan[2], Yuliang Cai[3], Byungheon Jeong[4], Ádám Halász[1], and Srinjoy Das[1(✉)]

[1] West Virginia University, Morgantown, WV 26506, USA
{xb0002,th00027}@mix.wvu.edu, halasz@math.wvu.edu,
srinjoy.das@mail.wvu.edu
[2] Intel Corporation, Santa Clara, CA, USA
sumit.mohan@intel.com
[3] University of Southern California, Los Angeles, CA 90089, USA
caiyulia@usc.edu
[4] Coupa Software, San Mateo, CA, USA
joseph.jeong@coupa.com

Abstract. We propose a deep learning based novel prediction framework for enhanced bandwidth reduction in motion transfer enabled video applications such as video conferencing, virtual reality gaming and privacy preservation for patient health monitoring. To model complex motion, we use the First Order Motion Model (FOMM) that represents dynamic objects using learned keypoints along with their local affine transformations. Keypoints are extracted by a self-supervised keypoint detector and organized in a time series corresponding to the video frames. Prediction of keypoints, to enable transmission using lower frames per second on the source device, is performed using a Variational Recurrent Neural Network (VRNN). The predicted keypoints are then synthesized to video frames using an optical flow estimator and a generator network. This efficacy of leveraging keypoint based representations in conjunction with VRNN based prediction for both video animation and reconstruction is demonstrated on three diverse datasets. For real-time applications, our results show the effectiveness of our proposed architecture by enabling up to 2× additional bandwidth reduction over existing keypoint based video motion transfer frameworks without significantly compromising video quality.

Keywords: Motion transfer · Bandwidth reduction · Recurrent Neural Network · Variational Recurrent Neural Network · Variational Autoencoder · Keypoints

1 Introduction

In today's era, characterized by an increasing demand for ubiquitous services, telecommuting, immersive visual interactions and realistic simulations, there is

L. Iliadis et al. (Eds.): EANN 2024, CCIS 2141, pp. 134–151, 2024.
https://doi.org/10.1007/978-3-031-62495-7_11

a proliferation of applications such as video conferencing, augmented reality (AR), virtual reality (VR) gaming and remote medical monitoring [1–4]. Video motion transfer is a transformative technique which involves the transposition of motion from one context to another that has been proposed to efficiently implement such applications, and can be used to enhance user experiences as well as generate creative expressions. Keypoint based representations for the source image and driving videos have been previously used to enable motion transfer based applications [5,6]. Such architectures have been more successful in achieving high video quality while enabling a high degree of compression for bandwidth efficiency in comparison to traditional video codec based methods. Some examples of applications where real-time motion transfer can play a critical role are as described below:

- **Video Conferencing on Mobile Devices:** Implementing motion transfer with keypoints generated in real-time on devices such as cellphones enables efficient bandwidth utilization, particularly for streaming applications, live interactions, and video conferencing. This can ensure a fluid and high-quality user experience while conserving network resources.
- **VR Gaming:** In VR gaming, real-time motion transfer from human players to animated characters ensures precise and immediate in-game responses to users' physical actions, contributing to a more authentic and enjoyable gaming experience.
- **Medical Monitoring Privacy:** In the context of medical applications, where the care provider is often located remotely, maintaining patient privacy is of paramount concern. In such cases real-time motion transfer can be used to transmit critical patient information such as body movements without disclosing the identity of the subject.

In this paper we propose using Deep Learning based keypoint prediction in conjunction with motion transfer pipelines that use unsupervised generation of keypoints for performing video synthesis. We demonstrate our approach using the First Order Motion Model (FOMM) [6] to represent complex motion, augmented with time series prediction via Variational Neural Networks (VRNN) [7]. In comparison to existing keypoint based video motion transfer schemes, our architecture enables a higher bandwidth reduction for transmission, and lowers the compute requirements of resource constrained client devices such as mobile phones or AR/VR devices used in such applications. This results in a net 20x or higher bandwidth reduction, as the savings from our prediction framework are additive to the 10x or more bandwidth savings, that can be realized from existing video motion transfer schemes [1].

2   Related Works

Video prediction and motion transfer have been discussed and studied from several perspectives using a broad range of approaches. Some recent methods related to these areas are discussed in this section.

Video Prediction in Pixel and High Level Feature Spaces: In order to predict and synthesize videos using object dynamics at pixel level, several feature learning strategies have been developed using techniques such as adversarial training [8] and gradient difference loss functions [9]. An autoencoder style convolutional neural network has been used in [10] to learn pixel-wise long-term dependencies from time-lapse videos, whereas in [11] a multi-frequency analysis that decomposes images into different frequency bands has been utilized to deal with distortion and lack of temporal coherence. These prediction methods accumulate a large error due to variability in consecutive frames. In [12], pixels are generated using convolution with input patches by applying a predicted kernel which enables capturing spatio-temporal contextual information. However, such approaches still face challenges for tasks involving future prediction. Additionally, forecasting of small and slow-moving objects is often not accurate using pixel based methods. To overcome the problems of prediction in the high dimensional pixel space, several representation learning methods have been explored such as semantic segmentation, human pose estimation and using extracted keypoint coordinates. Before the advent of neural networks, pose parameters or Principal Component Analysis (PCA) [13,14] were used to reconstruct a video sequence using only the face boundaries. However applications of pose-guided prediction methods [15–18] have been limited to only those videos which include human presence. In semantic segmentation, semantic elements obtained from visual scenes are utilized instead of pixel level representations [19]. The prediction process is decomposed [20] into current frame segmentation and future optical flow prediction in conjunction with LSTM (Long-Short term Memory) [21] based temporal modeling. On the other hand, keypoint based representations contain particulars at the object level which produces better results for trajectory prediction and action recognition. In [22] future video frames are reconstructed using keypoints and a reference frame, thereby preventing the accumulation of errors in the pixel space by focusing on the dynamics within the keypoint coordinate space. For our work we employ the concept of keypoint prediction for both video reconstruction and animation using multiple datasets.

Video Motion Transfer: Motivated by the requirement of making high quality interactive and immersive video calling feasible for users with poor connectivity or limited data plans, keypoint based motion transfer models which enable reconstruction of objects in real-time have been developed in order to realize sufficient bandwidth savings. The Neural Talking Heads algorithm [23] initially applies meta-learning on a large video dataset and afterwards becomes capable of generating talking head models from just a few or even a single image of a person using adversarial training. With the help of a stream of landmarks/keypoints and an initial face embedding, the face of one person and the movement of another person can be integrated. The limitation of this approach is the necessity of landmark adaptation where the model underperforms if landmarks are used from a different person. A model using keypoint representations for synthesizing talking head videos using a source image for appearance and a driving video for motion has been proposed in [1]. This enables video conferencing with no perceptible change in video quality while providing significant reduction for the required bandwidth. Monkey-Net proposed in [5], is known as the first object-agnostic deep learning based model for video animation, since here the source image is animated based on the keypoint movements detected in the driving video that are learned in a self-supervised manner. The principal drawback is that Monkey-Net relies on a simplistic zeroth order keypoint model which results in poor generation quality when there are significant changes in the object's pose. To address this challenge, the FOMM [6] has been proposed that decouples appearances and motion information of video frames with the help of local affine transformations and coordinates of self learned keypoints. A novel end-to-end unsupervised framework for motion transfer using keypoints has been recently proposed in [24] in order to address challenges posed by significant pose differences between source and driving images in video animation. This thin-plate spline motion estimation is utilized to make the optical flow more adaptable, as well as provide enhanced restoration of features in missing areas using multi-resolution occlusion masks which leads to the generation of high-quality images. Our current work which utilizes the FOMM motion transfer pipeline is a significant extension and improvement of our earlier results reported in [25] using Monkey-Net. Our method is quite general and can be applied for realizing bandwidth savings in other keypoint based architectures such as [1, 24] which are used for tasks such as video reconstruction and motion transfer.

3   The Proposed Pipeline

We apply keypoint prediction within the FOMM motion transfer pipeline [6]. The architecture of our pipeline, enabling keypoint prediction and video synthesis, is illustrated in Fig. 1. Inputs to the pipeline consist of a source image **S** and a sequence of driving video frames **D**. In this architecture, keypoints are first extracted in an unsupervised manner by a keypoint detector [26] for both the source image **S** and the driving video frames **D**. The extracted keypoints are represented as keypoint locations and the parameters of local affine transformations, which model the motion around each individual keypoint. Using the affine transformations helps the FOMM capture more complex motions as compared to earlier models like Monkey-Net [5]. Following this detection network, forecasting of keypoints is performed using a Variational Recurrent Neural Network (VRNN) which has been shown to effectively deal with complex underlying dynamics of high dimensional time series data [7]. For comparison purposes we also perform forecasting of keypoints using a Recurrent Neural Network (RNN) [27] and a Variational Autoencoder (VAE) [28]. Following prediction of keypoints, a dense motion network is used to align the feature maps from the source image **S** to the driving video frames **D**. Finally a generator module is used to produce a video of the source object as per the dynamics in the driving video.

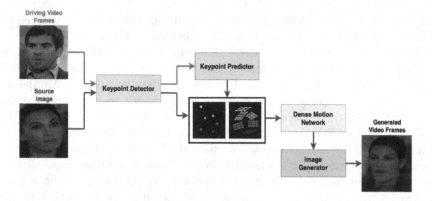

Fig. 1. Components of our proposed pipeline for keypoint prediction and video synthesis

In this work we use 10 keypoints for every video frame, each of which consists of coordinates x, y. The number of keypoints K is an important hyperparameter for our proposed pipeline involving keypoint prediction and video synthesis. In our empirical studies as described in Sect. 4, we found that setting K=10 is sufficient for generation of high quality video outputs while providing the targeted bandwidth savings. In addition, a dense motion field is used to align the keypoints captured for the source frame **S** and those captured for the object motions in driving frames **D**. In general this correspondence can be described by a function $\mathcal{T}_{S \leftarrow D}$. For simplicity of modeling, this function is linearized around each keypoint in which case it suffices to capture the 2×2 Jacobian matrix of the transformation $\mathcal{T}_{S \leftarrow D}$ which estimates the motion in the vicinity of each keypoint. Therefore the overall time series of keypoints for every video frame consists of 20 coordinates of the keypoints and 40 components from the Jacobian matrix. In the following subsections, we briefly discuss the underlying framework for the prediction of keypoint time series using the RNN, VAE and VRNN.

3.1 Recurrent Neural Network (RNN)

Keypoint prediction can be performed using an RNN [27] which is designed to handle sequential data $x = (x_1, x_2, \ldots, x_T)$ by introducing a hidden state h. At a given timestep t, the RNN updates its hidden state h_t based on input x_t as below:

$$h_t = f_\eta(x_t, h_{t-1}) \tag{1}$$

Here f is a nonlinear activation function and η is a set of learnable parameters of f. During prediction the RNN generates its output as below:

$$p(x_{t+1} | x_{<=t}) = g_\tau(h_t) \tag{2}$$

where g is a nonlinear function with learnable parameters τ that maps the hidden state h_t to a probability distribution p of outputs x_{t+1}. For our work given keypoints $x_1, x_2, \ldots x_T$ an RNN can be trained by minimizing the mean squared error loss between its predicted outputs and their corresponding ground truth values.

3.2   Variational Autoencoder (VAE)

Since the keypoints form a high-dimensional dataset, we can also consider performing prediction using the latent space of a generative model such as a VAE [28]. In a VAE at a given timestep t, the input x_t is initially fed into a probabilistic encoder q parameterized by weights ϕ. This is used to estimate the posterior distribution $q_\phi(z_t|x_t)$ which is chosen to be a Gaussian as below:

$$q_\phi(z_t|x_t) = \mathcal{N}(\mu_\phi(x_t), \sigma_\phi^2(x_t)) \tag{3}$$

Here z_t is the latent variable and $\mu_\phi(x_t)$, $\sigma_\phi^2(x_t)$ are the mean and variance of the Gaussian distribution respectively. The variable z_t is sampled using the reparameterization trick [29] as follows:

$$z_t = \mu_\phi(x_t) + \sigma_\phi(x_t) \odot \epsilon \tag{4}$$

where ϵ is a sample from a standard normal distribution, $\epsilon \sim \mathcal{N}(0, I)$ and $\odot$ denotes the element-wise product. The decoder parameterized by weights θ generates the reconstructed data x_t given a sampled latent variable z_t as below:

$$p_\theta(x_t|z_t) = \mathcal{N}(\mu_\theta(z_t), \sigma_\theta^2(z_t)) \tag{5}$$

where $p_\theta(x_t|z_t)$ is the likelihood of generating the data x_t given the latent variable z_t. The VAE can be trained by minimizing the loss function as below:

$$\mathcal{L}_{VAE} = -\mathbb{E}_{q_\phi(z_t|x_t)}[log\ p_\theta(x_t|z_t)] + KL[q_\phi(z_t|x_t)||p(z_t)] \tag{6}$$

Here θ and ϕ are the parameters of the decoder and encoder respectively and $p(z_t)$ is the prior distribution over the latent space which is usually a standard Gaussian distribution. The first term encourages the reconstruction of the input data x_t, and the second term is a regularizer which minimizes the Kullback-Leibler (KL) divergence between the prior distribution $p(z)$ over the latent space versus the posterior distribution $q_\phi(z|x)$.

Once trained a VAE can be used to perform reconstruction tasks where an input x_t can be reconstructed as x_t' as the output of the decoder. For our application given keypoints $x = (x_1, x_2, \ldots, x_T)$ the VAE can be trained so that the decoder can generate an output $x_{t+\tau}$ for a given lag $\tau = 1, 2, \ldots, k$ based on input x_t at time t.

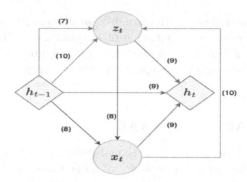

Fig. 2. Graphical representation of VRNN describing the dependencies between the variables in Eqs. (7)–(10). The green arrows correspond to the computations involving the (conditional) prior and posterior on z_t. The blue arrows show the computations involving the generative network. The computations for h_t are shown with red arrows. (Color figure online)

3.3 Variational Recurrent Neural Network (VRNN)

A VRNN [7] combines the principles of VAEs with RNNs to model sequential data. The VRNN consists of an RNN that contains a VAE at each time step.

Unlike a regular VAE, the prior z_t in a VRNN depends on the preceding inputs through h_{t-1} and is assumed to follow a Gaussian distribution with parameters $\mu_{0,t}, \sigma_{0,t}^2$ as below:

$$p(z_t) = \mathcal{N}(\mu_{0,t}, \mathrm{diag}(\sigma_{0,t}^2)), \text{where } [\mu_{0,t}, \sigma_{0,t}] = \varphi_\tau^{prior}(h_{t-1}) \tag{7}$$

The generating distribution of the data x_t parameterized by $\mu_{x,t}, \sigma_{x,t}^2$ is conditioned on the latent variable z_t and the hidden state h_{t-1} as follows:

$$p(x_t|z_t) = \mathcal{N}(\mu_{x,t}, \mathrm{diag}(\sigma_{x,t}^2)), \text{where } [\mu_{x,t}, \sigma_{x,t}] = \varphi_\tau^{dec}(\varphi_\tau^z(z_t), h_{t-1}) \tag{8}$$

The hidden state h_t of the RNN is updated using the recurrence equation:

$$h_t = f(\varphi_\tau^x(x_t), \varphi_\tau^z(z_t), h_{t-1}; \theta) \tag{9}$$

where f is a non-linear activation function. The approximate posterior $q(z_t|x_t)$ parameterized by $\mu_{z,t}, \sigma^2{}_{z,t}$ is conditioned on both x_t and h_{t-1} as below:

$$q(z_t|x_t) = \mathcal{N}(\mu_{z,t}, \sigma^2{}_{z,t}), \text{where } [\mu_{z,t}, \sigma_{z,t}] = \varphi_\tau^{enc}(\varphi_\tau^x(x_t), h_{t-1}) \tag{10}$$

Here φ_τ^{prior} in Eq. (7), φ_τ^{dec} in Eq. (8), $\varphi_\tau^x, \varphi_\tau^z$ in Eqs. (9) and φ_τ^{enc} in Eq. (10) all refer to non-linear functions that can be realized using Deep Neural Networks. A graphical representation of these computations for the VRNN is shown in Fig. 2 [30].

For our application given keypoints $x_1, x_2, \ldots x_T$ the VRNN is trained using a loss function which combines KL divergence with the reconstruction loss as below:

$$\mathcal{L}_{VRNN} = \mathbb{E}_{q(z_{\leq T}|x_{\leq T})} \left[\sum_{t=1}^{T} \left(KL(q(z_t|x_{\leq t}, z_{<t}) || p(z_t|x_{<t}, z_{<t})) - log \ p(x_t|z_{\leq t}, x_{<t}) \right) \right]$$
(11)

3.4 Training and Inference

Our proposed pipeline offers two operational modes: reconstruction and transfer. In reconstruction mode, the source image **S** and the sequence of driving video frames **D** are sourced from the same video. For instance, if video A consists of k frames, the source image **S** corresponds to the first frame of video A, and the driving video frames encompass frames 2 through k from video A. On the other hand, in transfer mode, the source image **S** and the sequence of driving video frames **D** originate from different videos. The pipeline is first trained end-to-end for video reconstruction, i.e., without keypoint prediction. The keypoint detector from the trained model is then utilized to generate keypoints, which are then employed to train the RNN, VAE, and VRNN separately based on their respective loss functions as described earlier.

During inference in either reconstruction or transfer mode, a source image **S** and a sequence of driving video frames **D** are input to the keypoint detector during the initial M frames of a video sequence. Subsequently, no inputs are provided for the following N frames. During this phase, the RNN, VAE, and VRNN predict the keypoints, after which the optical flow and generator networks are employed to synthesize the next N video frames. Although our model is trained in reconstruction mode, inference can be carried out in either mode to obtain the generated video sequence. In transfer mode, where there is no ground truth video for reference, we generate this using the FOMM pipeline without keypoint prediction and employ it as the ground truth during prediction.

4 Experimental Results

We present our experimental results to analyze the performance of the three networks introduced in Sect. 3 using our proposed keypoint prediction and video synthesis pipeline as shown in Fig. 1. Our experiments are conducted using three different networks for prediction: RNN, VAE, and VRNN across three diverse datasets: Mgif [5], Bair [31] and VoxCeleb [32], in both reconstruction and transfer mode. In the following subsections, we will provide an introduction to the three datasets and present our experimental results. We demonstrate the superior performance of VRNN compared to RNN and VAE across all three datasets in both reconstruction and transfer mode.

4.1 Datasets

We assess the quality of video generation using three datasets.

- **Mgif dataset:** We employ 284 training and 34 testing videos from the Mgif dataset, which captures periodic movements of various animals. The videos exhibit varying frame counts, ranging from a minimum of 168 frames to a maximum of 10,500 frames, capturing the diverse distribution of the data. This dataset enables a comprehensive analysis of the model's capacity to capture a range of animal movements with distinct patterns.
- **Bair dataset:** We use 5001 training and 256 testing videos from the Bair dataset. Each video contains a fixed set of 30 frames and consists of robotic arms in motion to capture different objects. This dataset is helpful for evaluating the proposed architecture's performance in complex environments characterized by diverse backgrounds and irregular movements.
- **VoxCeleb dataset:** We utilize 3884 training and 44 testing videos from the VoxCeleb dataset, which contains diverse interview scenes with celebrities. Within the dataset, the number of frames in each video varies, ranging from a minimum of 72 frames to a maximum of 1228 frames. This dataset tests the model's capability to capture subtle facial changes, a crucial aspect for applications such as videoconferencing where conveying delicate expressions is essential.

4.2 Evaluation Procedures

We compare the predictive capabilities of RNN, VAE, and VRNN across the Mgif, Bair, and VoxCeleb datasets, considering both reconstruction and transfer modes. For both modes, we take a block of k frames (where $k \geq 1$) of ground truth keypoints as input and predict the following block of k frames of keypoints. We then iterate this process over the entire video sequence until the remaining number of frames are less than $2k$. This is done for each video in their respective daatset, during training and inference.

In reconstruction mode, the network takes the source image **S** and driving video frames **D** from the same video A. The Mean Squared Error (MSE) and Frechet Video Distance (FVD) [33] between the reconstructed video A_r and the corresponding original ground truth video A are then calculated to evaluate the prediction performance. Lower values of MSE and FVD indicate lower amount of degradation versus the corresponding ground truth and therefore superior video quality. In transfer mode, the network operates with the source image **S** from video B and driving video images **D** from video A. In this mode, there is no ground truth corresponding to the generated video B_t. To address this we generate video B_t' by performing inference using the FOMM pipeline without Deep Learning based networks for keypoint prediction. This is then used in lieu of the ground truth for evaluating the performance in transfer mode.

4.3   Results on Mgif Dataset

To evaluate the performance of our prediction using the Mgif dataset, we perform long and short horizon predictions in both reconstruction and transfer mode. Specifically, for long horizon prediction, we set $k = 12$, i.e., we use the first 12 frames of ground truth as input to predict next 12 frames and repeat this process for the full video; while for short horizon prediction, we choose $k = 6$, i.e., we apply the first 6 frames of ground truth as input to predict the next 6 frames and repeat this for the full video.

The prediction performance of VRNN, RNN and VAE for the Mgif dataset in case of long and short horizon scenarios are shown in Tables 1 and 2 respectively. The results demonstrate that across all cases, VRNN consistently outperforms RNN and VAE in tasks involving both reconstructing ground truth videos and generating motion transfer videos. This superiority is evident through both assessment metrics, MSE and FVD. The qualitative results for selected videos are shown in Fig. 3.

Table 1. MSE and FVD results of Mgif dataset in reconstruction mode

Predicted results for reconstruction mode						
Prediction type	MSE			FVD		
(# input frames, # output frames)	VRNN	RNN	VAE	VRNN	RNN	VAE
(6, 6)	**0.0340**	0.0392	0.0380	**7.8469**	9.1903	8.8407
(12, 12)	**0.0338**	0.0388	0.0382	**7.7835**	8.8653	8.8571

Table 2. MSE and FVD results of Mgif dataset in transfer mode

Predicted results for transfer mode						
Prediction type	MSE			FVD		
(# input frames, # output frames)	VRNN	RNN	VAE	VRNN	RNN	VAE
(6, 6)	**0.0171**	0.0230	0.0215	**3.7741**	5.1614	4.7917
(12, 12)	**0.0164**	0.0227	0.0215	**3.5933**	5.0911	4.7714

4.4   Results on Bair Dataset

For the Bair dataset, given that each video consists of 30 frames, we perform both long and short horizon predictions by selecting $k = 15$ and $k = 5$, respectively. The prediction results for the Bair dataset are shown in Tables 3 and 4. Observing the outcomes, it is evident that for this dataset characterized by complex robotic motion, VRNN consistently outperforms RNN and VAE across both long and short horizon prediction tasks. The qualitative results for selected videos are shown in Fig. 4.

Table 3. MSE and FVD results of Bair dataset in reconstruction mode

Predicted results for reconstruction mode						
Prediction type (# input frames, # output frames)	MSE			FVD		
	VRNN	RNN	VAE	VRNN	RNN	VAE
(5, 5)	**0.0660**	0.0752	0.0749	**10.8439**	13.8028	13.7585
(15, 15)	**0.0717**	0.0732	0.0759	**13.0483**	13.1366	14.1428

Table 4. MSE and FVD results of Bair dataset in transfer mode

Predicted results for transfer mode						
Prediction type (# input frames, # output frames)	MSE			FVD		
	VRNN	RNN	VAE	VRNN	RNN	VAE
(5, 5)	**0.0133**	0.0305	0.0267	**2.3951**	6.7901	5.8773
(15, 15)	**0.0206**	0.0290	0.0299	**4.2714**	6.4359	6.6828

4.5   Results on VoxCeleb Dataset

For the VoxCeleb dataset, similar to the Mgif dataset, we conduct both long and short horizon prediction experiments with $k = 12$ and $k = 6$, respectively. The prediction results for the VoxCeleb dataset are shown in Table 5 and 6. We notice that, even in this scenario involving a more intricate dataset with diverse scenes, VRNN based prediction consistently exhibits superior performance compared to RNN and VAE. The qualitative results for selected videos are shown in Fig. 5.

Table 5. MSE and FVD results of VoxCeleb dataset in reconstruction mode

Predicted results for reconstruction mode						
Prediction type (# input frames, # output frames)	MSE			FVD		
	VRNN	RNN	VAE	VRNN	RNN	VAE
(6, 6)	**0.0483**	0.0564	0.0602	**3.7120**	4.6684	5.3585
(12, 12)	**0.0471**	0.0649	0.0651	**3.5917**	6.1379	6.2279

Table 6. MSE and FVD results of VoxCeleb dataset in transfer mode

Predicted results for transfer mode						
Prediction type (# input frames, # output frames)	MSE			FVD		
	VRNN	RNN	VAE	VRNN	RNN	VAE
(6, 6)	**0.0097**	0.0202	0.0245	**0.2325**	0.8705	1.2542
(12, 12)	**0.0086**	0.0285	0.0292	**0.1969**	1.6624	1.7347

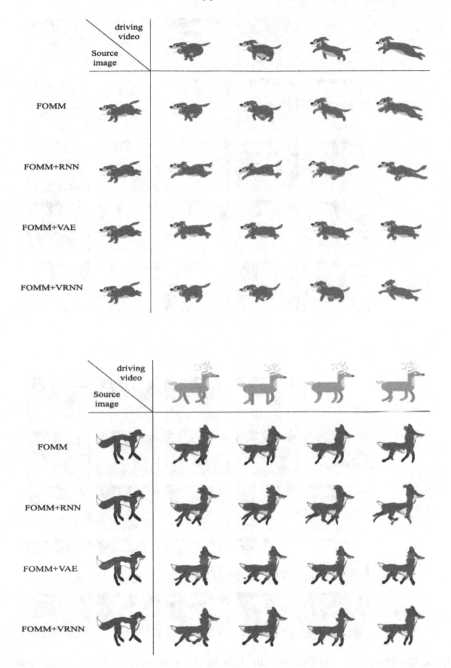

Fig. 3. Qualitative results for the Mgif dataset in reconstruction mode (upper panel) and transfer mode (lower panel). In each panel, consecutive frames generated using only FOMM are shown in the second row, and FOMM with keypoints prediction using RNN, VAE, and VRNN are shown in the third, fourth and fifth rows respectively. For reconstruction mode, the first row serves as the ground truth whereas for transfer mode the second row serves as the ground truth.

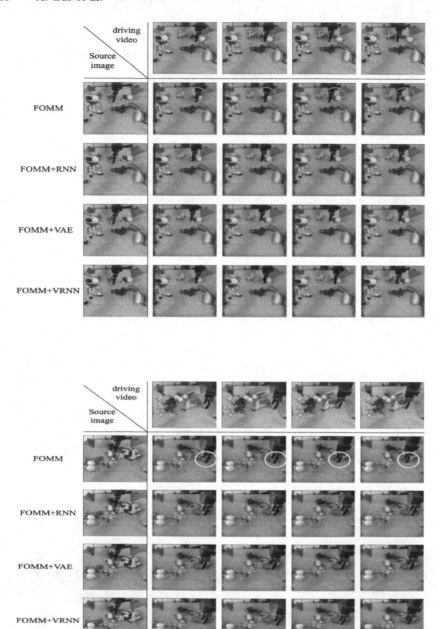

Fig. 4. Qualitative results for the Bair dataset in reconstruction mode (upper panel) and transfer mode (lower panel). In each panel, consecutive frames generated using only FOMM are shown in the second row, and FOMM with keypoints prediction using RNN, VAE, and VRNN are shown in the third, fourth and fifth rows respectively. For reconstruction mode, the first row serves as the ground truth whereas for transfer mode the second row serves as the ground truth. The circles in both figures are examples of regions where VRNN performs better than RNN and VAE.

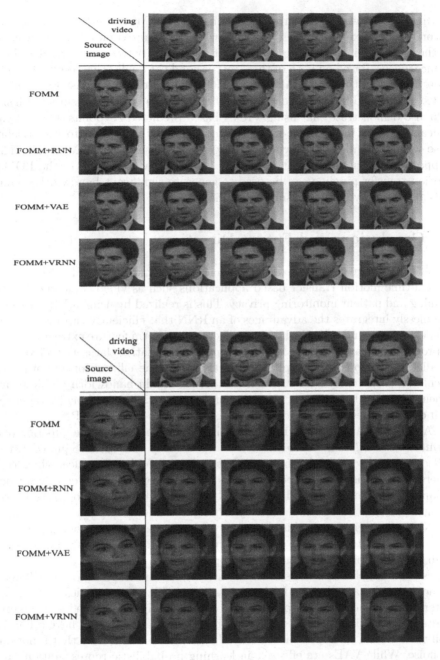

Fig. 5. Qualitative results for the VoxCeleb dataset in reconstruction mode (upper panel) and transfer mode (lower panel). In each panel, consecutive frames generated using only FOMM are shown in the second row, and FOMM with keypoints prediction using RNN, VAE, and VRNN are shown in the third, fourth and fifth rows respectively. For reconstruction mode, the first row serves as the ground truth whereas for transfer mode the second row serves as the ground truth.

In this work we use two error metrics namely the MSE which focuses primarily on pixel to pixel differences and FVD which is a more comprehensive measure of the difference in the distribution of feature vectors between generated and reference videos. Based on both of these metrics and the qualitative results it can be seen that the outputs generated from VRNN consistently demonstrate superior video quality and temporal coherence. Morever, our qualitative results in Figs. 3, 4, 5 also demonstrate that using VRNN based predicted keypoints does not significantly affect the quality of the output videos as compared to the baseline case when the full set of keypoints are generated using the FOMM only. This supports our contention that predicting keypoints with VRNN in the FOMM motion transfer pipeline can be used to generate significant bandwidth savings without seriously compromising video quality.

5   Conclusions and Future Directions

In this paper, we propose a novel approach for enhancing bandwidth savings in real-time motion transfer based applications such as video conferencing, VR gaming and patient monitoring privacy. This is realized by using a VRNN which seamlessly integrates the advantages of an RNN that efficiently captures temporal dependence and a VAE which can effectively perform feature extraction using a probabilistic latent space. By employing representative datasets and varying prediction horizons, our empirical analysis shows the efficacy of our proposed architecture in achieving a $2\times$ additional reduction in bandwidth requirements when compared to cases where prediction is omitted. This is done by replacing half of the frames using their predicted counterparts from the VRNN.

Across all datasets, our results consistently demonstrate the superior performance of VRNN in video prediction. Specifically, the Mean Squared Error, reflecting pixel-to-pixel differences, and the Frechet Video Distance, which considers both spatial and temporal aspects of videos, exhibit smaller values when compared to those obtained with RNN and VAE based methods. As it was pointed out in the original work by Chung et al. (2015) [7] who introduced VRNN for natural speech, this type of network is well-suited for modeling sequential data characterized by a complex structure, high intrinsic variability and a high signal-to-noise ratio. The typical application of VRNN is described as time series that exhibit high and sudden variations that are *not* due to noise. This is an accurate characterization for keypoints, which follow trajectories that are not deterministic or completely predictable but are highly constrained by geometry and are not significantly affected by position uncertainty. RNNs have a limited ability to deal with sudden variations and randomness in the data that is not due to noise. While VAEs are effective in learning probabilistic representations and generating diverse samples, they may face problems in capturing the temporal dependencies and sudden variations present in the data. Therefore, the incorporation of structured output functions in VRNNs, coupled with their ability to represent complex non-linear data, positions them as a superior choice for the type of applications that is the focus of this work. For applications such as video conferencing we plan to perform more detailed studies in future in order to determine how well our proposed pipeline generalizes to different subjects as well as its robustness to variations in the quality of the input videos. Our future research will also focus on using methods such as Transformers [34] for keypoint forecasting over longer horizons to realize a higher degree of bandwidth savings for motion transfer applications.

Acknowledgements. Xue Bai was supported for this work by an Intel grant. The authors would like to acknowledge the Pacific Research Platform, NSF Project ACI-1541349, and Larry Smarr (PI, Calit2 at UCSD) for providing the computing infrastructure used in this project.

Samples of Generated Videos
Selected videos from reconstruction and transfer and example code are provided at: https://github.com/xuebai95/Motion-Transfer-Keypoints-Prediction.

Author contributions. Xue Bai: Code development, simulations on all datasets and original draft. **Tasmiah Haque**: Literature studies and simulations. **Byungheong Jeong**: Computing infrastructure and feedback on manuscript. **Yuliang Cai and Adam Halasz**: Feedback on manuscript. **Sumit Mohan**: Conceptualization and feedback on manuscript. **Srinjoy Das**: Conceptualization, resources, supervision, methodology and original draft.

References

1. Wang, T.C., Mallya, A., Liu, M.Y.: One-shot free-view neural talking-head synthesis for video conferencing. In: Proceedings of the IEEE/CVF Conference on Computer Vision and Pattern Recognition, pp. 10039–10049 (2021)
2. Chan, C., Ginosar, S., Zhou, T., Efros, A.A.: Everybody dance now. In: Proceedings of the IEEE/CVF International Conference on Computer Vision, pp. 5933–5942 (2019)
3. McDonald, K.: Dance x machine learning: first steps (2019). https://medium.com/@kcimc/discrete-figures-7d9e9c275c47. Accessed 21 Mar 2019
4. Yang, H.C., Rahmanti, A.R., Huang, C.W., Li, Y.C.: How can research on artificial empathy be enhanced by applying deepfakes? J. Med. Internet Res. **24**(3), e29506 (2022)
5. Siarohin, A., Lathuilière, S., Tulyakov, S., Ricci, E., Sebe, N.: Animating arbitrary objects via deep motion transfer. In: Proceedings of the IEEE/CVF Conference on Computer Vision and Pattern Recognition, pp. 2377–2386 (2019)
6. Siarohin, A., Lathuilière, S., Tulyakov, S., Ricci, E., Sebe, N.: First order motion model for image animation. In: Advances in Neural Information Processing Systems, vol. 32 (2019)
7. Chung, J., Kastner, K., Dinh, L., Goel, K., Courville, A.C., Bengio, Y.: A recurrent latent variable model for sequential data. In: Advances in Neural Information Processing Systems, vol. 28 (2015)
8. Luc, P., et al.: Transformation-based adversarial video prediction on large-scale data. arXiv preprint arXiv:2003.04035 (2020)
9. Mathieu, M., Couprie, C., LeCun, Y.: Deep multi-scale video prediction beyond mean square error. arXiv preprint arXiv:1511.05440 (2015)

10. Zhou, Y., Berg, T.L.: Learning temporal transformations from time-lapse videos. In: Leibe, B., Matas, J., Sebe, N., Welling, M. (eds.) ECCV 2016. LNCS, vol. 9912, pp. 262–277. Springer, Cham (2016). https://doi.org/10.1007/978-3-319-46484-8_16

11. Jin, B., et al.: Exploring spatial-temporal multi-frequency analysis for high-fidelity and temporal-consistency video prediction. In: Proceedings of the IEEE/CVF Conference on Computer Vision and Pattern Recognition, pp. 4554–4563 (2020)

12. Reda, F.A., et al.: SDC-Net: video prediction using spatially-displaced convolution. In: Proceedings of the European Conference on Computer Vision (ECCV), pp. 718–733 (2018)

13. Lopez, R., Huang, T.S.: Head pose computation for very low bit-rate video coding. In: Hlaváč, V., Šára, R. (eds.) CAIP 1995. LNCS, vol. 970, pp. 440–447. Springer, Heidelberg (1995). https://doi.org/10.1007/3-540-60268-2_327

14. Koufakis, I., Buxton, B.F.: Very low bit rate face video compression using linear combination of 2D face views and principal components analysis. Image Vis. Comput. **17**(14), 1031–1051 (1999)

15. Tang, J., Hu, H., Zhou, Q., Shan, H., Tian, C., Quek, T.Q.: Pose guided global and local GAN for appearance preserving human video prediction. In: 2019 IEEE International Conference on Image Processing (ICIP), pp. 614–618. IEEE (2019)

16. Villegas, R., Erhan, D., Lee, H.: Hierarchical long-term video prediction without supervision. In: International Conference on Machine Learning, pp. 6038–6046. PMLR (2018)

17. Villegas, R., Yang, J., Zou, Y., Sohn, S., Lin, X., Lee, H.: Learning to generate long-term future via hierarchical prediction. In: International Conference on Machine Learning, pp. 3560–3569. PMLR (2017)

18. Walker, J., Marino, K., Gupta, A., Hebert, M.: The pose knows: video forecasting by generating pose futures. In: Proceedings of the IEEE International Conference on Computer Vision, pp. 3332–3341 (2017)

19. Ranzato, M., Szlam, A., Bruna, J., Mathieu, M., Collobert, R., Chopra, S.: Video (language) modeling: a baseline for generative models of natural videos. arXiv preprint arXiv:1412.6604 (2014)

20. Terwilliger, A., Brazil, G., Liu, X.: Recurrent flow-guided semantic forecasting. In: 2019 IEEE Winter Conference on Applications of Computer Vision (WACV), pp. 1703–1712. IEEE (2019)

21. Hochreiter, S., Schmidhuber, J.: Long short-term memory. Neural Comput. **9**(8), 1735–1780 (1997)

22. Minderer, M., Sun, C., Villegas, R., Cole, F., Murphy, K.P., Lee, H.: Unsupervised learning of object structure and dynamics from videos. In: Advances in Neural Information Processing Systems, vol. 32 (2019)

23. Zakharov, E., Shysheya, A., Burkov, E., Lempitsky, V.: Few-shot adversarial learning of realistic neural talking head models. In: Proceedings of the IEEE/CVF International Conference on Computer Vision, pp. 9459–9468 (2019)

24. Zhao, J., Zhang, H.: Thin-plate spline motion model for image animation. In: Proceedings of the IEEE/CVF Conference on Computer Vision and Pattern Recognition, pp. 3657–3666 (2022)

25. Cai, Y., Mohan, S., Niranjan, A., Jain, N., Cloninger, A., Das, S.: A manifold learning based video prediction approach for deep motion transfer. In: Proceedings of the IEEE/CVF International Conference on Computer Vision, pp. 4231–4238 (2021)

26. Jakab, T., Gupta, A., Bilen, H., Vedaldi, A.: Unsupervised learning of object landmarks through conditional image generation. In: Advances in Neural Information Processing Systems, vol. 31 (2018)
27. Salehinejad, H., Sankar, S., Barfett, J., Colak, E., Valaee, S.: Recent advances in recurrent neural networks. arXiv preprint arXiv:1801.01078 (2017)
28. Kingma, D.P., Welling, M.: Auto-encoding variational bayes. arXiv preprint arXiv:1312.6114 (2013)
29. Rezende, D.J., Mohamed, S., Wierstra, D.: Stochastic backpropagation and approximate inference in deep generative models. In: International Conference on Machine Learning, pp. 1278–1286. PMLR (2014)
30. Ullah, S., Xu, Z., Wang, H., Menzel, S., Sendhoff, B., Bäck, T.: Exploring clinical time series forecasting with meta-features in variational recurrent models. In: 2020 International Joint Conference on Neural Networks (IJCNN), pp. 1–9. IEEE (2020)
31. Ebert, F., Finn, C., Lee, A.X., Levine, S.: Self-supervised visual planning with temporal skip connections. In: CoRL 12, p. 16 (2017)
32. Nagrani, A., Chung, J.S., Zisserman, A.: VoxCeleb: a large-scale speaker identification dataset. arXiv preprint arXiv:1706.08612 (2017)
33. Unterthiner, T., Van Steenkiste, S., Kurach, K., Marinier, R., Michalski, M., Gelly, S.: Towards accurate generative models of video: a new metric & challenges. arXiv preprint arXiv:1812.01717 (2018)
34. Vaswani, A., et al.: Attention is all you need. In: Advances in Neural Information Processing Systems, vol. 30 (2017)

Enhancing Natural Language Query to SQL Query Generation Through Classification-Based Table Selection

Ankush Chopra[ID] and Rauful Azam[✉][ID]

Bangalore, India
{ankush.chopra,rauful.azam}@tredence.com

Abstract. In recent years, the convergence of natural language processing (NLP) and large language models (LLMs) has propelled the development of solutions enabling users to interact seamlessly with structured databases using natural language queries (NLQs). Existing NLQ-to-SQL models primarily approach this as a translation problem, converting NLQs into SQL queries for database interaction. However, challenges arise when dealing with extensive databases containing numerous tables, necessitating a robust approach for table selection to improve the efficiency of downstream NLQ-to-SQL models.

This paper introduces a classification-based method for table selection, addressing limitations in existing embedding-based approaches. By predicting the necessity of tables in query formulation, the proposed approach offers a more meaningful interpretation of model scores, facilitating the determination of a universal threshold for table selection. To validate this innovative approach, a custom dataset was curated, leveraging the Spider dataset for NLQ-to-SQL tasks, and a comprehensive set of experiments was conducted using various language models, including GPT-4, GPT-3.5, and DeBERTa.

Results demonstrate the effectiveness of the fine-tuned DeBERTa model in consistently outperforming other models across key metrics, showcasing its advancements in table selection tasks. This research not only addresses the challenge of context length in NLQ-to-SQL models but also highlights the potential of smaller LLMs when fine-tuned for specific tasks. The proposed classification-based approach offers a practical solution for improving the accuracy and efficiency of NLQ-to-SQL models, paving the way for enhanced interactions between users and structured databases.

Keywords: TableQA · Natural Language Interfaces · Context Length · Vector DB · Fine-tuning · SQL Query Generation · DeBERTa · GPT2 · GPT4 · GPT3.5

1 Introduction

In recent years, substantial efforts have been directed towards building a solution that lets users interact with structured databases (DBs) with natural language queries (NLQ). The recent advancement in the NLP and LLM research have fueled this further. These solutions aim to enable seamless interaction with databases for non-SQL users. These

© The Author(s), under exclusive license to Springer Nature Switzerland AG 2024
L. Iliadis et al. (Eds.): EANN 2024, CCIS 2141, pp. 152–165, 2024.
https://doi.org/10.1007/978-3-031-62495-7_12

solutions approach this as translation problem, where they convert the NLQ to SQL and get the desired output by querying the database with generated SQL queries.

To achieve this, most of the recent models rely on table schema or table content as input for converting NLQ to SQL queries. Using the table schema is more commonplace when the NLQs warrant the answers to come from multiple tables that may contain large number of rows. In most cases, where answer needs to come from multiple tables, using table data directly for answer generation is impractical as the content of these tables along with the metadata will not fit into the context window of language models used for answer or SQL query generation.

Even while using just the metadata, the challenge arises when dealing with an extensive database containing multitudes of schemas and numerous tables. This in fact is quite common in most of the practical applications where organizations store their data in hundreds if not thousands of tables. Passing the metadata of all the tables to model is not possible due to the context length limitations of the language models. Moreover, passing the metadata of irrelevant table would impact the performance of model responsible for query generation both in terms of response time and quality. In such scenarios, supplying the required tables manually to model could be one approach, but will not work out in most practical scenario since it would necessitate the user to know about tables present in the DB. Another more practical and adopted solution is usage of embedding similarity for table selection.

Embedding based methods work by converting the table metadata into the semantic embedding representations using LLMs like sentence-transformer [25] or OpenAI embedding models [16] in offline fashion. The same model is then used for generating the representation of the user question and similarity between the question and table metadata representations is calculated. In turn, a threshold is applied either in terms of number of tables to be selected or a similarity score. These approaches for table selection, however, suffer from few limitations.

First, although objective is to identify the tables that are required to formulate the query to answer the NLQ, this approach seeks similarity between table metadata and question. This makes the similarity score less reliable and identification of a universal threshold for table selection impossible. In Fig. 1, it is evident that even with a slight modification in the question, the meaning remains the same; however, the threshold for retrieving the same table varies. This variability poses a challenge in determining a universal threshold above which we can confidently assert that all tables are required for query formulation.

Second, if a conservative threshold is applied in terms of top-N tables, one could miss tables that might be needed for query generation, and liberal threshold might lead to selection of unnecessary or incorrect tables.

This entails a need for a more robust system for table selection for NLQ to SQL models. To this end, we propose a classification-based method for table selection. The proposed approach tries to predict the need of table in query formulation given the NLQ. By doing this, we model the problem objective in its original form, leading to more meaningful interpretation of model scores leading to ease of universal threshold selection. This innovative approach offers a practical solution to the context length challenge, introducing a novel perspective on improving the efficiency of downstream NLQ-to-SQL models.

> author : aid (Unique identifier for each author), oid (Foreign key referencing the organization the author belongs to), homepage (URL of the author's personal website), name (Name of the author)
> writes : aid (Foreign key referencing the author table's primary key), pid (Foreign key referencing the publication table's primary key).
> publication : year (The year of publication), cid (The ID of the conference where the publication was presented), citation_num (The number of citations received by the publication), jid (The ID of the journal where the publication was published), pid (The unique ID of the publication), reference_num (The number of references cited by the publication), title (The title of the publication), abstract (The abstract of the publication).

*** examples of three tables along with their column name and description.

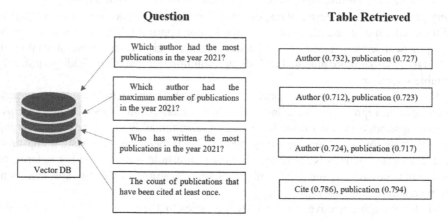

Fig. 1. Variation in similarity scores with minor changes in question, and between questions

2 Related Work

The landscape of research in natural language interfaces to databases has witnessed several notable contributions, such as Tapas [9], Tapex [13], Picard [26], Tablequery [1], Hybridqa [3], TableQA [5] and others [2, 10, 11]. These works revolve around the task of generating SQL queries from questions, employing various methodologies. While some leverage the table schema for query formulation, others delve into utilizing the actual content of tables. However, a critical aspect that has remained relatively unexplored in the existing literature is the challenge posed by the context limit in language models.

Various methods have been proposed to enhance the capabilities of Text-to-SQL LLMs. For example, Diverse Demonstrations Improve In-context Compositional Generalization [12] has highlighted the advantages of incorporating diverse demonstrations for better compositional generalization. Additionally, Learning to Retrieve Prompts for

In-Context Learning [24]; SYNCHROMESH [19] have demonstrated the effectiveness of similarity-based demonstration retrieval in the cross-domain setting. Furthermore, DIN-SQL [20] and Teaching Large Language Models to Self-Debug [4] incorporate intermediate steps in prompts and unlock LLMs' capability of self-correcting their predictions.

Notably, none of the works focuses explicitly on addressing the issues arising from context length limitations when dealing with many database tables. This research aims to fill this gap by proposing innovative approaches for table reduction inspired by RAG [18] which explore a general-purpose fine-tuning recipe, SIMLM [31] Similarity matching with Language Model pre-training and RocketQAv2 [23] novel joint training approach for dense passage retrieval and passage reranking. Strategically selecting essential tables to mitigate context length challenges and enhance the efficiency of natural language interfaces in the context of SQL query generation.

3 Methodology

In this section we will discuss the proposed approach. We will start off by describing the problem statement, which will be followed by the dataset description. Later, we will discuss the proposed solution in detail.

3.1 Problem Statement

Given a question(q) and all the available tables of database d = {T1, T2.... Tk}, we need to select all the tables (Ti, ..., Tj) which are required for the formulation of SQL queries for a given natural language question (q).

$$f(q, d) \rightarrow \{Ti \ldots Tj\} \in \{Ti \ldots Tj\} \subseteq d, d = \{T1, T2 \ldots Tk\} \tag{1}$$

3.2 Dataset

In the absence of publicly available data for this specific task, a custom dataset was meticulously curated. The dataset comprises of questions, table metadata, and labels. The labels are binary, where '1' signifies that a particular table is necessary to answer the given question, and '0' indicates that the table is not required. A sample dataset can be seen in Table 2. Sample dataset. This curated dataset was used for model training and validation. For the unbiased evaluation of the models, separate test data was considered.

Training Data Preparation. We have created this dataset using the Spider dataset [35]. This is a well-known dataset for NLQ to SQL generation task. It consists of 10,181 questions and 5,693 unique complex SQL queries on two hundred databases with multiple tables covering 138 different domains. Spider, however, lacks the metadata for the constituent tables. The missing metadata includes description of schema, tables, and columns.

Since metadata is a necessary requirement for our approach, we augmented the Spider data by adding the required metadata. Additionally, we need the required tables extracted from the SQL queries to create the modelling data. Lastly, we created negative examples (Label '0') to enable effective training of the classification models.

We considered a diverse set of ninety-one databases for generating the required dataset. These databases were selected randomly from available two hundred databases. We have made this dataset[1] available to everyone for further research on this topic.

Table Metadata Generation. We applied a two-step approach for metadata augmentation. First, we tried a few open and closed source LLMs in few-shot learning setting. Then, we manually validated and modified the generated metadata to ensure correctness. We selected ChatGPT [15] generated metadata after empirically analyzing the quality. The example prompt used for ChatGPT can be found in Fig. 2.

> Please generate the description of each table of the given schema.
> please generate the description in this format " driver: This table contains information
> about drivers. It includes the following columns: Driver_ID (Unique identifier for each
> driver), Name (Name of the driver), Party (Political party affiliation, if any),
> Home_city (Driver's hometown), Age (Age of the driver). It belongs to school_bus
> schema."
> Given schema: school_bus: driver: Driver_ID, Name, Party, Home_city, Age |
> school: School_ID, Grade, School, Location, Type | school_bus: School_ID,
> Driver_ID, Years_Working, If_full_time

Fig. 2. Example prompt for metadata generation

Query-Based Table Extraction. We used GPT-4 [17] with few-shot learning for extracting the tables from the queries. The example prompt can be found in Fig. 3.

> Context:
> - Provided a SQL query.
> Instructions:
> - Please return the table name used in SQL query.
> - If there are multiple tables used in SQL query, please return all of them in a
> single list.
> SQL query: SELECT Team FROM elimination GROUP BY Team
> HAVING COUNT(*) > 3

Fig. 3. Example prompt for table extraction

By utilizing the prompt, we obtained the required tables for each question. Example data can be found in Table 1.

Data Compilation. With questions, table metadata, the required table for each question and all available tables in a database, we compiled our training dataset. To enhance the

---

[1] https://github.com/raufulazam/Enhancing-NLQ-to-SQL-Query-Generation-through-Classific ation-Based-Table-Selection/tree/main.

Table 1. Example of extracted required table.

Question	Query	Required Table
Show teams that have suffered more than three eliminations	SELECT Team FROM elimination GROUP BY Team HAVING COUNT(*) > 3	["elimination"]
Which airlines offer flights from LAX to ORD?	SELECT DISTINCT {airline.airline_name, airline.airline_code} FROM flight JOIN airline ON flight.airline_code = airline.airline_code WHERE flight.from_airport = 'LAX' AND flight.to_airport = 'ORD';	['flight', 'airline']
What is the minimum amount of time required for a connecting flight at JFK Airport?	SELECT minimum_connect_time FROM airport WHERE airport_code = 'JFK';	['airport']

efficacy of our models, we deliberately created a robust negative set within our dataset. We designated instances as class 0 if the associated table were not required to answer the corresponding question within the same database context. For example, for a given question if the required table is "[driver]" and available tables within the same database context are "[driver, school, school_bus]". The resulting dataset structure, exemplified in Table 2.

Table 2. Sample dataset

Question	Table Metadata	Class
What is the count of drivers with an age below 30?	driver: This table contains information …………	1
What is the count of drivers with an age below 30?	school: This table stores details about ……	0
What is the count of drivers with an age below 30?	school_bus: This table indicates the ……	0

Dataset Size. Our approach resulted in the creation of a comprehensive training dataset comprising 21,458 datapoints. The dataset is partitioned into training and validation encompassing 17,166 and 4,292, respectively.

Test Data. The test dataset consists of 175 unique questions originating from seven new schemas, incorporating a total of 84 tables. This test data has been taken from sqlcoder [6] evaluation framework. Notably, these schemas were not included in the training and validation sets. This deliberate separation ensures that the models undergo evaluation on unseen instances, providing a rigorous assessment of their generalization capabilities.

3.3 Solution Approach

The problem at hand involves the estimation of a model or function tasked with determining the necessity of a table for formulating an SQL query based on the provided table metadata and user question. Given the inherent binary nature of this task, we employ a binary classification approach to address and resolve the specified objective. In addressing our research objective, we employed transformer [25] models, leveraging their established effectiveness in text classification, as demonstrated in numerous recent publications. Specifically, encoder-only models like BERT [7] and DeBERTa [8] emerged as suitable choices for our task, given their pretraining on text pairs.

While models like NSQL [14], fine-tuned versions of decoder-only models such as GPT-2 [27], are primarily designed for SQL generation tasks, we sought to explore their potential in the domain of table selection, despite their non-preference for classification tasks. This exploration aimed to assess whether the fine-tuning for SQL generation imparts efficiency to these models in the context of table selection.

The illustrative usage of these models in classification setting is given in Fig. 4 and Fig. 5.

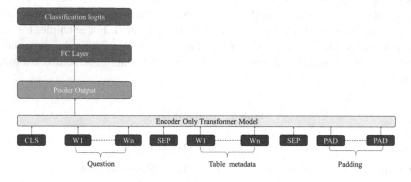

Fig. 4. Model architecture of encoder only models

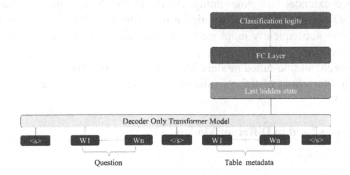

Fig. 5. Model architecture of decode only models

4   Experiments

In our research, we conducted several experiments to assess various methods for reducing or selecting tables. To gauge how well the models performed, we used standard metrics like mean average precision (MAP) and normalized discounted cumulative gain (NDCG). Additionally, we considered the number of questions where the model successfully selected all the necessary tables (Selected all required tables), the number of questions answered by selecting 5 tables or fewer (Within Top 5), and the number of questions answered by selecting 6 tables or more (more than 5) in our test dataset, which included 175 questions.

To compute MAP and NDCG scores, we created a rank list based on the total number of selected tables by model and the required number of tables. Rank ordering of the tables is done by considering the model output probability. For example, if the required tables are "[driver, school]", and the selected tables by model are "[driver, student, school, school_bus]", then the resulting rank list would be [1, 0, 1]. In this list, '1' signifies the presence of the required table at that position, while '0' indicates its absence. We constructed this list until all the required tables were identified. Subsequently, we employ this rank list to calculate the MAP and NDCG scores.

To assess the performance of our fine-tuned model, we conducted experiments using GPT-4 and GPT-3.5 for comparative analysis. Further information regarding these experiments is available under the prompt-based experiments section.

The outcomes of all experiments can be found in the "Results" section, detailed in Table 4.

4.1   Fine-Tuned Based Experiments

We performed fine-tuning on the DeBERTa-V2-xlarge model for classification capabilities using our training data. Similarly, the GPT2-Large model underwent fine-tuning for classification on our training dataset. Additionally, we explored the base GPT2 model, fine-tuning it to assess its performance relative to the larger GPT2-Large model.

Further, we extended our fine-tuning efforts to the NSQL model, specifically designed for SQL copilot tasks, and applied it to our training data. The resulting fine-tuned model was subsequently employed to extract all requisite tables essential for answering the questions.

In our research, all fine-tuned models demonstrated satisfactory performance when evaluated with a threshold of 0.5 on validation set. The best hyperparameters can be found at Table 3.

Hyperparameters Used in Different Models

Table 3. Hyperparameters used for different models.

Model Name	Learning Rate	Train Batch Size	Epochs	L.R Scheduler	Optimizer	Weight decay	Warmup Steps	Gradient Accumulation Steps
DeBERTa V2 xlarge	5e−5	12	10	Linear	Adam	0.01	100	4
GPT2 Large	2e−5	20	20	Linear	Adam	0.01	100	4
GPT2	2e−5	20	20	Linear	Adam	0.01	100	4
NSQL	2e−5	40	30	Linear	Adam	0.01	100	4

4.2 Prompt Based Experiments

We employed GPT-4 as a baseline, passing both the question and tables description as a prompt. The model's primary objective was to identify and return all the tables essential for answering a given question. The example prompt can be found in Fig. 6.

We passed all the available tables of the database. However, this approach encounters limitations, especially in situations where the database contains many tables, potentially surpassing the context limit of the model. It is noteworthy that in our current experiments, this issue did not arise since the test data only involved 84 tables. Consequently, we were able to bypass this challenge and pass all table metadata as a prompt without exceeding the context limit. Our solution does not suffer from this limitation in most cases since we classify one table at a time. In cases where tables contain many columns, encoder-only model with larger context window can be considered. Additionally, using GPT models in RAG [18] setting can help fight the context length limitation.

We also used GPT-3.5 to evaluate its performance and compare it against the results obtained with GPT-4.

Context:
- The provided table schema was given as the answer to the provided question.
Instructions:
- Please return all the tables which will be used to form the SQL query for given question.
- Please select all possible tables which can be used and don't select unnecessary tables.
- Please do not leave any possible tables which can be used.
- Please return the table along with the description in the list.
Question: How does the ratio of the cruising speed to the payload of an aircraft vary across different aircraft manufacturers?
Table: ['city: This table stores information about cities, ...', 'days: This table contains data about days of the week ....', ...] # description of tables in list

Fig. 6. Example prompt for table retrieval

5   Results and Discussion

The evaluation results on the test dataset, comprising 175 questions, for our fine-tuned models, GPT-4, and GPT-3.5 for the table selection task are summarized in Table 4. We empirically selected 0.5 as threshold to evaluate the performance. Threshold can be considered as a hyperparameter that can be optimized using a part of validation set.

Table 4. Experiments results

Model	Threshold value	Selected all required tables	Within Top 5	More than 5	NDCG	MAP
GPT-2 Large	0.50	149	133	16	0.905	0.894
GPT-2	0.50	151	115	36	0.894	0.878
DeBERTa V2 xlarge	0.50	**159**	**144**	15	**0.947**	**0.938**
GPT-4		134	132	2	0.727	0.714
GPT-3.5		117	117	0	0.712	0.710
NSQL	0.50	123	52	71	0.637	0.601

Both GPT-4 and GPT-3.5 exhibit lower performance compared to DeBERTa and GPT-2 Large models. The fine-tuned DeBERTa and GPT-2 Large model consistently outperformed GPT-4 and GPT-3.5 across various metrics. The fine-tuned DeBERTa model emerges as a robust solution, showcasing significant advancements over both GPT-4 and GPT-3.5 in the context of table selection tasks, emphasizing the effectiveness of fine-tuning strategies.

We tried multiple prompts while experimenting with prompt-based models, and selected the ones that worked the best on train and validation data. While we may have selected the best performing prompt based on our experiments, it is possible to get some improvement in results with more prompt-tuning.

NSQL model performed worst among the models that we tried, hinting at the fact that NLQ-to-SQL finetuning did not help in further learning the table selection task. The reasons behind which will be interesting to investigate in future.

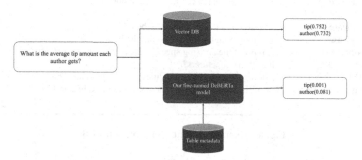

Fig. 7. Comparison of similarity-based score with classification model

The results presented in Table 4 are calculated at threshold of 0.5. This threshold seems to work well for the validation set and test set we considered for the experiments, and we believe that it'll generally work well. We suggest that a sample can be analyzed to ascertain the right threshold if the nature of question or the metadata doesn't conform to general practice.

In the Fig. 7 we attempted to compare table selection output for a question from data present in the training-set database. For question, "What is the average tip amount each author gets?"; when employing similarity-based method, it is selecting two tables – 'tip' and 'author' – with notably high scores due to keyword matches. However, when using the model based on proposed methodology, these tables received considerably lower scores, aligning more accurately with the fact that these tables are not sufficient for answering the question in consideration. Schema details for the mentioned table are given in Appendix.

6 Conclusion

Our research investigated the effectiveness of a fine-tuned model for table selection, comparing its performance to established models such as GPT-4 and GPT-3.5. Through careful fine-tuning, we improved the model's ability to choose relevant tables for query formulation, addressing challenges related to context length in scenarios with large number of tables. This work not only tries to solve the table selection problem, but the results of our experiments also underscore the effectiveness of smaller LLMs when finetuned with the right data for a specific task.

Lastly, although the proposed method performs well on table selection it might be a little slower when the number of candidate tables goes beyond a few hundred. To solve this problem one could combine the proposed method with embedding based similarity. Filtering tables with a liberal threshold of similarity with the question will help reduce the number of tables that are input to the classification model making the system fast enough to be used for real-time applications.

Appendix

The schema of academic database:

"cite : cited, citing | author : aid, oid, homepage, name | domain : did, name | writes : aid, pid | journal : jid, homepage, name | keyword : kid, keyword | conference : cid, homepage, name | publication : year, cid, citation_num, jid, pid, reference_num, title, abstract | organization : oid, continent, homepage, name | domain_author : aid, did | domain_journal : did, jid | domain_keyword : did, kid | domain_conference : cid, did | domain_publication : did, pid | publication_keyword : pid, kid"

The schema info of yelp database:

"tip : year, tip_id, month, user_id, business_id, text | users : uid, user_id, name | review : rating, rid, year, month, text, business_id, user_id | checkin : cid, count, business_id, day | business : review_count, is_open, rating, bid, city, latitude, longitude, state, business_id, name, full_address | category : id, business_id, category_name | neighbourhood : id, business_id, neighbourhood_name"

"tip" table belongs to yelp database and "author" table belongs to academic database. But when we used similarity-based approach although the given question "What is the average tip amount each author gets?" can't get answered but it is selecting two tables – 'tip' and 'author' – with high scores due to keyword match. And with our proposed model, these tables receive considerably lower scores, aligning more accurately with the fact that they are not applicable for answering the query within the provided schema.

References

1. Abraham, A., Rahman, F., Kaur, D.: TableQuery: querying tabular data with natural language. ArXiv abs/2202.00454 (2022)
2. Chen, W., Chang, M.W., Schlinger, E., Wang, W.Y., Cohen, W.W.: Open question answering over tables and text. ArXiv abs/2010.10439 (2021)
3. Chen, W., Zha, H., Chen, Z., Xiong, W., Wang, H., Wang, W.Y.: HybridQA: a dataset of multi-hop question answering over tabular and textual data. In: FINDINGS (2020)
4. Chen, X., Lin, M., Scharli, N., Zhou, D.: Teaching large language models to self-debug. ArXiv abs/2304.05128 (2023)
5. Cho, M., Amplayo, R.K., Hwang, S.W., Park, J.: Adversarial TableQA: attention supervision for question answering on tables. In: PMLR (2018)
6. Defog. SQLCoder (2023). https://defog.ai/sqlcoder-demo/
7. Devlin, J., Chang, M.W., Lee, K., Toutanova, K.: BERT: pre-training of deep bidirectional transformers for language understanding. ArXiv abs/1810.04805 (2019)
8. He, P., Liu, X., Gao, J., Chen, W.: DeBERTa: decoding-enhanced BERT with disentangled attention. Arxiv abs/2006.03654 (2021)
9. Herzig, J., Nowak, P.K., Müller, T., Piccinno, F., Eisenschlos, J.M.: TAPAS: weakly supervised table parsing via pre-training. ArXiv abs/2004.02349 (2020)
10. Katsis, Y., et al.: AIT-QA: question answering dataset over complex tables in the airline industry. ArXiv abs/2106.12944 (2021)

11. Lei, F., et al.: TableQAKit: a comprehensive and practical toolkit for table-based question answering. ArXiv abs/2310.15075 (2023)

12. Levy, I., Bogin, B., Berant, J.: Diverse demonstrations improve in-context compositional generalization. ArXiv abs/2212.06800 (2023)

13. Liu, Q., et al.: TAPEX: table pre-training via learning a neural SQL executor. ArXiv abs/2107.07653 (2022)

14. NSQL. Numbers Station Text to SQL model code. GitHub - NumbersStationAI/NSQL: Numbers Station Text to SQL model code (2023)

15. OpenAI. Introducing chatgpt (2022). https://openai.com/blog/chatgpt

16. OpenAI. Embeddings (2022). https://platform.openai.com/docs/guides/embeddings/what-are-embeddings

17. OpenAI. GPT-4 technical report. ArXiv, abs/2303.08774 (2023)

18. Piktus, A., et al.: Retrieval-augmented generation for knowledge-intensive NLP tasks. ArXiv abs/2005.11401 (2021)

19. Poesia, G., Polozov, O.: Synchromesh: reliable code generation from pre-trained language models. ArXiv abs/2201.11227 (2022)

20. Pourreza, M., Rafiei, D.: DIN-SQL: decomposed in-context learning of text-to-SQL with self-correction. ArXiv abs/2304.11015 (2023)

21. Prasad, A.: Enhancement of natural language to SQL query conversion using machine learning techniques. Int. J. Adv. Comput. Sci. Appl. **11**, 494–503 (2020). https://doi.org/10.14569/IJACSA.2020.0111260

22. Radford, A., Wu, J., Child, R., Luan, D., Amodei, D., Sutskever, I.: Language models are unsupervised multitask learners. https://d4mucfpksywv.cloudfront.net/better-language-models/language-models.pdf

23. Ren, R., et al.: RocketQAv2: a joint training method for dense passage retrieval and passage re-ranking. ArXiv abs/2110.07367 (2023)

24. Rubin, O., Herzig, J., Berant, J.: Learning to retrieve prompts for in-context learning. ArXiv abs/2112.08633 (2022)

25. SBERT.net. Sentence transformers (2022). https://www.sbert.net/

26. Scholak, T., Schucher, N., Bahdanau, D.: PICARD: parsing incrementally for constrained auto-regressive decoding from language models. ArXiv abs/2109.05093 (2021)

27. Sun, W., et al.: Is ChatGPT good at search? Investigating large language models as re-ranking agents. ArXiv abs/2304.09542 (2023)

28. Sun, Y., et al.: Semantic parsing with syntax- and table-aware SQL generation. ArXiv abs/1804.08338 (2018)

29. Vaswani, A., et al.: Attention is all you need. ArXiv abs /1706.03762 (2023)

30. Wang, B., Shin, R., Liu, X., Polozov, O., Richardson, M.: RAT-SQL: relation-aware schema encoding and linking for text-to-SQL parsers. In: ACL (2020)

31. Wang, L., et al.: SimLM: pre-training with representation bottleneck for dense passage retrieval. ArXiv abs/2207.02578 (2023)

32. Wang, P., Shi, T., Reddy, C.K.: Text-to-SQL generation for question answering on electronic medical records. ArXiv abs/1908.01839 (2020)

33. Yang, J., Gupta, A., Upadhyay, S., He, L., Goel, R., Paul, S.: TableFormer: robust transformer modeling for table-text encoding. ArXiv abs/2203.00274 (2022)

34. Yu, T., Li, Z., Zhang, Z., Zhang, R., Radev, D.R.: TypeSQL: knowledge-based typeaware neural text-to-SQL generation. In: NAACL (2018)

35. Yu, T., et al.: Spider: A large-scale human-labeled dataset for complex and cross-domain semantic parsing and text-to-SQL task. In: EMNLP (2018)

36. Zayats, V., Toutanova, K., Ostendorf, M.: Representations for question answering from documents with tables and text. In: EACL (2021)

37. Zhong, W., et al.: Reasoning over hybrid chain for table-and-text open domain QA. ArXiv abs/2201.05880 (2022)
38. Zhu, F., et al.: TAT-QA: a question answering benchmark on a hybrid of tabular and textual content in finance. In: ACL (2021)

Exploiting LMM-Based Knowledge for Image Classification Tasks

Maria Tzelepi[✉] and Vasileios Mezaris

Information Technologies Institute (ITI), Centre for Research and Technology Hellas (CERTH), Thessaloniki, Greece
{mtzelepi,bmezaris}@iti.gr

Abstract. In this paper we address image classification tasks leveraging knowledge encoded in Large Multimodal Models (LMMs). More specifically, we use the MiniGPT-4 model to extract semantic descriptions for the images, in a multimodal prompting fashion. In the current literature, vision language models such as CLIP, among other approaches, are utilized as feature extractors, using only the image encoder, for solving image classification tasks. In this paper, we propose to additionally use the text encoder to obtain the text embeddings corresponding to the MiniGPT-4-generated semantic descriptions. Thus, we use both the image and text embeddings for solving the image classification task. The experimental evaluation on three datasets validates the improved classification performance achieved by exploiting LMM-based knowledge, delivering for example on the UCF-101 dataset an improvement of almost 2%.

Keywords: Large multimodal models · MiniGPT-4 · Vision language models · CLIP · Embeddings · Representations · Image classification

1 Introduction

Large Language Models (LLMs) [14,24], such as GPT-3 [4] and GPT-4 [1], trained on vast amounts of data, have demonstrated exceptional performance in several downstream tasks over the recent few years, placing them squarely at the center of the research activity on Natural Language Processing (NLP) [7] and computer vision [5]. Considering vision recognition downstream tasks, in particular, the emergence of Vision-Language Models (VLMs), such as BLIP-2 [10] and CLIP [15], allowed for connecting image-based vision models with LLMs, forming Large Multimodal Models (LMMs) (also known as Multimodal Large Language Models) [20,23]. For example, MiniGPT-4 [28] aligns a frozen visual encoder with a frozen LLM using a single projection layer. Besides, it is noteworthy that CLIP, which apart from achieving remarkable zero-shot performance on various downstream tasks through prompting, is a powerful feature extractor, has been extensively used in the recent literature for various applications [2,18,21].

In this work, our goal is to address image classification tasks (i.e., tasks of assigning a class label to an image based on its visual content), harnessing the emerging technology of LLMs/LMMs, in order to achieve improved performance in terms of classification accuracy. Particularly, we focus on action/event recognition tasks [6]. To achieve this goal, we pursue the direction of utilizing CLIP, proposing to further incorporate knowledge encoded in powerful foundation models such as MiniGPT-4. More specifically, CLIP is commonly utilized as a feature extractor for fitting a linear classifier on the extracted image embeddings and evaluating the performance on various datasets. In this paper, we propose to use MiniGPT-4 for obtaining semantic textual descriptions for each sample of the considered dataset, and then to use the extracted descriptions for feeding them to the textual encoder of CLIP and obtaining the corresponding text embeddings. Thus, instead of using only the image encoder of CLIP to obtain image embeddings, we also use its text encoder to obtain text embeddings that capture LLM-extracted knowledge. As we experimentally show, the extracted LMM knowledge is indeed useful for the downstream image classification task, providing increased classification performance.

In the recent literature, as discussed in the subsequent section, there have been some efforts for introducing LLM-based knowledge in image and video classification tasks, using the CLIP vision-language model [15]. However, to the best of our knowledge, this is the first work that utilizes GPT-4 (MiniGPT-4 in particular) in a multimodal fashion for downstream image classification tasks. More specifically, relevant approaches utilize either the unimodal GPT-3 model for textual prompting (e.g., [19]) or the multimodal GPT-4 model again for textual prompting (e.g., [11]). On the contrary, in this work we prompt the MiniGPT-4 model both with text and images. Furthermore, in the literature approaches the LLM is prompted to extract information about the classes of the problem (e.g., [19]). On the contrary, in this paper, we obtain sample-specific information from the LMM.

The rest of the paper is organized as follows. Section 2 briefly presents related works. Section 3 presents in detail the proposed methodology for image classification tasks. Subsequently, Sect. 4 provides the experimental evaluation of the proposed methodology. Finally, conclusions are drawn in Sect. 5.

2   Prior Work

In this section we present previous relevant works, involving CLIP and LLMs/LMMs for classification tasks. First, in [27] the authors address a challenge associated with the deployment of VLMs, such as CLIP, that is, identifying the right prompt. To do so, they propose a method, called Context Optimization (CoOp), for adapting such models for downstream image recognition tasks, exploiting recent advances in prompt learning in NLP. Specifically, they model the context words of a prompt with learnable vectors, keeping the entire pretrained parameters frozen. Next, in [26] the authors aim to improve the generalization ability of the aforementioned learned context, by proposing a method called Conditional Context Optimization (CoCoOp). More specifically, they extend CoOp by introducing a lightweight neural network so as to produce an input-conditional token for each image, which is combined with the learnable context vectors.

In another recent work [19], the authors propose a method called Language Guided Bottlenecks (LaBo) building upon concept bottleneck models [8], aiming to develop interpretable-by-design classifiers. To do so, they combine the GPT-3 language model [4] and the CLIP vision-language model. More specifically, they prompt GPT-3 to produce candidate concepts describing each of the problem's classes. A submodular optimization is used then to select a subset of discriminating concepts, which are then aligned to images using the CLIP model. A linear layer is applied on the similarity scores of concepts and images in order to learn weight matrix that represents the importance of each concept in the classification task.

Finally, in [11] the authors utilize the GPT-4 language model [1] for generating text that is visually descriptive. Then they use this information in order to adapt the CLIP model to downstream tasks. In this way, they can achieve considerable improvements in zero-shot CLIP accuracy, compared to the default CLIP prompt. Furthermore, they propose a self-attention based few-shot adapter, called CLIP-A-self, for exploiting this additional information, providing improved performance over the aforementioned CoCoOp method [26]. More specifically, CLIP-A-self learns to select and aggregate the most relevant subset of the visually descriptive text in order to produce more generalizable classifiers.

3   Proposed Method

In this section we present the proposed pipeline, briefly presenting first the two main components involved in the pipeline, i.e., CLIP and MiniGPT-4.

3.1   MiniGPT-4

Following the evolution of LLMs, GPT-4 is the first model to accept both text and image input, producing text output. With the technical details behind GPT-4 remaining undisclosed, MiniGPT-4 was subsequently proposed. MiniGPT-4 aligns a frozen visual encoder with a frozen LLM, utilizing a projection layer. Specifically, MiniGPT-4 uses the Vicuna LLM, while for the visual perception it uses a ViT-G/14 from EVA-CLIP and a Q-Former network. MiniGPT-4 has been utilized in the recent literature for several applications, e.g., [3,22,25].

3.2   CLIP

Even though VLMs have been emerged since 2015 [17], CLIP is the first, most popular VLM, trained with natural language supervision at large scale. CLIP comprises of an image encoder and a text encoder, and it is trained with (image, text) pairs for predicting which of the possible (image, text) pairings actually occurred. To do so, it learns a multimodal embedding space by jointly training the image and text encoders to maximize the cosine similarity of the corresponding image and text embeddings of the real pairs in the batch, while minimizing at the same time the cosine similarity of the embeddings of the incorrect pairings. CLIP provides outstanding zero-shot classification performance, using the class labels of the dataset of interest in the text encoder. Another approach to exploit CLIP for classification tasks is to use the CLIP image encoder for extracting the corresponding image representations and use them with a linear classifier (linear probe) achieving exceptional classification performance. Other approaches focus on fine-tuning on a dataset of interest.

3.3   Combining Image Embeddings and MiniGPT-4 Descriptions

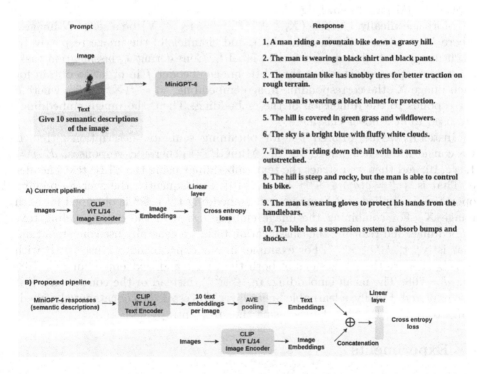

Fig. 1. Proposed pipeline for image classification tasks. We first prompt the MiniGPT-4 model for obtaining 10 semantic descriptions of each image of the dataset. While the current pipeline (A) uses the image encoder of CLIP to extract the image embeddings, we propose to exploit the knowledge extracted from the MiniGPT-4 (B). To do so, we also extract the text embeddings of the MiniGPT-4 semantic descriptions using the text encoder of CLIP, followed by the average pooling operation. Finally, the two embeddings for each image are concatenated and propagated to a linear layer for performing the classification task.

In this paper, we aim to exploit knowledge encoded in the MiniGPT-4 model for achieving advanced classification performance in terms of accuracy. To do so, as illustrated in Fig. 1, we first use the MiniGPT-4 for obtaining semantic descriptions for each image of the dataset. That is, we prompt the model with the image along with the text "*Give 10 semantic descriptions of the image*". Subsequently, we introduce the acquired responses to the CLIP's textual encoder (i.e., 10 semantic descriptions for each image of the dataset) and obtain the text embeddings at the final layer of the text encoder. Next, a pooling operation is applied on the aforementioned text embeddings, resulting to a unique embedding for each image. We finally use these embeddings along with the corresponding image embeddings, obtained from the image encoder of CLIP, to feed a single linear layer with a cross entropy loss for performing classification. That is, instead of simply using the image embeddings from the CLIP's image encoder to perform classification, we additionally use the CLIP's text embeddings that capture LMM-based knowledge.

More specifically, let $\mathcal{X} = \{\mathbf{X}_i \in \Re^{h \times w \times c} | i = 1, \ldots, N\}$ be a set of N images, where h, w, c denote the height, width, and channels of the image respectively. Each image $\mathbf{X}_i$ is linked with a class label l_i. Considering a classification task, a common approach is to use the CLIP image encoder f in order to obtain for each image $\mathbf{X}_i$ the corresponding image embedding, $\mathbf{y}_i = f(\mathbf{X}_i) \in \Re^d$, where d corresponds to the dimension of the embedding. Then, the image embeddings are used to fit a linear classifier.

Instead, we use MiniGPT-4 for obtaining semantic descriptions, that is we consider for each image $\mathbf{X}_i$ the MiniGPT-4-generated responses, $d_i^j, j = 1, \ldots, 10$, and then we extract the text embeddings using the CLIP text encoder g. That is, $\{\mathbf{t}_i^j = g(d_i^j) \in \Re^d | j = 1, \ldots, 10\}$. Subsequently, the average pooling operation is applied and a unique text embedding $\mathbf{t}_i^M \in \Re^d$ is obtained for each image $\mathbf{X}_i$. For combining the image embeddings with the corresponding text embeddings and realizing the classification task, we generally use concatenation, that is $[\mathbf{y}_i^\top, \mathbf{t}_i^{M\top}]^\top \in \mathbb{R}^{d+d}$. For example, in our experiments we use CLIP with ViT-L-14, were the dimensions of both the image and text embeddings is 768, i.e., $d = 768$. The mean embedding, $\mathbf{m}_i \in \Re^{768}$, instead of the concatenated, is also explored. Finally, a learnable linear layer processes the concatenated embeddings to predict the class labels, using the cross entropy loss.

4   Experiments

In this section we present the experiments conducted in order to evaluate the proposed methodology for image classification. First, the utilized datasets are presented followed by the evaluation metrics. Subsequently, the implementation details are presented followed by the experimental results.

4.1   Datasets

We use three datasets to evaluate the effectiveness of the proposed methodology, i.e., UCF-101 [16], Event Recognition in Aerial videos (ERA) [12], and Biased

Action Recognition (BAR) [13]. UCF-101 is an action recognition dataset, containing 101 classes. We derive the middle frame from each video and we follow the same protocol as in [16] for forming the training and test sets of the 13,320 extracted frames. ERA is an event recognition dataset in unconstrained aerial videos. It consists of 1,473 training images and 1,391 test images, divided into 25 classes. BAR is a real-world image dataset with six action classes which are biased to distinct places, consisting of 1,941 training images and 654 test images.

4.2 Evaluation Metrics

We use test accuracy to evaluate the performance of combining LMM-based features with image features for image classification tasks. Qualitative results of the MiniGPT-4 responses are also provided.

4.3 Implementation Details

As previously described, MiniGPT-4 is used as the source of LLM-based knowledge. We use MiniGPT-4 with Vicuna-13B locally. For image and feature extraction we use the ViT-L-14 CLIP version, since this is among the powerful encoders. For the classification task, a single linear layer is used, with output equal to the number of classes of each dataset. Models are trained for 500 epochs, and the learning rate is set to 0.001. Experiments are conducted using the Pytorch framework on an NVIDIA GeForce RTX 3090 with 24 GB of GPU memory.

4.4 Experimental Results

In this section we present the experimental results of the proposed methodology for addressing image classification tasks. We first provide the evaluation results of the proposed methodology of using both CLIP image embeddings and the CLIP text embeddings that reflect the MiniGPT-4 descriptions for the classification task, against the baseline approach of merely using the CLIP image embeddings, in Table 1. Best performance is printed in bold. As demonstrated, combining LMM knowledge with image embeddings provides considerably advanced classification performance in all the utilized datasets. Correspondingly, in Figs. 2, 3 and 4 we provide the test accuracy throughout the training epochs for the two compared approaches on the three utilized datasets, where the steadily advanced performance of the proposed approach is validated.

Table 1. Test accuracy.

Method	UCF-101	ERA	BAR
CLIP (image) [15]	89.981	84.472	94.801
CLIP (image & MiniGPT-4 descriptions)	**91.753**	**85.909**	**95.566**

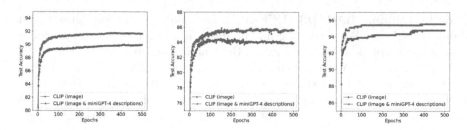

Fig. 2. UCF-101 dataset: **Fig. 3.** ERA dataset: Test **Fig. 4.** BAR dataset: Test Test accuracy throughout accuracy throughout the accuracy throughout the the training epochs.   training epochs.   training epochs.

Subsequently, an ablation study is performed on the UCF-101 dataset. We present in Table 2 the evaluation results. More specifically, we first evaluate the performance of each of the components individually. That is, the classification performance using only the CLIP image embeddings is firstly presented, which serves as the main comparison approach. Evidently, this approach provides exceptional performance. Next, we present the classification performance using only the text embeddings. That is, we only use the MiniGPT-4 knowledge to represent the images of the dataset. This approach performs, as expected, worse, however it achieved remarkable performance. Subsequently, we use both the image and text CLIP embeddings, concatenated. As it is shown, using the proposed methodology we can accomplish significant improvement over the approach of using only the image embeddings. Besides, as it was previously mentioned, we also explore the mean embedding of image and text embeddings instead of the concatenated, which as it is demonstrated also considerably improves the baseline performance, being however slightly worse as compared to the concatenation approach. The aforementioned remarks are validated through Fig. 5, where the test accuracy throughout the training epochs is provided for all the compared approaches.

Table 2. UCF-101: Ablation study.

Method	Test Accuracy
CLIP (image) [15]	89.981
CLIP (MiniGPT-4 descriptions)	80.333
CLIP (image & MiniGPT-4 descriptions - CONCAT)	**91.753**
CLIP (image & MiniGPT-4 descriptions - MEAN)	**91.277**

In Table 3 we present the comparisons of the proposed methodology against state-of-the-art methods. More specifically, the most relevant and straightforward comparison is against the CLIP model utilizing only the image emebeddings. However, we also include relevant works that include CLIP and LLMs/LMMs. The compared LLM/LMM based methods, use either the GPT-3

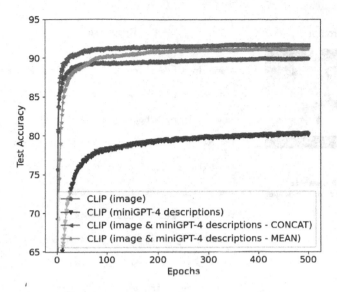

Fig. 5. Ablation - UCF-101 dataset: Test accuracy throughout the training epochs.

Table 3. UCF-101: Comparisons with CLIP-based approaches.

Method	Test Accuracy
CLIP-zero shot [15]	76.20
CLIP-A-self [11]	84.1
CoOp [27]	84.69
CoCoOp [26]	82.33
LaBo [19]	90.67
CLIP - Linear Probe [19]	90.11
CLIP (image) [15]	89.981
CLIP (image & MiniGPT-4 descriptions)	**91.753**

or the GPT-4 model. In our work, as mentioned, we use the recent MiniGPT-4 model since it allows both visual and textual input, however, it should be noted, that as stated in [11] other models, such as GPT-3.5 and OpenAssistant [9], are as capable as GPT-4 in producing meaningful textual information for image recognition tasks. All the models, as described in the Prior Work Section, include training. Finally, even though we do not proceed in a zero-shot approach, we also report the CLIP zero-shot classification performance for completeness. As it is demonstrated the proposed approach achieves the best performance.

Finally, in Figs. 6, 7, 8 and 9 we provide some qualitative results of the knowledge encoded in the MiniGPT-4 model. More specifically, we present the responses of the model, prompted with the image and the text "*Give 10 semantic descriptions of the image*". As it can be observed, accurate and meaningful descriptions are generally obtained.

Prompt   **Response**

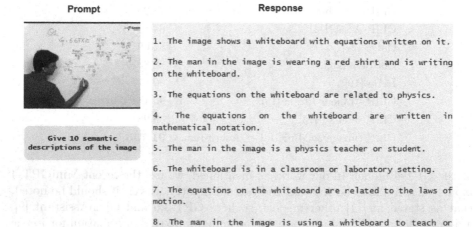

1. A man in a red shirt is bowling in a bowling alley.

2. The man is wearing a red shirt and black pants.

3. He is holding a bowling ball in his hand.

4. The man is in the process of releasing the ball.

5. The ball is about to hit the pins.

Give 10 semantic descriptions of the image

6. The pins are lined up in a row.

7. The man is wearing black shoes.

8. The bowling alley has a wooden floor.

9. There are other people watching in the background.

10. The image is in color.

Fig. 6. Example of MiniGPT-4 response for a test image of the class *Bowling*.

Prompt   **Response**

1. The image shows a whiteboard with equations written on it.

2. The man in the image is wearing a red shirt and is writing on the whiteboard.

3. The equations on the whiteboard are related to physics.

4. The equations on the whiteboard are written in mathematical notation.

Give 10 semantic descriptions of the image

5. The man in the image is a physics teacher or student.

6. The whiteboard is in a classroom or laboratory setting.

7. The equations on the whiteboard are related to the laws of motion.

8. The man in the image is using a whiteboard to teach or learn about physics.

9. The image shows a teacher or student teaching or learning about physics.

10. The whiteboard in the image is used for writing equations and solving problems related to physics.

Fig. 7. Example of MiniGPT-4 response for a test image of the class *Writing on board*.

Prompt

Give 10 semantic
descriptions of the image

Response

1. A female athlete performing a pole vault

2. The athlete is performing a pole vault

3. The athlete is in the process of jumping over the bar

4. The athlete is wearing a black and white outfit

5. The athlete is holding a pole in her hand

6. The athlete is performing the pole vault event

7. The athlete is in the air while performing the pole vault

8. The athlete is a female competing in the pole vault event

9. The athlete is wearing a black and white top

10. The athlete is performing the pole vault event in a stadium

Fig. 8. Example of MiniGPT-4 response for a test image of the class *Pole vaulting.*

Prompt

Give 10 semantic
descriptions of the image

Response

1. A man walking his dog on a dirt road in the woods.

2. A man walking his golden retriever on a trail in the fall.

3. A man walking his dog on a path in the forest.

4. A man walking his pet dog in the woods on a sunny day.

5. A man walking his dog on a trail in the forest during autumn.

6. A man walking his dog on a path in the woods.

7. A man walking his golden retriever on a trail in the fall foliage.

8. A man walking his dog on a trail in the forest during the fall season.

9. A man walking his pet dog in the woods on a sunny day in the fall.

10. A man walking his dog on a path in the forest during the fall.

Fig. 9. Example of MiniGPT-4 response for a test image of the class *Walking with dog.*

5　Conclusions

In this paper we deal with image classification tasks exploiting knowledge encoded in LMMs. Specifically, we use the MiniGPT-4 model to extract sample-specific semantic descriptions. Subsequently, we use these description for obtaining the text embeddings from the CLIP's text encoder. Then, we use the aforementioned text embeddings along with the corresponding image embeddings obtained from the CLIP's image encoder for the classification task. As it is experimentally validated, incorporating LMM-based knowledge to the image embeddings achieves considerably improved classification performance.

Acknowledgements. This work was supported by the EU Horizon Europe program, under grant agreement 101070109 TransMIXR.

References

1. Achiam, J., et al.: GPT-4 technical report. arXiv preprint arXiv:2303.08774 (2023)
2. Ao, T., Zhang, Z., Liu, L.: GestureDiffuCLIP: gesture diffusion model with CLIP latents. arXiv preprint arXiv:2303.14613 (2023)
3. Aubakirova, D., Gerdes, K., Liu, L.: PatFig: generating short and long captions for patent figures. In: Proceedings of the IEEE/CVF International Conference on Computer Vision, pp. 2843–2849 (2023)
4. Brown, T., et al.: Language models are few-shot learners. In: Advances in Neural Information Processing Systems, vol. 33, pp. 1877–1901 (2020)
5. Fu, D., et al.: Drive like a human: rethinking autonomous driving with large language models. In: Proceedings of the IEEE/CVF Winter Conference on Applications of Computer Vision, pp. 910–919 (2024)
6. Gkalelis, N., Daskalakis, D., Mezaris, V.: ViGAT: bottom-up event recognition and explanation in video using factorized graph attention network. IEEE Access **10**, 108797–108816 (2022)
7. Jiao, W., Huang, J.T., Wang, W., Wang, X., Shi, S., Tu, Z.: ParroT: translating during chat using large language models. arXiv preprint arXiv:2304.02426 (2023)
8. Koh, P.W., et al.: Concept bottleneck models. In: International Conference on Machine Learning, pp. 5338–5348. PMLR (2020)
9. Köpf, A., et al.: Openassistant conversations-democratizing large language model alignment. In: Advances in Neural Information Processing Systems, vol. 36 (2024)
10. Li, J., Li, D., Savarese, S., Hoi, S.: BLIP-2: bootstrapping language-image pretraining with frozen image encoders and large language models. arXiv preprint arXiv:2301.12597 (2023)
11. Maniparambil, M., Vorster, C., Molloy, D., Murphy, N., McGuinness, K., O'Connor, N.E.: Enhancing CLIP with GPT-4: harnessing visual descriptions as prompts. In: Proceedings of the IEEE/CVF International Conference on Computer Vision, pp. 262–271 (2023)
12. Mou, L., Hua, Y., Jin, P., Zhu, X.X.: ERA: a data set and deep learning benchmark for event recognition in aerial videos. IEEE Geosci. Remote Sens. Mag. **8**(4), 125–133 (2020)
13. Nam, J., Cha, H., Ahn, S., Lee, J., Shin, J.: Learning from failure: de-biasing classifier from biased classifier. In: Advances in Neural Information Processing Systems, vol. 33, pp. 20673–20684 (2020)

14. Naveed, H., et al.: A comprehensive overview of large language models. arXiv preprint arXiv:2307.06435 (2023)
15. Radford, A., et al.: Learning transferable visual models from natural language supervision. In: International Conference on Machine Learning, pp. 8748–8763. PMLR (2021)
16. Soomro, K., Zamir, A.R., Shah, M.: UCF101: a dataset of 101 human actions classes from videos in the wild. arXiv preprint arXiv:1212.0402 (2012)
17. Vinyals, O., Toshev, A., Bengio, S., Erhan, D.: Show and tell: a neural image caption generator. In: Proceedings of the IEEE Conference on Computer Vision and Pattern Recognition, pp. 3156–3164 (2015)
18. Wu, H.H., Seetharaman, P., Kumar, K., Bello, J.P.: Wav2CLIP: learning robust audio representations from clip. In: ICASSP 2022-2022 IEEE International Conference on Acoustics, Speech and Signal Processing (ICASSP), pp. 4563–4567. IEEE (2022)
19. Yang, Y., Panagopoulou, A., Zhou, S., Jin, D., Callison-Burch, C., Yatskar, M.: Language in a bottle: language model guided concept bottlenecks for interpretable image classification. In: Proceedings of the IEEE/CVF Conference on Computer Vision and Pattern Recognition, pp. 19187–19197 (2023)
20. Yin, S., et al.: A survey on multimodal large language models. arXiv preprint arXiv:2306.13549 (2023)
21. Yu, W., Liu, Y., Hua, W., Jiang, D., Ren, B., Bai, X.: Turning a CLIP model into a scene text detector. In: Proceedings of the IEEE/CVF Conference on Computer Vision and Pattern Recognition, pp. 6978–6988 (2023)
22. Yuan, Z., Xue, H., Wang, X., Liu, Y., Zhao, Z., Wang, K.: ArtGPT-4: artistic vision-language understanding with adapter-enhanced MiniGPT-4. arXiv preprint arXiv:2305.07490 (2023)
23. Zhang, D., et al.: MM-LLMs: recent advances in multimodal large language models. arXiv preprint arXiv:2401.13601 (2024)
24. Zhao, W.X., et al.: A survey of large language models. arXiv preprint arXiv:2303.18223 (2023)
25. Zhou, J., et al.: SkinGPT-4: an interactive dermatology diagnostic system with visual large language model (2023)
26. Zhou, K., Yang, J., Loy, C.C., Liu, Z.: Conditional prompt learning for vision-language models. In: Proceedings of the IEEE/CVF Conference on Computer Vision and Pattern Recognition, pp. 16816–16825 (2022)
27. Zhou, K., Yang, J., Loy, C.C., Liu, Z.: Learning to prompt for vision-language models. Int. J. Comput. Vis. **130**(9), 2337–2348 (2022)
28. Zhu, D., Chen, J., Shen, X., Li, X., Elhoseiny, M.: MiniGPT-4: enhancing vision-language understanding with advanced large language models. arXiv preprint arXiv:2304.10592 (2023)

HEADS: Hybrid Ensemble Anomaly Detection System for Internet-of-Things Networks

Zeeshan Ahmad[1]([✉]) [iD], Andrei Petrovski[1] [iD], Murshedul Arifeen[1] [iD],
Adnan Shahid Khan[2] [iD], and Syed Aziz Shah[3] [iD]

[1] National Subsea Centre, Robert Gordon University, Aberdeen, UK
{z.ahmad1,a.petrovski,m.arifeen}@rgu.ac.uk
[2] Faculty of CS and IT, Universiti Malaysia Sarawak, Kota Samarahan, Sarawak, Malaysia
skadnan@unimas.my
[3] Research Centre for Intelligent Healthcare, Coventry University, Coventry, UK
syed.shah@coventry.ac.uk

Abstract. The rapid expansion of Internet-of-Things (IoT) devices has revolutionized connectivity, facilitating the exchange of extensive data within IoT networks via the traditional internet. However, this innovation has also increased security concerns due to the presence of sensitive nature of data exchanged within IoT networks. To address these concerns, network-based anomaly detection systems play a crucial role in ensuring the security of IoT networks through continuous network traffic monitoring. However, despite significant efforts from researchers, these detection systems still suffer from lower accuracy in detecting new anomalies and often generate high false alarms. To this end, this study proposes an efficient Hybrid Ensemble learning-based Anomaly Detection System (HEADS) to secure an IoT network from all types of anomalies. The proposed solution is based on a novel hybrid approach to improve the voting strategy for ensemble learning. The ensemble prediction is assisted by a Random Forest-based model obtained through the best F1 score for each label through dataset subset selection. The efficiency of HEADS is evaluated using the publicly available CICIoT2023 dataset. The evaluation results demonstrate an F1 score of 99.75% and a false alarm rate of 0.038%. These observations signify an average 4% improvement in the F1 score while a reduction of 0.7% in the false alarm rate comparing other anomaly detection-based strategies.

Keywords: Anomaly Detection System · Ensemble-based learning · Gradient Boosting Machine · Internet-of-Things · Machine Learning

1 Introduction

The Internet-of-Things (IoT) has transformed a wide range of technological sectors, such as smart transportation, homes, healthcare, and logistics, to name a few [1]. IoT is an innovative computing paradigm consisting of a network of numerous IoT devices called "Things". These devices are equipped with sensors, actuators, limited storage, and communication capabilities to exchange and share data over the traditional internet

L. Iliadis et al. (Eds.): EANN 2024, CCIS 2141, pp. 178–190, 2024.
https://doi.org/10.1007/978-3-031-62495-7_14

[2]. However, the presence of the sensitive nature of data in IoT networks such as the health records of patients in the healthcare sector and the road safety information in the transportation domain, demands robust security measures. Different traditional security mechanisms such as firewalls, authentication methods, encryption schemes, etc. are employed as the first defensive shield against IoT anomalies. However, they are often insufficient to protect IoT against evolving anomalies (that are either novel or the mutation of an old anomaly). To enhance IoT security, intrusion detection systems (IDSs) can be deployed, that act as a second defensive shield against IoT network anomalies [3].

An IDS secures the IoT network by detecting anomalies through continuous network traffic monitoring for any suspicious behavior. IDS can be either host-based or network-based depending upon its deployment strategy. Additionally, It can be signature-based, anomaly detection-based, specification-based, or hybrid detection-based depending upon the type of detection scheme it adopts [4]. Our primary focus in this study is to propose a security solution for IoT networks based on a network-based IDS deployment strategy. This proposed methodology aims to secure the entry points of the IoT network by utilizing the anomaly-based detection strategy.

The rapid expansion of the IoT network has also led to a proportional increase in frequently evolving new anomalies. As a result, the performance of anomaly detection-based IDS methodology (AIDS) employing a network-based deployment strategy has observed a decline in detection accuracy and an increase in false alarm rates (FAR). The researchers have addressed these limitations by integrating artificial intelligence (AI) techniques such as machine learning (ML) and deep learning (DL) within AIDSs. AI-based AIDSs employ different ML schemes such as Decision Tree (DT), Random Forest (RF), Support Vector Machine (SVM), and Gradient Boosting Machine (GBM), among others. Further, the effectiveness of ML-based AIDS can be boosted through ensemble-based approaches, which combine learning from multiple models to enhance anomaly detection in IoT networks.

Ensemble approaches enhance the model's robustness by employing strategies such as bagging, boosting, and stacking [5]. Bagging involves training multiple models on different subsets of data and then combining their predictions to reduce variance and enhance generalization. Whereas, boosting utilizes an iterative process to adjust the weights of misclassified data points to improve the model's performance [6]. Also, stacking combines the predictions from different base models using a meta-learner, allowing the ensemble to utilize the strength of each individual model [7]. All these strategies enhance the performance and robustness of ensemble models by combining the predictive learning of base models.

Additionally, the final prediction of the ensemble methods is often drawn by utilizing the voting mechanisms such as hard and soft voting, that combine the predictions of all individual models [8]. In hard voting, each model's prediction is counted as an individual vote and the final prediction is based on majority votes. Whereas, in soft voting, the final prediction is derived based on the highest average probability of a label across all models [8]. The robustness of these ensemble methods by mitigating the model's overfitting makes them ideal for preventing IoT networks from all types of anomalies.

To this end, this study focuses on proposing an effective AIDS-based security solution for IoT networks by refining the voting strategy for ensemble learning.

The main contributions of this research are 3-fold. (1) To extensively discuss the state-of-the-art ensemble-based approaches for IoT networks. (2) To propose an efficient Hybrid Ensemble Anomaly Detection System (HEADS) by enhancing the voting strategies to improve anomaly detection in IoT networks. (3) To evaluate the performance of HEADS on the publicly available dataset CICIoT2023 [9] and compare its performance against various ML-based and ensemble AIDS methodologies.

The rest of the paper is organized as; Sect. 2 provides the state-of-the-art relevant work on ensemble-based AIDS methodologies for IoT networks. Section 3 details the preliminary concepts and the proposed methodology. Section 4 presents the dataset and experimental results with a discussion. Finally, Sect. 5 concludes this article.

2 Related Work

The researchers have widely explored ensemble-based techniques based on ML and DL methods to propose effective anomaly detection schemes for the IoT. This section discusses some notable ensemble-based IDSs proposed in the literature.

Cao et al. [7] proposed an efficient IDS strategy utilizing stacked ensemble learning models and the tree-structured Parzen estimator-based optimization method. The proposed model demonstrated superior performance, achieving an average accuracy rate of 99.99% on the N-BaIoT dataset and 99.37% on the UNSW-NB15 dataset. These results emphasize the model's potential to enhance the security of IoT networks.

Luo et al. [10] proposed an ensemble DL-based web attack detection system (EDL-WADS) designed to identify anomalous queries within IoT networks. They employed MRN, LSTM, and CNN models in parallel to generate intermediate vectors. These vectors are then fed into the comprehensive check and an MLP model, that acts as an ensemble classifier to combine all intermediate vectors to make the final decision. The proposed solution is evaluated on the synthetic dataset. The results showed demonstrated the model's efficiency by achieving an accuracy of 99.47%.

Alghanam et al. [11] proposed an enhanced pigeon-inspired optimization approach for the feature selection. The optimization block is then followed by an ensemble methodology based on multiple one-class classifiers such as one class support vector machine (OC-SVM), Isolation Forest (IF), and Local Outlier Factor (LOF) for the IDS. The proposed solution exhibited effectiveness by achieving impressive accuracy scores of 99.82%, 94.7%, 94.45%, and 97.37% on the KDDCup99, NSL-KDD, UNSW-NB15, and BoT-IoT datasets respectively.

Verma et al. [12] proposed a binary classification approach that is developed from the ML ensemble method. It is aimed at filtering and isolating malicious traffic to safeguard IoT networks. The ensemble approach used the GBM and RF models to improve the classification accuracy of individual models to 98.27% on the CSE-CIC-IDS2018-V2 dataset.

Abbas et al. [13] proposed a new ensemble-based IDS model for the IoT. Their proposed ensemble method used three supervised classification models such as DT, naïve Bayes, and logistic regression followed by a stacking classifier employing hard voting. The proposed model was evaluated on the CICIDS2017 dataset and exhibited an accuracy of 88.92% and 88.96% for the binary and multiclass classification scenarios.

Thakkar et al. [14] proposed a highly effective IDS designed specifically for IoT networks. Their approach relies on a bagging-Deep Neural Network (DNN)-based ensemble learning strategy, which is designed to tackle the challenge of class imbalance issues in IDS applications. The DNN classification capabilities are enhanced by integrating the bagging technique with carefully calibrated class weights to address the skewed class distribution in the training set. The proposed methodology exhibited model efficiency across different datasets, highlighting accuracy scores of 98.9%, 98.74%, 96.70%, and 98.99% across the NSL-KDD, CIC-IDS2017, UNSW-NB-15, and BoT-IoT datasets respectively.

This study adopts a slightly different approach by proposing a novel hybrid ensemble-based methodology for detecting anomalies in IoT networks. The ensemble prediction is assisted by the prediction of the RF model obtained through the best F1 score for each label through dataset subset selection. The final ensemble prediction then employs the hybrid hard and soft voting strategy to enhance prediction capability for effective IoT protection.

3 Proposed Solution

This section outlines the preliminary concepts, followed by the details of the proposed HEADS for the IoT network.

3.1 Base ML Models

The ensemble learning approach involves combining predictions from multiple individual base models to make a final decision based on certain voting criteria. To achieve this, we utilized RF, GBM, Extreme GBM (XGB), Light GBM (LGBM), and Category Boosting (CB) as our base models.

Random Forest (RF)
RF is a powerful ML-based ensemble learning approach used for both classification and regression tasks. It operates by constructing numerous DTs (forest) during the training phase. Each tree in the forest independently predicts the output. The final prediction is then obtained by a majority vote or averaging, depending on the task [15]. RF's capability to effectively mitigate overfitting and handle high-dimensional data makes it a popular choice for AIDS-based methodologies.

Gradient Boosting Machine (GBM)
GBM is another technique that sequentially constructs an ensemble of DTs. In the process, each subsequent tree aims to correct the errors made by the previous ones [6]. By optimizing a differentiable loss function through gradient descent, GBM gradually minimizes residuals. Hence it captures the complex relationships in data and achieves high predictive accuracy. However, GBM is sensitive to overfitting and requires careful tuning of hyperparameters to prevent it.

Extreme Gradient Boosting Machine (XGB)
XGB is an efficient variant of GBM, that is used for both classification and regression tasks. It improves model generalization by applying many regularization techniques to mitigate overfitting [16]. It is famous for its speed and performance by outperforming other ML algorithms working on structured and tabular data. It is highly customizable and allows fine-tuning of parameters to achieve optimal results.

Light GBM (LGBM)
LGBM is a gradient-boosting framework developed by Microsoft. It aims to achieve high efficiency and speed by using a novel tree-growing algorithm, which can handle large-scale datasets efficiently [17]. It can deal with categorical features directly without requiring one-hot encoding. It employs leaf-wise tree growth and histogram-based algorithms to achieve faster training times and lower memory usage.

Category Boosting (CB)
CB is also a powerful gradient-boosting-based ML technique [18]. It automatically handles missing data and does not require manual encoding of categorical features. It integrates advanced techniques for faster convergence. It also utilizes GPU acceleration for faster training when handling large datasets.

To sum up, RF, GBM, XGB, LGBM, and CB are all ensemble learning techniques that take advantage of the decision trees as base learners. They are effective in handling complex datasets and can capture nonlinear relationships between features and targets. However, they differ in their underlying algorithms and optimizations.

3.2   Methodology

In this study, we propose an efficient ensemble-based methodology HEADS for securing the IoT networks, as depicted in Fig. 1. The proposed solution consists of two phases, (1) Data Interception and Preparation Phase and (2) Hybrid Ensemble Anomaly Detection Phase.

Data Interception and Preparation Phase
The first stage of HEADS is the Data Interception and Preparation Phase, which provides the framework for the important task of intercepting data from IoT networks and preparing it to be in a suitable format for the ML process. The various steps performed in this phase include:

Step-1: The network traffic is captured using network sniffing tools such as tcpdump, which offer platforms for acquiring, examining, analyzing, and visualizing network packets [2, 19]. The sniffer thoroughly analyzes the captured network flows to generate raw packet features. These features are then stored to create an IoT Network dataset.
Step-2: The collected data undergoes a cleaning process that begins with the removal of redundant instances containing infinite or empty fields. Then all the categorical features excluding the target labels are encoded using a one-hot encoding scheme. Then each feature value is normalized between 0 and 1 using Min-Max scaling [2].

Step-3: The pre-processed IoT Network Dataset is then split into 80% Train Dataset for training the ML model and 20% Test Dataset for the evaluation on unseen data.

Hybrid Ensemble Anomaly Detection Phase.
This is the main anomaly detection phase designed for the detection of network anomalies within an IoT network. The main approach adopted here involves implementing hard and soft voting concepts within a hybrid setting to enhance model efficiency. The various steps performed in this phase are:

Step-4: We utilized five base models RF, GBM, XGB, LGBM, and CB. Each of these models is individually trained using the Train dataset to create trained models. Afterward, these trained models are independently tested using the Test Dataset to predict the test labels. For each instance in the Test Dataset, we recorded the predicted label and the corresponding confidence score of each model in the Predictions. The confidence score is the probability value of each model in predicting the label, to show its confidence in the prediction.

Step-5: To assist the ensemble prediction, we opted for the RF model and further trained and evaluated it using subsets of both the Train and Test datasets. Our main objective is to store the predictions made by the RF model, corresponding to the best F1 score for each label in the dataset. To accomplish this, we extracted a subset of the dataset containing only two labels. Following this, we trained the RF model on this subset and then tested the trained model to obtain the F1 scores. The predicted label and its associated confidence score from the RF model are also recorded in the Predictions for each label that corresponds to the highest F1 score.

Step-6: After obtaining predictions and confidence scores for each test instance in steps 4 and 5, we determine the final predictions using a hybrid approach involving both hard and soft voting:

    i) If all classifiers predict the same label, the final predicted label follows the hard voting rule and adopts that label.

    ii) However, if the classifiers do not reach a consensus on a single label, we employ a soft voting strategy. In this case, the final predicted label is selected based on the one with the highest average confidence score.

    iii) If there is a tie in the highest average confidence score, the final predicted label is the one with the highest individual confidence score.

4 Experimental Results and Analysis

This section details the dataset, evaluation metrics, experimental setup, and a comprehensive analysis of the obtained experimental results.

4.1 Dataset Description

To evaluate the performance of the HEADS with other ML-based AIDSs, we used the publicly available CICIoT2023 dataset [9]. This dataset is collected by the Canadian Institute for Cybersecurity, University of New Brunswick, Canada from the real IoT topology composed of 105 devices. The dataset contains network flows for the Benign

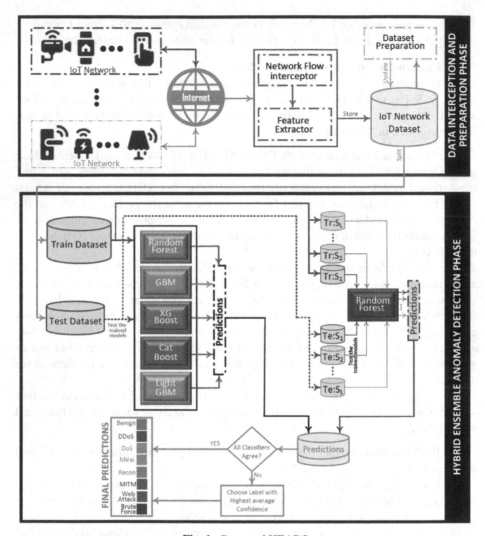

Fig. 1. Proposed HEADS

traffic and 33 attacks on IoT devices which are classified into seven categories, namely DDoS, DoS, Mirai, Reconnaissance, Spoofing, Web-based, and Brute force. The dataset files are publicly available in the PCAP and CSV formats. The CSV file contains 46 numerical features and one categorical label feature. For this study, we randomly selected instances for each label, ensuring that instances for all 33 types of attacks are included. The total number of instances considered in this study are detailed in Table 1.

Table 1. Dataset Distribution

Label	Instances	Train dataset	Test dataset
Benign	50000	39979	10021
DDoS	25000	20018	4982
DoS	15000	12049	2951
Mirai	10000	7930	2070
Reconnaissance	8000	6340	1660
Spoofing	7000	5656	1344
Web-based	3000	2417	583
Brute Force	2000	1711	289
Total Flows	*120000*	*96100*	*23900*

4.2 Evaluation Metrics

In this study, the performance evaluation of the HEADS and other ML/DL models considers evaluation metrics such as Accuracy, Precision, Recall, F1 score, and False Alarm Rate (FAR). All these metrics are calculated from various elements of the confusion matrix [19] and are given as,

$$\text{Accuracy} = \frac{TP + TN}{TP + TN + FP + FN} \tag{1}$$

$$\text{Precision} = \frac{TP}{TP + FP} \tag{2}$$

$$\text{Recall} = \frac{TP}{TP + FN} \tag{3}$$

$$\text{F1 score} = \frac{2(\text{Pr})(\text{Re})}{\text{Pr} + \text{Re}} \tag{4}$$

$$\text{FAR} = \frac{FP}{FP + TN} \tag{5}$$

where, the correctly predicted Anomaly and Benign instances are represented as True Positive (TP) and True Negative (TN) respectively. Also, the incorrectly predicted labels as Benign and Anomaly are given as False Negative (FN) and False Positive (FP) respectively.

4.3 Experimental Setup

All performance evaluation experiments were conducted on an HP laptop featuring an Intel Core i9-10885H processor, 32 GB RAM, and a 64-bit Windows 10 operating system. Python (version 3.10.12) served as the main programming language to implement and evaluate all AIDS methodologies within the Google Colab environment.

4.4 Results and Discussion

In this research, the performance of the HEADS is compared with five supervised ML approaches such as RF, XFB, LGBM, CB, and GBM, followed by their ensemble models employing the hard and soft voting strategies. Each experiment is performed 5 times, with a random selection of train and test split each time to obtain evaluation metric scores.

Table 2 presents the average evaluation metric score in percentages for all the considered ML-based AIDS models. We can observe that all models, including the ensembles, perform well, with accuracy scores ranging from approximately 95.7% to 96.1%. However, our proposed methodology HEADS performs exceptionally well by obtaining an accuracy of 99.75%, highlighting its effectiveness in correctly predicting network instances. Additionally, the precision, recall, and F1 scores obtained by HEADS indicate its effectiveness in identifying both positive and negative instances with minimal FP and FN. Also, the lower FAR further confirms the reliability of the HEADS, which is a crucial factor for the performance of AIDS. Overall, our proposed HEADS methodology exhibited better performance over other considered ML-based AIDS approaches.

Table 2. Performance Evaluation Metric Score [%]

ML Model	Accuracy	Precision	Recall	F1 score	FAR
RF	95.667	95.589	95.667	95.458	0.813
XGB	95.929	95.850	95.929	95.805	0.735
LGBM	95.792	95.678	95.792	95.654	0.761
CB	95.963	95.884	95.963	95.828	0.739
GBM	95.696	95.642	95.696	95.507	0.818
Ensemble (Hard)	96.029	95.971	96.029	95.870	0.748
Ensemble (Soft)	96.063	96.009	96.063	95.915	0.738
HEADS	**99.750**	**99.752**	**99.750**	**99.751**	**0.038**

The results depicted in Fig. 2 illustrate the percentage improvement of the HEADS compared to other ML-based AIDS methodologies for all the considered performance evaluation metrics. HEADS highlighted approximately 3.7% to 4.1% improvement in terms of accuracy and 3.8% to 4.3% in terms of F1 score comparing other methodologies. Additionally, HEADS obtained improvement in FAR reduction of around 0.7% comparing the other AIDS methodologies. Overall HEADS achieves higher accuracy, precision, recall, and F1 score compared to the other models, while also maintaining a lower FAR. These results highlight the effectiveness and superiority of the HEADS in accurately predicting the label with minimized FAR.

Figure 3 depicts the confusion matrices for the ensemble learning approaches employing hard/soft voting and HEADS. Comparing these results, we observe distinct patterns in the performance of different models. Across all three models, we observe

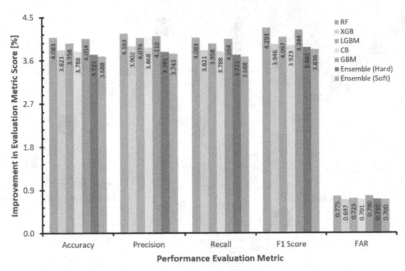

Fig. 2. Percentage improvement in the HEADS performance over other ML models.

the correct classification of instances labeled as Benign, DDoS, DoS, and Mirai, as indicated by high percentage values along the diagonal. However, both ensemble approaches exhibit degraded performance in correctly classifying instances labeled as Reconnaissance, Spoofing, web-based, and brute force, indicated by the higher misclassification rates reflected in off-diagonal percentage values. In contrast, the HEADS demonstrate higher percentage scores in the diagonal and significantly fewer off-diagonal percentages which indicate its superior accuracy in predicting class labels. Furthermore, comparing the HEADS to the ensemble approaches, we observe notable improvements in the correct classification percentages: Benign by 0.6%, DDoS by 0.1%, DoS by 0.07%, Reconnaissance by 19%, Spoofing by 16.8%, Web-based by 25.6%, and brute force by 36.5%. These results underscore the enhanced performance of the HEADS compared to the ensemble-based approaches across various labels.

Table 3 details the comparison of results in this study directly with the results obtained in DL-BiLSTM [20] and Blending [21] based AIDS approaches, on the CICIoT2023 dataset. F1 score and Accuracy are selected as the evaluation metric. We notice that the DL-BiLSTM model achieves a reasonable F1 score of 91.94% and an accuracy of 93.13%. The Blending model outperforms DL-BiLSTM significantly, achieving an impressive F1 score of 99.07% and an accuracy of 99.51%. In contrast, the HEADS surpasses both DL-BiLSTM and the Blending approach. It achieved an exceptional F1 score of 99.751% and an accuracy of 99.750%. These results highlight the effectiveness and superiority of the HEADS in accurately predicting class labels, making it a promising approach for detecting anomalies in IoT networks.

To sum up, the proposed HEADS improves AIDS performance by enhancing the voting strategy for ensemble learning. The proposed solution performed exceptionally well to not only improve the detection accuracy but also reduce FAR. However, this improvement comes at the expense of more complexity. In an IoT network scenario,

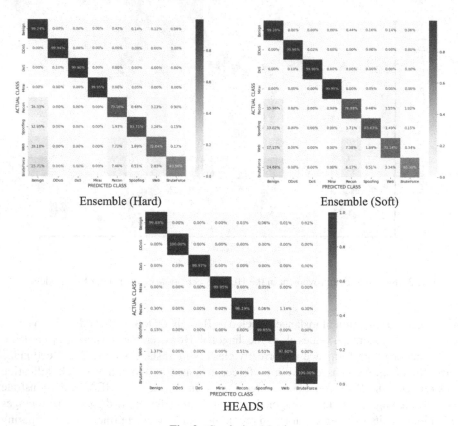

Fig. 3. Confusion Matrix

Table 3. Comparison with other studies [%]

Model	F1 score	Accuracy
DL-BiLSTM [20]	91.94	93.13
Blending [21]	99.07	99.51
HEADS [This Study]	**99.751**	**99.750**

where computing resources are limited, the possible solution will be the deployment of the HEADS at the cloud edge.

5   Conclusions

This paper proposes an effective Hybrid Ensemble-based Anomaly Detection System to strengthen the security at the entry points of the IoT network through monitoring the network traffic. The proposed solution improves ensemble learning by introducing a novel hybrid approach by combining the hard and soft voting strategies. Additionally, the detection accuracy is improved by including the predictions of the RF model corresponding to the best F1 score for each label obtained using the dataset subset selection. The proposed methodology is evaluated on the publicly available CICIoT2023 dataset, which exhibits the model's effectiveness by achieving high evaluation metric scores in correctly detecting the network anomalies while minimizing the FAR.

For future research, we aim to extend this work by implementing and evaluating HEADS performance in real-time IoT scenarios. Additionally, we also plan to explore the hybrid ensemble concept employing unsupervised ML/DL methodologies.

References

1. Ahmad, F., Ahmad, Z., Kerrache, C.A., Kurugollu, F., Adnane, A., Barka, E.: Blockchain in Internet-of-Things: architecture, applications and research directions. In: 2019 International Conference on Computer and Information Sciences, ICCIS 2019 (2019). https://doi.org/10.1109/ICCISCI.2019.8716450
2. Ahmad, Z., et al.: S-ADS: spectrogram image-based anomaly detection system for IoT networks. In: Proceedings - AiIC 2022: 2022 Applied Informatics International Conference: Digital Innovation in Applied Informatics During the Pandemic, pp. 105–110 (2022). https://doi.org/10.1109/AIIC54368.2022.9914599
3. Chaabouni, N., Mosbah, M., Zemmari, A., Sauvignac, C., Faruki, P.: Network intrusion detection for IoT security based on learning techniques. IEEE Commun. Surv. Tutor. **21**, 2671–2701 (2019). https://doi.org/10.1109/COMST.2019.2896380
4. Khan, A.S., Ahmad, Z., Abdullah, J., Ahmad, F.: A spectrogram image-based network anomaly detection system using deep convolutional neural network. IEEE Access **9**, 87079–87093 (2021). https://doi.org/10.1109/ACCESS.2021.3088149
5. Keshk, M., Koroniotis, N., Pham, N., Moustafa, N., Turnbull, B., Zomaya, A.Y.: An explainable deep learning-enabled intrusion detection framework in IoT networks. Inf. Sci. **639**, 119000 (2023). https://doi.org/10.1016/J.INS.2023.119000
6. Louk, M.H.L., Tama, B.A.: Dual-IDS: a bagging-based gradient boosting decision tree model for network anomaly intrusion detection system. Expert Syst. Appl. **213**, 119030 (2023). https://doi.org/10.1016/J.ESWA.2022.119030
7. Cao, Y., Wang, Z., Ding, H., Zhang, J., Li, B.: An intrusion detection system based on stacked ensemble learning for IoT network. Comput. Electr. Eng. **110**, 108836 (2023). https://doi.org/10.1016/J.COMPELECENG.2023.108836
8. Mohammed, A., Kora, R.: A comprehensive review on ensemble deep learning: opportunities and challenges. J. King Saud Univ. Comput. Inf. Sci. **35**, 757–774 (2023). https://doi.org/10.1016/J.JKSUCI.2023.01.014
9. Neto, E.C.P., Dadkhah, S., Ferreira, R., Zohourian, A., Lu, R., Ghorbani, A.A.: CICIoT2023: a real-time dataset and benchmark for large-scale attacks in IoT environment. Sensors **23**, 5941 (2023). https://doi.org/10.3390/S23135941
10. Luo, C., Tan, Z., Min, G., Gan, J., Shi, W., Tian, Z.: A novel web attack detection system for Internet of Things via ensemble classification. IEEE Trans. Ind. Inform. **17**, 5810–5818 (2021). https://doi.org/10.1109/TII.2020.3038761
11. Abu Alghanam, O., Almobaideen, W., Saadeh, M., Adwan, O.: An improved PIO feature selection algorithm for IoT network intrusion detection system based on ensemble learning. Expert Syst. Appl. **213**, 118745 (2023). https://doi.org/10.1016/J.ESWA.2022.118745
12. Verma, P., et al.: A novel intrusion detection approach using machine learning ensemble for IoT environments. Appl. Sci. **11**, 10268 (2021). https://doi.org/10.3390/APP112110268

13. Abbas, A., Khan, M.A., Latif, S., Ajaz, M., Shah, A.A., Ahmad, J.: A new ensemble-based intrusion detection system for Internet of Things. Arab. J. Sci. Eng. **47**, 1805–1819 (2022). https://doi.org/10.1007/S13369-021-06086-5/TABLES/12
14. Thakkar, A., Lohiya, R.: Attack classification of imbalanced intrusion data for IoT network using ensemble-learning-based deep neural network. IEEE Internet Things J. **10**, 11888–11895 (2023). https://doi.org/10.1109/JIOT.2023.3244810
15. Ahmad, I., Basheri, M., Iqbal, M.J., Rahim, A.: Performance comparison of support vector machine, random forest, and extreme learning machine for intrusion detection. IEEE Access **6**, 33789–33795 (2018). https://doi.org/10.1109/ACCESS.2018.2841987
16. Saheed, Y.K.: Performance improvement of intrusion detection system for detecting attacks on Internet of Things and edge of things. In: Misra, S., Kumar Tyagi, A., Piuri, V., Garg, L. (eds.) Artificial Intelligence for Cloud and Edge Computing. IT, pp. 321–339. Springer, Cham (2022). https://doi.org/10.1007/978-3-030-80821-1_15
17. Tang, C., Luktarhan, N., Zhao, Y.: An efficient intrusion detection method based on LightGBM and autoencoder. Symmetry **12**, 1458 (2020). https://doi.org/10.3390/SYM12091458
18. Kayode Saheed, Y., Idris Abiodun, A., Misra, S., Kristiansen Holone, M., Colomo-Palacios, R.: A machine learning-based intrusion detection for detecting internet of things network attacks. Alex. Eng. J. **61**, 9395–9409 (2022). https://doi.org/10.1016/J.AEJ.2022.02.063
19. Ahmad, Z., Khan, A.S., Zen, K., Ahmad, F.: MS-ADS: multistage spectrogram image-based anomaly detection system for IoT security. Trans. Emerg. Telecommun. Technol. **34**, e4810 (2023). https://doi.org/10.1002/ett.4810
20. Wang, Z., Chen, H., Yang, S., Luo, X., Li, D., Wang, J.: A lightweight intrusion detection method for IoT based on deep learning and dynamic quantization. PeerJ Comput. Sci. **9**, e1569 (2023). https://doi.org/10.7717/PEERJ-CS.1569/SUPP-1
21. Le, T.T.H., Wardhani, R.W., Catur Putranto, D.S., Jo, U., Kim, H.: Toward enhanced attack detection and explanation in intrusion detection system-based IoT environment data. IEEE Access **11**, 131661–131676 (2023). https://doi.org/10.1109/ACCESS.2023.3336678

HEDL-IDS²: An Innovative Hybrid Ensemble Deep Learning Prototype for Cyber Intrusion Detection

Anastasios Panagiotis Psathas[1](✉) (iD), Lazaros Iliadis[1] (iD), Antonios Papaleonidas[1] (iD), and Elias Pimenidis[2] (iD)

[1] Department of Civil Engineering-Lab of Mathematics and Informatics (ISCE), Democritus University of Thrace, 67100 Xanthi, Greece
{anpsatha,liliadis,papaleon}@civil.duth.gr
[2] University of the West of England, Bristol BS16 1QY, UK
Elias.pimenidis@uwe.ac.uk

Abstract. The growing volume of online activities exposes users to potential cyber-attacks. Consequently, the scientific community aims to develop pioneering approaches capable to mitigate the risk. To address this challenge, the authors introduce the second version of the *Hybrid Ensemble Deep Learning* (HEDL) *Intrusion Detection System* (IDS), that successfully detects nine serious cyber-attacks. The architecture of the introduced Ensemble comprises of four *Deep Neural Networks (DNN)*, four *Convolutional Neural Networks* (CNN) and four *Recurrent Neural Networks* (RNN) using *Long-Short Term Memory* (LSTM) layers, running in parallel. The final classification of each Ensemble employs a *Custom Vote* process, following the *Weighted Vote* and the *Majority Vote* principles. The HEDL-IDS² was successfully employed on the *UNSW-NB15* dataset, achieving extremely high-performance indices (*Accuracy, Sensitivity, Specificity, Precision and F-1 Score*) in all Training, Validation and Testing phases. This multiclass classification effort followed the One-Versus all Strategy.

Keywords: Hybrid · Ensemble · CNN · DNN · RNN · LSTM · Cyber Attacks · Cyber Intrusion Detection · Multi Class

1 Introduction

Technology has been developing rapidly during the last 20 years. Our postmodern societies are strongly depended on the Internet, and by the smooth operation of information and communication systems [16]. Cyberspace used to be a place of entertainment, information and of communication globally. However, over the years, as science progressed and evolved, the internet became a tool which is currently used globally and serves millions of users daily [17]. Internet services are provided, either publicly or privately, by mobile and information companies for the purpose of facilitating and simplifying the operations of organizations [18]. The international trade the storage of data, the management of financial and material resources run through the cyberspace/

© The Author(s), under exclusive license to Springer Nature Switzerland AG 2024
L. Iliadis et al. (Eds.): EANN 2024, CCIS 2141, pp. 191–206, 2024.
https://doi.org/10.1007/978-3-031-62495-7_15

However, the rapid internet development, and the desire to meet peoples' companies' and businesses' needs in due time, has led to many threats that exploit vulnerabilities [19]. Cyberattacks may focus in *Personal Identification Information* (PII) (e.g., credit card details) [21], and in illegal access on databases and Critical Infrastructure Facilities (hospitals, energy providers, water, and gas distributors) [22].

Cyber and network security also evolves rapidly. Nevertheless, the existing solutions are still inadequate to deal with all kinds of attacks in order to secure computer networks and interconnected devices [1]. A vital technology towards countering cyberattacks' risk, is the *Intrusion Detection System* (IDS) [46]. IDS is a system for monitoring and analyzing the events that take place in wide range of computer networks. The goal is to detect indications of potential intrusion attempts, which often reveal traces confidentiality violations and block of information resources' availability [47].

In this paper, the authors introduce a novel IDS for Cyber Intrusion Detection (CID). This manuscript extends a previous research effort of the authors, entitled "HEDL-IDS: *A Hybrid Ensemble Deep Learning Approach for Cyber Intrusion Detection*" [48] in which the authors proposed a novel *Hybrid Ensemble* IDS. The innovative IDS, consists of four *Multi-Layer Perceptrons* (MLPs), four *Convolutional Neural Networks* (CNNs) and four *Recurrent Neural Networks* (RNNs) with *Long-Short Term Memory* (LSTM) layers. All twelve Deep Learning (DL) Algorithms have different architectures, and they use different parameters' and hyperparameters' values. The aforementioned models are combined through a custom voting process in order to classify a given instance. The proposed approach was tested with the well-know and widely used *UNSW-NB15* Dataset [2]. The dataset includes network packets related to nine (9) different types of cyber-attacks (*Analysis, Backdoor, Denial of Service (DoS), Exploits, Fuzzers, Generic, Reconnaissance, Shellcode, Worms*) and a *normal flow*.

This ongoing research significantly improves the architecture of the model, offering more robust results. The main differences compared to the initial approach are listed below:

- The four additional features, namely Source *IP address, Source port number, Destination Ip address, and Destination port number* have been used as independent variables. Thus, in this research effort the total number of features were 47, in contrast to the initial research effort which considered only 43 features.
- The new architecture employs an *Ensemble* containing four DL Neural Networks of each type, in contrast to the initial architecture which consists of three Deep Learning (DL) Neural Networks of each kind.
- The authors use a custom vote of the aforementioned 12 Neural Networks (NNs) in order to classify an observation into the corresponding class, improving even further the accuracy and robustness of the results. The previous used the majority vote approach.
- In the initial manuscript, the authors dealt with a binary cyberattack problem, trying to distinguish the malicious flow from the normal one. In this paper, the authors deal with the multi class classification aspect of the same problem.

The rest of the paper is organized as follows: Sect. 2 emphasizes the research efforts in Cyber-Security. Sections 3 describes the dataset. Section 4 presents in detail the architecture of the proposed model. Section 5 demonstrates and discusses the results of the proposed approach. Finally, Sect. 6 concludes the paper.

2 Literature Review

This section describes some of the most remarkable ML and DL approaches and research efforts on the cybersecurity domain. Furthermore, it describes the development of robust models on using the *UNSW-NB15* Dataset.

In 2011, Damopoulos et al. [30], dealt with the Intrusion Detection Problem on mobile devices. They deployed four well-known ML techniques, *Bayesian Networks (BN), Support Vector Machines (SVM) classifiers with a Radial Basis Function (RBF) kernel, k-Nearest Neighbors (k-NN) and Random Forest* (RF) to achieve an overall accuracy of 98.9% for the detection of malicious packets. In 2012, Li et al. [3], presented an approach, capable to stamp out, some well-known cyber-attacks such as *DoS, Probe or Scan, User to Root* (U2R), *Root to Local* (R2L). Li et al., exploited the KDD'99 cup dataset, one of the most popular datasets for Cyber Attacks, by using the hyperplane based SVM classifier with a RBF kernel. The obtained accuracy was as high as 98.6249%. Also in 2015, Elekar [31], used Decision Trees (DT), Random Forest (RF) and J48 Tress on the KDDcup99 and NSL-KDD datasets, in order to detect the DoS, Probe, U2R and R2L Attacks. They achieved an overall accuracy of 92.62%. Similar research that have used ML techniques for the CID can be found in [32–36].

In 2015, Pascanu et al. [28], deployed an innovative hybrid IDS for the detection of malicious traffic using a combination of RNNS, MLPs and Logistic Regression (LR) techniques to achieve a *True Positive Rate* (TPR) of 98.3% and a False Positive Rate (FPR) of 0.1%. In 2017, Mizano et al. [29], used the HTTP headers of a NetFlow in order to identify malicious activity, achieving an overall precision of 97.1%, and at the same time the FPR was as low as 1%. These results were achieved using a *Neural Network* with two hidden layers [8]. In 2021, Psathas et al. [49], presented a hybrid Intrusion Detecting System (IDS) comprising of a 2-Dimensional *CNN* (2-D CNN), a RNN and a MLP for the detection of nine Cyber Attacks versus normal flow. The timely *Kitsune Network attack* dataset was used in this research. The proposed model achieved an overall accuracy of 92.66%, 90.64% and 90.56% in the train, validation and testing phases respectively. In 2022, Psathas et al. [50], extended their original work achieving greater accuracy for the *Kitsune Network Attack* Dataset and more robust results. Furthermore, they proposed a novel holistic approach that captures the packets of a network flow in the form of Packet Capture files, it stores them, and it classifies them either in one of the 9 cyberattacks provided by the *Kitsune* Dataset or in the normal class. Similar research that uses DL techniques for the CID can be found also in [37–41].

In 2016, Moustafa and Slay [27], used various ML techniques trying to achieve a high performance in the UNSW-NB15. More specifically, the ML algorithms that were used are Decision Trees (DT), Logistic Regression (LR), Naïve Bayes (NB) Artificial Neural Networks (ANNs) and Expectation Maximization Clustering (EM Clustering) achieved an accuracy of 85.56%, 83.15%, 82.07%, 81.34% and 78.47% respectively. In 2018, Potluri et al. [23] proposed an IDS based on CNN. In this research effort, they have used both the NSK-KDD and the UNSW-NB15 datasets. To exploit the full extent of the CNN, they also converted the packets into images. Thereafter, they developed a CNN with three convolution layers. They achieved and overall accuracy of 91.14% on the NSL-KDD and 94.9% on the UNSW-NB15. Finally, they performed a comparison with the well-known deep networks ResNet 50 and GoogleNet, highlighting the superiority of their models. In 2018, Hajisalem and Babaie [26], proposed a hybrid approach combining the Artificial Bee Colony (ABC) algorithm with the Artificial Fish Swarm (AFS) algorithm. They also applied the Fuzzy C-Means Clustering (FCM) and the Correlation-based Feature Selection (CFS) techniques to divide the training dataset and to remove the irrelevant features, respectively. In addition, *"If-Then"* rules were generated through the Classification and Regression Tree (CART) technique, according to the selected features, in order to distinguish the normal and the anomaly class records. The authors of this research effort have achieved an average accuracy of 97.5% for the testing set. In 2020, Zhang et al. [24], presented an innovative approach combining a Multiscale Convolutional Neural Network (MSCNN) with Long Short-Term Memory (LSTM). Their model was compared with Lenet-5, a simple MSCNN and the HAST-IDS achieving an overall accuracy of 95.6% in train data and 89.9% in test data. In 2020, Hassan et al. [25], presented a novel IDS consisting of a CNN network (to extract the features from the dataset) and a weight-dropped, long short-term memory (WDLSTM) network (to retain long-term dependencies among extracted features to prevent overfitting on recurrent connections), achieving an overall accuracy of 96.975% using the 10-fold cross validation technique. Similar research on the UNSW-NB for the CID can be found also in [42–44].

3 Dataset

3.1 Dataset Description

In this research, the UNSW-NB15 network intrusion public dataset [2] has been examined. The dataset comprises of raw network packets associated with nine distinct types of attacks. It was developed in 2015 at the University of New South Wales, within the Australian Defense Force Academy Canberra, Australia [5]. The IXIA *PerfectStorm* tool [6] was employed to generate a blend of normal and abnormal network traffic, incorporating real-time updates on new attacks from a CVE site [7]. CVE, a repository of publicly disclosed cybersecurity vulnerabilities, is accessible for searching, utilization, and integration into products and services, as per its terms of use. The simulation covered a period of 16 h of the 22nd of January 2015 and 15 h of the 17th of February 2015, with a total data volume of 100 GBs captured.

The overall number of packets in the dataset are 2,540,044. The malicious traffic comprises of nine different *Cyber Attacks* (*Fuzzers, Analysis, Backdoors, DoS, Exploits, Generic, Reconnaissance, Shellcode and Worms*) and contains 321,283 packets. The rest of the traffic records consist of 2,218,761 instances of *benign flow*. Nevertheless, the initial dataset is rather unbalanced something very well expected and typical for the specific case (*Cyber Attacks* are only 12.5% of the original dataset). Thus, the developers of the dataset, provided a more balanced subset of the *UNSW-NB15*. The subset contains a total of 257,673 records, 164,673 of which correspond to *malicious* traffic (including nine cyber-attacks) and 93,000 correspond to benign flow (Table 1). Nevertheless, there is still an internal "minority-class" problem, in the Cyber-Attacks' class (e.g., *Worms* and *Shellcode* are a small portion of the *"minority"* classes records). Thus, the authors had to cope with this challenge. The name and description of all the 48 features of the subset UNSW-NB15, has been omitted due to the limited length of the manuscript, but they can be found in [2]. There are 47 independent variables in the dataset, where the 48th variable contains the name of each category (if the packets characterizes and attack, it states the name of the attack, else it is filled with the string Normal).

Table 1. Description of the nine (9) Cyber Attacks and normal flow considered in this research effort.

Type	# Subset's Packets	# Dataset Packets	Label
Normal	93,000	2,218,761	0
Fuzziers	24,246	24,246	1
Analysis	2,677	2,677	2
Backdoors	2,327	2,329	3
DoS	16,353	16,353	4
Exploits	44,525	44,525	5
Generic	58,871	215,481	6
Reconnaissance	13,987	13,987	7
Shellcode	1,511	1,511	8
Worms	174	174	9
Total	257,673	2,540,044	

3.2 Dataset Pre-processing

The features *proto, state, service,* and *attack_cat* were stored as strings (sequences of characters). Thus, they were transformed by the authors from nominal to numeric. The transformations are presented in the following Tables 2 and 3.

Table 2. Service with the corresponding label.

service	-	dhcp	dns	ftp	ftp-data	http	irc	pop3	radius	smtp	snmp	ssh	ssl
service label	1	2	3	4	5	6	7	8	9	10	11	12	13

Due to the fact that the *Proto* feature has 133 different elements, the table with the correspondence to the labels has been omitted. For further information about the feature extraction process and the features, refer to [5]. Furthermore, the features *srcip, sport,*

Table 3. State with the corresponding label.

state	CON	ECO	FIN	INT	PAR	REQ	RST	URN	no	ACC	CLO	-
state label	1	2	3	4	5	6	7	8	9	10	11	12

dstip, and *dsport* have been transformed to integers using the *ipaddress.py* [45] library (e.g., 192.168.0.1 → 3232235521). The rest of the 40 features have numerical (either integer or float) values.

The rest of the data handling (except of the python code *ipaddress.py* that was used) has been achieved by writing code from scratch in Matlab. The dataset had the shape of a 257,673 × 48 Table (47 columns contain the independent variables and 1 contains the respective target label). The data was divided in Training (60%) Validation 15% and Testing 25%. The dimensions of the training, validation and testing tables were 154,603X48 38,651 X 48 and 64,419 X 43 respectively. All tables contain records of all classes. The optimal division emerged through a trial-and-error process.

4   The HEDL-IDS Model

As it was stated before, HEDL-IDS[2] consists of four ANN with the following architectures: CNN, RNN with LSTM layers and MLP. Thus, the following paragraphs present a short and basic description of their mathematical foundations [8–10].

Multilayer Perceptrons (MLPs) represent a fundamental type of artificial neural network that comprises multiple layers of interconnected neurons, each layer communicating with the next in a feedforward manner. Unlike simpler Perceptrons, MLPs possess hidden layers, which allow them to model complex relationships within data. Training a MLP involves adjusting the weights and biases of its connections following the principles of the *backpropagation* algorithm and employing the gradient descent protocol. This iterative process enables the network to learn from input-output pairs and to improve its performance over time [8] (Fig. 1).

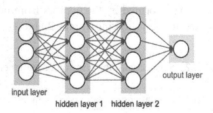

Fig. 1. The 4-layer DNN model architecture (1 input layer, 1 output layer and 2 hidden layers)

A CNN is characterized by its ability to extract features at a finer resolution and subsequently to transform them into more intricate features at a lower resolution, as depicted in Fig. 2. Hence, CNNs consist of three primary types of layers: *Convolutional, Pooling,* and *Fully Connected.* The arrangement of these layers forms the architecture of a CNN [11]. The feature value at the position (x, y) within the kth feature map of the Mth layer can be computed as follows:

$$feature^M_{x,y,k} = W^{M^T}_k X^M_{x,y} + b^M_k \tag{1}$$

where $X^M_{x,y}$ is the input patch centered at location (x, y), W^M_k is the weight vector of the kth filter, and b^M_k is the bias term of the Mth layer. The activation value $activate^M_{x,y,k}$ and the pooling value $pool^M_{x,y,k}$ of convolution feature $feature^M_{x,y,k}$ can be calculated as follows:

$$activate^M_{x,y,k} = activation(feature^M_{x,y,k}) \tag{2}$$

$$pool^M_{x,y,k} = pooling(feature^M_{a,c,k}), \quad \forall (a, c) \in N_{x,y} \tag{3}$$

where $N_{x,y}$ is a local neighborhood at location (x, y). The nonlinear activation functions are ReLU, Sigmoid, and Tangent Hyperbolic (Tanh). The Pooling operations employed are *Average* and *Max Pooling*.

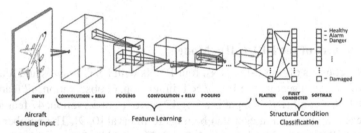

Fig. 2. CNN model architecture with 2 Convolution Layer, 2 Maxpooling Layer, one Flatten, 1 Fully Connected Layer and 1 Softmax Layer.

The output generated by RNNs in each phase relies on the output computed in the preceding state, repeating the same task for every element of the sequence. Essentially, RNNs leverage their inherent memory to retain previously calculated information [12]. However, RNNs encounter difficulty in retaining information over extended periods, due to the issue of vanishing or exploding gradients during backpropagation. This leads to notable fluctuations in training weights. This challenge has been addressed by *Long Short-Term Memory* (LSTM) networks.

An LSTM unit typically consists of three gates: an input gate, an output gate, and a forget gate. These gates regulate the flow of information into and out of the memory cell. The *input* gate determines the proportion of input to influence the cell's state value, while the *forget* gate manages the retention of information within the memory cell. Meanwhile, the *output* gate controls the accessibility of information from the memory cell to compute the output activation of the LSTM unit [13]. The architecture of an LSTM node is depicted in Fig. 3, where X_t represents the input, h_t denotes the output of the LSTM node, h_{t-1} signifies the output of the preceding LSTM node, C_t and C_{t-1} refer to the cell states at time t and t − 1 respectively. Furthermore, σ represents the *sigmoid* function used to decide what information to forget, *tanh* signifies the *hyperbolic tangent* function employed to assign weights, and *b* denotes the bias term. The notation "x" denotes the application of information scaling, while the symbol "+" indicates the process of adding information [14].

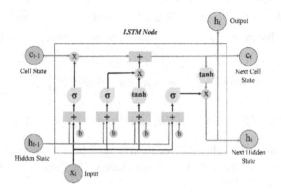

Fig. 3. Structure of an LSTM node.

4.1 Architecture of the HEDL-IDS Model

HEDL-IDS[2] consists of four 2-D CNNs, four RNNs with LSTM layers and four DNNs. The input of CNN is a vector with $1 \times 47 \times 1$ dimension, (1 observation, 47 features, and 1 channel). DNN's and RNN's input is a 1×47 vector (1 observation, 47 features). The output of each model is an integer that belongs to interval [0, 9]. The number of filters applied in the CNNs were 2^n, where $n = 1, 2\ldots 8$. The *stride* value was set to 1. The sizes of the kernel tested were 2, 3, 4, and 5. The number of neurons used in each LSTM and DNN layer was 50, 100, 150, 200, 250 and 300 nodes. The last layer for all 12 models was a *Dense Layer* with 1 node. Furthermore, the penultimate layer of the CNN models (after the *Flatten Layer*) is a Dense Layer with 20 nodes. To avoid overfitting, dropout layers were added after each *Flatten, LSTM* and *Dense* Layer. Additional training using 15% of the dataset (*validation* set) also decreased the probability of overfitting. The values tested were 0.1, 0.2, 0.3, 0.5 and 0.8. All parameters and hyperparameters were set after a trial-and-error process. The architecture of the twelve models, alongside the used parameters is displayed in the following Table 4. The Dropout Layer's rate was equal to 0.2. The input of each layer is the output of the previous one. Figure 4 presents the architecture of the HEDL-IDS[2] model.

All experiments have been performed in *Python*, using a computer with an Intel Core i9-9900 CPU (3.10 GHz) processor, DDR4 memory (32 GB) and GPU NVIDIA GeForce RTX 2070 Super (8 GB). The *Keras* and *Tensorflow* libraries have been employed to build the model's architecture. Based on the literature, in all layers, the *Categorical Crossentropy*, the *Adam Optimizer* and the *ReLU* functions were employed as the *Loss Function*, the *Optimizer* and the *Activation Function* respectively. The *Softmax Activation Function* has been used in the last dense layer of each model.

Table 4. Layers and Parameters Set for the 12 HEDL-IDS Models

NN	Layer	Parameters Set
1st CNN	2-D Covolution	(filters, kernel size, strides) = (32, 3, 1)
	2-D Maxpooling	Pool size=(1,2)
	Flatten	-
2nd CNN	2-D Covolution	(filters, kernel size, strides) = (16, 3, 1)
	2-D Maxpooling	Pool size=(1,2)
	2-D Covolution	(filters, kernel size, strides) = (64, 3, 1)
	2-D Maxpooling	Pool size = (1,2)
	Flatten	-
3rd CNN	2-D Covolution	(filters, kernel size, strides) = (8, 3, 1)
	2-D Maxpooling	Pool size=(1,2)
	2-D Covolution	(filters, kernel size, strides) = (32, 3, 1)
	2-D Maxpooling	Pool size = (1,2)
	2-D Covolution	(filters, kernel size, strides) = (128, 3, 1)
	2-D Maxpooling	Pool size = (1,2)
	Flatten	-
4th CNN	2-D Covolution	(filters, kernel size, strides) = (4, 3, 1)
	2-D Maxpooling	Pool size=(1,2)
	2-D Covolution	(filters, kernel size, strides) = (16, 3, 1)
	2-D Maxpooling	Pool size = (1,2)
	2-D Covolution	(filters, kernel size, strides) = (64, 3, 1)
	2-D Maxpooling	Pool size = (1,2)
	2-D Covolution	(filters, kernel size, strides) = (256, 3, 1)
	2-D Maxpooling	Pool size=(1,2)
	Flatten	-

NN	Layer	Parameters Set	NN	Layer	Parameters Set
1st RNN	LSTM	Nodes = 100	1st DNN	Dense	Nodes = 100
2nd RNN	LSTM	Nodes = 150	2nd DNN	Dense	Nodes = 150
	LSTM	Nodes = 50		Dense	Nodes = 50
3rd RNN	LSTM	Nodes = 250	3rd DNN	Dense	Nodes = 250
	LSTM	Nodes = 150		Dense	Nodes = 150
	LSTM	Nodes = 50		Dense	Nodes = 50
4th RNN	LSTM	Nodes = 300	4th DNN	Dense	Nodes = 300
	LSTM	Nodes = 200		Dense	Nodes = 200
	LSTM	Nodes = 100		Dense	Nodes = 100
	LSTM	Nodes = 50		Dense	Nodes = 50

* After each Flatten Layer always a Dense Layer with 20 nodes
** Last Layer of all Models is a Dense Layer with 1 node
*** Dropout Layer after each Flatten, LSTM and Dense Layer

4.2 Custom Vote

For the purposes of this research effort, the authors proposed a custom vote for the final prediction, combining the weighted vote and the majority vote of the ensemble models. Initially, all algorithms were trained and tested separately on the aforementioned dataset.

The following Table 5, presents weights for each classification algorithm according to the accuracy achieved in testing.

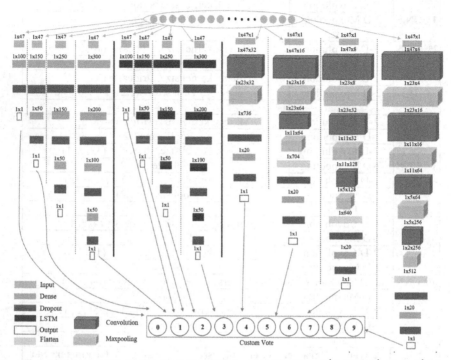

Fig. 4. Architecture of the HEDL-IDS. From left to right 1st DNN, 2nd DNN, 3rd DNN, 4th DNN, 1st RNN, 2nd RNN, 3rd RNN, 4th RNN, 1st CNN, 2nd CNN, 3rd CNN, 4th CNN.

Table 5. Evaluation Indices for the HEDL-IDS and for the Machine Learning Algorithms

Model	CNN	RNN	MLP
1 Layer	0.915	0.855	0.729
2 Layers	0.928	0.866	0.735
3 Layers	0.929	0.873	0.789
4 Layers	0.93	0.875	0.79

In order to form the custom vote, the accuracy result of each of the 12 algorithms were summed. The accuracy of each algorithm was divided with the sum to calculate the weight of each algorithm in the final classification of each instance. This is indicated in the following Table 6. The sum of all weights of all algorithms should sum up to 1.

Everythime the algorithm makes a prediction for a record, a 1 × 10 matrix is formed. Each column represents one label of the target variable. The value in each cell is the sum of the weights of the algorithms that classified the record in the specific class. If no

Table 6. Weights for the HEDL-IDS and the Machine Learning Algorithms

Model	CNN	RNN	MLP
1 Layer	0.0895	0.0837	0.0713
2 Layers	0.0908	0.0847	0.0719
3 Layers	0.0909	0.0854	0.0772
4 Layers	0.091	0.0856	0.0773

model classified the record in a class, the corresponding cell fills with the value 0. The predicted class of the instance is the number of the column with the highest value.

As it is easily understood from both Table 4 and Fig. 4, the complexity of the models increases as their number increases. For example, the 1st RNN has one LSTM layer, the 2nd RNN has two LSTM layers and so on. Thus, if the algorithm consists of five RNNs, then the 5th will have 5 LSTM layers. The algorithm has been developed to allow editing of the number of models. One can choose to deploy 1 DNN, 4 RNN and 2 CNN.

5 Evaluation and Experimental Results

The Accuracy is the overall evaluation index of the developed Machine Learning models. However, four additional performance indices have been used to estimate the efficiency of the algorithms. Due to the fact that we are dealing with a *multiclass* classification problem the *One-versus-All* Strategy has been used. Table 7 presents the name, abbreviation and the calculation method of each index.

Table 7. Calculated indices for the evaluation of the classification approach

Index	Abbreviation	Calculation
Sensitivity (also known as True Positive Rate or Recall)	SNS, REC, TPR	SNS = TP/(TP + FN)
Specificity, (also known as True Negative Rate)	SPC, TNR	SPC = TN/(TN + FP)
Accuracy	ACC	ACC = (TP + TN)/(TP + FP + FN + TN)
F1 Score	F1	F1 = 2*(Precision*Sensitivity)/(Precision + Sensitivity)
Precision (also known as Positive Predictive Value)	PREC, PPV	PREC = TP/(TP + FP)

The training of the model was performed for 100 *epochs* for all twelve models. The HEDL-IDS[2] performs very well in training, by correctly classifying the majority of the records. The overall accuracy in Training was equal to 98.85% and in the Validation 98.8%. The results look very promising in Testing Data too, where the ability of the model to generalize is high. The *Confusion Matrix* and the corresponding indices for the Testing Data are presented in Tables 8 and 9 respectively. The overall accuracy in Testing is as high as 97.5%.

Table 8. Confusion Matrix for the Testing Data

	Predicted Class									
Label	0	1	2	3	4	5	6	7	8	9
Actual Class 0	**22669**	96	8	18	84	153	187	28	7	0
1	148	**5910**	0	0	0	1	3	0	0	0
2	17	0	**652**	0	0	0	0	0	0	0
3	15	0	0	**567**	0	0	0	0	0	0
4	99	1	0	0	**3986**	0	2	0	0	0
5	271	2	0	0	1	**10853**	3	1	0	0
6	358	6	0	0	0	4	**14350**	0	0	0
7	85	1	0	0	0	0	1	**3410**	0	0
8	9	0	0	0	0	0	0	0	**369**	0
9	1	0	0	0	0	0	0	0	0	**43**

Table 9. Evaluation Indices for the Testing Data

Index	0	1	2	3	4	5	6	7	8	9
SNS	0.975	0.974	0.974	0.974	0.975	0.975	0.974	0.975	0.976	0.977
SPC	0.975	0.998	0.999	0.999	0.998	0.996	0.995	0.999	0.999	1
ACC	0.975	0.995	0.999	0.999	0.997	0.993	0.991	0.998	0.999	0.999
F1	0.966	0.978	0.981	0.971	0.977	0.98	0.98	0.983	0.978	0.988
PREC	0.957	0.982	0.987	0.969	0.979	0.985	0.986	0.991	0.981	1

Although the tables are more than satisfactory to assume that the model works with great success, one can make the following observations. The model can generalize with high accuracy and performs exceptionally well with first time seen data. It seems that the model can overcome the minority classes problem, as it perfectly classifies the *Worms* attack and almost perfectly the *Shellcode* attack. All indices' values are above 0.96. The major issue is the incorrectly classified normal packets as Cyber-attacks and vice versa. There are 581 *benign* packets that have been classified as *Cyber-Attacks*. These incorrectly classified packets are not much of an issue, as they cannot cause much of a harm. However, the 1003 *malicious* packets that were classified as *normal* flow is a problem, and it is a very strong goal for further extension of this work.

Additionally, Table 10 reminds the performance of our first model, which performs binary classification of the traffic in *malicious* and *benign* packets. As it is indicated by the Tables 9, and 10, the revised version of HEDL-IDS performs better, even performing a multilabel classification [48].

Table 10. Evaluation Indices for the Testing Data for HEDL-IDS

Model	SNS	SPC	ACC	F1	PREC
HEDL-IDS	0.945	0.973	0.962	0.948	0.952

6   Conclusions and Future Work

In this manuscript the authors propose the second version of the *Hybrid Ensemble Deep Learning Intrusion Detection* System (HEDL-IDS^2). The architecture of this hybrid approach comprises of four CNNs, four RNNs with LSTM layers and four DNNs running in parallel. For each record, the output space is the majority vote from the nine models. The model was trained and evaluated using the *UNSW-NB15* dataset [2]. The dataset consists of packets form 9 distinct Cyber Attacks and Benign Flow. The parameters and the layers of the hybrid model were determined through a trial and error process. The overall accuracy for the training, validation and testing data was as high as 98.85%, 98.8% and 97.5% respectively. The values of the performance indices were above 0.96 for both benign and malicious traffic all classes. Furthermore, except the innovative model, the authors introduce a custom vote process for ensemble models that combines the weighted vote and the majority vote principles.

The extension of the research effort is already ongoing. For future work, the authors will test the model using k-fold cross validation. Furthermore, they are going to modify the custom vote process. Finally, the authors will try to automate the process that decides the best combination of CNN, DNN and RNN model. More specifically, the model is going to automatically choose the optimal algorithms to be used in each model and the optimal number of layers. In the future, the authors will try to incorporate more architectures like *Gated Recurrent Networks* (GRU) or even the well-known AlexNet model.

References

1. Mohammadi, S., Mirvaziri, H., Ghazizadeh-Ahsaee, M., Karimipour, H.: Cyber intrusion detection by combined feature selection algorithm. J. Inf. Secur. Appl. **44**, 80–88 (2019)
2. The UNSW-NB15 Dataset. https://research.unsw.edu.au/projects/unsw-nb15-dataset

3. Li, Y., Xia, J., Zhang, S., Yan, J., Ai, X., Dai, K.: An efficient intrusion detection system based on support vector machines and gradually feature removal method. Expert Syst. Appl. **39**(1), 424–430 (2012)

4. Demertzis, K., Iliadis, L., Tziritas, N., Kikiras, P.: Anomaly detection via blockchained deep learning smart contracts in industry 4.0. Neural Comput. Appl. **32**(23), 17361–17378 (2020)

5. Moustafa, N., Slay, J.: UNSW-NB15: a comprehensive data set for network intrusion detection systems (UNSW-NB15 network data set). In: 2015 Military Communications and Information Systems Conference (MilCIS), pp. 1–6. IEEE (2015)

6. The IXIA PerfectStorm tool. http://www.ixiacom.com/products/perfectstorm

7. CVE. https://cve.mitre.org/

8. Yeung, D.S., Li, J.C., Ng, W.W., Chan, P.P.: MLPNN training via a multiobjective optimization of training error and stochastic sensitivity. IEEE Trans. Neural Netw. Learn. Syst. **27**(5), 978–992 (2015)

9. Baek, J., Choi, Y.: Deep neural network for predicting ore production by truck-haulage systems in open-pit mines. Appl. Sci. **10**(5), 1657 (2020)

10. Liu, W., Wang, Z., Liu, X., Zeng, N., Liu, Y., Alsaadi, F.E.: A survey of deep neural network architectures and their applications. Neurocomputing **234**, 11–26 (2017)

11. O'Shea, K., Nash, R.: An introduction to convolutional neural networks. arXiv preprint arXiv: 1511.08458 (2015)

12. Martin, E., Cundy, C.: Parallelizing linear recurrent neural nets over sequence length. arXiv preprint arXiv:1709.04057 (2017)

13. Mahdavifar, S., Ghorbani, A.A.: Application of deep learning to cybersecurity: a survey. Neurocomputing **347**, 149–176 (2019)

14. Le, X.H., Ho, H.V., Lee, G., Jung, S.: Application of long short-term memory (LSTM) neural network for flood forecasting. Water **11**(7), 1387 (2019)

15. Chawla, N.V., Bowyer, K.W., Hall, L.O., Kegelmeyer, W.P.: SMOTE: synthetic minority over-sampling technique. J. Artif. Intell. Res. **16**, 321–357 (2002)

16. Prasad, R., Rohokale, V.: Cyber Security: The Lifeline of Information and Communication Technology. Springer, Cham (2020)

17. Bezahaf, M., Hutchison, D., King, D., Race, N.: Internet evolution: critical issues. IEEE Internet Comput. **24**(4), 5–14 (2020)

18. Lubis, F., Lubis, M.: Internet provider service value delivery index problem: case study of the NetHost. In: Journal of Physics: Conference Series, vol. 1566, no. 1, p. 012081. IOP Publishing (2020)

19. Zhang, X., Xie, H., Yang, H., Shao, H., Zhu, M.: A general framework to understand vulnerabilities in information systems. IEEE Access **8**, 121858–121873 (2020)

20. Statista. https://www.statista.com/statistics/273575/average-organizational-cost-incurred-by-a-data-breach/

21. Dash, B., Sharma, P., Ali, A.: Federated learning for privacy-preserving: a review of PII data analysis in Fintech. Int. J. Softw. Eng. Appl. **13**(4), 1–13 (2022)

22. CI Cybersecurity: Framework for improving critical infrastructure cybersecurity (2018). https://nvlpubs.nist.gov/nistpubs/CSWP/NIST.CSWP.04162018

23. Potluri, S., Ahmed, S., Diedrich, C.: Convolutional neural networks for multi-class intrusion detection system. In: Groza, A., Prasath, R. (eds.) MIKE 2018, pp. 225–238. Springer, Cham (2018). https://doi.org/10.1007/978-3-030-05918-7_20

24. Zhang, J., Ling, Y., Fu, X., Yang, X., Xiong, G., Zhang, R.: Model of the intrusion detection system based on the integration of spatial-temporal features. Comput. Secur. **89**, 101681 (2020)

25. Hassan, M.M., Gumaei, A., Alsanad, A., Alrubaian, M., Fortino, G.: A hybrid deep learning model for efficient intrusion detection in big data environment. Inf. Sci. **513**, 386–396 (2020)

26. Hajisalem, V., Babaie, S.: A hybrid intrusion detection system based on ABC-AFS algorithm for misuse and anomaly detection. Comput. Netw. **136**, 37–50 (2018)
27. Moustafa, N., Slay, J.: The evaluation of Network Anomaly Detection Systems: statistical analysis of the UNSW-NB15 data set and the comparison with the KDD99 data set. Inf. Secur. J. Glob. Perspect. **25**(1–3), 18–31 (2016)
28. Pascanu, R., Stokes, J.W., Sanossian, H., Marinescu, M., Thomas, A.: Malware classification with recurrent networks. In: 2015 IEEE International Conference on Acoustics, Speech and Signal Processing (ICASSP), pp. 1916–1920. IEEE (2015)
29. Mizuno, S., Hatada, M., Mori, T., Goto, S.: BotDetector: a robust and scalable approach toward detecting malware-infected devices. In: 2017 IEEE International Conference on Communications (ICC), pp. 1–7. IEEE (2017)
30. Damopoulos, D., Menesidou, S.A., Kambourakis, G., Papadaki, M., Clarke, N., Gritzalis, S.: Evaluation of anomaly-based IDS for mobile devices using machine learning classifiers. Secur. Commun. Netw. **5**(1), 3–14 (2012)
31. Elekar, K.S.: Combination of data mining techniques for intrusion detection system. In: 2015 International Conference on Computer, Communication and Control (IC4), pp. 1–5. IEEE (2015)
32. Ganeshkumar, P., Pandeeswari, N.: Adaptive neuro-fuzzy-based anomaly detection system in cloud. Int. J. Fuzzy Syst. **18**(3), 367–378 (2016)
33. Meidan, Y., et al.: N-BaioT—network-based detection of IoT botnet attacks using deep autoencoders. IEEE Pervasive Comput. **17**(3), 12–22 (2018)
34. Soe, Y.N., Feng, Y., Santosa, P.I., Hartanto, R., Sakurai, K.: Machine learning-based IoT-botnet attack detection with sequential architecture. Sensors **20**(16), 4372 (2020)
35. Zhang, C., Jiang, J., Kamel, M.: Intrusion detection using hierarchical neural networks. Pattern Recogn. Lett. **26**(6), 779–791 (2005)
36. Dash, T.: A study on intrusion detection using neural networks trained with evolutionary algorithms. Soft. Comput. **21**, 2687–2700 (2017)
37. Cordonsky, I., Rosenberg, I., Sicard, G., David, E.O.: DeepOrigin: end-to-end deep learning for detection of new malware families. In: 2018 International Joint Conference on Neural Networks (IJCNN), pp. 1–7. IEEE (2018)
38. Gibert Llauradó, D.: Convolutional neural networks for malware classification. Master's thesis, Universitat Politècnica de Catalunya (2016)
39. Loukas, G., Vuong, T., Heartfield, R., Sakellari, G., Yoon, Y., Gan, D.: Cloud-based cyber-physical intrusion detection for vehicles using deep learning. IEEE Access **6**, 3491–3508 (2017)
40. Thamilarasu, G., Chawla, S.: Towards deep-learning-driven intrusion detection for the internet of things. Sensors **19**(9), 1977 (2019)
41. Shone, N., Ngoc, T.N., Phai, V.D., Shi, Q.: A deep learning approach to network intrusion detection. IEEE Trans. Emerg. Top. Comput. Intell. **2**(1), 41–50 (2018)
42. Patil, R., Dudeja, H., Modi, C.: Designing an efficient security framework for detecting intrusions in virtual network of cloud computing. Comput. Secur. **85**, 402–422 (2019)
43. Khammassi, C., Krichen, S.: A GA-LR wrapper approach for feature selection in network intrusion detection. Comput. Secur. **70**, 255–277 (2017)
44. Moustafa, N., Slay, J., Creech, G.: Novel geometric area analysis technique for anomaly detection using trapezoidal area estimation on large-scale networks. IEEE Trans. Big Data **5**(4), 481–494 (2017)
45. Pypi. https://pypi.org/project/ipaddress/. Accessed 10 Mar 2024
46. Ahmim, A., Derdour, M., Ferrag, M.A.: An intrusion detection system based on combining probability predictions of a tree of classifiers. Int. J. Commun. Syst. **31**(9), e3547 (2018)
47. Scarfone, K., Mell, P.: Guide to intrusion detection and prevention systems (IDPS). NIST Special Publication 800-94 (2007)

48. Psathas, A.P., Iliadis, L., Papaleonidas, A., Bountas, D.: HEDL-IDS: a hybrid ensemble deep learning approach for cyber intrusion detection. In: Maglogiannis, I., Iliadis, L., Macintyre, J., Cortez, P. (eds.) AIAI 2022, pp. 116–131. Springer, Cham (2022). https://doi.org/10.1007/978-3-031-08333-4_10
49. Psathas, A.P., Iliadis, L., Papaleonidas, A., Bountas, D.: A hybrid deep learning ensemble for cyber intrusion detection. In: Iliadis, L., Macintyre, J., Jayne, C., Pimenidis, E. (eds.) EANN 2021. PINNS, vol. 3, pp. 27–41. Springer, Cham (2021). https://doi.org/10.1007/978-3-030-80568-5_3
50. Psathas, A.P., Iliadis, L., Papaleonidas, A., Bountas, D.: COREM^2 project: a beginning to end approach for cyber intrusion detection. Neural Comput. Appl. **34**, 19565–19584 (2022)

Intelligent Framework for Monitoring Student Emotions During Online Learning

Ayoub Sassi[1], Safa Chérif[1(✉)], and Wael Jaafar[2]

[1] ESPRIT School of Engineering, Ariana, Tunisia
{ayoub.sassi,safa.zhiouacherif}@esprit.tn
[2] École de Technologie Supérieure (ÉTS), Montreal, QC, Canada
wael.jaafar@etsmtl.ca

Abstract. The prominence of online engineering education has notably increased. Various factors contribute to its effectiveness and relevance, making it a valuable facilitator of continuous learning and professional development in the dynamically evolving engineering field. To tackle this challenge, we introduce an intelligent framework that combines deep learning methods for the real-time detection of students' emotions during online learning and the assessment of their mental states regarding the taught content. Our framework comprises three modules. The first module employs a novel lightweight machine learning method, known as convolutional neural network-random forest (CNN-RF), to efficiently identify students' basic emotions during online courses. The second module involves mapping these basic emotions to an education-aware state of mind based on the Plutchik wheel. The third module is a visualization dashboard that provides educators with insights into students' emotional dynamics, enabling the identification of learning difficulties with high precision and offering informed recommendations for improvements in course content and online teaching methods. The proposed model has been trained and tested on the FER-2013 dataset, which is an open-labeled dataset for emotion recognition but not dedicated to a learning context. In this paper, we propose further experiments on a real learning situation. To assess the results of the framework, two evaluation questionnaires are proposed. The alignment between the reported outcomes and the results obtained from administered questionnaires serves to affirm the potential efficacy of our proposed model as a valuable support tool for establishing a good adaptive learning strategy.

Keywords: Computer vision · emotion recognition · online course

1 Introduction

Online engineering education has gained significant importance, especially after the outbreak of the COVID-19 crisis, due to various factors that contribute to

L. Iliadis et al. (Eds.): EANN 2024, CCIS 2141, pp. 207–219, 2024.
https://doi.org/10.1007/978-3-031-62495-7_16

its effectiveness and relevance [5]. According to the International Association of Universities Global Survey report [5], two-thirds of Higher Education Institutions (HEIs) successfully transitioned to online teaching, while the remaining one-third faced challenges. Nevertheless, in a rapidly evolving field like engineering, online engineering education facilitates continuous learning and professional development [1].

However, it's essential to ensure the credibility of the education received. Indeed, it has been observed that achieving comprehension during online learning is not always successful, regardless of the considerable efforts that tutors invest in creating materials for their remote courses. Consequently, minimal attention has been directed toward identifying and addressing the emotional stress associated with these teaching methods [11]. Therefore, there is a clear imperative to customize the learning process to align with the student's state of mind during online classes.

On the other hand, cutting-edge artificial intelligence has made significant contributions to the field of education, marking substantial progress and gaining momentum. In [6], authors underscore the significant role of AI in supporting and advancing education. Notably, the study emphasizes the role of these technologies in enabling continued education during the COVID-19 pandemic, ensuring that societies can progress in education even amidst challenging circumstances.

In this context, we introduce an intelligent framework that combines advanced artificial intelligence methods for real-time detection of students' emotions during online learning and the assessment of their mental states regarding the taught content. Previous studies aimed to connect emotion recognition with the learning environment [9,12,15]. However, these efforts may fall short in addressing specific emotions tailored to the dynamic nature of online learning. They often lack explicit representation of emotions and education-aware states of mind. Motivated by these shortcomings, we introduce a pioneering framework designed to perform real-time video traffic analysis for detecting students' emotions and evaluating their states of mind during online learning [13]. The framework comprises three key components: 1) recognition of facial expressions (basic emotions), 2) a mapping system correlating basic emotions with states of mind, and 3) a dynamic visualization dashboard.

The key contributions of this paper include the experimental validation of our framework to monitor students' emotions in a real e-learning setting. Indeed, in our previous work [13], the framework was tested on a public dataset not necessarily intended for an e-learning context. In contrast, the current work aims to rigorously assess the inference capabilities of our proposed framework through systematic testing procedures. To do so, additional experiments are conducted in a real online learning environment to evaluate the framework's ability to derive accurate conclusions or predictions from real data. First, we construct a novel dataset that reflects real-world scenarios relevant to online courses. To assess the effectiveness of the framework, two evaluation questionnaires are introduced. The first questionnaire is administered to students after the completion of video-based lessons, aiming to determine their mental state during the course visualization. The second questionnaire is provided to the tutor, soliciting his evaluation of the student's mental state throughout the course. Next, we test our framework on this new (real) dataset and measure its performance using appropriate evaluation metrics tailored to this inference task. Furthermore, we conduct a comparative analysis against the results obtained from the tutor's assessment. This comparative evaluation between the results of the framework and those obtained from the tutor provides insights into our approach's relative strengths and weaknesses and highlights its potential advantages over alternative solutions.

The remainder of the paper is organized as follows. Section 2 reviews the proposed framework steps. Section 3 presents the model architecture and training. Section 4 describes the proposed experiments' implementation. In Sect. 5, results are presented. In Sect. 6, we discuss the recommendations drawn from this experience. Finally, Sect. 7 concludes the paper.

2 Background

Continuous improvement through regular assessment and feedback is essential to refine and enhance educational practices. Students are key actors in program evaluation [7]. However, with the spread of online courses, traditional tools to measure student engagement are insufficient. The lack of interaction during these courses makes it difficult to assess student engagement. For this reason, other intelligent tools are needed to detect student behavior during these courses.

In this section, we present the main functionalities of our framework. The details of the models and algorithms used for emotion recognition and state-of-mind prediction are described in [13].

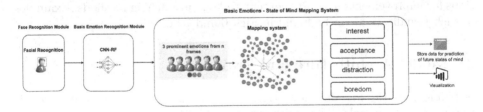

Fig. 1. Proposed emotion recognition framework [13].

Our framework comprises three modules, as shown in Fig. 1. The first module employs a novel lightweight machine learning method, a.k.a., convolution neural network-random forest (CNN-RF), to efficiently identify students' basic emotions during online courses. As described in [4], Ekman defined six basic emotions which are anger, surprise, disgust, happy, fear, and sadness. For better training of the model when using the FER-2013 dataset [10], we added a seventh emotion which is neutral. Our approach outperforms existing benchmarks' accuracies (over 71%) on the FER-2013 dataset while maintaining lower complexity by using fewer parameters compared to existing methods which is a crucial feature for real-time analysis.

In our context, basic emotions are not sufficiently representative of a student's state in a learning situation. This serves as the primary impetus for the forthcoming module.

The second module involves mapping these basic emotions to an education-aware state of mind. Unlike previous works, we propose a mapping system inspired by the Plutchik wheel, as shown in Fig. 2, which better reflects the relationship between combinations of basic emotions and resulting states of mind. In fact, according to Plutchik's theory, these emotions collaborate to form a state of mind, often determined by the combination of basic emotions. Assessing these states of mind may provide insights into how a student perceives an online course. To ascertain the student's state of mind, we associate the three primary emotions with the third level of Plutchik's wheel of emotions. Considering the overall relevance of e-learning environments, we have identified four specific states of mind: Interest, Acceptance, Distraction, and Boredom. For example, the dominance of the emotion "Happy" as the primary emotion suggests a state of Acceptance. Alternatively, if the second prominent emotion is "Surprise", in conjunction with the primary emotion "Happy", it indicates a state of "Interest". Furthermore, the positions of other considered basic emotions, warrant a nuanced exploration into the second and even third prominent emotions to define the associated state of mind precisely. This exhaustive analysis results in a comprehensive mapping of thirty-six unique combinations linking the selected basic emotions to distinct states of mind [13].

The third module is a visualization dashboard that provides educators with insights into students' emotional dynamics over time, enabling the identification of learning difficulties with high precision and offering informed recommendations for improvements in course content and online teaching methods. Examples of such visualization can be found in Figs. 6 and 7 below.

3   Model Architecture and Training

Expanding on the foundational layer of our framework, the emotion recognition module is pivotal in classifying students' facial expressions into seven basic emotions: anger, disgust, fear, happiness, neutrality, sadness, and surprise. This module integrates a Convolutional Neural Network (CNN) with a Random Forest (RF) classifier, creating a synergy that enhances the accuracy and efficiency of emotion detection. The architecture consists of multiple convolutional and pooling layers that extract significant features from facial expressions, followed by a Random Forest classifier that interprets these features to predict the corresponding emotion, as depicted in Fig. 3.

The training of this model was conducted using the FER-2013 dataset, selected for its diverse representation of facial emotions. To adapt this dataset for our e-learning context, we applied data augmentation techniques including

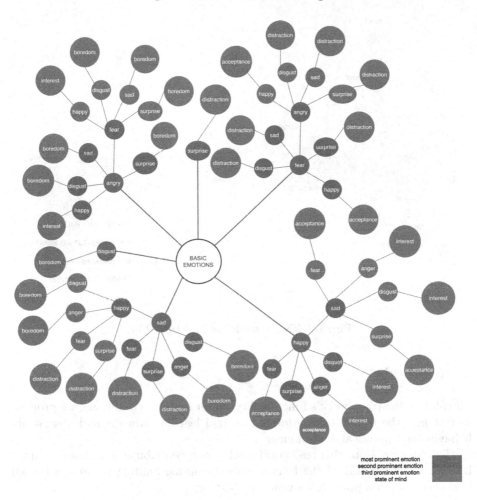

Fig. 2. Mapping of basic emotions to states of mind [13].

horizontal mirroring, rotation, and shifts. The model underwent extensive hyper-parameter optimization, with settings such as a learning rate of 0.001 and 310 epochs, following the experimental insights from Vulpe-Grigoraşi et al. [14]. This meticulous process ensured that our model achieved superior performance in recognizing basic emotions, thereby setting a new benchmark for accuracy in the domain of online learning analytics.

Given the dynamic nature of emotional changes during learning, our model employs a sequence analysis strategy. Acknowledging that emotions evolve over a period, we analyze a set of images captured sequentially over six seconds to calculate the average probability for each emotion, facilitating a nuanced understanding of the student's emotional state.

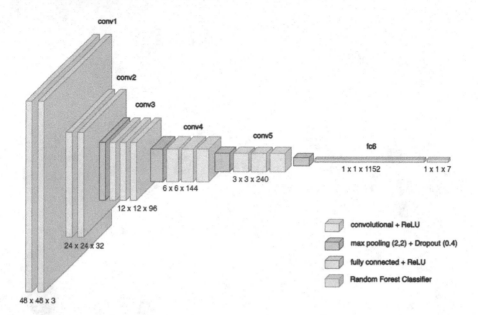

Fig. 3. CNN-RF model architecture [13].

4 Methods

To validate the framework's functionality under realistic conditions, we propose to test how the framework performs in a real learning context and observe its behavior in a practical environment.

The findings from this real-world testing can contribute to a more comprehensive understanding of the framework's strengths, limitations, and potential improvements in a practical educational setting.

4.1 Data Collection

For this experiment, we use video records of 3 students when attending an online course. The videos in the dataset capture student faces and gestures as students visualize the online course. A standard webcam from the student computer is used for video acquisition. Each sequence lasts approximately 60 min. These videos are then analyzed in three ways:

4.2 Self-assessment Labeling

Students are asked after watching the video recorded to identify their state of mind (interest, acceptance, distraction, boredom) during a specific period of time. The results are saved in a simple .xls table.

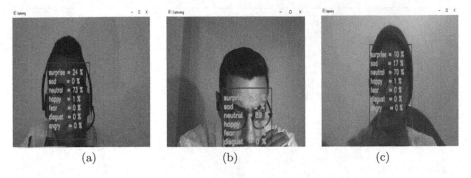

Fig. 4. Basic emotions detected by the framework for 3 students (a) Subject A, (b) Subject B, and (c) Subject C.

4.3 External Assessment

A tutor was asked to label the video records during specific periods. Thanks to his pedagogical expertise, the tutor analyzes the student's behavior and assesses the student's state of mind during the online course.

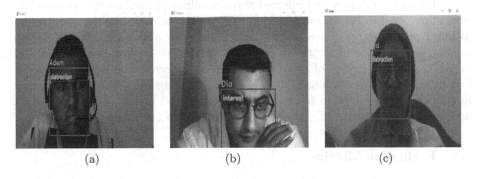

Fig. 5. State of minds detected by the framework for 3 students (a) Subject A, (b) Subject B, and (c) Subject C.

4.4 Framework Classification

The records have been fed into the proposed framework for intelligent analysis through the integration of the emotion recognition module and the state-of-mind estimation [13]. Figure 4 illustrates the proposed method's proficiency in detecting students' facial expressions and providing corresponding probability distributions for recognized basic emotions.

In Fig. 5, the proposed method extrapolates the student's states of mind from a video stream by leveraging the previously determined probability distributions.

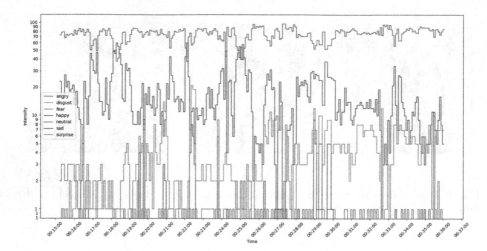

Fig. 6. Intensity (in percentage) for each emotion over time.

These basic emotions and state-of-mind predictions are subsequently depicted in Figs. 6 and 7, with time mapped on the X-axis and the probabilities of occurrence for basic emotions and inferred state-of-minds plotted on the Y-axis. Figures allow for the observation of varied fluctuations in basic emotions and state-of-minds, hence showcasing students' reactions during online learning and fostering the identification of emotional patterns and the establishment of correlations between students' states of mind at specific junctures in the learning process. For instance, between minutes 40 and 45 in Fig. 7, an important distraction is noticed. This may be due to the student being tired at the end of the course and/or the presentation of complex principles within the course.

4.5   Evaluation Metrics

Building upon the results of the three preceding assessments, we evaluate the effectiveness of the framework based on two criteria. First, we assess its performance by comparing its results to the self-assessed results. Then, we extend the results' comparison to an external assessment realized by a teacher. Specifically, we contrast the two to analyze their results differences, and similarities.

Performances are evaluated in terms of accuracy α, precision ϕ, recall ρ, and F1-score δ, defined respectively by

$$\alpha = \frac{TP + TN}{TP + TN + FP + FN}, \tag{1}$$

$$\phi = \frac{TP}{TP + TN}, \tag{2}$$

$$\rho = \frac{TP}{TP + FN}, \tag{3}$$

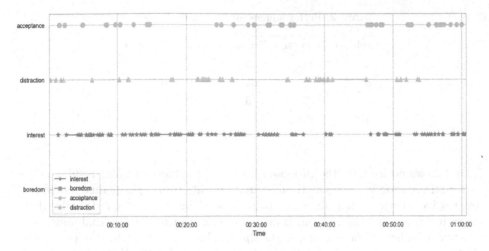

Fig. 7. Fluctuation of states of mind detected over time.

Table 1. Performances of the proposed framework

Subject	Accuracy	Precision	Recall	F1-score
A	0.67	0.55	0.67	0.81
B	0.6	0.6	0.6	0.58
C	0.47	0.77	0.47	0.36
All	0.58	0.59	0.58	0.52

and

$$\delta = \frac{2\,TP}{2\,TP + FP + FN}, \tag{4}$$

where TP, TN, FP, and FN indicate respectively true-positive, true-negative, false-positive, and false-negative outcomes.

5   Results

We strategically implemented a time synchronization approach to facilitate a comprehensive comparison between our framework's classification and the outcomes of the external assessment. This involved selecting data points at uniform two-minute intervals across the entirety of the collected dataset. By using this regular interval, we sought to examine results while keeping the observations well-balanced thoroughly.

For a more detailed evaluation, we present the metrics' results corresponding to each assessment scenario. Table 1 provides the performance metrics, including accuracy, precision, recall, and F1-score, for our framework compared to the self-assessment. Similarly, Table 2 details the corresponding metrics for the external assessment compared to the self-assessment. Based on the results within Tables

Table 2. Performances of the external assessor

Subject	Accuracy	Precision	Recall	F1-score
A	0.43	0.53	0.43	0.71
B	0.56	0.61	0.56	0.58
C	0.37	0.43	0.36	0.35
All	0.45	0.50	0.45	0.51

1 and 2, we notice that the proposed framework achieves similar results to the external assessor for Subject B. This may be due to a high-quality image and expressive emotions that allow one to recognize the states of mind easily. However, for Subjects A and C, our framework outperforms the external assessor.

For a holistic view, we aggregate the results across the three experiments. Figure 8.a presents a consolidated confusion matrix for the Framework classification, comparing the combined self-assessment data to our framework, while Fig. 8.b encapsulates a unified confusion matrix for the external assessment across all three experiments. Looking into the matrices' diagonals, we notice how well the proposed framework performs in identifying "distraction" and "interest", while it performs poorly in identifying "acceptance" compared to a human assessor.

Table 3 furnishes comprehensive metric results. The proposed framework performs better than an external assessor on all data, with a significant improvement of 9% and more for the accuracy, precision, and recall metrics.

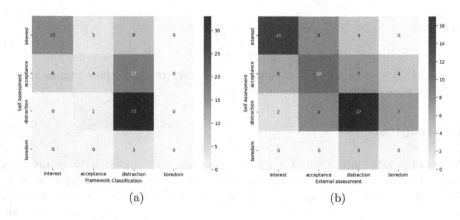

(a)   (b)

Fig. 8. Confusion matrices of (a) Proposed framework and (b) External assessor.

Table 3. Comparison of performances (Framework classification vs. External assessment)

Method	Accuracy	Precision	Recall	F1-score
Proposed framework	**0.58**	**0.59**	**0.58**	**0.52**
External assessment	0.45	0.50	0.45	0.51

6   Discussion and Insights

To the best of our knowledge, publicly available datasets explicitly tailored for the recognition of students' emotions are currently lacking. Despite the limited number of observations within the proposed dataset, the outcomes of this experiment underscore the strengths of our approach and point towards potential refinements in both the model and the experimental protocol employed for data collection and annotation. The proposed framework offers significant advantages in automatically monitoring student behavior during online courses. It provides a state-of-mind estimation every 6 s in real-time video streams, a notably brief interval aligned with human perception. Furthermore, as shown in Table 3 our framework's performance surpasses the proficiency of tutors in discerning the student's state of mind.

However, the accuracy observed in these experiments remains lower compared to results obtained with basic emotions (71.86% on FER2013). This decline in performance could be attributed to various factors. One potential factor is the annotation of the dataset. Assigning labels to the state of mind involves a level of personal interpretation and judgment. Individuals may hold distinct perspectives, opinions, or interpretations of the same content. This discrepancy is evident when comparing the labels provided by students with those provided by instructors. Students might not be fully cognizant of their 'learning behavior' while studying, whereas tutors may emphasize certain features or aspects based on their subjective understanding or interpretation. Mitigating this subjectivity may involve posing more specific questions to students that better capture their state of mind.

In addition, it is notable that certain students exhibit greater expressiveness than others. Indeed, the varying levels of expressiveness among students introduce a potential bias in the research findings. This variability in expression can be influenced by diverse factors such as personality traits, cultural background, and the comfort levels experienced in an environment monitored by cameras. Addressing this issue may involve enhancing diversity and expanding the size of the dataset, thus helping to ease the potential impact of individual expressiveness on the results.

Furthermore, facial expressions are certainly the best descriptor for recognizing emotion. However, when we investigate student behavior, we deduce that more features play a crucial role in enhancing the efficiency of the frameworks. Several measures can be considered as suggested by researchers in [3]. Incorporating eye tracking and head position data could lead to more effective results in analyzing and understanding student behavior.

In future research, exploring additional datasets, such as those introduced in [2,8] and collected with Asian students, could offer valuable insights and opportunities for further investigation. Indeed, analyzing such data could help uncover culturally specific patterns in emotion expressions and perception leading to the development of more robust and culturally sensitive emotion recognition models.

7 Conclusion

In this paper, we presented an intelligent framework that could detect and monitor student emotions and states of mind during online courses. The framework has been tested in a real online learning environment. The performance of the framework outperformed the assessment given by a human expert. Hence, an AI educational framework can be a powerful tool to provide personalized learning experiences through immediate feedback and adapting to individual needs. Managers and tutors of a Learning Management System could be the primary users of this framework. Their role will involve analyzing course success and identifying key factors for enhancing the overall quality of online teaching.

In summary, while intelligent frameworks can be powerful tools in education, they are not likely to completely replace the unique qualities and emotional intelligence that human tutors bring to the learning experience. The most effective educational approaches might involve a thoughtful combination of both, i.e., intelligent frameworks and human guidance.

References

1. Berglund, A.: Online courses for teaching engineering professionalism. In: Proceedings of the 19th International CDIO Conference. Trondheim, Norway, 26–29 June 2023
2. Dai, X., Wei, P., Zeng, Y., Zhang, Q.: Students' facial expression recognition based on multi-head attention mechanism. J. Phys.: Conf. Ser. **2493**(1), 012004 (2023). https://doi.org/10.1088/1742-6596/2493/1/012004
3. Delgado, K., et al.: Student engagement dataset. In: 2021 IEEE/CVF International Conference on Computer Vision Workshops (ICCVW), pp. 3621–3629 (2021)
4. Ekman, P.: An argument for basic emotions. Cogn. Emot. **6**(3–4), 169–200 (1992)
5. García-Morales, V.J., Garrido-Moreno, A., Martín-Rojas, R.: The transformation of higher education after the COVID disruption: emerging challenges in an online learning scenario. Front. Psychol. **12** (2021)
6. Gürdür Broo, D., Kaynak, O., Sait, S.M.: Rethinking engineering education at the age of industry 5.0. J. Ind. Inf. Integr. **25**, 100311 (2022)
7. Lassudrie, C., Kontio, J., Rouvrais, S.: Managing the continuous improvement loop of educational systems: students as key actors in program evaluation. In: CDIO2013: 9th International Conference: Engineering Leadership in Innovation and Design. Cambridge, MA, United States, June 2013

8. Lyu, L., et al.: Spontaneous facial expression database of learners' academic emotions in online learning with hand occlusion. Comput. Electr. Eng. **97**, 107667 (2022). https://doi.org/10.1016/j.compeleceng.2021.107667, https://www.sciencedirect.com/science/article/pii/S0045790621005899

9. Megahed, M., Mohammed, A.: Modeling adaptive e-learning environment using facial expressions and fuzzy logic. Expert Syst. Appl. **157** (2020)

10. Mollahosseini, I.M., Chan, D., Mahoor, M.H.: Face emotion recognition in context. In: IEEE Conference on Computer Vision and Pattern Recognition Workshops (CVPRW) (2016)

11. Sadeghi, M.: A shift from classroom to distance learning: advantages and limitations. Int. J. Res. Engl. Edu. (2019)

12. Saganowski, S., Dutkowiak, A., Dziadek, A., Dziezyc, M., Komoszynska, J., Michalska, W., et al.: Emotion recognition using wearables: a systematic literature review-work-in-progress. In: Proceedings of the International Conference on Pervasive Computing and Communications Workshops (PerCom Workshops), pp. 1–6, March 2020

13. Sassi, A., Jaafar, W., Cherif, S., Abderrazak, J.B., Yanikomeroglu, H.: Video traffic analysis for real-time emotion recognition and visualization in online learning. IEEE Access **11**, 99376–99386 (2023)

14. Vulpe-Grigoraşi, A., Grigore, O.: Convolutional neural network hyperparameters optimization for facial emotion recognition. In: Proceedings of the International Symposium on Advanced Topics in Electrical Engineering (ATEE), pp. 1–5 (2021). https://doi.org/10.1109/ATEE52255.2021.9425073

15. Yan, F., Wu, N., Iliyasu, A., et al.: Framework for identifying and visualising emotional atmosphere in online learning environments in the COVID-19 era. Appl. Intell. **52**, 9406–9422 (2022). https://doi.org/10.1007/s10489-021-02916-z

Leveraging Diverse Data Sources for Enhanced Prediction of Severe Weather-Related Disruptions Across Different Time Horizons

Hussain Otudi[iD], Shelly Gupta[iD], and Zoran Obradovic[(✉)][iD]

Center for Data Analytics and Biomedical Informatics Temple University,
Philadelphia, PA, USA
{hussain.otudi,shelly.gupta,zoran.obradovic}@temple.edu

Abstract. In recent years, shifts in weather patterns have become increasingly apparent, leading to a rise in the frequency and severity of severe weather-related disruptive events across the globe. These events, which can include floods, storms, heavy rain, high winds, winter storms, heavy snow, and blizzards, pose a significant threat to public health and safety, as well as having negative economic impacts on key sectors such as agriculture, critical infrastructure, and emergency management. To address this challenge, our paper proposes a multi-modal learning approach for predicting and estimating risk for disruptions, by integrating weather- related data from multiple sources, including text and sensor recordings. Through experimental evaluation on a dataset of hourly weather data from three different climates - Alaska, Nevada, and Pennsylvania - we demonstrate that our approach outperforms alternatives that rely solely on weather recordings.

Keywords: Multi-modal learning · Data fusion · Data scarcity · Severe weather event prediction

1 Introduction

Severe weather events occur frequently as depicted in Fig. 1, posing significant risks to human lives and the economy, particularly in terms of property damage. Timely and accurate forecasts of these events are crucial for facilitating timely evacuations, efficient resource allocation, and minimizing the impact on affected communities. Forecasts made 12, and 24 h in advance can significantly improve response strategies, thereby reducing environmental and human impacts through the optimization of Early Warning Systems (EWSs) on a global scale. Previous studies have proposed data-driven methods for event prediction utilizing Deep Learning techniques such as feed-forward neural networks like Convolutional Neural Networks (CNNs) [24,25], Recurrent Neural Networks (RNNs), Autoencoders [23], and attention-based networks [13]. However, these methods

L. Iliadis et al. (Eds.): EANN 2024, CCIS 2141, pp. 220–234, 2024.
https://doi.org/10.1007/978-3-031-62495-7_17

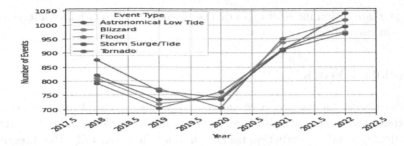

Fig. 1. The number of severe weather-related disruptions for five types of events over five years in Alaska (AK), Nevada (NV), and Pennsylvania (PA).

encounter challenges due to the highly imbalanced nature of severe weather event datasets and their reliance solely on weather data for predictions. Weather data sourced from platforms like ASOS often contain numerous instances of missing data attributable to sensor malfunctions and cloud disturbances, both of which are prevalent during severe weather events. Consequently, depending solely on this method is not advisable. Previous studies have explored alternative data sources to address the gaps in information concerning extreme events. One effective method involves utilizing simulations to produce additional examples of complex phenomena. However, this approach demands a significant investment of time and resources [19]. Furthermore, most of these studies overlook regional disparities, often concentrating on limited geographical areas or employing a single model for multiple states simultaneously [20]. For instance, when examining states such as Alaska and Pennsylvania, it is evident that severe weather patterns differ significantly. Alaska frequently reports blizzards, with 4,587 occurrences recorded from 2018 to 2022, whereas Pennsylvania and Nevada document fewer blizzards during the same time frame. This emphasises the necessity of considering regional variations in deployment strategies. Thus, the challenge persists in creating models that can effectively identify and forecast disruptive events across diverse weather conditions.

This work addresses these shortcomings by presenting a framework designed to detect and predict infrequent meteorological phenomena. Our approach addresses three critical aspects: (1) managing partially observed meteorological data, (2) integrating a rich source of explanatory texts with meteorological measurements, and (3) mitigating the challenge of imbalance weather data. Our proposed model harnesses expert-authored annotations detailing the nature and severity of disruptive weather events. Our methodology revolves around a robust multi-classification model tailored specifically for rare weather occurrences. We employ a Bidirectional Long Short-Term Memory (LSTM) neural network to learn sequences in two directions, forward and backward, to address classification problems, and adopt a multimodal strategy that integrates additional data sources. To address data imbalance, we utilize the focal loss function. Our innovative approach offers a comprehensive solution for classifying rare weather events, leveraging late fusion integration of diverse data sources to enhance analysis and prediction capabilities.

2   Related Work

The related work for the proposed methodology encompasses three main components that need to be discussed before presenting the background of the current study: firstly, weather prediction using unimodal data; secondly, the integration of social data with weather datasets; and thirdly, the development of a multimodal model for classifying severe weather-related events.

2.1   Severe Weather-Related Event Prediction Using Uni-Modal Data

Multiple studies have utilized Automated Surface Observing System (ASOS) as their weather data source [16]. Predicting severe weather events using data from ASOS presents challenges even though a ceilometer at an ASOS weather station scans the sky and can detect clouds up to 3.6 km high [14]. Data gaps can occur during sensor malfunctions or in regions affected by extreme weather, compromising the accuracy and reliability of forecasts. Previous studies have highlighted the need for enhanced weather measurement techniques and impact-based forecasting methods [7,18]. The use of data collected by unmanned aircraft was proposed to improve model validation [5]. Issues such as data consistency and the difficulty of tracking cloud cover have also been pointed out [2,4,22]. These studies highlight the significance of developing more effective data collection methods, and refining forecasting techniques. Our study aims to address these issues by incorporating detailed analyses based on expert descriptions of severe weather-related events [11], thereby improving the accuracy and reliability of disruption prediction. One source suggests that while weather simulations are essential for forecasting severe events, they face challenges, including inaccuracies in modeling the probabilities of such occurrences [3]. Alternatively, event description logs about severe weather events are suggested to sometimes be more useful than traditional weather forecasts [10].

2.2   Severe Weather-Related Event Prediction Using Social Data

Many studies have examined severe weather events using either weather data or data from social data [21], however, social media data may be cluttered with noise, lack verification, and potentially include misleading information. Another limitation of utilizing social data is that during extreme weather conditions, there tends to be an uptick in speculative or exaggerated content, which can compromise the reliability of analyses based on social data [21]. Our study advocates for utilizing expert logs instead of tweets, thus reducing potential biases.

2.3 Developing a Multi-modal Model for the Classification of Severe Weather-Related Events

The diverse nature of severe weather events highlights the necessity for accurate risk assessment. In prior studies risk for severe weather-related disruptions was estimated using the C4.5 classifier [8], as well as accounting for different frequency of occurrence for different variables [9]. Both of these prior studies highlight the importance of multi-class classification in the analysis of weather events. This approach allows for a more nuanced and accurate understanding of the complex and varied nature of severe weather events. Our study applied Bi-LSTM on integrated datasets for rare event detection, notably outperforming other models by employing the focal loss function to prioritize infrequent classes, marking an improvement over the traditional loss function. Additionally, our study employs analysis of severe local weather events for better understanding. It includes event narrative analysis for extracting meaningful information from textual event structures and flow, aiding in predictions and event sequencing. Moreover, we use BERT for assessing the effectiveness of external event text before integration, yielding promising results that strengthen its combination with weather data.

3 Datasets

3.1 Weather Data and Severe Weather-Related Events

The weather dataset used in our study spans five years (2018–2022), collected from ASOS stations across the U.S., and reported at 1-minute and 5-minute intervals. Preprocessing includes cleaning, handling missing values through imputation or removal, normalizing to a standard range for model efficiency, and aggregating data hourly for disruptive event prediction. Weather variables include temperature, humidity, wind speed, and proximity to events. The collected dataset comprises historical weather data from 205 weather stations (134 in AK, 22 in NV, and 49 in PA) as shown in Fig. 2, spanning from 2018 to 2022. It encompasses different weather variables recorded over time. Despite the vast amount of data, some severe weather-related disruptive events do not exist in consecutive years, adding challenges to understanding the long-term temporal dependence.

3.2 Events Log

Severe weather has caused widespread disruptions across diverse climates. The Storm Events Database, managed by the National Centers for Environmental Information (NCEI), provides a log of severe weather-related disruptive incident [11]. A few examples of event logs with the respective event type are illustrated in Table 1. By integrating local weather data and relevant texts with expert insights through a multi-modal strategy, we can predict and prepare for severe weather disruptions. This approach allows for proactive disaster preparedness, potentially reducing the impact of such events.

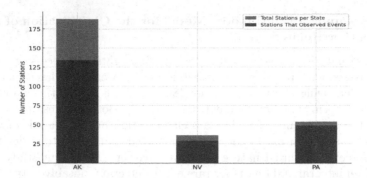

Fig. 2. Weather-related disruptions were observed at a fraction of locations across AK, NV, and PA.

Table 1. Examples of episode narratives describing the impact of severe weather-related disruptive events in Alaska

Episode Narrative	Event
Around 2 in. of snow fell, including near West Sadsbury and West Caln	Winter weather
An ice jam formed on the Kobuk River below Kobuk on May 18th, 2023	Flood
Significant snow fell along the north slopes of the Brooks Range from the Dalton Highway eastward. The University of Alaska Toolik Field Camp SNOTEL reported 13 in. of snow in less than 24 h and the Alaska DOT reported very poor driving conditions along the Dalton Highway	Astronomical low tide

4 Background

Weather stations often contain gaps in information due to two main issues: missing data and the rare occurrence of certain severe weather events. This section explores these challenges in greater detail. We distinguish three types of scenarios:

Scenario 1: The weather dataset contains recordings of infrequent but highly disruptive weather events, such as astronomical low tides, illustrated in the left panel Fig. 3.

Scenario 2: There are also records of disruptive weather events that are overall infrequent but are more common at specific locations. One such example is avalanche, illustrated in the middle panel of Fig. 3.

Scenario 3: The weather dataset also contains records of disruptive weather events that are more frequent at a larger region, such as blizzards as shown in the

Astronomical Low Tide
(A severe infrequent event)

Avalanche
(A severe less infrequent event)

Blizzard
(A severe frequent event)

Fig. 3. Examples of rare, infrequent, and frequent severe weather-related disrup- tions in Alaska.

right panel of Fig. 3. We address the challenge of learning rare types of events by collecting and processing data across longer time and space shown in Fig. 5. This strategy improves data availability for infrequent events, enabling more accurate predictions and analyses by covering a broader spectrum of occurrences.

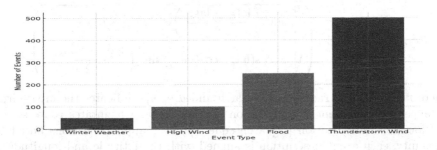

Fig. 4. Frequency of four severe weather-related events over one year (2018) across AK, NV, and PA.

5   Methodology

5.1   Feature Extraction from Weather Stations

We preprocessed weather variables into a vector of explanatory features con- sisting of temporal features (temperature, relative humidity, precipitation wind speed, and dew point), and static features (longitude, latitude, nearest weather station and distance from the station). Temporal features were constructed by considering lagged variables to encapsulate weather conditions leading up to a severe event, providing context and historical perspective for the model's pre- dictions. Statistical summaries for each variable were constructed by computing the mean, maximum, minimum, and standard deviation of weather variables over specific periods. The variability and severe values of weather conditions are captured, enriching the input space with valuable information. The mapping

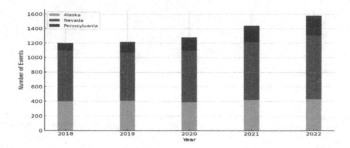

Fig. 5. Frequency of severe weather-related disruptive events in five years across AK, NV and PA.

function M: E -> S is used to assign each event to the nearest weather station. This mapping is determined by the Haversine formula, which approximates the geodesic distance d between the location of event e_i and station s_j:

$$d(e_i, s_j) = 2r \arcsin \left(\sqrt{ \sin^2 \left(\frac{\text{lat}_{e_i} - \text{lat}_{s_j}}{2} \right) + \cos(\text{lat}_{e_i}) \cos(\text{lat}_{s_j}) \sin^2 \left(\frac{\text{lon}_{e_i} - \text{lon}_{s_j}}{2} \right) } \right) \quad (1)$$

where r signifies the radius of the Earth and $d(e_i, s_j)$ indicates the great-circle distance between event e_i and station s_j, this formula facilitates route search and location identification [17]. Consequently, by mapping locations based on proximity, each event description is aligned with the latitude and longitude of the nearest weather station. This approach measures event proximity to weather stations, enhancing the model's emphasis on relevant data.

Additionally, we normalized the features separately and encoded the labels accordingly. For the spatial features encompassing event and station latitude/longitude, we implemented scaler transformation to derive representative values for the geographical locations. This procedure was also extended to weather features and the event distance to the nearest weather station, to ensure consistency across our dataset.

5.2 Feature Extraction from Disruption Narrative

In analyzing disruptive events narratives, we use BERT since it is well known for its capability to grasp context and subtlety in natural language [1]. By fine-tuning BERT using labeled datasets, our goal is to refine its parameters, thereby decreasing classification errors and boosting its capability to accurately analyze complex narratives. This process was applied to datasets for each climate AK, NV, and PA prior to integrating such a knowledge representation with the weather recordings dataset.

Described mulit-modal data is concatenated to integrate diverse features, including spatial, temporal, and event embeddings. This integration was performed after addressing missing values. After normalization, we adopted late fusion as discussed in Subsect. 5.3 to boost our LSTM-based model's performance.

5.3   Concatenation Procedure

Text embeddings were integrated with feature sequences before being passed for training the model, providing a fuller input representation. By combining numerical and contextual embeddings before learning starts, our model gains from a more integrated context. This approach improves joint learning from various data types, leading to a more unified grasp of severe weather-related events. The integration of sequential data features (X), embedding features (E), and labels (Y) in a mathematical way, we represent as $W_t = [w_{t,1}, \ldots, w_{t,n}]$, with $n = m + k + p$ representing the total feature count post-concatenation.

$$W_t = [x_{t,1}, \ldots, x_{t,m}, e_{t,1}, \ldots, e_{t,k}, y_{t,1}, \ldots, y_{t,p}]$$

where:

- X_t as the sequential data features at time t, where $X_t = [x_{t,1}, \ldots, x_{t,m}]$ and m represents the number of sequential features.
- At time t, E_t represents the embedding features with $E_t = [e_{t,1}, e_{t,2}, \ldots, e_{t,k}]$ where k is the dimensionality of the embedding features; Y_t denotes the labels with $Y_t = [y_{t,1}, y_{t,2}, \ldots, y_{t,p}]$ and p is the number of label dimensions.

Therefore, the concatenated input W_t consists of the sequential data feature X_t, embedding features E_t, and labels Y_t. This concatenated input W_t with labels is then fed into the disruptive events predictions model.

5.4   Model Architecture

The diagram shown in Fig. 6 illustrates the design of our proposed approach, which incorporates inputs from multiple weather stations and informative text over time. The proposed LSTM model processes batches of 8 samples each to update its internal parameters, utilizing a dropout rate of 0.5 after each LSTM layer to prevent overfitting. The model architecture includes bidirectional LSTM layers with 100 and 200 units, supplemented by a tanh-activated dense layer and a softmax output layer, to capture complex temporal dependencies within the integrate data. The rationale for selecting bidirectional LSTMs is to improve the understanding of sequence data by processing it from both directions. This dual-direction approach allows the model to capture context from both the past and the future in a given sequence and is relatively more efficient in terms of memory and computation compared to Transformer-based models. Transformer-based models can be computationally expensive, especially for long sequences,

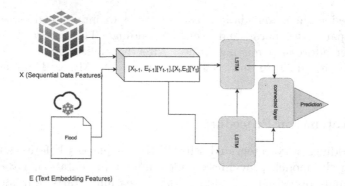

Fig. 6. Methodology for forecasting disruptions risk using integrated local weather data records and narratives containing expert insights.

due to the self-attention mechanism. The proposed approach for multimodal data integration is defined as follows:

$$y = \text{softmax}\left(D\left(\text{Dropout}\left(\text{Concat}\left(LSTM_{\text{fw}}\left(X_{\text{seq}}\right), LSTM_{\text{bw}}\left(X_{\text{seq}}\right)\right)\right)\right)\right) \quad (2)$$

where:

- X_{seq} represents the input sequences created from combining normalized features X_{norm} and embeddings X_{embed}.
- $LSTM_{\text{fw}}$ and $LSTM_{\text{bw}}$ denote the forward and backward Long Short-Term Memory operations, respectively.
- Concat refers to the concatenation of the outputs from $LSTM_{\text{fw}}$ and $LSTM_{\text{bw}}$.
- Dropout is applied for regularization, and D represents the dense layers, with the final layer utilizing a softmax function to predict the output y.

Several studies have demonstrated the effectiveness of highlighting strategies to combat class imbalance and overfitting. These strategies include the use of multi-class focal loss and the integration of multi-resolution feature maps from various aerial sources [12]. In this model, we adapt the focal loss function to pay more attention to classes that are hard to classify, as defined.

$$FL(p_t) = -\alpha_t(1 - p_t)^\gamma \log(p_t)$$

Focal loss which consists of gamma (γ) and alpha (α), enhances sensitivity to minority classes by adjusting loss for hard-to-classify examples. In large, diverse datasets, the choice between default loss and Focal Loss, along with model architecture, is critical due to imbalanced frequencies across time and space.

5.5   Evaluation Process

Our method for analyzing severe weather disruptions combines historical weather data with event descriptions from nearby weather stations. By integrating spatial and textual information, we aim to enhance weather prediction and description of disruptions. This multimodal approach is designed to offer a detailed and comprehensive model for accurately forecasting weather-related events. The proposed model is evaluated using real-world data collected over five years in AK, PA, and NV, including local weather information and descriptions of disruptive events. All models are trained on data from years 2018 to 2021 and evaluated on year 2022 data to prevent information leakage. The evaluation is based on measuring macro F1 score when predicting categories of severe weather-related disruptive events across 12, and 24-hour time horizons.

The macro average is essential for rare event prediction models because it ensures that the performance on rare classes is not ignored in the evaluation process [6], it measures the reliability of the model's predictions for severe weather conditions, showing the percentage of accurate forecasts among all the predicted events. Macro-Average F1-score (F_{macro}) is defined as follow:

$$F_{\mathrm{macro}} = \frac{1}{C} \sum_{i=1}^{C} F_i \tag{3}$$

where F_i is the F1-score associated with class i, and C indicates the overall number of classes.

Environment- Data preprocessing and experiments were conducted on a 64-bit processor, an Intel Xeon(R) Gold CPU @ 2.10 GHz with forty cores and 64.0 GB RAM. As for the platform, we employed TensorFlow, one of the most widely used deep learning libraries, to predict severe weather-related disruptions across various time horizons. The model was trained using a learning rate of 0.001 and up to 100 epochs.

6   Results

The initial experiments of our study evaluated the effectiveness of the proposed models, namely Bi-LSTM-AK -Floss (model trained using focal loss) and Bi-LSTM-AK- Closs (model trained on default loss). These models were evaluated in comparison to baseline models. Table 2 presents the outcomes of event predictions with forecast decisions made 12 and 24 h before severe weather events are reported in Alaska. As reported in Table 2, Baseline Model 1 and Model 2 are trained using unimodal (weather data alone) utilizing default and focal loss, respectively. These baseline models, utilizing unimodal data, exhibited inferior performance compared to models that leverage multimodal data sources.

The Bi-LSTM-AK-2 -Floss multimodal model, which utilizes multimodal data and focal loss, was the most effective, slightly outperforming the Bi-LSTM-AK-1 with default loss which uses multimodal data with the default loss. Baseline Model 3, trained with limited multimodal data (one year vs three years) and the use of focal loss, showed much better predictive performance as compared to Models 1 and 2. Building on this, the consistent outperformance of LSTM-AK-Floss and Bi- LSTM-AK-default-loss models over the baseline models, regardless of the loss function used, shows the advanced capability of multi-modal data integration and larger training data in refining the accuracy of event forecasts 12 h and 24 h in future, as reported at Table 2.

Table 2. Macro-average F1 score the proposed BiLSTM models vs. alternatives when predicting events 12 h and 24 h in future (F1-12H and F1-24H) on unseen year 2022 data in Alaska. Note: focal loss (i.e. F-loss) default loss(i.e. D-loss).

Early Multi-modal Data Fusion	F1-12 H	F1-24 H
Bi-LSTM-AK-2 with F-loss trained on larger multimodal data	0.79	**0.78**
Bi-LSTM-AK-1 with D-loss trained on larger multimodal data	0.79	0.77
Baseline Model 3 trained on less multimodal data using F-loss	0.73	0.68
Baseline Model 2 trained on unimodal weather data with F-loss	0.64	0.70
Baseline Model 1 trained on unimodal weather data alone	0.28	0.28

Next, we evaluate our proposed model architecture for the states of Pennsylvania and Nevada. For each of the states, we train the proposed BiLSTM model with focal loss and report results in Table 3. The Alaska (AK) model, with five classes, exhibits a solid performance with a precision of 0.85 and a recall of 0.80, resulting in an F1-score of 0.77. Alaska model's lower performance can be attributed to the distance between stations in Alaska. The stations in Alaska are more spread out and therefore, have more distance between them unlike Nevada in Pennsylvania, where the stations are more densely packed and situated near to each other. The Nevada (NV) model, encompassing a more complex model with nine classes, demonstrates balanced precision and recall, both at 0.86, and achieves an F1-score of 0.84. Remarkably, the Pennsylvania (PA) model, with four classes, outperforms the others by achieving near-perfect precision at 0.96 and recall at 0.98, which results in an impressive F1-score of 0.97.

Table 3. Comparison of 24 h ahead predictive performance of the BiLSTM model with focal loss on unseen year 2022 in AK, NV, and PA. In reported experiments expert narratives on the observed events were missing for the most recent 12 h and for the most recent 24 h.

State	Precision	Recall	F1-Score
AK (5 classes)	0.85	0.80	0.77
NV (9 classes)	0.86	0.86	0.84
PA (4 classes)	0.96	0.98	0.97

The objective of our next experiments was to evaluate the benefits of the proposed model when the updated narratives containing expert insights on observed events are not available at the prediction time, but such information from several hours earlier exists. Such scenarios are quite common during severe weather and the question we study is if useful early warnings for approaching disruptions could be learned even in such conditions based on partial information. Therefore, we conducted further experiments to evaluate the model's effectiveness in situations where the availability of textual narratives about the event is obstructed by storms or other incidents, leading to missing expert narratives about such events. Table 4 show macro-averaged F1 scores along with precision and recall for ahead prediction horizons without the most recent 12 (F1-12H) and 24-hour (F1-24) data, assessed on unseen 2022 data. It shows that the model's predictive accuracy declines when less recent data is used, with PA achieving the highest F1 score at a 12-hour horizon and all locations showing reduced scores at a 24-hour horizon. The results provide evidence that the model's predictive accuracy declines when less recent data is used for forecasting, but quality of the risk models was still useful with PA achieving the highest F1 score of 0.83 at a 12-hour horizon and all locations showing reduced scores at a 24-hour horizon.

Table 4. Macro-average metrics-based results of the BiLSTM model with focal loss for AK, PA, and NV models evaluated on unseen data from the year 2022.

States	12 h			24 h		
	Precision	Recall	F1-Score	Precision	Recall	F1-Score
AK	0.73	0.71	0.67	0.57	0.65	0.60
NV	0.80	0.77	0.78	0.69	0.67	0.67
PA	0.83	0.85	0.84	0.74	0.75	0.74

Next, we check the efficacy of the model in term of severity prediction (refer to Fig. 7). For all three state models, the predictions are grouped in three risk level categories (high-risk for probability greater that 0.7, medium-risk for probability between 0.3 an 0.7, and low-risk for probability less than 0.3). In this grouping the high-risk category includes 2,738 hourly events in a single year (710 for AK, 1173 for NV and 855 for PA). Next, we measure the F1-score for these groups. As visualized in Fig. 7, for PA and NV, we see a clear decline in F1 score as risk prediction decreases which is expected because the assumption is that when the model predicts low-risk, the event is less likely to happen as compared to high-risk prediction. This shows that model is able to differentiate between high-risk and low-risk events successfully. Note that in Alaska, we see that F1 score for medium-risk events is actually slightly higher than for high-risk events and this suggests that the quality of the data with medium-risk is better for AK than at other states. In summation, these results suggest that the approach proposed in our study could be beneficial for developing more confident early warning systems for approaching weather- related disruptions.

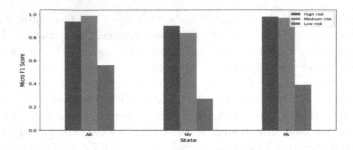

Fig. 7. Risk estimation for severe weather-related events across AK, NV, and PA by the BiLSTM model.

7 Conclusions

The unpredictability of severe weather-related disruptive events underscores the crucial need for more accurate predictions to aid in monitoring and pre- preparedness efforts. This study has contributed a novel approach to forecasting disruptive events that outperforms considered alternatives by integrating weather data and expert narratives describing observed events. One drawback of our approach is its reliance on event logs for prediction. If event logs are absent due to typical weather conditions, the model needs to rely on older narratives, which we showed in this study, could also be quite useful. Alternatively, the model can adopt an unimodal approach and utilize a weather-dependent model after applying feature engineering. Additionally, the model can leverage real-time social media data in conjunction with historical weather data to predict severe weather events, as demonstrated in our previous work [15]. Our method enhances server event prediction by integrating weather measurements from multiple locations, as well as textual descriptions of such events, to account for the intricate dynamics across three different climates. For future research, avenues include exploring spatial correlation and incorporating additional data sources to further enhance predictive capabilities. Future research aimed at analyzing severe weather events and their relation to climate change can benefit from collecting and examining data on these events over time.

Acknowledgements. This research was sponsored by the U. S. Army Engineer Research and Development Center (ERDC) and was accomplished under Cooperative Agreement Number W9132V-23-2-0002. The views and conclusions contained in this document are those of the authors and should not be interpreted as representing the official policies, either expressed or implied, of the U.S. Army Research Engineer and Development Center (ERDC) or the U.S. Government. During this work, Mr. H. Otudi was funded by the College of Computer Science and Information Technology at Jazan University in Saudi Arabia.

References

1. Chanda, A.K.: Efficacy of BERT embeddings on predicting disaster from Twitter data. arXiv preprint arXiv:2108.10698 (2021)
2. Dai, A., Karl, T.R., Sun, B., Trenberth, K.E.: Recent trends in cloudiness over the United States: a tale of monitoring inadequacies. Bull. Am. Meteorol. Soc. **87**(5), 597–606 (2006)
3. Frame, J.M., Kratzert, F., Klotz, D., Gauch, M., Shalev, G., Gilon, O., Qualls, L.M., Gupta, H.V., Nearing, G.S.: Deep learning rainfall-runoff predictions of extreme events. Hydrol. Earth Syst. Sci. **26**(13), 3377–3392 (2022)
4. Free, M., Sun, B.: Time-varying biases in us total cloud cover data. J. Atmos. Oceanic Technol. **30**(12), 2838–2849 (2013)
5. Frew, E.W., Elston, J., Argrow, B., Houston, A., Rasmussen, E.: Sampling severe local storms and related phenomena: using unmanned aircraft systems. IEEE Robot. Autom. Mag. **19**(1), 85–95 (2012)
6. Gowda, T., You, W., Lignos, C., May, J.: Macro-average: rare types are important too. arXiv preprint arXiv:2104.05700 (2021)
7. Gultepe, I., et al.: A review of high impact weather for aviation meteorology. Pure Appl. Geophys. **176**, 1869–1921 (2019)
8. Hasan, N., Uddin, M.T., Chowdhury, N.K.: Automated weather event analysis with machine learning. In: 2016 International Conference on Innovations in Science, Engineering and Technology (ICISET), pp. 1–5. IEEE (2016)
9. de Lima, G.R.T., Stephany, S.: A new classification approach for detecting severe weather patterns. Comput. Geosci. **57**, 158–165 (2013)
10. Matsueda, M., Nakazawa, T.: Early warning products for severe weather events derived from operational medium-range ensemble forecasts. Meteorol. Appl. **22**(2), 213–222 (2015)
11. National Centers for Environmental Information: National centers for environmental information homepage (2024). https://www.ncei.noaa.gov. Accessed 21 Feb 2024
12. Nemoto, K., Hamaguchi, R., Imaizumi, T., Hikosaka, S.: Classification of rare building change using CNN with multi-class focal loss. In: IGARSS 2018-2018 IEEE International Geoscience and Remote Sensing Symposium, pp. 4663–4666. IEEE (2018)
13. Niu, Z., Yu, Z., Tang, W., Wu, Q., Reformat, M.: Wind power forecasting using attention-based gated recurrent unit network. Energy **196**, 117081 (2020)
14. Olteanu, A., Castillo, C., Diaz, F., Kıcıman, E.: Social data: biases, methodological pitfalls, and ethical boundaries. Front. Big Data **2**, 13 (2019)
15. Otudi, H., Gupta, S., Albarakati, N., Obradovic, Z.: Classifying severe weather events by utilizing social sensor data and social network analysis. In: Proceedings of the 2023 IEEE/ACM International Conference on Advances in Social Networks Analysis and Mining. Kusadasi, Turkey (November 2023, in press)
16. Powell, M.D.: Wind measurement and archival under the automated surface observing system (ASOS): user concerns and opportunity for improvement. Bull. Am. Meteorol. Soc. **74**(4), 615–624 (1993)
17. Prasetya, D.A., Nguyen, P.T., Faizullin, R., Iswanto, I., Armay, E.F.: Resolving the shortest path problem using the haversine algorithm. J. Crit. Rev. **7**(1), 62–64 (2020)
18. Schroeter, S., et al.: Forecasting the impacts of severe weather. Aust. J. Emerg. Manag. **36**(1), 76–83 (2021)

19. de Souza, C.V.F., Barcellos, P.D.C.L., Crissaff, L., Cataldi, M., Miranda, F., Lage, M.: Visualizing simulation ensembles of extreme weather events. Comput. Graph. **104**, 162–172 (2022)

20. Sparkman, R.M.: Regional geography, the overlooked sampling variable in advertising content analysis. J. Curr. Issues Res. Advert. **18**, 53–57 (1996). https://api.semanticscholar.org/CorpusID:129491273

21. Styve, L., Navarra, C., Petersen, J.M., Neset, T.S., Vrotsou, K.: A visual analytics pipeline for the identification and exploration of extreme weather events from social media data. Climate **10**(11), 174 (2022)

22. Sun, B.: Cloudiness over the contiguous united states: contemporary changes observed using ground-based and ISCCP D2 data. Geophys. Res. Lett. **30**(2) (2003)

23. Wang, L., Tao, R., Hu, H., Zeng, Y.R.: Effective wind power prediction using novel deep learning network: stacked independently recurrent autoencoder. Renew. Energy **164**, 642–655 (2021)

24. Yu, R., et al.: Scene learning: deep convolutional networks for wind power prediction by embedding turbines into grid space. Appl. Energy **238**, 249–257 (2019)

25. Zhu, R., Liao, W., Wang, Y.: Short-term prediction for wind power based on temporal convolutional network. Energy Rep. **6**, 424–429 (2020)

Machine Learning-Based Detection and Classification of Neurodevelopmental Disorders from Speech Patterns

El Omari Mouad$^{(\boxtimes)}$ (ID), Belmajdoub Hanae (ID), and Minaoui Khalid (ID)

LRIT Laboratory, Faculty of Sciences in Rabat, Mohammed V University, Rabat, Morocco

{mouad.elomari,k.minaoui}@um5r.ac.ma, hanae_belmajdoub@um5.ac.ma

Abstract. Neurodevelopmental disorders represent a significant global health challenge due to their widespread prevalence and profound impact on individual lives. The conventional diagnostic process, reliant on behavioral observations and clinical assessments, is often time-intensive and fraught with limitations. This article delves into an approach, utilizing voice and speech analysis for the identification of neurodevelopmental disorders, promising to enhance diagnostic efficiency, reduce costs, and improve patient outcomes. Our research focuses on employing machine learning techniques to create an automated system capable of early disorder detection based on vocal characteristics. We tested multiple classifiers, among which Random Forests and Decision Trees emerged as the most effective, each achieving an accuracy of 82%. This study not only underscores the potential of machine learning in medical diagnostics but also paves the way for more accessible and efficient screening methods for neurodevelopmental disorders.

Keywords: neurodevelopmental disorders · voice · speech · machine learning

1 Introduction

Neurodevelopmental disorders (NDDs) present a spectrum of cognitive, behavioral, and neurological challenges stemming from atypical brain development. These disorders cover various conditions such as Attention Deficit Hyperactivity Disorder (ADHD), cerebral palsy, and a range of learning disorders, each characterized by complex causes that can include genetic factors interacting with environmental elements [1]. This broad category encapsulates diverse manifestations and etiologies, highlighting the intricate nature of brain development and its susceptibility to numerous influences.

The conventional detection and diagnosis of NDDs have historically relied on a combination of behavioral observation and a suite of medical and psychological assessments [2]. While these traditional approaches have provided foundational insights, they are hampered by inherent subjectivity, prohibitively high

L. Iliadis et al. (Eds.): EANN 2024, CCIS 2141, pp. 235–246, 2024.
https://doi.org/10.1007/978-3-031-62495-7_18

costs, extensive time requirements, and uneven global accessibility, which in turn intensify the disparities in diagnosis and treatment across different populations.

The advent of Artificial Intelligence (AI) presents a transformative potential in the realm of NDD identification, leveraging machine learning and deep learning techniques to surpass the aforementioned constraints of conventional methods. Pioneering research has already begun to harness advanced computational models, utilizing modalities such as neuroimaging [3], quantitative eye movement analysis [4], and nuanced analysis of speech prosody to identify and categorize NDDs with increasing precision. Characteristic speech anomalies observed in affected children ranging from atypical articulation patterns to distinctive prosodic features such as unusual intonation, rhythm, and phonation can serve as salient biomarkers for early detection [5–9].

One study [10] undertook a comprehensive critique of prosody within the context of ADHD, scrutinizing a corpus of 16 studies published between 1980 and 2002. The findings, albeit inconsistent, underscored the scarcity of focused research and provided a critical impetus for subsequent, more granular investigations into the prosodic variances exhibited by children with ADHD.

The research by [11] explores machine learning for diagnosing neurodevelopmental disorders, notably Autism Spectrum Disorder (ASD) and Parkinson's, by analyzing vocal characteristics. Examining children aged 9 to 18, the study gauges features like pitch and voice quality. Advanced models led to a 2.3% boost in ASD detection and a 2.8% improvement in classification, underscoring the value of acoustic analysis in diagnosis.

Furthering this line of inquiry, another study [12] explored the utility of domestic audio recordings, analyzed through a machine learning framework, to discern early signs of developmental disorders. Employing the innovative "Guess What?" mobile application, researchers amassed a sizable dataset comprising 77 video recordings from 58 children. The analytical models deployed-ranging from random forest classifiers to convolutional neural networks, and even the more sophisticated wav2vec 2.0-demonstrated predictive accuracies as high as 79.3%, showcasing the potential of AI in early-stage screening for developmental disorders.

Highlighting the nuanced complexities of speech in neurodevelopmental disorders, [13] conducted a thorough analysis on a corpus of Italian-speaking children with autism. The study compiled 28 audio files, balanced between autistic children and controls, aged 6 to 10. Leveraging the openSMILE tool with the eGeMAPS feature set, researchers extracted 88 acoustic features and rigorously selected the most statistically significant through the Mann-Whitney U test. For feature validation, four machine learning algorithms were employed, with decision trees, random forests, and support vector machines showcasing an impressive accuracy of 83%. These encouraging outcomes suggest the potential for early diagnostic tools in identifying neurodevelopmental disorders.

Moreover, a subsequent investigation [14] criticized the utilization of traditional predefined features in speech-based identification of developmental disorders, recommending instead the implementation of knowledge-driven speech features combined with SVM classifiers. This shift resulted in a noteworthy enhancement in detection accuracy, achieving a notable rate of 91.25%. However, the study also brought to light the challenge of classification bias arising from the size and distribution of the sample, underscoring the imperative for larger and more diverse datasets to effectively train robust AI systems.

The [15] study utilized machine learning with the SmartSpeech biometric dataset to identify neurodevelopmental disorders (NDs) in children, blending speech and language responses with biometric measures like eye tracking and heart rate. A variety of algorithms were employed, with a Grammatical Evolution variant (GenClass) showing promise, enhancing ND identification accuracy and providing significant clinical diagnostic support.

Our study contributes to this field by developing and refining an AI-based methodology for nuanced NDD detection and classification using speech sample analysis. Our approach is to integrate sophisticated speech and voice analysis techniques with state-of-the-art machine learning models. The aim is to provide an accessible, accurate, and non-invasive diagnostic tool. We will detail our methodology, from the construction of a small speech database to the meticulous extraction and selection of phonetic and prosodic features, the deployment of advanced classification algorithms, and the implementation of rigorous evaluation measures to validate our models.

In the subsequent sections of the article, we will delve into the intricate system architecture of our AI models, thoroughly discuss the empirical results obtained from our research, and provide a critical analysis of the study's strengths and potential limitations. Finally, we will outline prospective research avenues, envisioning future enhancements in the diagnosis and understanding of neurodevelopmental disorders.

2   Methodology

In this section, we will present our proposed approach to identify neurodevelopmental disorders using machine learning. This approach involves several essential steps, as illustrated in Fig. 1. A detailed analysis of each phase of our methodology will be presented in the following sections:

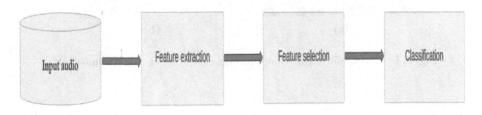

Fig. 1. Sequence of steps to train a machine learning model

2.1 Database

The dataset utilized in this research comprises speech audio recordings from children aged 4 to 10 years. It includes 54 distinct speech samples, evenly distributed between two cohorts: one consisting of individuals with various neurodevelopmental disorders and the other of typically developing children. These recordings were collected in a clinical setting, providing a standardized context for the assessment of communication and social behaviors associated with neurodevelopmental disorders. Each audio file was digitized at 16-bit resolution and sampled at a 44.1 kHz rate. These recordings encompass a wide range of speech characteristics, such as tone, pitch, and speech patterns, thus facilitating a comprehensive and nuanced analysis. The dataset is pivotal in both training and validating machine learning models designed for the early detection and classification of neurodevelopmental disorders. The durations of these recordings range between 19 to 29 s, providing extensive auditory data for in-depth analysis of vocal interactions within these groups. Additionally, we offer a visual representation of the distinct vocal characteristics of children with neurodevelopmental disorders in comparison to their typically developing peers. This is achieved by presenting spectrograms in Fig. 2. These spectrograms are crucial in enabling a detailed examination of specific acoustic features, including tone, pitch, and speech patterns. By providing a thorough graphical perspective, they facilitate comparative analysis and enhance the understanding of the subtle differences in speech interactions between the two cohorts of children. It is important to note that this dataset is private, in order to maintain the confidentiality of the participants.

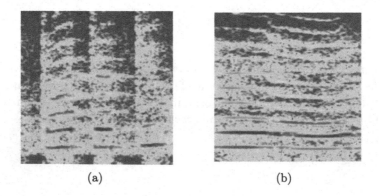

(a)   (b)

Fig. 2. Spectrogram of (a): Neurodevelopmental child (b): Normal child

2.2 Feature Extraction

In our research, we utilized openSMILE version 2.1, a tool specifically developed for the Interspeech challenge, as documented in [16]. This open-source software is extensively employed for extracting vocal features from audio signals, offering a wide array of capabilities for voice analysis. Its applications span various fields, including speech recognition, emotion detection, and voice classification. Among its feature sets are GeMAPS (Geneva Minimalistic Acoustic Parameter Set), eGeMAPS, and ComParE [17,18]. We selected eGeMAPS for its specific design aimed at paralinguistic and clinical speech analysis.

Our choice of eGeMAPS over other options was guided by several considerations. We avoided ComParE due to its extensive feature space (n = 6376), which could lead to overfitting in our machine learning models given our dataset's size-a scenario we aimed to prevent. Contrarily, we preferred eGeMAPS over GeMAPS, as the former includes features linked to psychological changes in vocal production [17]. This approach has demonstrated effectiveness in prior studies [19–25]. In our study, we extracted 88 acoustic features, focusing on key aspects like frequency, energy, amplitude, and their distribution across the spectrum.

2.3   Feature Selection

In machine learning, the inclusion of irrelevant features can adversely affect model accuracy. To address this, we applied the Mann-Whitney U test, also known as the Mann-Whitney-Wilcoxon test or Wilcoxon U test [26,27]. This non-parametric statistical test is ideal for comparing two independent groups to ascertain if they originate from the same population or if their distributions significantly differ. It is particularly effective with non-normal data distributions or small sample sizes. The test assesses whether one group's values are systematically higher or lower than the other's.

We employed this test to analyze the feature distributions of two sample groups: children with neurodevelopmental disorders and typically developing children, using the eGeMAPS parameter set. Our objective was to identify features with significantly different distributions between the groups, aiding in the classification of children with neurodevelopmental disorders.

The test revolves around two central hypotheses: the null hypothesis (H0) and the alternative hypothesis (H1).

Null Hypothesis (H0): This assumes no significant difference in the tested feature between the groups, implying the samples derive from the same population or observed differences are random.

Alternative Hypothesis (H1): This posits significant distribution differences in the tested feature between the groups, indicating the samples do not originate from the same population, and observed differences are statistically significant.

For our analysis, we calculated two critical parameters: the test statistic **U test**, reflecting the difference between the groups' average ranks, and the **p-value**, indicating the probability of the observed group differences occurring by chance. These parameters are crucial for deciding whether to accept or reject H0 in favor of H1.

1. **High Test Statistic, Low p-value ($p < 0.05$):** This suggests statistically significant differences between the groups, leading to the rejection of H0 in favor of H1.
2. **High Test Statistic, High p-value ($p > 0.05$):** Although the test statistic is high, the high p-value indicates insufficient evidence to reject H0. Observed differences could be random.
3. **Low Test Statistic, Low p-value:** This combination implies the groups' differences are not statistically significant, and H0 cannot be rejected due to weak evidence for H1.
4. **Low Test Statistic, High p-value:** Here, both low values suggest the groups' differences are not statistically significant, leading to insufficient evidence to reject H0.

Ultimately, this rigorous analytical approach enabled us to identify 15 acoustic features with significant differences between the two groups. These findings are essential for classifying children with neurodevelopmental disorders in comparison to typically developing children.

2.4   Classification

In our study, we initially employed a range of supervised machine learning methods, including Decision Trees (DT), k-Nearest Neighbors (KNN), Random Forests (RF), and Support Vector Machines (SVM), each chosen for their specific strengths in classification and regression tasks. Figure 3 provides an overview of the method proposed in this study.

- **Decision Trees**: DTs are a type of supervised learning algorithm, primarily used for classification tasks. In a decision tree, each internal node represents a test on an attribute, branches represent outcomes of these tests, and leaf nodes hold class labels. The structure is akin to an organizational chart [28].
- **k-Nearest Neighbors**: KNN is a fundamental supervised learning method, applicable for both classification and regression. It operates on the principle that similar data points are proximal to each other. The choice of 'K', the number of nearest neighbors, is crucial for minimizing prediction error. KNN typically uses Euclidean distance to measure similarity between data points [29].
- **Random Forests**: RF improves classification accuracy by constructing an ensemble of decision trees and aggregating their predictions. This method enhances predictive accuracy and prevents overfitting by subsampling the dataset for each tree in the ensemble [30].
- **Support Vector Machines** : SVMs are versatile, capable of linear and non-linear classification, regression, and outlier detection. They are particularly effective for complex datasets of small to medium size. SVMs function by finding the optimal hyperplane that maximizes the margin between different classes [31].

The mathematical representation of the SVM model can be expressed as:

$$\widehat{y} = \Theta_0 + \Theta_1 \times X_1 + \Theta_2 \times X_2 + \ldots + \Theta_n \times X_n \tag{1}$$

where: $\hat{y}$ is the predicted output, Θ_0 are the model parameters, and $\times X_i$ are the feature values.

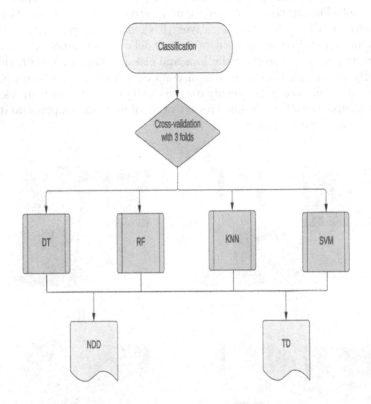

Fig. 3. The architecture used in this study

Prior to applying these methods, we meticulously preprocessed the data, which involved feature selection and normalization, to ensure the data was optimally formatted for effective model training.

We then adopted a stratified k-fold cross-validation approach with k = 3 for training our models, a strategy that not only enhances the robustness of our models by mitigating overfitting risks but also ensures comprehensive learning from the data. This process was executed by dividing our dataset, with an 80%-20% split between the training and testing sets, respectively.

Such a structured approach, from method selection through data preparation to model training, was instrumental in achieving accurate and reliable results, demonstrating the effectiveness of our chosen algorithms in handling the complexities of the dataset.

2.5   Evaluation Metrics

We assessed the performance of our system using key metrics: accuracy, precision, recall, F1 score, and the area under the curve (AUC). Central to our evaluation was the confusion matrix, comprising true positives (TP), true negatives (TN), false positives (FP), and false negatives (FN). This matrix was instrumental in providing a detailed assessment of our model's performance, enabling us to differentiate between correct predictions and classification errors effectively (see Fig. 4). By leveraging these metrics, in conjunction with the confusion matrix analysis, we could accurately evaluate our system's proficiency in identifying different sample classes, including the detection of neurodevelopmental disorders and other classification tasks.

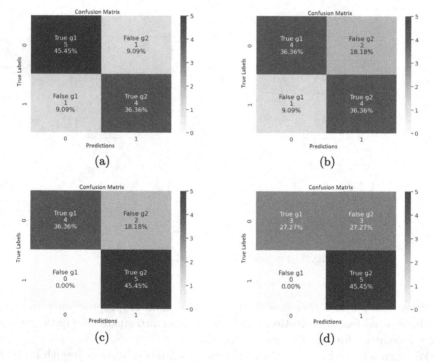

Fig. 4. Confusion matrix for (a): DT (b): KNN (c): RF (d): SVM

The metrics were defined as follows:

- **Accuracy**: The proportion of true results (both true positives and true negatives) in the total data set, calculated as:

$$\text{Accuracy} = \frac{\text{TP} + \text{TN}}{\text{TP} + \text{TN} + \text{FP} + \text{FN}} \tag{2}$$

- **Precision**: The ratio of true positives to all positive results, reflecting the model's ability to identify only relevant instances, expressed as:

$$\text{Precision} = \frac{\text{TP}}{\text{TP} + \text{FP}} \tag{3}$$

- **Recall**: Also known as sensitivity, it measures the proportion of actual positives correctly identified, formulated as:

$$\text{Recall} = \frac{\text{TP}}{\text{TP} + \mathbf{FN}} \tag{4}$$

- **F1 Score**: The harmonic mean of precision and recall, providing a balance between the two, calculated by:

$$\text{F1 Score} = 2 \cdot \frac{\text{Precision} \times \text{Recall}}{\text{Precision} + \text{Recall}} \tag{5}$$

- **AUC**: Represents the area under the ROC curve, a graphical representation of the model's diagnostic ability, denoted as:

$$\text{AUC} = \int_{a}^{b} f(x)\, dx \tag{6}$$

These metrics collectively provided a comprehensive understanding of our system's performance across various aspects of classification accuracy and error sensitivity.

3 Result and Discussion

Our study's results are detailed in Table 1, which presents the performance of the most effective model from each classifier, assessed using various metrics such as accuracy, precision, recall, F1 score, and the AUC. Additionally, the confusion matrices for each classifier are displayed in Fig. 4.

Table 1. Performance models for test data

Methods	Acc (%)	Rec (%)	Prec (%)	F1-sc (%)	AUC (%)
DT	82	80	80	80	82
KNN	73	80	67	73	73
RF	82	100	71	83	83
SVM	73	100	62	77	75

The results, derived from the test set reveals that RF emerge as the most effective model for our dataset. The RF classifier not only achieved a high accuracy rate of 82%, which is indicative of its overall performance, but also demonstrated an outstanding recall of 100%. This recall rate is particularly significant as it reflects the model's capability to flawlessly identify all relevant acoustic features in children with neurodevelopmental disorders. Moreover, with an AUC of 83%, the RF model exhibited superior discriminative ability compared to the other classifiers, effectively distinguishing between neurodevelopmental disorders and typical development.

Although DT displayed a similarly high accuracy rate of 82% and an AUC of 82%, they slightly lagged behind RF in terms of recall, achieving 80%. On the other hand, KNN and SVM models, while presenting certain strengths, fell short in overall performance with lower accuracy rates of 73% and AUC scores of 73% and 75%, respectively.

The outstanding performance of the Random Forests model can be attributed to its ensemble approach, leveraging multiple decision trees to enhance classification accuracy and mitigate overfitting. This characteristic renders RF exceptionally capable of handling the complex and nuanced nature of our dataset, which involves the intricate task of diagnosing neurodevelopmental disorders through speech analysis.

Our findings highlight the superiority of the Random Forests model in addressing the specific challenges posed by our dataset. With its high accuracy, perfect recall, and excellent AUC, RF emerges as the most suitable model among those evaluated for speech-based diagnosis of neurodevelopmental disorders. These insights pave the way for future research and practical applications, suggesting a strong preference for Random Forests in similar tasks.

4   Conclusion and Future Work

In conclusion, this study has demonstrated the potential of machine learning techniques for the detection and classification of neurodevelopmental disorders through speech analysis. Our results indicate that Random Forests are a particularly effective model, achieving high levels of accuracy and recall. The success of these techniques is heavily dependent on precise feature extraction and selection, highlighting the importance of a well-designed preprocessing pipeline.

We acknowledge the limitations posed by the limited size of our dataset and the relatively simple machine learning approaches used. However, this research contributes to the field by offering a new non-invasive diagnostic tool and highlighting the potential of AI in medical diagnostics.

Future work will focus on addressing these limitations by expanding the dataset, possibly through collaboration with other institutions or the collection of additional samples. We also plan to explore more advanced techniques such as deep learning and transfer learning, which have shown promise in other areas of speech analysis. Additionally, we aim to evaluate the generalizability of our model in real-world diagnostic scenarios, ensuring that it can be effectively applied in clinical settings. By pushing the boundaries of our current methodology, we hope to further improve the performance and applicability of our model, ultimately contributing to more accessible and efficient screening methods for neurodevelopmental disorders.

References

1. Thapar, A., Cooper, M., Rutter, M.: Neurodevelopmental disorders: definition, types, causes, symptoms, and treatments. The diamond luxury rehab in Thailand (2023)
2. Sharma, S.R., Gonda, X., Tarazi, F.I.: Autism spectrum disorder: classification, diagnosis and therapy. Pharmacol. Ther. **190**, 1–104 (2018)
3. Khodatars, M., et al.: Deep learning for neuroimaging-based diagnosis and rehabilitation of autism spectrum disorder: a review. Comput. Biol. Med. **139**, 104949 (2021)
4. Liu, W., Li, M., Yi, L.: Identifying children with autism spectrum disorder based on their face processing abnormality: a machine learning framework. Autism Res. **9**(8), 888–898 (2016)
5. Pillai, L.G., Sherly, E.: A deep learning based evaluation of articulation disorder and learning assistive system for autistic children. Int. J. Nat. Lang. Comput. **6**(5), 9–36 (2017)
6. Diehl, J.J., Paul, R.: Acoustic differences in the imitation of prosodic patterns in children with autism spectrum disorders. Res. Autism Spectr. Disord. **6**(1), 123–134 (2012)
7. Fusaroli, R., Lambrechts, A., Bang, D., Bowler, D.M., Gaigg, S.B.: Is voice a marker for autism spectrum disorder? A systematic review and meta-analysis. Autism Res. **10**(3), 384–407 (2017)
8. Lyakso, E., Frolova, O., Grigorev, A.: Perception and acoustic features of speech of children with autism spectrum disorders. In: Karpov, A., Potapova, R., Mporas, I. (eds.) SPECOM 2017. LNCS (LNAI), vol. 10458, pp. 602–612. Springer, Cham (2017). https://doi.org/10.1007/978-3-319-66429-3_60
9. Bone, D., et al.: Spontaneous-speech acoustic-prosodic features of children with autism and the interacting psychologist. In: Thirteenth Annual Conference of the International Speech Communication Association (2012)
10. McCann, J., Peppé, S.: Prosody in autism spectrum disorders: a critical review. Int. J. Lang. Commun. Disord. **38**(4), 325–350 (2003)
11. Pahwa, A., Aggarwal, G., Sharma, A.: A machine learning approach for identification & diagnosing features of neurodevelopmental disorders using speech and spoken sentences. In 2016 International Conference on Computing, Communication and Automation (ICCCA), pp. 377–382. IEEE (2016)
12. Chi, N.A., et al.: Classifying autism from crowdsourced semistructured speech recordings: machine learning model comparison study. JMIR Pediatr. Parent. **5**(2), e35406 (2022)
13. Beccaria, F., Gagliardi, G., Kokkinakis, D.: Extraction and classification of acoustic features from Italian speaking children with autism spectrum disorders. In: Proceedings of the RaPID Workshop-Resources and Processing of Linguistic, Paralinguistic and extra-linguistic Data from People with Various forms of Cognitive/Psychiatric/Developmental Impairments-within the 13th Language Resources and Evaluation Conference, pp. 22–30 (2022)
14. Lee, S., Yeo, E. J., Kim, S., Chung, M., et al.: Knowledge-driven speech features for detection of Korean-speaking children with autism spectrum disorder. Phon. Speech Sci. **15**(2), 53–59 (2023)
15. Toki, E.I., Tatsis, G., Tatsis, V.A., Plachouras, K., Pange, J., Tsoulos, I.G.: Employing classification techniques on smartspeech biometric data towards identification of neurodevelopmental disorders. Signals **4**(2), 401–420 (2023)

16. Schuller, B., et al.: The interspeech 2013 computational paralinguistics challenge: social signals, conflict, emotion, autism. In: Proceedings INTERSPEECH 2013, 14th Annual Conference of the International Speech Communication Association, Lyon, France (2013)

17. Eyben, F., et al.: The geneva minimalistic acoustic parameter set (GeMAPs) for voice research and affective computing. IEEE Trans. Affect. Comput. **7**(2), 190–202 (2015)

18. Schuller, B., et al.: The interspeech 2016 computational paralinguistics challenge: deception, sincerity & native language. In: 17TH Annual Conference of the International Speech Communication Association (Interspeech 2016), Vols. 1–5, vol. 8, pp. 2001–2005. ISCA (2016)

19. Julião, M., Abad, A., Moniz, H.: Comparison of heterogeneous feature sets for intonation verification. In: Quaresma, P., Vieira, R., Aluísio, S., Moniz, H., Batista, F., Gonçalves, T. (eds.) PROPOR 2020. LNCS (LNAI), vol. 12037, pp. 13–22. Springer, Cham (2020). https://doi.org/10.1007/978-3-030-41505-1_2

20. Lee, J.H., Lee, G.W., Bong, G., Yoo, H.J., Kim, H.K.: Deep-learning-based detection of infants with autism spectrum disorder using auto-encoder feature representation. Sensors **20**(23), 6762 (2020)

21. Marchi, E., et al.: Typicality and emotion in the voice of children with autism spectrum condition: evidence across three languages (2015)

22. Memari, N., Abdollahi, S., Khodabakhsh, S., Rezaei, S., Moghbel, M.: Speech analysis with deep learning to determine speech therapy for learning difficulties. In: Kahraman, C., Cevik Onar, S., Oztaysi, B., Sari, I.U., Cebi, S., Tolga, A.C. (eds.) INFUS 2020. AISC, vol. 1197, pp. 1164–1171. Springer, Cham (2021). https://doi.org/10.1007/978-3-030-51156-2_136

23. Pokorny, F.B., et al.: Earlier identification of children with autism spectrum disorder: an automatic vocalisation-based approach (2017)

24. Ringeval, F., et al.: Automatic analysis of typical and atypical encoding of spontaneous emotion in the voice of children. In: Proceedings INTERSPEECH 2016, 17th Annual Conference of the International Speech Communication Association (ISCA), pp. 1210–1214 (2016)

25. Schmitt, M., Marchi, E., Ringeval, F., Schuller, B.: Towards cross-lingual automatic diagnosis of autism spectrum condition in children's voices. In: Speech Communication; 12. ITG Symposium, pp. 1–5. VDE (2016)

26. Mann, H.B., Whitney, D.R.: On a test of whether one of two random variables is stochastically larger than the other. Ann. Math. Stat. 50–60 (1947)

27. Wilcoxon, F.: Some uses of statistics in plant pathology. Biom. Bull. **1**(4), 41–45 (1945)

28. Hemdan, E.E.D., El-Shafai, W., Sayed, A.: CR19: a framework for preliminary detection of COVID-19 in cough audio signals using machine learning algorithms for automated medical diagnosis applications. J. Ambient Intell. Humaniz. Comput. **14**(9), 11715–11727 (2023)

29. Raj, S., Masood, S.: Analysis and detection of autism spectrum disorder using machine learning techniques. Procedia Comput. Sci. **167**, 994–1004 (2020)

30. Breiman, L., Cutler, R.A.: Random forests machine learning. J. Clin. Microbiol. **2**, 199–228 (2001)

31. Géron, A.: Hands-on Machine Learning with Scikit-Learn, Keras, and TensorFlow: Concepts, Tools, and Techniques to Build Intelligent Systems. O'Reilly Media, Inc., Sebastopol (2019)

Neural SDE-Based Epistemic Uncertainty Quantification in Deep Neural Networks

Aabila Tharzeen[1][(✉)], Shweta Dahale[2], and Balasubramaniam Natarajan[1]

[1] Electrical and Computer Engineering, Kansas State University,
Manhattan, KS, USA
{aabilatharzeen,bala}@ksu.edu
[2] Eaton Research Labs, Cleveland, CO, USA
shwetaddahale@eaton.com

Abstract. Deep learning tools are now widely used across various areas due to the increasing interest in applied machine learning. While these tools demonstrate exceptional performance in prediction and classification tasks, they are often deployed as black-box inferencing entities without any precise measure of uncertainty associated with their outputs. Uncertainty quantification is essential for ensuring reliability and robustness, particularly in safety-critical applications. However, accurately quantifying model/epistemic uncertainty in machine learning-based regression and classification tasks is challenging. In this paper, we provide an analytical approach to quantify the epistemic uncertainty related to deep neural network models using neural stochastic differential equations. Through experiments carried out on synthetic data, we demonstrate that our proposed framework successfully addresses the challenge of representing uncertainty in deep neural network-based regression and classification without the computational complexity associated with the classic Monte Carlo dropout method.

Keywords: Uncertainty quantification · deep neural network · Neural stochastic differential equation

1 Introduction

Deep neural networks, or DNNs, have become highly effective models for handling challenging problems. They exhibit exceptional performance in areas including speech recognition, image classification, and natural language processing. However, despite their remarkable success, DNNs face several challenges that limit their reliability and interoperability [1]. These challenges include their vulnerability to adversarial attacks, their tendency to overfit the training data, and the lack of transparency in understanding their decision-making process. These limitations can have significant implications, particularly in safety-critical applications such as healthcare and autonomous vehicles, where incorrect predictions or unreliable decisions can lead to severe consequences [20]. Researchers have

L. Iliadis et al. (Eds.): EANN 2024, CCIS 2141, pp. 247–258, 2024.
https://doi.org/10.1007/978-3-031-62495-7_19

developed uncertainty quantification (UQ) methods for estimating and quantifying the uncertainty associated with DNN predictions. These methods aim to go beyond providing point estimates and instead provide measures of uncertainty, such as confidence intervals or probability distributions over the predictions. Quantifying uncertainty in DNNs enables better decision-making, risk assessment, and model interpretability in real-world applications.

Despite the growing importance of uncertainty quantification for DNNs, the field is still in its early stages [8], and several challenges need to be addressed. One key challenge is developing scalable and efficient UQ methods that can handle large datasets and complex models. Additionally, there is a need for UQ methods that can provide interpretable uncertainty estimates, allowing users to understand and trust the predictions made by DNNs [20]. Furthermore, it is essential to integrate UQ methods seamlessly into existing DNN architectures to ensure practical applicability.

In this paper, we propose a novel framework that can analytically quantify the epistemic uncertainty of a neural network. Specifically, we use a surrogate neural stochastic differential equation (Neural SDE) framework that allows the derivation of the output mean and covariance along all neural network layers. We present a paradigm that can capture and measure epistemic uncertainty effectively, offering useful insights into the predictability of neural networks. This improved understanding of uncertainty will contribute to improved decision-making and foster trust in the application of neural networks in various domains.

The main contributions of this paper can be summarized as follows:

- We propose a generic framework that quantifies the epistemic uncertainty of deep neural networks with the help of a neural SDE framework as a surrogate model applicable across various tasks and domains.
- The framework allows for uncertainty propagation through all the layers of the target neural network model, and the analytical results capturing the uncertainty (output mean and covariance) along each neural network layer are derived.
- It can be applied to pre-trained networks using the analytical method, which eliminates the need for any computationally demanding uncertainty quantification procedures.
- The effectiveness of the proposed framework is demonstrated using synthetic data for classification and regression tasks and the results show up to 88.45% reduction in UQ computational complexity relative to the state-of-the-art Monte Carlo dropout method.

2 Background and Related Work

Deep neural networks (DNNs) are a type of artificial neural network trained using large datasets, and optimization algorithms to learn the parameters that map input data to output predictions. However, a significant challenge in deploying DNNs lies in dealing with uncertainty. Various methods have been proposed to quantify uncertainty in DNNs. Existing uncertainty quantification techniques can be divided into (1) Bayesian approaches or (2) sampling-based techniques. A classic neural network model with input x and output y and network parameter θ can be written probabilistically as $p(y|x, \theta)$. The posterior distribution obtained by applying Bayes' theorem can be written as follows:

$$p(\theta|x, y) = \frac{p(y|x, \theta)p(\theta)}{\int p(y|x, \theta)p(\theta)d\theta} \tag{1}$$

Existing approaches use Bayesian inference to estimate the posterior distribution over model parameters instead of treating the model parameters as fixed [3]. However, finding the posterior distribution over all possible model parameters can be intractable. There exists variation inference-based techniques that approximate the posterior probabilities rather than finding the exact value [6]. The process involves finding a simple distribution that is as close to the actual distribution. Using this technique training takes longer and inference is slower as approximating posterior probability requires several samples to be drawn from the posterior distribution. Laplace approximation is also used in Bayesian inference, focusing on the region around the maximum of the posterior distribution. By leveraging a Taylor-series expansion, it provides an approximation of the distribution in the vicinity of this maximum [15]. This method can only capture the local behavior of the distribution, which implies that the approximation may significantly differ from the true distribution in other areas. Among sampling-based techniques, another efficient technique for approximating inference is the Monte Carlo Markov chain (MCMC) method, which involves applying a stochastic transition to a random draw from a distribution. [10]. Despite the success of the MCMC method, the method convergences slowly. Monte Carlo dropout is yet another technique that uses dropout as a Bayesian Approximation to calculate the intractable posterior distribution [5]. Monte Carlo (MC) dropout, which involves running inference multiple times with different dropout masks during testing can be used to estimate the epistemic uncertainty. Although dropout is a widely used technique, it is an empirical approach that gets computationally expensive for larger networks. The Deep Ensembles method proposed in [11] involves training multiple DNNs on the same dataset and combining their predictions to obtain the mean and variance of the predictions and can be used as a metric for the uncertainty. However, the existing methods are time-consuming and require maintaining many copies of the model parameters to quantify uncertainty, which can be costly for large NNs. In [9], stochastic differential equations (SDEs)-based techniques were employed to train the SDE model using out-of-distribution (OOD) data for training in order to quantify total uncertainty. However, the method falls short in its ability to assess uncertainty in a rigorous and principled manner.

In this paper, we aim to address these challenges and propose a novel approach to uncertainty quantification in neural networks (UQ-Net) using a neural SDE framework. Our objective is to develop a method that provides a rigorous and principled way to measure epistemic uncertainty. By leveraging the neural

SDE framework, our approach overcomes the limitations of existing methods and offers a more efficient and scalable solution for quantifying uncertainty in large neural networks.

3   Proposed UQ-Net Approach

This section presents a detailed outline of the problem statement along with an introduction to the main elements of our suggested structure.

3.1   Problem Statement

Given a training dataset $D = (x_j, y_j)_{j=1}^{N}$, where x_j represents the input data and y_j corresponds to the corresponding ground truth labels, we can train a model $\mathbf{M}$ parameterized by θ to make predictions on new test cases. The predictive uncertainty originates from two sources as described earlier. Our goal is to analytically quantify the epistemic uncertainty of the neural network model with reduced computational time in comparison to the existing methods.

3.2   Uncertainty Quantification with UQ-Net

Given a target neural network model that performs a regression or classification task on a set of data, the UQ-Net works as a surrogate network and helps to measure how uncertain the neural network model's predictions are. As shown in Fig. 1, the UQ-Net, which has an input, output, and a hidden layer, helps in propagating the uncertainty in the corresponding layers of the target neural network. As shown in Fig. 2, the UQ-Net architecture consists of input and output linear layers of deep neural networks at both the input and output stages. The neural SDE layer within UQ-Net corresponds to the hidden layer of the deep neural network. Since neural SDEs preserve dimensionality, the input and output layers of the network serve as reshaping layers before and after the hidden layer. These reshaping layers facilitate the seamless integration of the neural SDE layer into the overall network structure and help UQ-Net propagate the mean and covariance analytically from input to output. Each component of UQ-Net is further elaborated in the following sections, along with the analytical derivation of the output mean and covariance.

3.3   Neural SDE

Traditional neural networks typically consist of multiple stacked hidden layers that map input $\mathbf{x}$ to output $\mathbf{y}$. However, recent research has shown that these hidden representations can be interpreted as the states of a continuous dynamical system rather than discrete layers [4]. For instance, in the case of a residual neural network (a deep learning model in which each layer learns residual functions with respect to their input) [7], the transformation between layers can be expressed as

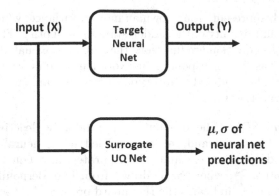

Fig. 1. Neural network with uncertainty quantification module (UQ-Net)

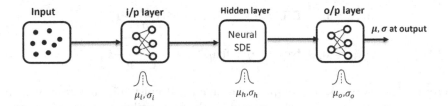

Fig. 2. UQ-Net

$$\mathbf{h}_{t+1} = \mathbf{h}_t + \mathbf{f}(\mathbf{h}_t, \theta) \tag{2}$$

Here, $\mathbf{h}_t$ represents the hidden features at depth t, and $\mathbf{f}$ is a neural network function approximation. The continuous limit of the residual neural network structure is expressed as

$$\mathbf{h}_{t+1} = \mathbf{h}_t + \int_t^{t+1} \mathbf{f}(\mathbf{h}_\tau, \tau, \theta) d\tau \tag{3}$$

The Eq. (3) is the continuous approximation of the transformations in residual neural network architecture and also the solution to an ordinary differential equation (ODE) problem. The neural ordinary differential equation (Neural ODE) method [4] parameterizes $\mathbf{f}(\mathbf{h}_\tau, \tau, \theta)$ with a neural network and leverages an ODE solver to evaluate the hidden states during the continuous transformation. However, the deterministic nature of neural ODEs is not suitable to model epistemic uncertainty. To address this, we employ the neural SDE model [13], which augments a neural ODE with a stochastic term. Thus, neural SDE incorporates a diffusion term to model randomness using the Brownian motion component [13]. Thus Eq. (3) can be rewritten as follows:

$$d\mathbf{h}_t = \underbrace{\mathbf{f}(\mathbf{h}_t, t; w)dt}_{\text{drift}} + \underbrace{\mathbf{g}(\mathbf{h}_t, t; v)d\mathbf{B}_t}_{\text{diffusion}} \tag{4}$$

Here, $\mathbf{g}(\mathbf{h}_t, t; v)d\mathbf{B}_t$ represents the Brownian motion variance, which helps to capture the epistemic uncertainty of the hidden state $\mathbf{h}_t$ at depth t. The drift and diffusion terms from the equation are functions that are approximated via neural networks with w and v as the corresponding network parameters. Equation (4) is a general form that can be modified to incorporate existing randomness models, such as dropout in neural networks.

Dropout Using Neural SDE: The dropout term randomly deactivates some neurons in the neural network and can be modeled using neural SDE [14]. Mathematically, the dropout rate can be incorporated into equation (3) as $\mathbf{h}_{t+1} = \mathbf{h}_t + \mathbf{f}(\mathbf{h}_t, t; w) \odot \frac{\gamma_n}{p}$, where γ_n is drawn from i.i.d Bernoulli distribution with parameter p and $\odot$ indicates the Hadamard product. Furthermore, the above hidden state dynamic can be simplified as,

$$\mathbf{h}_{t+1} = \mathbf{h}_t + \mathbf{f}(\mathbf{h}_t, t; w) + \mathbf{f}(\mathbf{h}_t, t; w) \odot (\frac{\gamma_n}{p} - \mathbf{I}),$$

$$= \mathbf{h}_t + \mathbf{f}(\mathbf{h}_t, t; w) + \mathbf{f}(\mathbf{h}_t, t; w) \odot \sqrt{\frac{1-p}{p}} \mathbf{z}_n. \tag{5}$$

where $\mathbf{z}_n \overset{\text{i.i.d.}}{\sim} \mathcal{N}(0, 1)$. To compare the quantified epistemic uncertainty with the state-of-the-art Monte Carlo dropout method, we utilize Eq. (5), which unifies dropouts under the neural SDE framework. Here, $\sqrt{\frac{1-p}{p}} \mathbf{f}(\mathbf{h}_t, t; w)$ represents the diffusion term and $q = \sqrt{\frac{1-p}{p}}$ controls the strength of regularization. It determines the scaling factor of the diffusion term and affects the magnitude of the injected noise or uncertainty. By adjusting the value of q, one can balance the trade-off between regularization and the expressiveness of the model. q can be treated similarly to the dropout probability term in the MC dropout method [5].

3.4   UQ-Net

As discussed above, the mean and covariance are computed from the input layer and subsequently propagated through the hidden layer, effectively carrying the uncertainty measures to the output layer with the help of UQ-Net. The input and output layers can be linear or nonlinear functions depending on the presence of an activation function.

Uncertainty Estimation in Input/Output Layer: Quantification of uncertainty for a non-linear input/output layer can be achieved by computing the statistics of the linearized approximation of the nonlinear function [2]. Suppose that for a nonlinear function $\mathbf{f}$ and a random vector $\mathbf{x}$ with expected value $\hat{\mathbf{x}}$ and covariance $\mathbf{C}_{xx}$, the expected value $\hat{\mathbf{y}}$ of the output $\mathbf{y} = \mathbf{f}(\mathbf{x})$ can be written as a Taylor series expansion around the mean as $\hat{\mathbf{y}} \approx \mathbf{f}(\hat{\mathbf{x}})$

Here $\nabla_x \mathbf{f}$ is the Jacobian of the function $\mathbf{f}$ at the operating point $\mathbf{x}$. Theorem 1 below can be used to evaluate the expected value of the mean and covariance of the output from the input/output layers of the neural network.

Theorem 1. Let $\mathbf{y} = \mathbf{f}(\mathbf{x}, \theta)$ be the output of the neural network layer denoted by $\mathbf{f}$, with the network layer parameter θ. The estimation of expected value $(\hat{\mathbf{y}})$ and the associated covariance can be calculated as,

$$\hat{\mathbf{y}} = \mathbf{f}(\hat{\mathbf{x}}, \theta),$$

$$\mathbf{C}_{yy} = (\nabla_x f)\mathbf{C}_{xx}(\nabla_x f)^{\mathsf{T}} \tag{6}$$

Here, the expected value of the input is $\mathbb{E}[\mathbf{x}] = \hat{\mathbf{x}}$ and its associated covariance is $\mathbf{C}_{xx}$ and $\mathbf{C}_{yy}$ is the covariance associated with the output of the neural network layer.

The uncertainty estimates obtained using Theorem 1 are propagated through the input layer and are passed to the hidden layer. Theorem 1 can also be applied to uncertainty estimation at the output layer.

Uncertainty Estimation in Hidden Layer: Uncertainty quantification of the hidden layer of the neural network is achieved using Gaussian assumed density approximation of Neural SDE [18]. By utilizing linearization techniques, we can compute the statistics of nonlinear neural SDE. Specifically, the nonlinear neural SDE can be linearized via Taylor series approximation. The drift term can be approximated by linearizing around the mean $\mathbf{m}$ and at depth t as follows:

$$f(\mathbf{h}, t) \approx f(\mathbf{m}, t) + \mathbf{F_h}(\mathbf{h}, t)(\mathbf{h} - \mathbf{m}) \tag{7}$$

And the diffusion term can be linearized as:

$$g(\mathbf{h}, t) \approx g(\mathbf{m}, t) + \mathbf{G_h}(\mathbf{h}, t)(\mathbf{h} - \mathbf{m}) \tag{8}$$

Here $\mathbf{F_h}$ and $\mathbf{G_h}$ are the Jacobian of f and g with respect to the hidden state $\mathbf{h}$ and the statistics of the hidden state can be calculated using Theorem 2.

Theorem 2. Consider a neural SDE as shown in Eq. (4), a linearization-based approximation to neural SDE can be obtained by integrating the equation,

$$\frac{d\mathbf{m}}{dt} = f(\mathbf{m}, t) \tag{9}$$

$$\frac{d\mathbf{C}}{dt} = \mathbf{C}\mathbf{F_h^{\mathsf{T}}}(\mathbf{m}, t) + \mathbf{F_h}(\mathbf{m}, t)\mathbf{C} + \mathbf{G_h}(\mathbf{m}, t)\mathbf{Q}\mathbf{G_h^{\mathsf{T}}}(\mathbf{m}, t) \tag{10}$$

where $\mathbf{m}$ and $\mathbf{C}$ are the mean and covariance of the states of the neural SDE at depth t and $\mathbf{Q}$ is the diffusion matrix.

Equations (9) and (10) enable the analytical determination of the mean and covariance of the hidden layer output in the neural network. It is to be noted that the diffusion term, denoted as g, is proportional to the function $\mathbf{f}$ in our particular context and is defined as $g = \sqrt{\frac{1-p}{p}} f(h_t, t; w)$. Thus, the uncertainty quantification of a deep neural network can be achieved analytically using UQ-Net.

4 Experimental Results

In this section, we conduct a comprehensive evaluation of our proposed uncertainty quantification method through experiments on two synthetic datasets and two real-world datasets: two designed for regression tasks and the other two for classification tasks. Detailed descriptions of these datasets are provided below:

Synthetic Regression Dataset: This dataset is generated synthetically and is intended for regression tasks. It comprises of a single feature **x** and consists of randomly generated homoscedastic data.

Half Moon Dataset: This synthetic dataset consists of two features and is specifically designed for performing classification tasks. Each data point in the dataset can be classified into one of two distinct classes.

Housing Dataset: The dataset is drawn from the 1990 U.S. Census reflecting real-world data. It consists 8 distinct features and is utilized to forecast the median house value within California districts [16].

Ionoshpehere Dataset: This real-world dataset consists of 34 feature which classifies radar returns from the ionosphere into three different categories [19].

By utilizing these datasets, we aim to assess the performance and effectiveness of our proposed uncertainty quantification method. To assess the effectiveness of our proposed uncertainty quantification method, we compare its performance against the widely adopted Monte Carlo dropout technique. All training and evaluation experiments are performed on a computer with an Intel i7 processor running at 2.80 GHz with 12 GB memory and 12 GB RAM. The learning rate set was 0.001 and the Adam optimizer was used.

Regression Task. The regression task is performed on the single feature synthetic regression dataset. The uncertainty estimates obtained using UQ-Net is compared with the MC dropout method using the expected normalized calibration error (ENCE) metric [12]. The ENCE metric serves as an indicator of the reliability of the confidence scores provided by the methods. The ENCE metric is utilized to calibrate the regressor by aligning the mean square error (MSE), representing the expected error, with the predicted uncertainty, denoted by the standard deviation σ. To assess the calibration of the regressor, the standard deviation axis is divided into bins, and the ENCE metric is calculated using the following formula:

$$\text{ENCE} = \frac{1}{N} \sum_{j=1}^{N} \frac{|\text{RMV}(j) - \text{RMSE}(j)|}{\text{RMV}(j)} \tag{11}$$

Here, Bj is a bin that represents the standard deviation axis interval, root mean variance(RMV) and root mean square error (RMSE) are obtained using the following equations:

$$\text{RMV}(j) = \frac{1}{|B_j|} \sum_{t \in B_j} \sigma_t^2 \tag{12}$$

$$\text{RMSE}(j) = \frac{1}{|B_j|} \sum_{t \in B_j} (y_t - \hat{y}_t)^2 \tag{13}$$

A lower ENCE value indicates a better-calibrated model. To assess the performance of UQ-Net, we calculate the ENCE score for various values of p, and the results are shown in Table 1. Similar experiments are conducted for the MC Dropout method, and the corresponding results are also presented in Table 1. From the table, it becomes evident that by adjusting the values of p, both methods effectively quantify the epistemic uncertainty and exhibit a similar trend. However, the advantage of UQ-Net lies in its analytical nature, resulting in significantly reduced computational time required to obtain uncertainty estimates compared to the empirical MC Dropout approach. The computational time required for both methods is summarized in Table 3.

For achieving optimal performance, the commonly chosen dropout value for hidden layers using MC Dropout is 0.5. However, the optimal dropout value may vary depending on various factors such as data size, model architecture, etc. [17]. Similarly, in the case of UQ-Net, there can be an optimal value of q that can be chosen to yield a lower ENCE score, making the choice of hyperparameters crucial for obtaining reliable uncertainty quantification results. We further asses the performance of our framework using real-world data from the California housing dataset. The results are detailed in Table 2. The trend observed in Table 1 for regression tasks is similarly evident in the evaluation using real-world datasets shown in Table 2. The computational time needed for assessing both UQ-Net and MC dropout is illustrated in Table 4.

Table 1. ENCE scores obtained using two methods for regression and classification task for synthetic dataset

p	Regression		Classification	
	UQ-Net	MC dropout	UQ-Net	MC dropout
0.1	0.760	0.804	0.779	2.685
0.2	0.758	1.608	0.632	1.981
0.3	0.767	0.656	0.693	0.977
0.4	0.747	2.423	0.916	0.992
0.5	0.77	0.300	0.990	0.426
0.6	0.718	0.401	0.607	0.439
0.7	0.246	0.184	0.692	0.638
0.8	0.150	0.492	0.755	0.338
0.9	0.607	0.516	1.343	0.476

Table 2. ENCE scores obtained using two methods for regression and classification task for real-world dataset

p	Regression		Classification	
	UQ-Net	MC dropout	UQ-Net	MC dropout
0.1	0.43	6.14	0.48	12.08
0.2	0.60	4.35	0.72	9.64
0.3	0.57	3.60	0.51	6.75
0.4	0.59	3.02	0.59	4.70
0.5	0.62	2.65	0.50	4.14
0.6	0.63	2.09	0.64	6.21
0.7	0.67	1.72	0.93	3.82
0.8	0.65	1.13	0.38	1.81
0.9	0.61	0.76	1.50	1.29

Table 3. Computation time in seconds required for regression and classification task for synthetic dataset

Regression		Classification	
UQ-Net	MC dropout	UQ-Net	MC dropout
0.83 sec	4.88 s	0.41 s	6.47 s

Table 4. Computation time in seconds required for regression and classification task for real-world dataset

Regression		Classification	
UQ-Net	MC dropout	UQ-Net	MC dropout
8.79 s	79.07 s	0.37 s	3.46 s

Classification Task. In the classification task, we utilize the half-moon dataset with two features. Just like in the regression experiments, we compare the uncertainty estimates obtained using UQ-Net with those from the MC Dropout method. While the ENCE score is used for evaluating uncertainty in regression tasks, it cannot be applied directly to classification tasks, as the RMSE loss is not relevant for classification. However, classifiers can predict continuous scores that are often transformed into class labels through a thresholding process during the final step of classification. To evaluate uncertainty estimates in our specific framework, we utilize the continuous output prior to this final step. Thus, the ENCE score is suitable for our specific case in evaluating uncertainty estimates for classification tasks.

Similar to the regression task, ENCE scores are calculated for various values of p for both UQ-Net and MC Dropout, and the results are depicted in Table 1. As previously discussed, an optimal value of p can be selected based on a lower

ENCE score. Similarly, an optimal value of q can also be chosen. The computational time required for both methods is presented in Table 3 and similar to the case of regression task there is up to 94% reduction in computation time compared to MC dropout method.

We also evaluate our framework's performance for classification using real-world data from the ionosphere dataset. The results are presented in Table 2. The trend observed in Table 1 for classification tasks is also evident in the evaluation using real-world datasets, as shown in Table 2. The computational time required for assessing both UQ-Net and MC dropout is provided in Table 4.

5   Conclusions

Uncertainty quantification plays a critical role in safety-critical applications involving deep neural networks. This paper presents a theoretical approach to uncertainty quantification in neural networks using a neural stochastic differential equation framework. The proposed framework allows for the analytical quantification of epistemic uncertainty in DNNs for various tasks like classification and regression. The results were compared with the state of art MC dropout uncertainty quantification technique. The results obtained highlight the effectiveness of UQ-Net in accurately quantifying uncertainty while offering the advantage of reduced computational time compared to MC Dropout. This further demonstrates the practicality and efficiency of our proposed analytical approach in uncertainty quantification tasks. Future work includes exploring the use of parametric dynamic models instead of neural SDEs for uncertainty quantification, which can potentially improve the interpretability and scalability of the methods.

Acknowledgements. The research was funded by National Science Foundation CNS 2039014.

References

1. Abdar, M., et al.: A review of uncertainty quantification in deep learning: techniques, applications and challenges. Inf. Fusion **76**, 243–297 (2021)
2. Amini, A., Liu, G., Motee, N.: Robust learning of recurrent neural networks in presence of exogenous noise. In: 2021 60th IEEE Conference on Decision and Control (CDC), pp. 783–788. IEEE (2021)
3. Blundell, C., Cornebise, J., Kavukcuoglu, K., Wierstra, D.: Weight uncertainty in neural network. In: International Conference on Machine Learning, pp. 1613–1622. PMLR (2015)
4. Chen, R.T., Rubanova, Y., Bettencourt, J., Duvenaud, D.K.: Neural ordinary differential equations. Adv. Neural Inf. Process. Syst. **31** (2018)
5. Gal, Y., Ghahramani, Z.: Dropout as a Bayesian approximation: representing model uncertainty in deep learning [eb/ol]. arXiv preprint arxiv:1506.02142 (2015)
6. Graves, A.: Practical variational inference for neural networks. Adv. Neural Inf. Process. Syst. **24** (2011)

7. He, K., Zhang, X., Ren, S., Sun, J.: Deep residual learning for image recognition (2015). corr abs/1512.03385 (2015)
8. He, W., Jiang, Z.: A survey on uncertainty quantification methods for deep neural networks: an uncertainty source perspective. arXiv preprint arXiv:2302.13425 (2023)
9. Kong, L., Sun, J., Zhang, C.: SDE-Net: equipping deep neural networks with uncertainty estimates. arXiv preprint arXiv:2008.10546 (2020)
10. Kupinski, M.A., Edwards, D.C., Giger, M.L., Metz, C.E.: Ideal observer approximation using Bayesian classification neural networks. IEEE Trans. Med. Imaging **20**(9), 886–899 (2001)
11. Lakshminarayanan, B., Pritzel, A., Blundell, C.: Simple and scalable predictive uncertainty estimation using deep ensembles. arXiv preprint arXiv:1612.01474 (2016)
12. Levi, D., Gispan, L., Giladi, N., Fetaya, E.: Evaluating and calibrating uncertainty prediction in regression tasks. Sensors **22**(15), 5540 (2022)
13. Liu, X., Xiao, T., Si, S., Cao, Q., Kumar, S., Hsieh, C.J.: Neural SDE: stabilizing neural ode networks with stochastic noise. arXiv preprint arXiv:1906.02355 (2019)
14. Liu, X., Xiao, T., Si, S., Cao, Q., Kumar, S., Hsieh, C.J.: How does noise help robustness? Explanation and exploration under the neural SDE framework. In: Proceedings of the IEEE/CVF Conference on Computer Vision and Pattern Recognition, pp. 282–290 (2020)
15. Murphy, K.P.: Machine Learning: A Probabilistic Perspective. MIT Press, Cambridge (2012)
16. Pace, R.K., Barry, R.: Sparse spatial autoregressions. Stat. Probab. Lett. **33**(3), 291–297 (1997)
17. Pauls, A., Yoder, J.: Determining optimum drop-out rate for neural networks. In: Midwest Instructional Computing Symposium (MICS) (2018)
18. Särkkä, S., Solin, A.: Applied Stochastic Differential Equations, vol. 10. Cambridge University Press, Cambridge (2019)
19. Sigillito, V., W.S.H.L., Baker, K.: Ionosphere. UCI Machine Learning Repository (1989). https://doi.org/10.24432/C5W01B
20. Wilkins, N., Johnson, M., Nwogu, I.: Regression with uncertainty quantification in large scale complex data. In: 2022 IEEE International Conference on Systems, Man, and Cybernetics (SMC), pp. 827–833. IEEE (2022)

Robust Traffic Prediction Using Probabilistic Spatio-Temporal Graph Convolutional Network

Atkia Akila Karim[✉] and Naushin Nower

Institute of Information Technology, University of Dhaka, 1209 Dhaka, Bangladesh
msse1760@iit.du.ac.bd, naushin@iit.du.ac.bd

Abstract. Accurate traffic forecasting is crucial for the effective functioning of intelligent transportation systems (ITS). It helps in urban traffic planning, traffic management, and traffic control. Although deep neural networks have made significant progress in traffic forecasting, their effectiveness is compromised by noise and missing data due to sensor malfunctions, communication errors, and many more. While various missing data imputation techniques exist, they often apply pre-processing before prediction which creates an extra processing step. In addition, the spatio-temporal nature of traffic makes missing data handling more challenging since data can be lost at the temporal axis or on a spatial axis(missing data at multiple sensors). Thus, there is a need for a robust model that can inherently handle missing data and noise in traffic forecasting. In this paper, we proposed a Robust Probabilistic Spatio-temporal Graph Convolutional Network model that can handle noisy and missing data using the proposed probabilistic adjacency matrix and node-specific learning. Two real-world datasets with noisy and missing data are used to evaluate the performance of our proposed model. Our model surpasses baseline models in accurately forecasting traffic data, even in the presence of noise and missing data. The source code of our model is available at https://github.com/atkia/RPSTGCN.

Keywords: Traffic forecasting · Graph Convolutional network · Robustness · Missing data · Probabilistic adjacency matrix · Graph convolutional network

1 Introduction

Traffic prediction involves forecasting future traffic patterns within a specific road network by analyzing both historical and current data [1]. It plays a crucial role in intelligent transportation systems (ITS), aiding users and systems in making effective decisions. Thus, accurate traffic forecasting is vital for effective transportation management and urban planning. However, traffic prediction remains a challenging task due to its complex spatio-temporal relationships, sudden incidents, inaccurate/noisy traffic data, and other factors [2].

© The Author(s), under exclusive license to Springer Nature Switzerland AG 2024
L. Iliadis et al. (Eds.): EANN 2024, CCIS 2141, pp. 259–273, 2024.
https://doi.org/10.1007/978-3-031-62495-7_20

In recent decades, there has been a shift in prediction techniques owing to advancements in big data and computational tools. As traffic data expands and computational power improves, forecasting methods are transitioning from traditional statistical approaches like the autoregressive integrated moving average model (ARIMA) [3] and the Kalman filter method (KF) [4] to more efficient machine learning techniques. Recently, machine learning-based methods, particularly deep learning, have propelled traffic forecasting research due to their capability to handle the dynamic nature of traffic.

Among these methods, the Graph Convolutional Network (GCN) has garnered attention from researchers for its ability to capture the spatial properties of road traffic through its graph structure [5]. Additionally, recurrent neural networks (RNNs) and their variants such as Gated Recurrent Unit (GRU) and Long Short-Term Memory (LSTM) are employed to capture the temporal features of traffic networks. Recent studies have explored combinations of GCN with GRU [6] or GCN with LSTM [7] to simultaneously capture spatial-temporal features. While deep learning models exhibit outstanding performance, they are heavily reliant on traffic data, which often suffers from issues like overfitting, noise, and data shortages [8]. Consequently, to address real-world scenarios, traffic prediction models must not only be accurate but also robust enough to handle data imperfections. In existing literature, missing values and noise are either ignored or addressed before the training process using imputation techniques. For example, Tian et al. employed a smoothing method to preprocess noisy data [9], while Chen et al. utilized a tensor-based method for imputing missing data [10]. However, these methods require a two-step processing approach and substantial datasets and computational resources for imputation and model training.

Additionally, some researchers have utilized recurrent neural network-based models [9,11] for this purpose. However, these models fail to capture the spatial features of traffic networks, considering only the temporal features in traffic data. Furthermore, some existing prediction methods completely ignore the missing data and noise thus hindering the performance in the noisy environment. Therefore, a robust prediction model is necessary to handle the missing data during prediction and provide better results than two-step processing.

To solve the problems mentioned above, in this study, we have proposed a robust probabilistic spatio-temporal Graph Convolutional Network (R-PST-GCN) model that can predict in a noisy environment. In the R-PST-GCN, we have proposed a modified GCN to capture the spatial characteristics and GRU and attention mechanism to capture the temporal characteristics in traffic data. Rather than using a static adjacency matrix in GCN, we used a probabilistic adjacency matrix that helps the model learn the dynamic spatial characteristics of traffic networks and helps to handle the missing data. We also used node-specific learning to learn the unique characteristics of the connected roads. Those modifications in GCN make our model capable of handling noisy data without any imputation or preprocessing of data. To evaluate the performance of our model we experimented with two real-world datasets. We used one city road dataset and one highway dataset as both have different patterns. Experimental results show that our model outperforms baseline methods while handling noisy or missing data. The performance of our model is steady throughout the different noisy data. The contributions of our paper are summarized below:

- We proposed a modified GCN that takes a probabilistic adjacency matrix and can learn node-specific characteristics. It helps the model learn dynamic spatio-temporal dependencies and handle missing data/noise more accurately.
- Our Robust Probabilistic Spatio-temporal Graph Convolutional Network model can handle missing data inherently and give a highly accurate prediction.
- The experimental results on two real-world datasets demonstrate that our proposed model performs better than baseline models in traffic forecasting, even when the data contains noise or missing values.

2 Related Work

In the era of ITS, traffic flow prediction has become more and more important over the past decades, leading experts to conduct focused research. Various prediction methods have already been developed by researchers and in this section, we discuss the traffic prediction techniques in two aspects i) Traffic forecasting without considering missing value and ii) Traffic forecasting method with missing value.

Traffic Forecasting Methods: Recently deep learning networks have been popular for their ability to process vast datasets and extract intricate traffic features through multiple layers. Initial deep learning models focused on Recurrent neural network (RNN) and its variant GRU [12] and LSTM [13] which can efficiently handle the temporal features of traffic data. However, they overlooked spatial aspects in traffic data. Some models combine CNN for space and LSTM for time [14]. However, CNN struggles with complex road structures, leading to the use of Graph Convolutional Networks (GCN) in newer models. GCN represents traffic networks as graphs, capturing spatial dependencies within the road network more accurately. As a result, GCN is used widely to capture the spatial features of traffic data. For example, the SGCN model [15] stacked GCN to give a long-term prediction. It uses GCN to capture spatial features and stacking GCN helps the model to capture the temporal features. TGCN model [6] uses GRU to capture temporal features and GCN for spatial features. After that, the attention mechanism is incorporated on top of TGCN to make A3TGCN [16] which can capture the global trend and sudden incidents of traffic flow. Some models [7,17] aggregate external data such as weather data, date, point of interest (POI) information, etc. to make the prediction. All of the above-discussed GCN-based models used static adjacent matrices that failed to capture the dynamic spatial features of traffic. In real life, the impact of adjacent roads does not remain the same at all times. As a result to learn neighboring nodes better LocGCLSTM model [18] used a trainable matrix with an adjacency matrix. AGCRN [19] model used node adaptive learning and adaptive adjacency matrix to better learn the neighboring node's dynamic impact. [20] also used an adaptive adjacency matrix in their model. Recently, DCGCN [21] used a correlation-based adjacency matrix based on GCN to learn the spatial feature better. All of these forecasting techniques perform well on clean data and assume that the environment is noise-free. However, these methods don't work well when the traffic data has missing value or the environment is harsh and noisy. This is because these methods are unable to handle missing data inherently and do not incorporate imputation or data pre-processing steps.

Traffic Forecasting with Missing Values. The performance of traffic forecasts can be significantly impeded by the missing data. Many techniques for data imputation have been developed to address the problem. Chen et al. [10] used a tensor-based model to extract latent features from a traffic dataset and, through decomposition and completion fill in the missing blanks. Kazemi et al. [22] used a generative adversarial network for an imputation task. However, for tuning the model large number of data is needed. Cui et al. [8] proposed a GMN model that infers traffic state step by step using the graph Markov process. Tian et al. [9] used LSTM with multi-scale temporal smoothing to infer missing data. One drawback of those methods they need pre-processing procedures like imputation techniques or intentional management of missing values because they are unable to handle missing data naturally. These actions may add biases and complexity.

To solve that problem, we proposed a robust model that can handle missing and noisy data inherently. It doesn't require pre-processing of data or any imputation techniques. The performance of our model is consistent while managing noisy and missing data.

3   Methodology

In this study, we want to predict a specified time of traffic data based on available historical data. The traffic network can be represented as a graph, $G = (V, E)$, where $V = \{v_1, v_2..., v_N\}$ is a set of nodes. Sensors or traffic segments can be considered as nodes and N is the number of nodes. E is a set of edges that represent connections between nodes. The connectivity between nodes is stored in an adjacency matrix, $A \in R^{N \times N}$. The traffic features are stored in $X \in R^{N \times P}$, where P is the historical time length. Thus, the problem can be formulated as finding a mapping function, f that predicts future k time steps based on past n time steps.

$$[X_{t+1}, ...X_{t+k}] = f(G; (X_t, X_{t-1}, ...X_{t-n})) \tag{1}$$

3.1   Proposed Robust Probabilistic Graph Convolutional Network

To solve the described prediction problem we proposed a robust probabilistic graph convolutional network. We used a modified GCN that uses a probabilistic adjacency matrix and node-specific learning to capture spatial features. For the temporal feature, we used GRU and attention mechanism so that our model can capture both local and global trends of traffic networks. Then a fully connected layer is used to give the final prediction. The framework of our proposed model is shown in Fig. 1. In the below section, we have described the module of our proposed model in detail.

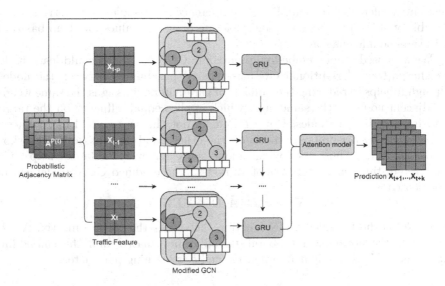

Fig. 1. The framework of our proposed R-PST-GCN model.

Probabilistic Graph Convolutional Network. Graph convolutional network (GCN) is widely used for extracting spatial features as it aggregates information from its neighboring nodes. However traditional GCN has some drawbacks since it uses a predefined adjacency matrix, A. Traditional GCN-based methods use binary values in a static adjacency matrix indicating whether the nodes have a connection or not. Those matrices result in predefined graphs which can not properly represent the dynamic spatial dependencies. Moreover, it introduces potential bias unrelated to prediction task [19]. Thus, to overcome those problems we proposed a probabilistic adjacency matrix rather than a predefined adjacency matrix. We used transitional probability with Bayesian inference to calculate the probability of traffic propagation. The probability of traffic in road segment i at time t is $P(i|X(t))$ based on observed traffic data $X(t)$. The conditional probability of traffic on road segment j at time t is $P(j|i,t)$ given that the traffic flow was initially on road segment i. From this, we can calculate the probability of traffic propagation from i to j as:

$$P(i \rightarrow j|X(t)) = P(j|i,t) \odot P(i|P(X(t))$$ (2)

Using this equation we calculated the adjacency matrix, $A^p(t)$ of time t given the previous traffic data. We have used Bayesian inference in the adjacency matrix since it can handle missing data naturally and flexibly. In Bayesian inference, missing data is interpreted as unknown parameters with a probability distribution that is inferred using the available information and the prior beliefs. As a result, we do not have to discard or impute the missing data, as it is in frequentist inference. Instead, Bayesian inference can handle the uncertainty and variability of the missing data, and generate plausible values for them based on the available information.

We also used a node embedding matrix in GCN so that it could learn node-specific patterns. Traditional GCN use shared parameters between the nodes. Though it helps in reducing the number of parameters, it assigns the same weight to adjacent nodes in the same layer which implies equal influence on the target road for all adjacent nodes. However, that's not the case in real life, adjacent nodes can show dissimilar patterns on the other hand disjoint nodes can show similar patterns. Thus, employing unique space for every node can help GCN learn the distinct characteristics of all nodes. The modified GCN model can be represented as:

$$GC(X) = \sigma(\tilde{D}^{\frac{1}{2}} \tilde{A}^p \tilde{D}^{-\frac{1}{2}} XE\tilde{W} + Eb) \tag{3}$$

Here, GC is the modified GCN function that takes the feature matrix, X, $\tilde{A}^p$ represents the normalized probabilistic adjacency matrix and the embedding matrix is E. $\tilde{W}$ is a weight pool matrix and b is learning parameter.

Temporal Feature Modeling Using GRU and Attention Mechanism.
Traffic data has spatial and temporal features. GCN can only capture the spatial feature. To capture the temporal feature we used GRU and attention mechanism. GRU is used for capturing the local trend of traffic features and the attention mechanism is used for capturing the global trend. Probabilistic GCN and GRU both are used at a time to capture the spatial-temporal feature and their correlation in traffic data.

$$u_t = \sigma(GC(X_t), h_{t-1}]W_u + b_u) \tag{4}$$

$$r_t = \sigma(GC(X_t), h_{t-1}]W_r + b_r) \tag{5}$$

$$c_t = \tanh(GC(X_t), r_t \odot h_{t-1}])W_c + b_c) \tag{6}$$

$$h_t = u_t \odot h_{t-1} + (1 - u_t) \odot c_t \tag{7}$$

Here, u, r, and c are the gates of GRU named update gate, reset gate, and current gate respectively. X_t is the input value at t time in GCN and the output from GCN is used as input in GRU. $W_u, W_r, W_c, b_u, b_r, b_c$ are learning parameters of the gates. $\odot$ denotes element-wise multiplication. Hidden states, $H = h_1, h_2, ..., h_n$ are generated for the previous n timestamp input. The attention mechanism gives weight to the previous state. The weight is calculated using the below equation:

$$\alpha_i = softmax(w_2(w_1 \odot h_i + b_1) + b_2) \tag{8}$$

$$c_t = \sum_{i=1}^{n} \alpha_i \odot h_i \tag{9}$$

Then a context vector c_t is calculated to detail the global variation of the traffic data. Finally, using the fully connected layer, forecasting results are produced.

3.2 Loss Function

Real traffic data and predicted traffic data are represented respectively as X and $\hat{X}$. We aim to minimize errors between real data and predicted data. We also used normalization so that the model doesn't overfit. We used L2 regularization denoted as L_{reg} and a hyperparameter λ. The loss function for our model can be formulated as:

$$loss = \sum_{i=t+1}^{i=t+k} ||X_i - \hat{X}_i|| + \lambda L_{reg} \tag{10}$$

4 Experiment Analysis

In this section, we will evaluate the effectiveness of our proposed method by comparing it with the baseline prediction methods.

4.1 Dataset Description

To demonstrate the effectiveness of our suggested method, we conducted experiments on two types of datasets one is the city road SZ-taxi [6] dataset and another is the highway PeMSD7 [23] dataset. These data sets have been utilized in previous studies to compare performance and are commonly used in traffic forecasting research.

SZ-taxi: This dataset contains the taxi trajectory data for Shenzhen, China from January 1 to January 31, 2015. The traffic data for 156 roadways are included in the collection. Traffic speed is captured at 15-min time intervals.

PeMSD7: PeMSD7 is traffic data from 228 sensors measuring the speed of traffic in District 7 of California from May to June 2012 (only weekdays). Traffic speed is stored with a 5-min interval total of 12671 timestamps from the highway.

4.2   Experimental Setup and Hyperparameters

The datasets are split into training and testing with an 8:2 size ratio. For the random missing dataset, we randomly sat values in the input set to 0 depending on the ratio of the missing rate. In the experiment process, the input values of training and testing are normalized. For the SZ-taxi dataset, we used batch size 64, hidden layer 100, and training epoch 3000. For the PeMSD7 dataset, we used batch size 32, hidden layer 64, and training epoch 500. The learning rate and embedding dimension for both datasets are 0.0001 and 10. We used Adam Optimizer for training the model. All experiments are done using NVIDIA T4 GPU and implemented using TensorFlow.

4.3   Performance Metrics and Baseline Methods

To measure the performance of the models we used mean absolute error (MAE), root mean square error (RMSE), accuracy, coefficient of determination (R^2), and variance score (var). To evaluate the effectiveness of our proposed model for traffic prediction, we compared it with some recent forecasting models and some models that can handle missing data. A brief description of those models is given below.

1. GCN [5]: Graph Convolutional Network captures spatial features by aggregating characteristics from neighboring nodes.
2. GRU [12]: Gated Recurrent Unit captures temporal features from sequential time-series data.
3. TGCN [6]: Temporal Graph Convolutional Network captures both spatial and temporal features simultaneously using GCN and GRU.
4. A3TGCN [16]: Attention Temporal Graph Convolutional Network uses attention mechanism to capture the global trend of traffic network.
5. AGCRN [19]: Adaptive Graph Convolutional Recurrent Network uses adaptive adjacency matrix and node adaptive parameter to capture spatial and temporal features.
6. DCGCN [21]: Dynamic Spatio-temporal Deep Learning Model uses a correlation-based adjacency matrix in GCN to better capture spatial features with GRU. For convenience, we called their model DCGCN.
7. LSTM-M [9]: LSTM-M utilizing LSTM performs traffic prediction with missing data. It employs a multi-3scale temporal smoothing technique to infer missing values.
8. GRU-D [11]: GRU-D, derived from GRU, performs prediction tasks by integrating masking information and incorporating the time intervals of missing values as input.
9. GMN [8]: GMN considers traffic networks as a graph Markov process and infers missing values step by step.

4.4 Result Discussion

Prediction Result Without Perturbation: First, we performed a prediction task for different horizons using two real-world datasets. Baseline models and our model predicted traffic speed for the next 15, 30, and 60 min based on previous one-hour traffic data. From Table 1, we can see that our model outperforms baseline models in both datasets except MAE of the PeMSD7 dataset for 15 min. AGCRN in both datasets shows the second-best performance. AGCRN learns through node adaptive learning and adaptive adjacency matrix. In both datasets for all time horizons, GCN has the largest RMSE and the lowest accuracy when compared to other approaches. This makes sense since it is limited to capturing only spatial patterns. TGCN and A3TGCN exhibit high RMSE when the time interval is minimal, which indicates high temporal resolution data. This is because these models rely on a static adjacency matrix. The static adjacency matrix performs worst when the time interval is very low as it contains high variability making it hard to predict accurately. TGCN and A3TGCN predict better on the SZ-taxi dataset than the PeMSD7 dataset because data with a lower temporal resolution, like the SZ-taxi dataset, are smoother owing to aggregating traffic observations of a comparatively longer horizon. However, as our model, AGCRN, and DCGCN employ a data-driven dynamic adjacency matrix, it can capture the traffic flow more accurately, even at low time intervals. Compared to models that employ static adjacency matrices, GRU has a lower

Table 1. The overall prediction results of baseline methods and our model

Time	Model	SZ-taxi					PeMSD7				
		RMSE	MAE	Accuracy	R^2	var	RMSE	MAE	Accuracy	R^2	var
15 min	GCN	6.0141	4.4683	0.5811	0.6681	0.6682	12.1832	8.9170	0.7960	0.2189	0.2212
	GRU	4.3054	2.8171	0.7000	0.8299	0.8299	3.7234	2.1488	0.9376	0.9270	0.9271
	TGCN	4.1094	2.7812	0.7137	0.8450	0.8452	9.9978	6.8702	0.8326	0.4740	0.4741
	A3TGCN	4.0883	2.7768	0.7148	0.8462	0.8463	9.8651	6.6965	0.8348	0.4879	0.4891
	AGCRN	4.0840	2.7600	0.7155	0.8469	0.8470	3.4139	2.0732	0.9428	0.9386	0.9386
	DCGCN	4.286	2.8866	0.7014	0.8314	0.8314	3.6073	**1.9802**	0.9396	0.9315	0.9315
	Ours	**4.0055**	**2.6660**	**0.7210**	**0.8530**	**0.8532**	**3.4033**	2.0273	**0.9430**	**0.9390**	**0.9391**
30 min	GCN	6.0126	4.472	0.5811	0.6683	0.6684	12.1834	8.9311	0.7960	0.2193	0.2220
	GRU	4.3602	2.8485	0.6963	0.8256	0.8256	5.0128	2.8016	0.9160	0.8678	0.8680
	TGCN	4.1429	2.8225	0.7114	0.8425	0.8426	9.7613	6.6534	0.8365	0.4988	0.50009
	A3TGCN	4.0792	2.7396	0.7158	0.8473	0.8474	9.5860	6.5601	0.8394	0.5167	0.5169
	AGCRN	4.1398	2.8084	0.7116	0.8428	0.8429	4.6203	2.8452	0.9226	0.8877	0.8878
	DCGCN	4.3217	2.8879	0.6989	0.8286	0.8286	4.94032	2.6954	0.9172	0.8716	0.8736
	Ours	**4.0257**	**2.6686**	**0.7196**	**0.8513**	**0.8514**	**4.4765**	**2.6451**	**0.9250**	**0.8946**	**0.8948**
60 min	GCN	6.0476	4.5016	0.5787	0.6645	0.6646	12.2024	8.9210	0.7956	0.2177	0.2199
	GRU	4.4044	2.8599	0.6932	0.8220	0.8226	6.70139	3.7495	0.8877	0.7640	0.7642
	TGCN	4.1894	2.8647	0.7081	0.8390	0.8393	10.0478	6.9842	0.8317	0.4695	0.4701
	A3TGCN	4.1298	2.7866	0.7123	0.8435	0.8439	10.6701	7.3645	0.8213	0.4018	0.4020
	AGCRN	4.1860	2.8551	0.7084	0.8393	0.8393	5.7984	3.6053	0.9028	0.8233	0.8246
	DCGCN	4.4317	2.9901	0.6912	0.8198	0.8199	6.4646	3.5409	0.8917	0.7804	0.7834
	Ours	**4.0473**	**2.6950**	**0.7174**	**0.8491**	**0.8493**	**5.6699**	**3.3784**	**0.9050**	**0.8311**	**0.8315**

RMSE since it does not use an adjacency matrix. Our model decreased RMSE by 0.31% compared to AGCRN and 5.66% compared to DCGCN.

Random Missing Perturbation: We have conducted traffic predictions for 15 min using one-hour historical traffic data from the SZ-taxi dataset under various missing rates. For the PeMSD7 dataset, we used the previous 10 times-tamps to predict the next timestamp. In Table. 2 we displayed the result for both datasets. We can see that under random missing perturbation, our model outperforms baseline models. Our model has the lowest RMSE compared to other models for different missing rates. * means that the values are too small indicating poor performance of GRU-D. LSTM-M and GMN showed better performance on the PeMSD7 dataset compared to the SZ-taxi dataset due to the smaller size of the SZ-taxi dataset.

Although GMN showed consistent results, it has a higher RMSE than our model. DCGCN performed well on prediction tasks but it can not handle missing data well. The reason is that DCGCN depends on node correlation thus if the missing rate goes higher its error rate also goes up. Conversely, our model's probabilistic adjacency matrix mitigates the impact of missing values, resulting in stable performance even with increasing missing rates. This is because Bayesian inference incorporates uncertainty into the analysis to deal with missing data. Our proposed probabilistic adjacency matrix treats missing data as additional parameters, estimating their distribution based on observed data. It refines the estimation using iterative updating, thus producing a comprehensive understanding of both observed and missing values. This flexibility provides a more realistic representation of uncertainty and contributes to robust decision-making in the presence of missing/incomplete information.

Noisy Perturbation: To evaluate the robustness of our proposed approach we have used different Gaussian and Poisson noise levels in the SZ-taxi and PeMSD7 datasets. One noise follows the Gaussian distribution $N \in (0, \sigma^2)$, where $\sigma \in (0.2, 0.4, 0.8, 1, 2))$ and other follows the Poisson distribution $P(\lambda)$, where $(\lambda \in (1, 2, 4, 8, 16))$ and then normalized the noise matrix. Figure 2 displays the outcome of noisy perturbation on the SZ-taxi dataset. The outcomes of introducing Gaussian noise are displayed in 2a, with the y-axis representing several evaluation metrics in different colors and the x-axes representing various σ values. Similarly, Fig. 2b, displays the prediction outcomes of in the Poisson noisy environment. Regardless of changes in σ/λ, the values of assessment measures stay the same. Figure 3, shows the outcome of introducing noise to the PeMSD7 dataset as well. We can see that for both datasets performance of our prediction model remains consistent for different noise. As we see from Fig. 2b and Fig. 3 the value of RMSE, MAE, Accuracy, R^2, and var remain the same with increasing levels of noise. Thus we can conclude that our model is noise-resistant and robust in terms of handling noise issues.

Table 2. Performance comparison with various missing rates.

Missing rate	Model	SZ-taxi					PeMSD7				
		RMSE	MAE	Accuracy	R^2	var	RMSE	MAE	Accuracy	R^2	var
10%	GCN	6.1379	4.5645	0.5724	0.6541	0.6542	12.2355	8.9008	0.7953	0.2102	0.2112
	GRU	4.9357	3.2604	0.6561	0.7763	0.7778	8.3511	5.9427	0.8603	0.6321	0.6327
	TGCN	4.2558	2.9380	0.7035	0.8337	0.8337	10.6125	7.2897	0.8224	0.4058	0.4079
	A3TGCN	4.2408	2.8865	0.7046	0.8349	0.8349	10.3493	7.1063	0.8269	0.4350	0.4358
	AGCRN	4.2684	2.9312	0.7026	0.8327	0.8327	4.1401	2.6431	0.9307	0.9095	0.9105
	DCGCN	4.9136	3.3604	0.6577	0.7783	0.7789	3.9407	2.2971	0.9341	0.9181	0.9182
	LSTM-M	6.9719	4.6873	0.6145	0.6884	0.6908	5.6291	3.4282	0.8023	0.8158	0.8160
	GRU-D	7.7023	5.4650	0.5147	0.4643	0.4699	12.9229	9.2897	*	*	*
	GMN	7.3423	4.9671	0.6017	0.6169	0.6338	5.3890	3.5264	0.8501	0.8404	0.8410
	Ours	**4.0981**	**2.7426**	**0.7145**	**0.8458**	**0.8460**	**2.8697**	**1.8523**	**0.9524**	**0.9573**	**0.9579**
20%	GCN	6.2466	4.6383	0.5648	0.6417	0.6420	12.2606	8.9405	0.7949	0.2070	0.2083
	GRU	5.4116	3.7098	0.6230	0.7311	0.7319	9.8438	7.1996	0.8353	0.4888	0.4895
	TGCN	4.2969	2.9761	0.7006	0.8305	0.8305	10.6767	7.3622	0.8214	0.3987	0.3990
	A3TGCN	4.3117	2.9890	0.6996	0.8293	0.8295	10.8265	7.3679	0.8189	0.3817	0.3840
	AGCRN	4.3117	2.9890	0.6996	0.8293	0.8295	4.55279	2.8768	0.9238	0.89065	0.8907
	DCGCN	4.9894	3.5872	0.6524	0.7714	0.7717	4.2467	2.5555	0.9290	0.9049	0.9050
	LSTM-M	7.2885	4.9308	0.6552	0.6692	0.6704	6.3077	3.8010	0.7656	0.7670	0.7675
	GRU-D	7.7842	5.3798	0.3987	0.4081	0.4280	12.9291	9.1756	*	*	*
	GMN	7.5934	5.1103	0.4981	0.5900	0.6091	5.4478	3.6624	0.8043	0.8357	0.8358
	Ours	**4.1474**	**2.7830**	**0.7111**	**0.8421**	**0.8423**	**3.1132**	**2.0112**	**0.9479**	**0.9489**	**0.9502**
40%	GCN	6.6705	4.9104	0.5353	0.5915	0.5918	12.2739	8.8665	0.7947	0.2053	0.2055
	GRU	6.4535	4.6824	0.5504	0.6176	0.6176	11.6429	8.6497	0.8052	0.2849	0.2857
	TGCN	4.4080	3.1549	0.6929	0.8216	0.8229	10.8774	7.3501	0.8180	0.3758	0.3816
	A3TGCN	4.3852	3.0946	0.6945	0.8234	0.8250	10.7750	7.2574	0.8197	0.3875	0.3890
	AGCRN	4.4013	3.0287	0.6934	0.8221	0.8222	5.6731	3.6947	0.9050	0.8302	0.8303
	DCGCN	5.5758	4.1052	0.6115	0.7146	0.7150	5.6163	3.3714	0.9060	0.8336	0.8336
	LSTM-M	8.1514	5.5630	0.5502	0.6150	0.6166	7.0997	4.2704	.6958	0.7032	0.7039
	GRU-D	7.8258	5.4817	0.4437	0.4778	0.4810	12.9674	9.1651	*	*	*
	GMN	8.2432	5.5723	0.4983	0.5178	0.5466	5.6909	4.0070	0.8012	0.8191	0.8194
	Ours	**4.1541**	**2.7810**	**0.7106**	**0.8416**	**0.8418**	**3.8334**	**2.4361**	**0.9359**	**0.9225**	**0.9230**

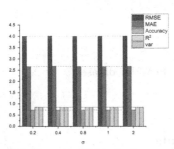

(a) Gaussian Perturbation

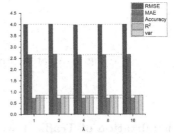

(b) Poisson Perturbation

Fig. 2. Perturbation analysis on SZ-taxi dataset.

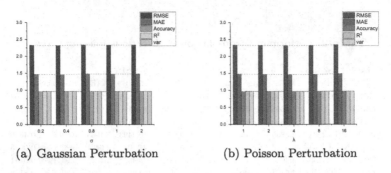

(a) Gaussian Perturbation   (b) Poisson Perturbation

Fig. 3. Perturbation analysis on PeMSD7 dataset.

4.5 Ablation Study

To better understand the impact of the probabilistic adjacency matrix and node-specific learning in handling missing data, we conducted an ablation study. We evaluated the performance of our model without the probabilistic adjacency matrix and performed prediction tasks for different missing rates on the PeMSD7 dataset. We also did the same for node-specific learning. In Fig. 4, we can see that if we use a static adjacency matrix rather than a probabilistic adjacency matrix, the RMSE of the model increases a lot. Taking out the node-specific learning module also increased RMSE, although not as significant as when we removed the probabilistic adjacency matrix. This indicates that the probabilistic adjacency matrix strongly influences managing missing data.

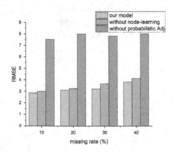

Fig. 4. Ablation study on PeMSD7 dataset.

4.6 Visualization of Traffic Forecasting

In Fig. 5, we visualize prediction for 15 min by our proposed model on the PeMSD7 dataset. We can see that our model can capture the trend of the traffic data. Using traditional GCN in the model can result in unsatisfactory prediction results because of its smoothing effect [6]. In our proposed model we modified the GCN which can learn unique characteristics of nodes and can capture dynamic spatial dependencies. Those modifications in GCN help our model to capture the peak. First, we visualize our prediction result without perturbation in Fig. 5a. Then we used noisy data for the prediction task. Under Gaussian noise for $\sigma = 0.4$, we visualize the prediction result in Fig. 5b. We also did the prediction task for Poisson noise ($\lambda = 4$) in Fig. 5c. We can see that our model captured the traffic flow and gave accurate performance for both noises. We also visualized performance for the 10% missing rate in Fig. 5d. It shows the robustness of our proposed model in handling abnormal or disrupted data.

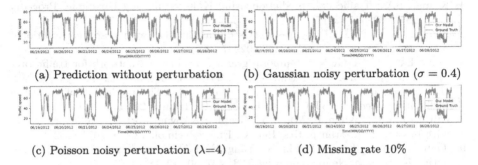

(a) Prediction without perturbation   (b) Gaussian noisy perturbation ($\sigma = 0.4$)

(c) Poisson noisy perturbation (λ=4)   (d) Missing rate 10%

Fig. 5. Visualization of predictions on the PeMSD7 dataset without perturbation, and with perturbation involving noise and missing data.

5   Conclusion

In this study, we proposed a Robust Probabilistic Spatio-temporal Graph Convolutional Network to forecast traffic information in a harsh environment. By combining GCN and GRU, our proposed model effectively captures both spatial and temporal characteristics of traffic networks. We introduced a dynamic probabilistic adjacency matrix, allowing the model to adapt to changing spatial dependencies over time. Our modifications to GCN enable the learning of node-specific patterns, enhancing the model's ability to handle noisy data without requiring extensive preprocessing or imputation. Adding an attention mechanism helps our model to capture the global trend of traffic networks. We focus on the inherent resilience of the model itself, rather than resorting to laborious and sub-optimal methods to address dataset shortcomings, a common approach in many other studies. Evaluation of real-world datasets, including city roads and highways, demonstrates the superior performance of our model compared to baseline approaches, even under challenging conditions with noisy or missing data. Importantly, our model exhibits consistent performance across varying levels of data imperfections, highlighting its robustness and practical utility in real-world scenarios. In the future, we plan to examine the robustness of our proposed method under complex scenarios and settings. Additionally, we aim to conduct experiments using other publicly available datasets.

References

1. Rahman, M.M., Nower, N.: Attention based deep hybrid networks for traffic flow prediction using google maps data. In: Proceedings of the 2023 8th International Conference on Machine Learning Technologies, pp. 74–81 (2023)
2. Lana, I., Olabarrieta, I.I., Velez, M., Del Ser, J.: On the imputation of missing data for road traffic forecasting.: new insights and novel techniques. Transp. Res. Part C: Emerg. Technol. **90**, 18–33 (2018)
3. Shahriari, S., Ghasri, M., Sisson, S.A., Rashidi, T.: Ensemble of ARIMA: combining parametric and bootstrapping technique for traffic flow prediction. Transp. A: Transp. Sci. **16**(3), 1552–1573 (2020)
4. Kumar, S.V.: Traffic flow prediction using Kalman filtering technique. Procedia Eng. **187**, 582–587 (2017)
5. Kipf, T.N., Welling, M.: Semi-supervised classification with graph convolutional networks. arXiv preprint arXiv:1609.02907 (2016)
6. Zhao, L., et al.: T-GCN: a temporal graph convolutional network for traffic prediction. IEEE Trans. Intell. Transp. Syst. **21**(9), 3848–3858 (2019)
7. Hou, F., Zhang, Y., Xinli, F., Jiao, L., Zheng, W.: The prediction of multistep traffic flow based on AST-GCN-LSTM. J. Adv. Transp. **2021**, 1–10 (2021)
8. Cui, Z., Lin, L., Ziyuan, P., Wang, Y.: Graph Markov network for traffic forecasting with missing data. Transp. Res. Part C: Emerg. echnol. **117**, 102671 (2020)
9. Tian, Y., Zhang, K., Li, J., Lin, X., Yang, B.: LSTM-based traffic flow prediction with missing data. Neurocomputing **318**, 297–305 (2018)
10. Chen, X., He, Z., Sun, L.: A Bayesian tensor decomposition approach for spatiotemporal traffic data imputation. Transp. Res. Part C Emerg. Technol. **98**, 73–84 (2019)
11. Che, Z., Purushotham, S., Cho, K., Sontag, D., Liu, Y.: Recurrent neural networks for multivariate time series with missing values. Sci. Rep. **8**(1), 6085 (2018)
12. Guo, J., Wang, Z., Chen, H.: On-line multi-step prediction of short term traffic flow based on GRU neural network. In: Proceedings of the 2nd International Conference on Intelligent Information Processing, pp. 1–6 (2017)
13. Kang, D., Lv, Y., Chen, Y.Y.: Short-term traffic flow prediction with LSTM recurrent neural network. In: 2017 IEEE 20th International Conference on Intelligent Transportation Systems (ITSC), pp. 1–6. IEEE (2017)
14. Wu, Y., Tan, H.: Short-term traffic flow forecasting with spatial-temporal correlation in a hybrid deep learning framework. arXiv preprint arXiv:1612.01022 (2016)
15. Atkia Akila Karim and Naushin Nower: Long-term traffic prediction based on stacked GCN model. Knowl. Eng. Data Sci. **6**(1), 92–102 (2023)
16. Bai, J., et al.: A3T-GCN: attention temporal graph convolutional network for traffic forecasting. ISPRS Int. J. Geo-Inf. **10**(7), 485 (2021)
17. Zhu, J., Wang, Q., Tao, C., Deng, H., Zhao, L., Li, H.: AST-GCN: attribute-augmented spatiotemporal graph convolutional network for traffic forecasting. IEEE Access **9**, 35973–35983 (2021)
18. Chen, Z., et al.: Spatial-temporal short-term traffic flow prediction model based on dynamical-learning graph convolution mechanism. Inf. Sci. **611**, 522–539 (2022)
19. Bai, L., Yao, L., Li, C., Wang, X., Wang, C.: Adaptive graph convolutional recurrent network for traffic forecasting. Adv. Neural. Inf. Process. Syst. **33**, 17804–17815 (2020)
20. Junhua, G., Jia, Z., Cai, T., Song, X., Mahmood, A.: Dynamic correlation adjacency-matrix-based graph neural networks for traffic flow prediction. Sensors **23**(6), 2897 (2023)

21. Li, B., Yang, Q., Chen, J., Yu, D., Wang, D., Wan, F., et al.: A dynamic spatio-temporal deep learning model for lane-level traffic prediction. J. Adv. Transp. **2023** (2023)

22. Yuan, Y., Zhang, Y., Wang, B., Peng, Y., Yongli, H., Yin, B.: STGAN: spatio-temporal generative adversarial network for traffic data imputation. IEEE Trans. Big Data **9**(1), 200–211 (2022)

23. Huang, R., Huang, C., Liu, Y., Dai, G., Kong, W.: LSGCN: long short-term traffic prediction with graph convolutional networks. In: IJCAI, vol. 7, pp. 2355–2361 (2020)

Support Vector Based Anomaly Detection in Federated Learning

Massimo Frasson[ID] and Dario Malchiodi[✉][ID]

Department of Computer Science, University of Milan,
Via Celoria 18, 20133 Milan, Italy
dario.malchiodi@unimi.it, massimo.frasson@studenti.unimi.it

Abstract. Anomaly detection plays a crucial role in various domains. However, traditional centralized approaches often encounter challenges related to data privacy. In this context, Federated Learning emerges as a promising solution. This work introduces two algorithms that leverage Support Vector Machines for anomaly detection in a federated setting. In comparison with the Neural Networks typically used in this field, these algorithms emerge as potential alternatives, as they can operate with small datasets and incur lower computational costs. The algorithms are tested in various configurations, yielding promising initial results Specifically, we attain comparable results to the centralized counterpart when the distributed system simulates a centralized setting. A trade-off emerges between split bias and client fraction, indicating that higher client fractions are necessary for optimal performance in scenarios with high bias.

Keywords: Anomaly Detection · Federated Learning · SVM

1 Introduction

Machine Learning (ML) has become increasingly pervasive in contemporary life, manifesting in diverse applications within business and consumer products. A plethora of algorithms exist, tailored to specific tasks. Among these tasks, Anomaly Detection (AD) received particular attention during the past few decades [25]. Initially conceived to spot low-quality measurements in experimental outcomes, AD swiftly found broader applications due to the intrinsic value of anomalies, events characterized by unexpected and abrupt occurrences. Anomalies, by their nature, are infrequent and often entail significant costs when they do transpire. Consider for instance continuous systems: being able to detect anomalous behaviors as they develop, for instance, within a piece of industrial equipment, or in the human body, enables engineers, in the first case, and physicians, in the second one, to act proactively. By their nature, anomalies escape formal definitions (excluding, of course, that of not behaving as in normal conditions), therefore it is very difficult to find them by using traditional algorithmic methods. Indeed, AD is typically rooted in statistical techniques: notably, ML

L. Iliadis et al. (Eds.): EANN 2024, CCIS 2141, pp. 274–287, 2024.
https://doi.org/10.1007/978-3-031-62495-7_21

proved to be effective in detecting or foreseeing them [18]. However, the classical supervised approach in ML is not well suited: this is because data describing anomalies are typically scarce, resulting in a strong class imbalance. This makes AD different from binary classification, and thus requiring different approaches. The more obvious option is that of unsupervised ML [3,10]. However, a significant drawback pervades the existing paradigm of AD when the objects to be analyzed live in a distributed world. Conventional algorithms require the centralization of all available data. Besides the obvious logistical challenges posed by the transmission and storage of substantial data volumes, this introduces serious privacy concerns. The potential data leakage, either during transmission or as the effect of cyber attacks to the server, raises severe business issues, particularly concerning sensitive domains like those involving medical records, culminating in costly fines, such as the ones regulated by the GDPR [26].

Given the practical benefits of ML in our society, the imperative arises to derive equivalent value from data involving AD, yet removing privacy concerns from the equation. Enter Federated Learning (FL), a paradigm introduced by [5,14,15]. FL is defined as a loose federation of devices (clients) participating in a ML process, under the coordination of a central server. FL adopts a protocol ensuring that the dataset of each client remains completely undisclosed, even to the server itself. Indeed, clients share with the central server only model updates computed via training on their local observations. The server simply receives these updates and aggregates them to build a global update which is subsequently distributed to all clients, so that they can enrich their performances without compromising privacy. Within the FL domain, all challenges in the realm of distributed systems related to handling device federations over the Internet are addressed at a lower layer of abstraction. This abstraction is provided by the platform executing the decentralized learning process, enabling developers to focus on devising algorithms that perform comparably to their centralized counterparts within the federated framework. One of the first studies in which FL was introduced [15] also proposed the first federated algorithm, called *FederatedAveraging*, devoted to training Neural Networks and applied to the problem of predicting the next typed word using smart keyboards in mobile devices [12].

In general, Neural Networks are at the forefront of contemporary ML models, being able to capture complex and nonlinear relations among data. They have been extensively applied also to the AD domain (see, for instance, [1] for a recent review). As highlighted in [19], the privacy concerns inherent in FL do not guarantee the availability of sufficient data to effectively train neural models on every single device. A trending solution in the literature is leveraging transfer learning. This involves training a general-purpose model on the central server and then fine-tuning it locally to provide a tailored model to each client, thereby protecting privacy and ensuring good personalized performance. However, this solution still necessitates data availability on a central server, which is not always guaranteed in privacy-sensitive environments. Training Neural Networks is computationally expensive, and while high-end smartphones currently available in the market are equipped with processors expressly designed for neural operations, they are more suited for querying complex networks, or fine-tuning them, rather than for a full training process [6]. This gap is further pronounced when considering the broader realm of IoT and edge devices [24]. These challenges leave room to explore alternatives. Support Vector Machines (SVMs) have long been used as a counterpart w.r.t. Neural Networks, because of their ability to generalize without overfitting data, in the meanwhile possibly compressing the dataset onto a small set of *support vectors* (SVs) that fully describe a learnt model. SVMs have been successfully applied to anomaly detection, modeling the region containing normal observations in two different ways: respectively, learning a hyperplane separating normal data and outliers [22], or building a small hypersphere enclosing normal observations [23]. The two approaches are equivalent under specific choices for the related hyper parameters, as shown in [22].

This work aims to integrate FL and the Support Vector Domain Description (SVDD) technique introduced in [23], proposing two possible strategies for solving the AD problem in the federated context: Support Vector Election and Ensemble SVDD, sketched here below.

- In the Support Vector Election approach, each client is tasked with the application of SVDD on its own data, subsequently applying a special noise addition mechanism inspired by differential privacy [7], sampling in the vicinity of each SV in order to obtain a replacement which can be sent to the central server without privacy concerns. The server trains a new SVM on the accumulated support vectors, potentially discarding superfluous ones.
- The Ensemble SVDD approach also requires each client to apply SVDD on its local data, now transmitting the entire learned model (that is SVs, their weights, and the hyper parameter values) to the central server. Functioning as a relay, the server distributes the incoming models to all clients. The classification of new observations is done via ensemble voting, using all models. When at least one of them predicts that the observation is an inlier, it is classified as such. When all models detect an outlier, the observation is classified as anomalous. To ensure privacy, before transmitting the model, each client generates a synthetic dataset, and trains SVDD a second time on this dataset, to derive SVs that do not originate from the client's data.

Experimental assessments are conducted to evaluate the effectiveness of the proposed approaches and of the related noise addition mechanisms. To maintain a comprehensive perspective and to facilitate meaningful comparisons, the experimental methodology aligns with that adopted in [10], based on the OC-SVM approach [22], whose performances are used as a (centralized) baseline. By replicating and validating the related results, a seamless connection is established between the novel approaches presented here and the existing state-of-the-art methods.

This work is structured as follows: Sect. 2 describes the main approaches used in the literature to address the AD problem, while Sect. 3 is devoted to briefly describe the FL setting. Section 4 details the two proposed approaches for a federated-based anomaly detection, and Sect. 5 illustrates the related experimental campaign, discussing the obtained results. Some concluding remarks end the paper.

2 Anomaly Detection

Anomaly (or outlier) detection is a well-studied problem in ML and data mining. Its goal is to identify data points that behave in a significantly different way w.r.t. the distribution modeling the usual behavior of a system. Detecting such points is important to spot malfunctions (such as damages in a mechanical system, or bugs in software), to notice illicit use of resources (e.g., frauds in financial transactions of healthcare), or to get aware of the emergence of novel phenomena.

One of the fundamental algorithms addressing AD is Local Outlier Factor (LOF) [4], based on scoring a point $\mathbf{x}$ using the ratio of the average density of its k nearest neighbors to the density of $\mathbf{x}$ itself. Points with a high LOF score are considered outliers. The effectiveness of this approach has been experimentally established, although its sensitivity to parameter selection and its high computational complexity have also been pointed out [10]. Analogous drawbacks are suffered by CBLOF [13], based on a more refined clustering procedure. Statistical approaches, such as that adopted by HBOS [9], evaluate anomalies by separately analyzing the various data features (typically via histogram analysis), subsequently aggregating the results into an outlier score. The obtained results outperform methods such as LOF, but this method assume that features are i.i.d., a property seldom satisfied by real-world datasets.

The most known adaptations of SVMs to AD are called One-Class SVM (OC-SVM) [22] and Support Vector Data Description (SVDD) [23], both exhibiting advantageous results w.r.t. alternative approaches in scenarios involving sparse or complex datasets. The common approach in these algorithms consists in considering images of the data in a high-dimensional space $\mathcal{H}$, yet discriminating anomalies from normal data in two different ways: OC-SVM learns a hyperplane, whereas SVDD learns a sphere. In the setting considered here, given a set $\{\mathbf{x}_1, \ldots, \mathbf{x}_n\}$ of normal points, SVDD finds the multiplier values $\beta_1, \ldots, \beta_n$ minimizing $\sum_{i,j} \beta_i \beta_j k(\mathbf{x}_j, \mathbf{x}_j)$, where k denotes a Gaussian kernel, under the constraints $\sum_i \beta_i = 1$ and $0 \leq \beta_i \leq C \; \forall i = 1, \ldots, n$. A new point $\mathbf{x}$ is classified in function of the distance between its image in $\mathcal{H}$ and the center of the learnt sphere, amounting to

$$R^2(\mathbf{x}) = 1 - 2 \sum_j \beta_j K(\mathbf{x}_j, \mathbf{x}) + \sum_{i,j} \beta_i \beta_j k(\mathbf{x}_i, \mathbf{x}_j). \tag{1}$$

It turns out that most of the optimal multipliers nullify, thus R^2 only depends on a small number of the original points, called support vectors. A crisp classification typically involves a comparison with the radius of the sphere, in turn obtained computing (1) on any support vector.

Despite their potential, the above-mentioned techniques for outlier detection may face practical challenges in distributed and privacy-sensitive settings. In many real-world scenarios, data is scattered across multiple sources or entities, and it may not be feasible or desirable to centralize it. The main contribution of this work (cfr. Sect. 4) is to propose two extensions of the SVDD algorithm that are privacy-sensitive and distributed. Both of them are deeply rooted in the FL framework, introduced in the next section.

3   Federated Learning

The FL setting [5] has been introduced to enhance the user experience in smartphones, using data collected via the latter to train ML models meanwhile preserving user privacy. The core idea is to keep data on the devices and leverage their computing power to locally train a model. The involved devices can subsequently transmit their model updates to a central server. This server is in charge of aggregating these updates into a global model that is broadcast to all clients. This results, in principle, in a privacy-preserving learning methodology that gives each smartphone predictive capabilities obtained by exploiting the data of all users[1]. FL is characterized by the following properties:

- *non-i.i.d.*: it is unlikely that data used in a local training procedure is representative of the entire user population;
- *imbalance*: different users may exhibit varying behaviors and data generation patterns;
- *massive distribution*: targeting mobile devices involves a huge number of clients;
- *limited communication*: mobile devices may be offline, have limited data usage, or experience slow connections or low power charge.

Training within the FL framework typically takes place using *FederatedAveraging*, an adaptation of Stochastic Gradient Descent that uses averaging to aggregate the weight updates of several neural networks having the same architecture, where each update has been locally learned by a single device using its own data batch. The average update is applied to the server's global model, repeating the process until a stopping condition is met. At that time, the global model is sent to all clients. The algorithm has been applied to the fields of image classification and language models [5], yielding impressive results.

The adoption of FL to perform AD has been predominantly done in the Internet of Things (IoT) domain, for instance in order to detect abnormal computation in complex systems behind augmented buildings [21], by considering the logs of indoor sensors and energy usage and focusing on an LSTM architecture. An analogous approach was applied to the identification of network attacks [16], combining GRUs learnt from the single devices so as to obtain an ensemble voting system. Finally, [17] addresses the issue of AD in FL under the assumption that clients might not agree on which the "normal" label is: after each client have executed OC-SVM on its data, pairs of clients exchange their models, and each uses the received model to classify its local data. In case of high accuracy, the

---

[1] For the sake of brevity, this description of the learning protocol is given in a simplified form. Some concern about the users privacy remain, as improperly crafted updates can leak information from the device, and this is handled in FL by adopting a *secure aggregation* technique, together with encrypted communications and, possibly, differential privacy.

Algorithm 1. Ensemble SVDD

Require: F (client fraction), K (num. clients)
   $t \leftarrow \max(F \cdot K, 1)$
   $S \leftarrow$ selectRandomClients(t)
   for each client $k \in S$ **in parallel do**
      $X \leftarrow$ retrieveData(k)
      $V, B, \gamma, C \leftarrow$ SVDD(X)
      $X' \leftarrow$ syntheticDataset(V, B, X)
      $m_k \leftarrow$ SVDD(X')
   end for
   $M \leftarrow$ mergeModels($m_1, \ldots, m_t$)
   sendToAllClients(M)

---

two models agree about what is to be detected as normal: autoencoders can be trained separately on this data, subsequently applying *FederatedAveraging*[2].

In general, the research around AD in FL is focused only on Neural Networks, leaving unexplored other fundamental model types. The next section proposes the direct use of SVMs in the FL framework.

4 The Proposed Methods

This section describes the main contribution of this work: two federated learning algorithms for AD using SVMs. Replacing Neural Networks with SVMs removes the need to perform multiple rounds during training, thus these methods aim at attaining a better time complexity, possibly also improving prediction performances. The proposed algorithms are Ensemble SVDD (ESVDD), in which each client locally runs SVDD and the resulting models are used from the central server to obtain an ensemble learner, and Support Vector Election (SVE), whose clients select representative points via SVDD, to be sent to the server for a second-round learning phase, still using SVDD. The proposed algorithms are built upon the foundation established by [23], though using most of the notation from [2], which fits better the proposed learning algorithms.

4.1 Ensemble SVDD

ESVDD recognizes that each client may have a distinct representation of the region containing normal points, due to local biases. Therefore, the algorithm uses an ensemble approach to leverage the collective insights of all clients, as detailed in Algorithm 1. ESVDD initially selects a subset S of clients for training, corresponding to a fraction F of the total K available clients. Each client k independently trains a SVDD model on its local data X. The resulting model

---

[2] Note that in this learning protocol there is a subtle violation of the FL paradigm: OC-SVM describes the learnt hyperplane using support vectors, that are points coming from the training set. The transmission of the model implies therefore the disclosure of some client data.

Algorithm 2. Support Vector Election

Require: F (client fraction), K (num. clients), γ (kernel width), C (slackness factor),
$\quad\sigma$ (standard dev. for anonymisation), τ (threshold for difference between distances)
$\quad t \leftarrow \max(F \cdot K, 1)$
$\quad S \leftarrow \text{selectRandomClients}(t)$
$\quad$**for** each client $k \in S$ **in parallel do**
$\quad\quad X \leftarrow \text{retrieveData}(k)$
$\quad\quad V, B \leftarrow \text{SVDD}(X, \gamma, C)$
$\quad\quad V_k' \leftarrow \emptyset$
$\quad\quad$**for** $\mathbf{v} \in V$ **do**
$\quad\quad\quad \mathbf{q} \leftarrow \text{gaussian}(\mathbf{v}, \sigma)$
$\quad\quad\quad R^2 \leftarrow \text{distanceFromCenter}(V, B)$
$\quad\quad\quad$**while** $|R^2(\mathbf{v}) - R^2(\mathbf{q})| > \tau$ **do**
$\quad\quad\quad\quad \mathbf{q} \leftarrow \mathbf{q} - \epsilon(\mathbf{q} - \mathbf{v})$
$\quad\quad\quad$**end while**
$\quad\quad\quad V_k' \leftarrow V_k' \cup \{\mathbf{q}\}$
$\quad\quad$**end for**
$\quad$**end for**
$\quad V' \leftarrow \cup_k V_k'$
$\quad M \leftarrow \text{SVDD}(V', \gamma, C)$
$\quad \text{sendToAllClients}(M)$

---

is described by the hyper parameter values (C and γ), the support vector set V and the multiplier set B. Note that outputting a prediction in the learnt model is related to the computation of (1), which involves all SVs, which are points from the training set. This means that clients cannot directly send their models to the central server without contradicting the FL principle prohibiting data from leaving the client's domain. To avoid this, ESVDD relies on a noise addition mechanism: after the local training, each client generates a synthetic dataset by drawing a sample from the input space and isolating the points within the learnt sphere[3]. This process yields a new set of inliers on which SVDD is rerun, resulting in a new model with synthetic SVs not originating from the initial training set. This model can be therefore transmitted to the central server. The server redistributes the received models to all the clients (including the ones not participating in training) as an ensemble, which will classify a new point as normal if and only if it is predicted as such by at least one among the sent models. As argued in [10], it is better to address the prediction problem by assigning a score to the data points rather than a binary "inlier"/"outlier" label, as some of the outliers might be more critical than others. This is already done by each model in the ensemble. Thus the overall score is computed as follows: if a point is predicted as an inlier, ESVDD returns the maximum score among

---

[3] More precisely, sampling is based on a mixture of a normal distribution fitted to the dataset and several normal distributions of small variance, centered around SVs. The latter distributions are introduced to avoid that sampling be focused only on the densest regions of the dataset.

Table 1. Performances of the considered algorithms, in terms of mean and standard deviation of AUC over several experiments with different C values, over the considered datasets (first column, denoting for sake of brevity each dataset using its initial letter). Only the best and worst performing results over the various configurations adopted for SVE and SVDD, respectively marked with $+$ and $-$, are reported. Boldface highlights the configurations in which a federated approach is either in line with the centralized algorithms, or outperforms them.

D	OC-SVM	SVDD	SVE (+)	ESVDD (+)	SVE (−)	ESVDD (−)
B	0.98 ± 1E-3	0.93 ± 5E-3	0.95 ± 2E-2	**0.96 ± 1E-2**	0.63 ± 3E-1	0.68 ± 3E-1
P	0.94 ± 3E-2	0.79 ± 4E-4	0.80 ± 2E-2	0.88 ± 1E-2	0.48 ± 2E-1	0.60 ± 2E-1
L	0.59 ± 4E-3	0.56 ± 1E-4	0.57 ± 1E-2	**0.79 ± 4E-3**	0.48 ± 4E-2	0.51 ± 5E-2
S	0.91 ± 6E-3	0.77 ± 1E-4	0.79 ± 2E-2	**0.88 ± 2E-3**	0.53 ± 2E-1	0.62 ± 2E-1

all clients' score assignments; conversely, it returns the sum of scores from all clients. The latter strategy heavily penalizes points that deviate significantly from many clients.

4.2   Support Vector Election

Conceptually speaking, SVDD can be seen as an election process, selecting SVs as representatives for the entire dataset. Leveraging this observation, SVE adopts an election mechanism to select a small number of points transmitted to the central server, as detailed in Algorithm 2. Each client k uses its local data X to train a model via SVDD[4]. The resulting support vector set V and multiplier set B are then used to compute the function R^2 mapping points to the squared distance from the center of the learnt sphere in feature space. All SVs are then anonymised using a technique inspired by the Gaussian Mechanism [8]: each support vector $\mathbf{v}$ is replaced by a new point $\mathbf{q}$ drawn from a Gaussian distribution centered around the vector itself. But in the case under study, this new point should also lie on the surface of the sphere learnt by SVDD. This problem is addressed by guiding sampled points towards the original support vector: if the initially drawn point lies too far from the surface, it is moved towards the original support vector, iterating the procedure until a satisfactory point is obtained. The result is a set V_k' of anonymised support vectors, whose elements are transmitted to the central server, which merges them into a collective set V'. An SVDD run is subsequently run on this set, obtaining a model M whose description is transmitted to all clients, which will use it in order to compute outlierness scores for new observations.

5   Experiments and Results

Both ESVDD and SVE score the test data, with higher scores indicating a greater likelihood of the point being an inlier. This score is converted into a crisp

---

[4] Note that, in this case, the central server imposes uniform hyper parameter values (C and γ) for all clients, and these values remain fixed throughout the algorithm.

classification via a threshold, and the evaluation of performances is done using the Area Under the Receiving Operator Curve (AUC). All experiments were conducted on the datasets Breast Cancer (367 objects, 30 features, 2.72% outliers), Pen Global (809 objects, 16 features, 11.1% outliers), Letter (1600 objects, 32 features, 6.25% outliers) and Satellite (5100 objects, 36 features, 1.49% outliers) introduced in [10], employing min-max normalization to all features. The federated infrastructure was simulated within a single machine equipped with an Apple M1 CPU and 16 GB of main memory. The Federated Learning process was simulated entirely locally and sequentially, computing updates for individual clients one at a time and subsequently performing server aggregation. We utilized scikit-learn [20] to conduct experiments and evaluations. SVDD was implemented by us using Gurobi [11] as the optimization framework for the SVM problem.

5.1 Evaluating Plasticity

The first part of the experiments concerns the ability of the proposed algorithms to be able to suitably adapt the learnt model to the provided dataset. In other words, the research question is: "does FL preserve the ability of SVM methods for AD to avoid underfitting the data they process?". As the experiments are not aimed at evaluating generalization ability (see Sect. 5.2 for this part), there is no separation between training and test set, meaning the whole dataset is used for training and evaluating a model. To answer the research question, a comparison is made with two baselines: (i) OC-SVM and (ii) SVDD (both the algorithms are described in the Introduction). Note that the considered baselines likely represent an upper bound to the performance achievable with federated techniques, as centralizing all data should provide them an unfair advantage w.r.t. FL. Following the methodology adopted in [10], the hyper parameter space is sampled, running each time the learning process and reporting the results in terms of mean and standard deviation of the AUC. The goal is to highlight the impact of the hyper parameter choice on these results. Concerning OC-SVM, the baseline is obtained sampling ν (a hyper parameter strictly related to C in the modelisation adopted here) uniformly in $[0.2, 0.8]$ and employing an automatic tuning for γ. Due to limited computational resources, the experiments reported here only replicate the first hyper parameter sampling, fixing γ at 1. The performances of SVDD, ESVDD, and SVE are replicated under the same setting. In all cases, 10 hyper parameter samples were collected. For computational constraints, ESVDD is run so that all client shared the values for C and γ, and the two additional hyper parameters of SVE are fixed so that $\sigma = 1$ and $\tau = 10^{-3}$ (the latter serving as a measure of the surrogate's quality of anonymised support vectors). All the combinations of the total number of clients $K \in \{2, 5, 10\}$ and of the client fraction $F \in \{0.5, 1\}$ are systematically tested. It is worth underlying that ESVDD and SVE are run both with and without using their anonymisation mechanisms, to discern the amount to which the latter impact in performance. Finally, the distribution of data w.r.t. clients is tested under two extreme scenarios: *i.i.d.*, where the dataset is shuffled and evenly partitioned among clients, and *Biased*,

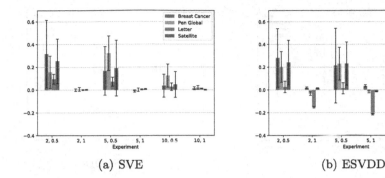

(a) SVE   (b) ESVDD

Fig. 1. Impact on the performance of SVE (a) and ESVDD (b) of the data split distributions for diffcrent combinations of K and F, shown in the X axis. The chart shows mean and standard deviation on several runs of the AUC difference, with positive values favoring i.i.d. over biased splits, and vice versa.

where observations are distributed across clients on the basis of KMeans clustering. Table 1 reports the obtained results. It is evident that SVE can match the performance of the baseline under optimal conditions (highlighted in bold in the table), although its performances w.r.t. the centralized counterparts significantly decrease under less favorable conditions. Similar considerations apply to ESVDD, with a remarkable difference: unexpectedly, this algorithm even outperforms the baseline under optimal conditions. Recall that the analyzed conditions refer to the following variables: degree of bias in the data distribution, client fraction, and total number of clients. Figures 1 and 2 analyze the configuration scenarios more in depth. More precisely, Fig. 1 depicts the AUC difference between experiments conducted in the *i.i.d.* and *Biased* settings, in function of the possible combinations of K and F. In general, the difference is negligible when the client fraction is set to 1, but the impact becomes substantial when $F = 0.5$. This behavior is expected because with a client fraction of 0.5, only half of the clients are used in training: this is not problematic with i.i.d. data, whereas uncertainty and mismodeling can significantly affect performance when the data is strongly biased. However, it is worth nothing an interesting exception arising on the letter dataset: when $F = 1$ the biased experiments always outperform those with i.i.d. data, and when $F = 0.5$ the difference between the two settings is almost negligible. Analogously, Fig. 2 illustrates the impact of the client fraction when the client amount and bias are fixed. Also in this case, we observe as expected that: (i) i.i.d. data do not result in meaningful differences in performances, but a biased split have a considerable impact on the reported AUC values, and (ii) this impact tends to be less evident as F grows, especially when using SVE. It is intriguing to highlight that, also in this experiment, the Letter dataset behaves in a different way w.r.t. the remaining datasets: using only a subset of the data leads to a result which is not dramatically worse than using all data, though this fact happens now in conjunction with SVE. Figure 3 illustrates the impact of the anonymisation technique. It is evident that the use

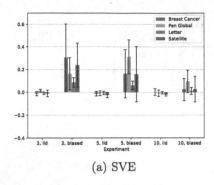 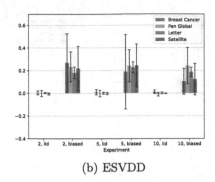

(a) SVE   (b) ESVDD

Fig. 2. Impact on the performance of SVE (a) and ESVDD (b) of the client fraction F, for different combinations of K and of the data split type. Same notation as in Fig. 1, with positive values favoring the usage of all data over a subset, and vice versa.

of anonymisation has minimal to no impact in most cases. However, in the likely worst-case scenario (i.e., $F = 0.5$ and biased split) the difference in performance becomes more pronounced and uncertain. Rather than to anonymisation, this is likely due to the random client selection during training: indeed, experiments with and without noise may have selected different training clients, resulting in performance disparities. Overall, the impact of anonymisation remains relatively constant, although, unexpectedly, it tends to lead to better results. Finally, the experiments don't identify discernible patterns for the impact of the client number.

5.2   Evaluating Generalization Ability

In order to assess the generalization ability of the proposed algorithms, a second set of experiments is conducted for each combination of the total number of clients $K \in \{2, 5, 10\}$ and the client fraction $F \in \{0.5, 1\}$ using a nested cross-validation process, with 3 outer folds used to estimate the test error and 3 inner folds devoted to the model selection phase. More precisely, the best value for C is found using a randomized search, uniformly sampling 10 values in the range $[0.2, 0.8]$. The results are shown in Table 2, using the same notations as in Table 1 (although now the standard deviation refers to the different folds of the outer cross-validation). The performances are in line with those shown in the previous section. Instances in which AUC in Table 2 (highlighted in bold) is higher than in Table 1 are frequent. This trend is rational since the former set of experiments involved averaging over multiple hyper parameter choices, some of which might have been sub-optimal. In the latter experiments, C is optimized for each training set, resulting in better performances. Of particular interest are the unexpected results for breast cancer, which exhibit markedly improved performances compared to the previous experiments. This suggests that the initial experiments might have been disadvantaged due to unfortunate choices of C and the clients participating in the training. In conclusion, the proposed methods, especially ESVDD, succeed in generalizing to unseen data.

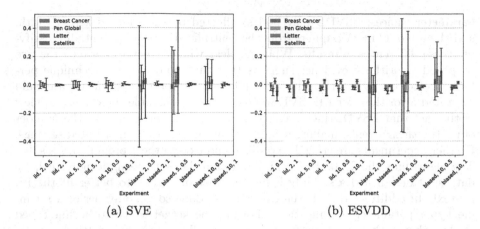

(a) SVE   (b) ESVDD

Fig. 3. Impact of the anonymisation technique on the performance of SVE (a) and ESVDD (d), for each combination of K, F and split bias. Same setting as in the previous figures, with positive values favoring using original data over applying anonymisation.

Table 2. Mean and standard deviation over outer cross-validation folds of the AUC values of the experiments described in Sect. 5.2, using the same notations as in Table 1. Bold values highlight better results w.r.t. Table 1.

D	OC-SVM	SVDD	SVE (+)	ESVDD (+)	SVE (−)	ESVDD (−)
B	0.98 ± 7E-3	0.96 ± 3E-2	**0.99 ± 5E-3**	**0.98 ± 9E-3**	**0.71 + 2E-1**	**0.86 ± 1E-1**
P	0.96 ± 1E-2	0.79 ± 6E-2	**0.84 ± 8E-3**	0.88 ± 1E-2	**0.55 ± 2E-1**	0.50 ± 3E-2
L	0.59 ± 4E-2	0.57 ± 3E-2	**0.59 ± 2E-2**	0.78 ± 2E-2	**0.51 ± 5E-2**	**0.54 ± 2E-2**
S	0.92 ± 8E-3	0.78 ± 8E-2	**0.82 ± 4E-2**	**0.89 ± 3E-2**	**0.56 ± 2E-1**	**0.68 ± 2E-1**

6   Conclusions

The objective of this study is to adapt SV-based learning algorithms for AD to the FL context, proposing two novel algorithms named ESVDD and SVE. In both cases, the privacy requirements set by FL are addressed using special anonymisation techniques. A first comparison with state-of-the-art (that is, centralized) methods is conducted focusing on the total number of clients available for training, the fraction of clients actually participating in the learning process, and the degree of bias among client data. While centralized approaches generally exhibit the highest performance across datasets, the FL results are closest to this baseline when mimicking a centralized setting, i.e., all clients are used and data are split in an i.i.d. fashion. A trade-off emerges between split bias and fraction of clients, indicating that higher client fractions are needed for optimal performance in high bias scenarios. In some instances, the decentralized approach of FL even outperforms the centralized algorithms; this could be attributed to hyper parameter choices: ESVDD may be less affected by the adopted kernel width, and the use of C in SVE differs from the centralized version, potentially justifying these differences in results. While no clear winner emerges between the two proposed algorithms, evidence suggests that the anonymisation technique performs better on SVE. In conclusion, while both proposed approaches are valid federated algorithms for AD, SVE stands out as a preferable choice, also in view of the fact that ESVDD increases its model size proportionally to the number of participating clients, making it impractical for massively distributed settings. Further experiments are crucial to confirm and extend these preliminary results. The algorithms should be tested on additional datasets, using a more realistic data split design and a sensibly higher number of clients, to better fit the FL context. In addition to that, the experiments done so far only perform a simple hyper parameter optimization: allowing the kernel width to be fine-tuned might enhance the overall performance, especially in high-bias settings; analogously, ESVDD could benefit from allowing each client to freely choose its hyper parameters, meanwhile filtering out or merging the models it receives in order to bar its inherent space complexity. Moreover, SVE might entail several training rounds, as in [5], in which clients collaborate in finding the best hyper parameters. Finally, SVE lends itself to a formal Differential Privacy proof, a necessary step for comparing it with other privacy-preserving algorithms.

Disclosure of Interests. The authors declare that they have no competing interests.

References

1. Albuquerque Filho, J.E.D., Brandão, L.C.P., Fernandes, B.J.T., Maciel, A.M.A.: A review of neural networks for anomaly detection. IEEE Access **10**, 112342–112367 (2022). https://doi.org/10.1109/ACCESS.2022.3216007
2. Ben-Hur, A., Horn, D., Siegelmann, H., Vapnik, V.: Support vector clustering. J. Mach. Learn. Res. **2**, 125–137 (2001). https://doi.org/10.1162/15324430260185565
3. Boukerche, A., Zheng, L., Alfandi, O.: Outlier detection: methods, models, and classification. ACM Comput. Surv. **53**(3) (2020). https://doi.org/10.1145/3381028
4. Breunig, M.M., Kriegel, H.P., Ng, R.T., Sander, J.: LoF: identifying density-based local outliers. In: Proceedings of the 2000 ACM SIGMOD International Conference on Management of Data, SIGMOD 2000, pp. 93–104. Association for Computing Machinery, New York (2000). https://doi.org/10.1145/342009.335388
5. Chen, M., Shlezinger, N., Poor, H.V., Eldar, Y.C., Cui, S.: Communication-efficient federated learning. Proc. Natl. Acad. Sci. **118**(17), e2024789118 (2021)
6. Das, A., Kwon, Y.D., Chauhan, J., Mascolo, C.: Enabling on-device smartphone GPU based training: Lessons learned. In: 2022 IEEE International Conference on Pervasive Computing and Communications Workshops and other Affiliated Events (PerCom Workshops), pp. 533–538 (2022). https://doi.org/10.1109/PerComWorkshops53856.2022.9767442
7. Dwork, C.: Differential privacy. In: Bugliesi, M., Preneel, B., Sassone, V., Wegener, I. (eds.) ICALP 2006. LNCS, vol. 4052, pp. 1–12. Springer, Heidelberg (2006). https://doi.org/10.1007/11787006_1

8. Dwork, C., Roth, A.: The algorithmic foundations of differential privacy. Found. Trends Theor. Comput. Sci. **9**(3–4), 211–407 (2014). https://doi.org/10.1561/0400000042
9. Goldstein, M., Dengel, A.: Histogram-based outlier score (HBOS): a fast unsupervised anomaly detection algorithm. In: KI-2012: Poster and Demo Track, vol. 1, pp. 59–63 (2012)
10. Goldstein, M., Uchida, S.: A comparative evaluation of unsupervised anomaly detection algorithms for multivariate data. PLoS ONE **11**(4), 1–31 (2016). https://doi.org/10.1371/journal.pone.0152173
11. Gurobi Optimization, LLC: Gurobi Optimizer Reference Manual (2023). https://www.gurobi.com
12. Hard, A., et al.: Federated learning for mobile keyboard prediction. arXiv preprint arXiv:1811.03604 (2018)
13. He, Z., Xu, X., Deng, S.: Discovering cluster-based local outliers. Pattern Recogn. Lett. **24**(9), 1641–1650 (2003). https://doi.org/10.1016/S0167-8655(03)00003-5
14. Konečný, J., McMahan, H.B., Ramage, D., Richtárik, P.: Federated optimization: distributed machine learning for on-device intelligence. arXiv preprint arXiv:1610.02527 (2016)
15. Konečný, J., McMahan, H.B., Yu, F.X., Richtárik, P., Suresh, A.T., Bacon, D.: Federated learning: strategies for improving communication efficiency. arXiv preprint arXiv:1610.05492 (2016)
16. Mothukuri, V., Khare, P., Parizi, R.M., Pouriyeh, S., Dehghantanha, A., Srivastava, G.: Federated-learning-based anomaly detection for IoT security attacks. IEEE Internet Things J. **9**(4), 2545–2554 (2022). https://doi.org/10.1109/JIOT.2021.3077803
17. Nardi, M., Valerio, L., Passarella, A.: Anomaly detection through unsupervised federated learning (2022)
18. Nassif, A.B., Talib, M.A., Nasir, Q., Dakalbab, F.M.: Machine learning for anomaly detection: a systematic review. IEEE Access **9**, 78658–78700 (2021)
19. Park, J., Choi, Y., Byun, J., Lee, J., Park, S.: Efficient differentially private kernel support vector classifier for multi-class classification. Inf. Sci. **619**, 889–907 (2023). https://doi.org/10.1016/j.ins.2022.10.075
20. Pedregosa, F., et al.: Scikit-learn: machine learning in Python. J. Mach. Learn. Res. **12**, 2825–2830 (2011)
21. Sater, R.A., Hamza, A.B.: A federated learning approach to anomaly detection in smart buildings (2021)
22. Schölkopf, B., Platt, J.C., Shawe-Taylor, J., Smola, A.J., Williamson, R.C.: Estimating the support of a high-dimensional distribution. Neural Comput. **13**(7), 1443–1471 (2001)
23. Tax, D.M., Duin, R.P.: Support vector domain description. Pattern Recogn. Lett. **20**(11–13), 1191–1199 (1999)
24. Thakur, D., Saini, J.K., Srinivasan, S.: Deepthink IoT: the strength of deep learning in internet of things. Artif. Intell. Rev. **56**, 14663–14730 (2023). https://doi.org/10.1007/s10462-023-10513-4
25. Thudumu, S., Branch, P., Jin, J., Singh, J.J.: A comprehensive survey of anomaly detection techniques for high dimensional big data. J. Big Data **7**(42) (2020). https://doi.org/10.1186/s40537-020-00320-x
26. Voigt, P., von dem Bussche, A.: Enforcement and fines under the GDPR. In: Voigt, P., von dem Bussche, A. (eds.) The EU General Data Protection Regulation (GDPR), pp. 201–217. Springer, Cham (2017). https://doi.org/10.1007/978-3-319-57959-7_7

Towards Digitisation of Technical Drawings in Architecture: Evaluation of CNN Classification on the Perdaw Dataset

Alexandru Filip[(✉)] and Stella Graßhof

IT University of Copenhagen, Copenhagen, Denmark
alfi@zmei.eu, stgr@itu.dk

Abstract. In a highly digitalised world, this paper aims at closing the gap towards automatic digitisation from 2D architectural drawings. We present the new image dataset *Plan, and Elevation Representations of Doors And Windows* (Perdaw) which provides a baseline for different classification problems with varying complexity. We investigate the performance of three machine learning models in distinguishing different types of doors and windows in their plan and elevation views. Our findings show that Inception V3 slightly outperforms MobileNet V2, which suggests that the latter solves the same classification tasks with less computational resources with only a minimal compromise in accuracy. Among the three investigated models, ResNet50 yields the lowest quality metrics within a small margin. Overall, all models perform better at classifying building components in their elevation views compared to their plan views. We consistently observed that the models yield the best results with 100% accuracy for the binary classification problems, and dropped to close to 70% accuracy for the 40-class classification problems.

Keywords: Deep Learning · Convolutional Neural Networks · Object Classification · Technical Symbols · Architectural Symbols

1 Introduction

Many technical drawings still only exist on paper, thus necessitating digitisation for use with modern computer programs. This digitisation is difficult and time-consuming, requiring significant human effort. While automated text and pattern extraction methods are improving, much work remains in applying these to technical drawings [9]. Another desired outcome based on 2D floor plans are 3D reconstructions, which are of high interest for the Architecture, Engineering and Construction (AEC) industry and hence an active area of research [3,5,8]. Some potential future applications are in the field of automated technical drawing analysis and element quantification.

Current state-of-the-art covers a wide variety of research efforts aimed at digitising complex engineering drawings and architectural floor plans, with a

L. Iliadis et al. (Eds.): EANN 2024, CCIS 2141, pp. 288–300, 2024.
https://doi.org/10.1007/978-3-031-62495-7_22

clear focus on object detection, symbol recognition, and classification through various methodologies. [1,9,14] delve into the digitization of engineering drawings, addressing challenges such as symbol variation and complex layouts. These works emphasize preprocessing, symbol detection, and classification, while leveraging deep learning, particularly CNNs, and other image processing methods. [1,9] both discuss the integration of deep learning techniques, including the use of Faster R-CNN and YOLO models for symbol recognition, while [14] propose a framework for automatic detection and classification using legends and template symbols. [4,12] employ CNNs and the YOLO architecture, respectively, for recognizing symbols in network-like diagrams and spotting symbols in digital architectural floor plans. [4] proposes a semi-automatic method involving symbol recognition, localization, and connectivity analysis, trained on manual and synthetic annotations. [12] focuses on detecting building components and furniture, showcasing high precision rates and the effectiveness of deep learning for symbol-specific detection. [10] addresses the detection and recognition of objects and text in large-scale technical drawings, utilizing a combination of Faster R-CNN for object detection and character-based recognition modules. This study illustrates the scalability of such systems aimed at handling intricate details and diverse layouts in technical drawings, emphasizing the role of data augmentation for improved performance.

In conclusion, current work emphasizes the importance of digitising engineering drawings, facing challenges like symbol variation, complex layouts, and the need for accurate classification and contextualization. Robust, efficient frameworks for the digitisation of complex drawings are critical for various applications, including automated design verification and high-quality architectural 3D reconstruction. While the advancements in deep learning, particularly through CNNs, YOLO, and Faster R-CNN models, are promising and demonstrate significant potential for improving digitisation accuracy, there is currently no technological solution available. Furthermore, is no dataset available which offers both plan and elevation views, e.g. the data used in [12] is unavailable, and the data used in [17] and limited to floor plans, hence not having enough information from which to attempt 3D reconstructions.

In this work, we contribute to a solution for this problem by offering a dataset, and careful evaluation of different methods for classifying elements in architectural drawings. In our proposed publicly available dataset *Plan, Elevation Representations of Doors And Window*, in short Perdaw, we provide a carefully crafted collection containing images of doors and windows varying in type and view. The dataset was created from 20 3D objects, namely 10 doors and 10 windows, and consists of a total of 28,800 images, see Sect. 3 for details.

The main contributions of this work are the following:

- A new publicly available dataset of doors and windows represented in their floor and elevation views.[1]
- Evaluation of deep learning models classifying very similar objects in the architectural domain.

---

[1] https://zenodo.org/records/10823907.

2   Machine Learning Models

In the following we will shortly describe the machine learning models employed in this work. We chose three models which are well-established in research and commercial applications.

2.1   ResNet50

[6] introduces *ResNet* which won the *ImageNet Competition* in 2015. Around that time, neural network architectures were scaling up rapidly, i.e. becoming *deeper*. However, significant increases in layers were yielding disproportionately small gains in accuracy or even decrease from a point onward, known as the *degradation problem*. The main contribution of ResNet is showing that residual connections can significantly reduce the size of the model while still increasing accuracy.

2.2   MobileNet V2

MobileNet V2 [13] is an improved version of the MobileNet [7]. The goal of this CNN architecture is to use as few computational resources as possible, hence allowing for usage on mobile devices. MobileNet V2 introduces inverted residuals, which instead of gradually increasing the number of channels throughout the network, start with a narrow bottleneck layer, expand the number of channels, and then reduce them back to the original size. By expanding the channels and then reducing them back, the network can capture richer feature representations with fewer parameters and computations. This inversion of channel expansion and reduction distinguishes inverted residuals from traditional residual blocks used in ResNet50 [6]. Through this process, MobileNet V2 manages to reduce the computational cost while maintaining, or even improving the representation capacity of the model.

2.3   Inception V3

In [16] Inception v3 was introduced as an extension of the original Inception [15] architecture (also known as GoogLeNet) specifically designed for image classification tasks. The key feature is the *Inception module* which allows for efficient and parallel processing of image data at different scales. These modules consist of convolutional layers with different filter sizes (1×1, 3×3, and 5×5), where smaller convolutions replace the 5×5 ones. These filter sizes are pooled, which are then concatenated together. Inception V3 also incorporates other techniques to improve performance, such as batch normalisation, regularisation, and factorised convolutions, which reduce the number of parameters and computational complexity.

3   Data

Architectural drawings, including floor plans and elevations, are essential for representing buildings at various scales, detailing everything from wall organization to the positioning of windows and doors. Floor plans show the layout from above, while elevations provide front or back views, crucial for illustrating facades and interior details [2]. For high quality 3D reconstruction, both plan and elevation views are necessary to capture an object's dimensions and spatial relationships from different angles, enabling the creation of a comprehensive 3D model. This dual-perspective approach is vital as each view alone offers a limited projection. Given the lack of datasets featuring both views, we decided to create one.

3.1   The Perdaw Dataset

The *Plan, Elevation Representations of Doors And Windows* (Perdaw) dataset comprises a total of 28,800 images of door and window elements initially developed as digital 3D objects. We designed 20 3D objects: 10 doors and 10 windows, and projected them onto their plan (top view) and elevation (front/back view). An overview of the different types of doors and windows is provided in Table 1.

For the plan view of each object, two sets of images were created, one with finer lines and another with thicker lines, in order to enhance object classification robustness. Each set spawned 360 additional images through a 1-degree incremental rotation, totaling 720 images per element.

In contrast to that, for the elevation views, we initially only chose six views per element: the front view, the back view, and four corresponding 45-degree side views. This is due to occlusions and redundancies introduced by different view angles. To achieve a balanced dataset, i.e. the same number of images for the elevation view, we employed mirroring, cropping, and shearing on the initial six images. Finally, to enhance processing efficiency and reduce storage requirements, all images were converted from PNG to JPG format.

The Doors. The dataset only contains hinged doors due to their prevalence as the predominant type of doors found in buildings. The selection of doors encompasses different sizes and types, including single doors as seen in Fig. 1a, one-and-a-half doors as seen in Fig. 1b and double doors as seen in Fig. 1c. Moreover, the dataset comprises doors with a glass variation, as seen in Fig. 1d, Fig. 1e and Fig. 1f. Examples of doors without glass panels are shown in Fig. 1g, Fig. 1h and Fig. 1i. A detailed overview of the types of doors is provided in Table 1a.

The Windows. The dataset provides hinged and awned windows as they represent the prevailing usage in contemporary architectural practices. The aim was to encompass various window sizes, including conventional proportions, as well as larger dimensions such as potential curtain wall components. The dataset contains the following types of hinged windows: single-framed, double-framed Fig. 2d, and triple window-framed Fig. 2e. The double and triple ones contain the corner window variation as seen in Fig. 2f and Fig. 2g. Additionally, the dataset

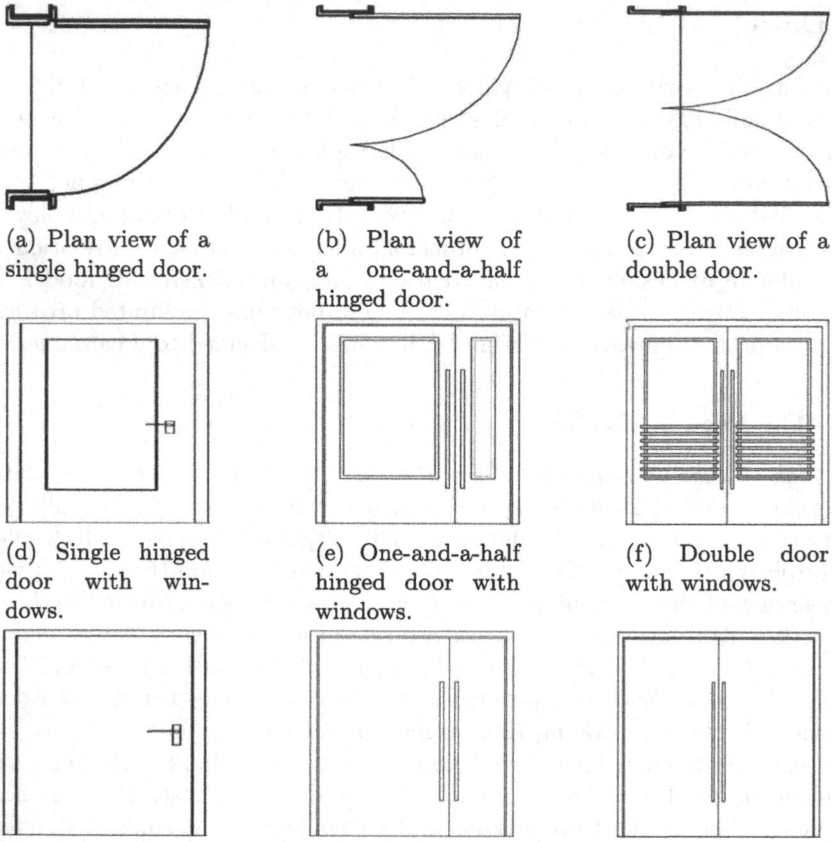

(a) Plan view of a single hinged door.

(b) Plan view of a one-and-a-half hinged door.

(c) Plan view of a double door.

(d) Single hinged door with windows.

(e) One-and-a-half hinged door with windows.

(f) Double door with windows.

(g) Single hinged door without windows.

(h) One-and-a-half hinged door without windows.

(i) Double door without windows.

Fig. 1. Illustration of different types of doors in plan view and elevation view.

provide more oversized windows with independent awned variations, both single and double as seen in Fig. 2h and Fig. 2i. Three representations in plan view are shown in Fig. 2a–Fig. 2c. A detailed overview of the windows can be observed in Table 1b.

4   Experiments

The experimental design focuses on evaluating the performance of three machine learning models across distinct dataset partitions. To investigate how the models perform on broader vs. more fine-grained categories, we divide the dataset into different subsets that represent different aspects and vary in complexity. The aim is to identify which model performs best on which of the classification problems.

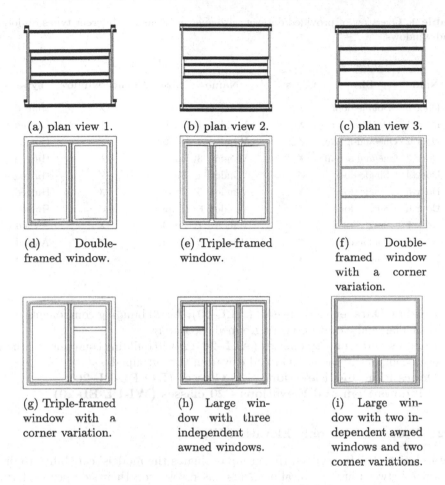

(a) plan view 1.   (b) plan view 2.   (c) plan view 3.

(d)   Double-framed window.

(e) Triple-framed window.

(f)   Double-framed window with a corner variation.

(g) Triple-framed window with a corner variation.

(h) Large window with three independent awned windows.

(i) Large window with two independent awned windows and two corner variations.

Fig. 2. Illustration of different types of windows.

These range from architectural components shown in different views, to those views being grouped together to represent the entirety of the building component. We expect the models to perform better on simpler, binary classifications compared to multi-class scenarios.

4.1 Datasets Featuring both Plan and Elevation Views

This grouping is intended to test the models' ability to recognize and classify architectural elements when provided with a comprehensive representation that includes both plan and elevation views. The rationale is that including both perspectives could potentially provide the models with a richer set of features to improve classification accuracy, and to test its ability to correctly classify the building components using both views. Dataset partitions:

Table 1. Overview of provided dataset with specifications for different types of doors and windows.

<table>
<tr><th colspan="3" align="center">(a) Doors.</th><th colspan="4" align="center">(b) Windows.</th></tr>
<tr><th>Name</th><th>Size</th><th>Glass</th><th>Name</th><th>Size</th><th>Corner window</th><th>Type</th></tr>
<tr><td>Door 0</td><td>Double-door</td><td>✓</td><td>Window 0</td><td>Single</td><td>✗</td><td>Hinged</td></tr>
<tr><td>Door 1</td><td>Double-door</td><td>✗</td><td>Window 1</td><td>Double</td><td>✗</td><td>Hinged</td></tr>
<tr><td>Door 2</td><td>One-and-a-half</td><td>✓</td><td>Window 2</td><td>Double</td><td>✓</td><td>Hinged</td></tr>
<tr><td>Door 3</td><td>One-and-a-half</td><td>✗</td><td>Window 3</td><td>Double</td><td>✗</td><td>Hinged</td></tr>
<tr><td>Door 4</td><td>Single-door</td><td>✓</td><td>Window 4</td><td>Single</td><td>✓</td><td>Hinged</td></tr>
<tr><td>Door 5</td><td>Single-door</td><td>✗</td><td>Window 5</td><td>Triple</td><td>✗</td><td>Hinged</td></tr>
<tr><td>Door 6</td><td>Single-door</td><td>✗</td><td>Window 6</td><td>Triple</td><td>✓</td><td>Hinged</td></tr>
<tr><td>Door 7</td><td>Single-door</td><td>✓</td><td>Window 7</td><td>Single</td><td>✗</td><td>Awned</td></tr>
<tr><td>Door 8</td><td>Double-door</td><td>✗</td><td>Window 8</td><td>Triple</td><td>✗</td><td>Awned</td></tr>
<tr><td>Door 9</td><td>Single-door</td><td>✗</td><td>Window 9</td><td>Triple</td><td>✓</td><td>Awned</td></tr>
</table>

- **Perdaw Dataset - 40 classes (ALL-40):** All 20 building components with their plan and elevation views grouped separately.
- **Perdaw Dataset - 20 classes (ALL-20):** All 20 building components where each component has its plan and elevation view grouped.
- **Doors Plan and Elevations - 20 Classes (DO-PL-EL-20)**
- **Windows Plan and Elevations - 20 classes (WI-PL-EL-20)**

4.2 Datasets with only Elevation Views

By isolating elevation views, this group evaluates the models' capability to distinguish between architectural elements based solely on their side perspectives. This assesses whether models can effectively identify features and classify elements without the plan view context, relying on the distinct characteristics visible in elevation views.

- **Only Elevation Views - 20 Classes (ELEV-20)**
- **Doors - Elevation View - 10 classes (DO-EL-10)**
- **Windows - Elevation View - 10 classes (WI-EL-10)**

4.3 Datasets with only Plan Views

Focusing solely on plan views, this category aims to assess the models' performance in scenarios where the classification must rely on information presented only in a singular, flat representation. This tests the models' ability to extract and utilize features specific to plan views for classification, with the purpose of understanding if using different models specialised only in one particular view would yield better performance compared to models which were trained on both views, or only on the elevation views.

- Only Plan Views - 20 classes (PLAN-20)
- Doors - Plan View - 10 classes (DO-PL-10)
- Windows - Plan View - 10 classes (WI-PL-10)

4.4 Binary Classifications on Plan Views

Based on the outputs of the plan view multi-class classifications, the decision was taken to further explore these potential causes of those returns through 2 binary classifications. The results are further elaborated in Sect. 5 and Sect. 6.

- Doors versus Windows - Plan View - 2 classes (DO-WI-PL-2)
- Single versus Double Doors - Plan View - 2 classes (SDO-DDO-PL-2)

4.5 Implementation Details

To train and evaluate the models we split the data in the following 80% training, 10% validation, and 10% test. For each classification problem, we selected the same number of samples per class, hence ensuring a balanced setting. In addition to the models' pre-trained frozen layers, we added 5 additional layers, which we trained using the Perdaw dataset. During training, only the new layers were trained while the remainder of weights remained frozen. We employed the categorical cross-entropy for multi-class classification, and the binary cross-entropy for binary classification problems, respectively. To compute the metrics described in Sect. 4.6 we used sklearn [11]. For all models, we use the following hyperparameters:

- batch size 32,
- maximum number of epochs 100,
- the initial learning rate of 0.1 is halved if the validation loss has not changed in 3 epochs.

4.6 Metrics

For evaluation and comparison of models we employ common the metrics accuracy, precision, recall, and F1 score. For multi-class classification problems, there are different definitions available. For this work, we chose the Macro definition for the metrics, because we are by design working with a balanced dataset. For multi-class classification, we define *true positive* (TP), *false positive* (FP), *false negative* (FN) per class as:

- TP_c: number of correctly classified samples of class c.
- FP_c: number of samples incorrectly assigned to class c.
- FN_c: number of samples not classified as class c, although they belong to class c.

The *accuracy* measures the proportion of correct predictions, the model makes over the total number of predictions. It is calculated by dividing the number of correctly classified instances by the total number of instances as

$$\text{Accuracy} = \frac{1}{N} \#\{\text{correctly classified samples}\}, \tag{1}$$

where N is the number of all samples in the dataset.

Precision is defined as the ratio of correctly classified samples of class c, over all samples which were classified as belonging to class c, hence

$$\text{Macro Precision} = \frac{1}{C} \sum_{c=1}^{C} \frac{\text{TP}_c}{\text{TP}_c + \text{FP}_c}. \tag{2}$$

Recall is defined as the ratio of the number of samples in a class that the model correctly classified over all instances of the class

$$\text{Macro Recall} = \frac{1}{C} \sum_{c=1}^{C} \frac{\text{TP}_c}{\text{TP}_c + \text{FN}_c}. \tag{3}$$

Finally, the macro F1-score is computed as the mean over the class-wise F1-scores, which are defined as the harmonic mean of precision and recall, hence

$$\text{Macro F1} = \frac{1}{C} \sum_{c=1}^{C} \frac{2\text{TP}_c}{2\text{TP}_c + \text{FP}_c + \text{FN}_c}. \tag{4}$$

5   Results

An overview of the results of the previously described experiments is presented in Table 2, where **Acc** stands for Accuracy, **Prec** stands for Precision, **Rec** for Recall, and finally **F1** for the model's F1 Score as defined in Sect. 4.6. In the following we elaborate on the different observations and trends.

As can be seen in Table 2, overall, MobileNet V2 and Inception v3 frequently outperform ResNet50 in terms of accuracy, precision, recall, and F1 score. This suggests that for the tasks at hand, MobileNet V2 and Inception v3 are generally more capable of distinguishing between architectural elements than ResNet50. The best performances are observed in partitions focusing on elevation views (ELEV-20, DO-EL-10, WI-EL-10) across all metrics. This implies that elevation views provide clearer, more distinguishable features for these models to classify doors and windows accurately.

In the ALL-40 and ALL-20 partitions, MobileNet V2 and Inception v3 perform almost alike, both outperforming ResNet50. This similarity in performance suggests that when dealing with a mixture of views (plans and elevations together), the architectural elements' complexity doesn't significantly affect these two models' ability to classify them accurately. When comparing the results DO-PL-10 and DO-EL-10, we observe that the metrics drop significantly for plan views. This indicates that the plan views hinder the overall performance

Table 2. Overview of the results for the classification problems for all models.

Partition Name	ResNet50				MobileNet v2				Inception v3			
	Acc	Prec	Rec	F1	Acc	Prec	Rec	F1	Acc	Prec	Rec	F1
ALL-40	0.54	0.54	0.54	0.51	**0.68**	0.68	**0.68**	0.66	**0.68**	**0.69**	**0.68**	**0.68**
ALL-20	0.53	0.55	0.53	0.53	**0.67**	**0.68**	**0.67**	0.66	**0.67**	**0.68**	**0.67**	**0.67**
PLAN-20	0.51	**0.53**	0.51	**0.50**	**0.55**	0.51	**0.55**	0.47	0.50	0.51	0.50	0.49
ELEV-20	0.72	0.73	0.72	0.71	**0.89**	**0.90**	**0.89**	**0.89**	0.88	0.89	0.88	0.88
DO-PL-EL-20	0.51	0.52	0.51	0.49	0.64	0.65	0.64	0.63	**0.65**	**0.66**	**0.65**	**0.64**
DO-PL-10	0.30	0.22	0.30	0.23	**0.50**	**0.49**	**0.50**	**0.46**	0.46	0.49	0.46	0.45
DO-EL-10	0.73	0.75	0.73	0.73	0.83	0.87	0.83	0.82	**0.88**	**0.88**	**0.88**	**0.88**
WI-PL-EL-20	0.63	0.67	0.63	0.58	0.70	0.60	0.70	0.63	**0.73**	**0.73**	**0.73**	**0.72**
WI-PL-10	0.52	0.49	0.52	0.45	**0.56**	**0.55**	**0.56**	**0.54**	0.54	0.53	0.54	0.53
WI-EL-10	0.76	0.78	0.76	0.76	**0.93**	**0.94**	**0.93**	**0.93**	0.89	0.90	0.90	0.89
DO-WI-PL-2	**1.00**	**1.00**	**1.00**	**1.00**	1.00	1.00	1.00	1.00	1.00	1.00	1.00	1.00
SDO-DDO-PL-2	0.98	0.98	0.99	0.98	1.00	1.00	1.00	1.00	1.00	1.00	1.00	1.00

in mixed settings, also seen in the inferior values for DO-PL-EL-20 (composed of DO-PL-10 and DO-EL-10). This is also confirmed by the corresponding confusion matrices in Fig. 3, where we observe that ResNet50 shown in Fig. 3a often incorrectly classifies *Dr 1 Plan*, and *Dr 9 Plan* as *Dr 5 plan*. Additionally, comparing Fig. 3a with Fig. 3b shows that ResNet50 and Inception v3 both confuse *Dr 0 Plan* for *Dr 6 Plan*.

In the partitions focusing on plan views (PLAN-20, DO-PL-10, WI-PL-10), we observe more variance in model performance. ResNet50 generally underperforms compared to the other two models, which suggests a lesser ability to extract and utilize features from plan views. We illustrate this trend for the results of PLAN-20, in a comparison of the corresponding confusion matrices of ResNet50 Fig. 3c and Inception v3 Fig. 3d, where the latter shows less misclassifications.

As can be seen in the last two rows of Table 2, all three models achieve perfect scores in binary classification tasks, i.e. they can distinguish doors from windows in plan views (DO-WI-PL-2), and single from double doors in plan views (SDO-DDO-PL-2).

6 Discussion

In the analysis of building component classification, using various deep learning models, the investigation reveals consistent trends with a few surprises. A critical finding pertains to the performance in plan views. Here, models struggle significantly, a phenomenon attributed to the inherent difficulty in distinguishing architectural features from plan views alone. This challenge is not merely a hurdle but points to a nearly insurmountable problem in classifying the same building components of the same type based on plan views, highlighting a limitation in current model capabilities.

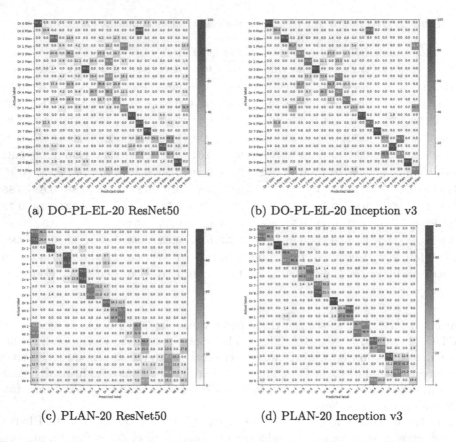

(a) DO-PL-EL-20 ResNet50   (b) DO-PL-EL-20 Inception v3

(c) PLAN-20 ResNet50   (d) PLAN-20 Inception v3

Fig. 3. Selected examples of confusion matrices from the different classification problems.

Moreover, the study observes that increasing the amount of data—via adding more views or complexities—does not linearly translate to better model performance. This observation is particularly evident when comparing the ALL-20 and ALL-40 partitions, where no notable improvement is seen, despite the increased data diversity. This suggests a diminishing return on information gain from added views, indicating that models fail to leverage additional perspectives effectively.

The models do not show a marked improvement in identifying building components when their plan and elevation views are grouped together in the same class. This is evidenced by the comparable outcomes in ALL-20 and ALL-40 partitions, where the grouping or the non-grouping of the different views of each building component does not yield significant performance differences.

However, in simpler classification tasks, such as distinguishing different building components or identifying variations of the same component (e.g., single versus double doors), models demonstrate remarkable effectiveness. This pattern underscores two fundamental insights: binary tasks are inherently less complex, allowing models to achieve high accuracy, and that perhaps these tendencies are further enhanced by the significantly different geometry of the two building components, or by the 2 different types of the same building component.

The dichotomy between task complexities underscores a nuanced understanding of model capabilities in architectural classification tasks.

7   Conclusion

In this study, we investigated the performance of three machine learning models on the task of classifying building components extracted from architectural drawings. The Perdaw dataset was specifically created for this study, with the intention to provide a valuable resource for future studies, and will be made available upon publishing of this work. The experiments involved partitioning the Perdaw dataset into different subsets and evaluating the performance of multiple machine-learning models in different classification tasks of varying complexity. Our analysis suggests that Inception v3 marginally outperforms MobileNet V2 as the best model for classifying architectural elements across different views, followed closely by MobileNet V2, with ResNet50 yielding the lowest performance metrics with a small margin.

Elevation views offer substantial advantages for model performance in classifying architectural elements, suggesting that elevation views might contain more distinctive features than plan views. Meanwhile, the effective classification in combined view partitions underscores the value of utilizing comprehensive datasets that include multiple perspectives for training machine learning models in architectural applications.

In conclusion, the results suggest a tailored approach for digitizing technical drawings, recommending separate models for plan and elevation views due to the distinct challenges each presents. Specifically, models exhibit limitations in distinguishing between doors of the same type but different sizes in plan views, although they perform admirably in differentiating between doors and windows, as well as doors of different types. This analysis indicates that while current models are adept at handling specific, less complex classification tasks, they struggle with more nuanced, detailed discriminations in architectural drawings, pointing to the need for specialized approaches depending on the view type and classification complexity.

References

1. Bhanbhro, H., Hooi, Y.K., Hassan, Z.: Modern approaches towards object detection of complex engineering drawings. In: 2022 International Conference on Digital Transformation and Intelligence (ICDI), pp. 01–06. IEEE (2022)
2. Ching, F.D.: Architectural Graphics, 4th edn. Wiley, Hoboken (2003)
3. Fathi, H., Dai, F., Lourakis, M.: Automated as-built 3D reconstruction of civil infrastructure using computer vision: achievements, opportunities, and challenges. Adv. Eng. Inform. 29(2), 149–161 (2015)

4. Fu, L., Kara, L.B.: From engineering diagrams to engineering models: visual recognition and applications. Comput. Aided Des. **43**(3), 278–292 (2011)
5. Han, X.F., Laga, H., Bennamoun, M.: Image-based 3D object reconstruction: state-of-the-art and trends in the deep learning era. IEEE Trans. Pattern Anal. Mach. Intell. **43**(5), 1578–1604 (2019)
6. He, K., Zhang, X., Ren, S., Sun, J.: Deep residual learning for image recognition. In: Proceedings of the IEEE Conference on Computer Vision and Pattern Recognition, pp. 770–778 (2016)
7. Howard, A.G., et al.: Mobilenets: efficient convolutional neural networks for mobile vision applications. arXiv preprint arXiv:1704.04861 (2017)
8. Ma, Z., Liu, S.: A review of 3D reconstruction techniques in civil engineering and their applications. Adv. Eng. Inform. **37**, 163–174 (2018)
9. Moreno-García, C.F., Elyan, E., Jayne, C.: New trends on digitisation of complex engineering drawings. Neural Comput. Appl. **31**, 1695–1712 (2019)
10. Nguyen, M.T., Pham, V.L., Nguyen, C.C., Nguyen, V.V.: Object detection and text recognition in large-scale technical drawings. In: Proceedings of the 10th International Conference on Pattern Recognition Applications and Methods ICPRAM - Volume 1 (2021)
11. Pedregosa, F., et al.: Scikit-learn: machine learning in Python. J. Mach. Learn. Res. **12**, 2825–2830 (2011)
12. Rezvanifar, A., Cote, M., Albu, A.B.: Symbol spotting on digital architectural floor plans using a deep learning-based framework. In: Proceedings of the IEEE/CVF Conference on Computer Vision and Pattern Recognition Workshops, pp. 568–569 (2020)
13. Sandler, M., Howard, A., Zhu, M., Zhmoginov, A., Chen, L.C.: Mobilenetv2: inverted residuals and linear bottlenecks. In: Proceedings of the IEEE Conference on Computer Vision and Pattern Recognition, pp. 4510–4520 (2018)
14. Sarkar, S., Pandey, P., Kar, S.: Automatic detection and classification of symbols in engineering drawings. arXiv preprint arXiv:2204.13277 (2022)
15. Szegedy, C., et al.: Going deeper with convolutions. In: Proceedings of the IEEE Conference on Computer Vision and Pattern Recognition, pp. 1–9 (2015)
16. Szegedy, C., Vanhoucke, V., Ioffe, S., Shlens, J., Wojna, Z.: Rethinking the inception architecture for computer vision. In: Proceedings of the IEEE Conference on Computer Vision and Pattern Recognition, pp. 2818–2826. IEEE (2016)
17. Ziran, Z., Marinai, S.: Object detection in floor plan images. In: Pancioni, L., Schwenker, F., Trentin, E. (eds.) ANNPR 2018. LNCS (LNAI), vol. 11081, pp. 383–394. Springer, Cham (2018). https://doi.org/10.1007/978-3-319-99978-4_30

YOLOv5 and Residual Network for Intelligent Text Recognition on Degraded Serial Number Plates

Amos Yu Xuan Tham and Cheng Siong Chin(✉)

Faculty of Science, Agriculture, and Engineering, Newcastle University in Singapore,
Singapore 599493, Singapore
Cheng.chin@newcastle.ac.uk

Abstract. Optical character recognition (OCR) categorizes text in images, such as license plate numbers. However, the industrial sector avoids OCR due to model training limitations with specific data, complicating the handling of incoming images. Industrial settings introduce noise to images, impacting quality and classification. This paper seeks to boost machine learning by constructing models with diverse datasets. Focusing on deteriorated serial plates in ship engine rooms, the study employed color inversion and two You Only Look Once (YOLOv5) models for object detection. Subsequently, the Residual Network 152 (ResNet-152) model classified the alphanumeric characters on the plates, achieving 90% accuracy in alphanumeric character classification on deteriorated serial plates.

Keywords: YOLOv5 · ResNet-152 · Classification · Custom Dataset · Noise · Serial Plate

1 Introduction

In a ship's engine room, the serial plate faces deterioration due to maintenance, wear, tear, and oil stains, making alphanumeric characters hard to read. Identifying the correct serial number is crucial for obtaining fitting spare parts, as installing the wrong component can damage the machine and endanger the crew. Ordering the wrong part can cause delays and financial loss. Text recognition, including Optical Character Recognition (OCR), has advanced, but challenges exist in industrial settings with varied conditions. Scene text recognition (STR), a sub-branch of OCR, faces complexity in images with diverse backgrounds. Traditional STR methods were computationally heavy, but technological advancements, especially in deep learning, have increased interest. A study on banknote serial number recognition [1] employs knowledge distillation and Bayesian optimization to detect regions of interest and classify serial numbers efficiently. While achieving high accuracy, this method requires a specific image format. Document text recognition with deep learning algorithms, like convolutional neural network (CNN), is effective, but challenges arise from diverse text patterns and backgrounds [2].

Residual Networks (ResNets) and Densely Connected Convolutional Networks (DenseNet) replace older OCR models due to automatic feature learning, but combining

L. Iliadis et al. (Eds.): EANN 2024, CCIS 2141, pp. 301–314, 2024.
https://doi.org/10.1007/978-3-031-62495-7_23

them with sequence modeling, like Bidirectional Long Short-Term Memory Network (BiLSTM), can be computationally intensive. Unattended and Monitored methods for text region detection in images were discussed, highlighting the effectiveness of ResNet in addressing degradation issues.

Another paper on Automatic License Plate Recognition (ALPR) [3] reviews various pre-processing methods. A recent study [4] presents a real-time ALPR system using YOLOv5 for license plate detection and EasyOCR for recognition, achieving 98% accuracy. The paper suggests incorporating vehicle specification information for improved resilience. In a recent paper [5, 6], an OCR model aims to identify serial numbers in challenging industrial settings. YOLOv5 is used for Region of interest (ROI) identification, and Transformation-Resnet-None-Attention (TRNA) is employed for classification, achieving a Levenshtein distance of 93. ResNet-152 is proposed for text classification to prevent issues with deteriorating license plates.

While ResNet-152 successfully recognizes text, challenges arise in diverse image conditions. Engineers taking photos may introduce variations in brightness and background noise. The proposed OCR method combines YOLOv5 for background noise removal, plate identification, and alphanumeric character classification, allowing engineers to input photos for automatic character classification.

2 Methodology

This paper will denote the initial YOLOv5 model as model (1) and the subsequent as model (2). Drawing from studies on YOLO [7–10], newer versions such as YOLOv6 and YOLOv7 surpass YOLOv5 in both speed and accuracy. YOLOv8 is available in various sizes for hardware integration. Nonetheless, these newer versions are subject to frequent updates and may not be compatible with older libraries. While YOLOv5 offers easier configuration and faster training than its predecessor, its mosaic model grants an edge in detecting smaller objects, like the diminutive characters on a serial plate. Therefore, the superiority of the YOLOv5 model is evident over others. As depicted in Fig. 1, the study will adhere to the proposed steps to attain optimal classification outcomes.

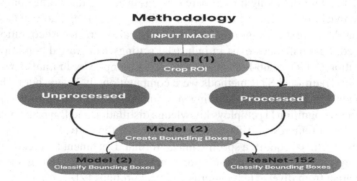

Fig. 1. Proposed methodology for reviewing classification models

2.1 Dataset

Neural networks are often trained on custom datasets for a specific use case only. This model can classify images like the custom dataset but suffers when there is a font style variation [2, 11]. Training the neural network with a combination of different images is vital to create a more robust classification system [12]. Roboflow, is an application to streamline the annotation and augmentation process. Custom datasets can be easily annotated and augmented to create a larger sample size without collecting more images.

A vehicle license plate public dataset [13] containing 350 annotated images of US license plates with the following classes: license plate and vehicle parts were used for training. This study utilized this dataset because the vehicle body's license plate is like a serial plate on a machinery body. As such, training on this dataset will serve as a good base for identifying the rectangular features of a plate mounted on a piece of machinery. The dataset has been augmented to create a total of 840 images, splitting into 735 for training, 70 for validation, and 35 for testing. The classes were also remapped in Roboflow from license plate to Serial Plate and vehicle part to machine part. The base dataset can be found at the following URL (https://public.roboflow.com/object-det ection/license-plates-us-eu). Two different custom datasets were collected to train the YOLOv5 models.

Model (1) Dataset
The first custom dataset mainly consists of random serial number plates from random types of machinery or parts. The dataset was gathered and annotated. The focus is to annotate the plate portion only such that model (1) can identify the serial plate portion with its distinct sharp edges and rectangular shape. The first dataset, in total, consisted of 470 images and was augmented to comprise 1134 images in total. 996 images were split for training, 91 for validation, and 47 for testing. This final dataset was named OCRFYP.

Model (2) Dataset
The second custom dataset mainly consists of marine machinery types usually found on board. The popular engines from MAN, B&W, and CAT were chosen to align with this project's goal. The dataset was created and annotated. The dataset consists of both deteriorated and good-condition serial plates. The annotation focused on only annotating the individual serial characters. Only necessary text, such as model name, will be annotated. This annotation technique will prevent the model from creating unnecessary bounding boxes, as the serial characters usually differ from other characters on the plate. The annotation labels will be created for 0–9, and A-Z as this model will also be used to train the ResNet-152 model. Since the alphanumeric characters are small compared to the plate, it is of utmost importance to collect high-quality images at high-resolution sizes. There are two primary issues encountered with the collected dataset. Firstly, only 184 images were gathered due to the limited availability of online resources, as no previous researchers have classified serial number plates. Additionally, it was observed during the training of model (2) that overfitting occurred. Another challenge arises from the difficulty reading some characters on the plates, leading to complications during the annotation phase. To address these issues, preprocessing steps are necessary to augment the dataset size and improve the readability of the alphanumeric characters. The forthcoming section

will provide a description of these preprocessing steps. In total, 736 images underwent augmentation through techniques such as color inversion, contrast enhancement, and a combination of both. Consequently, the dataset was expanded to include 1,500 images for training, 38 images for validation, and 15 images for testing purposes. Throughout the annotation process, extra labels were inadvertently created due to typographical errors, which were subsequently removed to prevent potential training inaccuracies. The resulting dataset was saved under the name "Alphanumeric Characters.

MNIST and A-Z Dataset

The code will export the datasets directly to the working environment and directory. Before exporting the dataset, a function was set to transform the data to suit the ResNet-152 training format using Pytorch. The first function transfers the image from a PIL format to a NumPy array, then transforms it to a Pytorch tensor representing the image's colour channels and spatial dimension. The second function will normalize the color channel independently such that the pixel values are in the range from -1 to 1, ensuring consistent scale and improving the convergence during training. This dataset will be used for training the ResNet-152 model to aid in classifying the alphanumeric characters on the license plate [5]. The MNIST dataset consists of 70,000 in total. The A-Z Dataset contains 26 labels, each containing 1,260 grayscale images, totaling up to 32,760 images. Both datasets are combined using the ConcatDataset module in Pytorch, where other libraries, such as data loaders, can work with the combined dataset, allowing efficient batching and parallel loading. Both the MNIST and A-Z datasets were combined, and since the MNIST datasets contain the labels 0–9, the A-Z labels must occupy the 11th position to avoid mislabelling. The combined dataset is split into 80% of training and 20% of validation data.

3 Pre-processing Methods

During the collection and training of model (2), it was observed that despite adequate training, the model could have achieved better performance on unseen datasets. To enhance the robustness of the model, various pre-processing methods were investigated based on studies [5, 14, 15] and implemented to augment the original dataset. The selected pre-processing techniques detailed in the following subsections will contribute to expanding the dataset and facilitating further annotation in Roboflow. These subsections will showcase different methods aimed at identifying and emphasizing the most effective techniques for accentuating character features. Considering the diverse range of serial plates in the dataset, it's challenging to apply a one-size-fits-all processing approach. Therefore, the study will focus on the most common type of serial number plate, characterized by engraved letters with a color similar to the background. This approach aims to create a custom dataset optimized for ResNet-152. The study found that the ResNet-152 model trained on MNIST, and A-Z datasets performed worst in the classification of serial plate alphanumeric characters compared to Model (2) classification. Hence, to build a more robust ResNet-152 model, the Model was fine-tuned and trained on custom datasets already annotated in Roboflow to save time. In Roboflow, there are no options to export datasets in ResNet-152 format. When exporting in Pytorch format, the images and labels are in different folders. ResNet-152 requires images and labels to be nested within their label folder. To counter this folder structure issue, a code was written to read all images, cropped each character individually, and assigned them to their respective folder. The.txt label file was also amended to remove additional labels that did not fit the characters being cropped out.

4 Training

The initial neural network, a YOLOv5 object detector classifier, identifies and crops a Region of Interest (ROI) on machinery, specifically serial plates. The cropped ROI is then input into a second YOLOv5 neural network, functioning as an object detector for creating bounding boxes around alphanumeric characters. Finally, the image and bounding boxes undergo classification using a ResNet-152 model, focusing on characters within the bounding boxes. The selection of specific hyperparameters, such as the number of epochs or batch size, was determined through trial and error. Increasing batch sizes can accelerate computation but may sacrifice generalization. Conversely, smaller batch sizes facilitate consistent learning and improved convergence. This study utilizes mini-batch gradient descent with a batch size of 16, adjusted as required.

The second hyperparameter, known as the number of epochs, dictates the total number of gradient updates. Typically initialized at 300 epochs, decisions regarding increments or decrements are guided by training loss diagrams and model-specific features such as early stopping. The third hyperparameter involves the selection of initial weights. Utilizing pre-trained weights accelerates convergence by capitalizing on previous knowledge. Transfer learning can take place through various methods, such as feature extraction or retraining on a new dataset.

Datasets like OCRFYP and Alphanumeric Characters, annotated in YOLOv5 PyTorch format, underwent augmentation in Roboflow. These datasets, exported with an API key, comprise train, valid, and test subfolders containing images and labeled files. A data.yaml file delineates image paths and labels for YOLOv5 training. CUDA plays a crucial role in facilitating GPU support during neural network training. In this study, all networks were trained on an Intel® Core™ i5-10300H @ 2.50 GHz CPU and NVIDIA GEFORCE RTX 2060 GPU.

4.1 Model (1) - Cropping Image

Model (1) represents the inaugural YOLOv5 model specialized in isolating the serial plate segment from machinery. This initial model will undergo two distinct stages of training. In the first stage, training will be conducted on a publicly available dataset containing US license plates, utilizing the pre-trained weights from yolov5s.pt. Following this stage, the model's optimal new weights will be saved and further trained using the custom dataset OCRFYP. The YOLOv5 framework was integrated with pre-trained weights from yolov5s.pt specifically for the vehicle-license dataset. These weights correspond to the smallest variant of YOLOv5 and were initially trained on a diverse array of objects within the COCO dataset, encompassing 80 different object classes. The yolov5s.pt weight is tailored to extract fundamental features such as edges and corners from input images, attributes particularly pertinent to serial plates, which typically possess these features. However, as the COCO dataset did not undergo specific training for classifying the Region of Interest (ROI) pertaining to the serial plate, the model will undergo fine-tuning using the serial plate dataset, necessitating updates to all layers accordingly.

Vehicle License Dataset

Fine-tuning YOLOv5 can be accomplished with a single code line. The code set the image at 416×416 with a batch size 16 and 300 epochs. The training lasted 0.758 h, achieving an overall precision score of 88.3% and a recall score of 75.9% based on 70 images. For serial plates, precision reached 92.8% and recall 82.2%, while machine parts prediction scored 83.8% precision and 69.7% recall. These results demonstrate the model's efficacy in serial plate detection. Though more epochs may improve performance, current cropping results suffice since weights will fine-tune to the custom dataset.

OCRFYP Dataset

The unique dataset contains only one class, serial plate, indexed as 0, aligning with the license plate dataset. No adjustments to class labels are needed. Following the same process, the code will utilize the best.pt weights instead of yolov5s.pt. In Fig. 2, best.pt's layers 0–10 constitute the backbone, comprising convolutional layers with increasing filters for low-level feature extraction. Layers 11–23 serve as the neck layers, transforming features from the backbone for the head in layer 24 for classification. Due to the custom dataset's similarity to the license plate dataset and smaller size, the study suggests retraining the neck and head of best.pt by freezing layer 11 during training. The one-line code for this training resembles the previous step but includes the added function ability to freeze the backbone (--freeze 10). With 200 epochs, the model achieved an overall precision score of 95.1% and a recall score of 92.4%.

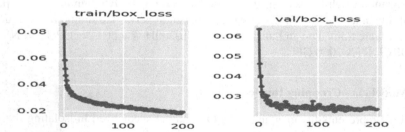

Fig. 2. Training and Validation loss graph of model (1) second training.

Looking at the training loss and validation graph, the training progress could have higher accuracy by increasing epochs. However, the validation loss graph shows signs of stagnation and the possibility of increased loss with increased epochs. During the test on 5 unseen images (for example), all 5 images were properly cropped out with varying sizes of the serial plate, as shown in Fig. 3.

Fig. 3. Testing model (1) on unseen images.

4.2 Model (2) – Bounding Box

Model (2) represents the second YOLOv5 model designed to generate bounding boxes for alphanumeric characters and perform text classification. Similar to the initial step in Model (1), the training concept for the second YOLOv5 model involves calling and training on the YOLOv5s.pt weight. However, in this case, the model will exclusively train on the custom dataset.

Alphanumeric Bounding Box Dataset
Despite the dissimilarity between identifying bounding boxes for alphanumeric characters and yolov5s.pt's training, utilizing pre-trained weights is still recommended for faster training and better convergence. Initially, the model trained on serial plates without unique pre-processing augmentations applied to images. Training parameters were set at 640 × 640 image size, 16-sample batches, and 500 epochs. Training duration was 5.538 h, achieving an overall precision score of 77.0% for 36 labels and 53% precision score. The training loss graph consistently decreased with increasing epochs, suggesting the model could benefit from more than 500 epochs. However, the validation loss graph showed a rising trend after around 300 epochs, indicating overfitting. Hence, augmentation techniques like color inversion, contrast enhancement, and their combination were applied to provide the model with more diverse data to learn.

Augmented Bounding Box Dataset
The dataset was retrained again, but this time, using the pre-trained weights of best.pt in previous training. The same hyperparameters were used. The total training was completed in 1.386 h, where early stopping was applied on 419th epochs. The overall precision score was 81% for the model, with a recall score of 69.4%. After the second training, the precision score improved by 4%. However, the validation graphs in Fig. 4 show signs of noise, which can be attributed to an imbalance in the class sample compared to the training dataset.

Faker Bounding Box Dataset
The third training on yolov5s.pt weights with a combination of serial and fake serial plates provided better results training on 500 epochs taking 2.183 h. Where overall precision was measured at 82.2%, it improved by 1.2% compared to the previous step. It also reaches a higher recall score of 72.1%. The validation loss in Fig. 5 improves by introducing more alphabets into the dataset, giving a less noisy graph. When using this model on a cropped image from model (1), the model correctly classified 86% of unseen

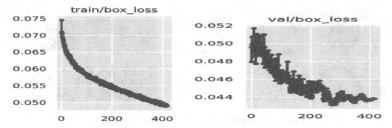

Fig. 4. Training and Validation loss graph of model (2) – second iteration.

images of good-condition serial plates. Interestingly, the YOLOv5 model could classify the alphanumeric characters correctly except for mistaking "G" for "C" in Fig. 6

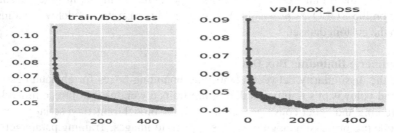

Fig. 5. Training and Validation loss graph of model (2) – third iteration

Fig. 6. Classification on unseen image using final iteration of model (2)

5 Residual Network 152 (ResNet-152)

ResNet is a residual network that aims to solve gradient issues using residual connections. This study uses ResNet-152 architecture, consisting of 152 layers, as the starting weight. The deep depth allows the model to capture abstract and intricate features of the alphanumeric characters. Since the ResNet-152 model was trained on a large dataset, it can provide a good starting point to speed up training time and improve generalization. In this study, the ResNet-152 model is fine-tuned to classify 36 classes in total. The first convolutional layer is modified with the correct parameters to read the input image. In this study, the input channel was set as "1" to read the grayscale images of the combined dataset and "3" for the custom dataset.

The output channels were set to 64 with a kernel size of 7×7. The padding was set to 3 to ensure the input dimensions matched the output feature's spatial dimension. The bias was set to false to prevent biased learning. As the ResNet-152 model was trained on 1000 classes, the fully connected layer will be replaced with a new linear layer. The new layer will be set as 36 output features which align with the 36 unique classes. The data loader is set up with a batch size of 32, with the shuffling of the training dataset set to true. The model was trained with 300 epochs. For the first training of 300 epochs, the training took about 22 h. Early stopping was observed at 131 epochs with a training accuracy of 99.98% and validation accuracy of 95.95% as seen in Fig. 7.

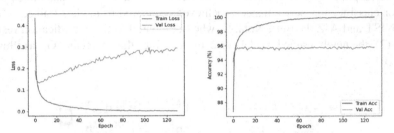

Fig. 7. Training and Validation loss graph on MNIST and A-Z datasets.

In the following testing on an unseen image, the Resnet-152 model could classify the characters within the bounding boxes classified by the model (2). But the results could have been better when model (2) outperformed the ResNet-152 model in classification as shown in Fig. 8. Since the Resnet-152 model trained on MNIST and A-Z dataset wasn't producing good results, the ResNet-152 model was retrained on the custom dataset instead with 500 epochs. The custom dataset was generated from the data used in the training of model (2). The new ResNet-152 model was trained with an 80% training split and a 20% validation split. The model achieved 80% accuracy but with high validation loss.

Fig. 8. Classification of unseen image using first iteration of ResNet-152 model.

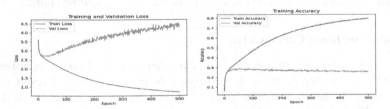

Fig. 9. Training and Validation loss graph of ResNet-152 trained on custom dataset.

Based on the training and validation loss graph depicted in Fig. 9, it is evident that the model could derive further benefit from additional epochs of training. However, indications of overfitting begin to emerge at approximately 80 epochs. Specifically, at this point, the model achieves an accuracy of only about 30%, indicating a failure to reach convergence and signalling the necessity for further training. In this study, the decision is made to persist with the ongoing training process rather than adopting the (2) augmentation technique proposed by the model, aiming to mitigate overfitting. This approach allows the model to gain a deeper understanding of the intricate features present in alphanumeric characters, encompassing various font styles and sizes found on the serial plate. With the ResNet-152 model newly trained on a customized dataset, superior classification performance is achieved compared to models trained solely on the MNIST and A-Z datasets. Notably, when compared to the classification results of model (2), the newly trained model correctly identifies the character "G," as illustrated in Fig. 10.

Fig. 10. Classification on unseen image using ResNet-152 model trained on Custom dataset.

6 Experiment on Unseen Dataset

In this section, models will be tested on unseen images to assess real-world accuracy. Emphasizing the study's focus, models will test on serial plates in poor condition due to rust or defacement. A total of 10 images unseen by the training model were selected, with 5 depicting various deterioration levels and 5 in good condition. The decision to limit the testing dataset stems from the need to maintain a balance between thorough evaluation and computational efficiency, ensuring practical feasibility in the testing process. These 10 images were cropped using Model (1), resulting in 10 additional images for testing, totaling 20. The testing dataset was compared in unprocessed and processed states. The processing method involved inversion of −0.5, contrast enhancement of −0.5, and a combination of inversion 1.5 and contrast enhancement 0.1, yielding optimal results.

6.1 Bounding Boxes Classification

The first and most important classification is the identification of bounding boxes using model (2). The higher accuracy in identifying bounding boxes will result in more alphanumeric characters being recognized and classified by the model (2) or ResNet-152. From Table 1, comparing 5 bad images and 5 bad cropped images, the uncropped images achieved better accuracy in classifying bounding boxes at 79%, while cropped images performed at 70%, which may not be too much of a difference. The classification results were the best when the uncropped image was processed with inversion achieving 92% of bounding box classification for uncropped images. Comparing 5 good images and 5 good, cropped images, on average, the uncropped images achieved better accuracy in classifying bounding boxes at 85%, while cropped images performed only 58%. The classification results were the best when the uncropped image was processed with inversion achieving 89% of bounding box classification for uncropped images. When looking at the overall results of the fifth row, both non-processed and image applied with inversion achieve satisfactory bounding box identification results for 87% and 90%, respectively. Poor bounding box classification mainly stems from improper ROI cropping from the model (1) as shown in Fig. 11, resulting in disappearing bounding boxes that should have been captured by the model (2).

Table 1. Results for identifying bounding boxes

Images	Normal	Inversion	Contrast	Inversion + Contrast	Avg
1. Five uncropped bad images	85%	92%	69%	69%	79%
2. Five cropped bad images	76%	80%	59%	66%	70%
3. Five uncropped good images	88%	89%	82%	81%	85%
4. Five cropped good images	71%	73%	42%	47%	58%
5. Five uncropped bad images and 5 Uncropped good images	87%	90%	76%	75%	82%
6. Five cropped bad images and 5 cropped good images	73%	76%	49%	55%	64%

Fig. 11. Improper ROI extraction by Model (1)

6.2 Alphanumeric Characters Classification

After creating the bounding box's ROI from the model (2), the bounding boxes are classified individually using model (2) and the ResNet-152 model.

Table 2. Results for classifying text in bounding boxes for YOLOv5 and ResNet-152 model

Bad images	Model	Normal	Inversion	Contrast	Inversion + Contrast	Avg
1. Five uncropped bad images	YOLO	89%	88%	87%	68%	83%
	ResNet	39%	48%	45%	20%	38%
2. Five cropped bad images	YOLO	92%	97%	94%	93%	94%
	ResNet	59%	53%	55%	63%	58%
3. Five uncropped good images	YOLO	85%	91%	81%	89%	86%
	ResNet	67%	64%	54%	55%	60%
4. Five cropped good images	YOLO	82%	84%	78%	80%	81%
	ResNet	71%	70%	73%	71%	71%
5. Five uncropped bad images and 5 Uncropped good images	YOLO	87%	89%	83%	80%	85%
	ResNet	55%	56%	50%	41%	51%
6. Five cropped bad images and 5 cropped good images	YOLO	87%	90%	86%	87%	88%
	ResNet	66%	62%	64%	67%	64%

From Table 2, ResNet-152 model exhibits lower accuracy in classifying bad images compared to YOLOv5. Conversely, cropped, unprocessed, and processed images demonstrate superior classification results overall. YOLOv5 model achieves 94% overall, while ResNet-152 achieves 58% overall as shown in Fig. 12. For classifying good images, YOLOv5 performs better on uncropped images at 86% compared to 81% for cropped images. In contrast, ResNet-152 excels in classifying cropped images at 71% compared to 60% for uncropped. Both unprocessed and preprocessing methods yield favorable results, with inversion processing slightly outperforming in accuracy. Overall, cropped images excel in classifying alphanumeric characters, with YOLOv5 achieving 88% and ResNet-152 achieving 64%. Conclusively, unprocessed and processed images yield desirable results with no standout techniques.

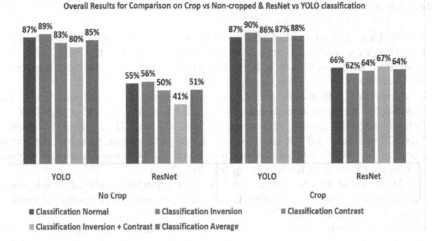

Fig. 12. Final text classification results for 20 images.

7 Conclusion

The principal findings for the unseen images reveal that YOLOv5 surpassed ResNet in text classification. Cropped images exhibited superior text classification compared to uncropped ones. Text classification performance reached 89% and 90% for non-cropped and cropped images with image inversion, respectively. The optimal text classification occurred with a cropped image using image inversion of −0.5, achieving 90%. The study suggests applying image inversion before feeding images into a combination of model (1) and model (2) to extract ROIs and classify serial plates. This approach achieved 90% accuracy in alphanumeric character classification. However, model (1) requires retraining on a larger dataset for improved ROI extraction, enhancing bounding box classification chances. Despite YOLOv5's reputation for object identification and secondary performance in alphanumeric character classification compared to ResNet, it was chosen for stability in this study.

ResNet-152 also exhibits promise, achieving 64% accuracy on cropped images despite training on an imperfect dataset. Future studies aim to compare ResNet's performance with YOLO in alphanumeric character classification on deteriorating serial plates. For future works, pre-processing techniques like color inversion and contrast enhancement to enhance character visibility on plates will be proposed. A newer YOLO version for potential differences in classification results and training speed can be used.

In summary, this paper presents backbone models and techniques for classifying deteriorating serial plates, ensuring better alphanumeric character identification, and minimizing human error in reading.

Acknowledgments. The authors gratefully acknowledge Newcastle University for their support and resources provided during the research conducted for this paper.

Disclosure of Interests. The authors have no competing interests.

References

1. Choi, E., Chae, S., Kim, J.: Machine learning-based fast banknote serial number recognition using knowledge distillation and Bayesian optimization. Sensors 1–18 (2019)
2. Desai, R.L., Kadam, B.P., Shinde, S.: Review on text detection methodology from images. Int. J. Adv. Res. Comput. Commun. Eng. **3**, 5581–5582 (2014)
3. Shashirangana, J., Padmasiri, H., Meedeniya, D., Perera, C.: Automated license plate recognition: a survey on methods and techniques. IEEE Access **9**, 11203–11225 (2020)
4. Vedhaviyassh, D.R., Sudhan, R., Saranya, G., Safa, M., Arun, D.: Comparative analysis of EasyOCR and TesseractOCR for automatic license plate recognition using deep learning algorithm. In: 6th International Conference on Electronics, Communication and Aerospace Technology, Coimbatore, India, 2022, pp. 966–971 (2022)
5. Hsu, M.M., Wu, M.-H., Cheng, Y.-C., Lin, C.Y.: An efficient industrial product serial number recognition framework. In: 2022 IEEE International Conference on Consumer Electronics – Taiwan, pp. 263–264. IEEE (2022)
6. Munter, J.: Number Recognition of Real-world Images in the Forest Industry, Mittuniveritetet, pp. 1–65 (2000)
7. Rekha, B.A., Marium, A., Srinivasan, D.G., Shetty, S.A.: Literature survey on object detection using YOLO. Int. Res. J. Eng. Technol. (IRJET) 3082–3088 (2020)
8. Liu, C., Tao, Y., Liang, J., Li, K., Chen, Y.: Object detection based on YOLO network. In: 2018 IEEE 4th Information Technology and Mechatronics Engineering Conference (ITOEC), pp. 799–803 (2018)
9. Li, C., et al.: YOLOv6: A Single-Stage Object Detection Framework for Industrial Applications, pp. 1–17 (2022)
10. Wang, C.Y., Bochkovskiy, A., Liao, H.-Y.M.: YOLOv7: trainable bag-of-freebies sets new state-of-the-art for real-time object detectors, pp. 1–15 (2022)
11. Jang, U., Suh, K.H., Lee, E.C.: Low-quality banknote serial number recognition based on deep neural network. J. Inf. Process. Syst. (JIPS) **16**(1), 224–237 (2020)
12. Chousangsuntorn, C., Tongloy, T., Chuwongin, S., Boonsang, S.: A deep learning system for recognizing and recovering contaminated slider serial numbers in hard disk manufacturing processes. Sensors **21**(18), 1–16 (2021)
13. Yousaf, U., et al.: A deep learning based approach for localization and recognition of pakistani vehicle license plates. Sensors **21**(22), 7696 (2021)
14. Jiang, P., Ergu, D., Liu, F., Cai, Y., Ma, B.: A review of yolo algorithm developments. Procedia Comput. Sci. **199**, 1066–1073 (2022)
15. Rashid, M.M., Musa, A., Rahman, M.A., Farahana, N., Farhana, A.: Automatic parking management system and parking fee collection based on number plate recognition. Int. J. Mach. Learn. Comput. 93–98 (2012)

Biomedical/Classification

A Spike Vision Approach for Multi-object Detection and Generating Dataset Using Multi-core Architecture on Edge Device

Sanaullah[1]([✉])[iD], Shamini Koravuna[2][iD], Ulrich Rückert[2],
and Thorsten Jungeblut[1][iD]

[1] Bielefeld University of Applied Sciences and Arts, Bielefeld, Germany
sanaullah@hsbi.de
[2] Bielefeld University, Bielefeld, Germany

Abstract. Spiking Neural Networks (SNNs) have gained significant attention in the field of neuromorphic computing for their potential to mimic the brain's spiking neurons, allowing event-driven processing based on exact spike timing. In this paper, we introduce a novel architecture that uses the power of SNN in combination with transfer learning to achieve real-time human presence detection and analysis using event-based cameras and compare it with non-event-based cameras. This architecture, which is deployed on edge computing devices, controls a comprehensive pipeline of components, seamlessly integrating various strategies. It combines object detection, transfer learning with SNN, human recognition, localizing and tracking, feature extraction, multi-core architecture, and run-time analysis. The application is initiated by extensively detecting objects and monitoring environments for motion events. Thus, transfer learning adjusts pre-trained Convolutional Neural Network (CNN) weights to SNNs upon detection, enabling event-driven processing. The utilization of multi-core processing speeds up the analytical workload while maintaining real-time operations. The architecture also keeps a valuable spike train dataset, which records important information about recognized objects. This dataset is useful for applications such as behavioral analysis and real-time monitoring.

Keywords: Spiking Neural Network · NVIDIA Jetson · Object Detection · Transfer Learning · Multi-Core Architecture · Real-time Tracking

This research was supported by the research training group "Dataninja" (Trustworthy AI for Seamless Problem Solving: Next Generation Intelligence Joins Robust Data Analysis) funded by the German federal state of North Rhine-Westphalia and the project SAIL. SAIL is funded by the Ministry of Culture and Science of the State of North Rhine-Westphalia under grant no. NW21-059B.

L. Iliadis et al. (Eds.): EANN 2024, CCIS 2141, pp. 317–328, 2024.
https://doi.org/10.1007/978-3-031-62495-7_24

1   Introduction

SNN offers the potential for efficient information processing and has garnered significant attention in the fields of computational neuroscience and artificial intelligence alike [10]. The SNN community frequently asks the following question: What makes SNNs differ from typical neural networks? One of the simplest answers is, that their approach to information encoding along with other differences including power consumption, computational efficiency, and most importantly SNN is inspired by the human brain [8,16]. Therefore, unlike traditional neural networks that use continuous-valued activations, SNNs mimic the behavior of biological neurons by encoding information in the form of discrete events known as spikes or action potentials to closely replicate the activity of actual neurons [4,23]. This discrete, event-based information encoding allows SNNs to more faithfully reflect the temporal dynamics of neural systems, making them particularly appropriate for tasks involving time-sensitive data processing, such as sensory perception, object detection, and autonomous driving control systems [20,24].

Furthermore, efficiently implementing SNN-based applications in real-time environments on edge computing (like NVIDIA Jetson or FPGA) provides a multidimensional challenge [30]. First and foremost, there is the question of hardware configurations. As described by [5], Learning processes are vital in enabling neuromorphic systems to adapt to specific applications, therefore, neuromorphic hardware is required for neuromorphic applications. Secondly, the combination of SNNs and event-based cameras, which similarly capture data to biological vision systems, adds another layer of complexity [17]. Therefore, the temporal dynamics necessary for real-time event processing include optimal network and sensory input integration, requiring balanced software-hardware synchronization [1]. To this end, we proposed a novel architecture based on a unique application of neuromorphic computing that manages a comprehensive pipeline of components designed to detect and analyze human presence in real-time using event-based cameras and deployed on edge computing devices [9]. As a result, our proposed architecture seamlessly integrates detection, enhanced object recognition through transfer learning, and the capabilities of SNNs. Because it gives immediate data regarding human presence and activity in a real-time environment, this application is powerfully dynamic and adaptive. Its applicability extends across a wide range of use cases, including security, surveillance, and cutting-edge behavioral research. Therefore, this full integration of the proposed architecture is the foundation of our novel solution.

2   Related Works

SNNs, with their sophisticated architecture and advanced learning algorithms, have gotten a lot of interest and research attention in recent years, as indicated by the large body of literature [18]. Hunsberger and Eliasmith [6] make an important contribution by delving into the use of spiking neurons within deep networks, demonstrating the feasibility of training deep SNNs via backpropagation. This important discovery not only sheds information on spiking neurons' capabilities but also highlights their potential for complicated learning tasks.

On the other hand, the study by Zhang et al. [31] is crucial in the field of spike-based learning. It investigates the integration of memory transverse arrays for neuromorphic computing, highlighting the importance of fast hardware implementations, particularly when dealing with large-scale spike train datasets. To further explore the capabilities of SNNs, researchers have investigated different learning algorithms and techniques. Mehonic et al. [11] provide an overview and learning algorithms for neuromorphic computing, discussing the challenges and opportunities in developing SNNs. Diehl and Cook [3] explore unsupervised learning of digit recognition using spike-timing-dependent plasticity (STDP), a biologically inspired learning rule that enables SNNs to learn from temporal spike patterns.

In the context of transfer learning of pre-generated weights from CNN to SNN, Wu and Feng et al. [27], investigate the use of SNNs to evaluate electroencephalogram (EEG) data, with an emphasis on upgrading the NeuCube SNN architecture for EEG-based pattern identification. It uses transfer learning to align EEG data covariance matrices, optimizes hyperparameters for feature extraction, and uses a weighted transfer support vector machine to improve the output classifier. Similarly, in the context of edge hardware platforms such as the NVIDIA Jetson series. Paolucci and Ammendola et al. [14], compare the performance of a distributed SNN simulator (DPSNN-STDP) on an embedded platform with dual-socket quad-core ARM architecture and a server platform with quad-core dual-socket Intel architecture.

To validate the effectiveness of the proposed approach, experimental results are crucial. Bzdok et al. [2] emphasize the importance of learning from the brain through computational approaches, providing insights into the validation and evaluation of neural models. Additionally, Wang et al. [25] review various spike learning rules for training deep SNNs and discuss the evaluation methods used to assess the performance of these networks. The results obtained from the proposed system are provided in the paper, showcasing significant improvements and state-of-the-art performance in various visual processing tasks [2, 25]. The achievements in generating large-scale spike train datasets and the advancements in SNN models have significant implications.

3   Discussion and Results

The foundation of the "Proposed Architecture" is built on the strategic incorporation of an SNN. SNN is inspired by the workings of the human brain, specifically in terms of neural behavior. Unlike traditional CNNs [19], SNN manipulates data using discrete spikes or pulses, simulating the firing of neurons in response to input signals [29]. This biologically inspired method provides the framework for the advanced capabilities of the architecture [10, 22]. Therefore, this architecture is designed with a specific and core objective: real-time detection and in-depth analysis of human presence.

Moreover, the proposed application architecture does not operate alone; by being distributed on edge computing devices (such as NVIDIA Jetson), it adopts a decentralized computing strategy. These edge devices are strategically placed closer to the data source, which reduces the requirement for data transfer to remote data centers [13]. Therefore, utilizing the capabilities of edge computing enables faster decision-making and action based on detected human presence, which makes it suited for applications where speedy reactions are critical or require different steps using parallel processing. Thus the basic flow of the proposed architecture can be seen in Fig. 1 and as explained above the proposed application architecture process involves major steps and allows users to freely integrate with different systems:

3.1   Data Acquisition

The proposed architecture of the neurocomputing application is designed to be adaptable in terms of data or input sources. It is capable of obtaining input data from a variety of sources, with a particular emphasis on event-based cameras (frames-based) and non-event-based cameras.

Non-Event-Based Camera Integration: We have taken a practical approach to incorporate non-event-based cameras into the proposed architecture, in our demonstration. We used a regular USB plug-in camera for this purpose. Within the architecture, a specific class has been integrated to manage the interaction with non-event-based cameras. The key innovation here is the introduction of a triggering mechanism that effectively modifies the behavior of the non-event-based camera input to closely mimic that of an event-based camera.

Initially, our architecture combines techniques such as frame differencing and contour detection to achieve a robust and accurate object detection system. Frame differencing allows us to compare consecutive frames and identify regions that have changed significantly, which is particularly useful for detecting moving objects. Let $I(t)$ and $I(t + 1)$ denote two consecutive frames of a video sequence. Subtracting $I(t) from I(t + 1)$ yields the difference image, $D(t) = I(t + 1) - I(t)$. The difference image highlights regions where significant changes have occurred between the two frames. Contour detection helps us identify the boundaries of objects in an image, enabling more precise localization. Edge detection algorithms such as Canny and Sobel apply to the difference image $D(t)$ [28]. These algorithms identify strong gradients in pixel intensities, which correspond to object boundaries. By thresholding and applying additional processing, we extract the contours that represent the spatial boundaries of the detected objects.

Event-Based Camera Integration: Event-based cameras, which are central to the design of this architecture, provide a dynamic and extremely efficient way of data collecting [9]. These cameras work on a novel basis, capturing and transmitting data only when substantial changes occur within their range of vision. The architecture has been methodically designed to capture and decode (frame-based) the different data streams generated by event-based cameras.

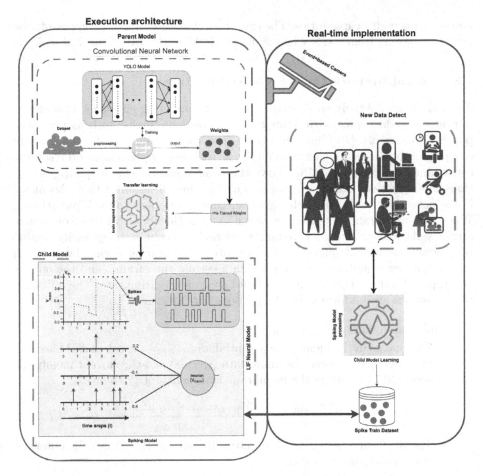

Fig. 1. The execution methodology of the proposed neuromorphic computing application.

3.2   Model Learning

Within the proposed architecture, the primary goal is to improve the architecture's recognition and understanding of complicated patterns and features, particularly in the context of object (human) identification and analysis. The motivation for using transfer learning in this context is rooted in the acknowledgment that developing an object detection algorithm that outperforms established models like YOLO (You Only Look Once) can be a difficult and challenging task [15]. YOLO has been extensively developed and optimized, transforming it into a powerful model in the domain of computer vision. Recognizing YOLO's outperform, the proposed architecture of the neurocomputing application adopts a novel approach it uses YOLO as the parent model, known as the pre-trained model, and a custom-designed SNN as the child model. This model hierarchy allows for dynamic collaboration between the two components and utilizing each's capabilities. The execution structure in Fig. 1, represents the transfer learning from a CNN to a Spiking Model of the LIF Neural Model.

3.3   Neural Network Core: SNN Architecture

The LIF [6] model truly succeeded in terms of computing efficiency. It achieved impressive performance with fewer computational resources, such as processor power and memory [7]. This efficiency is especially useful in situations where computing cost is a significant factor, such as real-time applications and resource-constrained environments. [18], shows the comparison of several spiking operations among different neural models. The LIF model assumes that the membrane potential of the neuron changes over time in response to the input stimuli. When the membrane potential crosses a certain threshold, the neuron generates a spike and undergoes a refractory period where it is temporarily unable to generate additional spikes. The firing rate of the neuron is calculated based on the number of spikes generated within a certain time frame, and the output is computed using a Poisson distribution based on the firing rate. The following LIF equations are performed by the proposed architecture:

- Membrane Potential ($V_{membrane}$):
  - The change in the membrane potential, $dv_{membrane}$, is calculated based on the difference between the input data (signals) and the current membrane potential, divided by the membrane time constant (τ_mem):

$$\frac{dv_{membrane}}{dt} = \frac{V_{membrane} + input\_data}{\tau_{membrane}} \tag{1}$$

  - The membrane potential is updated by adding the change in potential ($membrane\_capacitance$).

$$V_{membrane} + = \frac{dv_{membrane}.time\_step}{membrane\_capacitance} \tag{2}$$

- Spiking Threshold ($threshold$):
  - When the membrane potential crosses the threshold (th), indicating that a spike is generated, the spike train is incremented by 1 at the corresponding position.

$$spike\_train[V_{membrane} \geq threshold] + = 1 \tag{3}$$

- Refractory Period:
  - After a spike, the refractory period is simulated by setting the membrane potential to the reset potential for the neurons that have fired a spike and decrementing the spike train by 1.:

$$V_{membrane}[spike\_train > 0] = reset\_potential \tag{4}$$

$$spike\_train[spike\_train > 0] - = 1 \tag{5}$$

– Firing Rate and Output:
  • The firing rate of a LIF neuron is computed based on the number of spikes generated during the current time step:

$$firing\_rate = \frac{\sum spike\_train}{input\_data.size} \tag{6}$$

  • The output is generated based on the firing rate (firing_rate) by using a Poisson (P) distribution to randomly generate spike counts.

$$output \sim P(firing\_rate, size = input\_data.shape) \tag{7}$$

  • The firing rate is typically used to compute the output of the neuron.

These equations and notions describe the core dynamics of a proposed custom LIF neuron network class.

Spike-Timing-Dependent Plasticity (STDP): One of the significant features of the custom-build model is its implementation of STDP. STDP is a biological learning rule that adjusts the synaptic weights between neurons based on the timing of their spikes. The update_synaptic_weights function in the proposed algorithm modifies the synaptic weights associated with this neuron using the STDP rule. This method enables the SNN to adapt to and learn from new data.

Initialization and Integration: The proposed algorithm includes methods for initializing synaptic weights and running the neuron's dynamics using a given set of input data. The membrane potential is updated at each time step, and spike events are created when the threshold is crossed. The STDP rule is also used to alter the synaptic weights. This behavior integration occurs repeatedly, simulating the neurons' activity over time.

3.4 Spike Vision Approach for Generating Large-Scale Spiking Dataset

The proposed application spike vision approach for generating large-scale spike train dataset application is based on the real-time multi-object detection system using SNNs, which can mimic complicated neural activity and enable brain-inspired computation. Therefore, the Spike Train Dataset is the turning point of the proposed architecture and it acts as a repository for essential information related to detected objects, particularly humans. These datasets consist of sequences of spikes that mimic the firing patterns of neurons in response to visual signals. The proposed neurocomputing application spike vision approach and the resulting spike train datasets have the potential to be smoothly integrated into various applications other than object detection or recognition. Thus, the temporal information captured in the spike trains can be used to enable real-time interaction and coordination with other processes or systems.

324   Sanaullah et al.

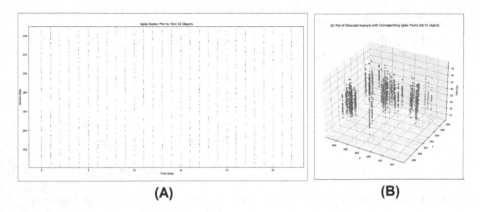

(A) **(B)**

Fig. 2. In (A), neurons are represented along the y-axis, and time is along the x-axis. Each spike (i.e., action potential) of a neuron is marked as a dot at its corresponding time of occurrence and (B), a 3D plot offers a visual representation of detected humans along with their corresponding spike trains.

For example, once spikes are formed as a result of object detection, they can be used as signals to initiate actions in robotic systems. The robot's control system can read these spike signals, allowing it to respond to and adapt to identified objects or their movements. This integration enables the robot to autonomously navigate its environment, avoid barriers, or perform specific tasks based on the visual information captured by the spike vision system [21]. The dataset includes a set of extracted characteristics related to the detected humans. Therefore, it is a repository of key features that are computed for each detected human object in the real-time environment. These features are essential for understanding and characterizing the detected object and are useful in a variety of neurocomputing applications. The spike train dataset repository consists of essential information about the detected object, such as Object Id, Bounding Box, Spike Train, and Computed Features (a more detailed explanation based on the proposed approach can be found in the appendix). Figure 2(A), shows the visualization of the spike trains dataset based on the activity of multiple neurons over time and Fig. 2(B), shows the spatial distribution of detected humans in the image (X and Y coordinates) and how the intensity (Z coordinate) varies for each detected human. X-Center and Y-Center represent the coordinates of the location of the bounding box of each detected human within the image. These coordinates enable us to precisely identify the spatial positioning of each individual. The intensity represents the cumulative spike counts for each detected human over time. It consists of the amount of neural activity, providing an estimate of the intensity of neural events connected with each human object.

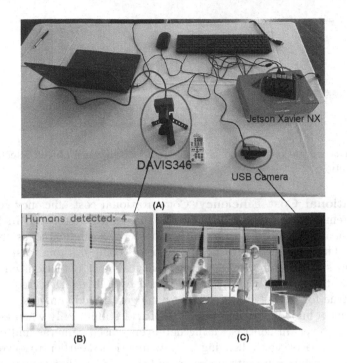

Fig. 3. The figure provides a general description of the setup.

3.5 Demonstration

In this section, we describe the demonstration of our neuromorphic computing application, which utilizes the power of SNNs for object detection on edge devices. Our study establishes a new standard in object detection by integrating advances in neuromorphic computing and traditional computer vision approaches.

In Real-Time Environment: To illustrate the case of the multi-object detection of the proposed architecture in a real-time demonstration, we used the lowest version of NVIDIA Jetson Xavier NX 8 GB developer kit [12] (Note: it reached EOL and is no longer available for purchase.), a DAVIS346 event-based camera, a USB camera, and a CPU-based system. The setup of the demonstration can be seen in Fig. 3(A). In the visualization of the practical output of the proposed neurocomputing application, Fig. 3(A–B), provides a detailed comparison of event-based and non-event-based cameras in the output visualization. Thus, Fig. 3(A) shows the frame-based output of an event-based camera, whereas Fig. 3(B) shows the output of a non-event-based camera. This demonstration showcases the detection ability of the proposed architecture, highlighting that the overlapping of objects (humans) does not affect the recognition ability of the application.

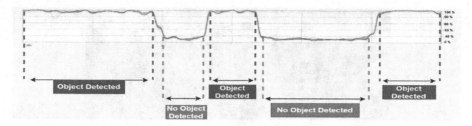

Fig. 4. The computational cost efficiency comparison between object detection and no object detection.

Computational Cost Efficiency: Computational cost efficiency comparison of the system between object detection and no object detection. In Fig. 4, the computational cost when no objects are detected is indicated as 'No Object Detected'. This demonstrates that the system's computational cost remains at a minimum state during periods of inactivity. Object detection, on the other hand, raises the computing cost, as indicated by 'Object Detected'. This finding holds true for both event-based and non-event-based cameras. Event-based cameras have a built-in functionality that provides input only when an object is detected. However, in contrast, using non-event-based cameras and controlling computational costs is a challenging task. As mentioned earlier, to solve this issue the proposed architecture introduces an additional class that acts as a filtration step for input data from non-event-based cameras, which acts as a flag to control the processing flow before engaging the detection part of the proposed architecture. Its benefit is particularly noticeable when the architecture is used with non-event-based cameras. But using this class introduces a new challenge where the detection algorithm in this case analyses each frame individually, which can result in several localizations for a single object, such as a human. The ability to distinguish individual frames complicates the detection process. To overcome this challenge, the proposed architecture includes an additional class specifically designed for preprocessing the detected bounding boxes. This class is responsible for managing overlaps between multiple bounding boxes corresponding to a single object.

4   Conclusion

In this study, we introduced a novel architecture that uses the power of neuromorphic computing to detect and analyze human presence in real-time utilizing event-based cameras. Our comprehensive solution combines a variety of strategies to create a dynamic and adaptive system. These strategies include object detection, transfer learning with SNN, human recognition, localization and tracking, feature extraction, multi-core processing, and real-time analysis. The proposed architecture begins operation by continuously monitoring the environment for detecting signals. It uses advanced computer vision techniques and unique algorithms to identify motion events, serving as the trigger for the rest of the algorithms. On the other side, the transfer learning approach, which combines pre-trained CNN weights with custom-designed SNNs, enables event-driven processing while closely simulating the complicated behavior of spiking neurons in the human brain.

Author contributions. Sanaullah designed and conducted all experiments evaluated the resulting data, and wrote the architecture code. Additionally, Sanaullah authored the manuscript. SK provided hardware support, while UR and TJ supervised the project, offering guidance to enhance and refine the outcomes.

Data Availibility Statement. All of the experiments have been performed using the proposed application and more detailed results and further information can be seen on the project webpage [26].

References

1. Brüderle, D., et al.: A comprehensive workflow for general-purpose neural modeling with highly configurable neuromorphic hardware systems. Biol. Cybern. **104**, 263–296 (2011)
2. Bzdok, D., Yeo, B.T.: Inference in the age of big data: future perspectives on neuroscience. Neuroimage **155**, 549–564 (2017)
3. Diehl, P.U., Cook, M.: Unsupervised learning of digit recognition using spike-timing-dependent plasticity. Front. Comput. Neurosci. **9**, 99 (2015)
4. Gerstner, W., Kistler, W.M., Naud, R., Paninski, L.: Neuronal Dynamics: From Single Neurons to Networks and Models of Cognition. Cambridge University Press, Cambridge (2014)
5. Hasler, J., Marr, B.: Finding a roadmap to achieve large neuromorphic hardware systems. Front. Neurosci. **7**, 118 (2013)
6. Hunsberger, E., Eliasmith, C.: Spiking deep networks with LIF neurons. arXiv preprint arXiv:1510.08829 (2015)
7. Ji, J., Tang, C., Zhao, J., Tang, Z., Todo, Y.: A survey on dendritic neuron model: mechanisms, algorithms and practical applications. Neurocomputing **489**, 390–406 (2022)
8. Kasabov, N.K.: Time-Space, Spiking Neural Networks and Brain-Inspired Artificial Intelligence. Springer, Heidelberg (2019). https://doi.org/10.1007/978-3-662-57715-8
9. Koravuna, S., Rückert, U., Jungeblut, T., et al.: A novel spike vision approach for robust multi-object detection using SNNs. Technical report, EasyChair (2024)
10. Maass, W.: Networks of spiking neurons: the third generation of neural network models. Neural Netw. **10**(9), 1659–1671 (1997)
11. Mehonic, A., Sebastian, A., Rajendran, B., Simeone, O., Vasilaki, E., Kenyon, A.J.: Memristors-from in-memory computing, deep learning acceleration, and spiking neural networks to the future of neuromorphic and bio-inspired computing. Adv. Intell. Syst. **2**(11), 2000085 (2020)
12. NVIDIA: NVIDIA Jetson Xavier NX (2023). https://developer.nvidia.com/embedded/learn/get-started-jetson-xavier-nx-devkit. Accessed 01 Mar 2023
13. Pan, S.J., Yang, Q.: A survey on transfer learning. IEEE Trans. Knowl. Data Eng. **22**(10), 1345–1359 (2009)
14. Paolucci, P.S., et al.: Power, energy and speed of embedded and server multi-cores applied to distributed simulation of spiking neural networks: ARM in NVIDIA Tegra vs Intel Xeon quad-cores. arXiv preprint arXiv:1505.03015 (2015)

15. Redmon, J., Divvala, S., Girshick, R., Farhadi, A.: You only look once: unified, real-time object detection. In: Proceedings of the IEEE Conference on Computer Vision and Pattern Recognition, pp. 779–788 (2016)
16. Sananullah, Koravuna, S., Rückert, U., Jungeblut, T.: Evaluation of spiking neural nets-based image classification using the runtime simulator RAVSim. Int. J. Neural Syst. 2350044–2350044 (2023)
17. Sanaullah, Koravuna, S., Rückert, U., Jungeblut, T.: SNNs model analyzing and visualizing experimentation using RAVSim. In: Iliadis, L., Jayne, C., Tefas, A., Pimenidis, E. (eds.) EANN 2022. CCIS, vol. 1600, pp. 40–51. Springer, Cham (2022). https://doi.org/10.1007/978-3-031-08223-8_4
18. Sanaullah, Koravuna, S., Rückert, U., Jungeblut, T.: Exploring spiking neural networks: a comprehensive analysis of mathematical models and applications. Front. Comput. Neurosci. **17**, 1215824 (2023)
19. Sanaullah, Koravuna, S., Rückert, U., Jungeblut, T.: Streamlined training of GCN for node classification with automatic loss function and optimizer selection. In: Iiadis, L., Maglogiannis, I., Alonso, S., Jayne, C., Pimenidis, E. (eds.) EANN 2023. CCIS, vol. 1826, pp. 191–202. Springer, Cham (2023). https://doi.org/10.1007/978-3-031-34204-2_17
20. Sanaullah, S.: A hybrid spiking-convolutional neural network approach for advancing machine learning models. In: Northern Lights Deep Learning Conference, pp. 220–227. PMLR (2024)
21. Tavanaei, A., Maida, A.S.: A minimal spiking neural network to rapidly train and classify handwritten digits in binary and 10-digit tasks. Int. J. Adv. Res. Artif. Intell. **4**(7), 1–8 (2015)
22. Ullah, S., Koravuna, S., Rückert, U., Jungeblut, T.: Design-space exploration of SNN models using application-specific multi-core architectures (2023)
23. Ullah, S., Koravuna, S., Rückert, U., Jungeblut, T.: Transforming event-based into spike-rate datasets for enhancing neuronal behavior simulation to bridging the gap for SNNs (2023)
24. Viale, A., Marchisio, A., Martina, M., Masera, G., Shafique, M.: CarSNN: an efficient spiking neural network for event-based autonomous cars on the loihi neuromorphic research processor. In: 2021 International Joint Conference on Neural Networks (IJCNN), pp. 1–10. IEEE (2021)
25. Wang, X., Lin, X., Dang, X.: Supervised learning in spiking neural networks: a review of algorithms and evaluations. Neural Netw. **125**, 258–280 (2020)
26. Project Webpage (2023). https://rao-sanaullah.github.io/neurocomputing_application/. Accessed 01 Mar 2023
27. Wu, X., et al.: Improving neucube spiking neural network for EEG-based pattern recognition using transfer learning. Neurocomputing **529**, 222–235 (2023)
28. Xian, R., Lugu, R., Peng, H., Yang, Q., Luo, X., Wang, J.: Edge detection method based on nonlinear spiking neural systems. Int. J. Neural Syst. **33**(01), 2250060 (2023)
29. Yamazaki, K., Vo-Ho, V.K., Bulsara, D., Le, N.: Spiking neural networks and their applications: a review. Brain Sci. **12**(7), 863 (2022)
30. Zhang, X., Wang, Y., Lu, S., Liu, L., Shi, W., et al.: Openei: an open framework for edge intelligence. In: 2019 IEEE 39th International Conference on Distributed Computing Systems (ICDCS), pp. 1840–1851. IEEE (2019)
31. Zhang, X., Huang, A., Hu, Q., Xiao, Z., Chu, P.K.: Neuromorphic computing with memristor crossbar. Physica Status Solidi (A) **215**(13), 1700875 (2018)

Ensembles of Bidirectional LSTM and GRU Neural Nets for Predicting Mother-Infant Synchrony in Videos

Daniel Stamate[1,2,3]([⊠]), Pradyumna Davuloori[1], Doina Logofatu[1,4],
Evelyne Mercure[5], Caspar Addyman[6], and Mark Tomlinson[6,7]

[1] Data Science & Soft Computing Lab, London, UK
d.stamate@gold.ac.uk
[2] Department of Computing, Goldsmiths, University of London, London, UK
[3] School of Health Sciences, The University of Manchester, Manchester, UK
[4] Faculty of Computer Science and Engineering, Frankfurt University of Applied Sciences,
Frankfurt, Germany
[5] Department of Psychology, Goldsmiths, University of London, London, UK
[6] Department of Global Health, Stellenbosch University, Stellenbosch, South Africa
[7] School of Nursing and Midwifery, Queens University, Belfast, UK

Abstract. The importance of positive, healthy and reciprocal interactions between mother and infant cannot be understated as it leaves a lasting impact on the rest of the infant's life. One way to identify a positive interaction between two people is the amount of nonverbal synchrony - or spontaneous coordination of bodily movements, present in the interaction. This work proposes a neural network and ensemble learning based approach to automatically labelling a mother-infant dyad interaction as high versus low by predicting the level of synchrony of the interaction. Bidirectional Long Short-Term Memory (BiLSTM) and Bidirectional Gated Recurrent Unit (BiGRU) models were trained and evaluated on a dataset consisting of 25 key body position coordinates of mother and infant extracted with an AI specialised tool called OpenPose, from 58 different videos. Ensembles of 30 such bidirectional recurrent neural network base models were built and then post-processed via ROC analysis, to improve prediction stability and performance, both of which assessed in a Monte Carlo validation procedure of 30 iterations. The prediction performances on the unseen test samples for the ensembles of BiLSTM and ensembles of BiGRU models include a mean AUC of 0.781 and 0.796, a mean precision of 0.857 and 0.899, and a mean specificity of 0.817 and 0.872, respectively. In particular our models predict higher probability scores for the high synchrony class versus the low synchrony class in 80% of cases. Moreover the achieved high precision level indicates that 90% of mother-infant dyads predicted to be in the high synchrony class are predicted correctly, and the high specificity level indicates a detection rate of the mother-infant dyads with low synchrony in 87% of cases, suggesting these models' high capability for automatically flagging cases that may be clinically relevant for further investigation and potential intervention.

P. Davuloori—Joint first-author

Keywords: Mother-infant synchrony detection · Recurrent neural networks · Bidirectional LSTM · Bidirectional GRU · Ensemble learning · Model post-processing optimisation · Monte Carlo validation · Video classification

1 Introduction

The relationship with their mother is arguably the most important one in a person's life. This relationship and the strength of it in infancy can shape the course of the person's social, emotional and mental wellbeing for the rest of their life. The early stages of life are paramount for babies' brain and emotional development, and the quality of interaction between mother and infant is critical in that period. If infants are denied attention and a positive interaction, they can struggle in later life with forming relationships, education and functioning in society [1, 10]. The strong bond and the early positive interactions between mother and infant can shape the social development of the latter [2]. On the other hand, infants who were neglected from the early stages of development face further social development difficulties [2, 21]. Moreover, authors of [22] found that parent-child closeness and affection are good predictors of adolescent mental health and self-worth.

One method to assess the quality of mother-infant interactions is nonverbal synchrony which is the spontaneous coordination of bodily movements. Synchrony can be a vital indicator of a positive, reciprocal mother-infant interaction and it also indicates a healthy relationship with familiarity between mother and infants, leading to positive developmental outcomes for the infant [9, 23]. In particular, research suggests that synchrony between the infant's behaviour and their caregivers play many functions in the infants' development, from co-regulations of exchanges in interactions to language acquisition [3]. A functional interaction between mother and baby is one in which the mother focuses her attention on the child and responds to their behaviour in a short time. Such an interaction can be described as synchronous. According to [4] synchrony between two people is defined as a state where they move together in the same or almost the same time with one another. Research suggests that synchrony in group interactions can have a later positive influence on forming social actions [5]. Synchrony is used to find patterns in movements of positive and negative interactions between mother and infant. Developing new methods for finding synchrony patterns can help to automate the process of assessing the mother-infant interaction quality.

One of the problems of interest in this context is the expert's assessment of the synchrony between mother and infant in videos capturing this interaction. Moreover, there is value in automating this assessment process using machine learning, as such automation could flag those videos which are more likely to capture a negative, lower synchrony between mother and infant. This would constitute a useful tool supporting specialists in an early intervention in problematic mother-infant interactions.

Predicting synchrony between participants in videos using machine learning models, was previously tackled in literature including works such as [6], in which the authors successfully trained a model based on Long Short-Term Memory (LSTM) recurrent neural networks, on facial expressions data that had been extracted from pre-recorded videos representing a group of three interacting people. The proposed approach was used to predict synchrony score on a scale of 1 to 5, and the recurrent neural model's predictions were validated by comparison with predictions based on a random permutations baseline. In another machine learning study proposing the prediction of synchrony between a human arm and a robot arm, the final position of the human arm was predicted also with recurrent neural networks based on LSTM models [7].

In the present study we propose an innovative machine learning approach to predicting the categorical level of dyadic synchrony – high versus low, for 58 mother-infant dyads, based on a dataset comprising 58 records with body part coordinates extracted from 58 videos capturing the interaction of these dyads. The approach proposed in this paper is based on Bidirectional Long Short-Term Memory and Bidirectional Gated Recurrent Unit neural network models [8, 13, 14], denoted BiLSTM and BiGRU, which are used as baseline models to build ensembles models, denoted BiLSTMens and BiGRUens, that enhance the base models' prediction performance and stability.

The rest of the paper is organised as follows: Sect. 2 provides a further discussion on synchrony related work. Section 3 introduces our proposed prediction modelling methodology, including data pre-processing, prediction models training and evaluation, and Monte Carlo validation. Section 4 presents and discusses our results, and Sect. 5 concludes the paper and indicates future research directions.

2   Related Work

Prior research has defined synchrony as the coordination of movements, patterns, rhythm and timing between two people in a well-established or budding relationship. It is known to aid in building rapport and understanding. Synchrony can also manifest itself as people imitating each other's speech patterns, through a phenomenon termed speech convergence (or linguistic convergence) [24]. [3] by Delaherche et al. offers valuable additional details about synchrony that merits consideration. The authors propose the following formal definition of synchrony: "Synchrony is the dynamic and reciprocal adaptation of the temporal structure of behaviours between interactive partners". A distinction is also made between mirroring and synchrony, stating that mirroring is the coordination of actions or behaviours, while synchrony is the coordination of behaviours at the same time. Mirroring and synchrony are interrelated, but not equal, with synchrony being more dynamic and fluid in time. With time being a pivotal factor for synchrony, the authors argue that there is but a limited window of time for a person to produce behaviour matching that of their partner, thereby achieving synchrony. Delaherche et al. [3] also delve into the topic of synchrony in mother-infant interactions. First, the authors state that a strong sense of synchrony with their mother is essential in early infancy as the infant uses these moments of connection with their mother to build confidence in their ability to interact with others. Synchrony with the mother also builds a sense of secure attachment in the infant and helps them learn languages.

Nguyen et al. [25] discuss neural synchrony between mother and infant. The authors define neural synchrony as "the temporal coordination of concurrent rhythmic brain activities between individuals". Related research stated by the authors showed neural synchronisation of the left inferior frontal cortex during conversations, measured through a technology named hyperscanning. The main focus of [25] was to understand neural synchrony between mother and infant during conversations and to study the impact of factors like turn-taking and conversation topics on said synchrony. Wavelet Coherence was used to calculate synchrony. The work found mother and child to have synchronised brain activity during conversations, with turn-taking proving a strong influence on increasing synchrony. This could be because, when the mother engages in proper turn-taking, she is listening intently and is allowing the child enough room to communicate and express themselves, thereby fostering good communication and synchrony. This study is enlightening on neural synchrony during mother-child conversations.

Egmose et al. in [26], investigated the impact of bodily movements including upper body, arms and head on synchrony between mothers and infants. The study included infants aged 4 months and 13 months old. An eight-camera optoelectronic motion registration system was used to capture the bodily movements of mothers and infants. The quality of interaction between the mother and infant was coded using the Coding Interactive Behaviour scale [27]. For data analysis purposes, Matlab and SPSS were used to process the data. The study found a few valuable insights. Firstly, it was found that when the mother coordinated her head movements with the infant's, the interaction had a higher rating for synchrony. Secondly, the correlation between bodily movements and synchrony ratings was higher for 4-month-old infants compared to 13-month-old infants.

3 Prediction Modelling Methodology

3.1 Data Pre-processing

This work was based on a sample of 60 videos from the SPEAKNSIGN dataset [20, 28], each lasting more than 10 min with 25 frames per second, capturing a session of free-play between 4–7-month-old infants and their mothers. The videos were scored by experts with a dyadic synchrony score ranging from 2 to 14. Out of the 60 videos available, 2 videos were discarded as they were lacking in clarity. The distribution of the synchrony scores of the remaining 58 videos is illustrated in Fig. 1.

The OpenPose library [19] was used to extract a 5D array including information such as the video number, camera number, frame number, number of people present in a video, pairs of x and y coordinates and their confidence intervals of 25 body keypoints. Figure 2 illustrates a single frame of a mother-infant dyad interaction video, with body part keypoints extracted with OpenPose.

Out of the 3 available cameras from which data was available for each video, only data from camera one was retained. Moreover, only data belonging to mother and infant were preserved in two separate arrays. To keep the shape of the data consistent for each video in these two arrays for mother and infant, a total of 9000 frames of data, starting from frame 500 and ending with frame 9,500 were retained and the rest of the frames were discarded. Moreover, the x and y coordinates of body keypoints were preserved while the confidence intervals for each coordinate, which were also estimated by OpenPose, were removed as they were not necessary for this study. 3D arrays were finally obtained for each, mother and infant, comprising the record number corresponding to each video, the frame number, and the sum aggregation of the x and y coordinates for body keypoints. Data cleaning included also the treatment of missing values which were imputed via linear interpolation [11], and the detection and removal of outliers using criteria based

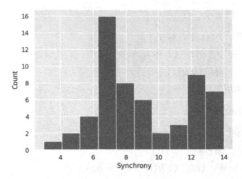

Fig. 1. Distribution of the mother-infant dyad synchrony scores.

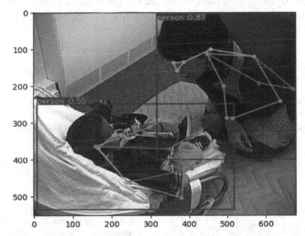

Fig. 2. Body part keypoints extracted with OpenPose from a single frame of an interaction video.

on the range of 0.025 or 0.975 quantiles [15, 16]. Data was normalised using the L2 norm.

Records corresponding to videos were categorized in two classes by using the dyadic synchrony scores: class 1 – high synchrony, and class 0 – low synchrony, containing the highest 60% scores and the lowest 40% scores in the dataset, respectively.

3.2 Classification and Model Post-processing via Receiver Operating Characteristic (ROC) Analysis and Optimisation

A bidirectional LSTM (BiLSTM) layer and bidirectional GRU (BiGRU) layer is a recurrent neural network layer that learns bidirectional long-term dependencies or patterns present in the input sequence data. They are based on Long Short-Term Memory (LSTM) and Gated Recurrent Unit (GRU) layers [12–14] whose computations are described by the equations below, which calculate the outputs y(t) from inputs x(t) as follows:

LSTM layer equations:

$$i(t) = \sigma(W_{xi}^{\mathsf{T}} x(t) + W_{hi}^{\mathsf{T}} h(t-1) + b_i)$$

$$f(t) = \sigma(W_{xf}^{\mathsf{T}} x(t) + W_{hf}^{\mathsf{T}} h(t-1) + b_f)$$
$$o(t) = \sigma(W_{xo}^{\mathsf{T}} x(t) + W_{ho}^{\mathsf{T}} h(t-1) + b_o)$$
$$g(t) = tanh(W_{xg}^{\mathsf{T}} x(t) + W_{hg}^{\mathsf{T}} h(t-1) + b_g)$$
$$c(t) = f(t) \otimes c(t-1) + i(t) \otimes g(t)$$
$$y(t) = h(t) = o(t) \otimes tanh(c(t))$$

GRU layer equations:

$$z(t) = \sigma(W_{xz}^{\mathsf{T}} x(t) + W_{hz}^{\mathsf{T}} h(t-1) + b_z)$$
$$r(t) = \sigma(W_{xr}^{\mathsf{T}} x(t) + W_{hr}^{\mathsf{T}} h(t-1) + b_r)$$
$$g(t) = tanh(W_{xg}^{\mathsf{T}} x(t) + W_{hg}^{\mathsf{T}} (r(t) \otimes h(t-1)) + b_g)$$
$$y(t) = h(t) = z(t) \otimes h(t-1) + (1 - z(t)) \otimes g(t)$$

where σ is the sigmoid function, W are the weight matrices, and b are the bias terms.

For illustration purposes, an LSTM cell which is a more complex version of a GRU cell, is depicted in Fig. 3 below [17]:

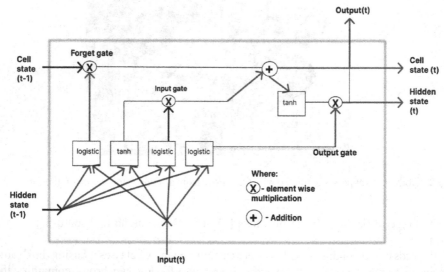

Fig. 3. An LSTM cell architecture where Input(t), Output(t), Cell state(t), and Hidden state(t) are the x(t), y(t), c(t), and h(t) quantities, respectively, appearing in the LSTM layer equations above.

Bidirectional LSTM (BiLSTM) and Bidirectional GRU (BiGRU) networks follow the general structure of a bidirectional recurrent neural network illustrated in Fig. 4 [13, 14].

The two types of recurrent neural network architectures employed in this work comprised, in this order, an input layer, 3 BiLSTM layers (3 BiGRU layers, respectively) with a number of units between 300 and 350 (the same for all 3 layers), and 1 hidden dense layer with a number of units between 50 and 70 and with *elu, gelu, mish,* or *swish* activations. The networks had an output layer with 1 unit with *sigmoid* activation for binary classification. As loss functions we employed *Binary focal crossentropy* with

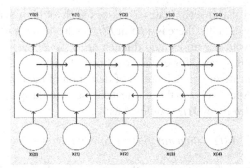

Fig. 4. A bidirectional recurrent neural network architecture, in which information from an input sequence data x is fed and processed in both directions as indicated by the horizontal arrows from left to right and from right to left, in order to compute the network's outputs y.

default parameter values. The *adam* optimiser with default parameter values was used, together with the exponential learning rate scheduling starting with the base learning rate of 0.003 which was decreased by a factor of 0.85 per epoch. To prevent overfitting, early stopping with 4 steps of *patience* was used on the validation set, and a *Gaussian noise layer* with standard deviation of 0, 0.01 and 0.02 was inserted after the input layer. To tune the hyperparameters for the respective value ranges mentioned above, we performed a random search with 10 iterations. Optimal hyperparameter values in the two architectures introduced above, are not constant and depended on the multiple non-test datasets used in the Monte Carlo procedure introduced in the next subsection. But some typical values were: (a) for the BiLSTM based architecture: 310 units for the BiLSTM layers, 62 units and *elu* activation for the dense layer, and a standard deviation of 0.1 for the Gaussian noise layer; and (b) for the BiGRU based architecture: 300 units for the BiGRU layers, 60 units and *elu* activation for the dense layer, and a standard deviation of 0 for the Gaussian noise layer.

Due to the relatively reduced number of records available in the dataset, i.e. 58, which may increase the variance of the model performance and hence negatively affect the model stability, we built ensembles of 30 BiLSTM models, and ensembles of 30 BiGRU models. We denote these ensemble models by BiLSTMens and BiGRUens, respectively. More precisely, BiLSTMens (BiGRUens) was built as follows: after splitting the dataset into test set and a non-test set, the base BiLSTM (BiGRU) models in each ensemble were obtained by first computing the optimal hyperparameter values using the non-test set as explained in the paragraph above, and then by further randomly splitting the non-test set into validation and train sets, 30 times, and by training 30 BiLSTM (BiGRU) models with the determined optimal hyperparameter values. The predicted probabilities were averaged among the 30 BiLSTM (BiGRU) models. Regarding data splitting, the following proportions were used: 25% test set, 75% non-test set. The non-test set was further split, 30 times, in 67% train and 33% validation.

For the BiLSTMens (BiGRUens) model post-processing, we utilised the *Youden index* maximisation method in a ROC analysis procedure [18, 29] for estimating the optimal probability threshold using the model's ROC curve calculated on the non-test (i.e. training plus validation) data set of records. For each generic probability threshold

$t \in [0, 1]$ of a model that discriminates 2 classes such as high synchrony versus low synchrony (t is 0.5 by default), there is a point $P(t)$ on the model's ROC curve computed on the non-test set, whose x and y coordinates are 1-$Specificity(t)$, and $Sensitivity(t)$, respectively [29]. In this case, for each probability threshold $t \in [0, 1]$, $Sensitivity(t)$ and $Specificity(t)$ indicate the model's rates of detection of the high synchrony and low synchrony classes, respectively, on the non-test dataset. Similarly to [29], the probability threshold based *Youden index* $Y(t)$ is defined as:

$$Y(t) = Sensitivity(t) + Specificity(t) - 1$$

We maximised the distance $D(t)$ from the point $P(t)$ to the main diagonal of the ROC curve ($D(t)$ is computed below and intuitively indicates how far our model is from the random guess model). Hence, we optimised the probability threshold t as follows:

$$D(t) = sin(\pi/4) \times Y(t); \quad p = argmax_{t \in [0,1]} D(t) = argmax_{t \in [0,1]} Y(t)$$

We employed the optimal probability threshold p and took $t = p$ to obtain the post-processed model, which was used to compute the test *accuracy, precision, sensitivity, specificity,* and *f1* performances [29]. Moreover, we computed *Cohen's kappa statistics* and *Matthews correlation coefficient MCC,* defined below, whose positive values, when sufficiently far from 0, indicate that the model predicts better than chance. In particular, *kappa* focuses more on the positive class while *MCC* treats classes equally.

$$kappa = 2 \times (TP \times TN - FN \times FP)/((TP + FP) \times (FP + TN) + (TP + FN) \times (FN + TN))$$

$$MCC = (TP \times TN - FP \times FN)/((TP + FP) \times (TP + FN) \times (TN + FP) \times (TN + FN))^{0.5}$$

The model's capability to predict better than chance was investigated also statistically, by running a one-side T-test, in order to prove that the model's general performance for binary classification, called Area Under ROC Curve, denoted simply by AUC, and defined with the conditional probability below, is significantly larger than 0.5 which is the performance of a random guess model. More precisely:

$$AUC = Pr(S(r_1) > S(r_2)|r_1 \in H, r_2 \in L)$$

where r_1 and r_2 are arbitrary records from the high synchrony class H, and low synchrony class L, respectively, and S is the score (i.e. probability to belong to the positive/high synchrony class) outputted by the model for each record.

3.3   Monte Carlo Validation for Assessing Models' Performance and Stability

To assess our models' predictive capability, we conducted a Monte Carlo validation based on 30 iterations, which allows to reliably evaluate the models' performance and stability.

3.4   Software and Hardware

Videos were initially processed with OpenPose library to detect the body keypoints coordinates. Data preprocessing and prediction modelling [17] were conducted in Python with Numpy, Scipy, Pandas, TensorFlow, Keras, Sklearn and Seaborn libraries, using 5 Linux servers with up to 128 GB RAM per machine, and Titan RTX 24GB, RTX 3090 24 GB, and RTX 4090 24 GB GPUs, for training the BiLSTM and BiGRU base models and building the BiLSTMens and BiGRUens ensemble models, as well as for assessing the models' performances and stability in computationally intensive Monte Carlo validation procedures of 30 iterations.

4   Results and Discussion

In this section we present and discuss the results of the analyses conducted following the lines of methodology introduced in Sect. 3.

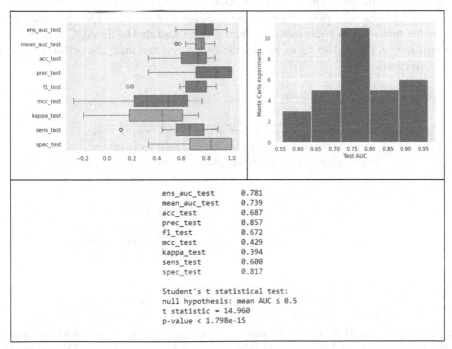

Fig. 5. Top: Boxplots (left) and histogram (right) of performances on the test data of Bidirectional LSTM ensemble models (BiLSTMens) in Monte Carlo validation of 30 iterations. Bottom: Mean performances, and one-tailed Student's t-test proving the alternative hypothesis: mean AUC > 0.5, demonstrating statistically the BiLSTMens models' prediction capability.

The distribution of classification performances of BiLSTMens models, provided as boxplots in Fig. 5 (top left), comprises performances computed in the 30 iterations of

Monte Carlo validation. More precisely they are evaluated using the 30 BiLSTMens models, each of which produced in 1 iteration of the Monte Carlo validation procedure, and the corresponding 30 test sets issued from the stratified splitting of the dataset. The performances evaluated are the AUC (ens_auc_test), accuracy (acc_test), precision (prec_test), f1 (f1_test), Matthews correlation coefficient MCC (mcc_test), kappa statistic (kappa_test), sensitivity (sens_test) and specificity (spec_test). Moreover, for comparison, we included also the distribution of the mean AUC of the 30 BiLSTM base models (mean_auc_test) which are the components of one BiLSTMens ensemble model. The means of the above mentioned performances are provided in Fig. 5 (bottom). On the other hand, the distribution of the AUC of the BiLSTMens models is represented additionally as a histogram in Fig. 5 (top right). The mean AUC of 0.781 represents a good capability of the BiLSTMens models to distinguish between mother-infant dyads with low vs. high synchrony. The distribution of AUC illustrated in Fig. 5 (top right) indicates a substantial variation of this performance across the Monte Carlo validation's 30 iterations, which may be explained by the relatively reduced number of records (videos) in the dataset that expectedly increases variance. When we conducted a one-tailed Student's t-test for the null hypothesis: mean AUC ≤ 0.5 (Fig. 5, bottom), we obtained the significant p-value $< 1.798e\text{-}15$ proving statistically that the BiLSTMens models predict better than random guess models, which is also illustrated by the AUC performance distributions in Fig. 5 (top right), and by the kappa_test and mcc_test performances in Fig. 5 (bottom).

exp	count	mean	std	min	25%	50%	75%	max
0	30.0	0.741975	0.055007	0.611111	0.722222	0.750000	0.777778	0.814815
1	30.0	0.756790	0.049531	0.574074	0.726852	0.759259	0.796296	0.814815
2	30.0	0.688272	0.034759	0.611111	0.666667	0.703704	0.722222	0.722222
3	30.0	0.640741	0.069902	0.518519	0.592593	0.648148	0.699074	0.740741
4	30.0	0.782099	0.100691	0.370370	0.759259	0.796296	0.833333	0.888889
5	30.0	0.812346	0.110442	0.425926	0.777778	0.824074	0.884259	0.981481
6	30.0	0.762346	0.080071	0.500000	0.740741	0.777778	0.810185	0.870370
7	30.0	0.635802	0.049912	0.462963	0.615741	0.648148	0.666667	0.685185
8	30.0	0.854321	0.040024	0.740741	0.837963	0.861111	0.870370	0.907407
9	30.0	0.782716	0.076111	0.629630	0.726852	0.777778	0.851852	0.907407
10	30.0	0.766358	0.050987	0.592593	0.759259	0.796296	0.796296	0.814815
11	30.0	0.863889	0.100114	0.370370	0.856481	0.870370	0.907407	0.944444
12	30.0	0.676543	0.067164	0.537037	0.634259	0.675926	0.722222	0.796296

Fig. 6. Sample of the Monte Carlo validation iterations: aggregation in 7 basic statistics, including mean, std, min, max and 25%, 50%, 75% quartiles of test AUC of the 30 BiLSTM base models grouped in one row, which are the components of one BiLSTMens model.

Figure 6 illustrates a sample of the 30 Monte Carlo iterations, each row representing the aggregation in 7 basic statistics including mean, standard deviation (std), min, max and the 25%, 50% and 75% quartiles, of test AUC of the 30 BiLSTM base models which are the components of each ensemble BiLSTMens model produced in the Monte Carlo procedure. Note the substantial std of AUC across the 30 base models, especially in rows such as 11 with std around 0.1, (see Fig. 6), and the min AUC around 0.37 which corresponds to a base model that is clearly counter-performing. On all rows of the table in Fig. 6, all the quartiles, max and mean values of AUC indicate figures substantially above 0.5 (which is the expected AUC of a random prediction model), but there are multiple rows with min AUC values under 0.5, which clearly demonstrates that a prediction modelling approach *based on a single base model* does not constitute a viable solution in this case. These aspects justify our choice to propose of a prediction modelling approach relying on *ensembles* of base models despite the higher volume of computation for training the 30 base models forming an ensemble. As Fig. 5 illustrates with the histogram of AUC of ensemble models, all AUC values are above 0.5 hence all ensemble models predict better than chance. Moreover, the ensemble models have a synergistic effect in this case, as their mean AUC of 0.781 is larger than the mean AUC of all the base models, which is 0.739 (see, in Fig. 5 bottom, ens_auc_test and mean_auc_test, corresponding to the ensemble models and base models, respectively).

The results from the conducted analysis regarding the BiGRU base models and the BiGRUens ensemble models, are summarised and presented in Fig. 7 below, similarly to the presentation of BiLSTM and BiLSTMens models in Fig. 5. The explanations regarding the results in Fig. 7 are similar to those provided for the results in Fig. 5. The main difference between the BiLSTMens and BiGRUens models is that the latter achieve better performances in the Monte Carlo validation procedure on this dataset. Indeed, the BiGRUens models showed a better prediction capability on the test sets compared with BiLSTMens, including a mean AUC of 0.796 vs 0.781, a mean accuracy of 0.729 vs 0.687, a mean precision of 0.899 vs 0.857, a mean f1 of 0.715 vs 0.672, a mean Matthews correlation coefficient MCC of 0.518 vs 0.429 (indicating models' performances are substantially different from just random prediction, from both classes' perspective), a mean kappa statistic of 0.479 vs 0.394 (indicating again that models' performances are substantially different from just random prediction), a mean sensitivity of 0.633 vs 0.6, and a mean specificity of 0.872 vs 0.817. In particular, the high AUC result of 0.796 entails that our BiGRUens models predict in average higher probability scores for the high synchrony class versus the low synchrony class in about 80% of cases. Moreover, the achieved high precision level indicates that 90% of mother-infant dyads predicted to be in the high synchrony class are predicted correctly. On the other hand, the high specificity level of 0.872 of these models indicates a detection rate of the mother-infant dyads with low synchrony in about 87% of cases, suggesting these models' high capability for automatically flagging cases that may be clinically relevant for further investigation and potential intervention.

As a further remark on the BiGRU based models, the ensemble models have a synergistic effect in this case too, as their mean AUC of 0.796 is larger than the mean AUC of all the base models, of 0.685 (see, in Fig. 7 bottom, ens_auc_test and mean_auc_test, corresponding to the ensemble models and base models, respectively).

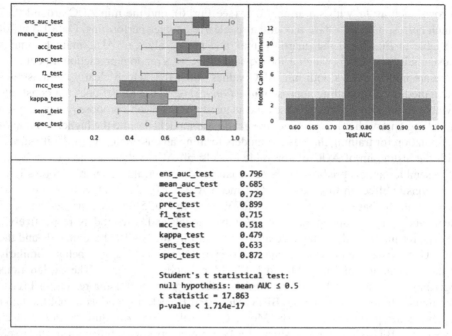

Fig. 7. Top: Boxplots (left) and histogram (right) of performances on the test data of Bidirectional GRU ensemble models (BiGRUens) in Monte Carlo validation of 30 iterations. Bottom: Mean performances, and one-tailed Student's t-test proving the alternative hypothesis: mean AUC > 0.5, demonstrating statistically the BiGRUens models' prediction capability.

5   Conclusion and Future Research Directions

In this paper we proposed a bidirectional LSTM and bidirectional GRU recurrent neural network approach to predicting mother-infant synchrony classes in 58 videos capturing the interaction between mother and their babies. To improve the level of prediction performance and stability, the base models have been integrated in ensemble models composed of 30 base models each, and we showed that this solution was an effective mitigation to the problem of substantial variation of the AUC performance of the base models due to the relatively reduced number of records (videos) in the dataset (i.e. 58). This research extends on previous work in [28] which proposed GRU ensemble based models for predicting high vs low mother-baby synchrony. In the new approach presented in this study, we explored bidirectional LSTM and bidirectional GRU base models and ensemble models, taking advantage of the bidirectional structure of these models which is suitable in this framework for analysing data extracted from the frames of the videos capturing the mother-infant interaction. Indeed, we detected better the patterns of synchrony in the mother-infant dyads by exploring, in both directions (i.e. in the normal sequence and reverse sequence of frames) the data extracted from the video. In the new approach presented here we improved the AUC, accuracy, precision, Matthews correlation coefficient, kappa statistics, and specificity, the latter of which ensuring in particular a better rate of detection of the mother-infant dyads with low synchrony from 83% in [28] to 87% in this study, suggesting a higher models' capability for automatically flagging cases that may be clinically relevant for further investigation and potential intervention.

Future research directions include: expanding the machine learning prediction modelling methodology with classes of autoencoders for (a) alternative, more effective feature extraction and representation, and for (b) researching an effective approach to synthetic data generation and data augmentation, given the relatively reduced number of videos (58) used in this research. Moreover, the methodology proposed here is to be further extended to the study of predicting the interaction between parents and children, in other activities such as book reading which makes the object of related research work we develop.

Acknowledgments. This work was supported by the Global Parenting Initiative (Funded by The LEGO Foundation), by University of London - Goldsmiths College, and by the University of Manchester. Data collection was supported by an ESRC Future Research Leader Fellowship to EM (ES/K001329/1). The authors would like to thank Harriet Bowden-Howl & Rudi Dallos for their expert rating of dyadic synchrony.

References

1. Winston, R., Chicot, R.: The importance of early bonding on the long-term mental health and resilience of children. London J. Primary Care **8**(1), 12–14 (2016)
2. Feldman, R.: The relational basis of adolescent adjustment: trajectories of mother–child interactive behaviors from infancy to adolescence shape adolescents' adaptation. Attachment Hum. Dev. **12**(1–2), 173–192 (2010)
3. Delaherche, E., Chetouani, M., et al.: Interpersonal synchrony: a survey of evaluation methods across disciplines. IEEE Trans. Affect. Comput. **3**(3), 349–365 (2012)
4. Merriam-Webster. "Synchrony". In Merriam-Webster.com dictionary (n.d.)
5. Wiltermuth, S., Heath, C.: Synchrony and cooperation. Psychol. Sci. **20**(1), 1–5 (2009)
6. Watkins, N., Nwogu, I.: Computational Social Dynamics: Analyzing the Face-level Interactions in a Group. arXiv preprint arXiv:1807.06124 (2018)
7. Chellali, R., Li, Z.: Predicting arm movements a multi-variate LSTM based approach for human-robot hand clapping games. In: Proceedings of 27th IEEE International Symposium on Robot and Human Interactive Communication (2018)
8. Cho, K., van Merrienboer, B., et al.: Learning phrase representations using RNN encoder-decoder for statistical machine translation. In: Proceedings of the 2014 Conference on Empirical Methods in Natural Language Processing (2014)
9. Leclère, C., Avril, M., Viaux-Savelon, S., Bodeau, N., Achard, C., Missonnier, S., et al.: Interaction and behaviour imaging: a novel method to measure mother–infant interaction using video 3D reconstruction. Transl. Psychiatry **6**(5), e816 (2016)
10. Guedeney, A., Matthey, S., Puura, K.: Social withdrawal behavior in infancy: a history of the concept and a review of published studies using the alarm distress baby scale. Infant Ment. Health J. **34**(6), 516–531 (2013)
11. Noor, M.N., Yahaya, A.S., Ramli, N.A., Al Bakri, A.M.M.: Filling missing data using interpolation methods: study on the effect of fitting distribution. Key Eng. Mater. **594–595**, 889–895 (2013)
12. Dey, R., Salem, F.M.: Gate-variants of Gated Recurrent Unit (GRU) neural networks. In: Proceedings of IEEE 60th International Midwest Symposium on Circuits and Systems (2017)

13. Aggarwal, C.: Neural Networks and Deep Learning. Springer, Cham (2018)
14. Goodfellow, I., Bengio, Y., Courville, A.: Deep Learning. MIT Press, Cambridge (2016)
15. Bishop, C.: Pattern Recognition and Machine Learning. Springer, New York (2006). https://doi.org/10.1007/978-0-387-45528-0
16. Hastie, T., Tibshirani, R., Friedman, J.: The Elements of Statistical Learning: Data Mining, Inference, and Prediction. Springer, New York (2009). https://doi.org/10.1007/978-0-387-84858-7
17. Geron, A.: Hands-on Machine Learning with Scikit-Learn, Keras, and TensorFlow: Concepts, Tools, and Techniques to Build Intelligent Systems. O'Reilly, Sebastopol (2019)
18. Unal, I.: Defining an optimal cut-point value in ROC analysis: an alternative approach. J. Comput. Math. Methods Med. **2017** (2017)
19. Cao, Z., Hidalgo, G., Simon, T., Wei, S.-E., Sheikh, Y.: OpenPose: realtime multi-person 2D pose estimation using part affinity fields. J. IEEE Trans. Pattern Anal. Mach. Intell. **43** (2021)
20. Rutkowska, K.: Automated measurement of nonverbal synchrony in infant-mother interaction using machine learning. MSc dissertation, Data Science & Soft Computing Lab and Computing Department, Goldsmiths College, University of London (2020)
21. Steinberg, L.: We know some things: parent-adolescent relationships in retrospect and prospect. J. Res. Adolesc. **11**(1), 1–19 (2001)
22. McAdams, T.A., et al.: Associations between the parent-child relationship and adolescent self-worth: a genetically informed study of twin parents and their adolescent children. J. Child Psychol. Psychiatry **58**(1), 46–54 (2017)
23. Leclère, C., et al.: Why synchrony matters during mother-child interactions: a systematic review. PLoS ONE **9**(12), e113571 (2014)
24. Wade, L.: What makes us subconsciously mimic the accents of others in conversation. The Conversation (2022)
25. Nguyen, T., Schleihauf, H., Kayhan, E., Matthes, D., Vrtička, P., Hoehl, S.: Neural synchrony in mother–child conversation: exploring the role of conversation patterns. Soc. Cogn. Affect. Neurosci. **16**(1–2), 93–102 (2021)
26. Egmose, I., et al.: Relations between automatically extracted motion features and the quality of mother-infant interactions at 4 and 13 months. Front. Psychol. **8**, 2178 (2017)
27. Stuart, A.C., Egmose, I., Smith-Nielsen, J., Reijman, S., Wendelboe, K.I., Væver, M.S.: Coding interactive behaviour instrument: mother-infant interaction quality, construct validity, measurement invariance, and postnatal depression and anxiety. J. Child Fam. Stud. **32**(6), 1839–1854 (2023)
28. Stamate, D., et al.: Predicting high vs low mother-baby synchrony with GRU-based ensemble models. In: Iliadis, L., Papaleonidas, A., Angelov, P., Jayne, C. (eds.) ICANN 2023. LNCS, vol. 14262, pp. 191–199. Springer, Cham (2023). https://doi.org/10.1007/978-3-031-44201-8_16
29. Kuhn, M., Johnson, K.: Applied Predictive Modeling. Springer, New York (2013). https://doi.org/10.1007/978-1-4614-6849-3

Feature Selection with L_1 Regularization in Formal Neurons

Leon Bobrowski[1,2]([⊠]) [iD]

[1] Faculty of Computer Science, Bialystok University of Technology, Wiejska 45A, Bialystok, Poland
l.bobrowski@pb.edu.pl
[2] Institute of Biocybernetics and Biomedical Engineering, PAS, Warsaw, Poland

Abstract. Designing classifiers on high-dimensional learning data sets is an important task that appears in artificial intelligence applications. Designing classifiers for high-dimensional data involves learning hierarchical neural networks combined with feature selection.

Feature selection aims to omit features that are unnecessary for a given problem. Feature selection in formal meurons can be achieved by minimizing convex and picewise linear (*CPL*) criterion functions with L_1 regularization. Minimizing *CPL* criterion functions can be associated with computations on a finite number of vertices in the parameter space.

Keywords: high-dimensional data sets · formal neurons with a margin · feature selection · CPL criterion functions · L_1 regularization

1 Introduction

Data sets consisting of a small number of high-dimensional vectors appear in many important problems [1]. High-dimensional data sets appear, for example, in bioinformatics or in the exploration of biochemical compounds [2].

Multidimensional feature vectors can be treated as an attempt to represent individual objects or phenomena based on the results of a large number of measurements of various types of features (characteristics).

Large number of measured features of individual objects may result in the use of too many parameters when building a classification or regression models, which may result in models overfitting [3]. Additionally, numerical difficulties arise when calculating in multidimensional parameter spaces, for example when inverting matrices the or solving eigenvalue problems [4]. For such reasons, feature selection procedures are implemented and unnecessary features are omitted.

In the case of high-dfimensional data sets, linear classification or regression models play a fundamental role [3]. This is because high-dimensional datasets can be separated by hyperplanes in the parameter space or located on certain hyperplanes.

Linear binary classifiers can be designed using a formal neuron model by minimizing convex and piecewise-linear (*CPL*) criterion functions. For this purpose, in particular,

L. Iliadis et al. (Eds.): EANN 2024, CCIS 2141, pp. 343–353, 2024.
https://doi.org/10.1007/978-3-031-62495-7_26

the perceptron criterion function with L_1 regularization is used [5]. L_1 regularization of this criterion fumctiom is used for feature selection and optimization of feature subsets [6].

Basis exchange algorithms allow for efficient and precise minimizing convex and piecewise-linear (CPL) criterion functions even in the case of numerous and multidimensional data sets. According to this algorithm, computations are performed at a finite number of vertices in the parameter space [7].

The article discusses the properties of basis exchange algorithms in the context of L_1 regularization. In particular, the article considers the design principles in the multidimensional feature space $F[n]$ ($m \ll n$) of two types of formal neurons: separating and representing.

Consider a set of m objects (patients, cases) $O_j(j = 1, \ldots, m)$ represented as feature vectors $\mathbf{x}_j[n] = \left[x_{j,1}, \ldots, x_{j,n}\right]^{\mathrm{T}}$ in the n-dimensional feature space $F[n]$ $\left(\mathbf{x}_j[n] \in F[n]\right)$, where $m \ll n$. The i-th component $x_{j,i}$ of the vector $\mathbf{x}_j[n]$ is a numerical result of the measurement of the i-th feature $X_i(i = 1, \ldots, n)$ on the j-th object $O_j\left(x_{j,i} \in \{0, 1\} \text{ or } x_{j,i} \in R^1\right)$. The feature space $F[n]$ is formed on the set $F(n)$ of n features $X_i(i = 1, \ldots, n)$:

$$F(n) = \{X_1, \ldots, X_n\} \tag{1}$$

Let us assume that m objects $O_j(j = 1, \ldots, m)$ have been divided into K classes ω_k ($k = 1, \ldots, K$) according to some a priori knowledge. Consequently, the feature vectors $\mathbf{x}_j$ can be labeled and related to particular categories $\square_k$. The k-th data set C_k contains m_k examples of feature vectors $\mathbf{x}_j(k) = \left[x_{j,1}, \ldots, x_{j,n}\right]^{\mathrm{T}}$ assigned to the k-th category ω_k:

$$(\forall k \in \{1, \ldots, K\}) \quad C_k = \{\mathbf{x}_i(k) : j \in J_k\} \tag{2}$$

where J_k is the set of indices j of m_k feature vectors $\mathbf{x}_j(k)$ assigned to the k-th class (category) ω_k.

The possibility of separating data sets C_k by hyperplanes $H(\mathbf{w}_k, \theta_k)$ (2) in the feature space $F[n]$ is investigated in pattern recognition tasks [1]:

$$H(\mathbf{w}_k, \theta_k) = \left\{\mathbf{x} : \mathbf{w}_k^{\mathrm{T}} \mathbf{x} = \theta_k\right\} \tag{3}$$

where $\mathbf{w}_k = \left[w_{k,1}, \ldots, w_{k,n}\right]^{\mathrm{T}} \in R^n$ is the k-th weight vector, $\theta_k \in R^1$ is the threshold, and $\mathbf{w}_k^{\mathrm{T}} \mathbf{x} = \sum_i w_{k,i} x_i$ is the inner product.

Definition 1: The data sets C_k are *linearly separable* in the feature space $F[n]$ if each of these sets can be fully separated from the sum of the remaining sets $C_{k'}\left(k' \neq k\right)$ by some hyperplane $H(\mathbf{w}_k, \theta_k)$:

$$(\forall k \in \{1, \ldots, K\}) \quad (\exists \mathbf{w}_k, \theta_k)(\forall \mathbf{x}_x(k) \in C_k) \quad \mathbf{w}_k \mathrm{T}^{\mathrm{T}} \mathbf{x}_j \geq \theta_k + 1,$$
$$and \ \left(\forall \mathbf{x}_j\left(k'\right) \in C_{k'}, k' \neq k\right) \mathbf{w}_k^{\mathrm{T}} \mathbf{x}_j \leq \theta_k - 1 \tag{4}$$

Data sets C_k are *high-dimensional* if the numbers m_k of feature vectors $x_j(k)$ are much smaller than the dimension n of these vectors ($m_k \ll n$). It can be expected, that the high-dimensional learning sets C_k are linearly separable [8]. The linear separabilty of learning sets C_k is related to linear independence of feature vectors from these sets.

Inequalities (4) describe the linear separation of the learning sets C_k with the margin $\delta(w_k) = 2/\|w_k\|$. The L_2 margin $\delta(w_k)_{L2}$ based on the Euclidean distance is determined as follows [1]:

$$\delta(w_k)_{L2} = 2/\left(w_k^T w_k\right)^{1/2} = 2/\left(\sum_i w_{k,i}^2\right)^{1/2} \tag{5}$$

The L_1 norm margin $\delta(w_k)_{L1}$ is determined similarly [8]:

$$\delta(w_k)_{L1} = 2/\left(\Sigma_i |w_{k,i}|\right) \tag{6}$$

The L_2 margins $\delta(w_k)_{L2}$ are used in support vector machines (*SVM*), the basic method of machine learning [9]. The maximum L_2 margins are obtained from data sets using quadratic programming. The maximum L_1 margins $\delta(w_k)_{L1}$ are obtained by minimizing the perceptron criterion function, which is a convex and piecewise linear function (*CPL*) [5]. In this case, the design algorithms are based on the basis exchange algorithm and vertex calculations [7].

The following classication rule can be associated with inequalities (4)

$$(\forall k \in \{1, \ldots, K\}) \left((\forall x \in F[n])\right.$$
$$if\ w_k^T x_j \geq \theta_k, then\ x \text{ is in the category } \omega_k \tag{7}$$
$$if\ w_k^T x_j < \theta_k, then\ x \text{ is not in the category } \omega_k$$

Increasing the margins $\delta(w_k)_{L2}$ (5) or $\delta(w_k)_{L1}$ (6) serves to increase the generalization power of the classification rule (7) [2]. The generalization power of a given classification rule is characterized by the frequency of incorrectly classified feature vectors $x_{j'}$ not belonging to the learning sets C_k. The generalization power is high when a large number of new vectors $x_{j'} \left(x_{j'} \notin \cup_k C_k\right)$ are classified correctly.

2 Convex and Piecewise Linear Criterion Functions

The family of convex and piecewise linear (*CPL*) criterion functions includes, among others, perceptron criterion function associated with beginning of neural networks theory [2]. The perceptron criterion function was defined in connection with the model of formal neuron $FN(w_k, \theta_k)$ with the below activation function $r(w_k, \theta_k; x)$ (7) [5]:

$$(\forall x \in F[n])$$
$$r = r(w_k, \theta_k; x) = \begin{array}{l} 1\ if\ w_k^T x \geq \theta_k \\ 0\ if\ w_k^T x < \theta_k \end{array} \tag{8}$$

According to function (8), the neuron $FN(w_k, \theta_k)$ is activated ($r = 1$) by the feature vector x, if and only if this vector is placed on the positive side of the hyperplane $H(w_k, \theta_k)$ (3).

The quality of the classication rule (7) depends on the parameters $\mathbf{w}_k = [w_{k,1}, \ldots, w_{k,n}]^T$ and θ_k of the neuron model $FN(\mathbf{w}_k, \theta_k)$ (8). The optimal parameters can be selected by minimizing the perceptron criterion function [5]. The perceptron criterion function is defined on feature vectors $\mathbf{x}_j$ constituting two learning sets G_k^+ and G_k^-.

The positive learning set $G_k^+(G_k^+ \subset C_k)$ contains $m_k^+(m_k^+ \leq m_k)$ labelled feature vectors $\mathbf{x}_j(k)$ selected from the data subset C_k representing the k-th category ω_k:

$$(\forall k \in \{1, \ldots, K\}) \quad G_k^+ = \{\mathbf{x}_j : j \in J_k^+\} \quad (9)$$

The negative learning set $G_k^-(G_k^- \subset \cup_{k' \neq k} C_{k'})$ contains m_k^- feature vectors $\mathbf{x}_j(k\prime)$ selected from the remaining subsets $C_{k'}$, where $k' \neq k$, and can be treated as the *context* of the category ω_k represented by the subset G_k^+ (4):

$$(\forall k \in \{1, \ldots, K\}) \quad G_k^- = \{\mathbf{x}_j : j \in J_k^-\} \quad (10)$$

Lemma 1: If the opposite learning sets G_k^+ (9) and G_k^- (10) consist of linearly independent feature vectors $\mathbf{x}_j(\mathbf{x}_j \in F[n])$, then these sets are linearly separable (4) with a zero threshold $\theta_k(\theta_k = 0)$ [8].

The perceptron penalty function $\varphi_j^+(\mathbf{w})$ is defined in the following manner for each element $\mathbf{x}_j$ of the learning set G_k^+ (5):

$$(\forall \mathbf{x}_j \in G_k^+) \quad \varphi_j^+(\mathbf{w}) = \max\{1 - \mathbf{x}_j^T \mathbf{w}, 0\} \quad (11)$$

Similarly

$$(\forall \mathbf{x}_j \in G_k^-) \quad \varphi_j^-(\mathbf{w}) = \max\{\mathbf{x}_j^T \mathbf{w} - 1, 0\} \quad (12)$$

The perceptron criterion function $\Phi_k(\mathbf{w})$ is defined as the sum of the penalty functions $\varphi_j^+(\mathbf{w})$ (11) and $\varphi_j^-(\mathbf{w})$ (12) [5]:

$$\Phi_k(\mathbf{w}) = \Sigma_j \varphi_j^+(\mathbf{w}) + \Sigma_j \varphi_j^-(\mathbf{w}) \quad (13)$$

where the summation (13) takes place over the indices j of all feature vectors $\mathbf{x}_j$ from the opposite learning sets G_k^+ (9) and G_k^- (10).

The criterion function $\Phi_k(\mathbf{w})$ (13) is related to the *error correction* algorithm, the basic algorithm of the *Perceptron* model [2]. The perceptron criterion function $\Phi_k(\mathbf{w})$ (13) is *convex and piecewise-linear* (*CPL*) function with a global minimum in the optimal vector $\mathbf{w}_k^*$:

$$(\exists \mathbf{w}_k^*)(\forall \mathbf{w} \in R^n)\Phi_k(\mathbf{w}) \geq \Phi_k(\mathbf{w}_k^*) = \Phi_k^* \geq 0 \quad (14)$$

The below theorem can be proved [5]:

Theorem 1: The minimum value $\Phi_k^* = \Phi_k(\mathbf{w}_k^*)$ (14) of the perceptron criterion function $\Phi_k(\mathbf{w})$ (13) is equal to zero ($\Phi_k^* = 0$) if the learning sets G_k^+ (9) and G_k^- (10) are linearly separable (4).

The proof of Lemma 1 and Theorem 1 can be based on vertexical linear equations described in the work [7]. In this approach, the optimal vertex $\mathbf{w}_k^*$ (15) is calculated as a solution of a system of m_k linear equations, where $m_k = m_k^+ + m_k^-$ is the number of feature vectors $\mathbf{x}_j$ with dimension n in the learning sets G_k^+ (9) and G_k^- (10) ($m_k << n$).

The regularized criterion function $\Psi_k(\mathbf{w})$ is defined as the sum of the perceptron criterion function $\Phi_k(\mathbf{w})$ (14) and the absolute values $|w_i|$ of weighs w_i, where $\mathbf{w} = [w_1, \ldots, w_n]^T$ [5]:

$$\Psi_k(\mathbf{w}) = \Phi_k(\mathbf{w}) + \sum_{i \in \{1,\ldots,n\}} |w_i| \tag{15}$$

The optimal vector $\mathbf{w}_k^*$ constitutes the global minimum $\Psi_k(\mathbf{w}_k^*)$ of the *CPL* criterion function $\Psi_k(\mathbf{w})$ (15) defined on elements $\mathbf{x}_j$ of the learning sets G_k^+ (9) and G_k^- (10):

$$\left(\exists \mathbf{w}_k^*\right)\left(\forall \mathbf{w} \in R^n\right) \Psi_k(\mathbf{w}) \geq \Psi_k\left(\mathbf{w}_k^*\right) > 0 \tag{16}$$

Minimizing the regularized criterion function $\Psi_k(\mathbf{w})$ (15) allows to find the largest L_1 margin $\delta(\mathbf{w}_k)_{L1}$ (6) [8]. A similar approach has also been used in the *relaxed linear separability* (*RLS*) method of selecting optimal feature subsets [6].

3 Vertices in the Parameter Space

The dual hyperplanes h_j^+ are defined in the parameter space R^n by feature vectors $\mathbf{x}_j$ from the positive learning set G_k^+ (9):

$$\left(\forall \mathbf{x}_j \in G_k^+\right) \ h_j^+ = \left\{\mathbf{w} \in R^n : \mathbf{x}_j^T \mathbf{w} = 1\right\} \tag{17}$$

Similarly, the dual hyperplanes h_j^- are defined by the elements $\mathbf{x}_j$ of the negative learning set G_k^- (10):

$$\left(\forall \mathbf{x}_j \in G_k^-\right) \ h_j^- = \left\{\mathbf{w} \in R^n : \mathbf{x}_j^T \mathbf{w} = -1\right\} \tag{18}$$

The dual hyperplanes h_j^0 are defined by unit vectors $\mathbf{e}_i$ [5]:

$$\left(\forall i \in (1,\ldots,n) \ h_i^0 = \left\{\mathbf{w} \in R^n : \mathbf{e}_i^T \mathbf{w} = 0\right\} = \{\mathbf{w} \in R^n : w_i = 0\}\right) \tag{19}$$

The vertex $\mathbf{w}_k(r)$ of the rank $r = m_k^+ + m_k^-$ based on all feature vectors $\mathbf{x}_j$ from the learning subsets G_k^+ (9) and G_k^- (10) is defined by the following system of n linear equations:

$$\left(\forall \mathbf{x}_j \in G_k^+\right) \ \mathbf{x}_j^T \mathbf{w}_k = 1$$
$$\left(\forall \mathbf{x}_j \in G_k^-\right) \ \mathbf{x}_j^T \mathbf{w}_k = -1 \tag{20}$$

and

$$\left(\forall i \in I_k(r)\right) \ \mathbf{e}_i^T \mathbf{w}_k = 0 \tag{21}$$

where $I_k(r) = \{i(1), \ldots, i(n - r)\}$ is the k-th subset of indices i defining $n - r$ unit vectors $\mathbf{e}_i$ with the hyperplanes h_i^0 (19) passing through the vertex $\mathbf{w}_k(r)$.

The linear Eqs. (20) and (21) can be written in a matrix form [7]:

$$\mathbf{B}_k(r)\mathbf{w}_k(r) = \mathbf{1}_k(r) \tag{22}$$

where $\mathbf{1}_k(r) = [+/-1, \ldots, +/-1, 0, \ldots, 0]^T$ is a vector in which the first r components are equal to 1 or -1 according to Eqs. (20), and the remaining n - r components are zero.

The square matrix $\mathbf{B}_k(r)$ in Eq. (23) contains r feature vectors $\mathbf{x}_j$ $(j = 1, \ldots, r)$ and can have the following structure when $m < n$ [7]:

$$\mathbf{B}_k(r) = \left[\mathbf{x}_1, \ldots, \mathbf{x}_r, \mathbf{e}_{i(r+1)}, \ldots, \mathbf{e}_{i(n)}\right]^T \tag{23}$$

where the symbol $\mathbf{e}_{i(l)}(i(l) \in I_k(r)(21))$ denotes an *inactive* unit vector forming the l-th row $(l = r + 1, \ldots, n)$ of the matrix $\mathbf{B}_k(r)$.

The non-singular matrix $\mathbf{B}_k(r)$ (23) formed by r feature vectors $\mathbf{x}_j$ from the learning sets G_k^+ (9) or G_k^- (10) and n - r unit vectors $\mathbf{e}_i(i \in I_k(r)(21))$ is the *basis* of the feature space $F[n]$ related to the vertex $\mathbf{w}_k(r)$:

$$\mathbf{w}_k(r) = \mathbf{B}_k(r)^{-1}\mathbf{1}_k(r) \tag{24}$$

Definition 2: The rank r of the vertex $\mathbf{w}_k(r)$ (24) is equal to the number of feature vectors $\mathbf{x}_j$ from the learning sets G_k^+ or G_k^- in the basis $\mathbf{B}_k(r)$.

*

The vertex $\mathbf{w}_k(r)$ (24) of the rank r in the parameter space $R^n (r < n)$ is located at the intersection of r hyperplanes h_j^+ (17) or h_j^- (18) and by $n - r$ hyperplanes h_i^0 (19), where $i \in I_k(r)$ (21).

As follows from the equations $\mathbf{w}_k(r)\mathbf{e}_i = 0$ (21), the last $n - r$ components $w_{k,i}$ of the vertex $\mathbf{w}_k(r) = \left[w_{k,1}, \ldots, w_{k,n}\right]^T$ (24) are equal to zero:

$$(\forall l \in \{r + 1, \ldots, n\}) \; w_{k,l} = 0 \tag{25}$$

Lemma 2: The value $\Phi_k(\mathbf{w}_k(r))$ of the perceptron criterion function $\Phi_k(\mathbf{w})$ (14) is equal to zero $\Phi_k(\mathbf{w}_k(r) = 0)$ at each vertex $\mathbf{w}_k(r)$ (25) based on all m_k vectors $\mathbf{x}_j$ forming the sets G_k^+ (9) and G_k^- (10).

The following relations occur at vertices $\mathbf{w}_k(r) = [w_1(r), \ldots, w_n(r)]^T$ (24):

$$(\forall \mathbf{w}_k(r)(24)) \quad \Psi_k(\mathbf{w}_k(r)) = \Sigma_i|w_i(r)| = ||\mathbf{w}_k(r)||_{L1} \tag{26}$$

The optimal vector $\mathbf{w}_k^*(r)$ (24) which is the global minimum $\Psi_k\left(\mathbf{w}_k^*(r)\right)$ (16) of the criterion function $\Psi_k(\mathbf{w})$ (15) has the smallest L_1 length $\mathbf{w}_k(r)_{L1}$ (26) among all vertices $\mathbf{w}_k(r)$ (24). We conclude from this that the L_+ margin $\delta(\mathbf{w}_k)_{L1} = 2/(\Sigma_i|w_{k,i}|)$ (9) has the largest value $\delta_{L1}\left(\mathbf{w}_k^*(r)\right)$ at the optimal vertex $\mathbf{w}_k^*(r)$ (24):

$$(\forall \mathbf{w}_k(r)(25)) \quad \delta_{L1}\left(\mathbf{w}_k^*(r)\right) \geq \delta_{L1}(\mathbf{w}_k(r)) \tag{27}$$

Basis exchange algorithms allow for efficient and precise finding of the optimal vertex $\mathbf{w}_k^*(r)$ (24) even in the case of numerous or multidimensional learning sets G_k^+ and G_k^- [5].

4 Selection of Separating Features Based on L_1 Regularization

The vertex $\mathbf{w}_k(r)$ (24) of the rank r is defined by the basis $\mathbf{B}_k(r)$ (24) composed of r feature vectors $\mathbf{x}_j\left(\mathbf{x}_j \in G_k^+ \cup G_k^-\right)$ and $n - r$ unit vectors $\mathbf{e}_i(i \in I_k(r)(21))$.

The *vertexical feature subset* $R_k(r)(R_k(r) \subset F(n)(1))$ consists of r features $X_{i(l)}$ that are active at the vertex $\mathbf{w}_k(r)$ (24) [8]. The subset $R_k(r)$ consists of r active features X_i that are not defined $((i \notin I_k(r))$ by disabling Eqs. (22) with inactive unit vectors $\mathbf{e}_i$:

$$R_k(r) = \left\{X_{i(1)}, \ldots, X_{i(r)}\right\} = \{X_i : i \notin I_k(r)\}. \tag{28}$$

where $I_k(r)$ (22) is a subset of indices i of r inactive features X_i.

Definition 3: The k-th *vertexical feature subspace* $F_k[r](F_k[r] \subset F[n])$ is based on r features $X_i(X_i \in R_k(r)$ (28) active at the vertex $\mathbf{w}_k(r)$ (24).

Mnimization (16) of the *CPL* criterion function $\Psi_k(\mathbf{w})$ (16) constrained to vertices $\mathbf{w}_k(r)$ (24) allows to determine the optimal vertex $\mathbf{w}_k^*(r)$ and the optimal set $R_k^*(r)$ (28) of r features X_i active at this vertex:

$$\left(\exists \mathbf{w}_k^*(r)\right)\left(\forall \mathbf{w}_k(r)(24)\quad \Psi_k(\mathbf{w}_k(r)) \geq \Psi_k\left(\mathbf{w}_k^*(r)\right) > 0 \tag{29}$$

The solution of the constrained minimization problem (29) can be achieved in steps, staring from the identity matrix $I = [\mathbf{e}_1, \ldots, \mathbf{e}_n]$ and the zero vertex $\mathbf{w}_k(0) = [0, \ldots, 0]^T$ (24) [4].

During the first r steps $l(l = 1, \ldots, r)$, unit vectors $\mathbf{e}_{i(l)}$ in the identity matrix I are gradually replaced by feature vectors $\mathbf{x}_j\left(\mathbf{x}_j \in G_k^+ \cup G_k^-\right)$ from the learning sets G_k^+ (9) and G_k^- (10). In the l - th step, the inverse of the basis matrix $\mathbf{B}_k(l) = \left[\mathbf{x}_1, \ldots, \mathbf{x}_l, \mathbf{e}_{i(l+1)}, \ldots, \mathbf{e}_{i(n)}\right]^T$ (23) is equal to:

$$\mathbf{B}_k(l)^{-1} = [\mathbf{r}_1(l) \ldots, \mathbf{r}_l(l), \ldots, \mathbf{r}_n(l)]^T \tag{30}$$

According to the Gauss-Jordan transformation, the columns $\mathbf{r}_i(l)$ of the inverse matrix $\mathbf{B}_k(l)^{-1}$ change as a result of the replacing of the unit vectors $\mathbf{e}_{i(l+1)}$ in the basis $\mathbf{B}_k(l) = \left[\mathbf{x}_1, \ldots, \mathbf{x}_l, \mathbf{e}_{i(l+1)}, \ldots, \mathbf{e}_{i(n)}\right]^T$ (23) by the vector $\mathbf{x}_{l+1}$ [5]:

$$\mathbf{r}_{l+1}(l + 1) = \left(1/\mathbf{r}_{l+1}(l)^T\mathbf{x}_{l+1}\right)\mathbf{r}_{l+1}(l) \tag{31}$$

and

$$(\forall i \neq l + 1)\quad \mathbf{r}_i(l + 1) = \mathbf{r}_i(l) - \left(\mathbf{r}_i(l)^T\mathbf{x}_{l+1}/\mathbf{r}_{l+1}(l)^T\mathbf{x}_{l+1}\right)\mathbf{r}_{l+1}(l) \tag{32}$$

The transformation (31) resulting from replacing the vector $\mathbf{e}_{i(l+1)}$ with the vector $\mathbf{x}_{l+1}$ in the basis $\mathbf{B}_k(l)$ (23) cannot be performed when the *collinearity condition* causing division by zero is

$$\mathbf{r}_{l+1}(l)^T\mathbf{x}_{l+1} = 0 \tag{33}$$

This problem can be reduced by rearranging the inactive unit vectors $\mathbf{e_i}(i \in I_k(l)(21))$ in the basis $\mathbf{B_k}(l) = [\mathbf{x_1}, \ldots, \mathbf{x_l}, \mathbf{e}_{i(l+1)}, \ldots, \mathbf{e}_{i(n)}]^T$ (23).

After performing r the steps above, the matrixs $\mathbf{B_k}(r)$ (23) is obtained, which contains all r feature vectors $\mathbf{x_j}$ from the learning sets G_k^+ (9) and G_k^- (10). As a consequence, the minimum value Φ_k^* (14) of the perceptron criterion function $\Phi_k(\mathbf{w})$ (13) is reduced to zero $(\Phi_k^* = 0)$.

In the next steps l $(l = r + 1, \ldots, L)$, selected unit vectors $\mathbf{e_i}$ in the matrix $\mathbf{B_k}(r) = [\mathbf{x_1}, \ldots, \mathbf{x_r}, \mathbf{e}_{i(r+1)}, \ldots, \mathbf{e}_{i(n)}]^T$ (23) are replaced. The replacing one of unit vectors $\mathbf{e_l}$ in the basis $\mathbf{B_k}(r)$ (23) by another unit vector $\mathbf{e_k}$ $(k \notin I_k(r)(21))$ causes the following changes of the columns $\mathbf{r_i}(r)$:

$$\mathbf{r_l}(l+1) = \left(1/\mathbf{r_l}(l)^T\mathbf{e_k}\right) \ \mathbf{r}_{l+1}(l) \tag{34}$$

and

$$(\forall i \neq l)\mathbf{r_i}(l+1) = \mathbf{r_i}(l) - \left(\mathbf{r_i}(l)^T\mathbf{e_k}/\mathbf{r_l}(l)^T\mathbf{e_k}\right)\mathbf{r_l}(l) \tag{35}$$

Transformation (34) cannot be performed when the condition causing division by zero is met [4]:

$$\mathbf{r_l}(l)^T\mathbf{e_k} = 0 \tag{36}$$

As in the case of condition (33), this problem can be avoided by changing the unit vector $\mathbf{e_k}$ entering the basis $\mathbf{B_k}(r)$ (23) [4].

Replacing the unit vector $\mathbf{e_l}$ with the vector $\mathbf{e_k}$ is only allowed if it reduces the value of the criterion function $\Psi_k \mathbf{w_k}(r))$ (26). It can be shown, the minimization based on the transformations (33) and (34) allows to find after a finite number L of steps l the optimal vertex $\mathbf{w_k^*}(r)$ of the rank r constituting the global minimum (29) of the criterion function $\Psi_k(\mathbf{w_k}(r))$ (26). This means that after a finite number L of steps l, the linear classifier (7) defined by the optimal vertex $\mathbf{w_k^*}(r)$ of the rank r and the threshold θ_k^* equal to zero $(\theta_k^* = 0)$ has the the largest L_1 margin $\delta(\mathbf{w_k^*}(r))_{L1}$ (6).

It means, that after a finite number L of steps l the linear classifier (7) with the the largest L_1 margin $\delta(\mathbf{w_k^*}(r))_{L1}$ (6) is defined by the optimal vertex $\mathbf{w_k^*}(r)$ of the rank r and the threshold θ_k^* equal to zero $(\theta_k^* = 0)$.

5 Selection of Collinear Features Based on L_1 Regularization

Subsets $R_k(r)$ (28) of r active features are selected from the set $F(n)$ of n features X_i $(i = 1, \ldots, n)$ in order to well separate opposing learning sets G_k^+ (9) and G_k^- (10). The collinear features X_i are selected from the set $F(n)$ (1) to represent only one learning set G_k^+ (9).

The collinearity criterion function was introduced to detect colinear subsets in data sets C_k (2) [10]. For this purpose, the collinearity penalty functions $\varphi_{k\,j}{}^1(\mathbf{w})$ are defined on elements $\mathbf{x_j}$ of the set G_k^+ (9):

$$(\forall \mathbf{x_j} \in G_k^+) \quad \varphi_{k,j}^1(\mathbf{w}) = \left|1 - \mathbf{x_j}^T\mathbf{w}\right| \tag{37}$$

where $\mathbf{w} = [w_1, \ldots, w_n]^T \in \mathbf{R}^n$.

The penalty function $\square_{k,j}^{\ 1}(\mathbf{w})$ (37) is zero if and only if the weight vector $\mathbf{w}$ lies on the dual hyperplane h_j^+ (17) in the parameter space $\mathbf{R}^n$.

The collinearity criterion function $\Phi_k^1(\mathbf{w})$ is defined as the sum of the penalty functions $\varphi_j^1(\mathbf{w})$ (37) determined on the k-th set $\mathbf{G}_k^+$ (2) [10]:

$$(\forall k \in \{1, \ldots, K\}) \quad \Phi_k^1(\mathbf{w}) = \Sigma_j \varphi_{k,j}^1(\mathbf{w}) \tag{38}$$

The collinearity criterion functions $\Phi_k^1(\mathbf{w})$ (38) are convex and piecewise linear (*CPL*) [10]. It has been shown that the minimum value $\Phi_k^1(\mathbf{w}_k^*)$ of the *CPL* criterion function $\Phi_k^1(\mathbf{w})$ (38) can be found at one of the vertices $\mathbf{w}_k$ (24) in the parameter space $\mathbf{R}^n$ [5]:

$$(\exists \mathbf{w}_k^*(24))(\forall \mathbf{w}) \quad \Phi_k^1(\mathbf{w}) \geq \Phi_k^1(\mathbf{w}_k^*) \geq 0 \tag{39}$$

Theorem 2: The minimum value $\Phi_k(\mathbf{w}_k^*)$ (39) of the collinearity criterion function $\Phi_k^1(\mathbf{w})$ (38), determined on m_k^+ elements $\mathbf{x}_j$ of the learning set $\mathbf{G}_k^+$ (9) is equal to zero $(\Phi_k^1(\mathbf{w}_k) = 0)$ if all feature vectors $\mathbf{x}_j$ from this set are located on the hyperplane $H(\mathbf{w}_k^*, 1)$ (3) with the threshold θ_k equal to one $(\theta_k = 1)$.

Proof of a similar theorem can be found in [10].

The regularized criterion function $\Psi_k^1(\mathbf{w})$ is defined similarly to (15) as the sum of the collinearity criterion function $\Phi_k^1(\mathbf{w})$ (38) and the absolute values $|w_i|$ of weighs w_i:

$$\Psi_k^1(\mathbf{w}) = \Phi_k^1(\mathbf{w}) + \sum_{i \in \{1, \ldots, n\}} |w_i| \tag{40}$$

The optimal vector $\mathbf{w}_k^*$ constitutes the global minimum $\Psi_k^1(\mathbf{w}_k^*)$ of the *CPL* criterion function $\Psi_k^1(\mathbf{w})$ (40) defined on elements $\mathbf{x}_j$ of the k-th learning sets $\mathbf{G}_k^+$ (4):

$$(\exists \mathbf{w}_k^*)(\forall \mathbf{w} \in \mathbf{R}^n)\Psi_k^1(\mathbf{w}) \geq \Psi_k^1(\mathbf{w}_k^*) > 0 \tag{41}$$

Minimizing the regularized function $\Psi_k^1(\mathbf{w})$ (40) allows finding the optimal vertex $\mathbf{w}_k^* = \left[w_{k,1}^*, \ldots, w_{k,n}^*\right]^T$ characterized by the smallest L_1 length $\left\|\mathbf{w}_k^*\right\|_{L1} = \Sigma_{i=1,\ldots,n}\left|w_{k,i}^*\right|$:

$$(\forall \mathbf{w}_k(r)(25))\Sigma_{i=1,\ldots,n}\left|w_{k,i}^*\right| \leq \Sigma_{i=1,\ldots,n}\left|w_{k,i}\right| \tag{42}$$

and the optimal subset $R_k^*(r)$ (28) of r features X_i active at this vertex.

Condition (42) have interesting connections with the biologically motivated principle of resources conservation [11].

6 Collinear Patterns

A collinear (flat) pattern $P_k(\mathbf{w}_k)$ is created by a large number r of feature vectors $\mathbf{x}_j$ from the set $\mathbf{G}_k^+$ (9) that lie on the hyperplane $H(\mathbf{w}_k, 1) = \{\mathbf{x} : \mathbf{w}_k^T \mathbf{x} = 1\}$ (3) [12]:

$$P_k(\mathbf{w}_k) = \left\{\mathbf{x}_j \in \mathbf{G}_k : \mathbf{w}_k^T \mathbf{x} = 1\right\} \tag{43}$$

Let us consider the hyperplane $H\left(\mathbf{w}_k^*(r), 1\right) = \left\{\mathbf{x} : \mathbf{w}_k^*(r)^\mathsf{T}\mathbf{x} = 1\right\}$ (3) defined by the optimal vertex $\mathbf{w}_k^*(r)$ (24) which is the minimum value $\Psi_k^1\left(\mathbf{w}_k^*\right)$ (41) of the *CPL* criterion function $\Psi_k^1(\mathbf{w})$ (40). In this case, the vertex $\mathbf{w}_k^*(r)$ (24) of the rank r ($r \le m_k^+$ (9)) in the parameter space $\mathbf{R}^n$ ($r < n$) is located at the intersection of r hyperplanes h_j^+ (17) and by $n - r$ hyperplanes h_i^0 (19) and defined by the system of n linear Eqs. (20) and (22):

$$\left(\forall \mathbf{x}_j \in G_k^+ \ (9)\right) \ \mathbf{x}_j^\mathsf{T}\mathbf{w}_k^*(r) = 1 \tag{44}$$

and

$$\left(\forall i \in I_k^*(r)\right) \ \mathbf{e}_i^\mathsf{T}\mathbf{w}_k^*(r) = 0 \tag{45}$$

The largest possible rank r of a vertex $\mathbf{w}_k^*(r)$ (24) based on the non-singular matrix $\mathbf{B}_k^*(r)$ (23) is equal to the number m_k^+ ($r = m_k^+$) of feature vectors $\mathbf{x}_j$ in the positive learning set G_k^+ (9). If the feature vectors $\mathbf{x}_j$ constituting the set G_k^+ (9) are linearly dependent, then the rank r is smaller than m_k^+ $\left(r < m_k^+\right)$. The linearly dependent feature vectors $\mathbf{x}_{r+1}$ cannot be entered into the basis $\mathbf{B}_k^*(r)$ (23) due to the condition (33).

Definition 3: The optimal vertex $\mathbf{w}_k^*(r)$ (24) of the rank r which is the minimum $\Psi_k^1(\mathbf{w}_k^*(r))$ (41) of the *CPL* criterion function $\Psi_k^1(\mathbf{w})$ (40) defines the k-th collinear pattern $P_k\left(\mathbf{w}_k^*(r)\right)$ (43) if the rank r is less than the number m_k^+ $\left(r \le m_k^+\right)$ of elements $\mathbf{x}_j$ of the set G_k^+ (9).

The search for a collinear pattern $P_k\left(\mathbf{w}_k^*(r)\right)$ (43) representing an individual category ω_k can be based on the selection of the learning set $G_{k(l)}^+\left(G_k^+ \subset C_k\right)$ with m_k^+ elements $\mathbf{x}_j(k)$ (9), which leads to the largest difference $m_k^+ - r$ at the optimal vertex $\mathbf{w}_k^*(r)$ (41) of rank r.

Based on the flat patterns $P_k\left(\mathbf{w}_k^*(r)\right)$ (43), it is possible, among others, designing models of linear interaction of many features (genes) X_i [12].

7 Concluding Remarks

The article discusses principles of designing separating and representing types of formal neurons $FN(\mathbf{w}_k, \theta_k)$ (8) in the high-dimensional feature space $F[n]$ ($m \ll n$).

The separating formal neurons $FN(\mathbf{w}_k, \theta_k)$ with $\theta_k = 1$ (8) aim to linearly classify different categories ω_k. The construction of the linear classifier (7) is based on the separation with the maximum margins $\delta_{L1}\left(\mathbf{w}_k^*(r)\right)$ (27) of pairs $\{G_k^+, G_k^-\}$ of the learning sets G_k^+ (9) and G_k^- (10). The optitmal vertex $\mathbf{w}_k^*(r)$ (16) determining the largest margin $\delta_{L1}\left(\mathbf{w}_k^*(r)\right)$ (27) is obtained by minimizing the perceptron criterion function $\Phi_k(\mathbf{w})$ (14) with the L_1 regularization $\sum_i |w_i|$ (15).

The second type of representing neurons $FN(\mathbf{w}_k, \theta_k)$ with $\theta_k = 1$ (8) aims to linearly represent one category ω_k. The optimal vertex $\mathbf{w}_k^*(r)$ with the minimal length $\|\mathbf{w}_k^*(r)\|_{L1}$ (42) is obtained by minimizing the collinearity criterion function $\Phi_k^1(\mathbf{w})$ (38) with the L_1 regularization $\sum_i |w_i|$ (40) determined on only one data set C_k (2).

Hierarchical neural networks can be designed from complex layers of formal neurons $FN(\mathbf{w}_k, \theta_k)$ (8). The separating and representing types of formal neurons $FN(\mathbf{w}_k, \theta_k)$ (8) can play complementary roles in hierarchical neural networks.

Acknowledgments. The presented study was supported by the grant WZ/WI-IIT/4/2023. From the Bialystok University of Technology and funded from the resources for research by the Polish Ministry of Science and Higher Education.

References

1. Duda, O.R., Hart, P.E., Stork, D.G.: Pattern Classification. J. Wiley, New York (2001)
2. Bishop, C.M.: Pattern Recognition and Machine Learning. Springer, Heidelberg (2006)
3. Johnson, R.A., Wichern, D.W.: Applied Multivariate Statistical Analysis. Prentice- Hall Inc., Englewood Cliffs (2002)
4. Bobrowski, L., Boldak, C.: Stepwise inversion of large matrices with the Gauss-Jordan vector transformation. J. Adv. Math. Comput. Sci. **37**(1), 28–39 (2022)
5. Bobrowski, L.: Data Exploration and Linear Separability, pp. 1–172. Lambert Academic Publishing (2019)
6. Bobrowski L., Łukaszuk, T.: Relaxed linear separability (*RLS*) approach to feature (Gene) subset selection. In: Xia, X. (ed.) Selected Works in Bioinformatics, pp. 103–108. INTECH (2011)
7. Bobrowski L.: Computing on vertices in data mining. In: Data Mining, pp. 1–19. Intech Open (2021)
8. Bobrowski, L.: Complex layers of formal neurons. In: Iliadis, L., Jayne, C., Tefas, A., Pimenidis, E. (eds.) Engineering Applications of Neural Networks: 23rd International Conference, EAAAI/EANN 2022, Chersonissos, Crete, Greece, June 17–20, 2022, Proceedings, pp. 81–89. Springer International Publishing, Cham (2022). https://doi.org/10.1007/978-3-031-082 23-8_7
9. Vapnik, V.N.: Statistical Learning Theory. J. Wiley, New York (1998)
10. Bobrowski, L., Zabielski, P.: Classification model with collinear grouping of features. J. Inf. Telecommun. **7**, 73–88 (2022)
11. Holmgreen, L., Tirone, V., Gerhart, J., Hobfoll, S.E.: Conservation of Resources Theory. J. Wiley, Hoboken (2017)
12. Bobrowski, L.: Collinear data structures and interaction models. In: Nguyen, N.T., Manolopoulos, Y., Chbeir, R., Kozierkiewicz, A., Trawiński, B. (eds.) Computational Collective Intelligence. ICCCI 2022, pp. 378–387. Springer, Heidelberg (2022). https://doi.org/10.1007/978-3-031-16014-1_30

Graph-Based Fault Localization
in Python Projects
with Class-Imbalanced Learning

Apoorva Anand Kulkarni[✉], Divya G. Niranjan, Noel Saju,
P. Rakshith Shenoy, and Arti Arya[iD]

PES University, Bangalore, India
apoorvakulkarni2001@gmail.com, artiarya@pes.edu

Abstract. Automated Program Repair (APR) is a domain of research
in software engineering that focuses on providing computationally-
generated fixes to buggy code. The primary objective is to alleviate the
challenges associated with identifying and rectifying errors that exist
within large-scale projects. Fault localization is a critical stage of the
APR pipeline, dedicated to identifying the locations of bugs within the
code. Despite Python now being one of the most popular programming
languages, most existing fault localization techniques are limited to real-
world Java and C repositories. This paper proposes a graph-based representation of buggy code that utilizes flow of control and data to capture
both semantic and syntactic information. We also present an analysis
of a novel approach, Class-Imbalanced Learning on Graphs (CILG) for
fault localization, as an alternative to conventional methods of calculating program element suspiciousness scores. The proposed approach is
trained and tested on a real-world dataset containing buggy Python code
snippets extracted from the PyTraceBugs dataset, achieving a notable
macro Area Under the Curve-Receiver Operating Characteristic (AUC-
ROC) score of 0.85. We have also provided a comparison with Graph
Neural Network (GNN) models and gpt-3.5-turbo to demonstrate the
effectiveness of our technique.

Keywords: Graph Neural Networks · Contrastive learning ·
Automated Program Repair · Fault Localization

1 Introduction

Automatic Program Repair (APR) refers to the field of study aimed at identifying and fixing faults in software projects without human intervention. As projects
grow in size, scale and complexity, the likelihood of introducing bugs and errors
into the project also increases manifold. This can lead to security vulnerabilities,
user dissatisfaction and system crashes. Apart from this, developers also have
to dedicate a substantial amount of time and effort to debugging. Introducing
APR into the software development process can help to produce more robust

L. Iliadis et al. (Eds.): EANN 2024, CCIS 2141, pp. 354–368, 2024.
https://doi.org/10.1007/978-3-031-62495-7_27

and reliable software systems. This leads to a reduction in the effort and time required to produce efficient and accurate code. Fault localization is a crucial stage within the process of automated software repair. The primary objective of fault localization is to accurately pinpoint the source of errors. Once faults are localized, subsequent stages of the APR process, such as patch generation, can be more effectively carried out. Hence, the performance of the automatic program repair process is directly impacted by the accuracy attained during fault localization.

The existing approaches for Fault Localization show several limitations that hinder their effectiveness. Primarily, the predominant focus on identifying bugs in Java or C restricts the applicability of these methods. There is a noticeable lack of fault localization techniques for Python, particularly for multi-fault real-world projects. Furthermore, fault localization for Python projects utilizes mostly statistical fault localization techniques [16] even though it has been demonstrated that learning-based techniques, particularly graph-based approaches, show better results for this task. This motivates the design of a new framework for fault localization in real-world Python projects. Hence, in this paper, we introduce a Class-Imbalanced Learning on Graphs (CILG) approach that utilizes a novel graph-based representation of buggy code.

The main contributions in this paper are as follows:

1. Development of a fault localization technique tailored specifically for real-world multi-fault Python projects.
2. Novel graph-based representation of code snippets by incorporating control flow information, data flow analysis and network embedding.
3. Node labelling by using a variant of the GumTree differencing algorithm.
4. CILG-based approach for node classification.
5. Comparison with traditional GNN models, i.e., GAT, GCN, GraphSAGE and directed GraphSAGE.
6. Comparison with LLM-based approach, i.e., gpt-turbo-3.5.

The subsequent sections of the paper are organized as follows: Sect. 2 highlights a survey of relevant literature. Section 3 provides a detailed explanation of the proposed approach. Section 4 highlights the research questions or gaps identified and Sect. 5 outlines experimentation, obtained results and interpretations of the results. Lastly, Sect. 6 concludes our findings and proposes a plan for future work.

2   Related Work

2.1   Statistical Fault Localization Techniques

Statistical techniques for fault localization can be categorized as spectrum-based fault localization (SBFL) and mutation-based fault localization (MBFL).

SBFL-based approaches [1] use program spectrum along with test case results for localization. Program spectrum refers to the code coverage data and results obtained from test case execution. An element exhibiting greater frequency in test cases that fail and lesser frequency in test cases that pass has a higher likelihood of being buggy. The two most widely employed SBFL methodologies are Ochiai and Dstar, both of which involve formulae designed to assess the "suspiciousness" of a statement.

Each statement can be written as a 3-value tuple (EX_f, EX_p, NX_f), where:

EX_f: Total count of failing test cases in which a given statement s is executed

EX_p: Total count of passing test cases in which a given statement s is executed

NX_f: Total count of failing test cases in which a given statement s is not executed

$$\text{Ochiai} = \frac{EX_f}{\sqrt{(EX_f + EX_p)(EX_f + NX_f)}} \tag{1}$$

$$\text{Dstar} = \frac{EX_f^2}{EX_p + NX_f} \tag{2}$$

The primary limitation associated with SBFL techniques is their reliance on code coverage information and the outcomes of test executions. This limitation makes it difficult to achieve higher accuracy when sufficient coverage information is absent.

MBFL-based techniques [12] involve the creation of mutated versions of the original program, each containing an artificial bug. Both the original program P and the set of mutant programs associated with P are tested using a test suite. Analyzing variations in the number of both failed and passed test cases for both P and all mutants proves to be an effective method for identifying faults within the code. MUSE and Metallaxis stand out as the two most widely utilized MBFL techniques for computing the "suspiciousness" scores of statements. The factors used in MUSE and Metallaxis include:

- $totalfailed$: Total count of failing test cases for original program P.
- $failed_{i,j}$: Total count of test cases that exhibit failure for original program P but exhibit success for mutant $m_{i,j}$.
- $passed_{i,j}$: Total count of test cases that exhibit success for original program P but exhibit failure for mutant $m_{i,j}$.
- $f2p$: Total count of test cases transitioning from failure to pass across any mutant.
- $p2f$: Total count of test cases transitioning from pass to failure across any mutant.

$$\text{MUSE}(s_i) = \frac{\sum_{m_{i,j} \in M_i} failed_{i,j} - \frac{f2p}{p2f} \cdot passed_{i,j}}{|M_i|} \tag{3}$$

$$\text{Metallaxis}(s_i) = \frac{\sum_{m_{i,j} \in M_i} \left(\frac{failed_{i,j}}{\sqrt{totalfailed \cdot (failed_{i,j} + passed_{i,j})}} \right)}{|M_i|} \tag{4}$$

While MBFL techniques are useful to obtain coverage information about statement execution, they are inefficient due to the vast computation cost.

2.2 Deep Learning-Based Fault Localization Techniques

Multiple deep learning based methodologies have also been explored for fault localization. DeepFL [7] outlines the utilization of Recurrent Neural Networks (RNN) and Multi-layer Perceptron (MLP), along with specialized model variants for fault localization. The features that DeepFL uses consist of suspiciousness-based features like SBFL and MBFL, fault proneness based features like code-complexity metrics, and textual-similarity-based features. DeepFL localized 213 faults within Top-1. On similar lines, the DEEPRL4FL paper [8] proposes another Fault Localization approach based on deep learning called DEEPRL4FL. It considers Fault Localization to be an image recognition task and faults are localized using a CNN model. It uses test case ordering to facilitate code representational learning and combines it with statement dependencies and the AST to generate representation vectors which are passed on as inputs to the CNN model for Fault Localization. The paper concludes by showing that the DEEPRL4FL approach outperforms existing fault localization models, with an average improvement of 12% in localizing buggy statements and methods. Similarly, CNN-FL [20] is a convolutional neural network based approach for localising faults. CNN-FL builds a customised CNN, trains it using test cases, and examines each statement's suspiciousness by testing the trained model on a virtual test set. The paper discusses the use of activation functions, pooling methods and learning rate in the context of deep learning for fault localization. The effectiveness of CNN-FL is assessed using two commonly used measures, exam and relative improvement (also known as RImp). The paper concludes that CNN-FL performs substantially better than ZhengFL, Dstar, Barinel, and Ochiai, demonstrating that fault localization becomes much more effective by integrating deep learning.

2.3 Graph Learning-Based Fault Localization Techniques

Recently, the usage of Graph Neural Networks (GNNs) for fault localization has gained prominence. For example, GNet4FL [13] gathers static and dynamic code information by using a combination of AST graphs and test case execution results. The approach then extracts the source code node representation using GraphSAGE. It preserves the graph's topological information while performing feature fusion on an entity made up of several nodes. The multi-layer perceptron is then used to train and rank entities using the representation of each entity as input. It has been demonstrated that the GNet4FL method performs better at locating faults than conventional methodologies. Similarly, [9] is another paper on GNN-based fault localization. This paper includes three steps which are collection of data, phase-1 fault localization and phase-2 fault localization. In the data collection phase, each program is expressed as a graph by combining both SBFL-based suspiciousness score and flow analysis. In phase-I localization, RankNet is used to rank at method-level granularity. A weight aware GNN is employed in phase-II localization to accurately localize intra-method statements. It receives the corresponding method graph as input with along with edge weights. This method successfully locates, on average, 114, 185, and 211 faults at the top-I, top-III, and top-V places for phase-I fault localization. This method successfully locates, on average, 91 at top-I, 206 at top-III, and 260 bugs at the top-V places for phase-II localization. Lastly, AGFL [14] is a GNN based method that leverages the AST's adjacency matrix and the word vector associated with each program token. This approach, inspired by Dstar, calculates the suspiciousness of statements and subsequently ranks them. AGFL's efficacy is demonstrated through experiments conducted on Defects4J. The experimental results reveal AGFL's impressive capability to pinpoint 178 among the 262 bugs that were studied within the Top-I ranking.

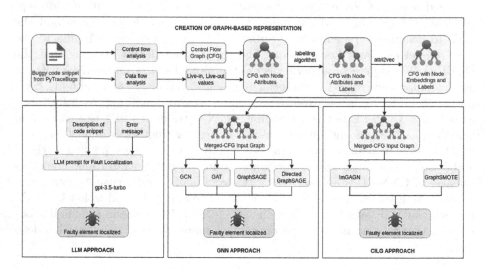

Fig. 1. Proposed Workflow for Fault Localization.

3   Proposed Approach

In this section, a detailed explanation of a fault localization technique specifically designed for real-world Python projects is provided. We introduce a novel graph-based representation of code snippets that incorporates control flow information, data flow analysis, and network embedding. Additionally, we propose a node labeling method using a variant of the GumTree differencing algorithm, and employ a CILG-based approach for node classification. The paper also includes a comparison with traditional Graph Neural Network (GNN) models such as GAT, GCN, GraphSAGE, and directed GraphSAGE, as well as a comparative analysis with a Large Language Model-based approach, namely gpt-turbo-3.5. A high-level view of our proposed approach and comparative analysis has been depicted in Fig. 1.

3.1   Dataset

PyTraceBugs. PyTraceBugs [2] dataset encompasses approximately 5.7 million correct as well as 24,000 buggy code snippets sourced from real-world Python programs. The construction of the dataset involves the extraction of buggy code snippets from GitHub, specifically from the "Issues" section of the Git repository, where issue names include keywords like "fix" or "error". The error types present in the dataset have been explained in Table 1. This dataset has been further divided into three categories: training, testing and validation code snippets.

Proposed Dataset. We have used 500 buggy code snippets from the training set of PyTraceBugs for our approach. Each snippet consists of a buggy function taken from a real-world Python repository, either containing a single fault or multiple faults. Unlike other graph-learning papers such as [13] and [14] which have focused on only single-fault programs, we have chosen both single-fault and multi-fault programs as most real-world scenarios require Fault Localization for both cases. The corresponding fixed snippet is also present for each buggy code snippet, which facilitates the process of labelling for node classification. Figure 2 is an example of a PyTraceBugs buggy code snippet, from the Binderhub Github repository, that we have used for our task.

```
def stream_logs(self):
    for line in self.api.read_namespaced_pod_log(
            self.name,
            self.namespace,
            follow=True,
            _preload_content=False):
        self.progress('log', line.decode('utf-8'))
```

Fig. 2. Buggy Code Snippet from PyTraceBugs.

Table 1. Some Most Common Error Types in PyTraceBugs

Error type	Percentage of snippets (%)
Type Error	15.9
Attribute Error	16.6
Value Error	10.2
Runtime Error	5.5
Key Error	8.2
Index Error	5.3
Others	38.3

3.2   Graph-Based Representation

Control Flow Graphs. Graphs are a fundamental paradigm for modelling software programs as they capture the inherent relationships that exist between various program elements. A Control Flow Graph (CFG) serves as a graphical representation illustrating the sequence of execution within a program.

The components of a CFG are:

- **Nodes**: Each node represents a basic block of code, which is a sequence of statements that are executed together, without any branching or jumping.
- **Edges**: Each edge represents the flow of control from one basic block to another.

Mathematically, a control flow graph is defined as $G = (I, E)$, where:

I denotes the set of nodes representing basic blocks.

E denotes the set of directed edges between basic blocks.

The control flow graph can be mathematically expressed as a tuple:

$$G = (I, E)$$

$$I = \{i_1, i_2, \ldots, i_k\}$$

$$E = \{(i_n, i_m) \mid \text{where flow of control is from } i_n \text{ to } i_m\}$$

In other papers such as [13] and [11], where GNN-based approaches were explored for fault localization in Java programs, abstract syntax tree (AST) was the predominant graph representation adopted. However, we suggest that CFGs are better than ASTs for fault localization because a CFG captures the dynamic execution flow of a program, enabling a more precise representation of control dependencies. By focusing on the actual paths taken during execution, CFG can more accurately pinpoint the source of faults, whereas AST primarily captures the syntactic structure.

CFG-Based Representation. CFG for each buggy code snippet from the proposed dataset was generated using `python-graphs` [17], an open source library that constructs graph representations of Python programs using static analysis. Figure 3 depicts an example of a buggy code snippet and its corresponding CFG generated by the above library. Each node in the CFG graph is also assigned a corresponding node type $t \in T$ where T is the set of all node types (e.g., Entry block, Exit block, True block, etc.). All of these individual CFGs are then merged to form the final merged-CFG graph. This final graph consists of 7068 nodes and 10585 edges.

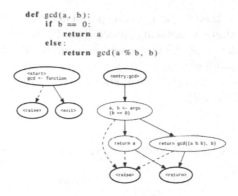

Fig. 3. Buggy Code Snippet and Corresponding CFG.

3.3 Data Flow Analysis for Node Features

Data flow analysis is a technique used in program analysis to provide information about the flow of data through a program. Data flow analysis is often applied to CFGs to analyze how data values are used and propagated within the program. Combining information on both flow of control and flow of data enables a rich syntactic and semantic representation that allows for better fault localization. By performing data flow analysis, the following node features are obtained:

- **Live-in value**: Live-in values at a particular node are the variables whose values are used within that block before being redefined. These values are live when entering the block.
- **Live-out value**: Live-out values at a particular node are the variables whose values are used in successor blocks before being redefined. These values are live when leaving the block.

3.4 Labelling Algorithm

In our approach, fault localization is treated as a node classification task, where each node is classified as "modified", "unmodified" or "inserted". To prepare labels for training, we employ a labeling algorithm inspired by the Gumtree AST differencing algorithm [3]. This algorithm, which takes the Control Flow Graphs (CFGs) of both the buggy and corresponding corrected code snippet as input, identifies and assigns labels to nodes. A similar labelling technique has been used in [11] as well. The labelling of unmodified, modified, and inserted nodes follows this process:

- Modified nodes are those that have been removed or have been changed. In the former case, nodes lacking correspondence from the buggy to the corrected version are identified. To detect content changes, nodes with altered content between the buggy and corrected versions are located.

– Inserted nodes are those lacking correspondence from the corrected version to the buggy version. Annotating inserted nodes proves challenging due to their absence in the buggy CFG. To address this, we identify the parent node that remains unmodified in the buggy version and label it.
– Unmodified nodes are those that remain the same in both the buggy and the corrected CFGs (Table 2).

Table 2. Number of Nodes in Merged-CFG for Each Label.

Label	Count
unmodified nodes	5792
modified nodes	697
inserted nodes	579

3.5 Network Embedding

Network embedding refers to the task of defining nodes in a network as vectors in a continuous vector space. The objective of network embedding is to determine the underlying relationships, patterns, and data in a network, allowing downstream machine learning tasks to be carried out with ease.

The paper "Attributed Network Embedding via Subspace Discovery" [19] describes a novel approach for network embedding utilising subspace discovery techniques. Unlike existing approaches, which focus solely on structural information, attri2vec takes into account both node properties and network architecture. The use of subspace discovery, which allows the extraction of underlying patterns from the network, is the fundamental innovation. Attri2vec provides more informative embeddings as opposed to node2vec [4] and word2vec [10]. It is appropriate for our task as it takes into account both control flow and data flow information.

To generate node embeddings using attri2vec, random walks were generated with four walks per node and a walk length of five. Batches of 200 samples each were processed for training. The model architecture included a single hidden layer with 128 neurons. Training spanned 50 epochs, employing the Adam optimizer which has a 0.001 learning rate and optimizing for binary cross-entropy loss. After running attri2vec on the dataset, each node is described by a 128-length feature vector.

3.6 Class-Imbalanced Learning on Graphs

Graph Neural Networks (GNNs) are a NN architecture specifically designed for processing data present in the form of graphs. In the context of fault localization, GNNs offer a powerful framework for capturing the relationships between program elements, facilitating the identification of buggy code.

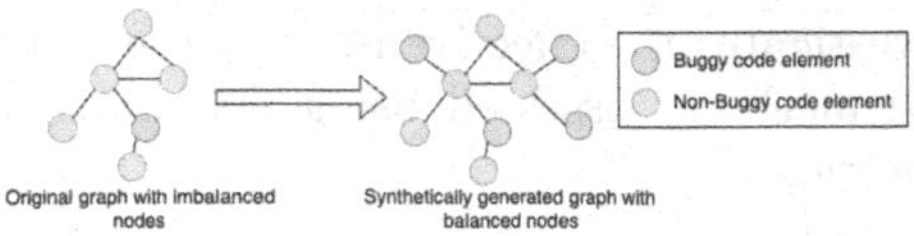

Fig. 4. Generation of Synthetic Networks in CILG techniques.

A typical graph neural network involves three fundamental operations: message passing, aggregation, and updating. In the context of a graph $G = (I, E)$, the state vector h_i for each node $i \in I$ evolves at the k-th step as follows:

$$h_i^{(k+1)} = \text{update}\left(h_i^{(k)}, \text{aggre}\left(h_j^{(k)}, \forall j \in N_i\right)\right) \tag{5}$$

N_i signifies the collection of neighboring nodes connected to node i. The function *aggre* encompasses various aggregation techniques like min, max, or avg, consolidating information from the neighbours for node i. Some of the popular models include graph attention networks (GAT) [18], graph convolution networks (GCN) [6] as well as graph sample and aggregation (GraphSAGE) [5].

Graph Neural Networks (GNNs) have outperformed standard statistical approaches in fault localization, such as SBFL and MBFL. Furthermore, GNNs outperformed a variety of other deep learning approaches. However, GNNs face significant challenges due to the disproportionate distribution of buggy and non-buggy code elements. As a result, their failure to successfully manage this imbalance remains a significant constraint, prompting further research into fault localization techniques to handle this.

Hence, the field of Class-Imbalanced Learning on Graphs (CILG) has rapidly gained prominence due to the widespread occurrence of imbalanced class distributions in graph data. The skewed distribution can bias conventional GNN models towards the majority class, resulting in suboptimal performance for the minority class. This approach, therefore, is useful for fault localization as it contains a disproportionate distribution of buggy and correct code snippets. Figure 4 highlights the generation of synthetic networks in CILG techniques.

The first CILG method used in this study is GraphSMOTE [21]. GraphSMOTE consists of four essential components that are Feature Extractor, Synthetic Node Generator, Edge Generator and GNN-based Classifier. The second CILG method explored in this research is ImGAGN [15]. ImGAGN consists of a Generator and a Discriminator. The original architechture of ImGAGN utilizes GCN as the discriminator. For our approach, we have created a modified ImGAGN architecture that uses GraphSAGE as the discriminator. This enables a better comparison with the GraphSAGE-based GraphSMOTE architecture mentioned in the above section.

4 Research Questions

This paper aims to answer the following research questions:

RQ1. How effective are the CILG-based approaches, and which among them exhibits optimal performance for fault localization?

This question investigates the effectiveness of approaching fault localization through CILG-based methods, assessed using accuracy and the macro AUC-ROC score as key metrics.

RQ2. How does the effectiveness of our proposed approach compare to that of conventional GNN models?

This question involves a comparative analysis between our method and GNN models like GAT, GCN, GraphSAGE, and directed GraphSAGE.

RQ3. How does the effectiveness of our approach compare to that of an LLM-based approach?

This question involves a comparative evaluation of our approach against results obtained from gpt-3.5-turbo.

5   Results and Discussion

5.1   Experimental Setup

The experiments are executed on a platform running Ubuntu 20.04 LTS equipped with an AMD Ryzen 5 CPU and 12GB RAM. This study employs the `python-graphs` library for extracting CFGs and conducting data flow analysis. Additionally, `attri2vec` is utilized to generate network embeddings, while GNN models are implemented using the `StellarGraphs` library. A standardized 70-15-15 split is adopted for training, testing, and validation across all models.

5.2   Metrics

In this paper, we assess and compare the effectiveness of several methods using the subsequent metrics:

Accuracy: Accuracy is a popular metric when evaluating the performance of ML models. Accuracy is intuitive and simple, but it might not be the best metric to use when datasets are imbalanced. A model may attain high accuracy in cases where one class greatly outnumbers the others just by correctly predicting the majority class more often, possibly ignoring the performance of minority classes. Therefore, when class imbalance is a major concern, alternate metrics are required in order to provide a better evaluation.

Macro AUC-ROC Score: Macro Area Under the Receiver Operating Characteristic curve (AUC-ROC) score is an important measure for assessing models, particularly in the case of imbalanced datasets. Macro AUC-ROC takes into account the model's discriminating capability for each class separately. This measure gives a thorough picture of the model's capacity to discriminate between various classes, regardless of how frequently they occur, by computing the AUC-ROC score for each class and then averaging over all classes.

5.3   RQ1: Effectiveness of CILG Approach

In our approach, we have explored the effectiveness of three CILG models (Table 3).

Table 3. Accuracy and AUC-ROC Score for CILG Models.

Model	Accuracy	AUC-ROC
ImGAGN	0.82	0.73
Modified ImGAGN	0.82	0.77
GraphSMOTE	0.82	0.85

GraphSMOTE with GraphSAGE as the base architecture gives the best performance with an AUC-ROC score of 0.85. In general, CILG models which include GraphSAGE in their architecture outperform those with GCN. Graph-SAGE's capacity for inductive learning, i.e. the ability to generalize to nodes that were not encountered during training, is one of its main advantages. GCN-based CILG models, on the other hand, are limited to predicting nodes that are present in the training graph due to their transductive nature.

5.4   RQ2: Comparison with Conventional GNN Models

Table 4. Accuracy and AUC-ROC Score for GNN Models.

Model	Accuracy	AUC-ROC
GAT	0.81	0.5
GCN	0.81	0.5
GraphSAGE	0.82	0.56
Directed GraphSAGE	0.82	0.63

The best GNN model is directed GraphSAGE with an AUC-ROC score of 0.63. Therefore, our CILG-based approach shows better results with a 35% improvement from the best GNN model. This proves our initial hypothesis that GNNs face challenges due to the disproportionate distribution of buggy and correct code elements and hence, may not be the best approach for this task (Table 4).

5.5   RQ3: Comparison with LLM-Based Approach

Given the advent of LLM-based techniques in APR, we leveraged the capabilities of GPT to conduct a comparative analysis between CILG-based approach and LLM-based approach. Our methodology involved sending the buggy code snippet, a natural language description of the buggy code snippet, and the corresponding error message to the GPT-3.5-turbo model as a prompt for fault localization. This approach successfully localized 118 bugs among 477 buggy code snippets, achieving an accuracy of 24.7%. The accuracy attained through the CILG approach surpassed that achieved by utilizing LLMs.

6 Threats to Validity

In this section, we will discuss the potential threats to the validity of our research.

Firstly, our approach does not include evaluation based on comparison with related works. This is because, to best of our knowledge, there is no paper focusing exclusively on fault localization for real-world Python projects. Hence, we have evaluated our approach using baseline GNN approaches and LLM-approach.

Secondly, we have provided only a preliminary analysis of using CILG for Fault Localization. The comparison with both the baseline approaches and the LLM approach indicate strongly that a CILG-based approach shows promising results. However, testing with a greater number of buggy code snippets is required in further stages of research.

7 Conclusion and Future Work

In conclusion, this paper has presented a preliminary analysis of a novel CILG-based approach for fault localization in the context of real-world Python projects. To validate the effectiveness of the proposed approach, comparisons were made with traditional graph neural network (GNN) models, including GAT, GCN, GraphSAGE, and directed GraphSAGE. Additionally, a comparative analysis with a language model-based approach, gpt-turbo-3.5, was conducted.

Although this work shows promising initial results, further evaluation is required. Firstly, it is important to train as well as test the model on a greater number of snippets in order to conclusively state that a CILG-based approach is the best approach. Further, the proposed approach could be trained on buggy code snippets from other languages as well in order to improve the applicability to other languages. Lastly, since each node is derived from multiple lines of source code, the proposed approach can be made more developer-friendly by incorporating a step that performs statement level Fault Localization in each buggy node.

References

1. Abreu, R., Zoeteweij, P., Van Gemund, A.J.: On the accuracy of spectrum-based fault localization. In: Testing: Academic and Industrial Conference Practice and Research Techniques-MUTATION (TAICPART-MUTATION 2007), pp. 89–98. IEEE (2007)
2. Akimova, E.N., et al.: Pytracebugs: a large python code dataset for supervised machine learning in software defect prediction. In: 2021 28th Asia-Pacific Software Engineering Conference (APSEC), pp. 141–151. IEEE (2021)
3. Falleri, J.R., Morandat, F., Blanc, X., Martinez, M., Monperrus, M.: Fine-grained and accurate source code differencing. In: Proceedings of the 29th ACM/IEEE International Conference on Automated Software Engineering, pp. 313–324 (2014)
4. Grover, A., Leskovec, J.: node2vec: Scalable feature learning for networks. In: Proceedings of the 22nd ACM SIGKDD International Conference on Knowledge Discovery and Data Mining, pp. 855–864 (2016)
5. Hamilton, W., Ying, Z., Leskovec, J.: Inductive representation learning on large graphs. Adv. Neural Inf. Process. Syst. **30** (2017)
6. Kipf, T.N., Welling, M.: Semi-supervised classification with graph convolutional networks. arXiv preprint arXiv:1609.02907 (2016)
7. Li, X., Li, W., Zhang, Y., Zhang, L.: Deepfl: integrating multiple fault diagnosis dimensions for deep fault localization. In: Proceedings of the 28th ACM SIGSOFT International Symposium on Software Testing and Analysis (2019)
8. Li, Y., Wang, S., Nguyen, T.: Fault localization with code coverage representation learning. In: 2021 IEEE/ACM 43rd International Conference on Software Engineering (ICSE), pp. 661–673. IEEE (2021)
9. Li, Z., Tang, E., Chen, X., Wang, L., Li, X.: Graph neural network based two-phase fault localization approach. In: Proceedings of the 13th Asia-Pacific Symposium on Internetware (2022)
10. Mikolov, T., Chen, K., Corrado, G., Dean, J.: Efficient estimation of word representations in vector space. arXiv preprint arXiv:1301.3781 (2013)
11. Nguyen, T.D., et al.: Ffl: fine-grained fault localization for student programs via syntactic and semantic reasoning. In: 2022 IEEE International Conference on Software Maintenance and Evolution (ICSME), pp. 151–162. IEEE (2022)
12. Papadakis, M., Le Traon, Y.: Metallaxis-fl: mutation-based fault localization. Softw. Test. Verificat. Reliabil. **25**(5–7), 605–628 (2015)
13. Qian, J., Ju, X., Chen, X.: Gnet4fl: effective fault localization via graph convolutional neural network. Autom. Softw. Eng. **30**(2), 16 (2023)
14. Qian, J., Ju, X., Chen, X., Shen, H., Shen, Y.: AGFL: a graph convolutional neural network-based method for fault localization. In: 2021 IEEE 21st International Conference on Software Quality, Reliability and Security (QRS), pp. 672–680. IEEE (2021)
15. Qu, L., Zhu, H., Zheng, R., Shi, Y., Yin, H.: Imgagn: imbalanced network embedding via generative adversarial graph networks. In: Proceedings of the 27th ACM SIGKDD Conference on Knowledge Discovery & Data Mining, pp. 1390–1398 (2021)
16. Sarhan, Q.I., Szatmari, A., Toth, R., Beszedes, A.: Charmfl: a fault localization tool for python (2021)
17. Sutton, C., et al.: Graph representations of python programs via source-level static analysis (2022)

18. Velickovic, P., Cucurull, G., Casanova, A., Romero, A., Lio, P., Bengio, Y., et al.: Graph attention networks. STAT **1050**(20), 10–48550 (2017)
19. Zhang, D., Yin, J., Zhu, X., Zhang, C.: Attributed network embedding via subspace discovery. Data Min. Knowl. Disc. **33**, 1953–1980 (2019)
20. Zhang, Z., Lei, Y., Mao, X., Li, P.: CNN-FL: an effective approach for localizing faults using convolutional neural networks. In: 2019 IEEE 26th International Conference on Software Analysis, Evolution and Reengineering (SANER), pp. 445–455. IEEE (2019)
21. Zhao, T., Zhang, X., Wang, S.: Graphsmote: imbalanced node classification on graphs with graph neural networks. In: Proceedings of the 14th ACM International Conference on Web Search and Data Mining, pp. 833–841 (2021)

HCER: Hierarchical Clustering-Ensemble Regressor

Petros Barmpas[1]([✉]), Panagiotis Anagnostou[1], Sotiris K. Tasoulis[1],
Spiros V. Georgakopoulos[2], and Vassilis P. Plagianakos[1]

[1] Department of Computer Science and Biomedical Informatics,
University of Thessaly, Volos, Greece
{petrosbarmpas,panagno,stasoulis,vpp}@uth.gr
[2] Department of Mathematics, University of Thessaly, Volos, Greece
spirosgeorg@uth.gr

Abstract. This paper studies the Hierarchical Clustering-Ensemble Regressor (HCER) framework, a novel and advanced approach in predictive analysis that combines hierarchical clustering with ensemble methods. The HCER framework is designed to leverage the intricate structures inherent in large-scale data, often overlooked by standard regression models. By identifying and utilizing sub-populations within datasets, this approach enables the discovery of unique predictive dynamics and enhances the accuracy of predictions. Our study extends the application of the HCER framework beyond its initial deployment in the ATHLOS dataset, exploring its versatility and effectiveness across various data domains. We highlight the capability of the framework to capture localized patterns in data, which might be lost in global models, thereby enriching the understanding of the data's underlying structure. This is crucial in fields where deep data comprehension is as essential as prediction accuracy. Additionally, we investigate the computational efficiency of the HCER framework, considering the growing need for scalable and efficient methods in the era of Big Data. Our findings indicate that the HCER framework contributes to the machine learning domain by enhancing prediction accuracy and offering a scalable solution suitable for large datasets. This comprehensive study positions the HCER framework as a potent predictive modeling tool capable of handling the diversity and complexity of contemporary data landscapes.

Keywords: Clustering · Ensemble learning · Regression · Prediction enhancement

1 Introduction

In the burgeoning field of data science, the quest for robust predictive models that can navigate the complexity of large-scale datasets is relentless. In a pre-

Financed by the European Union - NextGenerationEU through Recovery and Resilience Facility, Greece 2.0, under the call RESEARCH - CREATE - INNOVATE (project code: TAEDK-06185/T2EDK- 02800).

vious study in The ATHLOS project [3], the authors illuminated the potential of hierarchical clustering to enhance the predictive power of regression models within the context of health and aging studies. The project's innovative approach, encapsulated in the Hierarchical Clustering-Ensemble Regressor (HCER) framework, demonstrated that clustering could serve as a powerful preprocessing step, leading to more accurate predictions by exploiting the inherent structures within complex datasets.

The success of the HCER framework in the ATHLOS (Ageing Trajectories of Health: Longitudinal Opportunities and Synergies, http://athlosproject.eu/) project prompts a broader inquiry. "Can this methodology maintain its efficacy across diverse datasets and domains?" This follow-up study seeks to answer this question by applying the HCER framework to a variety of datasets and comparing its performance against other state-of-the-art regression approaches.

The rationale behind the HCER framework is grounded in the principle that data, particularly in large-scale studies, often exhibit intricate hierarchical structures that standard regression models may overlook. By integrating unsupervised learning through hierarchical clustering, the HCER framework allows for the discovery of sub-populations within the data, each with potentially unique predictive dynamics. Subsequent specialized models can then be trained on these clusters, capturing localized patterns that might be lost in a global model.

Recent advancements in machine learning have seen a surge in ensemble methods, which combine the strengths of multiple predictive models to improve accuracy and robustness [13,17]. The HCER framework contributes to this work by introducing a novel ensemble architecture that leverages the diversity of predictions from models trained on data clusters. This approach not only enhances prediction accuracy but also offers insights into the underlying structure of the data, which can be invaluable in fields where understanding the data is as crucial as making accurate predictions.

In this paper, we extend the application of the HCER framework beyond the ATHLOS dataset to investigate its versatility and effectiveness. We benchmark its performance against leading regression techniques, including Random Forests, Support Vector Machines, and Gradient Boosting Regression, representing the current state-of-the-art predictive analytics. We aim to establish the HCER framework as a competitive approach in the machine learning arsenal through a series of experiments across datasets with varying characteristics.

Moreover, we investigate the computational efficiency of the HCER framework. The original implementation within the ATHLOS project showcased a scalable method that could handle large datasets with a reduced computational burden compared to traditional ensemble methods. This study evaluates the framework's computational performance in broader scenarios, considering the increasing importance of scalability and efficiency in the era of Big Data.

In summary, this paper presents a comprehensive study of the HCER framework's generalizability, effectiveness, and efficiency. By exploring its application across different domains and comparing it with state-of-the-art methods, we aim to contribute a significant piece to the puzzle of predictive modeling in the age of data diversity and complexity.

2   Background and Related Work

The pursuit of accurate and robust predictive models has long been a corner-stone of statistical and machine learning disciplines [9]. Regression analysis, a statistical process for estimating the relationships among variables, has been extensively studied and applied across numerous fields. This section reviews the foundational and contemporary methodologies that inform our study's comparative analysis.

- *Linear regression*, one of the most fundamental and widely used statistical techniques, serves as a baseline for predictive performance due to its simplicity and interpretability [10]. Despite its limitations in handling non-linear relationships and interactions between variables, it remains a benchmark in regression analysis.
- *Lasso (Least Absolute Shrinkage and Selection Operator)* and Ridge Regression represent two regularization techniques that modify the least squares estimation to prevent overfitting. Lasso does this by adding a penalty equivalent to the absolute value of the magnitude of coefficients. In contrast, Ridge adds a penalty equivalent to the square of the magnitude of coefficients [20]. Both methods are instrumental when dealing with multicollinearity or when the goal includes feature selection.
- *Random Forest (RF)* is an ensemble learning method known for its high accuracy, parallel running capability, and overfitting robustness. By aggregating the predictions of numerous decision trees, RF can capture complex interaction structures in the data [4].
- *Support Vector Machines (SVM)* have been recognized for their effectiveness in high-dimensional spaces and flexibility through a kernel trick, allowing them to model non-linear boundaries [5].
- *Gradient Boosting Machines (GBM)* models are also included in our comparative analysis. GBM is a powerful ensemble technique that builds models sequentially to minimize residuals using gradient descent [11].

Additionally, we investigated the comparison of an approach that utilized KMeans as the clustering step, and then for each cluster node, again tailor a specialized model [2].

Each of these methods brings a unique set of strengths and assumptions to regression analysis. Our study aims to compare these methods with the HCER framework to evaluate its performance across different datasets and problem domains.

In the context of hierarchical clustering for regression, the literature suggests that while there is a rich history of clustering for classification, its application in regression problems needs to be explored more. The HCER framework's use of hierarchical clustering as a preprocessing step for ensemble regression presents a novel approach that warrants thorough investigation and benchmarking against these established methods.

Algorithm 1. Hierarchical Clustering-Ensemble Regressor (HCER)

Require: Dataset D, Number of clusters K
Ensure: Ensemble of predictive models $\{M_k\}_{k=1}^{K}$
 1: Perform hierarchical divisive clustering on D to form K clusters and extract the
    tree structure.
 2: **for** each cluster node C_{2k-1} **do**
 3:     Train a predictive model M_{2k-1} on C_{2k-1}
 4: **end for**
 5: **for** each new instance x **do**
 6:     Find the node path for x using the tree split criteria
 7:     Predict the outcome using the corresponding
        model for each node M_{2k-1}
 8:     Average the predictions from all models in the
        path to leaf for x
 9: **end for**

---

3   Methodology

The core of our study revolves around the HCER framework, which we posit as a versatile and potent tool for regression analysis across various domains. This section delineates the methodology employed in our investigation, including the HCER framework procedure description and algorithmic implementation in Algorithm 1.

The HCER framework, applied initially to the ATHLOS dataset for health trajectory prediction [3], is adapted in this study to cater to a broader range of datasets. The framework's adaptability lies in its hierarchical clustering approach, which can be fine-tuned to discern the unique structures within each dataset while requiring very little additional computational overhead.

The HCER framework operates on the principle of dividing the dataset into clusters using hierarchical clustering and then applying regression models tailored to each cluster. This approach allows for capturing the unique characteristics and patterns within different data segments, leading to more accurate and nuanced predictions.

The first step in the HCER framework is to perform hierarchical clustering on the dataset (Algorithm 1, line 1). Hierarchical clustering is a method of cluster analysis that seeks to build a hierarchy of clusters. In the context of this study, projection-based divisive clustering is employed utilizing a plethora of hierarchical approaches found in [1], where the dataset is initially considered as a single cluster, which is then recursively split into smaller clusters. This process continues until a predefined number of clusters or a specific cluster quality criterion is reached.

Once the clusters are formed, the next step is to train a regression model for each cluster (Algorithm 1, lines 2–3). In the scope of this study, we implemented linear regression models for comparison reasons, however, the choice of the regression model can vary depending on the characteristics of the data within each cluster. For instance, a linear regression model might be suitable for

Table 1. Mean Absolute Percentage Error (MAPE) metric for all methods (rows) in all datasets (columns). In each cell the values are scaled by a factor of 1000 for the sake of presentation.

MAPE Comparison ($\times 10^{-3}$)						
Method\Data	Diabetis	Real Estate	Apartment Rent	California Housing	YearPredictionMSD	WEC
LR	366.72	216.10	234.78	317.50	3.37	0.01
Cluster LR	336.41	170.35	228.75	301.79	3.30	0.01
KMEANS LR	341.81	170.85	226.91	301.47	3.29	0.01
Lasso	365.47	215.12	234.78	395.51	3.38	0.45
SVM	486.26	230.40	343.03	519.67	3.53	184.12
RF	382.22	151.53	179.29	189.24	3.37	8.97
XGboost	393.78	161.50	182.77	176.04	3.31	5.59

Table 2. Train Time metric for all methods (rows) in all datasets (columns). In each cell the values are scaled by a factor of 1000 for the sake of presentation.

Train Time Comparison ($\times 10^{-3}$)						
Method\Data	Diabetis	Real Estate	Apartment Rent	California Housing	YearPredictionMSD	WEC
LR	0.59	1.08	1.03	2.17	101.11	19.26
Cluster LR	6.42	11.24	14.88	25.15	400.20	105.53
KMEANS LR	9.57	10.64	27.90	44.92	617.30	157.53
Lasso	0.77	0.53	1.09	7.65	1248.34	10273.49
SVM	2.94	2.78	1144.78	5015.74	103930.31	11756.66
RF	255.85	148.05	2690.16	15094.20	114210.25	18704.15
XGboost	62.80	74.29	76.71	114.30	897.27	439.94

clusters with linear relationships. In contrast, more complex models like support vector regression or neural networks might be employed for clusters exhibiting non-linear patterns.

For a new data instance, the HCER framework first determines the most appropriate cluster node for this instance based on the clustering criteria after the sample is first projected into the appropriate projection vector (Algorithm 1, lines 5–9). The instance is then passed through the regression model associated with that cluster to generate a prediction. This process ensures that each prediction is tailored to the specific data segment, enhancing the overall accuracy and reliability of the model (Tables 1 and 2).

4   Experimental Setup

The experimental setup is crucial for validating the efficacy of the Hierarchical Clustering-Ensemble Regressor (HCER) framework across varied datasets and benchmarking it against established regression methods. This section depicts the selection criteria for the datasets and data preprocessing steps, the comparative methods and training procedures, the performance evaluation metrics, and the computing setup utilized in our experiments.

The benchmark datasets for this study are chosen based on their diversity in size and complexity to evaluate the HCER framework's performance. We include datasets from the UCI Machine Learning Repository, Kaggle, and other

Table 3. Dataset info

Dataset	Samples	Features
Diabetis	442	11
Real_Estate	414	6
Appartment_Rent	9950	7
California_Housing	20640	9
YearPredictionMSD	51535	91
WEC	28800	49

public domain sources, ensuring a mix of small to large datasets with varying feature types and complexity levels [8]. We deliberately did not include datasets that have thousands or millions of dimensions. The reasons are mainly twofold. Firstly, since the intention was to evaluate the performance of our methodology with classical regression methods, as well as state-of-the-art methods, the former would suffer from issues like multicollinearity, where features are highly correlated with each other. This correlation can lead to unstable estimates of regression coefficients, making it difficult to determine the effect of each individual feature [7]. Another issue would be the risk of overfitting. With a large number of features, a regression model can fit the training data, capturing noise rather than the underlying data pattern. This reduces the model's ability to generalize to new, unseen data [14].

The standardized preprocessing pipeline applied to each dataset is an essential step in ensuring the quality and comparability of data. This process involves several key stages. Initially, it addresses any missing values, which is crucial for maintaining data integrity and avoiding biases in the analysis. Following this, numerical features undergo normalization or standardization. This step is vital for bringing all variables to a standard scale, allowing for meaningful comparisons and analyses.

Additionally, categorical variables are encoded, which is a critical process for converting these non-numeric variables into a format that algorithms can efficiently process. Finally, the pipeline includes outlier detection and removal. This is a significant step, as outliers can skew results and lead to inaccurate conclusions. By systematically applying these procedures, the preprocessing pipeline ensures that the data is clean, consistent, and ready for further analysis, forming a solid foundation for any data-driven decision-making process [12]. The list of the datasets is presented in Table 3 (Fig. 1).

For a comprehensive comparison, we include a suite of established regression methods: Linear Regression (LR) [10], Random Forest (RF) [4], Support Vector Machines (SVM) [5], Lasso, and Ridge Regression [20]. These methods are selected for their prevalence in the literature and their representation of both traditional and modern approaches to regression. Additionally, we incorporate Gradient Boosting Regression (XGBoost) models to represent the cutting-edge regression techniques [11]. The comparative methods are trained following their standard protocols, using cross-validation on each dataset. This ensures that the

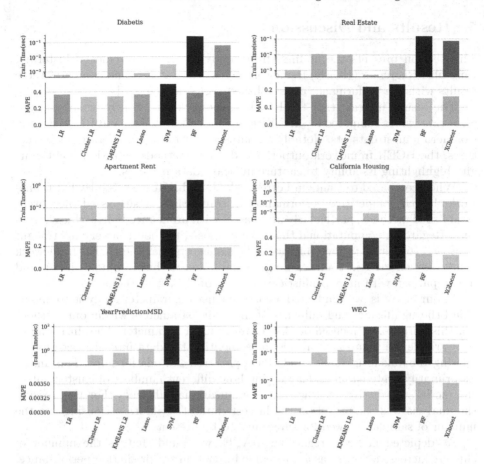

Fig. 1. Collective results from all methods in the four datasets. Each of the four figures presents a separate dataset; for each dataset, we evaluate the execution time (top plot) and the MAPE (bottom plot) of the algorithms. The x-axis presents the different methodologies used for comparisons, and the y-axis are the evaluated results metric used.

comparison is fair and that each method is given the best opportunity to perform well [15].

To evaluate the performance of the HCER framework against the comparative methods, we employ Mean Absolute Percentage Error (MAPE) [6] and collective Training Time needed [21]. These metrics provide a comprehensive view of the models' accuracy and computational cost of the model.

The computational experiments were conducted on a Ryzen 5900x-based system with 64GB of RAM. The implementation leverages programming languages and libraries well-suited for machine learning tasks, specifically Python and R. Scikit-learn was used for machine learning models, and HiPart [1, 16] was used for the clustering implementations.

5   Results and Discussion

This section presents the findings from applying the Hierarchical Clustering-Ensemble Regressor (HCER) framework across the datasets and compares these results with the performance of established regression methods.

The results indicate that the HCER framework consistently achieved lower error rate values compared to Linear Regression, SVM, Lasso, and Ridge Regression across most datasets. Notably, in datasets with complex hierarchical structures, the HCER framework outperformed other methods by a significant margin, highlighting its ability to capture intricate data patterns.

When compared to Random Forrest, SVM, and XGBoost, the HCER framework showed competitive performance. In some cases, it surpassed these well-established methods, particularly in datasets with pronounced hierarchical structure. Regarding computational time, the proposed method is a very lightweight approach compared to these methods. This suggests that the HCER framework is not only effective in traditional regression scenarios but also holds its ground in comparison with more sophisticated, state-of-the-art methods.

In our analysis, we conducted a comprehensive parameter analysis to understand the significance and influence of the main parameters within our method. For this purpose, we focused on the cluster number parameter. The cluster number variable plays an essential role in segmenting the data into distinct groups, offering valuable insights into underlying patterns and relationships. This analysis primarily centered on understanding how different numbers of clusters affect the model's predictive accuracy and computational efficiency. For this reason, the analysis was conducted on the largest dataset 'California Housing', as the number of samples allowed for subgroups to be present.

As depicted in Fig. 2 regarding MAPE, we found that as the number of clusters increased, there was a noticeable impact on the prediction performance. Firstly, there was a significant reduction in the prediction error, resulting in the cluster number range of 2 through 11. Afterward, the prediction performance declined, indicating potential overfit into local structures or noise. This finding was expected as the nature of the clustering approach leads to smaller and smaller groups. However, we can also see the method's ability to leverage the dataset's structure. In this study, we focused on something other than finding the optimal number of clusters for each dataset; however, this would be an easily applicable approach utilizing well-established methods such as the Elbow Method [19] and Silhouette Analysis [18].

Additionally, the time taken for computations was another vital aspect of our analysis. We monitored the time required for clustering and training for subsequent predictions as we varied the cluster numbers. It was observed that the computational time tended to increase linearly with a higher number of clusters. This was expected due to the additional complexity introduced by managing more clusters. The hierarchical clustering approach in this study also exhibited promising results, as anticipated. That is because we only needed to compute and train only two new models for each additional splitting step with only a small portion of the total population in contrast to using KMEANS, for example,

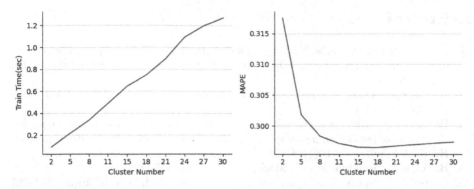

Fig. 2. Parameter evaluation on the main parameter of the methodology that is the number of clusters used to train the models upon. We evaluate the execution time (top plot) and the MAPE (bottom plot) of the proposed methodology. The x-axis presents the ascending number of clusters, and the y-axis depicts the evaluated results metric used.

where there is a need to work on the entire dataset for each different cluster number. However, the user must find a balance between the most computational efficiency and predictive accuracy.

6   Conclusion

In summary, the results from the experiments provide valuable insights into the efficacy of the HCER framework.

The superior performance of the HCER framework in datasets with complex structures can be attributed to its ability to exploit hierarchical relationships within the data. By creating specialized models for different data clusters, the framework can capture localized patterns effectively, a feature that general regression models often miss.

One of the HCER framework's key strengths is its adaptability to various data types and structures. However, in cases where such structures are not prominent or are incorrectly identified, the framework may not offer significant advantages over traditional methods.

Moreover, the presented parameter analysis allows us to understand that we can perform much better in the final regression results by parameterizing the clustering to better depict the intrinsic dataset structure.

For the next steps in our analysis, we will investigate more sophisticated regression methods as the base for our method. In our investigation, we will try to find, if possible, a comparable execution time with the HCER framework with better predictive accuracy. Lastly, we will investigate the possibility of an automated parametrization of the framework as the results of the parameter analysis we conducted present its importance.

References

1. Anagnostou, P., Tasoulis, S., Plagianakos, V.P., Tasoulis, D.: Hipart: hierarchical divisive clustering toolbox. J. Open Source Softw. **8**(84), 5024 (2023). https://doi.org/10.21105/joss.05024
2. Ari, B., Güvenir, H.A.: Clustered linear regression. Knowl.-Based Syst. **15**(3), 169–175 (2002)
3. Barmpas, P., et al.: A divisive hierarchical clustering methodology for enhancing the ensemble prediction power in large scale population studies: the athlos project. Health Inf. Sci. Syst. **10**(1), 6 (2022)
4. Breiman, L.: Random forests. Mach. Learn. **45**(1), 5–32 (2001)
5. Cortes, C., Vapnik, V.: Support-vector networks. Mach. Learn. **20**(3), 273–297 (1995)
6. De Myttenaere, A., Golden, B., Le Grand, B., Rossi, F.: Mean absolute percentage error for regression models. Neurocomputing **192**, 38–48 (2016)
7. Dormann, C.F., et al.: Collinearity: a review of methods to deal with it and a simulation study evaluating their performance. Ecography **36**(1), 27–46 (2013)
8. Dua, D., Graff, C.: Uci machine learning repository (2017). https://archive.ics.uci.edu/ml/index.php
9. Fernández-Delgado, M., Sirsat, M.S., Cernadas, E., Alawadi, S., Barro, S., Febrero-Bande, M.: An extensive experimental survey of regression methods. Neural Netw. **111**, 11–34 (2019)
10. Freedman, D.: Statistical Models: Theory and Practice. Cambridge University Press, Cambridge (2009)
11. Friedman, J.H.: Greedy function approximation: a gradient boosting machine. Ann. Stat. 1189–1232 (2001)
12. García, S., Luengo, J., Herrera, F.: Data preprocessing in predictive data mining. Knowl. Inf. Syst. **39**(1), 1–20 (2014)
13. Golalipour, K., Akbari, E., Hamidi, S.S., Lee, M., Enayatifar, R.: From clustering to clustering ensemble selection: a review. Eng. Appl. Artif. Intell. **104**, 104388 (2021)
14. Hawkins, D.M.: The problem of overfitting. J. Chem. Inf. Comput. Sci. **44**(1), 1–12 (2004)
15. Lessmann, S., Baesens, B., Mues, C., Pietsch, S.: An empirical comparison of model validation techniques for defect prediction models. IEEE Trans. Softw. Eng. **34**(4), 546–558 (2008)
16. Pedregosa, F., et al.: Scikit-learn: machine learning in python (2011). https://scikit-learn.org
17. Sagi, O., Rokach, L.: Ensemble learning: a survey. Wiley Interdisc. Rev. Data Min. Knowl. Disc. **8**(4), e1249 (2018)
18. Shi, C., Wei, B., Wei, S., Wang, W., Liu, H., Liu, J.: A quantitative discriminant method of elbow point for the optimal number of clusters in clustering algorithm. EURASIP J. Wirel. Commun. Netw. **2021**(1), 1–16 (2021)
19. Shutaywi, M., Kachouie, N.N.: Silhouette analysis for performance evaluation in machine learning with applications to clustering. Entropy **23**(6), 759 (2021)
20. Tibshirani, R.: Regression shrinkage and selection via the lasso. J. Roy. Stat. Soc.: Ser. B (Methodol.) **58**(1), 267–288 (1996)
21. Tibshirani, R.: Regression shrinkage and selection via the lasso: a retrospective. J. Roy. Stat. Soc.: Ser. B (Stat. Methodol.) **73**(3), 273–282 (2011)

Machine Learning Modeling in Industrial Processes for Visual Analysis

Antonio Morán[1]([⊠]) [iD], Serafín Alonso[1] [iD], Juan J. Fuertes[1] [iD],
Miguel A. Prada[1] [iD], Lidia Roca[2] [iD], and Manuel Domínguez[1] [iD]

[1] SUPPRESS Research Group, Escuela de Ingenierías, Universidad de León,
Campus de Vegazana, 24007 León, Spain
{a.moran,saloc,jj.fuertes,ma.prada,mdomg}@unileon.es
[2] CIEMAT-Plataforma Solar de Almería, Ctra. de Senés s/n, Tabernas,
04200 Almería, Spain
lidia.roca@psa.es
https://suppress.unileon.es

Abstract. The use of visualization tools makes it easy to analyze the operation of an industrial process. Given the large number of variables involved in today's industrial systems, it is necessary to use techniques that reduce both the size of the data and the number of samples. In addition, since industrial systems involve similar processes running in parallel, this information can be added to analyze the processes.

This paper proposes the use of a variant of self-organizing maps, Env-SOM, which allows conditioning the projection of these maps based on a set of variables. This variant is applied to operational data from AQUA-SOL II pilot plant located at the Plataforma Solar de Almería (PSA), which consists of several flat-plate collector loops that share a common water distribution pipe. Projecting the data in a conditional manner visualization maps are generated based on differences that allow to determine the existing differences between the heating loops.

Keywords: Environmental conditions · Data mining · Exploratory analysis · Self-Organizing Maps · envSOM

1 Introduction

Nowadays the complexity of the industrial process involves a great number of variables which are nonlinearly related. This complexity makes difficult to understand the dynamic and the behaviour of the industrial process. In this context, what is known as Industry 4.0 [6,11] comes into focus, since it involves the increase of industrial instrumentation that makes possible to acquire vast amount of data from many variables which can be used in order to analyze the process. For that reason, an analysis of the process by means of Knowledge Discovery and Data Mining (KDD) techniques [14] can lead to an easy and better comprehension of the process. Specially, visual data-mining techniques have proven to be very powerful techniques to manage large volumes of high-dimensional data and extract knowledge [8].

The dimensionality of the data is usually high, so it is necessary for visualizing the data to perform a dimensionality reduction [4]. Numerous algorithms have been proposed in order to visualize industrial process data via dimensionality reduction such as PCA or SNE among many others [7]. Usually industrial processes are composed of identical sub-processes that may run in parallel to guarantee a redundant operation or match the demand, so this information can be analyzed using deep autoencoders [12]. The problem of these techniques is that usually do not reduce the number of samples so the visualizations are difficult to handle. In addition, autoencoder architectures have long training times. On the contrary, we can highlight the Self-Organizing Map (SOM) [9], which is most suitable for visualizing large data sets, because it simultaneously reduces the number of samples and projects them onto a 2D map where the information can be easily interpreted [13]. The SOM has been used successfully in different industrial applications [3].

In this work, it is presented the application of visual data mining techniques based on SOM in order to analyze a real industrial process such as a solar thermal field based on flat-plate collectors. This process consists of several identical subprocess that will be compared to analyze the dissimilarities in the performance. The aim of this paper is to prove how interpretable visual information can be easily obtained and how the operation of the system can be inferred without extensive prior knowledge.

The paper is structured as follows: Sect. 2 describes the tools and algorithm used to create the visual maps to perform an inspection of the process; Sect. 3 explains the industrial process analyzed (AQUASOL-II pilot plant); Sect. 4 shows the results obtained with the different visualizations obtained from the process; and finally the conclusions are exposed in Sect. 5.

2   Comparative Analysis of Parallel Processes

The proposed methodology aims to perform a quick visual analysis of the dynamics of processes that involve a large number of variables and are composed of identical sub-processes. The Self-Organizing Map (SOM) is an excellent tool for pattern recognition and visualization [10] through the use of component planes or the u-matrix [15]. However, the organization of the neurons is not controllable when using self-organized maps. Thus, when multiple SOMs are trained for each sub-process, the arrangement of the neurons is not guaranteed to be organized in the same way, so they cannot be compared appropriately. The maps should be organized in a similar way, since the goal is to compare parallel processes that share variables. For that reason, a variant of SOM called *envSOM* [2] is used in this work. This modification allows a organization of the SOM maps conditioned on the common or environmental variables as seen in Fig. 1.

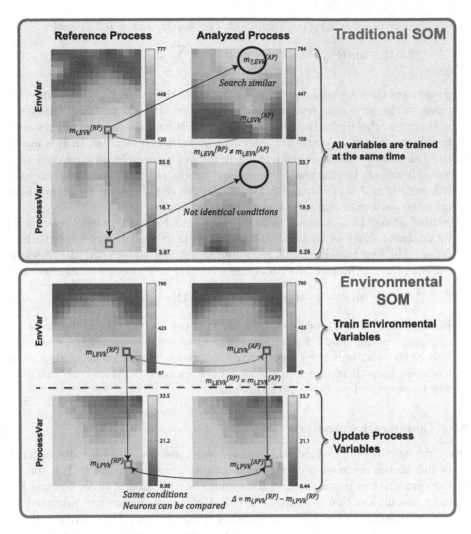

Fig. 1. Comparison of component planes using Self-Organizing Maps

2.1 Environmental Self-Organized Map

The environmental Self-Organized Map (envSOM) [2] is a variant of the traditional SOM [9] which comprises two consecutive trainings of the self-organizing map. It can be divided in two phases:

1. *First phase*: This phase consists of training a SOM using only the environmental or common variables for computing the best matching unit according to the following equation:

$$c(t) = \arg \min_i \|\mathbf{x}(t) - \mathbf{m}_i(t)\|_\omega \, , i = 1, 2, \ldots, M$$

$$\|\mathbf{x}(t) - \mathbf{m}_i(t)\|_\omega^2 = \omega \|\mathbf{x}(t) - \mathbf{m}_i(t)\|^2 = \sum_k \omega_k \left[x_k(t) - m_{ik}(t)\right]^2 \qquad (1)$$

$\mathbf{m}$ denotes the codebook vector and $\mathbf{x}$ refers to the current input sample. M refers to the number of neurons and t is the time of the sample. The equation is similar to the original one but in this case a binary mask, ω, is always used to indicate which variables are used for computing the winner. In this mask, the values are 1 or 0, depending on if the component is an environmental variable or not. In this phase, the update rule is not modified and therefore, it is similar to the traditional SOM. The result of this phase is a map where only the environmental components are organized.

2. *Second phase*: In this phase, a SOM is trained for each parallel process to be analyzed. Each of them are initialized with the codebooks from the first phase. The best matching unit is computed without considering the previous mask ω, but the update process is now modified following the next equation:

$$\mathbf{m}_i(t + 1) = \mathbf{m}_i(t) + \alpha(t)h_{ci}(t)\mathbf{\Omega}[\mathbf{x}(t) - \mathbf{m}_i(t)] \qquad (2)$$

In the second phase, a new binary mask $\mathbf{\Omega}$ is used so that its values are 0 for common variables and 1 for variables of the particular process to be analyzed. Using this mask only the process variables are updated whereas the common variables keep their values in the codebook vectors. This way, all variables will be organized properly after this phase.

2.2 Comparative Analysis

Once the envSOM is trained, the process variables are topologically ordered according to the common environmental conditions. As seen in Fig. 1, a spatial correspondence can be assumed so some maps can be used in order to compare visually the information encoded. Two kind of visualizations are proposed to analyze the similarities or differences among the processes [1]. A set of similarity features can be defined from the codebook vectors of the envSOM. These features are computed basically using the cityblock or L_1 distance between the codebooks of the envSOM of each process. Other metrics such as the Euclidean distance could be used but, in this case, it is important if the difference is positive or negative. A new codebook is generated by computing two kind of similarity features:

1. *Component-wise similarity feature*: this feature indicates the L_1 distances for a single process variable of the codebook vectors. One similarity feature is calculated for each one of the process variable by mean of the following equation:

$$m_{i,k}^{AP,RP} = L_1(AP_k, RP_k) = \left(m_{i,k}^{AP} - m_{i,k}^{RP}\right) \qquad (3)$$

where $m_{i,k}$ corresponds to the weights of the neuron i for the process component k. $m_{i,k}^{AP,RP}$ is a new codebook which size is the same as the process envSOM and it encodes the diference between the neuron weight of the Analyzed Process (AP) and the Reference Process (RP).

2. *Global similarity feature*: this feature summarizes the L_1 distances for each process component of codebook vectors. The similarity between the Analyzed Process (AP) and the Reference Process (RP) is calculated using the following equation:

$$m_{i,GS}^{AP,RP} = L_1(AP, RP) = \sum_k abs\left(m_{i,k}^{AP} - m_{i,k}^{RP}\right) \tag{4}$$

where $m_{i,GS}^{AP,RP}$ is a new feature which encodes the sum of the absolute values of similarity features.

3 Physical System and Dataset

The process to be analyzed is the solar field AQUASOL-II (Fig. 2) located at the Plataforma Solar de Almería (PSA) in Spain. This facility is a solar desalination process which makes use of the solar field to provide the thermal energy required for the operation of the desalination plant by heating water.

Fig. 2. AQUASOL-II solar field facility at PSA (Spain).

The solar field is composed of 60 stationary flat plate solar collectors (Wagner LBM 10HTF) which are connected to a thermal storage system through a heat exchanger. The solar collectors are divided in 4 loops with 14 flat plate collectors each with two rows connected in series per loop and one additional smaller loop with 4 collectors connected in parallel, which will not be used in this experiments due to its differences with regard to the other four as seen in Fig. 3.

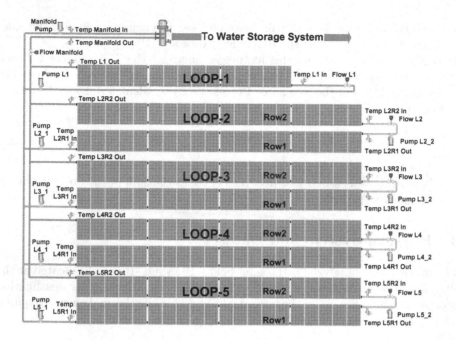

Fig. 3. Diagram of the Solar Field.

All the loops of the solar field are connected to a common manifold which delivers energy to the heat exchanger and it, in turn, to a water storage system (acting as a heat buffer). The stored hot water can be used to operate other facilities, such as a thermal desalination plant or steam generator. The manifold and each loop have a pumping system in charge of guaranteeing the flow. The solar collectors have a fixed position but they have an adjustable mirror whose angle can be modified to maximize the solar radiation that reach these collectors.

In this paper, the behaviour of this system is studied. For that, the data corresponding to the solar panel loops at AQUASOL-II will be used. More specifically, data from the loops 2, 3, 4 and 5 will be used. The loop 1 will be ignored due to the asymmetry of the panels, as it has a smaller number of panels. These loops can be considered as parallel process of the system which should operate in a similar way, while the common environment of the system is defined by manifold variables and meteorological data.

The normal operation cycle of the solar field is that the system is started up in the early morning to provide heat to the desalination plant. The operation setpoint is maintained throughout the day and the system is shut down in the late afternoon, leveraging the residual heat from the system. In normal operation, all the loops operate identically since the flow pump setpoint is the same, so the flow rate through each loop is expected to be the same, and as the panels are identical, the heat supplied to the fluid will be also the same.

Table 1. System Variables

Manifold Variable (Common Variables)		Loop Variables (Process Variables)	(Loops 2–5)
Hour		Loop N Row1 Tracker	Degrees
Humidity	%	Loop N Row2 Tracker	Degrees
Ambient Temperature	°C	Loop N Flow	m^3/s
Solar Radiation	W/m^2	Loop N Row 1 ΔTemp	°C
Manifold Flow	m^3/s	Loop N Row 2 ΔTemp	°C
Manifold ΔTemp	°C		

The variables listed in the Table 1 are used in the experiments. The inlet and outlet temperatures and flow rate in the manifold are used as common variables. Instead of using the inlet and outlet temperatures, the delta temperature in the manifold is computed (difference between inlet and outlet temperatures) because it is more promising for visualising the dynamics of the system. Additionally, humidity, ambient temperature, solar radiation and hour of the day are used as common variables for all loops in the solar field. Note that, the hour of the day is used as an indicator of whether the system is in a start-up, stationary or shut-down state. For each of the loops, two delta temperatures are computed, one for each row of collectors in the corresponding loop. Additionally, the flow rate circulating through the loop and the position of the tracking mirror in each row of collectors are used as process variables. Note that in loop 5, the both row trackers are switched off and so are not working.

In the experiments, we use data corresponding to operation cycles from the months of November, December and January. The number of operation cycles in these months is 42 and data are sampled every 10 s, so the total number of samples is 114,866. Data are preprocessed to eliminate the data corresponding to states in which the system is not operating (there are several periods in which the system is stopped), since the aim is to analyze only the operation of the system. These data are normalised to ensure that all data have the same scale, thus reducing the influence of the few data that may be outliers.

4   Results

Using the available dataset, an envSOM is trained for each loop, i.e., 4 envSOMs. Six environmental or common variables and five process variables specific to each of the loops are introduced to these envSOMs (see Table 1). In order to analyze the processes, dissimilarity features introduced in Sect. 2 will be calculated and visualized. Furthermore, traditional SOM visualizations such us the component planes, the distance matrix and the residual maps [5] will be used.

Loop 3 will be considered as the reference process (RP) since it is the most stable one and the other three loops (2, 4, 5) (AP) will be compared with regard

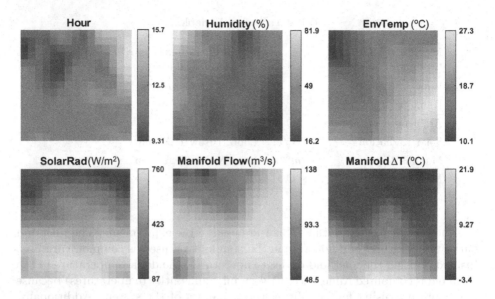

Fig. 4. EnvSOM component planes of the environmental variables for all processes.

to this loop 3. The main aim of the analysis is not obtain the optimal behavior of a heating loop but rather to find the working differences between loops. Figure 4 shows the component planes of the environmental variables. When using env-SOM, these visualizations are identical for all loops in the system, enabling the visual comparison of the process variables. As expected, a great heat transfer happens at high values of solar radiation at noon.

Figure 5 shows the component planes of the process variables from the loop 3 (RP). In this case, only the variables corresponding to the reference loop are shown because the main idea is to compare the identical processes. It can be seen that the heat flow delivered to the collectors is directly related to the heat flow in the manifold (see Figs. 4 and 5). The distance map for loop 3 (RP) is shown in Fig. 6 in order to analyze the dynamics of the process. Note that, this distance matrix is calculated with all variables (both environmental and process ones). As the process is continuous and only data from operation cycles are used, there are no marked areas in the distance plane, i.e., there are no large jumps in adjacent areas. Therefore, it does not provide relevant information on the dynamics of this process.

Before calculating the dissimilarity features, the residual maps are calculated for the loops 2, 4 and 5 (AP) with regard to loop 3 (RP). These residual maps are obtained by calculating the difference between the state estimated by the winning neuron in the envSOM corresponding to the loop 3 and the data corresponding to the loop to be analyzed (2, 4 and 5). These differences are presented as a continuous colour image, revealing differences in the analyzed process. As seen in Fig. 7, loops 4 and 5 have differences with regard to loop 3. These differences are particularly evident in the tracker variable of the loop 5, but the continuous

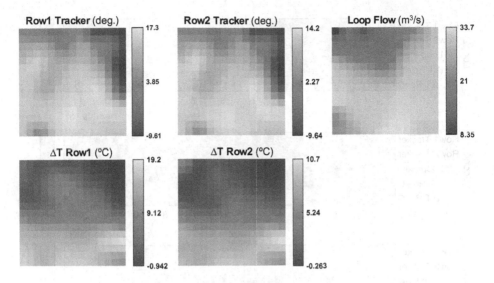

Fig. 5. EnvSOM component planes of the process variables corresponding to the loop 3.

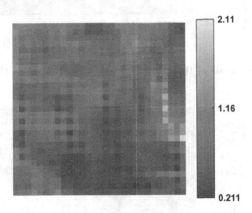

Fig. 6. Distance matrix of the Loop3 envSOM.

nature of this visualisation does not allow us to identify the moment at which these differences occur.

Finally, global and component-wise dissimilarity features are computed and the corresponding visualizations using these values are presented. On the one hand, the global difference maps for each analyzed loop (2, 4, and 5) are shown in Fig. 8. Analyzing these maps, it can be seen that the loop 2 shows few differences whereas the loop 5 has great divergences. The global map indicates the existence of differences but it does not reveal which variables are influential and determine these variations, so it is convenient to analyze each variable individually.

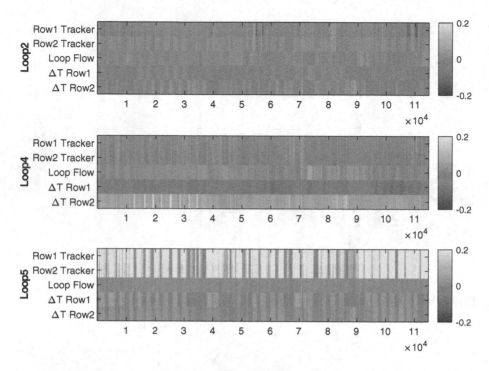

Fig. 7. Residuals of the loops 2, 4 and 5 referenced to the loop 3.

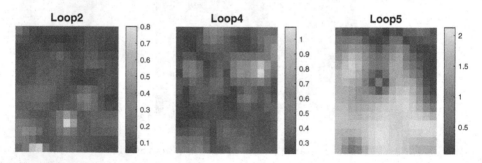

Fig. 8. Global similarity map for loop 2, 4 and 5 referred to loop3.

Figure 9 shows detailed maps of the differences by each component, giving us more information about the deviation in the behaviour of each of the loops (2, 4 and 5) with respect to the reference loop 3. These maps are centred on 0 and the difference is scaled to the maximum value and shown in percentage, so that they can be compared among variables. A green colour on a certain map indicates that there is no deviation for that variable, while a yellow colour indicates a positive deviation and a blue colour indicates a negative deviation. By analysing these maps together with the maps in Fig. 4, which shows the behaviour of the

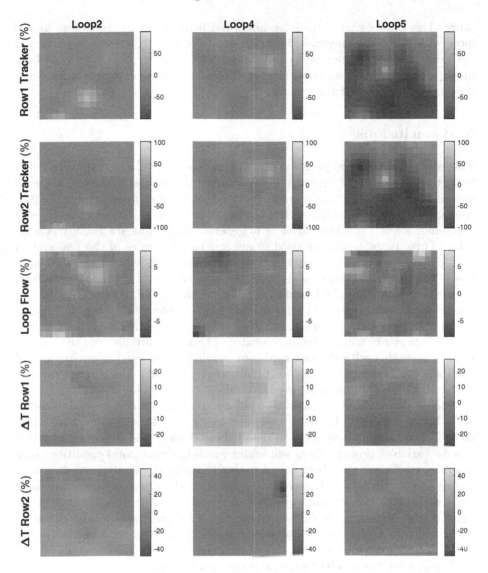

Fig. 9. Component-wise similarity map for loop 2, 4 and 5 referred to loop3.

common variables of the process, it is possible to determine at what time and conditions these deviations take place.

Focusing on maps corresponding to the loop 5 (see Fig. 9), it can be seen that the main differences happen in the solar trackers which confirms that these devices are turned off. Despite of this, the deviations that take place in the delta temperature are quite small. The most deviated temperature values appear in loop 4, where it can be seen that the first row of collectors provides a greater delta temperature while the second row provides a smaller increase of temperature. This proves that there is an abnormal behavior in the collectors in this loop, which should be reviewed by maintenance staff. Furthermore, a particular deviation in row 2 of the loop 4 can be observed. If it is correlated with the hour map (see Fig. 4), we can confirm that these deviations in temperature occur during the shutdown of the process.

5   Conclusions

This paper presents an application of a variant of self-organizing maps called env-SOM that makes use of common or environmental variables to achieve a spatial ordering of neurons during the training, with the aim of comparing identical processes. Moreover, it is proposed the computation of global and component-wise dissimilarity features which allow us to generate maps that are visually comparable. These maps have been used to analyze the dynamics of the real system and compare processes that are identical and are surrounded by the same conditions. The proposed methodology has been applied to real operation data from a solar field located at the Plataforma Solar de Almería (PSA) in Spain. It consists of four identical parallel solar heating loops in charge of producing energy which is delivered to a common manifold and then, used for desalination or o for produce steam with a steam generator. The main variables of the common manifold together with the meteorological conditions are used as environmental variables. Representative variables from each loop such as delta temperatures, flow and trackers are used as process variables.

Global similarity maps allow us to discover visually the existence of differences between each of the loops whereas component-wise similarity maps allow us to inspect and analyze more in detail these divergences, determining which process variables provoke them and under which environmental conditions take place them. The use of these visual tools facilitates the analysis of data in a simple and fast way since training and generating the maps requires little time.

Regarding to this system, operating deviations have been discovered in the loops 4 (the delta temperature corresponding to each row is totally different, likely due to a fault) and 5 (the solar trackers do not work, nevertheless the behavior of this loop is quite similar to the reference loop 3).

Future work will involve further automation of the process in order to achieve more accurate detection of faults and deviations in the process. Another improvement would be to incorporate other relevant information about the dynamics of the process in order to achieve a better understanding and comparison of the processes.

Acknowledgements. This work was supported by the Spanish State Research Agency, MCIN/ AEI/ 10.13039/ 501100011033 under Grant PID2020-117890RB-I00 and Grant PID2020-115401GB-I00.

References

1. Alonso, S., Domínguez, M., Prada, M.A., Sulkava, M., Hollmén, J.: Comparative analysis of power consumption in university buildings using envSOM. In: Gama, J., Bradley, E., Hollmén, J. (eds.) IDA 2011. LNCS, vol. 7014, pp. 10–21. Springer, Heidelberg (2011). https://doi.org/10.1007/978-3-642-24800-9_4
2. Alonso, S., Sulkava, M., Prada, M.A., Domínguez, M., Hollmén, J.: EnvSOM: a SOM algorithm conditioned on the environment for clustering and visualization. In: WSOM 2011 8th International Workshop on Self-Organizing Maps, Espoo, Finland (2011)
3. Bertolini, M., Mezzogori, D., Neroni, M., Zammori, F.: Machine learning for industrial applications: a comprehensive literature review. Expert Syst. Appl. **175**, 114820 (2021). https://doi.org/10.1016/j.eswa.2021.114820. https://www.sciencedirect.com/science/article/pii/S095741742100261X
4. Carreira-Perpiñán, M.Á.: A review of dimension reduction techniques. Technical Report. CS–96–09. Department of Computer Science, University of Sheffield (1996)
5. Cuadrado Vega, A.A., Díaz Blanco, I., Díez González, A.B., Obeso Carrera, F., González, J.A.: Visual data mining and monitoring in steel processes. In: Records of the Industry Applications Conference. 37th IAS Annual Meeting, vol. 1, pp. 493–500 (2002)
6. Fuertes, J.J., Prada, M.A., Rodríguez-Ossorio, J.R., González-Herbón, R., Pérez, D., Domínguez, M.: Environment for education on Industry 4.0. IEEE Access **9**, 144395–144405 (2021). https://doi.org/10.1109/ACCESS.2021.3120517
7. Joswiak, M., Peng, Y., Castillo, I., Chiang, L.H.: Dimensionality reduction for visualizing industrial chemical process data. Control Eng. Pract. **93**, 104189 (2019). https://doi.org/10.1016/j.conengprac.2019.104189. https://www.sciencedirect.com/science/article/pii/S0967066119301728
8. Keim, D.A., Sips, M., Ankerst, M.: Visual data-mining techniques. In: Visualization Handbook, pp. 831–843. Butterworth-Heinemann, Burlington (2005). https://doi.org/10.1016/B978-012387582-2/50045-9. https://www.sciencedirect.com/science/article/pii/B9780123875822500459
9. Kohonen, T.: Self-Organizing Maps, 3rd edn. Springer, Heidelberg (1995). https://doi.org/10.1007/978-3-642-56927-2
10. Kohonen, T., Oja, E., Simula, O., Visa, A., Kangas, J.: Engineering applications of the self-organizing map. Proc. IEEE **84**(10), 1358–84 (1996)
11. Lasi, H., Fettke, P., Kemper, H.G., Feld, T., Hoffmann, M.: Industry 4.0. Bus. Inf. Syst. Eng. **6**(4), 239–242 (2014)
12. Morán, A., Alonso, S., Prada, M.A., Fuertes, J.J., Díaz, I., Domínguez, M.: Analysis of parallel process in HVAC systems using deep autoencoders. In: Boracchi, G., Iliadis, L., Jayne, C., Likas, A. (eds.) EANN 2017. CCIS, vol. 744, pp. 15–26. Springer, Cham (2017). https://doi.org/10.1007/978-3-319-65172-9_2
13. Stefanovič, P., Kurasova, O.: Visual analysis of self-organizing maps. Nonlinear Anal. Model. Control **16**(4), 488-504 (2011). https://doi.org/10.15388/NA.16.4.14091. https://www.journals.vu.lt/nonlinear-analysis/article/view/14091
14. Venkatasubramanian, V., Rengaswamy, R., Kavuri, S., Yin, K.: A review of process fault detection and diagnosis part iii: process history based methods. Comput. Chem. Eng. **27**(3), 327–346 (2003)
15. Vesanto, J.: SOM-based data visualization methods. Intell. Data Anal. **3**(2), 111–126 (1999)

Machine Learning Modeling to Provide Assistance to Basketball Coaches

Eduardo Véras Argento[1]([✉]), Marley Vellasco[1], José Franco Amaral[2], Karla Figueiredo[2], and Meyer Nigri[1]

[1] Pontifical Catholic University of Rio de Janeiro, Rio de Janeiro, Brazil
eduardoverasargento@gmail.com
[2] Rio de Janeiro State University, Rio de Janeiro, Brazil
franco@eng.uerj.br

Abstract. This study proposes the development of decision-support systems, based on neural networks and k-Nearest Neighbors (kNNs) techniques. The goal is to evaluate, for each substitution during a match, which group of players on the court, known as lineup, has a higher probability of outperforming their opponent. The developed model was tested using a database obtained from Brazilian Basketball League (NBB) matches, involving players statistics, match details and different contexts. The model achieved an accuracy of 76,99% in projections of superiority between the playing lineups, demonstrating the potential of using computational intelligence methods in decision-making applied to professional sports. Finally, the study highlights the importance of using such tools in conjunction with human experience, encouraging future research for the development of even more sophisticated and effective models for decision-making in the sports field.

Keywords: Neural Networks · K Nearest Neighbours · Basketball · Sports analytics · Basketball analytics · Artificial intteligence · Lineup performance inference · Prediction · Decision support

1 Introduction

In light of the recent significant growth in technological capabilities and observed advancements in the field of computational intelligence, the latter has demonstrated potential for application across various sectors of society. In the context of extreme competitiveness and growing relevance in the most famous sports around the world, decision-support systems capable of enhancing the efficacy and consistency of team victories in championships are becoming increasingly frequent.

Professional sports, especially basketball, are increasingly driven by technological innovations and methodological advances, as shown in recent studies [7,8,14]. The complexity of basketball, with its dynamic gameplay and extensive data collection, offers an ideal opportunity for the application of machine learning techniques and computational intelligence [9]. This sport, characterized by highly competitive and unpredictable games, creates an environment where even small advantages can significantly impact a team's performance. The direct application of advanced data analysis for real-time decision-making represents an emerging and promising area of study [6,13].

A prominent demonstration of the application of intelligent systems within the sports domain, particularly in basketball, is illustrated by the study of [10], wherein the authors conduct a study applying neural networks in conjunction with fusion to predict the outcomes of future games, and compare this prediction with the opinions of various experts from the global basketball community. Another interesting application of neural networks in the basketball universe is observed in [3]. In the mentioned work, an advanced graph neural network is implemented, which is meticulously trained with a vast amount of data derived from the National Basketball Association (NBA). The primary goal of this implementation is to provide an auxiliary tool for the formation of basketball teams, aiming for a substantial improvement in team performance during games.

In this work, the focus is on developing and applying a machine learning-based predictive model to improve real-time decision-making in professional basketball. Based on the instant and accumulated statistics up to the moment of the match, the aim is to assist coaches in selecting the ideal lineup on the court. This study is conducted in the context of a Brazilian Basketball League (NBB), one of the main professional basketball leagues, providing a competitive and challenging environment for research. The use of such database for training and validating the models allows it's use in any other competitive context.

The project involved several critical stages: obtaining and evaluating a robust database, preprocessing the data, training and optimizing neural networks, and the practical application of the system. The data used includes over 270,000 records of ball possessions in games from 2013 to 2019, with 152 attributes related to the individual and collective performance of players, as well as details of ball possessions. Detailed manual work was carried out to select the most relevant variables and analyze the data in conjunction with sports experts, followed by an analysis of the key variable distributions and the output classes. During the process, some methods were used, such as variable selection, normalization and data fitting, and the application of computational intelligence mechanisms.

After preprocessing and selecting variables, as well as defining the prediction methods, the system was trained using the mentioned database. An exhaustive search was conducted to optimize the most relevant parameters of the system, such as the learning rate, the neural network structure, the number of neighbors in the kNN, among others. Finally, the system was applied to provide information on the best lineup to face a specific opposing lineup in real time, providing a valuable tool for coaches during games.

The main contribution of this work is to provide a new class of computational intelligence application in sports, combined with result optimization. The developed tools are valuable for increasing the competitiveness of the teams that use them, representing significant commercial value in the sports industry.

The main contributions include the classification of ball possession sequences, numerical predictions of results, and definitions of the best lineup in real time, assisting coaches in game strategies and increasing the teams' chances of success. This work also aims to contribute to the growing body of research on the application of machine learning and artificial intelligence in sports, highlighting the importance of balancing technology and human intuition in sports decisions [3,10,12].

2   System Conception

In developing machine learning models for basketball game analysis, data from individual ball possessions are structured and prepared. Basketball's balanced nature means a team's technical edge doesn't always lead to immediate scoring or defense success, presenting a challenge in predicting individual possession outcomes.

To enhance predictive accuracy, a data aggregation strategy groups sequences of possessions without player substitutions on either team. This allows assessing whether teams are balanced or if one has a consistent technical advantage, which could affect the game's outcome after a sequence of possessions.

The focus is on analyzing medium and long-term trends in the game, using the points balance from these possession sequences as the prediction target for machine learning models. The approach divides the models into two stages: the first categorizes a sequence of possessions into classes like "advantage," "disadvantage," or "equality," based on score differentials, which is the difference in scores between the two teams. The second stage forecasts the actual point differential for more accurate value predictions.

For both cases there are two methods implemented: Artificial neural networks (ANNs) and k-Nearest Neighbours (kNNs). A parameter optimization is evaluated in each model for each stage. As long as the best parameters are found, both models are trained and aggregated to the system.

This two-stage approach, illustrated in Fig. 1, creates a robust and versatile prediction system for basketball games, offering detailed insights into team performance and expected outcomes over sequences of possessions.

The database used in this work is provided by the Basketball Brazillian League, *"Novo Basquete Brasil"* (NBB). Which is structured with 273 lines of instantaneous and accumulated information for each ball possession of every match in the league from 2013 to 2019. The features include team and season identifications, time elapsed, number of possessions and other statistics such as points per possession, player and lineup, accumulated fouls, turnovers, among others.

One of the most important variables is player representation. It involves a factor analysis clusterization based on collective and individual player statistics resulting in 16 clusters. This information is inputted as one variable for each cluster, which value represents the number of players from each cluster in the court. In total, there are 61 input variables on the system.

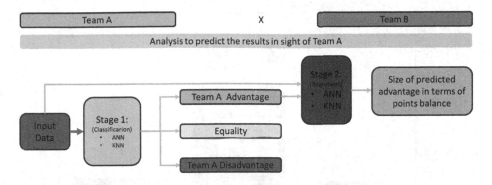

Fig. 1. Example of the stages working together in the system.

The original data presents the above features as input variables while considers the possession result as the target. Instead adopting this approach directly, a new database is first created through data transformation. It considers that each new observation is a sequence of original possessions where there has been no lineup change. The input values consider the first possession of each sequence, while the target value is determined by the balance of the score difference between the first and the last possession of the sequence. Using this reference adds robustness to the target forecasting.

The data is segmented into sequences with different granularity levels, considering smaller windows within larger sequences, to maximize data utilization. This method results in a comprehensive database with observations ranging from 2 to 30 consecutive possessions. While the first stage of the model doesn't include window size as an input, focusing instead on predicting a team's advantage, the second stage requires this input for estimating the point differential.

3   Results

Initially, it's noted that the representation of classes in the data is not equally represented, as observed in Fig. 2. This requires a strategy to balance the distribution. Considering the size of the dataset after prior processes, a technique of sub-sampling was chosen to equalize the representation of classes. This involves removing some entries from over-represented classes to achieve a more uniform distribution for model application, as observed in Fig. 3 and 4. The test data is maintained original in order to represent correctly the tested universe.

The implementation of this classification algorithm was based in two robust machine learning methods: Artificial Neural Networks and the k-Nearest Neighbors (kNN) algorithm. These methods were selected for their ability to handle multi-class classification problems and adaptability to various data structures [4].

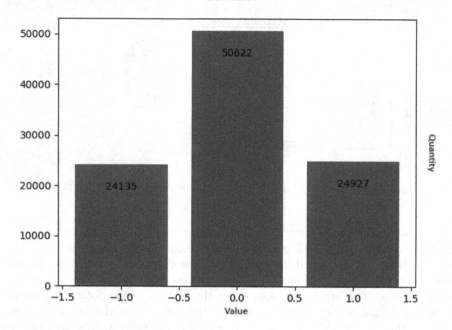

Fig. 2. Data distribution before class balancing.

The neural network was trained using different combinations of hidden layers with the ReLU activation function, while the kNN was implemented with neighbor number optimization through exhaustive search and cross-validation.

The performance evaluation of these models was primarily focused on accuracy. For optimal performance of the Neural Network, layers and neurons were selected using an exhaustive search algorithm, considering the accuracy results from validation.

As a secondary evaluation method, confusion matrices were employed for visual effect. Confusion matrices are powerful tools for evaluating machine learning model performance, particularly useful in the in-depth analysis of classification models. They visually display the model's performance in classification tasks, clearly showing the relationship between true classes and those predicted by the model [11].

3.1   Stage 1

To find the best neural network architectures, an exhaustive search algorithm was used, varying in a step of 5 neurons per layer, ranging from 10 to 80 neurons for a single hidden layer, and from 10 to 60 neurons for two hidden layers, with the second layer limited to the size of the first by heuristics [5]. A patience of 500 and a maximum of 20,000 epochs were set to ensure the algorithm had enough time to find the best weights before reaching the epoch limit. Due to a peculiarity

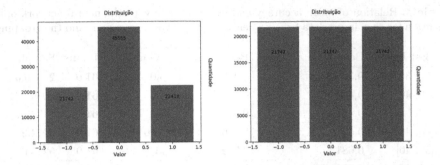

Fig. 3. Comparison between the training data distribution before and after the class balancing.

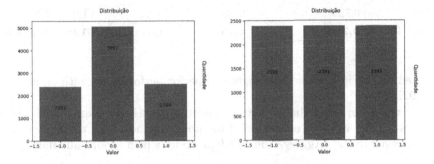

Fig. 4. Comparison between the validation data distribution before and after the class balancing.

of the Keras library, if the training stops due to reaching the maximum number of epochs before the patience criteria, the best weights are not saved. However, if the training is stopped by the patience criteria in early stopping, the best weights are preserved.

For both the neural network and kNN, Cross-Validation was employed, characterized by subdividing the dataset into smaller subsets or "folds". The model is then trained on k-1 of these folds and validated on the remaining k fold. This process is repeated multiple times, each time with a different set of folds for training and validation. This offers a more robust view of the model's performance.

The best neural network configuration was obtained with hidden layers [60, 40], as shown in Table 1, which presents the validation accuracy for choosing the network architecture. The accuracy for the test group in this configuration was 71.82%. The confusion matrix for this configuration is shown in Fig. 5.

For the kNN optimization, Grid Search Cross-Validation was used, a common technique for hyperparameter tuning [1]. It searches for the best parameter combination within a predefined set of options, such as the ideal number of neighbors for kNN. The confusion matrix for the kNN's optimized configuration

Table 1. Relation of mean accuracy and best accuracy with the neural network optimization for each input data from sequence of 5 to 15 ball possessions and the grouping.

Best Layers	Best mean accuracy	Best accuracy	Window	Inputs	Samples
[50, 30]	0,398	0,440	5,0	61,0	25686,0
[50, 40]	0,444	0,474	6,0	61,0	20162,7
[70]	0,471	0,517	8,0	61,0	13547,7
[55, 40]	0,678	0,716	10,0	61,0	5974,2
[60, 40]	0,681	0,712	11,0	61,0	5223,6
[55, 30]	0,691	0,724	13,0	61,0	2130,3
[50, 40]	0,709	0,756	15,0	61,0	1548,0
[50, 40]	0,716	0,755	14,0	61,0	1802,7
[80]	0,724	0,75	12,0	61,0	4383,9
[60, 40]	**0,753**	**0,762**	**Grouping**	**61,0**	**40794,3**

is presented in Fig. 6, showing a slightly superior performance with an accuracy of 73.92.

The results indicate that a more extended analysis of a team's performance provides a more accurate prediction of the point balance, with the highest accuracy achieved in the "Aggregation" configuration, which groups all analysis windows.

3.2   Stage 2

In the second stage of the predictive system, the focus is on quantifying the predicted class's magnitude, based on the result (advantage, disadvantage, or equality) determined in the first stage. The same Neural Network and kNN structures are employed with adjustments for the numeric nature of the problem. The goal is to predict the intensity of the advantage indicated in stage one, represented by the point difference.

A critical distinction in this stage is the inclusion of a variable representing the number of ball possessions in each sequence. This variable is crucial as it allows the model to capture the trend of a greater point differential in longer sequences compared to shorter ones.

This stage adds an extra layer of information to the predictions, enhancing the evaluation of the first stage's predictions' reliability. This two-step implementation allows a more detailed and refined analysis of team performance, providing not just a prediction of the winner of a set of possessions but also an estimate of the victory's magnitude.

A significant portion of the data shows low point balances, which fits the balanced nature of basketball. To adapt these results to a numerical universe, a piecewise linear normalization is used, matching each value or small group of values on the converted line to the same proportion represented in the database. This idea is explained on Fig. 7.

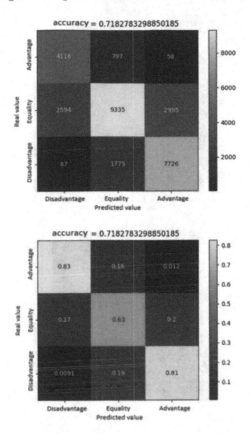

Fig. 5. Confusion matrix for the test group prediction obtained from the best neural network configuration according to optimization.

The MAPE (Mean Absolute Percentage Error) metric was used for model quality evaluation, calculated as the average of the absolute percentage differences between the forecast and the actual value, providing an idea of the error magnitude without considering direction [?]. Lower MAPE values indicate higher accuracy in model forecasts.

Scatter diagrams were used to visualize and understand how predictions align with actual values. These diagrams offer a clear visual representation of the relationship between model predictions and real outcomes, quickly identifying where the model is accurate or erring and any systematic trends in the model's errors.

In summary, the second stage of the system provides a more sophisticated and accurate assessment of team performance, significantly impacting team strategies and decision-making in basketball games.

Following a similar approach to the first stage, this stage differed primarily in the use of the MAPE metric for result evaluation.

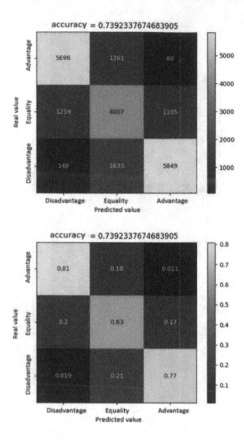

Fig. 6. Confusion matrix for the validation group prediction obtained from the kNN optimization.

Using the same optimization structure for neural network hidden layers, but with MAPE as the evaluation parameter, optimization results were documented. The results, shown in Table 2, considered segments from 10 to 15 ball possessions and a "Grouping" of segments. Shorter segments were excluded due to consistently low viable results. The findings indicated that broader analysis windows correlated with lower errors, suggesting that a comprehensive view of team performance enables more accurate point margin predictions. The "Grouping," encompassing all analysis windows, continued to exhibit the lowest error, implying that a larger data set significantly enhances model performance.

Table 2 provides insight into how the number of ball possessions in the analysis window affects the MAPE calculation in the model's prediction. This information is crucial for the system's continuous optimization.

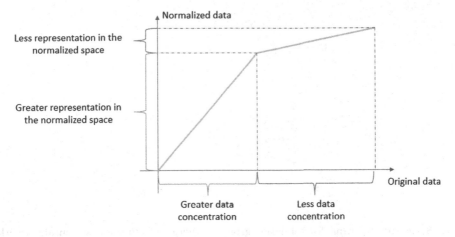

Fig. 7. Example of the functioning of piecewise linear normalization.

Table 2. Relation of average MAPE and best MAPE obtained with neural network optimization for each input data from sequences of 10 ball possessions to 15 and grouping of windows from 8 to 15.

Best layers	Sequence size (possessions)	Lowest average MAPE	Lowest MAPE
[65]	10	0,288	0,267
[50, 40]	11	0,310	0,289
[50, 40]	12	0,288	0,259
[65]	13	0,286	0,254
[45, 30]	14	0,272	0,249
[60, 40]	15	0,292	0,266
[60, 40]	Grouping	0,241	0,235

Scatter diagrams visualizing the best window combination from Table 2 are shown in Figs. 8 and 9, presenting validation and test results.

The best configuration for this stage was achieved with a grouping of 8 to 15 windows, resulting in a MAPE of 23.39%. The configuration choice was also based on scatter diagrams, with Figs. 8 and 9 showcasing the model's accuracy for forecasting both small and larger points balance values.

The kNN algorithm showed slightly lower performance. Using the grid search method, optimal hyperparameters "number of neighbors" and "type of weight" were determined. The best MAPE value for the same test group was 26.59%, using 9 nearest neighbors and distance-weighted. The "MAPE" results of the grouping and corresponding scatter diagram are in Table 3 and Fig. 10.

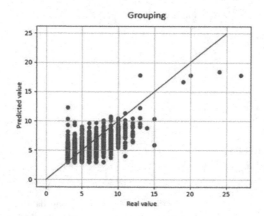

Fig. 8. Scatter diagrams for validation group predictions from the best neural network configuration, using the grouping of 8 to 15 ball possession windows.

Table 3. Relation of "MAPE" obtained with kNN optimization for each input data from the window 8 to 15 and the windows grouping.

Sequence size (possessions)	MAPE_Test (%)
8	26,59
9	26,37
10	26,01
11	55,84
12	37,74
13	54,03
14	51,1
15	35,51
Grouping	28,67

Observing the results demonstrated in this section, it is evident that Stage 1 yilds a relatively high accuracy. This provides an advantageous forecast that can assist coaches in visualizing lineup duels during the match.

However, considering that the first stage already provides an expectation about the situation in question, the interpretation of the second stage results becomes clearer. It provides a sense of the intensity of the difference observed in the first stage. Therefore, although the model's fluctuation may be more uncertain when it returns a low value, if the value is higher, it confirms the pointed advantage with greater certainty.

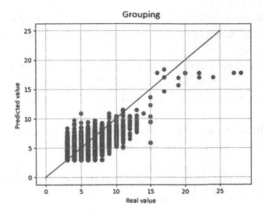

Fig. 9. Scatter diagrams for test group predictions from the best neural network configuration, using the grouping of 8 to 15 ball possession windows.

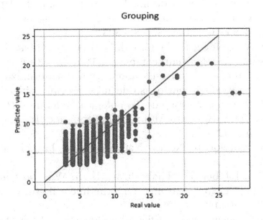

Fig. 10. Scatter diagrams test group predictions from the best kNN configuration, using the grouping of ball possession sequences.

4   Conclusion

This project developed an advanced decision-support system for basketball, using Neural Networks and k-Nearest Neighbors (kNN) algorithms. The system operates in two stages to predict basketball game outcomes: first, identifying which team has the advantage, and second, estimating the extent of this advantage. The innovative approach allows for ranking team combinations based on their likelihood of success in specific game scenarios.

Key findings include the importance of analyzing a broader range of ball possession data for more accurate predictions. The system's performance was enhanced by optimizing the kNN algorithm through Grid Search Cross-Validation, which helped fine-tune the model according to specific data trends.

Visual tools like confusion matrices and scatter diagrams aid in interpreting the predictive results, making the system practical for strategic planning in real-time basketball games.

Future enhancements might involve refining the model with new parameters and data types and exploring other machine learning techniques. The goal is to provide a more comprehensive tool for basketball coaching, potentially applicable to other sports.

Despite some limitations, this project demonstrates the potential of artificial intelligence in sports analytics and decision-making.

Acknowledgements. This work was supported in part by the Conselho Nacional de Desenvolvimento e Pesquisa (CNPq).

References

1. Adnan, M., Alarood, A.A.S., Uddin, M.I., Ur Rehman, I.: Utilizing grid search cross-validation with adaptive boosting for augmenting performance of machine learning models. PeerJ Comput. Sci. **8**, e803 (2022)
2. De Myttenaere, A., Golden, B., Le Grand, B., Rossi, F.: Mean absolute percentage error for regression models. Neurocomputing **192**, 38–48 (2016)
3. Diniz, E.M.F.: Diamond Hoop: uma abordagem para otimização na composição de equipes no basquetebol com o uso de inteligência artificial sobre estatísticas pregressas. B.S. thesis, Universidade Tecnológica Federal do Paraná (2023)
4. Han, J., Pei, J., Tong, H.: Data Mining: Concepts and Techniques. Morgan kaufmann, Burlington (2022)
5. Heaton, J.: Introduction to Neural Networks with Java. Heaton Research Inc., Chesterfield (2008)
6. Kapadia, K., Abdel-Jaber, H., Thabtah, F., Hadi, W.: Sport analytics for cricket game results using machine learning: an experimental study. Appl. Comput. Inf. **18**(3/4), 256–266 (2020)
7. Li, B., Xu, X.: Application of artificial intelligence in basketball sport. J. Educ. Health Sport **11**(7), 54–67 (2021)
8. Li, H., Zhang, M.: Artificial intelligence and neural network-based shooting accuracy prediction analysis in basketball. Mob. Inf. Syst. **2021**, 1–11 (2021)
9. Liu, Z.: Application of artificial intelligence technology in basketball games. In: IOP Conference Series: Materials Science and Engineering, vol. 750, p. 012093. IOP Publishing (2020)
10. Loeffelholz, B., Bednar, E., Bauer, K.W.: Predicting NBA games using neural networks. J. Quant. Anal. Sports **5**(1) (2009)
11. Monard, M.C., Baranauskas, J.A.: Conceitos sobre aprendizado de máquina. Sistemas inteligentes-Fundamentos e aplicações **1**(1), 32 (2003)
12. Pretorius, A., Parry, D.A.: Human decision making and artificial intelligence: a comparison in the domain of sports prediction. In: Proceedings of the Annual Conference of the South African Institute of Computer Scientists and Information Technologists, pp. 1–10 (2016)
13. Singh, N.: Sport analytics: a review. Learning **9**, 11 (2020)
14. Yang, Z.: Research on basketball players' training strategy based on artificial intelligence technology. In: Journal of Physics: Conference Series, vol. 1648, p. 042057. IOP Publishing (2020)

Understanding Users' Confidence in Spoken Queries for Conversational Search Systems

Youjing Yu[1]([✉]), Zhengxiang Shi[2], and Aldo Lipani[2]

[1] University of Cambridge, Cambridge, UK
yy471@cam.ac.uk
[2] University College London, London, UK
{zhengxiang.shi.19,aldo.lipani}@ucl.ac.uk

Abstract. The confidence level in users' speech has long been recognised as an important signal in traditional dialogue systems. In this work, we highlight the importance of user confidence detection in *queries* in conversational search systems (CSSs). Accurately estimating a user's confidence level in CSSs is important because it enables the CSSs to infer the degree of competency of a user on the queried topic and subsequently tailor its responses appropriately. This is especially important in CSSs since their responses need to be concise and precise. However, few prior works have evaluated user confidence in CSSs due to a lack of available datasets. We present a novel speech-based dataset named UNderstanding Spoken qUeRiEs (UNSURE) (Code and instructions on how to obtain this dataset is available at https://github.com/YoujingYu99/confidence_css), which contains confidence grading annotations of user queries in natural language conversations. Based on this dataset, we propose a multimodal approach to infer users' confidence in spoken queries as a baseline model. Preliminary experimental results demonstrate that our proposed fusion model is capable of achieving near human-level performance.

Keywords: user understanding · conversational search · conversational system

1 Introduction

Conversational search systems (CSSs) enable users to engage in mixed-initiative interactions by expressing their queries in natural language and interacting with the system through multiple turns of exchanges [9,15,24]. Compared to the use of written language, the use of speech in CSSs can make these interactions more convenient, as the use of hands is not required. However, the amount of information that CSSs can convey at any given turn is limited. This makes it crucial to present the user with not just the most relevant answer, but also an answer that is appropriate for the user's level of understanding and expertise [25,28].

© The Author(s), under exclusive license to Springer Nature Switzerland AG 2024
L. Iliadis et al. (Eds.): EANN 2024, CCIS 2141, pp. 405–418, 2024.
https://doi.org/10.1007/978-3-031-62495-7_31

Brennan and Williams [1] suggested that successful communication requires the person to accurately estimate and monitor not only this person's own knowledge state but also the knowledge state of their conversational partners. Inferring how well someone else knows something is termed as the Feeling of Another's Knowledge, or FOAK [1]. The listener's perception of a speaker's expressed confidence or FOAK allows the listener to infer the knowledge state of the speaker. If the speaker raises a query, the listener's perception of the speaker's confidence level in this query is important for the listener to infer about the speaker's knowledge state and subsequently make a decision on how and what to reply [19]. This is backed by many studies which find that there exists a positive relationship between confidence in a person's voice and their expertise in the field of the conversational topic [6, 18, 21]

In the context of CSSs, where the listener is the system, a successful evaluation of the perceived confidence level in the user's voice enables CSSs to obtain a deeper understanding of the user's desires, beliefs, and intentions as well as the situational and conversational context, and thus the search can be enhanced. For example, in the context of CSSs for education, if a user asks the system: "What does hypothesis mean?" and the system deems the user's confidence level to be high, the system may hence infer that the user has some expertise in the field of statistics and proceed to suggest the formal definition: "a supposition or proposed explanation made on the basis of limited evidence as a starting point for further investigation." In contrast, if the system deems the user's confidence level to be low, the system may infer that the user has limited prior knowledge in the field of statistics and suggest a simpler explanation: "a possible explanation that may not be correct."

Despite its importance, user confidence in CSSs has not been systematically studied, with few works assessing user confidence in conversations. The major challenge is the lack of appropriate datasets. A summary of the available datasets that focus on human confidence detection in speech is presented in Table 1. The existing datasets are mostly collected from Question Answering (QA) conversations. They focus on confidence detection in the speech of the person *answering* the question, which is mostly of assertive or declarative nature. On the other hand, there is no available dataset that specifically focuses on queries or interrogative speech. To tackle the aforementioned issues, we propose a new dataset named UNSURE, which stands for UNderstanding Spoken qUeRiEs. This dataset is based on the Spotify Podcast Dataset [3], which contains queries raised by either the interviewer or the interviewee during podcast sessions and their corresponding confidence scores annotated by Amazon Mechanical Turk (MTurk) workers. In addition, We propose a fusion (speech and text) model to predict the confidence scores as a baseline model for this task.

The rest of the paper is organised as follows: Sect. 2 outlines the related works in the field of emotion recognition in speech and confidence assessment. Section 3 describes the methodologies for the collection, labelling and processing of the dataset. Section 4 describes the confidence prediction task, and Sect. 5 describes the fusion model. Section 6 presents the results and discussions of the proposed fusion model. Finally, we conclude in Sect. 7.

Table 1. Summary of the statistics of the existing datasets and our proposed dataset **UNSURE**.

	Size	Raters	Score Range	Annotations Performed on	Other Limitations
Nair et al. [19]	254	3	0–100	Self-introductions	Size too small
Chanda et al. [2]	1 242	2	3 Categories	Audiovisual answers	Number of raters
Pon-Barry [23]	1 700	6	5 Categories	Answers to handwritten digits	Limited Topics
Martin et al. [16]	956	-	0–4	Answers to colour names	Limited Topics
UNSURE	4 542	3	0–5	Queries	-

2 Related Work

Nair et al. [19] conducted an initial investigation into the prediction of speakers' confidence and evaluated the performance of different neural network structures on this task. Their dataset consists of two parts: the first is based on recordings of university students' self-introductions, and the second is based on an audio dataset from Kaggle. Chanda et al. [2] also created an audiovisual dataset based on a collection of interviews, which contains the interviewees' answers to questions raised by interviewers. Pon-Barry [23] prepared The Harvard Uncertainty Speech Corpus, where participants view a train route illustration and answer a question about the train timings. The images of the digits presented to participants are taken from the handwritten MNIST dataset and vary in terms of ambiguity and legibility, representing a measure of certainty about the identity of the digit. However, the Harvard Uncertainty Speech Corpus is limited in scope to the topic of digits and does not provide a comprehensive understanding of confidence in the context of CSSs.

Another existing dataset is prepared by Martin et al. [16], where participants were asked to name the colour they saw, and the entropy level associated with each colour was calculated based on the number of unique names that participants have given each colour. Apart from the limited range of conversational topics, we point out another very important limitation here: while the calculation of confidence based on the number of names each colour has been called is a clear and well-defined approach for the domain of colour, it is very difficult to generalise this approach to other domains where the context is much more complicated. Most importantly, all of the aforementioned datasets are recordings of conversations, which mainly contain declarative speech rather than questions or queries. Hence their use is limited in CSSs, as the emphasis is placed on queries raised by users.

3 The UNSURE Dataset

We propose a new dataset built upon the Spotify Podcast Dataset, named UNSURE. The UNSURE dataset contains a total of 4 542 audio samples, each of which is one query sentence. We now describe the steps we took to generate this dataset.

3.1 Dataset Collection

Pre-processing. We first pre-process the Spotify Podcast Dataset with its word-level transcription files. Firstly, we selected podcasts within certain categories: Business, Government, History, News, Science, Religion & Spirituality, Society & Culture and Technology. This is done to make sure to cover a wide range of topics and to select queries that the users are more likely to ask CSSs. From the transcription files, we then *filter out* the podcasts and sentences based on the following criteria. At a podcast level, we removed (1) podcasts with only one speaker since we prefer conversations and not monologues; (2) podcasts that are clean of interjecting sounds (e.g., "hmm", "oh", etc.) since the absence of these sounds is a sign of edited podcasts; we want unedited podcasts to capture the authenticity of speech. This is backed by the study by Brennan and Williams [1] that confirmed that a listener's perceived confidence in the speaker is largely affected by the presence of fillers and interjecting sounds. At a sentence level, we removed (1) sentences which contain more than one speaker tag since multiple speakers in one audio clip may affect the consistency of the tonal quality when used for training and (2) sentences which are shorter than 2 seconds as these are deemed too short to provide enough context.

Annotation Process. A total of 7 919 audio clips are sampled and uploaded to MTurk for crowd-workers to grade the confidence of the audio clip from 0 to 5, with an interval of 0.5 (0 = very unconfident, 5 = very confident). Each MTurk Human Intelligence Task (HIT) is annotated by three crowd-workers. In the instructions section of the HIT, three sample audio clips are provided for reference, which the authors of this paper deem to have a confidence score of 0, 2.5 and 5. In the answers section, workers rate the confidence level of the speaker. In addition, they have to answer two questions: the first (Q1) to identify whether the speaker in the audio clip is asking a question and the second (Q2) to identify whether there are multiple speakers in the audio. These two questions are also used to verify the answers of the crowd workers.

Out of the 7 919 audio clips, 219 samples of audio clips are from the verification set we prepared for quality control purposes. The authors of this paper listened to each of the sample clips and gave answers to Q1 and Q2. Each HIT consists of 12 audio clips to which the crowd-worker gives a score and answers Q1 and Q2 for each clip. Two out of the 12 clips are from the verification set. Hence, we set a threshold of 50%, and workers who answered more than 50% of the verification questions wrong are deemed to be giving random answers instead of truthful answers and hence rejected. The rejected HITs are then republished for new workers to work on. After seven rounds of rejection and republishing, we collect the results, which are now deemed truthful.

Having gathered data for 7 919 audio clips, using Q1 and Q2, we filter out the clips which are not questions, contain more than one speaker and are assessed by fewer than 3 workers. The final dataset consists of 4 542 audio clips. Since the workers are given example audio clips and the associated confidence scores, and only results from workers deemed truthful are accepted, no normalisation is done

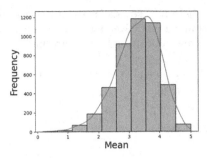 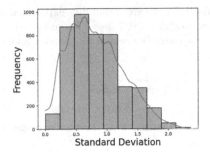

Fig. 1. Histograms for mean scores (left) and standard deviation (right) of each audio.

on the scores the workers gave to avoid introducing potentially artificial agreements. Table 1 compares our dataset with other datasets available for assessing user confidence. It is important to note that our dataset is not only relatively large with a suitable number of raters, but it is also entirely query-based, which is useful in the context of CSSs.

3.2 Dataset Analysis

Scores Distribution. For the average score of three scores given for 4 542 audio samples, the exact number of scores in each category is 16, 168, 1099, 2375 and 884. Half of the samples have a score between 3 and 4 (relatively confident), while very few samples have a score between 0 and 1 (extremely unconfident). The histogram for the mean and standard deviation of the scores per audio are plotted in Fig. 1. The mean for the audio scores centred around 3.5, which is slightly higher than the mean of the scoring range of 2.5. This is expected since the audio samples were extracted from podcasts; we would expect the speakers to have more confidence in their voice since the topic of conversation is usually in their domain of expertise. However, this also means that we have more samples which are fairly confident compared to samples which are not confident at all. The standard deviation for the audio follows averaged around 0.7, which means that the scores are fairly close together. However, the presence of many audio samples with a standard deviation greater than 1.0 indicates disagreement in the crowd-workers' judgement.

Rater Agreement. To understand and quantify how well the crowd-workers agree with each other, we measure the inter-rater reliability [12,27] using the Intraclass Correlation Coefficient (ICC) [7], the Pearson correlation coefficient (Pearson's r) [20] and Kendall's tau [14]. Table 2 shows the agreement scores for the dataset among the original three workers. All three values are less than 0.5, indicating limited agreement among the three workers. By inspecting the results closely, we notice many outliers in the scores, that is, cases when a worker's score is in strong contradiction with the scores given by two other workers. We recognise two possible explanations for such a limited agreement:

Table 2. Inter-rater reliability experiments, where ICC stands for the intraclass correlation coefficient. ICC has a range between −1 and 1 while Kendall's tau and Pearson's r have a range between 0 to 1, and a higher score indicates a better agreement.

	ICC	Pearson's r	Kendall's tau
Among 3-raters	0.181	0.306	0.040
Our vs 3-raters average	0.428	0.277	0.179
Our vs closer 2-raters average	0.339	0.205	0.117

1. The limited agreement among the workers is due to outliers in data, which results from the workers not giving truthful scores when rating the confidence of the speaker.
2. The limited agreement among the workers is not due to outliers in data. All scores given by the workers are truthful, and they are the result of individual confidence perception.

If the second explanation is deemed more likely, the three scores given by all three workers should be used. On the other hand, if the first explanation is deemed more likely, we should discard the outliers, which is the score furthest from the other two. Hence we only keep the two most similar scores and use the average of these two scores as the label.

We proceed to devise an experiment to test which reason is more likely. We first label a test set consisting of 492 speech samples ourselves. Note that this is the same set we used as the test set for model evaluation in Sect. 6. These labels are hence regarded as reliable and consistent and will be referred to as the expert validation set onwards. We then proceed to calculate the user agreement between our scores and the average between three raters (using all three scores) and two raters (discarding outliers), and the results are shown in Table 2. Interestingly, we see that the agreement between our score and the three-rater average is better than that between our score and the closer two-rater average. This suggests that the average of the three raters should be regarded as more reliable than the average between two raters. This indicates that the outliers are not a result of the workers giving random answers, and hence, we should keep all three scores and use their averages as the labels.

Through this experiment, we gain the important insight that it is inherently difficult for humans to agree much with each other on the confidence level of speech. The disagreement among raters on the confidence level of speech is likely not to result from poor quality of the data or untruthful answers provided by workers. Rather, it illustrates the difference in individual understanding of confidence assessment and the subjective nature of the hearer-centric affect labelling paradigm [23]. This is indeed very common in the labelling of subjective qualities. For instance, in the study by Flexer and Grill [8] where the participants were asked to grade whether the candidate song that was played to them was similar to a query song, their results only achieved a Pearson correlation of 0.40. Moreover, when Erkelens et al. [5] performed research where primary care experts were asked to listen to recorded emergency calls and rate the safety of triage of patients with chest discomfort, the ICC among the medical experts was reported to be only 0.16. Furthermore, Perski et al. [22] carried out another study where raters were asked to rate the top ten features from a pre-specified list that are most important for the reduction of alcohol consumption and they found that the overall ICC is only 0.15. These strengthen our argument that the limited rater agreement is not a problem but, rather, demonstrates the subjective nature of the rating of human confidence. Our measure of averaging the scores between three workers has served to mitigate this inherent disagreement between human ratings as much as possible.

4   Speech Confidence Prediction Task

4.1   Task Definition

The objective of this task is to learn a function, denoted as f, that can predict the level of uncertainty of a speaker when posed with an audio question, represented as x_s, along with its corresponding transcription in natural language form, represented as x_t. The model function can be expressed as:

$$y = f(x_s, x_t) \tag{1}$$

This equation indicates that the uncertainty score, denoted as y, is a function of the audio x_s and the transcription x_t. The value of y is expected to fall within the range of 0 to 5.

4.2   Evaluation Metrics

To evaluate the model's performance on this task, we use two metrics: (1) Mean Squared Error (MSE) and (2) a parameterized accuracy rate.

On the one hand, MSE is a measure of the average squared difference between the predicted values of a model and the ground-truth values. MSE provides a quantitative measure of the performance of the model, where a lower value of MSE indicates better predictive performance.

On the other hand, the accuracy considers a prediction to be correct if the uncertainty score falls within a range of ±0.5 (inclusive) of the ground-truth value. The decision to use a tolerance value of ±0.5 is based on our observations during the re-annotation process of the expert validation set. We found that when the same sample was annotated and re-annotated after a week, the scores assigned were typically within a margin of 0.5. As a result, we determine that a margin of ±0.5 would be an acceptable level of accuracy for the predicted scores.

Formally, given the ground-truth value, denoted as y_i, and the predicted result, denoted as $\hat{y}_i$, the equation for the accuracy metric is computed as follows:

$$Accuracy_{0.5} = \frac{1}{N} \sum_{i=1}^{N} \mathbb{1}_{[y_i-0.5, y_i+0.5]}(\hat{y}_i), \tag{2}$$

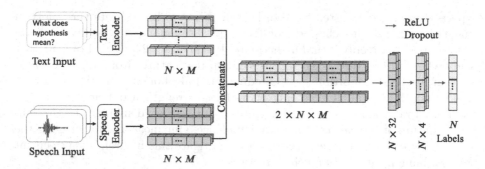

Fig. 2. Model architecture with three components, *text encoder*, *speech encoder* and *fusion module*. N represents the batch size and M stands for the dimension of the speech and text encoder outputs.

where N is the sample size and $\mathbb{1}$ is the indicator function that returns a value of 1 if the predicted score $\hat{y}$ falls within a range of ± 0.5 of the ground-truth score y, and a value of 0 otherwise.

5   The Proposed Method

This section outlines our proposed baseline model for the task of predicting the level of confidence exhibited by a user in response to an audio question and its corresponding transcriptions.

Our proposed model is composed of three major components: *text encoder*, *speech encoder* and *fusion module*. For the text encoder, we used the BERT$_{base}$ model [4] to convert the natural language transcription of the audio question into a contextual representation, and we specifically selected the CLS vector as the transcription representation, which typically contains 768 dimensions. Other text encoders can be used in place of BERT, but we chose BERT due to its simplicity and popularity. The resulting CLS vector is further processed through two dense layers and an activation layer as part of the text encoding process.

For the speech encoder, we utilised the pre-trained HuBERT$_{base}$ model, as outlined by Hsu et al. [13], to transform the raw audio signal of the user's speech into a continuous representation. The pooled output is further processed through two dense layers and an activation layer as part of the text encoding process.

Finally, the fusion module combines the encoded text and speech inputs to generate the predicted confidence score. The network structure for the fusion model is depicted in Fig. 2, with N representing the batch size. A fusion layer utilises the concatenated output from the speech encoder (dimension M) and the text encoder (dimension M). After the fusion layer, the concatenated output is processed through two dense layers and an activation layer.

Table 3. Test results for a random classifier, a naive average baseline classifier, experts, and our proposed fusion model. The top-performing results are highlighted in bold.

	$Accuracy_{0.5}$	MSE
Random Classifier	0.197	3.160
Experts	**0.416**	1.060
Fusion Model	0.411	**0.923**

In general, this proposed baseline model aims to serve as a foundational framework for subsequent development in the area of predicting user speech confidence.

6 Experiments and Results

In this section, we first compare the proposed model performance with those of random classifiers and expert validation. Additionally, we perform an ablation study on speech-only and text-only models. Our experimental results are presented in Table 3 and 4.

6.1 Main Results

To evaluate the performance of our fusion model, we compare it against two baseline models: (1) a random number generator that generates continuous values randomly between 0 and 5 (inclusive); and (2) expert labels provided in the expert validation set. Experiments are conducted using the same two metrics described in Sect. 6.1.

Accuracy. The accuracy of a random number generator simulated is 0.197, which is expected given that we have a tolerance of 1.0 on a scale from 0 to 5. However, this represents the worst-case scenario, and we anticipate that the model would have an accuracy higher than 0.200 if it is able to effectively extract useful features expressing confidence level from the speech and text. Note that the expert performance achieves an accuracy of only 0.416. This is promising as our model, with an accuracy of 0.411, is close to achieving human-level performance, reaching the upper bound in confidence score prediction. We argue that this limited accuracy level achieved by the fusion model does not imply a poor performance in this scenario since even human beings rarely agree with each other on the confidence level of a speaker, as demonstrated by the low accuracy of the expert performance. Rather, this result indicates that the model is able to extract similar relevant features for confidence detection as human beings, showcasing its effectiveness and usefulness.

MSE. We also calculate the MSE between the scores and ground-truth labels. The random number generator achieves the highest value for MSE, which is 3.160. The MSE between the expert performance and the labels is 1.060, and

Table 4. Test results for fusion model, speech-only model and text-only model. The top-performing results are highlighted in bold font.

	Accuracy$_{0.5}$	MSE
Speech-Only Model	0.405	1.015
Text-Only Model	0.274	1.932
Fusion Model	**0.411**	**0.923**

that between the model performance and the labels is 0.923. Although the model performs slightly worse in terms of accuracy compared to the expert, it performs slightly better in terms of MSE. This could be attributed to the fact that the model was directly optimised using the MSE loss function, and thus, it has learned to minimise the loss between the score and the predictions.

Summary. Our experimental results have highlighted the importance of utilising both the accuracy and MSE metrics when evaluating the performance of models in predicting human confidence levels in speech. The accuracy metric provides an indication of the proportion of correct predictions made by the model, while the MSE measures the average deviation between the predicted scores and the ground-truth labels. Therefore, it is advisable to consider both metrics as performance indicators when evaluating human confidence in speech.

6.2   Ablation Studies

To determine which input, speech or text, contains more information on the confidence level of the individual raising the query, we conduct further experiments by training the model on speech input only and then text input only while keeping the other input encoder frozen. Our hypothesis is that speech carries more information on human confidence compared to text. This is because speech encompasses various features that better depict our confidence level, such as the vocal volume [26], vocal pace [11], duration and frequency of disfluencies such as pauses or interjecting sounds [10].

The experimental results are presented in Table 4. The results show that the fusion model, which receives both speech and text inputs, outperforms the speech-only and text-only models in terms of accuracy and error, demonstrating the importance of incorporating both sources of information. However, the speech-only model outperforms the text-only model in terms of accuracy and MSE, which supports our prior belief that speech conveys more information on human confidence than text. It is worth noting that passing speech input alone into the model can achieve good accuracy, strengthening our prior argument that speech embeds much more information on human confidence expression than text.

7   Conclusion and Future Work

In this work, we propose UNSURE, a novel dataset for the task of human confidence evaluation in query-based speech, to facilitate further research on speech confidence in this field of the development of information retrieval and conversational systems. Through rater agreement analysis and expert validation on the UNSURE dataset, we gain the important insight that there is a fundamental difference in the human understanding of confidence, which remains a significant challenge in the evaluation of human confidence in speech. We also presented a fusion transformer-based model as a baseline model, which achieves an accuracy of 0.411 and a low mean squared error (MSE) of 0.923, comparable to the performance of human experts.

For future work, incorporating visual elements into the confidence detection model could be considered, such as collecting a query-based video dataset that incorporates facial expressions and body language of the user, which might provide additional information on the confidence level of the user [17]. With the emergence of multimodal avatars such as Botanic Human Machines which are equipped with webcams, a combination of input modes such as text, speech and video will potentially be better able to predict user confidence levels during interactive sessions. The proposed dataset and models may also help in the development of personalised chatbots. Specifically, accurately monitoring the confidence level in the user's speech enables the chatbot to monitor the knowledge state of the user throughout the conversational sessions. Future work can hence explore the possibility of user-aware chatbots which not only dynamically tailor their responses based on the user's confidence level, but also guide the user behaviour in the turn of conversations in an appropriate manner, hence maximising expected outcome and achieving a more balanced human-chatbot relationship.

A   Appendix

Dataset Details. The dataset, which contains 4, 542 instances, is split into the train, validation and test sets of size 3 600, 450, and 492 respectively. Given the imbalanced distribution of scores within the dataset, we employed upsampling on underrepresented instances prior to the training phase to guarantee an equal number of audio samples across all ranges. Additionally, we augmented the audio samples in the audio encoder and fusion module through random modifications to their pitch, pace, and loudness, as well as the introduction of white noise.

Table 5. Results for hyperparameter searching, where the bold texts highlights the best-performing results.

Learning Rate	Trainable Layers in BERT and HuBERT	Number of Dense Layers	Val Accuracy (%)	Val Loss
$5e^{-8}$	None	2	28.3	0.148
$5e^{-8}$	Last Hidden Layer	2	40.9	0.080
$1e^{-7}$	None	2	40.9	0.075
$1e^{-7}$	Last Hidden Layer	2	**41.1**	**0.071**
$1e^{-7}$	Last Hidden Layer	3	33.6	0.091
$5e^{-7}$	None	2	40.1	0.079
$5e^{-7}$	Last Hidden Layer	2	36.3	0.137
$5e^{-7}$	Last Hidden Layer	3	28.2	0.148
$5e^{-6}$	Last Hidden Layer	2	40.5	0.083
$5e^{-6}$	None	3	39.6	0.096

Training Details. To find the set of hyperparameters that give the optimal performance, we validated the learning rate, the number of layers to freeze in the pre-trained $BERT_{base}$ and $HuBERT_{base}$ models and the number of dense layers. The learning rate was explored between the range $5e^{-8}$ and $5e^{-6}$. We also experimented with freezing the first 10, 11 and all layers in the pre-trained models and two numbers of dense layers were tested (2 and 3) after the fusion layer. A total of 20 combinations of the hyperparameter settings were tested and the validation accuracy and loss for the 10 combinations which give the best results are shown in Table 5. The final model hyperparameters chosen are a learning rate of $1e^{-7}$ with a linear weight decay rate of $1e^{-9}$. We also freeze the first 11 layers of $BERT_{base}$ and $HuBERT_{base}$ models, and the two dense layers after the concatenation stage have 32 and 4 neurons respectively.

Tahn activation is used before the final layer. A dropout level of 50% is introduced after all the hidden layers and layer normalisation is applied to prevent overfitting. The number of total trainable parameters for the fusion module is hence 46 810 561. The loss function chosen is the Mean Square Error (MSE) loss. The batch size is kept at 16 and the number of epochs on average is 60. Each epoch runs for approximately 10 minutes on a 24 GB Nvidia Titan RTX.

References

1. Brennan, S.E., Williams, M.: The feeling of anothers knowing: prosody and filled pauses as cues to listeners about the metacognitive states of speakers. J. Memory Lang. **34**(3), 383–398 (1995). https://www.sciencedirect.com/science/article/pii/S0749596X85710170?via%3Dihub
2. Chanda, S., Fitwe, K., Deshpande, G., Schuller, B.W., Patel, S.: A deep audio-visual approach for human confidence classification. Front. Comput. Sci. **3**

(2021). https://doi.org/10.3389/fcomp.2021.674533, https://www.frontiersin.org/articles/10.3389/fcomp.2021.674533/full

3. Clifton, A., Pappu, A., Reddy, S., Yu, Y., Karlgren, J., Carterette, B., Jones, R.: The spotify podcast dataset. arXiv preprint arXiv:2004.04270 (2020). https://www.researchgate.net/publication/340541821_The_Spotify_Podcasts_Dataset

4. Devlin, J., Chang, M.W., Lee, K., Toutanova, K.: BERT: pre-training of deep bidirectional transformers for language understanding. In: Proceedings of the 2019 Conference of the North American Chapter of the Association for Computational Linguistics: Human Language Technologies, Volume 1 (Long and Short Papers), pp. 4171–4186. Association for Computational Linguistics, Minneapolis, Minnesota (2019). https://doi.org/10.18653/v1/N19-1423, https://aclanthology.org/N19-1423

5. Erkelens, D.C., et al.: Limited reliability of experts' assessment of telephone triage in primary care patients with chest discomfort. J. Clin. Epidemiol. **127**, 117–124 (2020). https://doi.org/10.1016/j.jclinepi.2020.07.016, https://www.sciencedirect.com/science/article/pii/S0895435620301839

6. Favazzo, L., Willford, J.D., Watson, R.M.: Correlating student knowledge and confidence using a graded knowledge survey to assess student learning in a general microbiology classroom. J. Microbiol. Biol. Educ. **15**(2), 251–258 (2014). https://www.ncbi.nlm.nih.gov/pmc/articles/PMC4278496/#:~:text=The%20moderate%20positive%20correlation%20observed,that%20confidence%20rises%20with%20knowledge

7. Fisher, R.A.: Statistical methods for research workers. In: Kotz, S., Johnson, N.L. (eds.) Breakthroughs in Statistics, pp. 66–70. Springer, New York (1992). https://doi.org/10.1007/978-1-4612-4380-9_6, https://psychclassics.yorku.ca/Fisher/Methods/chap6.htm

8. Flexer, A., Grill, T.: The problem of limited inter-rater agreement in modelling music similarity. J. New Music Res. **45**, 239–251 (2016)

9. Fu, X., Yilmaz, E., Lipani, A.: Evaluating the cranfield paradigm for conversational search systems. In: Proceedings of the 2022 ACM SIGIR International Conference on Theory of Information Retrieval, pp. 275–280. ICTIR 22, Association for Computing Machinery, New York, NY, USA (2022). https://doi.org/10.1145/3539813.3545126

10. Goberman, A.M., Hughes, S., Haydock, T.: Acoustic characteristics of public speaking: anxiety and practice effects. Speech Commun. **53**(6), 867–876 (2011)

11. Guyer, J.J., Fabrigar, L.R., Vaughan-Johnston, T.I.: Speech rate, intonation, and pitch: investigating the bias and cue effects of vocal confidence on persuasion. Pers. Soc. Psychol. Bull. **45**(3), 389–405 (2019)

12. Hallgren, K.A.: Computing inter-rater reliability for observational data: an overview and tutorial. Tutorials Quant. Methods Psychol. **8**(1), 23 (2012). https://www.ncbi.nlm.nih.gov/pmc/articles/PMC3402032/

13. Hsu, W.N., Bolte, B., Tsai, Y.H.H., Lakhotia, K., Salakhutdinov, R., Mohamed, A.: Hubert: self-supervised speech representation learning by masked prediction of hidden units. IEEE/ACM Trans. Audio, Speech, Lang. Process. **29**, 3451–3460 (2021). https://arxiv.org/abs/2106.07447

14. Kendall, M.G.: A new measure of rank correlation. Biometrika **30**(1/2), 81–93 (1938). https://www.jstor.org/stable/pdf/2332226.pdf

15. Liu, Z., Zhou, K., Wilson, M.L.: Meta-evaluation of conversational search evaluation metrics. ACM Trans. Inf. Syst. (TOIS) **39**, 1 – 42 (2021). https://www.semanticscholar.org/paper/Meta-evaluation-of-Conversational-Search-Evaluation-Liu-Zhou/05e4c6e0edd230accd1976f91a6350dfd470a1ab

16. Martin, L., Stone, M., Metze, F., Mostow, J.: A methodology for using crowd-sourced data to measure uncertainty in natural speech. In: 2014 IEEE Spoken Language Technology Workshop (SLT), pp. 95–99 (2014). https://doi.org/10.1109/SLT.2014.7078556, https://ieeexplore.ieee.org/document/7078556

17. Maslow, C., Yoselson, K., London, H.: Persuasiveness of confidence expressed via language and body language. Br. J. Soc. Clin. Psychol. **10**(3), 234–240 (1971)

18. Mudavanhu, Y., Zezekwa, N.: Relationship between confidence and knowledge of the nature of science: student-teachers perspective in zimbabwe. Young (2017). https://www.researchgate.net/publication/279853899_RELATIONSHIP_BETWEEN_CONFIDENCE_AND_KNOWLEDGE_OF_THE_NATURE_OF_SCIENCE_STUDENT-TEACHERS_PERSPECTIVE_IN_ZIMBABWE

19. Nair, S., Mohan, M., Rajesh, J., Chandran, P.: On finding the best learning model for assessing confidence in speech. 2020 The 3rd International Conference on Machine Learning and Machine Intelligence (2020). https://doi.org/10.1145/3426826.3426838, https://dl.acm.org/doi/10.1145/3426826.3426838

20. Pearson, K.: Note on regression and inheritance in the case of two parents. Proc. R. Soc. London Ser. I **58**, 240–242 (1895). https://royalsocietypublishing.org/doi/10.1098/rspl.1895.0041

21. Pell, M.D.: Cerebral mechanisms for understanding emotional prosody in speech. Brain Lang. **96**(2), 221–234 (2006)

22. Perski, O., Baretta, D., Blandford, A., West, R., Michie, S.: Engagement features judged by excessive drinkers as most important to include in smartphone applications for alcohol reduction: a mixed-methods study. DIGITAL HEALTH 4, 2055207618785841 (2018). https://doi.org/10.1177/2055207618785841. pMID: 31463077

23. Pon-Barry, H., Shieber, S.M., Longenbaugh, N.S.: Eliciting and annotating uncertainty in spoken language. In: Proceedings of the 2014 Language Resources and Evaluation Conference (2014). https://dash.harvard.edu/handle/1/12149963

24. Radlinski, F., Craswell, N.: A theoretical framework for conversational search. In: Proceedings of the 2017 Conference on Conference Human Information Interaction and Retrieval (2017). https://www.semanticscholar.org/paper/A-Theoretical-Framework-for-Conversational-Search-Radlinski-Craswell/ba3659ef1d5835c07ba0de91f61fe8c3611b3bf1

25. Salle, A., Malmasi, S., Rokhlenko, O., Agichtein, E.: Studying the effectiveness of conversational search refinement through user simulation. In: Hiemstra, D., Moens, M.-F., Mothe, J., Perego, R., Potthast, M., Sebastiani, F. (eds.) ECIR 2021. LNCS, vol. 12656, pp. 587–602. Springer, Cham (2021). https://doi.org/10.1007/978-3-030-72113-8_39

26. Scherer, K.R., London, H., Wolf, J.J.: The voice of confidence: paralinguistic cues and audience evaluation. J. Res. Pers. **7**(1), 31–44 (1973)

27. Tinsley, H.E., Weiss, D.J.: Interrater reliability and agreement. In: Handbook of Applied Multivariate Statistics and Mathematical Modeling, pp. 95–124. Elsevier (2000). https://www.sciencedirect.com/science/article/pii/B9780126913606500057

28. Trippas, J.R., Spina, D., Cavedon, L., Joho, H., Sanderson, M.: Informing the design of spoken conversational search: Perspective paper. In: Proceedings of the 2018 Conference on Human Information Interaction and Retrieval, pp. 32–41 (2018). https://doi.org/10.1145/3176349.3176387

Unsupervised Anomaly Detection Combining PCA and Neural Gases

Marco Vannucci[(✉)] [iD], Valentina Colla[iD], Antonella Zaccara,
Stefano Dettori[iD], and Laura Laid

TeCIP Institute, Scuola Superiore Sant'Anna, Pisa, Italy
{marco.vannucci,valentina.colla,antonella.zaccara,
stefano.dettori,laura.laid}@santannapisa.it

Abstract. Anomaly detection concerns the identification of patterns that deviate from normality in a dataset. It is a significant and common problem in a number of fields, and for this reason, a variety of methodologies, both standard and attributable to artificial intelligence, have been developed. The problem is complex due to the extreme variety of dataset and anomalies characteristics. In this paper, a new unsupervised approach to anomaly detection is presented. The algorithm is based on the combination of Principal Component Analysis and Neural Gases which, through the suitable vector quantization of the data, allows the calculation of an effective anomaly score. The method has been tested on numerous benchmarking datasets, reporting excellent results and outperforming other state-of-the-art algorithms for anomaly detection tasks.

Keywords: anomaly detection · neural gas · vector quantization · PCA

1 Introduction

Anomaly detection (AD), refers to the identification of unusual patterns or instances that deviate significantly from the norm within a dataset. These anomalies can represent events, behaviors, or data points that are rare, or potentially indicative of an abnormal behavior [4]. This technique is widely applied in various fields, including fraud detection in credit cards, Insurance, and healthcare, intrusion detection in cybersecurity. The terms *anomalies* and *outliers* are commonly used interchangeably in this context. The significance of AD lies in the fact that anomalies in data provide substantial and often critical actionable information across a diverse range of application domains. Illustratively, an irregular traffic pattern within a computer network may imply that a compromised computer is transmitting confidential data to an unauthorized destination. A deviation in a medical image could suggest the existence of malignant tumors. Aberrations within credit card transaction data might signal instances of credit card or identity theft, while irregular readings from an industrial machine sensor may denote a potential fault in a component of the production line [3].

Given the centrality of the problem, numerous algorithms for detecting anomalies in the data have been developed over the years and, in recent decades,

L. Iliadis et al. (Eds.): EANN 2024, CCIS 2141, pp. 419–432, 2024.
https://doi.org/10.1007/978-3-031-62495-7_32

techniques based on machine learning (ML) have played an important role, allowing the combination of data-driven approaches, statistics and, in some cases, expert knowledge in the various fields of application. Despite great effort, the problem remains critical and difficult to solve due to a number of interacting challenges:

- *imbalanced data*: anomalies are often rare events compared to normal instances, leading to imbalanced datasets. Traditional machine learning algorithms aiming to an overall performance maximization may struggle to distinguish anomalies from the majority class [28,29];
- *labeling*: while it's relatively straightforward to amass a substantial amount of normal data, the scarcity and unpredictability of anomalies pose a challenge in compiling a representative and well-labeled dataset for anomaly detection tasks [30];
- *overfitting*: AD methods may be prone to overfitting, especially when dealing with high-dimensional data and data imbalance. In those cases the scarcity of anomalous samples within a complex domain prevents the generalization of their distinctive characteristics [19,30];
- *scalability*: some AD algorithms do not scale efficiently to large datasets. The computational complexity of certain algorithms may make them impractical for many applications [6,13];
- *adversarial attacks*: AD models may suffer from adversarial attacks where malicious actors intentionally manipulate input data to prevent the detection of anomalies [1];

Despite the great efforts made by researchers belonging to diverse scientific communities, the challenges mentioned and the peculiarities of the different applications have so far prevented the development of a method that fits all applications [17]. Successful tasks often rely upon the careful selection and adaptation of methods to suit the unique characteristics of the data and the specific nature and requirements of the problem at hand.

In this paper, we present a new approach to unsupervised anomaly detection based on the combination of a popular dimensional reduction technique such as Principal Components Analysis (PCA) and Neural Gases (NG), a type of Neural Network (NN) inspired by Self-Organizing-Maps (SOM) and particularly suited to vector quantization and topology learning tasks. This combination aims to overcome the limitations highlighted by the other methods in performing satisfactorily on a large number of applications and datasets. The paper is organized as follows: in Sect. 2 an overview of state-of-the-art methods is provided, then in Sect. 3 the proposed approach is described in detail. The experimental set–up for method assessment is depicted in Sect. 4 while the achieved results are discussed in Sect. 5. The conclusive Sect. 6 is devoted to drawing conclusions and outlining the future perspectives of this approach.

2   Related Works

The great importance of the task and its transversality to several application areas have led to the development of multiple methodologies for AD. Prior to the advent of ML techniques, most of these methods were based on statistics that relied on assumptions regarding the distribution of non-anomalous data. In those cases, statistical models are built upon such assumptions and subsequently a statistical inference test can be employed to determine if an instance is part of this model. Various approaches exist for performing statistical AD (i.e. *Z-Score* is the most popular), encompassing proximity-based, parametric, non-parametric, and semi-parametric methods [21].

In the last two decades, ML methods have been the ones most investigated for the purpose of anomaly detection. The advantage of such approaches is to limit *apriori* assumptions about the distribution of data, which is often not available or can lead to a drop in performance if it is incorrect. Such methods aim to extract knowledge from the available training data for their tuning. ML methods for AD can be divided into three main categories with respect to the nature of data and the adopted learning function.

Unsupervised methods use unlabelled data. This circumstance is common in many real-world applications where the labelling process represents a cost and/or introduces uncertainties [30]. This context has resulted in unsupervised methods being the most developed and used in recent years. Such approaches build models of the distribution of samples based on training data and use different assumptions about it (i.e. anomalies are located in low-density regions; the relative rarity of anomalous versus normal samples) to identify anomalous samples. Within this category, a distinction can be made between shallow and deep methods (based on the use of deep NNs) [4]: the former offer greater interpretability of results while the latter are more suitable for dealing with complex multidimensional data.

Supervised methods exploit training data for which the ground truth label is available for each sample [8]. In general, classifiers such as NNs, decision trees or ensemble methods are adopted (as they are or are adapted on purpose). These approaches are subject to two main issues: the first concerns the reliability of the labels; the other the number of anomalous data, which is usually low and complicates characterization through the learning process of standard classifiers.

Semi-supervised methods assume that the training data only contains labeled instances for the normal class. The training process exclusively involves regular class instances and, as a result, any item not categorized as ordinary - exploiting some sort of distance metric - is identified as anomalous [31]. Due to their lack of dependence on anomaly class labels, these techniques are more common than supervised methods.

2.1 Unsupervised Approaches

The method proposed in this paper belongs to the unsupervised category. Within it, a number of algorithm families can be further distinguished on the basis of the metrics used to determine the anomalous data or, in most cases, the *anomaly score*, an index of the probability of each sample to be an anomaly (the higher the more probable). The methods shortly described below are used as terms of comparison in the experimental tests reported in Sects. 4 and 5. The largest family includes methods that make use of the distribution, either univariate or multivariate, of the data. Histogram-based outlier detection (HBOS) [7] uses different histogram types for the individual features that make up the data domain assuming their independence. The membership to extreme bins of these histograms determines the degree of *outlyingness*. Subspace Outlier Detection (SOD) [12] uses the distribution of projected data in subspaces that are (significantly) smaller than the original problem domain. By doing so, it avoids the so-called *curse of dimensionality* problem and guarantees applicability even in the case of large domains. Empirical-Cumulative-distribution-based Outlier Detection (ECOD) [15] and Copula Based Outlier Detector (COPOD) [14] are two hyperparameter free methods that take the multivariate distribution of the features and use it to determine the degree of extremeness of the various samples to which the degree of anomaly is then associated. Other approaches exploit the concept of clusters within data, assuming that anomalies lie far from other groups of data. The K-Nearest Neighbors (KNN) [20] approach considers the anomaly score of an input instance to be the distance to its kth nearest neighbor. Local Outlier Factor (LOF) [2] relates the anomaly score to the local deviation of the density of a given sample in relation to its neighbors. Clustering Based Local Outlier Factor (CBLOF) [10] works by initially assigning samples to clusters and then using the distance among clusters as anomaly scores. Connectivity-Based Outlier Factor (COF) [27] employs the ratio of the average chaining distance of data points to the average chaining distance of the kth nearest neighbor of the data point. Similarly, One-class Support–Vector–Machine (OCSVM) [23] exploits the idea of *distance from normality* to calculate the anomaly score. OCSVM uses a SVM to maximize the margin between origin and the normal samples, and defines the decision boundary as the hyperplane that determines the margin. Some methods use models capable of learning the data representation and then calculating the anomaly score in relation to the reconstruction error. PCA [24] is a method of linear dimensionality reduction that involves employing singular value decomposition on the data to project it into a lower-dimensional space. In the context of AD, PCA is applied to project the data into this reduced space, utilizing the reconstruction errors as the anomaly scores. Deep Support Vector Data Description (DeepSVDD) [22] and Deep Autoencoding Gaussian Mixture Model (DAGMM) [33] use deep autoencoders to generate a compact representation of the dataset. DeepSVDD trains a neural network by minimizing the volume of a hypersphere that encompasses the network representations of the data to extract the shared factors of variation. Both DeepSVDD and DAGMM associate the anomaly of individual samples to their reconstruction errors. Finally, approaches based on the use of ensemble methods include Lightweight On-line Detector of Anomalies (LODA) [18], which applies this methodology to the distribution of data within the dataset. Isolation Forest (IForest) [16] works through a Random Forest by randomly selecting features and creating splits, efficiently identifying anomalies as they require fewer splits to be isolated. To the best of our knowledge, no methods have been developed that adopt NG for AD (all the more so in combination with PCA or other decomposition methods). Examples can be found in the field of computer vision where they are used to highlight anomalies within images [26] or for the detection of drift in recordings obtained from sensors [25].

3 Proposed Approach

The method proposed in this paper is based on the combination of PCA and NG, hence the name, *PiCoNG*. It aims to exploit PCA's capabilities of capturing the underlying structure of the data while reducing its dimensionality, and exploit this projection in a vector quantization context via the NG.

PCA is widely employed in ML and statistical analysis to condense high-dimensional data into a lower-dimensional representation while preserving the underlying variability. PCA uncovers the principal components, linear combinations of the original features, and prioritizes them according to their capacity to explain the data's variance. The main purpose of PCA is to reduce the number of features (dimensions) in the dataset, thus it is often used for dealing with the curse of dimensionality and can lead to more efficient and computationally less demanding models. PCA aims to maximize the variance along the principal components. The first principal component captures the most variance, and each subsequent component captures the maximum remaining variance orthogonal to the previous ones. This latter property allows for the selection of a specific number of principal components, enabling to choose the level of dimensionality reduction based on the desired amount of variance retained, usually expressed as a percentage of the original one.

NG is a clustering algorithm used for data analysis and pattern recognition. It was introduced by Thomas Martinetz and Klaus Schulten in 1991 as a competitive learning algorithm, similar to SOMs. NG is particularly useful for organizing and grouping data in an unsupervised manner. Like other competitive learning algorithms, NG involves neurons - called *particles* in this particular context - that compete with each other to learn and represent patterns in the input data. During training, the neurons adjust their weights to better capture the distribution and structure of the input data. The activation of neurons decays with distance in the output space: neurons closer to the input data have higher activation and this activation decreases as the distance from the input data increases. This allows the algorithm to adapt more quickly to changing regions of input space. In addition NG incorporates a learning rate that adapts during the training process. Initially, the learning rate is higher, allowing for larger weight adjustments, but it gradually decreases over time to fine-tune the weights as the model converges. At the end of the training process, the neurons will be positioned in the domain in such a way as to faithfully represent the topology of the training data. Since the number of particles used is usually much smaller than that of the training samples, the NGs are said to learn the topology of the original data in a compact manner. For this reason they are often used in vector quantization applications such as data compression or signal preprocessing.

In this context, each original sample can be associated with the so-called *best-matching-unit* (BMU), the particle closest to it and, on this basis, the *quantisation error* (QE) can be calculated for each sample as the distance between the sample itself and its BMU. The idea behind PiCoNG is to exploit this last measure as the anomaly score of each sample. The method in fact uses an NG trained on the training data after their pre-processing through PCA. After training, the anomaly score of each sample is calculated as the QE of the sample in the space resulting from the projection defined by PCA. Under these assumptions, the samples characterised by high QE will in fact be those furthest away from their BMUs and, consequently, from the regions most densely populated by samples. The NG property of maintaining the distribution of the training data is crucial in this process, as it ensures that the particles obtained after training are indeed representative of the original topology and density of the data. More sample-populated regions will in fact be better represented by particles located in these areas of the domain and vice-versa. The training pipeline of PiCoNG is described through the following points, assuming to deal with a dataset D formed by n samples in the domain X whose dimension is m:

1. the original data is scaled by limiting the values of each feature in the range [0;1]. Each sample $d \in X$ is transformed scaled into $d_s \in X_s$ where X_s is $[0;1]^m$. Scaling is necessary to avoid bias due to the use of distances by dealing with measurements of several orders of magnitude. In the following, it is assumed to work with scaled data.
2. PCA application to transform each $d_s \in X_s$ into $d_{PCA} \in X_{PCA}$ where X_{PCA} is $[0;1]^r, r < m$.
3. training the NG with PCA data with determination of $k (k << n)$ NG particles p in the domain X_{PCA}.

PiCoNG uses two main hyper-parameters that determine its performance. The first is the explained variance (*exp.var*), which determines the number of principal components that are selected with PCA. If the value of this parameter is relatively high, the loss of information content in X_{PCA} with respect to X (and equivalently X_s) is acceptable. This loss has little impact in a context of measuring quantisation error with respect to the particles of a NG, as PCA minimises the loss of variance of the new components with respect to the original ones. The second hyper-parameter to be considered is the number k of particles used: a high value of k means a higher fidelity of the particle distribution to the training data, but it also entails a higher computational load and the low generalization capabilities of the resulting NG in terms of particles representativeness and vector quantization.

The reasons for using PCA are manifold. The first is to reduce the computational load of the training phase (both in terms of time and memory usage). Reducing the size of the domain in which the NG operates significantly reduces the complexity of the updates of the weights of the NG's particles, with an obvious effect on time and memory. Further, PCA reduces the noise in the transformed data allowing the NG to better group nearby samples and to associate them to the obtained particles.

NGs were selected as the method for vector quantisation because they prove more suitable for preserving the topology of the training data than similar clustering methods such as SOMs, k-means, hierarchical clustering methods that mainly focus on the minimization of the reconstruction error of the data representation as shown in [11]. Once the NG has been trained, the anomaly score can be calculated for any arbitrary sample, whether belonging to the training dataset or not. The calculation, starting from the original sample $d \in X$, involves an initial transformation by applying the normalisation and the PCA (whose parameters are defined during the training phase), then the BMU is calculated for this sample ($d_{PCA} \in X_{PCA}$) together with its quantization error and associated to the original sample. This measurement is adopted as an anomaly score and used for performance assessment in the next sections in line with most literature works. The so–calculated anomaly score is a real number in the range $[0; \infty)$ and, in line with other approaches, is proportional to the probability of a sample to be an anomaly.

4   Experimental Tests

This section describes the experimental set-up adopted for the evaluation of PiCoNG. The algorithm is tested on an extensive set of datasets commonly used as benchmarks [9] for AD algorithms and the results obtained are compared with those of other state-of-the-art approaches belonging to the category of unsupervised methods. The tests aim not only to show the general performance of PiCoNG but also to compare its performance relative to the main competitors and understand how the experimental conditions affect it. The performance of PiCoNG is compared to that of the 14 main and trending unsupervised methods for AD that have already been listed and briefly described in Sect. 2.1. The implementation of these algorithms used in this work comes from the popular PyOD (Python Outliers Detection) package [32]. We employ the default hyperparameters values specified in the original paper for fair comparison across all methods.

PiCoNG adopts mainly two hyper–parameters. The first one is the percentage of PCA-explained variance which is set to 90% in all these tests. This setting represents a very high value and is intended to minimise the potential loss of information resulting from this operation while reducing (often significantly) the number of features processed in subsequent stages. Furthermore, this is a conservative choice that aims to maximise the method's accuracy at the expense of the NG training time: other PiCoNG configurations may favour the latter. The second hyperparameter is the number of particles (k) forming the NG. This value is proportional to the number of samples in the training dataset. More in detail $k = n/Q$ where n is the number of samples forming the dataset and

$$Q = \begin{cases} 200 & \text{if } n > 5000 \\ 100 & \text{if } 1000 < n \leq 5000 \\ 50 & \text{if } n < 1000 \end{cases}$$

These values were empirically determined on the basis of some preliminary tests and the analysis of their influence on method performance, although interesting, was not addressed due to space constraints.

4.1 Datasets

The datasets employed for the tests are listed in Table 1 where the number of samples, features and the rate r of anomalies is reported. Since this test is focused on unsupervised methods, the *ground truth* label is used only in the evaluation phase of the outcomes of the tested algorithms and not during their training phase. The datasets come from the *AdBench* repository [9], which contains datasets specifically selected for the evaluation of AD algorithms and is becoming a standard for this purpose. They cover different fields (i.e. healtcare, engineering and more) and a variety of characteristics in terms of size (i.e. number of samples and features) and anomaly rates (according to ground truth) in order to allow the evaluation of the tested algorithms under different conditions. In addition to the benchmark datasets, an industrial one named *Alchimia-t* was included, provided by the Italian foundry *Fonderia di Torbole*, which produces brake discs and drums, castings and machined parts for the automotive sector. The dataset includes data related to the thermal analysis of cast iron in two different points of the production line that significantly affect the final product quality and the casting temperature. The objective of the industrial use case is to avoid the production of parts that do not conform to customer requirements and the application of data-driven models can help in predicting product quality by exploiting as input the information deriving from thermal and chemical analyses along the production line [5]. This dataset was found to be problematic for the detection of anomalies that undermine the following planned data-driven modelling steps. The problems encountered in this dataset led to the development of the PiCoNG method. In line with the other works about this topic and with literature surveys, since the unsupervised algorithms are developed for *transductive* settings (they calculate the anomaly score for the input data, not using the ground truth) there is no separation between training and test data but the dataset is processed entirely and the anomaly score is calculated for each sample. Each algorithm is run 10 times on each dataset and the average performance is reported in the results section.

4.2 Metrics

The assessment of AD model performance often relies on metrics such as the Area Under the Receiver Operating Characteristic curve (AUC-ROC) and Area Under the Precision-Recall curve (AUC-PR). The ROC curve illustrates the balance between sensitivity (*true positive rate*) and specificity (1 - *false positive rate*) at different anomaly score thresholds. AUC-ROC provides a comprehensive measure of the classification model's effectiveness across diverse threshold settings, with a higher value (approaching 1) signaling improved differentiation between normal and anomalous instances. On the other hand, the PR curve focuses on the

Table 1. Description of the characteristics of the datasets used within the pursued experimental tests in terms of number of samples, features and rate of anomalies (r).

Dataset	Samples	Features	r
annthyroid	7200	6	0.07
breastw	683	9	0.35
cardiotocography	2114	21	0.22
fault	1941	27	0.35
glass	214	7	0.04
internetads	1966	1555	0.19
landsat	6435	36	0.21
letter	1600	32	0.06
lymphography	148	18	0,04
magic.gamma	19020	10	0.35
mammography	11183	6	0.02
musk	3062	166	0.03
satellite	6435	36	0.32
shuttle	49097	9	0.07
spambase	4207	57	0.40
speech	3686	400	0.02
vowels	1456	12	0.03
waveform	3443	21	0.03
yeast	1484	8	0.34
alchimia-t	409	82	0.02

interplay between *precision* (true positives divided by total predicted positives) and *recall* (true positives divided by total actual positives). AUC-PR captures the model's precision-recall performance across various anomaly score threshold settings, with a higher value (closer to 1) indicating superior performance, particularly in scenarios with imbalanced datasets, a common occurrence in real world AD applications.

5   Results and Discussion

The performances obtained by PiCoNG and other methods are shown in Tables 2 and 3 in terms of AUC-ROC and AUC-RP respectively, in accordance with the experimental set-up described in Sect. 4.

The analysis of these results shows that the general performance of PiCoNG is very satisfactory: it obtains a high AUC-ROC value on all the datasets processed, highlighting its ability to detect a large number of anomalies, irrespective of the characteristics of the dataset in question, by means of the anomaly score defined.

Table 2. AUC-ROC obtained by the tested AD methods on the benchmarking datasets. Best performing method for each dataset in **bold**. Some names of the methods adopted have been abbreviated for reasons of space. The proposed PiCoNG approach is indicated as PCNG

	PCA	OCS.	LOF	CBL.	COF	HBOS	KNN	SOD	COP.	EC.	D.SVD	DAG.	LODA	IF	PCNG
breastw	0.93	0.80	0.41	0.98	0.39	**1.00**	0.99	0.94	0.99	0.98	0.66	0.00	0.97	0.97	0.97
cardiot.	0.75	**0.79**	0.59	0.65	0.53	0.61	0.57	0.51	0.68	0.68	0.51	0.61	0.72	0.68	0.69
fault	0.47	0.47	0.58	0.63	0.63	0.52	**0.72**	0.69	0.45	0.44	0.49	0.45	0.41	0.57	0.68
glass	0.66	0.35	0.68	0.82	0.71	0.79	0.81	0.73	0.74	0.76	0.40	0.76	0.72	0.76	**0.88**
internet	0.62	0.68	0.67	**0.72**	0.64	0.67	0.69	0.61	0.66	0.66	0.67	0.00	0.56	0.70	0.71
landsat	0.36	0.36	0.55	**0.64**	0.54	0.55	0.57	0.61	0.41	0.57	0.50	0.43	0.39	0.47	0.61
letter	0.50	0.45	0.83	0.76	0.80	0.60	**0.84**	**0.84**	0.55	0.52	0.38	0.51	0.51	0.62	0.82
lympho.	0.99	0.98	0.88	**1.00**	0.89	**1.00**	0.55	0.72	**1.00**	**1.00**	0.50	0.71	0.84	**1.00**	0.99
magicg.	0.66	0.61	0.69	0.74	0.67	0.70	0.82	0.77	0.68	0.65	0.49	0.58	0.69	0.73	**0.85**
mammog.	0.89	0.87	0.76	0.82	0.78	0.86	0.84	0.82	**0.93**	**0.93**	0.52	0.00	0.86	0.86	0.89
musk	0.98	0.80	0.41	**1.00**	0.39	**1.00**	0.71	0.74	0.92	0.96	0.50	0.75	0.96	0.99	0.91
satellite	0.58	0.60	0.55	0.73	0.54	**0.76**	0.66	0.65	0.62	0.74	0.52	0.61	0.63	0.70	0.67
spambase	0.54	0.52	0.44	0.54	0.41	0.65	0.53	0.52	0.69	0.67	0.51	0.00	0.41	0.65	**0.68**
speech	0.52	0.51	0.51	0.50	**0.56**	0.51	0.51	**0.56**	0.53	0.51	**0.56**	0.52	0.51	0.52	0.52
vowels	0.65	0.60	0.91	0.91	0.92	0.71	**0.99**	0.92	0.54	0.46	0.43	0.61	0.70	0.72	0.82
waveform	0.64	0.56	0.72	0.72	0.74	0.67	0.74	0.67	0.74	0.75	0.51	0.49	0.60	0.71	**0.80**
wdbc	**1.00**	0.99	0.89	0.97	0.94	**1.00**	0.94	0.91	**1.00**	0.96	0.72	0.77	0.97	0.98	0.97
yeast	0.41	0.40	0.46	0.46	0.44	0.39	0.39	0.42	0.37	0.40	**0.48**	0.40	0.45	0.38	**0.48**
alchimia-t	0.5	0.43	0.41	0.57	0.52	0.42	0.36	0.49	0.53	0.57	0.47	0.35	0.44	0.56	**0.58**

Table 3. AUC-PR obtained by the tested AD methods on the benchmarking datasets. Best performing method for each dataset in **bold**. Some names of the methods adopted have been abbreviated for reasons of space. The proposed PiCoNG approach is indicated as PCNG.

	PCA	OCS.	LOF	CBL.	COF	HBOS	KNN	SOD	COP.	EC.	D.SVD	DAG.	LODA	IF	PCNG
breastw	0.97	0.84	0.29	0.90	0.28	0.96	0.90	0.87	0.98	**1.00**	0.62	0.00	0.98	0.95	0.95
cardiot.	0.48	**0.53**	0.31	0.45	0.29	0.39	0.35	0.28	0.41	0.44	0.25	0.31	0.48	0.42	0.40
fault	0.33	0.39	0.39	0.44	0.42	0.36	**0.56**	0.48	0.30	0.31	0.35	0.34	0.30	0.41	0.50
glass	0.10	0.08	0.21	0.14	0.12	0.12	0.20	0.19	0.10	0.18	0.04	**0.25**	0.13	0.11	0.24
internet	0.33	0.55	0.40	**0.58**	0.39	0.53	0.42	0.28	0.51	0.52	0.34	0.00	0.23	0.49	0.39
landsat	0.16	0.16	0.24	0.30	0.25	0.22	0.25	0.26	0.18	0.25	0.21	0.24	0.19	0.20	**0.34**
letter	0.07	0.06	**0.35**	0.15	0.21	0.09	0.30	0.29	0.07	0.07	0.10	0.12	0.07	0.09	0.30
lympho	**0.97**	0.93	0.24	0.96	0.36	0.92	0.39	0.23	0.90	0.90	0.06	0.20	0.44	0.99	0.92
magicg.	0.59	0.52	0.55	0.68	0.54	0.62	0.76	0.69	0.60	0.54	0.36	0.46	0.59	0.66	**0.78**
mammog.	0.19	0.13	0.10	0.11	0.11	0.21	0.16	0.13	**0.40**	**0.40**	0.07	0.00	0.15	0.20	0.33
musk	**1.00**	0.11	0.03	**1.00**	0.03	0.98	0.09	0.08	0.34	0.35	0.05	0.32	0.48	**1.00**	0.61
satellite	0.60	0.57	0.38	0.60	0.39	**0.69**	0.51	0.46	0.57	0.66	0.33	0.58	0.63	0.67	0.57
spambase	0.41	0.40	0.34	0.41	0.34	0.51	0.41	0.40	0.56	0.54	0.40	0.00	0.36	0.51	**0.59**
speech	0.02	0.02	0.02	0.02	0.02	0.02	0.02	0.02	0.02	0.02	**0.05**	0.02	0.02	0.02	0.02
vowels	0.09	0.08	0.34	0.22	0.55	0.13	**0.65**	0.38	0.04	0.04	0.09	0.12	0.14	0.15	0.28
waveform	0.06	0.04	0.11	**0.19**	0.14	0.06	0.13	0.10	0.07	0.07	0.03	0.03	0.05	0.06	0.17
wdbc	0.74	0.70	0.15	0.80	0.51	**0.91**	0.43	0.35	0.83	0.57	0.15	0.18	0.65	0.80	0.82
yeast	0.30	0.30	0.32	0.32	0.32	0.33	0.29	0.30	0.30	0.32	0.33	0.30	**0.34**	0.30	**0.34**
alchimia-t	0.03	0.04	**0.11**	0.05	0.07	0.06	0.08	0.1	0.07	0.06	0.06	0.05	0.1	0.07	0.09

The AUC-PR value is equally satisfactory although in absolute terms lower than the other metric, but this behaviour is due to the nature of the index itself, which is affected by the inbalanced conditions of the dataset. The high AUC-PR value highlights the reliability of anomaly detections provided by the proposed method.

The validity of the proposed method is proven by comparison with other methods, as can be seen in Tables 2 and 3. In terms of ranking, PiCoNG ranks among the top-performers in most cases. In terms of AUC-ROC it is the best-performing method for 6 out of 14 datasets, and in the case of AUC-PR for 4 out of 14. To better compare the various methods used in this research, the performance percentiles (the closer to 100 the better) in which each approach ranks in terms of AUC-ROC and AUC-PR was calculated. The result of this analysis is shown in a combined manner in Fig. 1 where the percentiles of the various methods are plotted, one metric relative to the other. The figure shows that PiCoNG performs significantly better than all other methods for each of the two metrics in a similar manner, overcoming the 80th percentile for both criteria, significantly distancing the runner-up and the other methods.

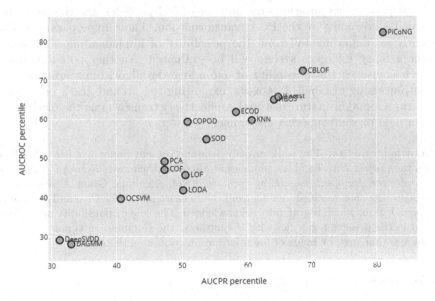

Fig. 1. Scatter-plot of AUC-ROC and AUC-PR performance percentiles for the tested approaches throughout the benchmarking datasets (the closer to 100 the better).

6   Conclusions and Future Works

In this work, a new algorithm for AD based on vector quantization belonging to the family of unsupervised methods was introduced. The method, PiCoNG, takes its name from the two methods it combines: NG and PCA. The NG has the task of quantizing the domain of the processed dataset by exploiting its well-known efficiency in terms of learning the topology of the training data. The preprocessing layer constituted by the PCA, on the other hand, has the task of extracting the main variance components of the data, reducing complexity to lower computational costs and reduce noise. The efficiency of the proposed method was evaluated by testing it on a set of datasets with varied character-istics commonly used for benchmarking AD algorithms with the addition of an industrial database. These tests revealed the excellent overall performance of PiCoNG in terms of sensitivity and specificity across the AUC-ROC and AUC-PR metrics, which are commonly used for such purposes. Although PiCoNG was not the best method according to the two metrics for the totality of the dat-sets, it markedly globally outperformed the other approaches tested. Further, the analysis of the results did not reveal any particular criticality with respect to the main characteristics of the processed datasets.

Despite the excellent results achieved, the development of the PiCoNG algo-rithm is only in its initial stages and several activities are planned for its improve-ment. The first concerns the possibility of automatically setting the value of the hyperparameters governing the number of NG *particles* and the percentage of explained variance by the PCA transformation. These hyperparameters are currently set experimentally, but the possibility of implementing a rule-based and/or a fuzzy inference system will be evaluated. Another potential line of research envisages the possibility of extending the algorithm's functionalities to the processing of labelled datasets, exploiting the ground–truth information about the anomalous nature of samples, effectively transforming the method into a supervised or semi-supervised approach.

Acknowledgements. The work described in the present paper has been developed within the project entitled "*Data and decentralized Artificial intelligence for a competitive and green European metallurgy industry*" (Ref. Alchimia, Grant Agreement No. 101070046) that has received funding from the Research Fund for Coal and Steel of the European Union, which is gratefully acknowledged. The sole responsibility of the issues treated in the present paper lies with the authors; the Commission is not responsible for any use that may be made of the information contained therein.

References

1. Alotaibi, A., Rassam, M.A.: Adversarial machine learning attacks against intrusion detection systems: a survey on strategies and defense. Future Internet **15**(2), 62 (2023)
2. Breunig, M.M., Kriegel, H.P., Ng, R.T., Sander, J.: LOF: identifying density-based local outliers. In: Proceedings of the 2000 ACM SIGMOD International Conference on Management of Data, pp. 93–104 (2000)
3. Cateni, S., Colla, V., Vannucci, M.: A fuzzy system for combining different outliers detection methods. In: Proceedings of the IASTED International Conference on Artificial Intelligence and Applications, AIA, vol. 2009, pp. 87–93 (2009)
4. Chandola, V., Banerjee, A., Kumar, V.: Anomaly detection: a survey. ACM Comput. Surv. (CSUR) **41**(3), 1–58 (2009)

5. Colla, V., Pietrosanti, C., Malfa, E., Peters, K.: Environment 4.0: how digitalization and machine learning can improve the environmental footprint of the steel production processes. Matériaux Tech. **108**(5–6), 507 (2020). https://doi.org/10.1051/mattech/2021007

6. Dromard, J., Roudiere, G., Owezarski, P.: Online and scalable unsupervised network anomaly detection method. IEEE Trans. Netw. Serv. Manage. **14**(1), 34–47 (2016)

7. Goldstein, M., Dengel, A.: Histogram-based outlier score (hbos): a fast unsupervised anomaly detection algorithm. KI-2012: poster and demo track **1**, 59–63 (2012)

8. Görnitz, N., Kloft, M., Rieck, K., Brefeld, U.: Toward supervised anomaly detection. J. Artif. Intell. Res. **46**, 235–262 (2013)

9. Han, S., Hu, X., Huang, H., Jiang, M., Zhao, Y.: Adbench: anomaly detection benchmark. Adv. Neural. Inf. Process. Syst. **35**, 32142–32159 (2022)

10. He, Z., Xu, X., Deng, S.: Discovering cluster-based local outliers. Pattern Recogn. Lett. **24**(9–10), 1641–1650 (2003)

11. Herrmann, M., Villmann, T.: Vector quantization by optimal neural gas. In: Gerstner, W., Germond, A., Hasler, M., Nicoud, J.-D. (eds.) ICANN 1997. LNCS, vol. 1327, pp. 625–630. Springer, Heidelberg (1997). https://doi.org/10.1007/BFb0020224

12. Kriegel, H.-P., Kröger, P., Schubert, E., Zimek, A.: Outlier detection in axis-parallel subspaces of high dimensional data. In: Theeramunkong, T., Kijsirikul, B., Cercone, N., Ho, T.-B. (eds.) PAKDD 2009. LNCS (LNAI), vol. 5476, pp. 831–838. Springer, Heidelberg (2009). https://doi.org/10.1007/978-3-642-01307-2_86

13. Laptev, N., Amizadeh, S., Flint, I.: Generic and scalable framework for automated time-series anomaly detection. In: Proceedings of the 21th ACM SIGKDD International Conference on Knowledge Discovery and Data Mining, pp. 1939–1947 (2015)

14. Li, Z., Zhao, Y., Botta, N., Ionescu, C., Hu, X.: COPOD: copula-based outlier detection. In: 2020 IEEE International Conference on Data Mining (ICDM), pp. 1118–1123. IEEE (2020)

15. Li, Z., Zhao, Y., Hu, X., Botta, N., Ionescu, C., Chen, G.: Ecod: unsupervised outlier detection using empirical cumulative distribution functions. IEEE Trans. Knowl. Data Eng. **35**, 12181–12193 (2022)

16. Liu, F.T., Ting, K.M., Zhou, Z.H.: Isolation forest. In: 2008 Eighth IEEE International Conference on Data Mining, pp. 413–422. IEEE (2008)

17. Pang, G., Shen, C., Cao, L., Hengel, A.V.D.: Deep learning for anomaly detection: a review. ACM Comput Surv. (CSUR) **54**(2), 1–38 (2021)

18. Pevný, T.: Loda: lightweight on-line detector of anomalies. Mach. Learn. **102**, 275–304 (2016)

19. Pimentel, T., Monteiro, M., Veloso, A., Ziviani, N.: Deep active learning for anomaly detection. In: 2020 International Joint Conference on Neural Networks (IJCNN), pp. 1–8. IEEE (2020)

20. Ramaswamy, S., Rastogi, R., Shim, K.: Efficient algorithms for mining outliers from large data sets. In: Proceedings of the 2000 ACM SIGMOD International Conference on Management of Data, pp. 427–438 (2000)

21. Rousseeuw, P.J., Hubert, M.: Anomaly detection by robust statistics. Wiley Interdisc. Rev. Data Min. Knowl. Disc. **8**(2), e1236 (2018)

22. Ruff, L., et al.: Deep one-class classification. In: International Conference on Machine Learning, pp. 4393–4402. PMLR (2018)

23. Schölkopf, B., Williamson, R.C., Smola, A., Shawe-Taylor, J., Platt, J.: Support vector method for novelty detection. In: Advances in Neural Information Processing Systems, vol. 12 (1999)

24. Shyu, M.L., Chen, S.C., Sarinnapakorn, K., Chang, L.: A novel anomaly detection scheme based on principal component classifier. In: Proceedings of the IEEE Foundations and New Directions of Data Mining Workshop, pp. 172–179. IEEE Press (2003)

25. Song, L., Zheng, T., Wang, J., Guo, L.: An improvement growing neural gas method for online anomaly detection of aerospace payloads. Soft. Comput. **24**, 11393–11405 (2020)

26. Sun, Q., Liu, H., Harada, T.: Online growing neural gas for anomaly detection in changing surveillance scenes. Pattern Recogn. **64**, 187–201 (2017)

27. Tang, J., Chen, Z., Fu, A.W., Cheung, D.W.: Enhancing effectiveness of outlier detections for low density patterns. In: Chen, M.-S., Yu, P.S., Liu, B. (eds.) PAKDD 2002. LNCS (LNAI), vol. 2336, pp. 535–548. Springer, Heidelberg (2002). https://doi.org/10.1007/3-540-47887-6_53

28. Vannucci, M., Colla, V.: Genetic algorithms based resampling for the classification of unbalanced datasets. In: Czarnowski, I., Howlett, R.J., Jain, L.C. (eds.) IDT 2017 Part II. SIST, vol. 73, pp. 23–32. Springer, Cham (2018). https://doi.org/10.1007/978-3-319-59424-8_3

29. Vannucci, M., Colla, V., Nastasi, G., Matarese, N.: Detection of rare events within industrial datasets by means of data resampling and specific algorithms. Int. J. Simul. Syst. Sci. Technol. **11**(3), 1–11 (2010)

30. Vázquez, F.I., Hartl, A., Zseby, T., Zimek, A.: Anomaly detection in streaming data: a comparison and evaluation study. Expert Syst. Appl. **233**, 120994 (2023)

31. Villa-Pérez, M.E., Alvarez-Carmona, M.A., Loyola-Gonzalez, O., Medina-Pérez, M.A., Velazco-Rossell, J.C., Choo, K.K.R.: Semi-supervised anomaly detection algorithms: a comparative summary and future research directions. Knowl.-Based Syst. **218**, 106878 (2021)

32. Zhao, Y., Nasrullah, Z., Li, Z.: Pyod: a python toolbox for scalable outlier detection. arXiv preprint arXiv:1901.01588 (2019)

33. Zong, B., et al.: Deep autoencoding gaussian mixture model for unsupervised anomaly detection. In: International Conference on Learning Representations (2018)

Deep Learning/Convolutional

A New Approach to Learn Spatio-Spectral Texture Representation with Randomized Networks: Application to Brazilian Plant Species Identification

Ricardo T. Fares⬤ and Lucas C. Ribas(✉)⬤

Institute of Biosciences, Humanities and Exact Sciences,
São Paulo State University (UNESP), São José do Rio Preto, SP, Brazil
{rt.fares,lucas.ribas}@unesp.br

Abstract. Texture and color are fundamental visual descriptors, each complementing the other. Although many approaches have been developed for color-texture analysis, they often lack spectral analysis of the image and suffer from limited data availability for training in various problems. This paper introduces a new single-parameter texture representation, which integrates spatial and spectral analyses by combining the weights of the output layers of randomized autoencoders applied on both the same and adjacent image channels. As our approach is not end-to-end, we can extract individual representations for each image independently of the dataset size and without the need of fine-tuning. The rationale behind this approach is to learn meaningful spatial and spectral information of color-texture images through a simple neural network architecture. The proposed representation was evaluated using four benchmark datasets: Outex, USPtex, 1200Tex and MBT. We also verify the performance of the proposed representation on a practical and challenging task of Brazilian plant species identification. The experiments reveal that our method has a competitive classification accuracy in both scenarios when compared to the other methods, including various complex deep learning architectures. This shows an important contribution to the color-texture analysis and serves as a useful resource for other areas of computer vision and pattern recognition.

Keywords: Color-texture · Representation learning · Randomized neural network

1 Introduction

Texture, a visual attribute known for its significant discriminatory properties, has been the subject of extensive study since the 1960s, in which it can be viewed as the spatial arrangement of intensity or visual patterns of the pixels within an image [15]. The texture is an object characteristic that allows them be distinguished not only by the visual perception of the living beings, but also

L. Iliadis et al. (Eds.): EANN 2024, CCIS 2141, pp. 435–449, 2024.
https://doi.org/10.1007/978-3-031-62495-7_33

by texture analysis and recognition approaches in digital images. They play a key role in various fields and problems, such as in botanic [6], material sciences [19], medicine [12,40], agriculture [3], and others.

In that sense, although for a period of time only the use of texture was needed, currently computer vision and pattern recognition applications are increasingly filled with colored images, demanding more powerful color-texture analysis approaches. Thereby, since it has been shown that the use of color, a powerful visual cue, enhances the overall image description in pattern recognition tasks, many color-texture methods have been proposed [5,15,28,33] . These works indicate that texture and color are fundamental visual elements within an image, functioning as foundational components across numerous applications and within various domains of computer vision [37].

Several approaches for color-texture analysis have been proposed in the literature. Most of these methods use the integrative approach which applies gray-level texture techniques on each color channel separately and combines these features to form the representation. Examples include integrative local binary pattern methods such as integrative CLBP [11], LETRIST [38], and LGONBP [36], with the latter two enhancing the noise robustness and rotation invariance, and complex network approaches such as integrative CNDT [4]. Additionally, deep convolutional neural networks (DCNNs) have been used for learning color-texture representations [39], although they still require large computational costs and still suffer from data availability. On the other hand, there are also pure color methods that ignore the spatial relationship of the pixels, such as color statistics methods. Hence, a widely used approach is to combine both methods for accounting texture and color attributes [9].

Further, over the past few years, it is noteworthy that many texture representation learning techniques, as presented in the literature [27,29–31], use randomized neural networks due to their simplicity, low computational cost, and high accuracies, allowing them to be applied in many tasks, especially real-time ones. However, these color-texture analysis approaches lack incorporation of spectral analysis of the image, applying only a parallel methodology [15] for acquiring texture representation. Thus, they overlook the potential benefits of employing spectral analysis, which can provide deeper insights into essential aspects of the image.

This paper proposes a new single-parameter texture representation that integrates spatial and spectral analysis using randomized networks. First, we divide each image channel into stretched 3×3 patches that sweep over every pixel of the image to assemble the input feature matrix. Next, we employ randomized neural network-based modules to conduct spatial and spectral analysis, using the same input and adjacent image channel input feature matrix as input and output, respectively. Thus, the proposed descriptor is composed by learned weights of the output layer, which extract spatial and spectral texture key information within and between color channels. In summary, the major contributions of the proposed approach are as follows: (i) A simple, fast, and single-parameter approach based on randomized neural networks. (ii) A texture descriptor containing key information about the relationship of the multispectral pixels obtained from spectral analysis. (iii) A texture representation demonstrating high performance in the practical application of identifying plant species utilizing images from foliar surfaces.

The paper is organized as follows. In Sect. 2, we describe the proposed texture representation. In Sect. 3 the experimental setup, parameter evaluation and the comparison of the results are shown, followed by the conclusion in Sect. 4.

2 Proposed Method

2.1 Randomized Neural Network

Randomized neural networks (RNNs) are one-pass artificial neural networks that were proposed in [14,24,25,34]. In their simplest form, they consist of a single hidden layer with randomly generated weights following some probability distribution. The primary objective is to non-linearly project the input data into another dimensional space, thereby enhancing the likelihood that the data will become linearly separable, as stated in Cover's theorem [10]. Ultimately, the learning is performed through the weights of the output layer, which can be calculated using the Moore-Penrose pseudoinverse [26].

Mathematically, consider the input matrix $X \in \mathbb{R}^{p \times N}$ composed of N samples of p-dimensional feature input vectors, and the output matrix $Y \in \mathbb{R}^{r \times N}$, comprising N samples of r-dimensional output vectors. To initiate the process, the hidden layer weight matrix $W \in \mathbb{R}^{Q \times (p+1)}$ is generated, with Q denoting the number of hidden neurons and p representing the number of attributes in each feature input vector.

Additionally, consider the row matrix $\mathbb{1}_N$ with N columns, each entry set to one. This allows the construction of the matrix $X' = \left[-\mathbb{1}_N^T \ X^T\right]^T$, where the first row corresponds to the bias. Subsequently, the forward pass of the hidden layer is computed as $U = \phi(WX')$, where ϕ denotes a sigmoid function, and in which the columns of matrix U represent the projected feature input vectors.

Further, defining $Z = \left[-\mathbb{1}_N^T \ U^T\right]^T$ as the matrix U augmented with the bias, we determine the learned weights for the output layer using:

$$M = YZ^T \left(ZZ^T\right)^{-1}, \qquad (1)$$

where $Z^T(ZZ^T)^{-1}$ represents the Moore-Penrose pseudoinverse [20,26]. It is worth noting that the matrix ZZ^T may become singular or nearly singular, leading to unstable outcomes. To mitigate such scenarios, Tikhonov's regularization [1,7] can be applied by modifying the formula to $M = YZ^T \left(ZZ^T + \lambda I\right)^{-1}$, where $\lambda > 0$, and I denotes the identity matrix.

Lastly, RNNs can function as a randomized autoencoder (RAE) by treating the input feature matrix X as the target output Y (i.e., $Y = X$). In this scenario, the model consists of a random encoder and a decoder based on least squares, capable of mapping the input data. Consequently, the weight matrix M serves as the transformation for projecting the randomly generated Q-dimensional space back into the original input data.

2.2   Learning Color-Texture Representations

In this paper, we propose to use as texture representation the weights of the output layer of randomized networks and autoencoders trained with information within and between image channels to conduct a spatio-spectral analysis.

For this, let I be a 3-channel image, with I_C denoting a channel of I, where $C \in \{R, G, B\}$. We define X_C as the matrix built by assembling stretched 3×3 windows that traverse the entirety of channel C, i.e., the window is centered in each pixel of the image and overlaps each other. The process to build the input feature matrix X_R for the red channel is illustrated in Fig. 1(a). Note that the X matrices are constructed from individual images, making the several randomized networks to be trained for each image in our approach. Further, the weight matrix W for the hidden layer is generated using a Linear Congruent Generator (LCG) with the equation $V(n + 1) = (aV(n) + b) \mod c$, where V has a length of $L = Q \cdot (p+1)$, and parameters $V(0) = L+1, a = L+2, b = L+3$, and $c = L^2$. Hence, the matrix W is formed by partitioning the vector V into Q segments, each of length $p + 1$. Furthermore, all values in matrix W undergo normalization through z-scoring. Ultimately, Tikhonov's regularization was used with $\lambda = 10^{-3}$ as commonly employed [28, 29, 31] to prevent singular matrices.

Therefore, we propose two learning modules to construct two texture representations:

- **Spatial Representation** $\vec{\Theta}_C(Q)$: This module is responsible for the spatial representation, which is built by stretching the weights of the output layer of a randomized autoencoder, using a z-scored version of X_C as input matrix and the X_C itself as output matrix, as shown in Fig. 1, conducting a spatial analysis. The spatial analysis enables the randomized network to learn the arrangement of the pixels in local neighborhoods, leading the trained weights of the output layer to capture essential details about the spatial relationship between the pixels.
- **Spectral Representation** $\vec{\Omega}_{C_1,C_2}(Q)$: This representation is obtained by stretching the weights of the output layer of a randomized network, using a z-scored version of X_{C_1} as input feature matrix and X_{C_2} itself as output feature matrix, as shown in Fig. 2, conducting a spectral analysis. C_1 and C_2 are two adjacent channels such as (R, G), (G, B) and (G, R). The spectral analysis provides the means for the randomized network to learn to predict the pixels of one channel based on the previous one, thus causing the trained weights of the output layer to contain key information about the spectral relationship between two channels.

Therefore, with the two constructed signatures, $\vec{\Theta}_C(Q)$ and $\vec{\Omega}_{C_1,C_2}(Q)$, which conduct spatial and spectral analyses, respectively, we combine both to create our proposed spatio-spectral texture representation using all channels:

$$\vec{\Psi}(Q) = \left[\vec{\Theta}_R(Q), \vec{\Theta}_G(Q), \vec{\Theta}_B(Q), \vec{\Omega}_{R,G}(Q), \vec{\Omega}_{G,B}(Q), \vec{\Omega}_{B,R}(Q)\right] \tag{2}$$

To conclude, the main steps of the proposed color-texture descriptor are summarized in a high-level module diagram in Fig. 3. The spatial and spectral

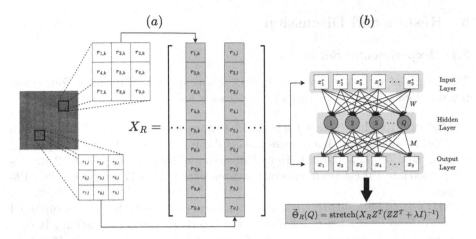

Fig. 1. Illustration of the proposed approach for conducting a spatial analysis. (a) Construction of X_R from assembling of stretched 3×3 windows of the red channel. (b) spatial representation $\vec{\Theta}_R(Q)$ from stretching the output layer weight matrix. (Color figure online)

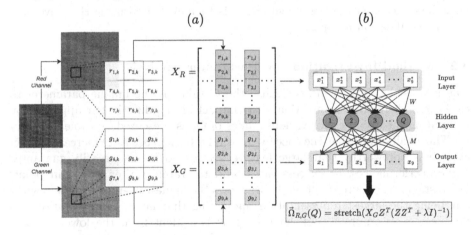

Fig. 2. Illustration of the proposed approach for conducting a spectral analysis. (a) Construction of X_R and X_G from assembling of stretched 3×3 windows of the red channel. (b) spectral representation $\vec{\Omega}_{R,G}(Q)$ obtained from stretching the output layer weight matrix. (Color figure online)

modules have been detailed previously, and are characterized by the Fig. 1 and 2. Each of these modules produces the spatial and the spectral representation, which will be concatenated later to form the proposed color-texture descriptor.

3 Results and Discussion

3.1 Experimental Setup

The proposed approach described in Sect. 2 was applied in images of four color-texture datasets. The structure of the datasets are described as follows:

- **Outex** [21]: This dataset contains 1360 images divided into 68 classes with 20 images per class. The images in this dataset has size of 128×128 pixels.
- **USPtex** [5]: This dataset, from University of São Paulo, has 2292 images divided into 191 classes of natural textures, each having 12 images of 128×128 pixels.
- **MBT** [2]: The Multi-Band Texture dataset is composed by images obtained from the combination of intraband and interband spatial variations. It contains 2464 images divided into 154 classes, each having 16 images of 160×160 pixels.

Finally, the texture representation is computed for each image, followed by a supervised classification using Linear Discriminant Analysis (LDA). Additionally, the performance of the classification is then evaluated using the leave-one-out cross-validation method.

3.2 Method Investigation and Parameter Analysis

The proposed approach in Sect. 2 has the Q value as the unique parameter to calibrate. Therefore, we investigate the impact of Q values in our approach by computing the accuracy for various values of Q, as presented in Table 1.

The results show that the success rates tend to increase as Q increases. However, it is noteworthy that large feature vectors do not necessarily guarantee higher performances, as success rates tend to stabilize after a certain point. For instance, the representation $\vec{\Psi}(13)$ shows the highest average accuracy without being the largest representation, indicating that larger representations do not necessarily improve performance. This is evident from the lower average accuracy obtained by the representation $\vec{\Psi}(15)$. Furthermore, the representation $\vec{\Psi}(03)$, comprising only 216 features, provides a good average accuracy with fewer features than $\vec{\Psi}(09)$, $\vec{\Psi}(13)$ and $\vec{\Psi}(15)$, indicating a representation with a good trade-off between number of features and performance.

Moreover, although we do not use the reconstruction error as guidance for obtaining higher accuracies, in Fig. 4 and Fig. 5, we provided a visualization of the reconstructed images using the spatial $\Theta_C(Q)$ and spectral $\Omega_{C_1,C_2}(Q)$ representations, respectively. As can be seen, the reconstructed images are very similar to the original ones. This suggests that the two proposed modules are capable of learning the texture properties, with the learned output weights (decoder) serving as valuable features to represent the images. Therefore, the capability of spatial and spectral representations (learned weights) to reconstruct the original image with good quality, as illustrated in the figures, provides clear evidence

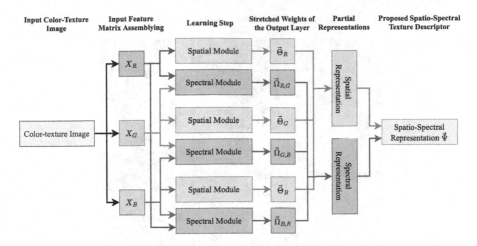

Fig. 3. A high-level diagram describing the proposed approach.

Table 1. Accuracies of the feature vector $\vec{\Psi}(Q)$ for various values of Q.

Q	No of Features	Outex	USPtex	MBT	Avg.
01	108	93.1	98.3	97.7	96.4
03	**216**	**96.0**	**98.7**	**98.9**	**97.9**
05	324	95.9	99.1	99.5	98.2
07	432	95.7	98.9	99.6	98.1
09	540	96.2	99.2	99.6	98.3
13	**756**	**96.8**	**99.1**	**99.8**	**98.6**
15	864	94.9	99.1	99.7	97.9

that the proposed descriptor captures rich information about the image. This highlights its potential as a highly discriminative and robust descriptor, capable of effectively distinguishing between different textures and colors in images.

3.3 Comparison and Discussions

In order to evaluate the effectiveness of the proposed approach, we compared our best representation $\vec{\Psi}(13)$ with other methods presented in the literature. Consistency was maintained across all methods with the use of the same experimental setup, employing the Linear Discriminant Analysis (LDA) classifier and using a leave-one-out cross-validation strategy. The results are shown in Table 2.

To begin with, our analysis compares the first section of methods which goes from Opponent-Gabor to SSR². In the Outex dataset, experimental results indicate that our proposed approach outperforms all compared methods in the section, except for SSR² in which both obtain 96.8%. In the USPtex dataset, our method achieves the third-best accuracy, being just 0.6% of difference from

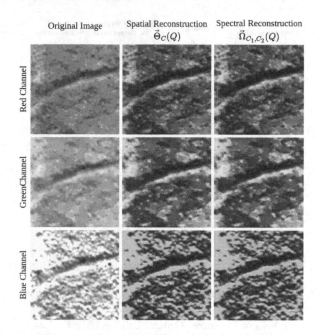

Fig. 4. Examples of the original images channels and the reconstructed images channels using the spatial $\Theta_C(Q)$ and spectral $\Omega_{C_1,C_2}(Q)$ representations, respectively, obtained from a sample of the 1200Tex dataset.

the highest accuracy obtained by SSN (φ^6_{WB}). For the MBT dataset, our approach stands out, nearly reaching 100% accuracy and exceeding the accuracy of the second-best method by 1.2%. Further, it is noteworthy that our approach surpasses existing literature methods in the field of plant species recognition, a real, complex, and demanding problem presented in Sect. 3.4.

In relation to deep learning models, we compared results against various deep convolutional neural network architectures (DCNNs), including AlexNet [18], VGG16 and VGG19 [35], ResNet50 and ResNet101 [13], and InceptionV3 [39]. These results were obtained from [33], where these DCNNs were initially pre-trained on the ImageNet dataset, and then their pre-tained layers were used as a feature extraction method. Due to the fixed input size of each DCNN, images from each dataset were resized and inputted, generating the feature vectors by applying the Global Average Pooling (GAP) to the convolutional layers. For a comprehensive description of this methodology, refer to [33].

The proposed method demonstrated higher accuracy than DCNN architectures in both Outex and MBT datasets. However, for the USPtex dataset, the ResNet50 model slightly outperformed our proposed approach. In the MBT dataset, our proposed method outperforms all the DCNNs architectures. Particularly, the AlexNet, which achieved the highest accuracy among DCNN models in the MBT dataset with 97.8%, was surpassed by our method which obtained 99.8%. The lower performance of these DCNNs on the MBT dataset can be

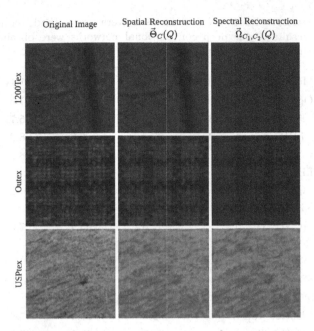

Fig. 5. Examples of the original images and their reconstruction using the spatial $\Theta_C(Q)$ and spectral $\Omega_{C_1,C_2}(Q)$ representations are along the columns. Each row contains a sample from a different dataset.

attributed to the absence of spectral analysis, an important component for MBT. This significance arises from the structure of the dataset, where each image channel is composed of different textural images, emphasizing the importance of spectral analysis. In the Outex dataset, our proposed method surpasses by over 5% when compared to the various DCNNs architectures, showing the inefficiency of these models due to the varying illumination conditions present in the Outex dataset. For instance, the ResNet50, which represents the highest accuracy among the DCNNs models, obtained 91.5% while our method obtained 96.8%, showing a significant improvement.

Considering the results obtained from methods based on randomized neural networks, namely RNN-RGB, SSR[1], and SSR[2], our proposed approach outperforms RNN-RGB and SSR[2] across all datasets. Furthermore, it surpasses the SSR[1] in the Outex and MBT datasets, though SSR[1] maintains a slight edge with 0.2% higher accuracy in the USPtex dataset. However, it is particularly noteworthy that our approach enhances the accuracy by 1.2% in the MBT dataset. Therefore, this comparative analysis illustrates the advantage of integrating features extracted from both the same and adjacent image channels, thereby enhancing the overall accuracy, and evidencing the effectiveness of a spatio-spectral analysis of images.

Table 2. Comparison of accuracies of different literature methods on 3 color-texture datasets. The results of the deep convolutional networks were obtained from [33]. Unavailable results of some methods are represented by empty cells.

Method	USPTex	Outex	MBT
Opponent-Gabor [16]	99.1	93.5	97.6
LPQ integrative [23]	90.4	80.1	95.7
CLBP integrative [11]	97.4	89.6	98.2
CNTD integrative [4]	97.9	92.3	98.5
LETRIST (gray-level) [38]	92.4	82.8	79.1
LGONBP (gray-level) [36]	83.3	83.5	74.2
Sá Junior et al. [17]	96.9	91.5	–
MCND [32]	99.0	95.4	97.0
RNN-RGB [31]	98.4	94.8	–
SSN (φ_{WB}^6) [33]	**99.7**	96.6	98.6
SSR^1 [28]	99.3	96.7	98.2
SSR^2 [28]	99.0	**96.8**	98.0
AlexNet [18]	99.6	91.4	97.8
VGG16 [35]	99.5	91.1	97.2
VGG19 [35]	99.5	90.7	96.3
InceptionV3 [39]	99.5	89.5	94.4
ResNet50 [13]	**99.7**	91.5	94.9
ResNet101 [13]	99.5	91.3	94.6
Proposed Method			
$\vec{\Psi}(13)$	99.1	**96.8**	**99.8**

3.4 Brazilian Plant Species Identification

To assess the practical application effectiveness of the proposed approach, we applied our method to plant species recognition. This poses challenges owing to the diverse spatial arrangements and color patterns found within a single plant leaf but also due to the resemblance in traits across different species [8]. Further, the plant species dataset [8], named 1200Tex, has 400 images divided into 20 classes, each having 20 images. However, for a leaf texture analysis, each image was cropped in three non-overlapping windows of 128×128 pixels, resulting in 1200 images. Figure 6 shows samples from different classes of the dataset. The experimental setup was the same one used in Sect. 3.1.

The results of the proposed approach $\vec{\Psi}(03)$ and other literature methods are shown in Table 3. The results show that our approach achieves the highest accuracy in recognizing plant species while maintaining the second-smallest texture representation size, comprising only 216 features. This shows an improvement over the second-best accuracy obtained by SSR^1, comprising 630 features, which uses a combination of graphs and randomized neural networks. Further, we also

Table 3. Comparison of accuracies of different literature methods in Brazilian plant species identification.

Method	Accuracy (%)
LPQ [23]	73.00
LBP [22]	72.00
CNTD [4]	83.33
$\vec{\Psi}(06, 08)_{04,14,19}$ [41]	87.00
SSN [33]	91.83
SSR^1 [28]	94.08
SSR^2 [28]	93.67
AlexNet [18]	84.92
VGG16 [35]	87.00
VGG19 [35]	83.92
ResNet101 [13]	93.42
Proposed Method	
$\vec{\Psi}(03)$	**94.50**

compare our representation with deep convolutional neural networks, such as AlexNet (256) [18], VGG16 (512) [35], VGG19 (512) [35] and ResNet101 (512) [13], in which the number in parentheses is the feature vector size, obtained by following the same feature extraction setup in [33]. Our proposed descriptor outperformed all compared DCNNs with an increase of 1.08% over the second-best DCNN accuracy, and with a lower feature vector size of 216 attributes, when compared to 512 features of ResNet101.

Finally, the SSR^1 and SSR^2 not only have higher feature vector size than $\vec{\Psi}(03)$ but also represent a multi-parameter method, contributing to the potential for time-consuming adaptation to newer situations due to the numerous possible combinations. On the other hand, our proposed approach has a smaller feature vector size, achieved the highest accuracy in the plant species recognition task and, primarily, it is a single-parameter method. These factors evidence the simplicity and effectiveness of our texture representation, indicating it to be a promising approach for computer vision and pattern recognition applications, such as plant species recognition.

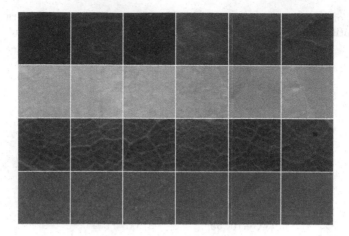

Fig. 6. Examples of samples from the 1200Tex dataset. This figure shows four different class with each row corresponding to six samples of the same class.

4   Conclusion

In this paper, we proposed a new method for color-texture analysis which introduces a single-parameter texture representation that conducts a spatio-spectral analysis from the image color channels. In each image six randomized networks (or autoencoders) are applied, the first three conduct spatial analysis in each color channel, and the last three perform spectral analysis among each combination of two color channels.

The proposed method yields a texture representation with spatio-spectral properties, providing a highly discriminative color-texture representation. This is substantiated by the results obtained from benchmark datasets, where our method outperformed various texture literature methods. Furthermore, the proposed approach also outperformed other literature methods in a practical and challenging application: Brazilian plant species identification. In this context, this paper demonstrates that the utilization of randomized network and autoencoder modules in color images holds significant potential for color-texture analysis and various computer vision tasks. As future work, we believe that our method can be adapted to other types of multi-channel images (e.g., hyperspectral) and other practical applications.

Acknowledgments. L. C. Ribas acknowledges support from São Paulo Research Foundation (FAPESP) (grants #2023/04583-2 and 2018/22214-6). This study was financed in part by the Coordenação de Aperfeiçoamento de Pessoal de Nível Superior - Brasil (CAPES) - Finance Code 001.

References

1. On the solution of ill-posed problems and the method of regularization. On the solution of ill-posed problems and the method of regularization **151**, 501–504 (1963)
2. Abdelmounaime, S., Dong-Chen, H.: New Brodatz-based image databases for grayscale color and multiband texture analysis. ISRN Mach. Vis. **2013**, 876386 (2013)
3. Babalola, E.O., Asad, M.H., Bais, A.: Soil surface texture classification using RGB images acquired under uncontrolled field conditions. IEEE Access **11** (2023)
4. Backes, A.R., Casanova, D., Bruno, O.M.: Texture analysis and classification: a complex network-based approach. Inf. Sci. **219**, 168–180 (2013)
5. Backes, A.R., Casanova, D., Bruno, O.M.: Color texture analysis based on fractal descriptors. Pattern Recogn. **45**(5), 1984–1992 (2012)
6. Boudra, S., Yahiaoui, I., Behloul, A.: Tree trunk texture classification using multi-scale statistical macro binary patterns and CNN. Appl. Soft Comput. **118**, 108473 (2022)
7. Calvetti, D., Morigi, S., Reichel, L., Sgallari, F.: Tikhonov regularization and the l-curve for large discrete ill-posed problems. J. Comput. Appl. Math. **123**(1), 423–446 (2000)
8. Casanova, D., de Mesquita Sá Junior, J.J., Bruno, O.M.: Plant leaf identification using gabor wavelets. Int. J. Imaging Syst. Technol. **19**(3), 236–243 (2009)
9. Cernadas, E., Fernandez-Delgado, M., González-Rufino, E., Carrión, P.: Influence of normalization and color space to color texture classification. Pattern Recogn. **61**, 120–138 (2017)
10. Cover, T.M.: Geometrical and statistical properties of systems of linear inequalities with applications in pattern recognition. IEEE Trans. Electron. Comput. **EC-14**(3), 326–334 (1965)
11. Guo, Z., Zhang, L., Zhang, D.: A completed modeling of local binary pattern operator for texture classification. IEEE Trans. Image Process. **19**(6), 1657–1663 (2010)
12. Gómez Flores, W., de Albuquerque Pereira, W.C., Infantosi, A.F.C.: Improving classification performance of breast lesions on ultrasonography. Pattern Recogn. **48**(4), 1125–1136 (2015)
13. He, K., Zhang, X., Ren, S., Sun, J.: Deep residual learning for image recognition. In: Proceedings of the IEEE Conference on Computer Vision and Pattern Recognition, pp. 770–778 (2016)
14. Huang, G.B., Zhu, Q.Y., Siow, C.K.: Extreme learning machine: theory and applications. Neurocomputing **70**(1), 489–501 (2006)
15. Humeau-Heurtier, A.: Color texture analysis: a survey. IEEE Access **10**, 107993–108003 (2022)
16. Jain, A., Healey, G.: A multiscale representation including opponent-color features for texture recognition. IEEE Trans. Image Process. **7**(1), 124–128 (1998)
17. Junior, J.J.D.M.S., Cortez, P.C., Backes, A.R.: Color texture classification using shortest paths in graphs. IEEE Trans. Image Process. **23**(9), 3751–3761 (2014)
18. Krizhevsky, A., Sutskever, I., Hinton, G.E.: ImageNet classification with deep convolutional neural networks. In: Advances In Neural Information Processing Systems, pp. 1–9 (2012)
19. Liu, H., Fang, J., Xu, X., Sun, F.: Surface material recognition using active multimodal extreme learning machine. Cogn. Comput. **10**(6), 937–950 (2018)

20. Moore, E.H.: On the reciprocal of the general algebraic matrix. Bull. Am. Math. Soc. **26**, 394–395 (1920)
21. Ojala, T., Mäenpää, T., Pietikäinen, M., Viertola, J., Kyllönen, J., Huovinen, S.: Outex - new framework for empirical evaluation of texture analysis algorithms. Object Recogn. Supported By User Interact. Serv. Robots **1**, 701–706 (2002)
22. Ojala, T., Pietikainen, M., Maenpaa, T.: Multiresolution gray-scale and rotation invariant texture classification with local binary patterns. IEEE Trans. Pattern Anal. Mach. Intell. **24**(7), 971–987 (2002)
23. Ojansivu, V., Heikkilä, J.: Blur insensitive texture classification using local phase quantization (2008)
24. Pao, Y.H., Takefuji, Y.: Functional-link net computing: theory, system architecture, and functionalities. Computer **25**(5), 76–79 (1992)
25. Pao, Y.H., Park, G.H., Sobajic, D.J.: Learning and generalization characteristics of the random vector functional-link net. Neurocomputing **6**(2), 163–180 (1994)
26. Penrose, R.: A generalized inverse for matrices. Math. Proc. Cambridge Philos. Soc. **51**(3), 406–413 (1955)
27. Ribas, L.C., Junior, J.J.D.M.S., Scabini, L.F., Bruno, O.M.: Fusion of complex networks and randomized neural networks for texture analysis. Pattern Recogn. **103**, 107189 (2020)
28. Ribas, L.C., Scabini, L.F., Condori, R.H., Bruno, O.M.: Color-texture classification based on spatio-spectral complex network representations. Physica A: Stat. Mech. Appl. 129518 (2024)
29. Ribas, L.C., Scabini, L.F., de Mesquita Sá Junior, J.J., Bruno, O.M.: Local complex features learned by randomized neural networks for texture analysis. Pattern Anal. Appl. **27**(1), 1–12 (2024)
30. Sá Junior, J.J.D.M., Backes, A.R.: ELM based signature for texture classification: Pattern Recogn. **51**, 395–401 (2016)
31. Sá Junior, J.J.D.M., Backes, A.R., Bruno, O.M.: Randomized neural network based signature for color texture classification. Multidimension. Syst. Signal Process. **30**(3), 1171–1186 (2019)
32. Scabini, L.F., Condori, R.H., Gonçalves, W.N., Bruno, O.M.: Multilayer complex network descriptors for color-texture characterization. Inf. Sci. **491**, 30–47 (2019)
33. Scabini, L.F., Ribas, L.C., Bruno, O.M.: Spatio-spectral networks for color-texture analysis. Inf. Sci. **515**, 64–79 (2020)
34. Schmidt, W., Kraaijveld, M., Duin, R.: Feedforward neural networks with random weights. In: Proceedings 11th IAPR International Conference on Pattern Recognition. Vol. II. Conference B: Pattern Recognition Methodology and Systems, pp. 1–4 (1992)
35. Simonyan, K., Zisserman, A.: Very deep convolutional networks for large-scale image recognition. CoRR **abs/1409.1556** (2014)
36. Song, T., Feng, J., Luo, L., Gao, C., Li, H.: Robust texture description using local grouped order pattern and non-local binary pattern. IEEE Trans. Circuits Syst. Video Technol. **31**(1), 189–202 (2020)
37. Song, T., Feng, J., Wang, Y., Gao, C.: Color texture description based on holistic and hierarchical order-encoding patterns. In: 2020 25th International Conference on Pattern Recognition (ICPR), pp. 1306–1312 (2021)
38. Song, T., Li, H., Meng, F., Wu, Q., Cai, J.: LETRIST: locally encoded transform feature histogram for rotation-invariant texture classification. IEEE Trans. Circ. Syst. Video Technol. **28**(7), 1565–1579 (2017)

39. Szegedy, C., Vanhoucke, V., Ioffe, S., Shlens, J., Wojna, Z.: Rethinking the inception architecture for computer vision. In: The IEEE Conference on Computer Vision and Pattern Recognition (CVPR) (2016)
40. R, X., et al.: Pulmonary textures classification via a multi-scale attention network. IEEE J. Biomed. Health Inform. **24**(7), 2041–2052 (2019)
41. Zielinski, K.M.C., Ribas, L.C., Scabini, L.F.S., Bruno, O.M.: Complex texture features learned by applying randomized neural network on graphs. In: 2022 Eleventh International Conference on Image Processing Theory, Tools and Applications (IPTA), pp. 1–6 (2022)

Application of Directional Vectors for Independent Subspaces in the Bio-Inspired Networks

Naohiro Ishii[1]($\boxtimes$), Kazunori Iwata[2], Kazuya Odagiri[3], and Tokuro Matsuo[1]

[1] Advanced Institute of Industrial Technology, Tokyo 140-0011, Japan
nishii@acm.org, matsuo@aiit.ac.jp
[2] Aichi University, Nagoya 453-8777, Japan
kazunori@aichi-u.ac.jp
[3] Sugiyama Jogakuen University, Nagoya 464-8622, Japan
kodagiri@isugiyama-u.ac.jp

Abstract. Machine learning, deep learning and neural networks are extensively developed in many fields, in which neural network architectures have shown a variety of applications. However, there is a need for explainable fundamentals in complex neural networks. It is important to know how the sensory information in neural networks develops to the higher-level processing for classification and learning. In this paper, it is shown that bio-inspired networks are useful for the explanation of network functions. First, the asymmetric network is created based on the biological retinal network with nonlinear functions. Second, the classification performance of the asymmetric network is compared to the conventional symmetric network. Prominent characteristic in the biological networks is sensitive to the motion intensity changes in their visual environments. Here, it is shown that the adjacent neurons create sensory directional information in the movements. Further, directional vectors are generated on the activities of the adjacent neurons caused by the intensity changes of the input. These vectors are useful for the generation of independent subspaces, which connect from the sensory information to the higher-level functions in networks.

Keywords: asymmetric and symmetric networks · classification performance of networks · generation of the directional vectors · independent subspaces

1 Introduction

Recently, there has been a great deal of excitement and interesting processing in deep neural networks, because they have achieved breakthrough results in areas as machine learning, computer vision, neural computations and artificial intelligence [1, 2]. Their networks are expected to be transparent, understandable and explainable in their successive processing in the multilayered structures [2]. It is important to know how the sensory information in neural networks connects to the higher-level processing as classification and learning [3]. Prominent characteristic in the biological networks is sensitive to the motion intensity changes in their visual environments, which is the most important function [4, 5]. Studies from motion direction and network mechanisms as sensory code are carried out [6]. Further, independent space codes as the basis set functions for spatial receptive fields are studied as sparse coding in the biological cortex [7, 8]. In this paper, it is shown that bio-inspired networks are useful for the explanation of network functions. In this paper, it is shown that bio-inspired network generates useful bases for the explanation of features classification. First, the asymmetric network with nonlinear functions is created based on the bio-inspired retinal network. From sensory information as the movement stimulus, we can analyze the movement behavior by using systematic approach. The computational results for the sensitivity of the movement stimulus are compared between the bio-inspired asymmetric network and the symmetric one [8–10]. The superiority of the asymmetric network is sensitive to the directional movement, which is shown computationally. Further, the classification performance is compared between the bio-inspired asymmetric network and the symmetric one. Then, the asymmetric network shows a better classification performance than the symmetric network. Their orthogonal bases in the asymmetric network show the same classification ability of the Fourier bases under the extended asymmetrical networks [13, 15]. Finally, the adjacent neurons create sensory directional information in the stimulus movements and the intensity changes of the input between adjacent neurons. Then, the activity between adjacent neurons is important to obtain the higher-level processing mechanisms. Directional vectors are proposed for activities of adjacent neurons. These vectors are useful for the generation of independent subspaces, which connect from the sensory information to the higher-level functions in networks. Sections 2 and 3 introduce the bio-inspired asymmetric and the symmetric networks. These networks are compared in the movement functions and classification performances in Sects. 4 and 5. Directional vectors are newly proposed in Sect. 6.

2 Bio-Inspired Neural Networks

2.1 Background of Asymmetric Neural Networks Based on the Bio-Inspired Network

In the biological neural networks, the structure of the network, is closely related to the functions of the network. Naka et al. [12] presented a simplified, but essential networks of catfish inner retina as shown in Fig. 1. The asymmetric neural network is extracted from the catfish retinal network [12]. The asymmetric structure network which composes of the pathway from the bipolar cell B to the amacrine cell N and that from the bipolar cell B, via the amacrine cell C to the N [12, 13]. It is shown that N cell response is realized by a linear filter. Thus, the asymmetric network in Fig. 1 is composed of a linear pathway and a nonlinear pathway with the cell C working as a squaring function.

2.2 Model of Asymmetric and Symmetric Networks

Models of the asymmetric and symmetric networks, both of which are the bio-inspired networks [8, 12, 13] are shown in Fig. 2(a) and (b), respectively, in which impulse

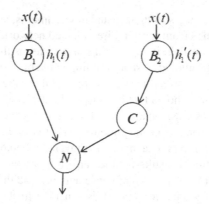

Fig. 1. Asymmetric network with linear and squaring nonlinear pathways

response functions of cells are shown in $h_1(t)$ and $h'_1(t)$. The $(\ )^2$ shows a square operation. The symmetric model called energy model is proposed [8–10] in the bio-inspired network for visual system.

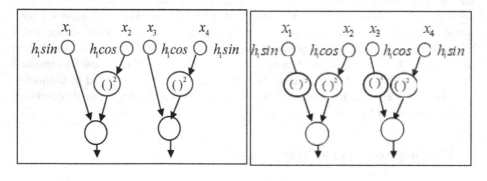

(a) Asymmetric network unit   (b) Symmetric network unit

Fig. 2. Asymmetric unit and symmetric unit in the 1st layer of the network

3   Basis Set in the Asymmetric Networks

3.1   Orthogonality and Independence of Bases in the Asymmetric Network Unit

We can compute the orthogonality of the network unit in Fig. 2. We assume here the input $\{x\}(x = x_i, i = 1 \sim 4)$ is same for the unit. Then, relation of the orthogonality of the bases of the asymmetric network unit are shown in the arc in Fig. 3. Only the orthogonality is not satisfied between cos^2x and sin^2x, which is indicated in $\times$ with the arc. Independence is also an important characteristic for classification and integration of features. We compare the asymmetric networks and the symmetric ones from the independence. Then, the following theorems are derived.

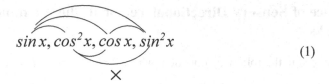

$$sin\,x,\,cos^2x,\,cos\,x,\,sin^2x \tag{1}$$

Fig. 3. Relations of orthogonality in the asymmetrical unit

Theorem 1. The bases set $\{sin\,x,\,cos^2x,\,cos\,x,\,sin^2x\}$ in the asymmetric network unit in Fig. 2(a), is independent.

This is proved using the following Eq. (2), where all the constant coefficients

$$\alpha_1 sin^2 x + \alpha_2 cos^2 x + \alpha_3 cos^2 x + \alpha_4 sin^2 x = 0 \tag{2}$$

$\alpha_i = 0, i = 1 \sim 4$ hold by setting $x = 0, x = (\pi/6), x = (\pi/3)$ and $x = (\pi/2)$ in Eq. (2). Then, the solution $\alpha_i = 0, i = 1 \sim 4$, $x \neq x', x \neq x''$, $x' \neq x''$ satisfy Eq. (2). Thus, the bases are independent in the asymmetric unit, while bases set in the symmetric network unit, is dependent in the following equation.

$$\alpha_1 sin^2 x + \alpha_2 cos^2 x + \alpha_3 cos^2 x' + \alpha_4 sin^2 x'' = 0 \tag{3}$$

By setting the same value of x in Eq. (3), $\alpha_i = 0, i = 1 \sim 4$ does not obtained. This shows the dependence of the bases set in the symmetric network.

3.2 Independence of Weights for Classification in the Network

Independence for classification in the network is important also with learning. The network performance for classification is evaluated using mean squared loss function, *Loss* in Eq. (4) between the inputs and outputs of the network [11].

$$Loss = \frac{1}{m}\|XW - Z\|^2 \tag{4}$$

where X and Z are the inputs and output matrices of the network, respectively W is the connection weight matrix between the inputs and outputs. The optimization of the loss function in Eq. (4) is realized by the derivative of Eq. (5) with respect to W

$$\frac{\partial}{\partial W}(\frac{1}{M}\|XW - Z\|^2) = \frac{1}{M}X^T(XW - Z) = 0 \tag{5}$$

By the differentiation in Eq. (5),

$$W = (X^TX)^{-1}X^TZ \tag{6}$$

is obtained. From Eq. (6), a sufficient condition for the existence of the weights is the matrix, X to be non-singular, i.e., the X consists of independence input vectors. For the classification of input vectors and the learning by the modified weight ΔW in the network, the sufficient condition implies the determinant of the matrix to be non-zero.

4 Existence of Sensory Directional Vector in the Asymmetric Networks

$X'(t)$, is described in the following equation, where $0 \le \alpha \le 1$ and $\beta = 1 - \alpha$ hold.

$$x'(t) = \alpha x(t) + \beta x''(t) \tag{7}$$

Let the power spectrums of $x(t)$ and $x''(t)$, be p and p'', respectively an equation $p'' = kp$ holds for the coefficient k. Figure 4 shows that the left slashed light is moving from the receptive field of B_1 cell to the right field of the B_2 cell in the schematic diagram.

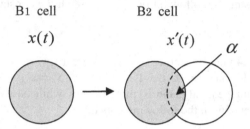

B1 cell   B2 cell

$x(t)$ $x'(t)$ α

Fig. 4. Schematic diagram of the preferred stimulus direction

First, on the linear pathway in Fig. 2(a), the input function is $x(t)$ and the output function is $y(t)$ are given.

$$y(t) = \int h_1'''(\tau)(y_1(t - \tau) + y_2(t - \tau))d\tau + \varepsilon \tag{8}$$

where $y_1(t)$ shows the linear information on the linear pathway, while $y_2(t)$ shows the nonlinear information on the nonlinear pathway and ε shows error value. The $y_1(t)$ and $y_2(t)$ are given, respectively as follows,

$$y_1(t) = \int_0^\infty h_1'(\tau)x(t - \tau)d\tau \tag{9}$$

$$y_2(t) = \int_0^\infty \int_0^\infty h_1''(\tau_1)h_1''(\tau_2)x'(t - \tau_1)x'(t - \tau_2)d\tau_1 d\tau_2 \tag{10}$$

We assume that the impulse response function $h1'''(t)$ is assumed to be value 1 without loss of generality.

4.1 Sensory Directional Equations from Optimized Conditions in the Asymmetric Network

Under the assumption that the impulse response functions, $h_1'(t)$ of the cell B_1, $h_1''(t)$ of the cell B_2 and moving stimulus ratio α in the right to be unknown, the optimization of the network is carried out. By the minimization of the mean squared value ξ using Eq. (8), the following necessary conditions for the optimization of equations are derived,

$$\frac{\partial \xi}{\partial h1'(t)} = 0, \frac{\partial \xi}{\partial h2''(t)} = 0, \frac{\partial \xi}{\partial \alpha} = 0 \tag{11}$$

Then, the following equations are derived for the optimization conditions satisfying Eqs. (11).

$$
\begin{aligned}
&E[y(t)x'(t-\lambda)] = \alpha p h_1'(\lambda) \\
&E[(y(t)-C_0)x'(t-\lambda_1)x'(t-\lambda_2)] = 2\{(\alpha^2+k\beta^2)p^2 h_1''(\lambda_1)h_1''(\lambda_2)\} \\
&E[(y(t)-C_0)x(t-\lambda_1)x(t-\lambda_2)] = 2\alpha^2 p^2 h_1''(\lambda_1)h_1''(\lambda_2) \\
&E[(y(t)-C_0)x''(t-\lambda_1)x''(t-\lambda_2)] = 2\beta^2(kp)^2 h_1''(\lambda_1)h_1''(\lambda_2)
\end{aligned}
\tag{12}
$$

where C_0 is the mean value of, $y(t)$ which is shown in the following. Here, Eqs. (12) can be rewritten by applying Wiener kernels[10], which are computed from input and output correlations. From the necessary optimization equations in Eq. (11), the following Wiener kernel equations are derived as shown in the following. First, we can compute the 1-st order Wiener kernel, $C_{11}(\lambda)$ the 2-nd order one $C21(\lambda 1 \lambda 2)$ as follows.

$$C_{11}(\lambda) = \frac{1}{p}E[y(t)x(t-\lambda)] = h_1'(\lambda) \tag{13}$$

$$C_{21}(\lambda_1, \lambda_2) = \frac{1}{2p^2}E[(y(t)-C_0)x(t-\lambda_1)x(t-\lambda_2)] = \alpha^2 h_1''(\lambda_1)h_1''(\lambda_2) \tag{14}$$

From Eqs. (12), (13) and (14), the ratio, α which is a mixed coefficient of $x(t)$ to $x(t)$ is computed through α as the amplitude of the second order Wiener kernel. Second, on the nonlinear pathway, we can compute the 0-th order kernel, C_0, the 1-st order kernel $C_{12}(\lambda)$ and the 2-nd order kernel by the $C_{22}(\lambda_1 \lambda_2)$ cross-correlations between $x(t)$ and $y(t)$.

$$C_{12}(\lambda_1, \lambda_2) = \frac{1}{p(\alpha^2+k\beta^2)}E[y(t)x'(t-\lambda)] = \frac{\alpha}{\alpha^2+k(1-\alpha)^2}h_1'(\lambda) \tag{15}$$

and

$$C_{22}(\lambda_1, \lambda_2) = h_1''(\lambda_1)h_1''(\lambda_2) \tag{16}$$

The second order kernels C_{21} and C_{22} are abbreviated in the representation in Eqs. (14) and (16).

$$(C_{21}/C_{22}) = \alpha^2 \tag{17}$$

Then, from Eq. (17), the ratio α is computed as follows

$$\alpha = \sqrt{\frac{C21}{C22}} \tag{18}$$

Equation (18) is called here α- equation, which implies the directional stimulus on the network. The directional equation from the left to the right, holds as shown in the following,

$$\frac{C_{12}}{C_{11}} = \frac{\sqrt{\frac{C_{21}}{C_{22}}}}{\frac{C_{21}}{C_{22}} + k(1 - \sqrt{\frac{C_{21}}{C_{22}}})} \tag{19}$$

Equation (19) shows the direction of the stimulus from the left to the right.

5 Evaluation in the Asymmetric and the Symmetric Networks

We assume the first 4-dimensional input as the $X_1 = (x_{11}\ x_{12}\ x_{13}\ x_{14})$ which is a component of the total input $X = [X_1\ X_2\ X_3\ X_4]$. The X is described in 4-dimensional input matrix. The output in Fig. 2(a) becomes $\{sin(x_1),\ cos^2(x_2),\ cos(x_3),\ sin^2(x_4)\}$ for the input $\{x_1, x_2, x_3, x_4\}$, in which h_1 to be 1 for the simplicity.

$$X = \begin{bmatrix} x_{11} & \cdots & x_{14} \\ \vdots & \ddots & \vdots \\ x_{41} & \cdots & x_{44} \end{bmatrix} \left(\equiv \begin{bmatrix} 1 & 0 & 0 & 1 \\ 0 & 1 & 1 & 0 \\ 0 & 0 & 1 & 1 \\ 1 & 1 & 0 & 0 \end{bmatrix} \right) \tag{20}$$

The determinant of the outputs of asymmetric networks for Eq. (20) is shown in Eq. (21), where we assume $a = sin(x_i)$ and $b = cos(x_j)$.

$$\|Asym.\|\ for\ Eq.(20) = \begin{Vmatrix} a & 1 & 1 & a^2 \\ 0 & b^2 & b & 0 \\ a & 1 & b & a^2 \\ 0 & b^2 & 1 & 0 \end{Vmatrix} \tag{21}$$

The determinant of the outputs of networks including Eq. (21) is represented as

$$\|Asym.\| = \left(a^3\right)\{(\pm b)[Z_1] + (\pm 1)[Z_2]\} \tag{22}$$

where $[Z_1]$ shows the summed determinants of matrices by the cofactor, variable $\pm b$ expansion across the 3rd column in Eq. (21) and $[Z_2]$ shows those by the cofactor ± 1 expansion. Similarly, the determinant of symmetric networks in Eq. (20) is in Eq. (23).

$$\|Sym.\|\ for\ Eq.(20) = \begin{Vmatrix} a^2 & 1 & 1 & a^2 \\ 0 & b^2 & b^2 & 0 \\ a^2 & 1 & b^2 & a^2 \\ 0 & b^2 & 1 & 0 \end{Vmatrix} \tag{23}$$

The determinant of the output of symmetrical networks including Eq. (23) is represented as

$$\|Sym.\| = \left(a^4\right)\{\left(\pm b^2\right)[Z_1] + (\pm 1)[Z_2]\} \tag{24}$$

Note here the determinant $\{[Z_1] + (\pm 1)[Z_2]\}$ is same in both Eqs. (23) and (24).

5.1 Conditions of Independence of $\|Asym.\|$ and $\|Sym.\|$

The independence in the asymmetric networks and the symmetric ones are evaluated based on the $\|Asym.\|$ and $\|Sym.\|$.

Theorem 2. Under the condition $[Z_1] \neq 0$, the determinant of asymmetric networks, $\|Asym.\| \neq 0$ holds.

This is proved as follows. The first term, $(\pm b)[Z_1]$ in the determinant of asymmetric networks in Eq. (22), have the odd order exponentiation of the variable b, while the second term $(\pm 1)[Z_2]$ have the even order exponentiation of the variable b. Thus, these terms do not generate the summation to be zero.

Lemma 3. The determinants $[Z_1]$ and $[Z_2]$ in the asymmetric and symmetric network are described in a quadratic polynomial of variable b in the following.

$$[Z_1] = mb^2 + l \text{ and } [Z_2] = kb^2 + n \tag{25}$$

where m, l, k and n are numerical coefficients.

This is proved from the definition of the matrix. Since $[Z_1]$ and $[Z_2]$ are computed by the cofactor of expansion across the 3rd column in the 4-demensional matrix, variable b^2 exists only in the 2nd column of the matrix. Since only one variable in the 2nd column is used in the each expansion term from the definition of the determinant, the expansion terms consist of the quadratic polynomial in Eq. (25).

Theorem 4. $\|Sym.\| = 0$ holds if and only if $m = 0$, $(l + k) = 0$ and $n = 0$ holds. Similarly, $\|Asym.\| = 0$ holds if and only if $m = 0$, $l = 0$, $k = 0$ and $n = 0$ holds.

Theorem 5. When $\|Sym.\| = 0$ holds, the parameters $l = -k \neq 0$ holds. Then, if $l = -k \neq 0$ holds, $\|Asym.\| \neq 0$ is satisfied.

Theorem 6. When $\|Sym.\| \neq 0$ holds, $\|Asym.\| \neq 0$ is also satisfied.

This is proved by the contradiction of the statement; if $\|Asym.\| = 0$ holds, then. $\|Sym.\| = 0$ holds. From Theorems 4, 5 and 6, the performances are compared.

Theorem 7. The performance of the classification of $|Asym.|$ include that of $|Sym.|$. This shows $|Asym.|$ is superior to $|Sym.|$ in the classification ability.

6 Application of Sensory Directional Vectors for Generation of Independent Subspaces

Directional vectors are applied to the evaluation for the generation of independent subspaces in the asymmetric networks.

$$
\begin{vmatrix} 1 & 1 & 0 & 0 \\ 0 & 0 & 1 & 1 \\ 1 & 1 & 1 & 0 \\ 0 & 1 & 1 & 1 \end{vmatrix}
\qquad
a^3 \begin{Vmatrix} 1 & b^2 & 1 & 0 \\ 0 & 1 & b & 1 \\ 1 & b^2 & b & 0 \\ 0 & b^2 & b & 1 \end{Vmatrix}
\qquad
\begin{Vmatrix} 1 \rightarrow b^2 & 1 \rightarrow 0 \\ 0 \leftarrow 1 & b \leftarrow 1 \\ 1 \rightarrow b^2 & b \rightarrow 0 \\ 0 \leftarrow b^2 & b \leftarrow 1 \end{Vmatrix}
$$

(A) Input matrix   (B) Determinant of (A)   (C) Arrow components of (B)

Fig. 5. Input matrix, determinant of the matrix and notations with arrow components

6.1 Independent Directional Vectors

Generation of directional vectors are made of the intensity change of the input in the following steps. First, the input matrix is given, in which the bases are set as $[\sin(x),$ $\cos(x)^2, \cos(x), \sin(x)^2]$ as shown in Sect. 4. We propose here the arrow components in Fig. 5(C). The arrow component, $1 \rightarrow b^2$ shows the intensity, 1 is larger than the intensity, b^2, then directed arrow is described from the left 1 to the right b^2.

The determinant of the matrix (B) in Fig. 5 based on the bases $[\sin(x), \cos(x)^2,$ $\cos(x), \sin(x)^2]$ becomes to be 0. We change bases $\cos(x)^2 \leftrightarrow \sin(x)^2$ in Fig. 5(B). Thus, a new bases become as $[\sin(x), \sin(x)^2, \cos(x), \cos(x)^2]$. Then, the replacement between the 2nd and the 3rd columns generates a new matrix Fig. 6 (A), which causes a new determinant in Fig. 6(B). Since the determinant in Fig. 5(B) is 0, the new determinant in Fig. 6(B) also becomes 0 by the replacement of two columns in Fig. 5(B).

$$
\begin{vmatrix} a & 0 & 1 & b^2 \\ 0 & a^2 & b & 1 \\ a & 0 & b & b^2 \\ 0 & a^2 & b & b^2 \end{vmatrix}
\qquad
a^3 \begin{Vmatrix} 1 & 0 & 1 & b^2 \\ 0 & 1 & b & 1 \\ 1 & 0 & b & b^2 \\ 0 & 1 & b & b^2 \end{Vmatrix}
\qquad
\begin{Vmatrix} 1 \rightarrow 0 & 1 \rightarrow b^2 \\ 0 \leftarrow 1 & b \leftarrow 1 \\ 1 \rightarrow 0 & b \rightarrow b^2 \\ 0 \leftarrow 1 & b \rightarrow b^2 \end{Vmatrix}
$$

(A) Matrix of Fig.5(A)   (B) Determinant of (A)   (C) Arrow components of (B)

Fig. 6. Matrix and determinant of new bases $[\sin(x), \sin(x)^2, \cos(x), \cos(x)^2]$

Since the determinant: Fig. 6(B) becomes 0, the following linear equation holds using column vectors in Fig. 6(A)

$$
\alpha \begin{pmatrix} 1 \\ 0 \\ 1 \\ 0 \end{pmatrix} + \beta \begin{pmatrix} b^2 \\ 1 \\ b^2 \\ b^2 \end{pmatrix} + \gamma \begin{pmatrix} 1 \\ b \\ b \\ b \end{pmatrix} + \delta \begin{pmatrix} b^2 \\ 1 \\ b^2 \\ b^2 \end{pmatrix} = 0 \tag{26}
$$

where α, β, γ and δ are coefficients and their values are 0 by the independence of vectors. Similarly, from the matrix of Fig. 6(A), the following equation holds.

$$
\alpha' \begin{pmatrix} 1 \\ 0 \\ 1 \\ 0 \end{pmatrix} + \beta' \begin{pmatrix} 0 \\ 1 \\ 0 \\ 1 \end{pmatrix} + \gamma' \begin{pmatrix} 1 \\ b \\ b \\ b \end{pmatrix} + \delta' \begin{pmatrix} b^2 \\ 1 \\ b^2 \\ b^2 \end{pmatrix} = 0 \tag{27}
$$

where α', β', γ' and δ' are coefficients and their values are 0 by the independence of vectors. Since the coefficients in Eqs. (26) and (27) are all zero, the following equation is derived by combining these equations.

$$\tilde{\alpha}\left\{\begin{pmatrix}1\\0\\1\\0\end{pmatrix}+\begin{pmatrix}b^2\\1\\b^2\\b^2\end{pmatrix}\right\}+\beta\left\{\begin{pmatrix}1\\b\\b\\b\end{pmatrix}+\begin{pmatrix}b^2\\1\\b^2\\b^2\end{pmatrix}\right\}+\tilde{\gamma}\left\{\begin{pmatrix}1\\0\\1\\0\end{pmatrix}+\begin{pmatrix}0\\1\\0\\1\end{pmatrix}\right\}+\tilde{\delta}\left\{\begin{pmatrix}1\\b\\b\\b\end{pmatrix}+\begin{pmatrix}b^2\\1\\b^2\\b^2\end{pmatrix}\right\}=0 \quad (28)$$

and coefficients $\tilde{\alpha}=0$, $\tilde{\beta}=0$, $\tilde{\gamma}=0$ and $\tilde{\delta}=0$ hold.

Here, we define the directional vector using adjacent column vectors of Fig. 5(C) and Fig. 6(C), whose notations of the arrow components are defined in Fig. 7 for the directional vectors.

Notation	Arrow comp.	Notation	Arrow comp.
B	; $b \leftarrow 1$	-bB	; $b \longrightarrow b^2$
C	; $1 \longrightarrow 0$	-C	; $0 \leftarrow 1$
bC	; $b \longrightarrow 0$	D	; $1 \longrightarrow b^2$
$-b^2C$	; $0 \leftarrow b^2$	E	; $1 \longrightarrow 1$

Fig. 7. Notations of the arrow components in the directional vectors

The directional vectors are shown using notations of the arrow components as follows,

$$\begin{pmatrix}D\\C\\C\\D\end{pmatrix},\begin{pmatrix}-C\\B\\-C\\B\end{pmatrix},\begin{pmatrix}D\\bC\\C\\-bB\end{pmatrix},\begin{pmatrix}-b^2C\\B\\-C\\-bB\end{pmatrix} \quad (29)$$

A linear equation using directional vectors in Eq. (29) is shown in the following.

$$\alpha\begin{pmatrix}D\\C\\C\\D\end{pmatrix}+\beta\begin{pmatrix}C\\B\\-C\\B\end{pmatrix}+\gamma\begin{pmatrix}D\\bC\\C\\-bB\end{pmatrix}+\delta\begin{pmatrix}-b^2C\\B\\-C\\-bB\end{pmatrix}=0 \quad (30)$$

where α, β, γ and δ are coefficients. Equation (30) is shown into the vector components equation, Eq. (31).

$$\begin{aligned}(\alpha+\gamma b)C+(\beta+\delta)B&=0\\(\alpha+\gamma b)C+(\beta+\delta)B&=0\\(\alpha-\beta+\gamma-\delta)C&=0\\\alpha D+(\beta-\gamma b-\delta b)B&=0\end{aligned} \quad (31)$$

In the fourth equation in Eq. (31), vectors D and B are directionally inverse. Thus, to satisfy the fourth equation, the following equations are obtained.

$$\alpha = 0, (\beta - \gamma b - \delta b) = 0 \tag{32}$$

The second equation in Eq. (31) shows vectors B and D are directionally inverse. Thus,

$$(\alpha + \gamma b) = 0, (\beta + \delta) = 0 \tag{33}$$

Using $\alpha = 0$ in Eq. (32), $\gamma = 0$ is derived from Eq. (33). From Eq. (33), $\beta = -\delta$ holds, which derives $\delta = 0$. Then, $\beta = 0$ is satisfied. Thus, all the coefficients α, β, γ and δ become to be0. This shows the directional vectors are linearly independent. Since the determinant in Fig. 5(C) is not zero, the input vectors are linearly independent. Since the input matrix is derived also from the arrow components in the directional vectors, a linear subspace generated from the directional vectors is same to that from the input matrix. This case of linear independence of inputs is generalized as follows.

Theorem 8. Independence of input matrix is satisfied if and only if the directional vectors between adjacent columns of the matrix are independent.

Proof of the necessary condition is derived similarly according to the above steps. The sufficient condition is shown by decomposing the above directional vectors to the arrow components. Two determinant matrices of Fig. 5(C) and Fig. 6(C) are zero.

6.2 Dependent Directional Vectors

First, the input matrix is given, in which the bases are set as $[\sin(x), \cos(x)^2, \cos(x), \sin(x)^2]$ as shown in Sect. 4. We show the arrow components in Fig. 8(C) and (D).

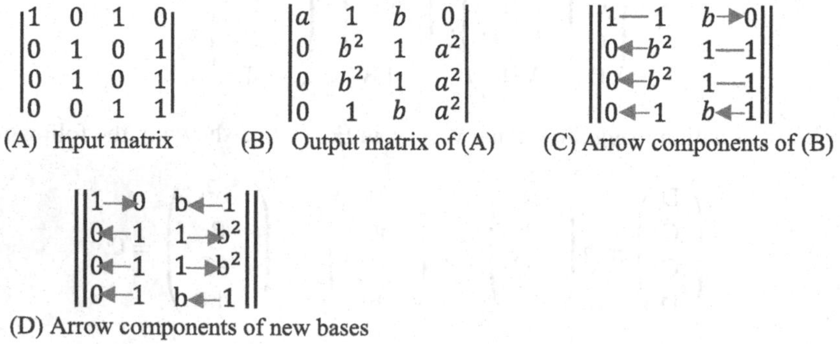

$$
\begin{vmatrix} 1 & 0 & 1 & 0 \\ 0 & 1 & 0 & 1 \\ 0 & 1 & 0 & 1 \\ 0 & 0 & 1 & 1 \end{vmatrix}
\qquad
\begin{vmatrix} a & 1 & b & 0 \\ 0 & b^2 & 1 & a^2 \\ 0 & b^2 & 1 & a^2 \\ 0 & 1 & b & a^2 \end{vmatrix}
\qquad
\begin{Vmatrix} 1-1 & b \to 0 \\ 0 \leftarrow b^2 & 1-1 \\ 0 \leftarrow b^2 & 1-1 \\ 0 \leftarrow 1 & b \leftarrow 1 \end{Vmatrix}
$$

(A) Input matrix   (B) Output matrix of (A)   (C) Arrow components of (B)

$$
\begin{Vmatrix} 1 \to 0 & b \leftarrow 1 \\ 0 \leftarrow 1 & 1 \to b^2 \\ 0 \leftarrow 1 & 1 \to b^2 \\ 0 \leftarrow 1 & b \leftarrow 1 \end{Vmatrix}
$$

(D) Arrow components of new bases

Fig. 8. Arrow components of the bases $[\sin(x), \sin(x)^2, \cos(x), \cos(x)^2]$

The directional vectors are created using notations of the arrow components in Fig. 7 with determinants in Fig. 8(C) and (D) as follows,

$$
\begin{pmatrix} E \\ bC \\ C \\ B \end{pmatrix},
\begin{pmatrix} -b^2C \\ E \\ -C \\ D \end{pmatrix},
\begin{pmatrix} -b^2C \\ E \\ -C \\ D \end{pmatrix},
\begin{pmatrix} -C \\ B \\ -C \\ B \end{pmatrix}
\tag{34}
$$

A linear equation using directional vectors in Eq. (34) is shown in the following.

$$\alpha \begin{pmatrix} E \\ bC \\ C \\ B \end{pmatrix} + \beta \begin{pmatrix} -b^2C \\ E \\ -C \\ D \end{pmatrix} + \gamma \begin{pmatrix} -b^2C \\ E \\ -C \\ D \end{pmatrix} + \delta \begin{pmatrix} -C \\ B \\ -C \\ B \end{pmatrix} = 0 \tag{35}$$

where α, β, γ and δ are coefficients. From Eq. (35),

$$\beta + \gamma = 0 \text{ and } \delta = \alpha = 0 \tag{36}$$

are derived, which satisfy the linear equation, Eq. (36). Thus, the directional vectors generate dependent subspace in case of the input matrix in Fig. 8(A).

7 Conclusion

Studies of machine learning, artificial intelligence and neural networks have been developed greatly. In this paper, starting from the bio-inspired neural networks, it is shown that the asymmetrical network with nonlinear functions have characteristics of orthogonal basis. The adjacent neurons create sensory direction information in the sensory movements and input patterns. The superiority of the asymmetric network is sensitive to the directional movement, which is shown computationally. Further, the classification performance is compared between the bio-inspired asymmetric network and the symmetric one. Then, the asymmetric network shows a better classification performance than the symmetric network. The activity between adjacent neurons is important to obtain the higher-level processing mechanisms. Directional vectors are proposed for the connected activities of adjacent neurons caused by the intensity changes of the input. These vectors are useful for the generation of independent subspaces, which will connect from the sensory information to the higher-level functions in networks.

References

1. Samek, W., Lapusckn, S., Anders, C.J., Mullci, K.-R.: Explaining deep neural networks and beyond: a review of methods and applications. Proc. of the IEEE 103(3), 247–278 (2021)
2. Peng, X., Li, Y., Tsang, I.W., Zhu, H., Lv, J., Zhou, J.T.: XAI beyond classification: interpretable neural clustering. J. Mach. Learn. Res. 23, 1–28 (2022)
3. Xu, X., Hanganu-Opatz, I.L., Bieler, M.: Cross-talk of low-level sensory and high-level cognitive processing: development, mechanisms, and relevance for cross-modal abilities of the brain. Front. Neurorobot. 14(7), 1–19 (2020)
4. Albright, T.D., Stoner, G.R.: Visual motion perception. Proc. Natl. Acad. Sci. U.S.A. 92, 2433–2440 (1995)
5. Ullman, S.: The measurement of visual motion. Trends Neurosci. 6, 177–179 (1983)
6. Lewis, J.E.: Sensory processing and the network mechanisms for reading neuronal population codes. J. Comp. Physiol. (A) 185, 373–378 (1999)
7. Olshausen, B.A., Field, D.J.: Sparse coding with an overcomplete basis set: a strategy employed by V1? Vision. Res. 37(23), 3311–3325 (1997)

8. Adelson, E.H., Bergen, J.R.: Spatiotemporal energy models for the perception of motion. J. Optical Soc. Am. A, 284–298 (1985)
9. Hyvarinen, A., Hoyer, P.: Emergence of phase-and shift invariant features by decomposition of natural images into independent feature subspaces. Neural Comput. **12**, 1705–1720 (2000)
10. Hashimoto, W.: Quadratic forms in natural images. Netw. Comput. Neural Syst. **14**(4), 765–788 (2003)
11. Zhao, G., Wang, T., Li, Y., Jin, Y., Lang, C., Ling, H.: The cascade forward algorithm for neural network training, arXiv:2303.09728v2, Cornell University, pp.1–12, (2023)
12. Naka, K.I., Sakai, H.M., Ishii, N.: Generation and transformation of second-order nonlinearity in catfish retina. Ann. Biomed. Eng. **16**, 53–64 (1988)
13. Ishii, N., Deguchi, T., Kawaguchi, M., Sasaki, H., Matsuo, T.: Orthogonal properties of asymmetric neural networks with Gabor filters. In: Pérez García, H., Sánchez González, L., Castejón Limas, M., Quintián Pardo, H., Corchado Rodríguez, E. (eds.) HAIS 2019. LNCS (LNAI), vol. 11734, pp. 589–601. Springer, Cham (2019). https://doi.org/10.1007/978-3-030-29859-3_50
14. Marmarelis P.Z., Marmarelis V.Z.: Analysis of Physiological Systems – The White Noise Approach, vol. 504 Springer, New York (2011)
15. Ishii, N., Iwata, K., Iwahori, Y., Matsuo, T.: Comparison of Fourier bases and asymmetric network bases in the bio-inspired networks. In: Rojas, I., Joya, G., Catala, A. (eds.) IWANN 2023, LNCS, vol. 14134, pp. 200–210. Springer, Cham (2023). https://doi.org/10.1007/978-3-031-43085-5_16

Assessing the Impact of Preprocessing Pipelines on fMRI Based Autism Spectrum Disorder Classification: ABIDE II Results

Fatima Ez-zahraa Bazay[(✉)] and Ahmed Drissi El Maliani

LRIT, Faculty of Sciences in Rabat, Mohammed V University in Rabat, Rabat, Morocco
{fatimaezzahraa.bazay,a.elmaliani}@um5r.ac.ma

Abstract. Resting-state functional MRI (rs-fMRI), a tool for assessing the brain's spontaneous activity, plays a crucial role in understanding functional connectivity, contingent on the precision of Blood Oxygen Level Dependent (BOLD) signal processing. At the forefront of this process lies preprocessing as a fundamental step in the analysis of resting-state fMRI data, enabling any subsequent investigations. This research focuses on assessing the impact of three distinct preprocessing methods on the classification of resting-state fMRI data, utilizing a range of classifiers including Support Vector Classifier with radial basis function (SVC-rbf), Linear Support Vector Classifier (LinearSVC), ridge, K-Nearest Neighbors (KNN), Logistic Regression (LR), Decision Trees (DT), Random Forests (RF), and Adaptive Boosting (AdaBoost). The objective is to understand how the order and efficiency of these preprocessing steps influence the classification of Autism spectrum disorder (ASD). We conduct standard preprocessing steps on the fMRI data, including slice-timing, realignment, segmentation, co-registration, normalization, and smoothing methods. Additionally, the brain was parcellated into AAL and CC200 atlases. The evaluation, involving 1076 subjects from the ABIDE II database, represents the first application of these preprocessing methods to this dataset. Results reveal that the choice and the order of preprocessing steps significantly impact the ability to classify ASD accurately. Notably, the preprocessing strategy involving dropping the first 10 volumes, realignment, slice timing, normalization, and smoothing, yielded the best accuracy with the Ridge classifier and AAL atlas, achieving an accuracy of 65.42%, specificity of 70.73%, and AUC of 68.04%. The findings highlight the significant impact of selected preprocessing methods on the accuracy of functional connectivity classifications, underlining the importance of strategic method selection to achieve the most favorable outcomes in ASD classification.

Keywords: resting-state fMRI · preprocessing · ABIDE II · motion correction · slice timing · normalization · smoothing · ASD classification

© The Author(s), under exclusive license to Springer Nature Switzerland AG 2024
L. Iliadis et al. (Eds.): EANN 2024, CCIS 2141, pp. 463–477, 2024
https://doi.org/10.1007/978-3-031-62495-7_35

1   Introduction

Autism Spectrum Disorder (ASD) involves communication and behavioral challenges, with potentially severe outcomes if diagnosis is delayed. Conventional diagnosis relies on subjective behavioral assessments, which are exhaustive and require specialized expertise not universally available. Brain imaging studies have linked ASD with altered brain connectivity, suggesting the possibility of more objective diagnostic criteria [1].

The human brain operates as an intricate network where different areas are linked through both structural and functional pathways, achieving highly efficient processing of information. This complexity can be explored using various neuroimaging methods such as Magnetic Resonance Imaging (MRI), Diffusion Tensor Imaging(DTI), Electroencephalography(EEG), Magnetoencephalography (MEG), functional Magnetic Resonance Imaging (fMRI), Positron Emission Tomography (PET), and Single Photon Emission Computed Tomography (SPECT), each offering unique insights into the brain's anatomy and functionality [2]. MRI plays a key role in non-invasively detecting brain development issues. fMRI builds on this by tracking signal changes linked to neuronal activity. Its safe, non-invasive nature makes it ideal for pediatric assessments.

In the realm of fMRI, the technique distinguishes different neural pathways by analyzing how the Blood Oxygen Level Dependent (BOLD) signal fluctuates over time across specific brain areas, culminating in four-dimensional imagery that elucidates both the anatomical structure and functional dynamics of the brain [3]. There are two primary applications for fMRI: resting-state and task-based studies. While task-based fMRI may offer superior precision in classification tasks, compiling extensive datasets for this approach is challenging, often involving fewer than 50 participants [4]. Moreover, it may not be appropriate for numerous individuals with ASD, especially those with more profound challenges or young children, due to the demands of active engagement in task-based assessments. Furthermore, resting-state fMRI does not necessitate a specific experimental framework or the active involvement of participants, which broadens its applicability. It has shown potential in detecting the interactive patterns among various brain regions, which could serve as markers for diagnosing neurological conditions [5].

Preprocessing fMRI data is crucial before any advanced analysis for several reasons. Initially, fMRI captures the variations in the BOLD signals, which correlate with brain activity. However, these signals also encapsulate contributions unrelated to neuronal activity, including head movements, physiological factors, external tissues, and artifacts introduced by the MRI process itself, alongside the desired neuronal information [6]. These extraneous elements can obscure the true interpretation of the fMRI data. Moreover, the integrity of fMRI data is significantly influenced by the parameters set during image capture. Variabilities in intensity values, matrix sizes, and image orientations can arise from the specific parameters chosen during the data acquisition phase. Consequently, it is imperative to implement preprocessing routines to address and mitigate these challenges.

The present study aims to expand the existing knowledge by applying three novel preprocessing approaches to the ABIDE II dataset for the first time. This innovative initiative represents a significant step forward in the utilization of neuroimaging data for ASD research. The structure of this paper is organized as follows: Sect. 2 delves into the various preprocessing techniques, feature extraction processes, and classifiers employed to assess the impact of different preprocessing on ASD classification. Section 3 presents the experimental results, discusses the findings, and provides a comprehensive analysis of the performance of the proposed methodologies. Finally, Sect. 4 offers a concise conclusion, summarizing our research outcomes.

1.1 Related Work

Given the crucial role of preprocessing in enhancing the interpretability and quality of fMRI data, significant strides have been made within the context of the Autism Brain Imaging Data Exchange II (ABIDE II) dataset. A spectrum of methodologies has been employed to refine neuroimaging data for ASD research. A notable study introduced rigorous preprocessing, encompassing slice timing correction, motion realignment, intensity normalization, and rigid registration to a standard template, and was further enhanced by applying specific filtering, signal standardization, and de-trending processes [7]. Another research effort utilized the Configurable Pipeline for the Analysis of Connectomes (CPAC) pre processing, integrating motion correction and global signal regression, along with specialized filtering [8]. Further research efforts have underscored the importance of removing initial volumes to stabilize magnetization, detailed adjustments for slice-timing discrepancies, and comprehensive motion correction to address spatial inconsistencies [9]. An additional study implemented a comprehensive set of preprocessing steps including realignment, coregistration, normalization, filtering, smoothing, and skull stripping, further enhanced by root mean square deviation analysis to ensure image alignment [10]. In a separate exploration, a study pursued a preprocessing path by first converting fMRI images into JPG format, then resizing these images to 224×224 pixels, and applying normalization to standardize the data [11].

1.2 Motivations and Contributions

As shown in the previous section, previous studies have explored various preprocessing methods within the ABIDE II dataset. Our approaches introduce unique modifications and enhancements, setting a new precedent in the analysis of fMRI data for understanding ASD. Distinct in their combination and sequence of methods, these tailored approaches are specifically designed to enhance the clarity and interpretability of fMRI data. The preprocessing strategies meticulously refine the data before subjecting it to classification analysis, ensuring the capture of the most relevant and subtle patterns indicative of ASD.

To rigorously test the efficacy of these preprocessing pipelines, we will employ a suite of advanced machine learning classifiers. The selection includes Ridge regression, Support Vector Classifier with radial basis function (SVC-rbf), Linear Support Vector Classifier (LinearSVC), K-Nearest Neighbors (KNN), Logistic Regression (LR), Decision Trees (DT), Random Forests (RF), and Adaptive Boosting (AdaBoost). Each of these classifiers has been chosen for its proven track record in pattern recognition and predictive modeling across various domains. The analysis will focus on two specific regions of interest within the brain, the CC200 and AAL regions, to investigate how preprocessing techniques influence classifier performance in these areas, thereby shedding light on their impact on ASD detection.

At the heart of the study is the exploration of the impact that preprocessing has on the accuracy of ASD classification. This key contribution involves a detailed examination of how different preprocessing techniques influence the effectiveness of machine learning models in detecting ASD. The goal is to identify which preprocessing methods most significantly improve classification accuracy, thereby elucidating the critical role of data preparation in the neuroimaging analysis of ASD. Through this endeavor, we aim to provide valuable insights into optimizing fMRI data processing for more accurate ASD detection, marking a significant step forward in the neuroscientific study of ASD.

Our main contributions in this paper are:

- Applying various preprocessing pipelines on the ABIDE II dataset.
- Evaluating the Impact of Preprocessing on ASD Classification.
- Identifying the Optimal Classifier for ASD Detection.

2   Material and Methods

In this study, we explore the effect of distinct fMRI data preprocessing pipelines on the classification of ASD, employing various preprocessing and feature extraction methods along with different machine learning classifiers on the AAL and CC200 atlases.

2.1   Pre-processing

Preprocessing in fMRI data analysis is crucial for ensuring reliable results [12]. In this study, the approach has been expanded by applying three distinct preprocessing pipelines using SPM12 [13], each employing varied methods. This comprehensive strategy was designed to not only prepare the data for accurate analysis but also to allow a comparative evaluation of different preprocessing methodologies. Specifically, we aim to determine how each preprocessing pipeline affects the classification accuracy of ASD.

Pre-processing 1
In fMRI data analysis, addressing head motion is crucial as it can significantly impact data quality, potentially leading to unreliable outcomes. The preprocessing pipeline is designed to mitigate these effects and enhance data integrity through a series of steps. The process begins with realignment to correct for any

head movements during scanning, ensuring consistent alignment of brain volumes across the session. Following realignment, slice-timing correction is employed to adjust for the timing differences in the acquisition of slices, setting the acquisition time of the first slice as the reference. This helps in synchronizing the timing across all slices for each brain volume. After addressing these initial concerns, co-registration is undertaken to align the functional images with corresponding high-resolution structural images, which aids in accurately localizing functional activities within anatomical regions. The next phase involves segmentation, dividing brain tissues into gray matter, white matter, and cerebrospinal fluid. This step is essential for distinguishing between signals of interest and artifacts. Following segmentation, spatial normalization resizes the images to a uniform voxel size of $2 \times 2 \times 2$ mm^3 and aligns them with the Montreal Neurological Institute (MNI) standard space to ensure consistent spatial dimensions across all samples. The final step in the preprocessing pipeline is spatial smoothing, applied with an $8 \times 8 \times 8$ mm^3 Full-Width Half-Maximum (FWHM) Gaussian kernel to enhance the signal-to-noise ratio, thus improving the overall quality of the data [14,15].

Pre-processing 2
It involved the removal of the initial ten volumes to ensure magnetization equilibrium. Subsequently, we applied slice timing correction, realignment, segmentation, and normalization with a voxel size of $3 \times 3 \times 3$ mm^3. This step aimed to align the data with consistent spatial dimensions and coordinates. Additionally, spatial smoothing was performed with a 6mm^3 Gaussian kernel to further enhance data quality and the signal-to-noise ratio in the fMRI analysis. To conclude the preprocessing sequence, one-zero normalization was performed. This final step involves scaling the entire dataset so that the minimum value across the data becomes zero, and the maximum value becomes one, ensuring that the data values are normalized within a standardized range [14,15].

Pre-processing 3
It involved removing the initial ten volumes, followed by realignment, slice timing correction, normalization with a voxel size of $3 \times 3 \times 3$ mm^3, and smoothing with

Table 1. Summary of Preprocessing Steps

Step	Preprocessing1	Preprocessing2	Preprocessing3
Drop First Volumes	0	10	10
Realignment	YES	YES	YES
Slice Timing	YES	YES	YES
Coregistration	YES	NO	NO
Segmentation	YES	YES	NO
Normalization	$2 \times 2 \times 2$mm^3	$3 \times 3 \times 3$mm^3	$3 \times 3 \times 3$mm^3
Smoothing	8mm	6mm	4mm
Normalization One and Zero	NO	Yes	NO

a 4 mm Gaussian kernel. This sequence ensured consistent spatial dimensions and coordinates in the data [14, 15] (Table 1).

2.2   Extracting Time-Series Data from Regions of Interest via Brain Atlas

fMRI technology maps brain activity by tracking changes in BOLD signals. Participants stay still and relaxed during scans as the device records BOLD signal fluctuations, producing a 4D dataset of spatial and temporal dimensions. Rather than analyzing the complete time series data from every voxel in the brain, this study focuses on specific regions of interest (ROIs) identified by selected brain atlases. The average BOLD signal intensities were extracted from voxels within these ROIs using the atlases. This research employed two widely recognized brain atlases for ROI extraction: the Craddock 200 (CC200) atlas [18], which are functional, alongside the Automated Anatomical Labeling (AAL) atlas [19], which is structural. The CC200, and AAL atlases identify 200, and 116 ROIs, respectively.

Utilizing a brain atlas on 4D fMRI scans can be likened to superimposing a set of 3D grids over the scans, serving as a filter to determine which voxels are analyzed at each moment in time. As a result, the original 4D fMRI data for an individual, with dimensions (H, W, D, T), is converted into 2D data with dimensions (T, N), where H, W, and D represent the height, width, depth (or number of slices), T denotes the time points of the image volume, and N is the number of ROIs. The task involves extracting average time-series data by applying a brain atlas to preprocessed resting-state fMRI (rs-fMRI) data. For our study, the average time-series data for ROIs defined by the CC200 and AAL atlases were sourced directly from the Preprocessed Connectomes Project (PCP) [16]. Consequently, the dimensions (T, N) varied among subjects, depending on the specific atlas and the individual scan durations.

2.3   Constructing a Matrix of Functional Connections

The data, with dimensions of (T, N), were transformed into a functional connectivity matrix, also known as a connectome, featuring dimensions of (N, N). These connectomes serve as matrices capturing the correlation coefficients between distinct brain regions of interest (ROIs), identified through specific brain atlases. The dimensions for these matrices were established as (116, 116), and (200, 200) for the AAL, and CC200 atlases, respectively. To construct these functional connectomes, the methodology centered around employing a correlation-based analysis to evaluate the interactions between the brain ROIs outlined by the respective atlases. This technique directly quantifies the relationships between the time series of various regions, thereby elucidating functional connectivity. For this purpose, we utilized the Nilearn library [17], a versatile tool for neuroimaging data analysis that facilitates the computation of correlation matrices in an efficient and standardized manner.

2.4 Converting a 2D Functional Connectivity Matrix into a Single-Dimensional Feature Vector

The correlation connectivity matrix was symmetric, meaning the values above the diagonal mirrored those below it. To streamline the data, we focused on the lower triangular section, excluding the upper triangular and diagonal elements. We then converted the selected lower triangular matrix into a one-dimensional (1D) vector. The length of this vector is determined by the formula 1:

$$S = \frac{N(N-1)}{2} \tag{1}$$

where N is the total number of Regions of Interest (ROIs). Applying this approach to the selected brain atlases resulted in 1D feature vectors with lengths of 6786, and 20100 for the AAL, and CC200 atlases, respectively, for each subject studied.

2.5 Data Dimensionality Reduction Using Principal Component Analysis

Following the transformation of functional connectivity matrices into one-dimensional feature vectors, we applied Principal Component Analysis (PCA) as a dimensionality reduction technique. This step, critical in the preprocessing pipeline, aimed to concentrate information by preserving 99% of the variance inherent in the functional connectivity vectors, thereby simplifying the dataset while enhancing computational efficiency and potentially boosting the classification accuracy of the models. The PCA transformation of the connectivity vectors into a reduced-dimensional space is mathematically represented as:

$$\mathbf{X}_{PCA} = \mathbf{W}^{T} \cdot \mathbf{X} \tag{2}$$

where:

- $\mathbf{X}$ denotes the original feature vector obtained from the connectivity matrix,
- $\mathbf{W}$ represents the matrix of eigenvectors
- $\mathbf{W}^{T}$ is the transpose of the eigenvector matrix,
- $\mathbf{X}_{PCA}$ is the feature vector transformed into the PCA space.

This formula highlights the projection of the original feature vector $\mathbf{X}$ onto the principal component space using the eigenvector matrix $\mathbf{W}^{T}$, resulting in a new, compact representation $\mathbf{X}_{PCA}$ that emphasizes the most significant patterns of brain connectivity. The first principal component captures the highest variance among connectivity patterns, with each subsequent component selected for its ability to explain the highest possible variance while being orthogonal to the previous components [20]. This strategic reduction ensures that the most informative features are retained, significantly reducing dimensionality while maintaining the essence of the original connectivity data for ASD classification.

After applying PCA to the feature vectors derived from the functional connectivity matrices for the AAL and CC200 atlases, the resultant PCA-transformed vectors had lengths of 723 and 855, respectively. This indicates a substantial reduction in dimensionality, focusing the analysis on the components that hold the most variance and, thus, the most information about brain connectivity patterns in ASD classification.

2.6   Classification Methods

Recent advancements in machine learning (ML) have showcased the potential of various classifiers in analyzing fMRI data for ASD detection [21]. Studies predominantly utilize supervised learning methods such as SVC-rbf, LR, RF, and others, reporting high classification accuracies in single-site studies. However, the accuracy often decreases in multi-site studies involving a larger cohort, presenting challenges in model generalization across diverse datasets. In this context, the study focuses on the influence of preprocessing on ASD classification, leveraging the ABIDE II dataset to explore the effectiveness of a range of ML classifiers. These include SVC-rbf, LinearSVC, Ridge regression, KNN, LR, DT, RF, and AdaBoost. The objective is to determine how different preprocessing strategies can optimize classification performance across multiple sites and a broad spectrum of subjects.

3   Results and Discussion

For preprocessing tasks, we utilized MATLAB's SPM12 toolbox. Subsequently, experiments were conducted in a Kaggle notebook environment, employing Python version 3.7. This cloud-based setup provided us with complimentary access to GPU computing resources and 16 GB of RAM, all powered by an Intel Core i7 processor. For further analyses, we leveraged a suite of Python libraries, including NumPy for handling numerical operations, Pandas for data management, and scikit-learn for deploying a range of machine learning classifiers and assessing their effectiveness.

3.1   ABIDE Dataset

The ABIDE initiative is divided into two collections: ABIDE I and ABIDE II. The focus is on ABIDE II because, unlike ABIDE I which offers preprocessed data, ABIDE II provides raw data that has not undergone preprocessing, allowing for custom data processing techniques to be applied. ABIDE II incorporates contributions from 19 international locations, offering resting-state fMRI, anatomical, and phenotypic data for community-wide research endeavors. [16]. Out of the 1125 participants, 11074 were identified as suitable for the analysis, thanks to their comprehensive phenotypic data. Among these selected individuals, there are 503 diagnosed with ASD and 571 typical controls.

3.2 Partition Data Using 5-Fold Cross-Validation

The study applied a detailed cross-validation grid search to identify optimal parameters for each classifier, ensuring peak efficiency. We used stratified 5-fold cross-validation for model testing and validation, maintaining a balanced representation of autism and control groups within the dataset. Specifically, we partitioned the dataset so that 20% served as the test set, with the remaining 80% allocated for training and validation purposes. From this latter portion, 80% of the data was used for training the models, while the remaining 20% was dedicated to validation. This structured approach allowed us to systematically assess the impact of preprocessing on ASD classification, employing a wide array of machine learning classifiers to ascertain which preprocessing pipeline optimally enhances classification performance.

3.3 Results

The study utilizes various preprocessing methods with AAL and CC200 atlases, assessing their impact on ASD classification. We optimized classifiers through grid search and measured their effectiveness using metrics like accuracy, precision, F1 score, specificity, sensitivity, and Area Under the Curve (AUC). This approach allows us to pinpoint the preprocessing strategies that most enhance classification accuracy (Tables 2, 3 and 4).

Table 2. Evaluation of the Effect of Preprocessing 1 in ASD Classification

Classifier	Atlas	Accuracy	Precision	F1 Score	Specificity	Sensitivity	AUC
SVC-rbf	AAL	62.79%	55.79%	55.76%	62.60%	63.04%	65.08%
	CC200	64.65%	59.75%	56.32%	73.17%	53.26%	67.97%
linearSVC	AAL	60.46%	53.93%	53.03%	66.66%	52.17%	63.19%
	CC200	64.18%	57%	61.30%	62.60%	66.30%	67.65%
Ridge	AAL	61.39%	55.69%	51.46%	71.54%	47.82%	63.02%
	CC200	62.79%	55.35%	60.78%	59.34%	67.39%	66.48%
K-Nearest Neighbors	AAL	58.13%	51%	53.12%	60.16%	55.43%	58.97%
	CC200	50.02%	45.54%	47.66%	55.28%	50%	51.65%
Logistic Regression	AAL	58.13%	50.86%	56.73%	53.65%	64.13%	58.16%
	CC200	64.65%	57.40%	62%	62.60%	67.39%	68.35%
Decision Tree	AAL	54.41%	47.05%	49.48%	56.09%	52.17%	56.92%
	CC200	56.27%	48.86%	47.77%	63.41%	46.73%	57.01%
Random Forests	AAL	63.72%	61.66%	48.68%	81.30%	40.21%	62.59%
	CC200	60%	56.81%	36.76%	84.55%	27.17%	56.05%
AdaBoost	AAL	59.06%	51.92%	55.10%	59.34%	58.69%	59.02%
	CC200	58.13%	51.08%	51.08%	63.41%	51.08%	57.25%

Table 3. Evaluation of the Effect of Preprocessing 2 in ASD Classification

Classifier	Atlas	Accuracy	Precision	F1 Score	Specificity	Sensitivity	AUC
SVC-rbf	AAL	60%	53%	55.20%	61.78%	57.60%	64.13%
	CC200	64.18%	52.17%	55.49%	73.17%	52.17%	67.17%
linearSVC	AAL	62.79%	56.38%	56.98%	66.66%	57.60%	67.67%
	CC200	60%	52.72%	57.42%	57.72%	63.04%	60.88%
Ridge	AAL	62.79%	56.97%	55.05%	69.91%	53.26%	67.60%
	CC200	60.93%	53.70%	58%	59.34%	63.04%	62.81%
K-Nearest Neighbors	AAL	59.53%	52.47%	54.92%	60.97%	57.60%	63.31%
	CC200	56.95%	47.05%	53.08%	48.78%	60.86%	57.16%
Logistic Regression	AAL	62.32%	55.91%	56.21%	66.66%	56.52%	61.03%
	CC200	56.27%	49.16%	55.66%	50.40%	64.13%	60.79%
Decision Tree	AAL	54.41%	45.83%	40.24%	68.29%	35.86%	51.80%
	CC200	56.27%	48.93%	48.46%	60.97%	50%	54.78%
Random Forests	AAL	60.46%	54.92%	67.85%	73.98%	42.39%	57.92%
	CC200	61.86%	57.14%	49.38%	75.60%	43.47%	58.36%
AdaBoost	AAL	54.88%	47.42%	48.67%	58.53%	50%	54.26%
	CC200	53.95%	46.39%	47.61%	57.72%	48.91%	53.31%

Table 4. Evaluation of the Effect of Preprocessing 3 in ASD Classification

Classifier	Atlas	Accuracy	Precision	F1 Score	Specificity	Sensitivity	AUC
SVC-rbf	AAL	63.55%	56.84%	58.06%	66.66%	59.34%	64.91%
	CC200	63.08%	55.88%	59.06%	63.41%	62.63%	66.67%
linearSVC	AAL	64.01%	57.60%	57.92%	68.29%	58.24%	67.79%
	CC200	61.68%	54.36%	57.73%	61.78%	61.53%	65.87%
Ridge	AAL	65.42%	59.55%	58.88%	70.73%	58.24%	68.04%
	CC200	59.81%	52.33%	56.56%	58.53%	61.53%	65.35%
K-Nearest Neighbors	AAL	56.07%	48.35%	48.35%	61.78%	48.35%	57.67%
	CC200	52.33%	45.13%	50%	49.59%	56.04%	53.19%
Logistic Regression	AAL	69.61%	56.17%	55.55%	68.29%	54.94%	64.75%
	CC200	58.41%	50.98%	53.88%	59.34%	57.14%	60.35%
Decision Tree	AAL	53.73%	45.83%	47.05%	57.72%	48.35%	51.41%
	CC200	54.20%	47%	52.88%	49.59%	60.43%	52.10%
Random Forests	AAL	63.08%	58.82%	50.31%	77.23%	43.95%	67.87%
	CC200	61.21%	56.89%	44.29%	79.67%	36.26%	61.20%
AdaBoost	AAL	53.27%	45.45%	47.36%	56.09%	49.45%	52.77%
	CC200	54.20%	47.05%	53.33%	48.78%	61.53%	55.15%

Effect of Initial Volume Removal on ASD Classification Performance
The removal of initial volumes, applied in preprocessings 2 and 3 to counter
artifacts from the initial instability of the fMRI signal, has a nuanced impact on
classifiers. While this technique aims to improve data quality, its effectiveness

can vary significantly among classifiers. For instance, AdaBoost shows a notable decrease in accuracy from 59.06% for the AAL atlas and 58.13% for CC200 without removal and numerical normalization in preprocessing 1, to 54.88% and 53.95% respectively, after the application of these methods in preprocessing 2. This reduction emphasizes that the removal of initial volumes and numerical normalization can remove crucial information for classification. A similar observation is noted with preprocessing 3, where despite the persistence of initial volume removal, accuracy does not significantly improve, reinforcing the idea that this removal could eliminate relevant data. The effects of preprocessing on other classifiers like SVC-rbf and Ridge also attest to the complexity of their influence. SVC-rbf, for example, shows a slight improvement in accuracy moving from preprocessing 1 to 3 for the AAL atlas but sees a reduction for CC200, suggesting a variable response that does not allow for definitive conclusions on the efficacy of initial volume removal and normalization. Ridge, on its part, demonstrates an increase in accuracy for AAL with preprocessing 1, while a decrease is observed for CC200 with preprocessing 3, indicating some sensitivity to preprocessing methods, influenced by the chosen atlas. Similarly, KNN undergoes a performance reduction following the removal of initial volumes, moving from 58.13% to 56.07% for AAL and from 53.02% to 52.33% for CC200 between preprocessing 1 and 3. This indicates that the elimination of the first acquisitions can remove beneficial information for classification. These observations highlight the need for a thorough evaluation of the effectiveness of preprocessing techniques, underscoring that their impact can greatly vary depending on the classifier and atlas used, and that a more nuanced approach may be necessary to optimize the quality and utility of fMRI data for classification.

Effect of Spatial Normalization on ASD Classification Performance
The incorporation of spatial normalization at varying resolutions has been critical in optimizing the processing and analysis of fMRI data across diverse preprocessing pipelines. In preprocessing approach 1, spatial normalization to a resolution of $2 \times 2 \times 2$ mm^3 enabled more precise characterization of brain structures by facilitating more accurate localization of regions of interest, leading to a notable improvement in classifier performance. For instance, the SVC-rbf classifier achieved an accuracy of 62.79% for the AAL atlas and 64.65% for CC200, showcasing the effectiveness of this normalization approach in reducing artifacts and enhancing data integrity. Transitioning to a spatial normalization resolution of $3 \times 3 \times 3$ mm^3 in preprocessing approaches 2 and 3 resulted in performance changes in classifiers, illustrating the impact of normalization resolution on the analysis. The accuracy of the SVC-rbf classifier slightly varied, moving to 60% for AAL and 64.18% for CC200 with preprocessing 2, and then to 63.55% for AAL and 63.08% for CC200 in the context of preprocessing 3. These variations suggest that while spatial normalization helps standardize fMRI data across participants, the chosen resolution can affect the classifiers' ability to finely detect relevant neuronal patterns. Similarly, Ridge, employing the same preprocessing framework, also demonstrated sensitivity to spatial normalization resolution. With preprocessing 1, an accuracy of 61.39% for AAL and 62.79% for CC200

was recorded, compared to 62.79% (AAL) and 60.93% (CC200) for preprocessing 2, and ultimately 65.42% (AAL) and 59.81% (CC200) for preprocessing 3. These findings emphasize the importance of carefully selecting the normalization resolution based on the specific objectives of the study and the sensitivity of the utilized classifiers.

Effect of Smoothing on ASD Classification Performance

The impact of spatial smoothing on fMRI classifier performance was significantly influenced by the choice of kernel size in various preprocessing approaches. In Preprocessing 1, where we utilized an 8mm smoothing kernel, we noted a marked improvement in classifier accuracy. This kernel size effectively reduced noise while preserving essential information for classification. For instance, with this smoothing approach, the SVC-rbf classifier achieved an accuracy of 62.79% for the AAL atlas and 64.65% for CC200, illustrating an optimal balance between noise reduction and preservation of relevant spatial details. In contrast, switching to a 6mm smoothing kernel for Preprocessing 2 led to a slight alteration in performance. Although this kernel size still aims to mitigate noise, it may not be as effective as the 8mm kernel at eliminating random variations while retaining critical information. With this setting, the accuracy of SVC-rbf slightly decreased, coming to 60% for AAL and 64.18% for CC200. This suggests that while 6mm smoothing remains beneficial for signal clarity, achieving the balance between noise reduction and information preservation may be more challenging. Preprocessing 3, which involved an even smaller 4mm smoothing kernel, allowed for the retention of more spatial detail, which might be advantageous for certain targeted analyses. However, this kernel size might not be optimal for overall noise suppression, as evidenced by the accuracy attained with SVC-rbf, which was 63.55% for AAL and 63.08% for CC200. Although this approach permits greater fidelity to fine spatial variations, it might also let through a higher level of noise, potentially impacting classification performance. These findings demonstrate that the size of the smoothing kernel plays a critical role in balancing noise reduction and the preservation of significant spatial information.

Performance Comparison of Machine Learning Methods

The study scrutinized classifier responses to fMRI preprocessing variations and atlas choices, underscoring the complexity of fMRI data classification. Notably, the Ridge classifier demonstrated optimal performance with preprocessing 3 and AAL atlas, achieving 65.42% accuracy and 68.04% AUC, highlighting the impact of strategic spatial normalization and smoothing on capturing neuronal intricacies. AdaBoost and SVC-rbf showed varied performance across preprocessing strategies, underscoring the importance of comprehensive preprocessing, especially with the CC200 atlas, for improving classification. AdaBoost achieved 59.06% accuracy and a 59.02% AUC in preprocessing 1, while SVC-rbf excelled with 64.65% accuracy and a 67.97% AUC. This highlights the critical role of precise preprocessing, including realignment and slice timing, in boosting support vector classifiers' accuracy in high-dimensional fMRI analysis. KNN classifier performance varied across preprocessing steps, showing the nuanced effect of these methods on classification. Starting with a 58.13% accuracy for AAL in preprocessing 1, adjustments in preprocessing 2 slightly improved it to 59.53%. Yet, a different approach in preprocessing 3 decreased accuracy to 56.07% for AAL. This suggests preprocessing impacts on KNN are not always predictable, highlighting the importance of selecting appropriate preprocessing strategies based on classifier and atlas specifics to enhance fMRI data classification. LR significantly benefited from preprocessing 1 with the CC200 atlas, achieving 64.65% accuracy and 68.35% AUC. This improvement indicates the effectiveness of precise spatial normalization and noise reduction, essential for classifiers sensitive to feature variations. This underlines the importance of careful preprocessing in enhancing classifier accuracy in neuroimaging data analysis. DT excelled with preprocessing 1 and the CC200 atlas, achieving 56.27% accuracy and 57.01% AUC. This highlights the advantage of not removing initial volumes or applying numerical normalization, suggesting that a full dataset enhances class differentiation. This sensitivity to initial data underscores the importance of strategic preprocessing for optimal classification. Random Forests demonstrated exceptional performance with preprocessing 1 and the AAL atlas, achieving 63.72% accuracy and 62.59% AUC. This underscores their ability to utilize comprehensively preprocessed data to identify complex fMRI patterns, emphasizing the benefit of preserving a diverse range of features. Overall, the Ridge classifier particularly when used in conjunction with preprocessing approach 3 and the AAL atlas, achieved the highest accuracy (65.42%), specificity (70.73%), and AUC (68.04%) among the tested classifiers. The variance in classifier performance across preprocessing setups highlights the nuanced impact of preprocessing on classifier success. No classifier universally outperforms across all setups. However, classifiers like SVC-rbf and linear SVC show strong results under certain conditions, suggesting the best classifier choice depends on specific preprocessing steps and atlas selection. The superior results with Ridge, especially with preprocessing 3 and AAL atlas, demonstrate its effectiveness in ASD classification.

4   Conclusion

In the exploration within the ABIDE II dataset, we observed a significant impact of preprocessing step selection on the classification of ASD. The comprehensive analysis reveals that the accuracy of functional connectivity classification is intricately linked to the chosen preprocessing strategies, underscoring the nuanced relationship between preprocessing choices and classification outcomes. While preprocessing 3, which involves the removal of the first ten volumes, realignment, slice timing correction, normalization, and smoothing, notably enhanced classification performance for the Ridge classifier using the AAL atlas, achieving an impressive accuracy of 65.42%, a specificity of 70.73%, and an AUC of 68.04%, the findings also indicate that different preprocessing configurations yielded the most favorable results for other classifiers. The results contribute valuable insights to the field, emphasizing the critical role of strategic preprocessing in leveraging neuroimaging data for ASD classification through machine learning algorithms. Moving forward, future work aims to apply several other preprocessing methods to further explore and potentially enhance the robustness and accuracy of ASD classification.

References

1. Anderson, J.S., et al.: Functional connectivity magnetic resonance imaging classification of autism. Brain **134**(12), 3742–3754 (2011)
2. Camprodon, J., Stern, T.: Selecting neuroimaging techniques: a review for the clinician. The Primary Care Companion CNS Disorders **15** (2013)
3. Benabdallah, F.Z., Drissi El Maliani, A., Lotfi, D., Jennane, R., El Hassouni, M.: An autism spectrum disorder adaptive identification based on the Elimination of brain connections: a proof of long-range underconnectivity. Soft Comput. **26**(10), 4701–4711 (2022)
4. Lau, W.K.W., Leung, M.K., Lau, B.W.M.: Resting-state abnormalities in autism spectrum disorders: a meta-analysis. Sci. Rep. **9**, 1–8 (2019)
5. Benabdallah, F.Z., Drissi El Maliani, A., Lotfi, D., El Hassouni, M.: A convolutional neural network-based connectivity enhancement approach for autism spectrum disorder detection. J. Imaging **9**(6), 110 (2023)
6. Murphy, K., Birn, R.M., Bandettini, P.A.: Resting-state fMRI confounds and cleanup. Neuroimage **80**, 349–359 (2013)
7. Pominova, M., Kondrateva, E., Sharaev, M., et al.: Fader networks for domain adaptation on fMRI: ABIDE-II study. In: Thirteenth International Conference on Machine Vision. SPIE, vol. 11605, pp. 570–577 (2021)
8. Khosla, M., Jamison, K., Kuceyeski, A., Sabuncu, M. R.: 3D convolutional neural networks for classification of functional connectomes. In International Workshop on Deep Learning in Medical Image Analysis, 137–145 (2018)
9. Aghdam, M.A., Sharifi, A., Pedram, M.M.: Diagnosis of autism spectrum disorders in young children based on resting-state functional magnetic resonance imaging data using convolutional neural networks. J. Digit. Imaging **32**, 899–918 (2019)
10. Ronicko, J.F.A., Thomas, J., Thangavel, P., Koneru, V., Langs, G., Dauwels, J.: Diagnostic classification of autism using resting-state fMRI data improves with full correlation functional brain connectivity compared to partial correlation. J. Neurosci. Methods **345**, 108884 (2020)
11. Husna, R.N.S., Syafeeza, A.R., Hamid, N.A., Wong, Y.C., Raihan, R.A.: Functional magnetic resonance imaging for autism spectrum disorder detection using deep learning. Jurnal Teknologi **83**(3), 45–52 (2021)
12. Jenkinson, M., Smith, S.M.: Pre-Processing of BOLD fMRI Data. Oxford University Centre for Functional MRI of the Brain (FMRIB) (2006)
13. Friston, K.J., Ashburner, J., Kiebel, S., Nichols, T., Penny, W.D. (eds.): Statistical Parametric Mapping: The Analysis of Functional Brain Images. Elsevier (2012)
14. Jaber, H.A., Aljobouri, H.K., Çankaya, İ, Koçak, O.M., Algin, O.: Preparing fMRI data for postprocessing: conversion modalities, preprocessing pipeline, and parametric and nonparametric approaches. IEEE Access **7**, 122864–122877 (2019)
15. Park, B.Y., Byeon, K., Park, H.: FuNP (fusion of neuroimaging preprocessing) pipelines: a fully automated preprocessing software for functional magnetic resonance imaging. Front. Neuroinf. **13**, 5 (2019)
16. Autism Brain Imaging Data Exchange. https://fcon_1000.projects.nitrc.org/indi/abide/. Accessed 10 Mar 2024

17. Nilearn. Statistical Analysis for NeuroImaging in Python-Machine Learning for NeuroImaging. https://nilearn.github.io/index.html. Accessed 10 Mar 2024
18. Tzourio-Mazoyer, N., et al.: Automated anatomical labeling of activations in SPM using a macroscopic anatomical parcellation of the MNI MRI single-subject brain. Neuroimage **15**, 273–289 (2002)
19. Craddock, R., James, G., Holtzheimer, P., Hu, X., Mayberg, H.: A whole brain fMRI atlas generated via spatially constrained spectral clustering. Hum. Brain Mapp. **33**, 1914–1928 (2011)
20. Bro, R., Smilde, A.K.: Principal component analysis. Anal. Methods **6**(9), 2812–2831 (2014)
21. Pereira, F., Mitchell, T., Botvinick, M.: Machine learning classifiers and fMRI: a tutorial overview. Neuroimage **45**(1), S199–S209 (2009)

Data-Driven Methods for Wi-Fi Anomaly Detection

Telma Garção$^{(\boxtimes)}$ (iD), Joana Sousa(iD), Luis André(iD), Carlos Alves, Nuno Felizardo,
Carlos Silva, and João Ferreira

NOS Inovação, Lisbon, Portugal
telma.garcao@nos.pt

Abstract. This paper presents a methodology based on data science techniques
and ML for detecting anomalies in Wi-Fi networks. The approach employs
dynamic time series analysis to identify anomalies by monitoring fluctuations
in signal strength, packet loss, and other network metrics. SARIMA, SARIMAX,
VARIMAX, and LSTM models were applied to address the challenge of forecasting anomalies. Subsequently, a SVM classifier is utilized to identify affected
routers at the detected timestamps. Furthermore, the paper explores a technique
to enhance the model's adaptability to different router types, considering potential variations in expected performance. This technique, constructed via PCA,
enhances the methodology's robustness across diverse network environments,
and facilitates its application in various settings. In addition, the paper takes initial efforts to comprehend and define anomalies in a broader sense and specifically explores the correlation with Wi-Fi metrics. This recurrent theme persists
throughout the entirety of the paper.

Keywords: Anomaly Detection · Machine Learning (ML) · Wi-Fi

1 Introduction

With the widespread integration of wireless networks across diverse domains, ensuring
the reliability and security of Wi-Fi networks has become paramount. To uphold reliable
data transmission and secure data storage in wireless networks and information security,
there is a pressing need for swift implementation of new safety methods, standardized
portability norms, open system interaction, and robust data security measures [1].

Expanding upon the imperative of ensuring reliability and security in Wi-Fi networks, the evolution of wireless technology has brought forth innovative solutions such
as wireless mesh networks. These networks offer a distributed architecture that enhances
coverage, scalability, and redundancy, thereby augmenting the reliability and security
of data transmission in diverse environments. By interconnecting multiple nodes seamlessly, wireless mesh networks provide robust connectivity and adaptability, essential
for modern network infrastructures. Wireless mesh networks (WMNs) consist of mesh
routers and mesh clients, where mesh routers have minimal hmobility and form the
backbone of WMNs [2].

L. Iliadis et al. (Eds.): EANN 2024, CCIS 2141, pp. 478–491, 2024.
https://doi.org/10.1007/978-3-031-62495-7_36

Amidst traditional mesh routers, the evolution of networking technologies has given rise to smart routers. These advanced routers offer a pivotal feature: the capability to deliver personalized broadband services. By harnessing customer data, home gateways (HGW), and customer behavior, both companies and customers stand to benefit from more sophisticated and tailored services. To achieve this, specific technical aspects have been identified for investigation and implementation, with one of them being the focus of this paper's theme. Challenges can emerge in two distinct environments: outside the customer's home and within the customer's home (at the HGW level or between HGW and connected devices). The methodology of this paper aims to leverage the vast amount of status information collected from a sample of routers and develop an algorithm to predict Wi-Fi anomalies in both HGW and device connections.

The paper is structured into several sections:

Section 1 serves to introduce the paper's theme.

Section 2 delves into the realm of anomaly detection, providing a theoretical framework about the definition of anomalies. It also discusses the reporting method, detailing how anomalies can be reported and labeled.

Section 3 explores data science techniques for anomaly detection. It provides an overview and discusses conventional techniques such as time series analysis, and spectral analysis. Additionally, it covers more data-driven techniques like supervised learning, and deep learning.

Section 4 presents the methodology, discussing data understanding and the implementation of algorithms.

Section 5 presents the results obtained from the study.

Section 6 is dedicated to discussion and outlines potential next steps and provides the conclusion of the paper.

2 Anomaly Detection

2.1 Theoretical Framework

Anomaly detection poses challenges across various domains and aims to identify unusual or unexpected patterns within captured data. Existing anomaly detection methods often require specialized understanding of both the method itself and the specific context of its application, tailored to individual use cases.

In IoT data analysis, there's a frequent requirement to pinpoint new or uncommon states within a monitored system, utilizing sensors deployed in its immediate surroundings. This analytical approach finds utility in diverse fields such as smart traffic management, remote healthcare, energy optimization, and industrial automation [3, 4].

2.2 Definition of Anomaly

Please note that the first paragraph of a section or subsection is not indented. The first paragraphs that follows a table, figure, equation etc. does not have an indent, either.

Subsequent paragraphs, however, are indented.

At its core, anomaly detection entails identifying patterns that do not adhere to the expected standard for the system. However, numerous factors contribute to the complexity of this fundamental interpretation [4, 5].

Although IoT data may share similarities with data collected from other domains, there are distinct aspects of the time series structure and the data production and analysis environment that could impact the effectiveness of an anomaly detection algorithm [5].

1. Environmental cues:
   1.1. Temporal Factor: Given that most IoT data appears in the form of time-series data, which can be sampled regularly or irregularly, there's an inherent suggestion of temporal correlation among observations. This implies that the reading at time 't' is connected to observations from prior times.
   1.2. Spatial Factor: Similarly, the deployment of multiple sensors to monitor a single system introduces an inherent spatial context that requires attention. This complexity increases with the expansion of the spatial context or when the sensors themselves become mobile through various means. For in-stance, let's consider a scenario where multiple sensors are deployed to monitor environmental conditions in an urban setting.
   1.3. External Factor: A subset of spatial context involves considering the external conditions surrounding the monitored system.
2. Dimensionality:
   It refers to the number of distinct data attributes recorded in each observation. The dimensionality of the data influences the selection of appropriate methods, as some techniques may not be suitable for high-dimensional data [5, 6]:
   2.1. Univariate data represents a sequence of observations gathered by a lone sensor. Usually, these data streams are structured as key–value pairs, with the key representing the observation's timestamp and the value indicating a scalar, nominal, or ordinal measurement of the monitored environment.
   2.2. Multivariate data consists of a sequence of observations collected by multiple sensors. These data streams are commonly organized as key–vector pairs, where multiple observations are logged at the same timestamp, each associated with a unique sensor or actuator monitoring a single system. These datasets represent a collection of univariate data streams that are temporally correlated.
3. Noise:
   In real-world systems, noise is a natural component. Noisy data reflects minor fluctuations in reported values that do not significantly alter the overall data structure. These fluctuations may arise from slight variations in detector sensitivity, unrelated events near the sensor, or transmission errors in the data management system [6].

Stationarity:
A stationary time series is characterized by consistent mean, variance, and autocorrelation over time. In contrast, real-world time series often display non-stationarity, where these statistical properties vary [6]. Non-stationarity in data poses challenges for IoT anomaly detection methods, as they are designed to detect patterns and deviations within stationary datasets. On the other hand, when dealing with stationary data, especially if it exhibits seasonal patterns, SARIMA (Seasonal AutoRegressive Integrated Moving Average) models become particularly relevant. SARIMA models extend the capabilities

of ARIMA models by incorporating seasonal components into the time series analysis. This allows SARIMA models to capture and account for seasonal variations in the data, making them suitable for detecting anomalies within seasonal patterns.

Concept drift is the change in statistical distribution of a data stream over time [7].

Seasonality refers to a special case of concept drift where cyclical changes occur over varying time scales of much higher period than the sampling resolution [6, 7].

Change points indicate either locally or globally permanent alterations in the normal state of a monitored system. Typically, these changes occur more abruptly than those observed in concept drift, indicating the swift transition to a new system state [7].

2.3 Reporting Method

There are two primary ways in which anomalous data may be reported [8].
Anomaly Score:
An anomaly score represents a quantified measure of how much a particular observation diverges from the anticipated value, as defined by the utilized anomaly detection model. Different algorithms employ distinct methods to derive these anomaly scores [7, 8].
Labels:
Each observation can be assigned a binary label indicating whether the detection algorithm has classified it as "normal" or "anomalous." While some algorithms directly provide this binary classification, it is often determined using a threshold applied to the initial score generated by the detection algorithm [8].

3   Data Science Techniques for Anomaly Detection

3.1 Overview

Traditionally, anomaly detection has been approached from a statistical perspective. However, the rise of machine learning (ML) has introduced new avenues for outlier detection, especially with the abundance of data available for model training. This presents opportunity, in domains like the IoT, where evolving data patterns pose challenges for static models [9].

3.2 Conventional Techniques

Time Series
Time series forecasting, a key component, predicts future data values, aiding in anomaly detection by comparing actual and expected values. Noteworthy techniques include cross-correlation analysis, auto-regressive moving average (ARMA), auto-regressive integrated moving average (ARIMA), Kalman filtering [9], as well as advanced models like Seasonal AutoRegressive Integrated Moving Average (SARIMA), Seasonal AutoRegressive Integrated Moving Average with exogenous variables (SARIMAX), and Vector AutoRegressive Moving Average with exogenous variables (VARMAX).In IoT anomaly detection, SARIMA, SARIMAX, and VARMAX models are frequently employed due to their ability to handle complex seasonal patterns and incorporate exogenous variables. These models enhance the robustness of anomaly detection engines,

allowing for more accurate predictions and anomaly identification in diverse IoT environments.

Spectral Techniques

The spectral approach focuses on dimensionality reduction by assuming that data can be embedded into a lower-dimensional subspace where normal and anomalous instances exhibit significant differences. Techniques often rely on Principal Component Analysis (PCA), a widely used method for projecting data into a lower-dimensional space [9]. Dimensionality reduction provided by spectral techniques is advantageous for handling high-dimensional data and can serve as a preprocessing step before applying other anomaly detection techniques on the subspace. However, drawbacks of spectral techniques may include high computational complexity and applicability limitations, particularly when anomalies cannot be distinguished from normal conditions in a lower-dimensional embedding of the data.

3.3 Data-Driven Techniques

Supervised Learning

Supervised learning denotes machine learning methodologies that train a model using a dataset comprising examples and corresponding target outputs (labels).

However, applying supervised learning to anomaly detection poses unique challenges. In practical scenarios, instances of rare samples are often scarce in the training dataset. To address this class-imbalanced situation, algorithms are modified to amplify the influence of rare instances on the models. One prevalent strategy involves employing cost-sensitive learning, where the training data is relabeled using associated costs. These adjustments have been integrated into common classification algorithms such as proximity-based classifiers, Support Vector Machines (SVMs), decision trees, and rule-based classifiers [9].

Deep Learning

Deep learning, an evolution from traditional artificial neural networks (ANNs), distinguishes itself primarily through its architectural depth. Unlike traditional ANNs, deep learning architectures feature numerous hidden layers, allowing them to delve deeper into data representations. Deep learning techniques can operate in both supervised and unsupervised modes. Various deep learning architectures have emerged, including Convolutional Neural Networks (CNNs), autoencoders, Restricted Boltzmann machines, and Recurrent Neural Networks (RNNs).

Moreover, sequential networks, such as Recurrent Neural Networks (RNNs), leverage temporal correlations between neurons for their operation. A notable addition to RNNs is the Long Short-Term Memory (LSTM) unit, which functions as a memory component during gradient descent. This addresses the inherent limitation of RNNs in capturing context as the number of time steps increases.

4 Methodology

4.1 Data Understanding

Since the paper focuses on anomaly detection in data reported by a sample of routers within a Wi-Fi network over a specific time frame, it is essential to discuss some of its metrics and indicators of good behavior.

Routers gather copious amounts of data, necessitating a reduction in the frequency of information collection to alleviate overhead, typically done on an hourly basis. This periodicity poses challenges for developing Wi-Fi proactive maintenance (PNM) due to the limited and sporadic data availability. To mitigate this constraint, the paper concentrates on gathering a select few critical pieces of information [10]:

1. PHY (Physical Data Rate): The physical data rate denotes the speed at which bits are transmitted by stations and access points (AP) during data frame transmission. It directly impacts network congestion and Wi-Fi utilization.
2. RSSI (Received Signal Strength Indicator): RSSI measures the strength of the device receiving a specific signal. While it may not be inherently useful on its own, when combined with other parameters, it becomes a potent metric. For instance, when correlated with adjacent-channel and non-Wi-Fi interference and coverage, RSSI can provide valuable insights into signal propagation and network performance.
3. SNR (Signal to Noise Ratio): SNR gauges how effectively the desired signal is discerned amidst background noise, which can originate from other Wi-Fi networks (e.g., adjacent-channel and co-channel interference) or other RF sources. Evaluating SNR aids in understanding signal clarity and potential interference issues.
4. Channel Utilization and Selection: Channel utilization measures how occupied a particular channel is, helping to identify congestion and optimize channel allocation for improved network performance.
5. Frame Retries: Frame retries indicate the number of times a frame is sent without receiving its corresponding acknowledgment (ACK).
6. Client Capabilities: Understanding user device specifications, such as Wi-Fi generation support, provides insights into network compatibility and potential performance limitations.

In their study [10], the authors proposed a method to assess Wi-Fi performance. They achieved this by configuring Access Points (APs) with specialized measurement and monitoring software, developed by the authors themselves, which communicates with a measurement controller. This approach addresses a problem and architecture like the one currently under research.

To quantitatively evaluate the quality of a wireless network, the authors introd0uced the Wi-Fi-Based TCP Throughput (Witt) metric. W0itt measures the probable TCP throughput between the client device and the AP, serving as a valuable indicator of network performance [10]. By focusing on TCP-based flows, which constitute a significant portion of internet traffic, this metric captures the user's experience when the wireless link acts as the bottleneck. Inspired by the TCP Throughput, we developed a metric that is the ratio between the difference of consecutive total number of outbound packets that could not be transmitted due to errors (SSID layer) and the difference between consecutive total number of packets transmitted out of the interface (SSID layer). We termed this metric ERR and established that if the ERR exceeded or equaled a threshold of 0.02, the router would report an anomaly; otherwise, it would operate according to the expected behavior. This threshold enables us to create a binary labeling for the anomalies.

The anomaly detection pipeline functions as a cohesive framework. The data undergoes treatment for missing values, followed by feature selection using Pearson correlation, and then normalization between 0 and 1 is applied. The forecasting of the variable ERR is performed with a lag of 6 for the next 6 h, using hourly data from 2024-01-09 00:00:00 to 2024-01-21 23:00:00. We implemented harmonic trans-formation to capture cyclic patterns inherent in the data and proceeded with the extraction of features such as hour cosine, hour sine, day cosine, day sine, week sine, and week cosine from the timestamp data. If the forecasted value of ERR crosses the threshold, it suggests a potential anomaly.

Subsequently, a Support Vector Machine (SVM) classifier is employed to predict and identify the unique MAC addresses of the router or routers marked as anomalous. It's noteworthy that the SVM classifier is tuned through grid search, a technique used to systematically explore a range of hyperparameters to optimize the model's performance and generalization ability, as described in Fig. 1.

However, if the time series does not detect an anomaly, it continues to operate with a lag of 6, aiming to predict the next 2 steps or hours from the current moment.

Algorithm 1 Grid Search for Choosing Hyperparameters with Precision (RBF Kernel)

1: Define hyperparameter grid G for C and γ values
2: Define performance metric M (e.g., precision)
3: Set best_score $\leftarrow -\infty$
4: Set best_param $\leftarrow$ None
5: **for** each parameter combination p in grid G **do**
6:     Train SVM model with hyperparameters p (RBF kernel)
7:     Evaluate model precision on validation set
8:     **if** precision $>$ best_score **then**
9:         Update best_score $\leftarrow$ precision
10:        Update best_param $\leftarrow p$
11:    **end if**
12: **end for**
13: **return** Best hyperparameters: best_param

Fig. 1. Grid Search.

4.2 Algorithms

Addressing Data Leakage

As mentioned previously, we employed the ERR metric as the basis for discerning the presence of anomalies. Given its association with anomaly detection, integrating ERR into the SVM model would inadvertently expose information about anomaly states. Therefore, we conducted an outlier study utilizing the interquartile range. Through this analysis, we identified the 75th percentile as a viable alternative to ERR, offering a suitable proxy without revealing excessive details. This approach reinforces the model's robustness while effectively addressing the challenge of anomaly detection.

Addressing Model Agnosticism

Dealing with the heterogeneous nature of data stemming from different router types presents a challenge in achieving model agnosticism. Variations in data distributions among different router models can impact the performance and generalizability of machine learning models trained on such data. Data preprocessing emerges as a crucial step in the pursuit of model agnosticism.

Initially, the process involves selecting the most relevant features. Subsequently, normalization techniques such as standardization and feature scaling are applied to ensure that data from different router models are brought to a comparable scale and distribution.

Lastly, PCA is utilized to reduce dimensionality by intentionally selecting the percentage of explained variance that must be retained. Figure 2 illustrates the algorithm.

Addressing Data Drift

Machine learning models are seldom static due to the dynamic nature of data. Data drift, which refers to changes in the data distribution over time, is a common phenomenon encountered in various applications [8].

These changes can stem from evolving user behaviors, shifts in environmental conditions, or updates in underlying systems. As a response to data drift and other variations in datasets, models may need to be retrained on slightly modified data to maintain their performance and adapt to new patterns. Additionally, retraining models on subsets of data can be valuable for uncertainty quantification, especially in scenarios where data distributions may change unpredictably.

To initiate the retraining process, we loaded the saved model and the initial predictions. Subsequently, we stratified the new data based on the target variable and proceeded with the retraining phase. We selected 1% of the total dataset based on the target variable and employed random sampling within this subset to obtain a representative sample. The 1% sample was then split into an 80/20 ratio for training and testing purposes. The model is currently undergoing training, and evaluations are being conducted to assess its performance.

Following this, the remaining 99% of the data was split into a 75/25 ratio for the test and train sets, respectively. The SVM p'arameters were set to $C = 10$ and gamma $= 0.1$. Priority is given to the precision of the label referring to the existence of anomalies.

Algorithm 2 Algorithm 2: Principal Component Analysis (PCA) with Explicability Threshold

---

Require: X: Dataset with dimensions ($n_{samples}$, $n_{features}$)
Ensure: PCA_scores: PCA scores retaining 70% explicability
    pca_model: Trained PCA model
    Initialize PCA model with desired number of components: k.
2: Compute the mean-centered dataset:

$$X_{mean} = X - \mu$$

where μ is the mean of each feature.
Compute the covariance matrix of X_{mean}:

$$\Sigma = \frac{1}{n_{samples}} X_{mean}^T X_{mean}$$

4: Compute the eigenvalues (λ) and eigenvectors (V) of the covariance matrix:

$$\Sigma V = \lambda V$$

Sort the eigenvalues in descending order and rearrange the corresponding eigenvectors accordingly.
6: Compute the explained variance ratio for each principal component:

$$explained\_variance\_ratio_i = \frac{\lambda_i}{\sum_{j=1}^{n_{features}} \lambda_j}$$

Determine the cumulative sum of explained variance ratios:

$$cumulative\_variance\_ratio_i = \sum_{j=1}^{i} explained\_variance\_ratio_j$$

8: Determine the minimum number of components needed to retain at least 70% of the explicability:

$$k = \min\{i : cumulative\_variance\_ratio_i \geq 0.7\}$$

Select the top k eigenvectors corresponding to the highest eigenvalues.
10: Project the mean-centered dataset X_{mean} onto the selected eigenvectors to obtain PCA scores:

$$PCA\_scores = X_{mean} V_{selected}$$

---

return PCA_scores, pca_model

Fig. 2. PCA Reduction.

5 Results

5.1 Time Series

Using sine and cosine functions in time series analysis offers advantages. They represent periodicity effectively, being inherently periodic and suitable for modeling cyclical patterns and the orthogonality enables independent representation of cyclical patterns with varying phases and amplitudes.

Figure 3 illustrates the decomposition of the time series into its trend, seasonality, and residuals components, as characterized by the target ERR. The Dickey-Fuller test yielded a p-value lower than the specified alpha confidence level, confirming the stationarity of ERR. Additionally, as depicted in Fig. 3, ERR exhibits seasonality. The target ERR achieved a correlation value of 0.53 with the sine transformation of the hour.

Figure 4 depicts a scatter plot between ERR and the sine transformation for each hour. It appears that the threshold to detect anomalies is crossed when the sine values reach 0.50 or higher. The sine function oscillates between −1 and 1 over one period, which is 2π radians. At the peak of the sine function, it equals 1, and at the trough, it equals −1. The mid-point, where it equals 0, happens halfway between the peak and

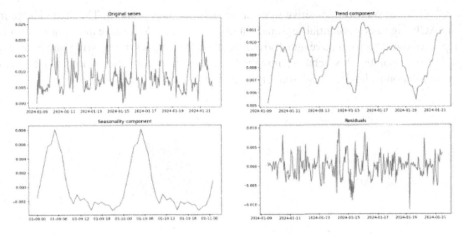

Fig. 3. Decomposition of ERR.

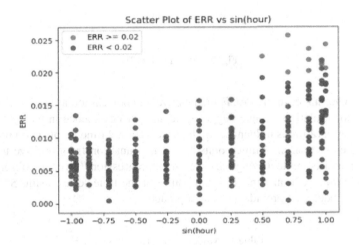

Fig. 4. Scatter Plot.

the trough. For a sine value of 0.5, it means we're at half of the amplitude of the sine function, which happens at a certain angle between 0 and $\pi/2$ (radians). Therefore, we need to find the angle (in radians) whose sine equals 0.5. We know that $\sin(\pi/6) = 0.5$. Now, we need to convert radians to hours since the original calculation was based on the hour of the day. There are 2π radians in 24 h, so $\pi/6$ radians correspond to

$$(24/(2\pi)) * (\pi/6) \text{ hours.} \tag{1}$$

A sine value of 0.5 corresponds to 20 min in the given formula. The analysis indicates that anomalies tend to occur around the 20th minute of each hour when the data was reported, as suggested by the scatterplot.

Figure 5 displays the Autocorrelation Function (ACF) and Partial Autocorrelation Function (PACF) of the hourly time series comprised of ERR. It can be observed that the

ACF changes sign from positive to negative between lags 4 and 5. The sign change in the ACF suggests a potential seasonal pattern in the data. A positive auto-correlation at lag 4 followed by a negative autocorrelation at lag 5 indicates a recur-ring pattern every 4 or 5 time points. This behavior implies correlation between observations at a lag of 4 or 5 time points, hinting at seasonality or periodicity with a period of 4 or 5.

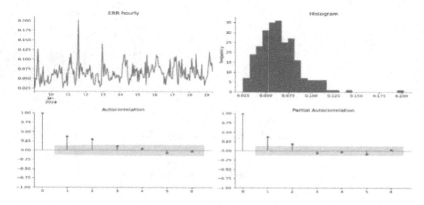

Fig. 5. ACF and PACF.

On the other hand, in the PACF, the positive autocorrelation at lag 2 followed by a negative autocorrelation at lag 3 suggests memory or persistence in the system. Here, the current observation is influenced by the observation 2 time points ago but inversely related to the observation 3 time points ago. This transition from positive to negative in the PACF assists in identifying the order of autoregression. Given the observed characteristics in the PACF and the seasonal nature of the time series, using SARIMA or SARIMAX models can provide a sound approach.

Table 1. Models and performance.

Model	Window	Lag	N Steps	MAPE
SARIMAX(1,0,3)*(4,0, [1-4],6)	24	6	24	25.71%
SARIMAX(5,0,3)*(4,0, [1-4],6)	24	6	24	22.57%
VARMAX(1,0,2)*(0,0,0,0)	24	6	24	9.78%
LSTM(128, batch_size = 64, lr = 0.001)	24	6	24	30.26%
SARIMAX(1,0,3)*(4,0, [1-4],6)	24	6	24	25.71%

Table 1 summarizes the performance of the models. The VARMAX model was implemented with the sine transformation of the hour included in the exogenous variable list. This inclusion resulted in a MAPE of 9.78%. This indicates that the predictions of the model deviate from the actual values by approximately 10% of the actual values.

The SARIMAX model with parameters (5,0,3)*(4,0, [1,2,3,4],6) achieved the best MAPE compared to the other SARIMAX model with a different parameter combination. This outcome is consistent with the fact that it also attained the lowest AIC (Akaike Information Criterion).

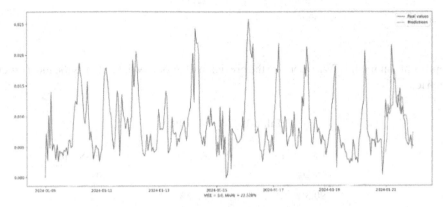

Fig. 6. Prediction.

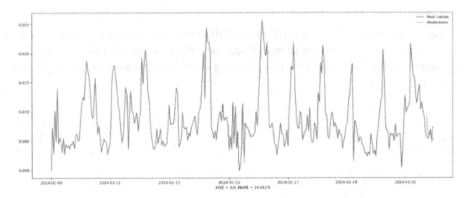

Fig. 7. Forecast.

Figure 6 illustrates the predictions made by the SARIMAX(5,0,3)*(4,0,[1,2,3,4],6) model. These predictions are based on observations from the test set, allowing for a comparison of the model's performance against the actual data. They were generated using a window of the last 24 h, with a lag of 6, and 24 steps ahead. Figure 7 displays the forecast for the next 6 h, starting from the last observation recorded in the dataset. It's important to note that this forecast extends beyond the data presented in the test set, incorporating additional data for future predictions.

5.2 SVM Classifier

Table 2 displays the SVM performance when the data was not yet subjected to PCA reduction. In this context, label 0 denotes non-anomalous observations, while label 1

Table 2. SVM prior to PCA.

Label	Precision	Recall	F1-Score
0	97.1%	99.5%	98.2%
1	93.5%	72.4%	81.6%
Accuracy	96.8%		

represents anomalies. We prioritize the precision of anomaly detection as the most crucial metric.

Table 3. SVM after PCA.

Label	Precision	Recall	F1-Score
0	97.4%	99.3%	98.3%
1	90.3%	71.9%	80.1%
Accuracy	96.9%		

Table 3 illustrates the SVM performance following the reduction of data to scores by PCA. Despite a slight increase in model accuracy, the precision of label 1 experienced a decrease, as did the recall, albeit to a lesser extent. This prompts further exploratory work in the future.

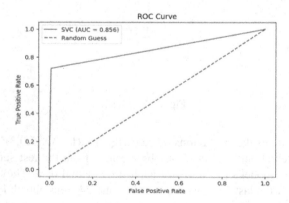

Fig. 8. ROC Curve.

In the context where anomalies are labeled as 1 and non-anomalies as 0, a ROC curve with an AUC (Area Under the Curve) of 0.856 signifies that the model exhibits strong discriminatory power in distinguishing between anomalies (label 1) and non-anomalies (label 0), as demonstrated in Fig. 8. With an AUC of 85.6%, the model correctly ranks a randomly chosen anomaly higher than a randomly chosen non-anomaly approximately 85.6% of the time.

6 Future Work and Conclusion

The results of PCA reduction appeared promising; however, future endeavors aim to test a variety of router types within a Wi-Fi network. Employing time series analysis can help determine the optimal timing for running the SVM model. VARMAX appears to be the most suitable approach for time series forecasting, incorporating the hour transformation alongside ERR. The threshold, set at 0.02, seemed well-calibrated. As evident in the scatterplot, there appears to be periodicity in the occurrence of ERR values equal to or above the threshold, which suggests a potential pattern of anomalies occurring approximately every 20th minute or more frequently on an hourly basis.

Considering our current findings and ongoing research objectives, it is important to contemplate the potential integration of online training methodologies for machine learning models in our future work. Online training strategies enable the continuous adaptation of models to the evolving data streams, facilitating real-time updates and refinements.

References

1. Kasimov, S., Bugibaev, E., Arzikulov, S.: Wireless networks and information security. In: Proceedings of the 2007 3rd IEEE/IFIP International Conference in Central Asia on Internet, pp. 1–4. IEEE (2007). https://doi.org/10.1109/CANET.2007.4401684
2. Redmore, J., Teckchandani, A.: Top key performance indicators in Wi-Fi. CableLabs Technical Brief, July 2016 (2016)
3. Cook, A.A., Mısırlı, G., Fan, Z.: Anomaly detection for IoT time-series data: a survey. IEEE Internet Things J. **7**(7), 6481–6494 (2020). https://doi.org/10.1109/JIOT.2019.2958185
4. Syafrudin, M., Alfian, G., Fitriyani, N.L., Rhee, J.: Performance analysis of IoT-based sensor, big data processing, and machine learning model for real-time monitoring system in automotive manufacturing. Sensors **18**, 2946 (2018). https://doi.org/10.3390/s18092946
5. Gaddam, A., Wilkin, T., Angelova, M.: Anomaly detection models for detecting sensor faults and outliers in the IoT - a survey. In: Proceedings of the IEEE International Conference on Software Testing, Verification and Validation Workshops, pp. 1–6 (2019). https://doi.org/10.1109/ICST46873.2019.9047684
6. Hinder, F., Artelt, A., Hammer, B.: A probability theoretic approach to drifting data in continuous time domains (2019). ArXiv, abs/1912.01969
7. Chinn, C.A., Brewer, W.F.: The role of anomalous data in knowledge acquisition: a theoretical framework and implications for science instruction. Rev. Educ. Res. **63**(1), 1–49 (1993). https://doi.org/10.2307/1170558
8. Erhan, L., et al.: Smart anomaly detection in sensor systems: a multi-perspective review. Inf. Fusion **67**, 64–79 (2021). https://doi.org/10.1016/j.inffus.2020.10.001
9. Ribeiro, M., Singh, S., Guestrin, C.: Model-agnostic interpretability of machine learning (2016). ArXiv, abs/1606.05386
10. Patro, A., Govindan, S., Banerjee, S.: Observing home wireless experience through WiFi APs. In: Proceedings of the 19th Annual International Conference on Mobile Computing & Networking (MobiCom 2013), pp. 339–350. ACM (2013)

Discrete-Time Replicator Equations on Parallel Neural Networks

Armen Bagdasaryan, Antonios Kalampakas[✉], and Mansoor Saburov

College of Engineering and Technology, American University of the Middle East,
Egaila 54200, Kuwait
antonios.kalampakas@aum.edu.kw

Abstract. In this paper, we are aiming to propose a novel mathematical model that studies the dynamics of synaptic damage in terms of concentrations of toxic neuropeptides (neurotransmitters) during neurotransmission processes. Our objective is to employ *"Wardrop's first and second principles"* within a neural network of the brain. Complete manifestations of Wardrop's first and second principles within a neural network of the brain are presented through the introduction of two novel concepts: *neuropeptide's (neurotransmitter's) equilibrium* and *synapses optimum*. In the context of a neural network within the brain, an analogue of the price of anarchy is *the price of cognition* which is *the most unfavorable ratio between the overall impairment caused by toxic neuropeptide's (neurotransmitter's) equilibrium in comparison to the optimal state of synapses (synapses optimum)*. Finally, we also propose an iterative algorithm (neurodynamics) in which *the synapses optimum* is eventually established during the neurotransmission process. We envision that this mathematical model can serve as a source of motivation to instigate novel experimental and computational research avenues in the fields of artificial neural networks and contemporary neuroscience.

Keywords: Price of cognition · neurotransmission · neurotransmitter's equilibrium · synapses optimum · neurodynamics

1 Introduction

Neurotransmissions are the intricate processes through which brain cells establish communication channels. It is now well-established within the domain of contemporary neuroscience that the *synapse* plays a critical role in a variety of cognitive neurotransmission processes, especially those involved with deep learning and memory. The *synapse* is the small pocket of space situated between two neurons which is essential to the transmission of electric nerve impulse from one neuron to another. A single neuron has the capacity to house thousands of *synaptic links*. The linkage space between a presynaptic fiber and a postsynaptic fiber is called the *synaptic cleft*. Neurotransmitters are essential neurochemicals that maintain synaptic and cognitive functions in humans by sending

L. Iliadis et al. (Eds.): EANN 2024, CCIS 2141, pp. 492–503, 2024.
https://doi.org/10.1007/978-3-031-62495-7_37

signals across presynaptic to postsynaptic neurons throughout the *unidirectional synaptic links.*

In the past, neuroscientists held the belief that all synapses remained *constant* in their functionality, operating consistently at a *uniform* level. However, contemporary understanding has evolved to acknowledge (see [1]- [5]) that synaptic *strength* can be modified by activity or inactivity, leading to strengthening or weakening of synapses or even *damaging* the functionality of synapses in the brain. The augmentation of synaptic strength occurs in direct proportion to its usage, thereby enhancing its capacity to exert a more substantial influence over its adjacent postsynaptic neurons. Contemporary neuroscientists believe (see [6]-[14]) that this strengthening of synapses constitutes a fundamental mechanism for facilitating the process of learning and, as a result, the formation of memories.

Due to the importance of knowing *damage* and *deterioration* of synapses in the brains of people with Alzheimer's disease, in this paper, we are aiming to propose a novel mathematical model that *studies the dynamics of synaptic damage in terms of concentrations of toxic neuropeptides (neurotransmitters) during neurotransmission processes.*

Our objective is to employ *"Wardrop's first and second principles"* in order to *enhance our understanding of the dynamics of toxic neuropeptides (neurotransmitters) during the neurotransmission process within a neural network of the brain.*

We first introduce the so-called *neuropeptide's (neurotransmitter's) equilibrium* concept that encapsulates the fundamental essence of Wardrop's first principle. Namely, the *neuropeptide (neurotransmitter) equilibrium* refers to *a distribution of toxic neuropeptides (neurotransmitters) that leads to uniform damage across all synaptic links.* Subsequently, we proceed to present a complete manifestation of Wardrop's second principle through the introduction of another so-called *synapses optimum* concept. *Synapses optimum is the most desirable distribution of toxic neuropeptides (neurotransmitters) that minimizes the cumulative damage experienced by all synapses.*

Consequently, within the context of a neural network of the brain, an analogue of the price of anarchy is *the price of cognition* which is *the most unfavorable ratio between the overall impairment caused by toxic neuropeptide's (neurotransmitter's) equilibrium in comparison to the optimal state of synapses (synapses optimum).* To put it differently, *the price of cognition* measures *the loss of cognitive ability resulting from increased concentrations of toxic neuropeptides (neurotransmitters).* Finally, we also present an iterative algorithm (neurodynamics) in which *the synapses optimum* is eventually established during the neurotransmission process.

Our model represents a sophisticated simplification and abstraction of the natural neurotransmission process involving two neurons. Nevertheless, we envision that this mathematically abstract model can serve as a catalyst and a source of motivation to instigate novel experimental research avenues in the fields of artificial neural networks and contemporary neuroscience.

2   The Price of Cognition

A *brain neural network* consists of a collection of neurons that are *chemically interconnected* or *functionally associated*. Within the brain neural network, *synapses* play a vital role in facilitating the transmission of nervous impulses from one neuron to another. The fundamental types of connections between neurons include both *chemical* and *electrical synapses*. An *electrical synapse*'s primary advantage lies in its ability to swiftly transmit signals from one neuron to the adjacent neuron. In the context of *chemical synapses*, it's important to note that there is a temporal delay in the neurotransmission process. Therefore, a part of the brain neural network that relies on chemical synapses for communication can be regarded as a *transportation network*.

Within this framework, the *impairment, deterioration, degradation*, or *decline* of the functionality of synapses, occurring due to elevated levels of toxic neuropeptides/neurotransmitters during the neurotransmission process, can be linked to a *traffic congestion* problem in a transportation network. From a theoretical standpoint, when investigating the dynamic relationship between synaptic damage and the concentration of toxic neuropeptides/neurotransmitters during the neurotransmission process, it is plausible to adapt "*Wardrop's first and second principles*". Although these principles were originally formulated to describe *optimal flow* distributions in transportation networks, we believe that they can be adapted and applied effectively within the framework of the neural network in the brain.

The network optimization problems have attracted much attention over the last decade for their ubiquitous appearance in real-life applications and the inherent mathematical challenges that they present, especially, in optimal transportation theory and communication networks (see [15–21]). Back in 1952, J. G. Wardrop (see [15]) formulated two principles of optimality of flows in networks that describe the circumstances of the *user equilibrium* and the *system optimum*. The first Wardrop principle states that *the costs of all utilized links are equal and less than the costs of those unutilized links for every fixed source-destination pair*. Meanwhile, the *system optimum* is *the optimal distribution of the flow for which the total cost of the system is minimal*.

The problems of finding the user equilibrium and system optimum are the topics of active research both in theory and practice. When making route choices in traffic networks, the network users frequently display selfish behavior, that is the fundamental principle of the first Wardrop principle, by selecting routes that minimize their individual travel costs.

It is widely recognized (see [16–19]) that selfish routing, in general, does not lead to a system optimum of the network that minimizes the total travel cost. The so-called *Price of Anarchy* (see [22,23]) is a quantitative measure of the inefficiency of the traffic network that was caused by the selfish behavior of the network users. Namely, *the price of anarchy is the worst-possible ratio between the total cost of a user equilibrium in comparison to the system optimum*.

The primary objective of this paper is to gain insight into specific mechanisms and phenomena within the neural network of the brain by applying methods originally designed for solving traffic assignment problems in transportation networks. For the sake of simplicity, we focus on examining the process of signal transmission between two neurons through chemical synapses.

Broadly speaking, there exist comprehensive *arrays* (*links*) of *synapses* between presynaptic and postsynaptic neurons that carry out the signal transmission process. In this scenario, let's assume that the presynaptic neuron releases *one-unit* of toxic *neuropeptides/neurotransmitters*. These toxic *neuropeptides/neurotransmitters* are subsequently absorbed by receptors located on the postsynaptic neuron across *unidirectional synaptic links* (Fig. 1).

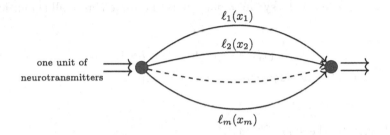

Fig. 1. The model of neurotransmission process between two neurons

We can visualize *two neurons connected by unidirectional synaptic links* as *a parallel network between two nodes*. Let $\mathbf{I}_m = \{1, 2, \ldots, m\}$ denote the set of the synaptic links between two neurons. We denote by $x_k \geq 0$, the concentration of toxic *neuropeptides/neurotransmitters* passing through the synaptic link k and $\mathbf{x} = (x_1, x_2, \ldots, x_m)$ denote a distribution of toxic *neuropeptides/neurotransmitters* over all synaptic links $\mathbf{I}_m = \{1, 2, \ldots, m\}$, where

$$\sum_{i=1}^{m} x_i = 1.$$

Within the framework of the neurotransmission process, increased levels of toxic neuropeptides/neurotransmitters damage the synaptic links. To investigate this correlation, we make the assumption that each synaptic link $k \in \mathbf{I}_m$ is associated with a *synaptic damage function*

$$\ell_k : [0, \infty) \to [0, \infty)$$

dependent on the concentration of toxic neuropeptides/neurotransmitters that measures the damage on the synaptic link k. This synaptic damage function ℓ_k, for each $k \in \mathbf{I}_m$, will be assumed to be a convex, strictly increasing, continuously differentiable function with $\ell_k(0) = 0$. We denote by

$$\mathbf{L}_m(\mathbf{x}) = (\ell_1(x_1), \ldots, \ell_m(x_m))$$

a *synaptic damage vector function* at $\mathbf{x} = (x_1, \ldots, x_m)$. Hence, a synaptic damage between two neurons can be identified with the synaptic damage vector function $\mathbf{L}_m(\cdot) = (\ell_1(\cdot), \cdots, \ell_m(\cdot))$.

In what follows, we use interchangeably the synaptic damage vector function and the neural network involving two neurons. The standard simplex is denoted by

$$\mathbb{S}^{m-1} = \{\mathbf{x} \in \mathbb{R}_+^m : \sum_{i=1}^m x_i = 1\}$$

and we define $\mathbf{supp}(\mathbf{x}) := \{i \in \mathbf{I}_m : x_i \neq 0\}$ and

$$\mathrm{int}\mathbb{S}^{m-1} = \{x \in \mathbb{S}^{m-1} : \mathbf{supp}(\mathbf{x}) = \mathbf{I}_m\}.$$

A distribution $\mathbf{x} = (x_1, \ldots, x_m) \in \mathbb{S}^{m-1}$ is called a *neuropeptide (neurotransmitter) equilibrium* if the synaptic damage is the same across all synaptic links, i.e.,

$$\ell_i(x_i) = \ell_j(x_j) \text{ for all } i, j \in \mathbf{I}_m.$$

The *cumulative damage* experienced by synapses at a distribution

$$\mathbf{x} = (x_1, \ldots, x_m) \in \mathbb{S}^{m-1}$$

is defined by the sum $\sum_{i=1}^m x_i \ell_i(x_i)$.

Obviously, the *neuropeptide/neurotransmitter equilibrium* that results in uniform damage across all synaptic links does not generally minimize the cumulative damage experienced by all synapses. The primary objective of experts in the domains of synapses and neurotransmitters of Alzheimer's disease is *to reduce and minimize the cumulative damage experienced by synapses in the brains of individuals afflicted with Alzheimer's disease.* Therefore, a distribution $\mathbf{x} = (x_1, \ldots, x_m) \in \mathbb{S}^{m-1}$ is called the *optimal state of synapses (synapses optimum)* if it minimizes the cumulative damage

$$\sum_{i=1}^m x_i \ell_i(x_i)$$

experienced by all synapses.

It has been well-established (see [16,18,19]) that if for each $k \in \mathbf{I}_m$ a synaptic damage function $\ell_k : [0, \infty) \to [0, \infty)$ with $\ell_k(0) = 0$ is a convex, strictly increasing, continuously differentiable function then there always exists a unique neuropeptide/neurotransmitter equilibrium $\mathbf{x}^{(\mathbf{ne})} \in \mathrm{int}\mathbb{S}^{m-1}$, as well as a unique synapses optimum $\mathbf{x}^{(\mathbf{so})} \in \mathrm{int}\mathbb{S}^{m-1}$. In general, we have that $\mathbf{x}^{(\mathbf{ne})} \neq \mathbf{x}^{(\mathbf{so})}$.

Consequently, within the context of a neural network of the brain, an analogous concept to *the price of anarchy* can be called as *the price of cognition.* This represents *the most unfavorable ratio between the overall impairment caused by toxic neuropeptide's (neurotransmitter's) equilibrium in comparison to the optimal state of synapses (synapses optimum).* To put it differently, *the price of cognition* measures *the loss of cognitive ability resulting from increased concentrations of toxic neuropeptides/neurotransmitters.* In terms of the mathematical formula, *the price of cognition* is defined as follows

$$\mathbf{PoC}(\mathbf{L}_m) := \frac{\mathbf{CD}(\mathbf{x}^{(\mathbf{ne})})}{\mathbf{CD}(\mathbf{x}^{(\mathbf{so})})}$$

where $\mathbf{x}^{(\mathbf{ne})} \in \mathrm{int}\mathbb{S}^{m-1}$ is the unique neuropeptide/neurotransmitter equilibrium, $\mathbf{x}^{(\mathbf{so})} \in \mathrm{int}\mathbb{S}^{m-1}$ is the unique synapses optimum, and

$$\mathbf{CD}(\mathbf{x}) = \sum\nolimits_{i=1}^{m} x_i \ell_i(x_i)$$

is the cumulative damage experienced by all synapses at a distribution $\mathbf{x} \in \mathbb{S}^{m-1}$.

Obviously, we always have that $\mathbf{PoC}(\mathbf{L}_m) \geq 1$. The case $\mathbf{PoC}(\mathbf{L}_m) = 1$ represents the most favorable and desirable circumstance for individuals afflicted with Alzheimer's disease. Indeed, if $\mathbf{PoC}(\mathbf{L}_m) = 1$ then we must have that

$$\mathbf{x}^{(\mathbf{ne})} = \mathbf{x}^{(\mathbf{so})}$$

due to the uniqueness of the neuropeptide/neurotransmitter equilibrium as well as synapses optimum. This means that *the neuropeptide/neurotransmitter equilibrium that leads to uniform damage across all synaptic links is also the optimal state of synapses which minimizes the cumulative damage experiences by them.* Under such circumstances, when two equilibria coincide $\mathbf{x}^{(\mathbf{ne})} = \mathbf{x}^{(\mathbf{so})}$, then it is referred to as *the optimal state of neurotransmitters-synapses (neurotransmitters-synapses optimum).*

3   The Mathematical Model

Within the domain of transportation networks, the significance of achieving a *price of anarchy* of 1 in a transportation network was emphasized by S. Dafermos as early as 1968, even before the concept of *the price of anarchy* itself was formally introduced. Namely, the problem proposed by S. Dafermos in her Ph.D. thesis [17] (see also [18]) seeks to identify the specific class of cost functions for a given network that lead to the emergence of identical equilibria according to Wardrop's first and second principles.

According to S. Dafermos, "*such networks are extremely desirable because the pattern created by the individuals acting in their own self interests coincides with the pattern most economical for the total society* (see [17,18]). She also provided a solution to her problem by specifying a family of cost functions in the form of monomial polynomials $\ell_i(x_i) = a_i x_i^k$ where $a_i > 0$ and $k \in \mathbb{N}$. This family of cost functions is capable of solving the problem for any given network (see [17,18]).

Recent empirical studies in real-world networks (see [24]), as well as theoretical studies (see [25,26]), show that the actual value of the price of anarchy is very close to 1. The price of anarchy in proximity to 1 indicates that *the user equilibrium is approximately socially optimal, thereby implying that the effects of selfish behavior are relatively benign.*

Moreover, theoretical studies on real-world networks also indicate (see [25,26]) that *the price of anarchy is approximately* 1 *in both light and heavy traffic conditions.* In addition, the price of anarchy for a broad range of cost functions, which includes all polynomials, tends to approach 1 in both heavy and light traffic, regardless of the network topology and the number of origin and destination pairs within the network.

Particularly, *the comprehensive asymptotic principle* for polynomial cost functions states (see [25,26]) that in networks where costs are polynomial, *the price of anarchy converges to 1 under both light and heavy traffic*. This implies that in light and heavy traffic congestion conditions, *a benevolent social planner with complete authority over traffic assignment would not do any better than the selfish behavior of users.*

On the other hand, parallel networks hold a unique status among other network types. Namely, *parallel networks are nontrivial classes of network topologies for which the price of anarchy is smaller than for any other networks* (see [27]). Among many other important results, one of the main results of the paper (see [27]) state that under weak assumptions on the class of cost functions, the price of anarchy for any multicommodity flow network is achieved by a *single-commodity instance* within a *network of parallel links*.

Consequently, for a given class of cost functions, the price of anarchy cannot be improved by any nontrivial constraint on the class of network topologies and/or the number of commodities. Therefore, *the lower value of the price of anarchy can always be attained by the simplest parallel network* (see [27]).

Despite its profound importance and practical applicability (see [24–26]), Dafermos's problem did not receive adequate attention from experts until more recently. All of these theoretical discoveries and empirical observations (see [24–26]) served as the driving force behind the exploration of the central and fundamental questions addressed recently in [28–30]:

- Can these observations be justified theoretically?
- Can we theoretically describe all cost functions associated with parallel networks in which the price of anarchy achieves its least value of 1?

Finally, Dafermos's problem has been fully solved for parallel networks in the papers (see [28–30]). For any prior given positive distribution

$$\mathbf{p} = (p_1, \ldots, p_m) \in \mathrm{int}\mathbb{S}^{m-1}$$

and for any convex, strictly increasing, continuously differentiable function $\ell : [0, \infty) \to [0, \infty)$ with $\ell(0) = 0$, we define the following cost vector function

$$\mathbf{\Phi}_m \left(\frac{\mathbf{x}}{\mathbf{p}} \right) = \left(\ell \left(\frac{x_1}{p_1} \right), \ldots, \ell \left(\frac{x_m}{p_m} \right) \right).$$

Among many other interesting results (see [28–30]), one of the main results states that the distribution $\mathbf{p} = (p_1, \ldots, p_m) \in \mathrm{int}\mathbb{S}^{m-1}$ is the *user equilibrium* as well as the *system optimum* of the parallel network $\mathbf{\Phi}_m$. In this case, the *price of anarchy* is equal to its least value that is 1. This shows that there are a vast class of parallel networks for which the *price of anarchy* is always equal to its least value that is 1.

Unlike Dafermos's example, there are also another interesting classes of parallel networks

$$\mathbf{L}_m(\frac{\mathbf{x}}{\mathbf{p}}) = \left(\ell_1(\frac{x_1}{p_1}), \ldots, \ell_m(\frac{x_m}{p_m}) \right)$$

generated by different degrees of polynomials for which the *price of anarchy* is always equal to 1, where

$$\ell_1(\frac{x_1}{p_1}) = \frac{x_1}{p_1},$$

$$\ell_2(\frac{x_2}{p_2}) = \frac{a_{22}}{2}\left(\frac{x_2}{p_2}\right)^2 + \frac{a_{21}}{1}\left(\frac{x_2}{p_2}\right) + \frac{a_{22}}{2},$$

$$\ell_3(\frac{x_3}{p_3}) = \frac{a_{33}}{3}\left(\frac{x_3}{p_3}\right)^3 + \frac{a_{32}}{2}\left(\frac{x_3}{p_3}\right)^2 + \frac{a_{31}}{1}\left(\frac{x_3}{p_3}\right) + \frac{2a_{33}}{3} + \frac{a_{32}}{2}$$

$$\vdots$$

$$\ell_i(\frac{x_i}{p_i}) = \sum_{k=1}^{i} \frac{a_{ik}}{k}\left(\frac{x_i}{p_i}\right)^k + \sum_{k=2}^{i} \frac{k-1}{k}a_{ik}$$

$$\vdots$$

$$\ell_m(\frac{x_m}{p_m}) = \sum_{k=1}^{m} \frac{a_{mk}}{k}\left(\frac{x_m}{p_m}\right)^k + \sum_{k=2}^{m} \frac{k-1}{k}a_{mk}.$$

and

$$\sum_{k=1}^{i} a_{ik} = 1 \quad \text{and} \quad a_{ik} > 0 \quad \text{for all} \quad 1 \le i \le m, \ 1 \le k \le i.$$

4   Simulations

In this section we will consider the case of a network with three parallel links with polynomial latency functions generated as described in the previous section. For this, we will consider a matrix of the form

$$A = \begin{bmatrix} u_{11} & & \\ a_{22} & a_{21} & \\ a_{33} & a_{32} & a_{31} \end{bmatrix}$$

such that the sum of elements in each row equals 1 and investigate the price of anarchy of the corresponding network $\mathbf{L}(\mathbf{x}) = (\ell_1(x_1), \ell_1(x_2), \ell_3(x_3))$, where

$$\ell_1(x_1) = x_1$$

$$\ell_2(x_2) = \frac{a_{22}}{2}x_2^2 + \frac{a_{21}}{1}x_2 + \frac{a_{22}}{2}$$

$$\ell_3(x_3) = \frac{a_{33}}{3}x_3^3 + \frac{a_{32}}{2}x_3^2 + \frac{a_{31}}{1}x_3 + \frac{2a_{33}}{3} + \frac{a_{32}}{2}.$$

For our simulation we choose the matrix:

$$A_1 = \begin{bmatrix} 1 \\ 0.2\ 0.8 \\ 0.3\ 0.2\ 0.5 \end{bmatrix}$$

and we obtain the network $L_{A_1}(\mathbf{x}) = \langle \ell_1(x_1), \ell_2(x_2), \ell_3(x_3) \rangle$, where

$$\ell_1(x_1) = x_1$$
$$\ell_2(x_2) = 0.1x_2^2 + 0.8x_2 + 0.1$$
$$\ell_3(x_3) = 0.1x_3^3 + 0.1x_3^2 + 0.5x_3 + 0.3$$

We consider the following discrete-time replicator equation $\mathcal{R} : \mathbb{S}^2 \to \mathbb{S}^2$

$$(\mathcal{R}(\mathbf{x}))_k = x_k \left[1 + \varepsilon \left(\ell_k \left(\frac{x_k}{p_k} \right) - \sum_{i=1}^{3} x_i \ell_i \left(\frac{x_i}{p_i} \right) \right) \right], \quad \forall\, k \in \mathbf{I}_3 \qquad (1)$$

where $\mathbf{p}$ is the interior flow $(0.2, 0.3, 0.5)$.

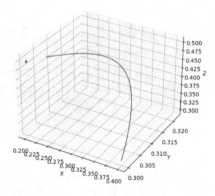

Fig. 2. 50 steps

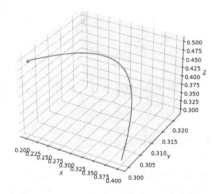

Fig. 3. 100 steps

Figures 2 and 3 depict the result of the iterative application of Eq. 1, for $\varepsilon = -0.05$ in three dimensions, on the network L_{A_1} starting from the initial point (0.4,0.3,0.3) after respectively 50 and 100 steps.

It turns out that, using replicator Eq. 1, with the described parameters, 50 steps are not enough to reach the desired equilibrium point. We can further assess the behavior of the network L_{A_1} by using as benchmark the uniform linear network with latency functions given by

$$\ell_i(x_i) = x_i, \quad i \in \mathbf{I}_3$$

and the uniform quadratic network with latency functions

$$\ell_i(x_i) = x_i^2, \quad i \in \mathbf{I}_3.$$

By taking the Manhattan distance of the resulting point at each step from the equilibrium point we observe that the network L_{A_1} is approaching the equilibrium point in a similar rate as the uniform linear network (Fig. 4).

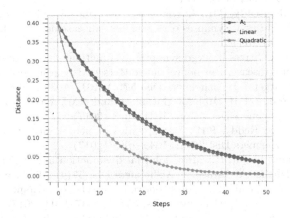

Fig. 4. Distance from the equilibrium

5   Conclusion

The primary objective of this paper was to gain insight into specific mechanisms and phenomena within the neural network of the brain by applying methods originally designed for solving traffic assignment problems in transportation networks. In this regard, the *impairment, deterioration, degradation,* or *decline* of the functionality of synapses, occurring due to elevated levels of toxic neuropeptides (neurotransmitters) during the neurotransmission process, can be linked to a *traffic congestion* problem in a transportation network. Therefore, when investigating the dynamic relationship between synaptic damage and the concentration of toxic neuropeptides (neurotransmitters) during the neurotransmission process, it is plausible to adapt *"Wardrop's first and second principles"*. Although these principles were originally formulated to describe *optimal flow* distributions in transportation networks, we believed that they could be applied effectively within the framework of the neural network in the brain. This was a novel approach adopted in this paper. Our model represents a high-level simplification and abstraction of the natural neurotransmission process involving two neurons. Nevertheless, we envisioned that this mathematical model could serve as a source of motivation to instigate novel experimental and numerical research avenues in the fields of artificial neural networks and contemporary neuroscience.

References

1. Della Sala, S.: Encyclopedia of Behavioral Neuroscience, 2nd Ed., Elsevier Science, (2021)
2. Fauth, M., Wörgötter, F., Tetzlaff, C.: The formation of multi-synaptic connections by the interaction of synaptic and structural plasticity and their functional consequences. PLoS Comput. Biol. **11**(1), 1–29 (2015)
3. Reddy, P.H.: A critical assessment of research on neurotransmitters in Alzheimer's disease. J. Alzheimers Dis. **57**(4), 969–974 (2017)
4. Rajmohan, R., Reddy, P.H.: Amyloid-beta and phosphorylated tau accumulations cause abnormalities at synapses of Alzheimer's disease neurons. J. Alzheimers Dis. **57**(4), 975–999 (2017)
5. Jha, S.K., et al.: Stress-induced synaptic dysfunction and neurotransmitter release in Alzheimer's disease: can neurotransmitters and neuromodulators be potential therapeutic targets? J. Alzheimers Dis. **57**(4), 1017–1039 (2017)
6. Wang, R., Reddy, P.H.: Role of glutamate and NMDA receptors in Alzheimer's disease. J. Alzheimers Dis. **57**(4), 1041–1048 (2017)
7. Kandimalla, R., Reddy, P.H.: Therapeutics of neurotransmitters in Alzheimer's disease. J. Alzheimers Dis. **57**(4), 1049–1069 (2017)
8. Guo, L., Tian, J., Du. H.: Mitochondrial dysfunction and synaptic transmission failure in Alzheimer's disease. J. Alzheimers Dis. **57**(4) 1071–1086 (2017)
9. Cai, Q., Tammineni, P.: Mitochondrial aspects of synaptic dysfunction in Alzheimer's disease. J. Alzheimers Dis. **57**(4), 1087–1103 (2017)
10. Tönnies, E., Trushina, E.: Oxidative stress, synaptic dysfunction, and Alzheimer's disease. J. Alzheimers Dis. **57**(4), 1105–1121 (2017)
11. Jiang, S., Bhaskar, K.: Dynamics of the complement, cytokine, and chemokine systems in the regulation of synaptic function and dysfunction relevant to Alzheimer's disease. J. Alzheimers Dis. **57**(4), 1123–1135 (2017)
12. Chen, K., Weng, Y., Hosseini, A.A., Dening, T., Zuo, G., Zhang, Y.: A comparative study of GNN and MLP based machine learning for the diagnosis of Alzheimer's Disease involving data synthesis. Neural Netw. **169**, 442–452 (2024)
13. Park, S., Hong, Ch.H., Lee, D-Gi., Park, K., Shin, H.: Prospective classification of Alzheimer's disease conversion from mild cognitive impairment. Neural Networks **164**, 335–344 (2023)
14. Ho, Ng-H., Yang, H.-J., Kim, J., Dao, D-Ph., Park, H.-R., Pant, S.: Predicting progression of Alzheimer's disease using forward-to-backward bi-directional network with integrative imputation. Neural Networks **150**, 422–439 (2022)
15. Wardrop, J.G.: Some theoretical aspects of road traffic research. Proc. Inst. Civil Eng. Part II **1**(3), 325–362 (1952)
16. Beckmann, M., McGuir, C., Winsten, C.: Studies in Economics of Transportation. Yale University Press, New Haven (1956)
17. Dafermos, S.: Traffic Assignment and Resource Allocation in Transportation Networks. Ph.D. Thesis, The Johns Hopkins University (1968)
18. Dafermos, S., Sparrow, F.T.: Traffic assignment problem for a general network. J. Res. Natl. Bureau Standards, Sect. B: Math. Sci. **73**(2), 91–118 (1969)
19. Patriksson, M.: The Traffic Assignment Problem: Models and Methods. VSP, The Netherlands (1994)
20. Acemoglu, D., Ozdaglar, A.: Competition and efficiency in congested markets. Math. Oper. Res. **32**(1), 1–31 (2007)

21. Acemoglu, D., Srikant, R.: Incentives and prices in communication networks. In: Algorithmic Game Theory. Nisan, N., Roughgarden, T., Tardos, E., Vazirani, V.V. (eds.), pp. 107-132, Cambridge University Press, Cambridge (2007)

22. Koutsoupias, E., Papadimitriou, C.: Worst-case equilibria. In: Proceedings of the 16th Annual Symposium on Theoretical Aspects of Computer Science, pp. 404–413, (1999)

23. Koutsoupias, E., Papadimitriou, Ch.: Worst-case equilibria. Comput. Sci. Rev. **3**(2), 65–69 (2009)

24. Monnot, B., Benita, F., Piliouras, G.: Routing games in the wild: efficiency, equilibration and regret. In: Devanur, N.R., Lu, P. (eds.) WINE 2017. LNCS, vol. 10660, pp. 340–353. Springer, Cham (2017). https://doi.org/10.1007/978-3-319-71924-5_24

25. Colini-Baldeschi, R., Cominetti, R., Mertikopoulos, P., Scarsini, M.: When is selfish routing bad? The price of anarchy in light and heavy traffic. Oper. Res. **68**(2), 411–434 (2020)

26. Wu, Z., Möhring, R,H., Chen, Y., Xu, D.: Selfishness Need Not Be Bad. Oper. Res. **69**(2), 410-435 (2021)

27. Roughgarden, T.: The price of anarchy is independent of the network topology. J. Comput. Syst. Sci. **67**(2), 341–364 (2003)

28. Bagdasaryan, A., Kalampakas, A., Saburov, M.: Dynamic traffic flow assignment on parallel networks. In: Karabegovic, I., Kovačević, A., Mandzuka, S. (eds.) New Technologies, Development and Application VI. NT 2023, LNNS, vol. 687, pp. 702–711. Springer, Cham (2023). https://doi.org/10.1007/978-3-031-31066-9_82

29. Bagdasaryan, A., Kalampakas, A., Saburov, M., Spartalis, S.: Optimal traffic flow distributions on dynamic networks. In: Iliadis, I., Maglogiannis, I., Alonso, S., Jayne, C., Pimenidis, E. (eds.) Engineering Applications of Neural Networks, EANN 2023, Communications in Computer and Information Science, vol. 1826, pp. 178–190. Springer, Cham (2023). https://doi.org/10.1007/978-3-031-34204-2_16

30. Kalampakas, A., Bagdasaryan, A., Saburov, M., Spartalis, S.: User equilibrium and system optimality conditions for flow distributions on congested networks. In: Iliadis, L., Maglogiannis, I., Alonso, S., Jayne, C., Pimenidis, E. (eds.) Engineering Applications of Neural Networks, EANN 2023, Communications in Computer and Information Science, vol. 1826, pp. 203–214 Springer, Cham (2023). https://doi.org/10.1007/978-3-031-34204-2_18

Evaluating Forecast Distributions in Neural Network HAR-Type Models for Range-Based Volatility

Michele La Rocca[ID] and Cira Perna[✉][ID]

Department of Economics and Statistics, University of Salerno, Via Giovanni Paolo II, 132, 84084 Fisciano, SA, Italy
{larocca,perna}@unisa.it

Abstract. In this paper, we focus on a range-based measure for volatility and present a forecasting tool combining the heterogeneous autoregressive model with feed-forward neural networks. Using a bootstrap scheme, we can also obtain the forecast distributions, which are useful to evaluate how much uncertainty is associated with each point forecast. An application to real data shows a significant contribution of the proposed methodology to improving forecast accuracy in terms of point forecasts and forecast distributions.

Keywords: Range-based volatility measures · HAR-type models · Feed-forward neural networks · Residual bootstrap

1 Introduction

Volatility plays a crucial role in many areas of financial econometrics, including derivative pricing, asset allocation, and investment decisions. As it quantiles the dispersion of returns, reliable forecasts of the volatility of the underlying assets and forecast intervals to account for uncertainty in the point forecasts are essential in risk analysis. However, since volatility is not directly observed, the first problem is obtaining a volatility measure. Generally, when daily closing prices are available, the natural proxy for the volatility can be obtained using the squared demeaned daily returns. This estimator, which is the most used in many volatility models, could be very inefficient because it employs only a single measurement of the price each period and hence contains no information about the price movement between each measurement. A more precise estimator can be obtained by using intraday high-frequency data. However, this data is often only available for short time horizons. In addition, the resulting volatility estimator is rather complex due to market microstructure effects [1].

Alternatively, the daily Open-High-Low-Close (OHLC) prices, readily available for many financial time series, can be used to construct valid alternative volatility proxies. In particular, among the numerous alternative estimators in the literature, we focus on the range volatility proposed in [2], a simple estimator

L. Iliadis et al. (Eds.): EANN 2024, CCIS 2141, pp. 504–517, 2024.
https://doi.org/10.1007/978-3-031-62495-7_38

which outperforms more complex range estimators [3]. It seems to be a superior choice for forecasting volatility compared to return-based estimators [4]. It is much less noisy than squared returns and is fairly robust toward microstructure effects [5]. Moreover, it is claimed to be more efficient for return-based estimators [6] and seems to outperform more complex range estimators [3].

In forecasting volatility using range estimators, some popular alternative model specifications have been employed in recent literature. They include some simple econometric models, such as autoregressive models [7], ARMA models (see [8]) and Exponentially Weighted Moving Average models [9] along with more complex models, such as GARCH-type models [10, 11], stochastic volatility models [12] and specific models for the range volatility time series [13]. Alternatively, to capture the high persistence observed in the volatility of many financial assets, the simple and easy-to-estimate Heterogeneous AutoRegressive (HAR) model [14] has arguably emerged as the preferred specification for realized volatility-based forecasting. Although it generally performs better than the forecasts from traditional parametric GARCH and stochastic volatility models, some nonlinear volatility features may remain unexplained in the model.

This paper presents and discusses a novel method for forecasting range-based volatility. The procedure uses a feed-forward neural network HAR-type model (NN-HAR) for range estimators to obtain point forecasts for the nonlinear dynamics of volatility and implement a bootstrap scheme to derive forecast distributions. Despite their simple structure, the implemented NN faces several characteristics that make it a valuable and attractive tool for forecasting. Indeed, NNs are data-driven self-adaptive methods and show good forecasting performance with high accuracy without suffering the so-called dimensionality curse. Moreover, for more complex neural network specifications, the NN-HAR model can reproduce the memory persistence observed in the data but, at the same time, remains parsimonious and easy to estimate. The proposed NN model allows us to easily implement a bootstrap scheme useful for obtaining forecast distributions and evaluating the uncertainty associated with each point forecast. In particular, we implement a standard bootstrap scheme from the residuals of the estimated NN-HAR model. The approach is in the spirit of neural network sieve bootstrap introduced in [15]. It is model-free within a general class of nonlinear processes and has a nice nonparametric property. It is also asymptotically justified and, in small samples, outperforms alternative bootstrap schemes for nonlinear time series [16].

The paper is organized as follows. Section 2 briefly introduces HAR-type models for range-based volatility. Section 3 discusses the proposed NN-HAR type model and presents the bootstrap scheme to obtain forecast distributions. Section 4 reports an application to the most significant stocks of SP&500, and the empirical findings are discussed. Some remarks in Sect. 5 close the paper.

2 HAR-Type Models for Range-Based Volatility

Classical methods measure volatility using squared returns based on daily opening or closing prices. Range-based measures use a stock's open-high-low-close price to calculate proxies of the volatility. Among the numerous proposals in the literature, this study focuses on the range estimator introduced by Garman and Klass [2]. It is defined as:

$$V_t = 0.51[\log(H_t) - \log(L_t)]^2 - 0.39[\log(C_t) - \log(O_t)]^2 \tag{1}$$

where O_t, H_t, L_t and C_t are the daily OHLC prices.

The Garman-Klass volatility uses the commonly available price information and extends Parkinson's volatility, which uses only the high and low daily prices. This range volatility estimator is based on the assumption that the asset price follows a driftless geometric Brownian motion, and it has also proven to be up to eight times more efficient than the close-to-close estimator. Moreover, the range estimator is not significantly biased and is robust to microstructure errors (see [5, 17]). This range estimator's relative efficiency and simplicity make a strong case for its use in volatility forecasting. However, for most financial assets, the range volatility shows a long-range dependence, a slowly decaying autocorrelation feature known as long memory. Forecasting models which exploit this long-memory property include FIGARCH and ARFIMA models [18].

An alternative approach to long-memory modelling views the long-memory feature of volatility as the result of data aggregation, breaks and filtration. Building on these ideas, the Heterogeneous AutoRegressive model (HAR) has been proposed [14]. The basic HAR model is an additive cascade model of different volatility components. It states that the conditional variance of discrete sampled returns is a linear function of the lagged squared return over the identical return horizon and the squared returns over longer or shorter return horizons. Compared with alternative models, the model is simple, parsimonious and easy to estimate. Furthermore, the empirical analysis shows excellent forecasting performance with respect to parametric GARCH and stochastic volatility models.

With the same formulation, the basic HAR model proposed for the Realized Variance can be used for the range volatility. In this case, the model is defined as:

$$V_t = \beta_0 + \beta_1 V_{t-1} + \beta_2 V_t^{(5)} + \beta_3 V_t^{(22)} + \varepsilon_t \tag{2}$$

where V_t is the range volatility defined in (1), $\varepsilon_t \sim NID(0, \sigma^2)$ and $V_t^{(5)}$ and $V_t^{(22)}$ are defined, respectively, as:

$$V_t^{(5)} = \frac{1}{5}(V_{t-1} + \ldots + V_{t-5}) \quad \text{and} \quad V_t^{(22)} = \frac{1}{22}(V_{t-1} + \ldots + V_{t-22}) \tag{3}$$

The HAR is a constrained AR(22) model, so the estimation and inference are straightforward when using autoregressive moving average modelling approaches. In addition to capturing long memory, the HAR model can also model other stylized features of financial returns [14].

However, range volatility can be subject to structural breaks and regime shifts, which are challenging to model using rigid parametric models. Hence, there is a need for a nonlinear adaptive modelling approach to improve the accuracy and efficiency of financial volatility forecasting.

In this context, deep learning techniques, and in general, artificial neural networks, have recently gained much traction in volatility forecasting (for a review, see [19]) due to their great flexibility and capability of providing models which fit any data with an arbitrary degree of accuracy. For the range-based proxies of volatility, in [20], the predictability of several range-based stock volatility estimates has been investigated using long short-term memory recurrent neural networks. The analysis shows that range-based estimates are more predictable than the estimate from daily closing values only.

In this study, we consider a possible extension of the basic HAR model for range volatility by including the possibility of a nonlinear relationship between the actual range volatility V_t and its lagged values over the same period $V_{t-1}, \ldots, V_{t-p}$ and over short and long horizons $V_t^{(5)}$ and $V_t^{(22)}$.

This approach has already been considered in [21]. However, this latter study focuses on realized volatility and in this context, assuming a Normal distribution for the NN parameters, parametric asymptotic confidence intervals are determined. Instead, in our study, a simple bootstrap scheme is implemented to obtain the entire forecast distribution. The approach is in the spirit of neural network sieve bootstrap introduced in [15] and, consequently, it is asymptotically justified and, in small samples, outperforms alternative bootstrap schemes for nonlinear time series [16].

3 Neural Network HAR-Type Models for Range Volatility

We assume the V_t, $t = 1, \ldots, T$ can be modeled as:

$$V_t = g\left(\mathbf{z}_t\right) + \varepsilon_t \tag{4}$$

where $\mathbf{z}_t$ is a vector of $r = p + 2$ variables, including p lagged values of V_t and average levels of volatility over the previous week and month. That is

$$\mathbf{z}_t' = \left(V_{t-1}, \ldots, V_{t-p}, V_t^{(5)}, V_t^{(22)}\right) \tag{5}$$

with $\mathbf{z}_t'$ denoting the transpose of the vector $\mathbf{z}_t$. As usual, all vectors are intended as column vectors. The error terms ε_t are assumed to be i.i.d. with mean zero and finite variance, and $g(\cdot)$ is an unknown (possibly nonlinear) function assumed to be continuously differentiable and defined on a compact subset of $\mathbb{R}^{p+2}$.

The function $g(\cdot)$ can be approximated with a single-layer feed-forward neural network with skip-layer connections between input and output layers, defined as:

$$f_s\left(\mathbf{z}_t; \boldsymbol{\theta}\right) = \boldsymbol{\beta}'\mathbf{z}_t + \sum_{j=1}^{s} c_j \psi\left(\boldsymbol{\alpha}_j'\mathbf{z}_t + \alpha_{j0}\right) + \beta_0 \tag{6}$$

in which $\boldsymbol{\theta}' = (\boldsymbol{\beta}', c_1, \ldots, c_s, \boldsymbol{\alpha}_1', \ldots, \boldsymbol{\alpha}_s', \alpha_{10}, \ldots, \alpha_{s0}, \beta_0)$ is the parameter vector of dimension $s(r + 2) + r + 1$, where s is the hidden layer size; $\{\boldsymbol{\alpha}_j' = (\alpha_{j1}, \ldots, \alpha_{jr}), j = 1, \ldots, s\}$ are the weight vectors of the connections between the input layer and the hidden layer; $\{c_j, j = 1, \ldots, s\}$ are the weights of the link between the hidden layer and the output neuron; $\beta' = (\beta_1, \ldots, \beta_r)$ is the vector of skip-layer connections; $\alpha_{10}, \ldots, \alpha_{s0}$, and β_0 are bias terms; $\psi(\cdot)$ is a properly chosen activation function for the hidden neurons.

In the following, we will refer to the model (6) with the specification of the input variables defined in (5) as the NN-HAR model. The implemented neural network in (6) uses skip connections, and therefore, it generalises the classical HAR model, which is nested in our NN-HAR model. Consequently, the novel model adds nonlinear components to the basic linear relationship and is expected to have a superior ability to learn more complex patterns from the data.

Once the hidden layer size s is fixed, the neural network model (6) can be estimated by using some learning algorithm (such as Gradient Descent or Broyden-Fletcher-Goldfarb-Shanno). So, the 1-step ahead forecast of V_{T+1} given the information available up to time T is:

$$\hat{V}_{T+1\,T} = f_s\left(\mathbf{z}_T; \hat{\boldsymbol{\theta}}\right) \tag{7}$$

where

$$\hat{\boldsymbol{\theta}} = \arg\min_{\boldsymbol{\theta}} \sum_{t=\ell+1}^{T} \mathcal{L}\left(V_t, f_s\left(\mathbf{z}_t; \boldsymbol{\theta}\right)\right) + \frac{\lambda}{2}\|\boldsymbol{\theta}\|^2 \tag{8}$$

with $\ell = 22$ when using daily financial data, $\mathcal{L}$ an appropriate loss function, $\|\cdot\|$ the L^2-norm and λ a regularization parameter which forces the weights to decay towards zero.

The forecast distribution for the future observation V_{T+1}, which is important in measuring the uncertainty of the model forecasts, can be obtained by using a bootstrap scheme from the residuals of the estimated NN(r, s) model. The bootstrap resampling scheme can be implemented as in Algorithm 1.

Algorithm 1. Bootstrap forecast distribution

Require: Define the input variables $\mathbf{z}_t$, fix the hidden layer size s and the weight decay λ by cross-validation.

1: Estimate the weights by using equation (8) and the BFGS algorithm.
2: Compute the centred residuals from the estimated network.
3: Let $\hat{F}(x)$ the ECDF of the centered residuals $\tilde{\varepsilon}_t$.
4: **for** b from 1 to B **do**
5:     Let $\varepsilon_{T+1}^{(b)}$ be a random draw from from $\hat{F}(x)$ Compute the future bootstrap observations as $\hat{V}_{T+1|T}^{(b)} = f(\mathbf{z}_T, \hat{\boldsymbol{\theta}}) + \epsilon_{T+1}^{(b)}$
6: **end for**
7: Estimate the unknown forecast distribution F_{T+1} of V_{T+1} through the ECDF

$$\hat{F}_{T+1|T}^*(x) = \frac{1}{B}\sum_{b=1}^{B} I\left\{\hat{V}_{T+1|T}^{*(b)} \le x\right\} \tag{9}$$

8: The $(1-\alpha)$ forecast interval for V_{T+1} is given by $\left[\hat{Q}^*(\alpha/2),\ \hat{Q}^*(1-\alpha/2)\right]$ where $\hat{Q}^*(.)$ is the quantile function of the estimated bootstrap distribution $\hat{F}_{T+1|T}^*$.

---

4   An Application to Real Data

In this application, our aim is to evaluate, on real datasets, the forecasting performance of proposed NN-HAR models and the bootstrap forecast distributions. We have considered the nine companies with the highest weight in the S&P500 index, a market-capitalization-weighted index of 503 large-cap U.S. stocks. These stocks are Apple (AAP), Amazon (AMZN), Alphabet Class C (GOOG), Alphabet Class A (GOOGL), Meta Platforms Class A (META), Microsoft (MSFT), NVIDIA (NVDA), Tesla (TSLA) and UnitedHealth Group (UNH) and they make up 28.7% of the index's market value as of Aug. 31, 2023. The time series was downloaded from Yahoo Finance and covered the period from 01/11/2021 to 31/12/2023. The time plots of the volatility V_t, defined in (1) for the selected nine stocks are reported in Fig. 1.

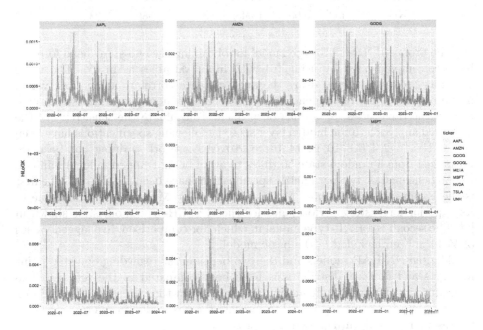

Fig. 1. Garman-Klass range volatility of the nine companies with the highest weight in the S & P500 index

First, we should verify if nonlinear features and conditional heteroscedasticity, the so-called ARCH effects, are present in volatility time series. To this aim, the Teraesvirta and the White tests have been used to test for linearity and the LM test for the ARCH effects [22]. The results in Table 1 show a clear rejection of linearity and ARCH effects in all nine series.

The first $T_0 = 500$ observations have been used as a training set, whereas the remaining $T - T_0 = 44$ observations have been used as a testing set.

Table 1. Test statistics and p-values for the Teraesvirta and White linearity tests and the LM test for ARCH effects for the range volatility of the nine selected stocks

Stock	Teraesvirta Test		White Test		LM Test	
	Statistic	p-value	Statistic	p-value	Statistic	p-value
AAPL	35.793	0.00	34.494	0.00	33.425	0.00
AMZN	19.241	0.00	19.663	0.00	34.755	0.00
GOOG	6.545	0.04	6.887	0.03	33.477	0.00
GOOGL	8.488	0.01	7.830	0.02	32.392	0.00
META	21.358	0.00	21.414	0.00	66.669	0.00
MSFT	12.226	0.00	13.054	0.00	4.287	0.12
NVIDA	19.583	0.00	17.850	0.00	7.073	0.03
TSLA	13.676	0.00	14.027	0.00	23.850	0.00
UNH	14.450	0.00	15.489	0.00	6.986	0.03

The proposed NN-HAR-type model for obtaining the one-step ahead forecast has been implemented by using (6) with input variables as in (5). The value of p has been determined using the auto distance correlation function, which measures the temporal dependence structure of a nonlinear time series [23]. For all the time series, $p = 5$ has been fixed. To evaluate the sensitivity of the proposed approach to the hidden layer size, the following specifications have been selected $s \in \{2, 4, 6, 8, 10, 12, 14, 16, 18, 20\}$. All network training has been re-initialized from a random state 50 times to avoid being trapped in local minima.

As benchmarks, two parametric specifications have been considered. The first is the Exponentially Weighted Moving Average (EWMA) model, chosen due to its superior forecasting performance for the GARCH-type models, as shown in [9]. The second is a HAR-type model in which, for comparison, five lagged values of V_t have been included in the basic model.

The ten NN-HAR models and the two benchmarks regarding one-step point forecasts and forecast distributions have been compared in the test set. The procedure involves gradually adding one value from the test set to the training set at a time and using the model to forecast the next value in the test set. This process is repeated until the entire test set has been considered, obtaining the one-step forecasted values $\hat{V}_{T_0+i|T_0}$ for $i = 1, \ldots, 44$. The forecast distributions have been obtained using the bootstrap procedure in Algorithm 1, with $B = 1999$ runs. The odd number is necessary to avoid any interpolation step when computing the percentiles of the bootstrap forecast distribution. All forecast intervals have been calculated with a nominal confidence level of 0.95.

The point forecast accuracy has been evaluated using the Root Mean Square Error (RMSE) and the Mean Percentage Absolute Error (MAPE), defined as:

$$\text{RMSE} = \sqrt{\frac{\sum_{i=1}^{T-T_0} \hat{e}_{T_0+i}^2}{T - T_0}} \quad \text{and} \quad \text{MAPE} = \frac{1}{T - T_0} \sum_{i=1}^{T-T_0} \frac{|\hat{e}_{T_0+i}|}{|V_{T_0+i}|} \tag{10}$$

Table 2. Forecast accuracy measures for the range volatility of AAPL, AMZN and GOOG stocks. The smallest value for each measure and stock is marked with an asterisk.

Stock	Model	RMSE	MAPE	WS	QS	CRPS
AAPL	EWMA	2.660	660.447	15.645	1.587	1.571
	HAR	0.661	164.119	7.912	0.562	0.557
	NN-HAR(02)	1.084	264.371	7.243	0.682	0.676
	NN-HAR(04)	0.819	196.484	6.054	0.533	0.528
	NN-HAR(06)	1.054	253.087	5.770	0.627	0.621
	NN-HAR(08)	0.648	145.349	5.096	0.429	0.425
	NN-HAR(10)	0.557	123.154	4.762	0.384	0.380
	NN-HAR(12)	0.640	142.976	4.460	0.402	0.399
	NN-HAR(14)	0.529	112.063	4.276	0.355	0.352
	NN-HAR(16)	0.576	117.079	4.255	0.364	0.361
	NN-HAR(18)	0.547	101.323	4.162	0.343	0.340
	NN-HAR(20)	0.518*	93.815*	4.145*	0.323*	0.320*
AMZN	EWMA	2.597	317.806	18.698	1.682	1.666
	HAR	4.052	479.079	17.290	2.398	2.375
	NN-HAR(02)	2.203	261.650	12.016	1.329	1.317
	NN-HAR(04)	2.623	317.879	11.739	1.557	1.543
	NN-HAR(06)	2.778	335.247	11.234	1.652	1.638
	NN-HAR(08)	2.575	310.690	10.575	1.517	1.503
	NN-HAR(10)	2.520	306.917	10.739	1.438	1.426
	NN-HAR(12)	1.977	239.480	9.392	1.139	1.129
	NN-HAR(14)	2.497	306.021	9.485	1.442	1.429
	NN-HAR(16)	2.425	298.965	10.507	1.310	1.299
	NN-HAR(18)	1.772*	207.424*	8.296*	1.015*	1.007*
	NN-HAR(20)	2.549	312.0985	8.720	1.483	1.470
GOOG	EWMA	2.880	394.541	20.865	1.822	1.805
	HAR	1.201	158.173	8.129	0.758	0.751
	NN-HAR(02)	1.142	143.760	7.299	0.709	0.703
	NN-HAR(04)	1.150	145.697	6.737	0.699	0.693
	NN-HAR(06)	1.192	154.761	6.150	0.710	0.704
	NN-HAR(08)	1.312	178.406	5.970	0.774	0.767
	NN-HAR(10)	1.173	150.033	5.614	0.691	0.685
	NN-HAR(12)	1.152	139.717	5.506	0.673	0.667
	NN-HAR(14)	1.162	140.575	5.315	0.678	0.672
	NN-HAR(16)	1.142	133.644*	5.442	0.666	0.660
	NN-HAR(18)	1.149	134.561	5.330	0.663*	0.658 *
	NN-HAR(20)	1.141*	138.694	4.747*	0.665	0.659

EWMA = Exponentially Weighted Moving Average model; HAR= HAR-type model with five lagged variables; NN-HAR = Neural network HAR model with five lagged variables and hidden layer size in parenthesis. The RMSE is reported as RMSE $\times 10^{-4}$ for readability. The same is true for WS, QS, and CRPS.

Table 3. Forecast accuracy measures for the range volatility of GGOGL, META and MSFT stocks. The smallest value for each measure and stock is marked with an asterisk.

Stock	Model	RMSE	MAPE	WS	QS	CRPS
GOOGL	EWMA	3.111	399.511	26.619	2.119	2.098
	HAR	1.268	155.284	8.251	0.790	0.783
	NN-HAR(02)	1.328	167.766	7.443	0.803	0.796
	NN-HAR(04)	1.394	179.977	6.822	0.830	0.822
	NN-HAR(06)	1.602	212.615	6.339	0.957	0.949
	NN-HAR(08)	1.443	186.271	5.948	0.859	0.851
	NN-HAR(10)	1.353	170.965	5.701	0.802	0.795
	NN-HAR(12)	1.367	172.640	5.452	0.810	0.803
	NN-HAR(14)	1.485	193.518	5.347	0.891	0.883
	NN-HAR(16)	1.256*	142.214*	5.060	0.729*	0.723*
	NN-HAR(18)	1.409	178.011	5.414	0.831	0.824
	NN-HAR(20)	1.372	172.250	4.981*	0.812	0.804
META	EWMA	19.995	1610.319	908.142	55.955	55.418
	HAR	2.868	249.518	16.885	1.750	1.733
	NN-HAR(02)	3.233	283.344	15.485	1.929	1.912
	NN-HAR(04)	3.687	320.885	15.077	2.193	2.173
	NN-HAR(06)	2.986	263.831	13.510	1.783	1.767
	NN-HAR(08)	2.794*	244.555*	13.236*	1.634*	1.620*
	NN-HAR(10)	3.417	300.102	13.711	1.986	1.969
	NN-HAR(12)	24.090	1632.872	67.632	7.871	7.801
	NN-HAR(14)	9.888	780.955	34.433	4.222	4.185
	NN-HAR(16)	8.770	717.791	21.090	5.473	5.424
	NN-HAR(18)	4.960	424.390	22.597	2.318	2.298
	NN-HAR(20)	9.135	738.889	23.015	5.158	5.112
MSFT	EWMA	1.242	266.747	10.211	0.845	0.837
	HAR	0.910	187.604	8.665	0.669	0.663
	NN-HAR(02)	0.910	183.835	7.647	0.628	0.623
	NN-HAR(04)	0.882	174.237	6.982	0.589	0.584
	NN-HAR(06)	0.873	172.051	6.451	0.568	0.563
	NN-HAR(08)	0.849	159.774	6.172	0.546	0.541
	NN-HAR(10)	0.814	141.960	5.925	0.517	0.513
	NN-HAR(12)	0.941	172.834	6.074	0.567	0.562
	NN-HAR(14)	0.722	121.216	5.673	0.472	0.468
	NN-HAR(16)	0.859	149.692	6.394	0.530	0.525
	NN-HAR(18)	0.825	133.847	5.661	0.509	0.505
	NN-HAR(20)	0.637*	111.221*	5.660*	0.442*	0.440*

EWMA = Exponentially Weighted Moving Average model; HAR= HAR-type model with five lagged variables; NN-HAR = Neural network HAR model with five lagged variables and hidden layer size in parenthesis. The RMSE is reported as RMSE $\times 10^{-4}$ for readability. The same is true for WS, QS, and CRPS.

Table 4. Forecast accuracy measures for the range volatility of NVDA, TSLA and UNH stocks. The smallest value for each measure and stock is marked with an asterisk.

Stock	Model	RMSE	MAPE	WS	QS	CRPS
NVDA	EWMA	2.992	178.838	14.296*	1.752	1.735
	HAR	2.583	134.205	24.346	1.878	1.860
	NN-HAR(02)	2.687	143.266	22.098	1.814	1.798
	NN-HAR(04)	2.539	131.546	19.266	1.652	1.637
	NN-HAR(06)	2.454	126.824	18.136	1.579	1.566
	NN-HAR(08)	2.375	117.059	17.424	1.493	1.480
	NN-HAR(10)	2.597	136.714	16.953	1.577	1.563
	NN-HAR(12)	2.536	128.096	16.936	1.540	1.526
	NN-HAR(14)	2.623	130.329	17.109	1.574	1.560
	NN-HAR(16)	2.565	127.589	16.623	1.534	1.521
	NN-HAR(18)	2.265*	85.870	17.353	1.361*	1.349*
	NN-HAR(20)	2.336	80.481*	18.473	1.495	1.482
TSLA	EWMA	4.639	119.702	32.127	2.937	2.909
	HAR	3.972	84.417	27.709	2.515	2.490
	NN-HAR(02)	3.999	86.230	24.017	2.417	2.396
	NN-HAR(04)	3.988	89.872	22.264	2.381	2.360
	NN-HAR(06)	4.085	93.187	21.264	2.395	2.374
	NN-HAR(08)	3.836	83.929	19.547	2.239	2.219
	NN-HAR(10)	3.820	84.064	19.855	2.228	2.208
	NN-HAR(12)	3.723	74.704	19.384*	2.144	2.126
	NN-HAR(14)	3.764	69.746	19.584	2.147	2.129
	NN-HAR(16)	3.664	61.660	19.739	2.097*	2.079*
	NN-HAR(18)	3.644*	60.675	19.468	2.106	2.087
	NN-HAR(20)	3.736	53.272*	20.606	2.152	2.133
UNH	EWMA	0.981	196.155	99.911	6.049	5.991
	HAR	0.843	152.798	6.262	0.549	0.544
	NN-HAR(02)	0.877	157.825	5.555	0.542	0.537
	NN-HAR(04)	0.874	156.702	5.025	0.528	0.523
	NN-HAR(06)	0.862	152.268	4.645	0.515	0.510
	NN-HAR(08)	0.864	154.712	4.379	0.512	0.507
	NN-HAR(10)	0.809	126.145	4.258	0.476	0.472
	NN-HAR(12)	0.800	126.257	4.018	0.467	0.463
	NN-HAR(14)	0.813	107.254	4.119	0.468	0.464
	NN-HAR(16)	0.776*	106.060	4.032	0.449	0.445
	NN-HAR(18)	0.782	99.175*	4.036	0.448*	0.444*
	NN-HAR(20)	0.818	124.863	3.822*	0.468	0.464

EWMA = Exponentially Weighted Moving Average model; HAR= HAR-type model with five lagged variables; NN-HAR = Neural network HAR model with five lagged variables and hidden layer size in parenthesis. The RMSE is reported as RMSE $\times 10^{-4}$ for readability. The same is true for WS, QS, and CRPS.

Table 5. Statistics and p-values for the Teraesvirta linearity test, the White linearity test and the LM test for ARCH effects for the residuals from the EWMA model, HAR model and the "best" NN-HAR model.

Stock	Model	Teraesvirta Test		White Test		LM Test	
		Statistic	p-value	Statistic	p-value	Statistic	p-value
AAPL	EWMA	20.139	0.00	17.095	0.00	22.470	0.00
	HAR	8.034	0.02	10.560	0.01	8.412	0.01
	NN-HAR(20)	0.475	0.79	0.061	0.97	0.703	0.70
AMZN	EWMA	10.803	0.01	10.911	0.01	5.895	0.05
	HAR	8.034	0.02	10.560	0.01	8.412	0.01
	NN-HAR(18)	3.032	0.22	2.075	0.35	0.802	0.67
GOOG	EWMA	15.252	0.00	12.856	0.00	17.473	0.00
	HAR	0.409	0.81	0.318	0.85	4.090	0.13
	NN-HAR(20)	1.013	0.60	0.850	0.65	0.695	0.71
GOOGL	EWMA	17.176	0.00	16.23	0.00	15.23	0.00
	HAR	0.723	0.70	0.200	0.90	2.794	0.25
	NN-HAR(16)	1.084	0.58	1.823	0.40	0.924	0.63
META	EWMA	22.613	0.00	26.404	0.00	54.021	0.00
	HAR	13.225	0.01	7.993	0.02	8.107	0.02
	NN-HAR(8)	1.270	0.53	0.175	0.92	0.021	0.99
MSFT	EWMA	4.369	0.11	6.844	0.03	0.134	0.94
	HAR	0.215	0.90	0.094	0.95	0.177	0.92
	NN-HAR(20)	0.121	0.94	1.1403	0.57	0.302	0.86
NVDA	EWMA	14.313	0.00	13.965	0.00	1.696	0.43
	HAR	9.830	0.01	8.857	0.01	2.917	0.23
	NN-HAR(18)	0.664	0.72	1.941	0.38	1.019	0.60
TSLA	EWMA	11.708	0.01	10.445	0.01	10.028	0.00
	HAR	3.310	0.19	2.897	0.23	6.299	0.04
	NN-HAR(18)	0.309	0.86	0.485	0.78	2.515	0.28
UNH	EWMA	41.839	0.00	33.374	0.00	17.034	0.00
	HAR	5.204	0.07	8.858	0.01	0.709	0.70
	NN-HAR(18)	1.378	0.50	0.787	0.67	0.580	0.75

where $\hat{e}_{T_0+i} = \hat{V}_{T_0+i|T_0} - V_{T_0+i}$, $i = 1, \ldots, 44$ is the one step forecast error.

The accuracy of the forecast distributions has been evaluated through the Winkler score (WS) [24], the Quantile Score (QS) [25], and the Continuous Ranked Probability Score (CRPS) [26].

The WS is designed to evaluate the accuracy of the forecasting interval. Given α, let $L(\alpha) = \left(\hat{Q}^*(1 - \alpha/2) - \hat{Q}^*(\alpha/2) \right)$ be the $(1 - \alpha)$ forecast interval width. The Winkler score is defined by averaging for $i = 1, \ldots, 44$ the following score:

$$WS_{\alpha,i} = \begin{cases} L(\alpha) + \frac{2}{\alpha}(\hat{Q}^*(1-\alpha/2) - V_{T_0+i}), & \text{if } V_{T_0+i} < \hat{Q}^*(\alpha/2) \\ L(\alpha), & \text{if } \hat{Q}^*(\alpha/2) < V_{T_0+i} < \hat{Q}^*(1-\alpha/2) \quad (11) \\ L(\alpha) + \frac{2}{\alpha}(V_{T_0+i} - \hat{Q}^*(1-\alpha/2)), & \text{if } V_{T_0+i} > \hat{Q}^*(\alpha/2) \end{cases}$$

The Quantile score is formulated to evaluate the quantile of the forecast distribution rather than the forecast interval. For a fixed α, it is defined by averaging for $i = 1, \ldots, 44$ the following score:

$$QS_{\alpha,i} = \begin{cases} 2(1-\alpha)(\hat{Q}^*(\alpha) - V_{T_0+i}), & \text{if } \hat{Q}^*(\alpha) > V_{T_0+i} \\ 2(1-\alpha)(\hat{Q}^*(\alpha) - V_{T_0+i}), & \text{if } \hat{Q}^*(\alpha) < V_{T_0+i} \end{cases} \quad (12)$$

where $\hat{Q}^*(\alpha)$ is the α-quantile of the forecast distribution at $T_0 + i$, obtained by using the bootstrap procedure illustrated in Algorithm 1.

Finally, the Continuous Ranked Probability Score is defined as:

$$CRPS(x) = \int_{-\infty}^{\infty} \left(\hat{F}^*_{T_0+1|T_0}(x) - H\{y \geq x\} \right)^2 dy \quad (13)$$

where $H(\cdot)$ is the Heaviside function, and the integral is approximated into a discrete finite sum.

Tables 3 and 4 report the five forecast accuracy measures for range volatility of the nine stocks of S & P500 index derived by using the proposed models. It is evident that, in most cases, the EWMA model has the worst performances, both in terms of point forecasts and forecast distributions. An exception is the case of the AMZN stock in which the RMSE and the MAPE have smaller values than the HAR model, highlighting better point forecast accuracy. The NN-HAR models perform better than the two competing models, regardless of the hidden layer size. However, when the hidden layer size is small ($s = 2$), they present, except AAPL and META, values very similar to those of the HAR model for point forecasts. However, the accuracy measures of the forecast distributions appear to be much worse. Furthermore, the performance of NN-HAR models improves as the hidden layer size increases. Among NN-HAR models, those with a higher value of the hidden layer size seem preferable, providing more accurate point forecasts and distributions. An exception is META, where all indices agree for an NN-HAR model with $s = 8$.

To evaluate if the identified NN-HAR model can capture the nonlinear features and the high persistence observed in the volatility of the range estimator, for each stock, the Teraesvirta test, the White test and the LM test have been performed on the residuals of the model. Also, a comparison with the two benchmark models has been considered in this case. The results are reported in Table 5. It is clear that, in most cases, the EWMA models leave neglected nonlinearities and are incapable of modelling the ARCH effects. The same happens for HAR-type models, except for the case of GOOG, GOOGL, and MSFT stocks, for which the residuals from the HAR-type models seem linear and not highly persistent. In the case of UNH, the residuals have no ARCH effects but still non-linearity features. For NN-HAR models, with the hidden layer identified through the forecasting accuracy measures, the residuals do not show any neglected nonlinearities and have no ARCH effect for all the stocks.

5   Concluding Remarks

In this paper, a novel method for forecasting range-based volatility has been presented and discussed. The procedure implements an NN-HAR type model for a range-based estimator to obtain point forecasts for the nonlinear dynamics of volatility. The approach also allows us to derive forecast distributions using a bootstrap scheme, which helps evaluate how much uncertainty is associated with each point forecast. An application to real data shows that the proposed approach improves point forecasts and forecast distribution accuracy.

However, several different aspects should be further explored. The proposed method should be calibrated with an appropriate model selection procedure to identify the "optimal" hidden layer. The advantages of using the NN-based approach over other range volatility measures and over models that generalize the HAR model to incorporate jumps, leverage, and other stylized volatility behaviours should also be evaluated. These topics are still under investigation.

References

1. Jacod, J., Li, Y., Zheng, X.: Statistical properties of microstructure noise. Econometrica **85**(4), 1133–1174 (2017)
2. Garman, M., Klass, M.: On the estimation of security price volatilities from historical data. J. Bus. **53**, 67–78 (1980)
3. Korkusuz, B., Kambouroudis, D., McMillan, D. G.: Do extreme range estimators improve realized volatility forecasts? Evidence from G7 stock markets. Finance Res. Lett. **55**, 103992 (2023)
4. Bali, T.G., Weinbaum, D.: A comparative study of alternative extreme-value volatility estimators. J. Futures Mark. Futures, Options, Other Deriv. Prod. **25**(9), 873–892 (2005)
5. Shu, J., Zhang, J.E.: Testing range estimators of historical volatility. J. Futures Mark. Futures, Opt. Other Derivat. Prod. **26**(3), 297–313 (2006)
6. Parkinson, M.: The extreme value method for estimating the variance of the rate of return. J. Bus. **53**, 61–65 (1980)
7. Li, H., Hong, Y.: Financial volatility forecasting with range-based autoregressive volatility model. Financ. Res. Lett. **8**(2), 69–76 (2011)
8. Jacob, J.: Vipul: estimation and forecasting of stock volatility with range-based estimators. J. Fut. Mark. **28**(6), 561–581 (2008)
9. Jiang, I.M., Hung, J.C., Wang, C.S.: Volatility forecasts: do volatility estimators and evaluation methods matter? J. Futur. Mark. **34**(11), 1077–1094 (2014)
10. Mapa, D.S.: A Range-Based GARCH Model for Forecasting Volatility, MPRA Paper 21323. University Library of Munich, Germany (2003)
11. Brandt, M.W., Jones, C.S.: Volatility forecasting with range-based EGARCH models. J. Bus. Econ. Stat. **24**(4), 470–486 (2006)

12. Chan, L., Lien, D.: Using high, low, open, and closing prices to estimate the effects of cash settlement on futures prices. Int. Rev. Financ. Anal. **12**(1), 35–47 (2003)
13. Chou, R.Y.: Forecasting financial volatilities with extreme values: the conditional autoregressive range (CARR) model. J. Money, Credit, Bank. **37**(3), 561–582 (2005)
14. Corsi, F.: A simple approximate long-memory model of realized volatility. J. Financ. Economet. **7**(2), 174–196 (2009)
15. Giordano, F., La Rocca, M., Perna, C.: Forecasting nonlinear time series with neural network sieve bootstrap. Comput. Stat. Data Anal. **51**(8), 3871–3884 (2007)
16. Giordano, F., La Rocca, M., Perna, C.: Properties of the neural network sieve bootstrap. J. Nonparametric Stat. **23**(3), 803–817 (2011)
17. Alizadeh, S., Brandt, M.W., Diebold, F.X.: Range-based estimation of stochastic volatility models. J. Financ. **57**, 1047–1091 (2002)
18. Andersen, T.G., Bollerslev, T., Diebold, F.X., Labys, P.: Modeling and forecasting realized volatility. Econometrica **71**(2), 579–625 (2003)
19. Ge, W., Lalbakhsh, P., Isai, L., Lenskiy, A., Suominen, H.: Neural network-based financial volatility forecasting: a systematic review. ACM Comput. Surv. (CSUR) **55**(1), 1–30 (2022)
20. Petneházi, G., Gáll, J.: Exploring the predictability of range-based volatility estimators using recurrent neural networks. Intell. Syst. Account. Finan. Manage. **26**(3), 109–116 (2019)
21. Kim, J., Baek, C.: Neural network heterogeneous autoregressive models for realized volatility. Commun. Stat. Appl. Methods **25**(6), 659–671 (2018)
22. Engle, R.F.: Autoregressive conditional heteroscedasticity with estimates of the variance of United Kingdom inflation. Econometrica **50**(4), 987–1007 (1982)
23. Zhou, Z.: Measuring nonlinear dependence in time-series, a distance correlation approach. J. Time Ser. Anal. **33**(3), 438–457 (2012)
24. Winkler, R.L.: A decision-theoretic approach to interval estimation. J. Am. Stat. Assoc. **67**(337), 187–191 (1972)
25. Hyndman, R.J., Athanasopoulos, G.: Forecasting: Principles and Practice (3rd ed), Monash University, Australia, vol. 23, no. 2 (2018)
26. Gneiting, T., Katzfuss, M.: Probabilistic forecasting. Ann. Rev. Stat. Appl. **1**, 125–151 (2014)

Machine Learning Classification of Water Conductivity Raw Values of "Faneromeni" Reservoir in Crete

Lazaros Iliadis, Nichat Kiourt[✉], Christos Akratos, and Antonios Papaleonidas

Department of Civil Engineering, Democritus University of Thrace, Komotini, Greece
{liliadis,nkiourt}@civil.duth.gr

Abstract. Water Conductivity is a measure of dissolved salts' concentration in the water. It depends on the concentration of ions and on water temperature. Assessment of the conductivity values is a priority, as the higher its values the more dangerous it becomes for humans. Therefore, the first purpose of this research is to evaluate and classify the water conductivity levels in the "*Faneromeni*" reservoir located in Crete. This was achieved by developing powerful Machine Learning models. The raw data from the survey area comprised of simple crisp conductivity measurements, which were successfully converted to labels by developing Quartiles, during preprocessing. This was followed by the development of Machine Learning models, which successfully yield four labels '*Low*', '*Medium*', '*High*' and '*Extreme*' assigned to each record. Subsequently, a comparative discussion was performed (for the first time in the literature) between the obtained outcome with the relative one from our previous research effort, concerning the reservoir of the '*Bramianon*' area of Crete.

Keywords: Water Conductivity · Machine Learning · Classification · Quartiles

1 Introduction

1.1 Problem Specification – Aim of This Research

The term *water quality* describes its physical, chemical, biological and aesthetic properties and determines its suitability for various types of use [1]. Water may contain microorganisms, viruses, protozoa and bacteria, inorganic pollutants from industrial processes and oil use, pesticides, and herbicides [1]. In rare cases it may even contain radioactive substances.

Water Conductivity (COw) is a measure of the concentration of salts in the water, such as *chloride, nitrate, sulfate, and phosphate* anions (ions that carry a negative charge) or *sodium, magnesium, calcium, iron, and aluminum* cations (ions that carry a positive charge). As such, it is related to the potential of water to conduct electricity, sound and heat. Water containing from 1 to 100 mg/l total dissolved solids is characterized by low COw value.

L. Iliadis et al. (Eds.): EANN 2024, CCIS 2141, pp. 518–529, 2024.
https://doi.org/10.1007/978-3-031-62495-7_39

The presence of dissolved substances - pollutants and the level of their concentration, affects its quality. High COw of *irrigation water*, results in the inability of the plant to compete with ions in the soil solution for water (physiological drought) which results in less available water for the plants even though the soil appears wet. The higher the Electrical Conductivity (EC), the less water is available to plants, even though the soil may appear wet. Plants are sensitive to electroconductivity for the absorption of nutrients and water.

Drinking water must be clean from a physical, biological, and microbiological point of view, as its consumption must not endanger human health. It should not have a high level of conductivity, organic substances, heavy metals or pathogenic parasites and microbes [2]. Organic substances might originate from decomposing tree leaves that fall into rivers and lakes, from sewage, from living organisms that live in water (e.g., fish) and from human waste. Inorganic substances can come from lead and copper in water pipes, from pesticides and generally from human activities. All these elements (organic and inorganic substances) contribute to the increase of water conductivity [3].

Machine Learning (ML) is a branch of Artificial Intelligence imitating the way humans are learning. It can employ a high spectrum of intelligent algorithms capable to develop powerful models having the capacity to learn and to make predictions by finding correct patterns. This can be achieved by considering high volumes of raw data [4].

This research paper is part of a broader effort to develop Machine Learning models capable to rationally classify with proper labels, the quality of the reservoir water resources of Greek dams used for irrigation. This first approach is considering COw concentrations that were measured in the *"Faneromeni"* reservoir, located in the regional entity of *Heraklion* in eastern Crete.

This research has proved that a robust Machine Learning classifier can be efficiently used in order to offer the capacity of continuous water quality monitoring, regarding water conductivity levels. Of course, such an approach will require periodic (seasonal) retraining of the model in order to obtain up to date classifiers. This process can be very useful especially in the case of sensor's malfunction.

Moreover, at second level, the results obtained herein are compared to the ones related to the *"Bramianon"* reservoir in the *"Ierapetra"* area of South-eastern Crete that were obtained in a previous research effort of our team [6]. A comparative presentation and analysis of the water quality and the classification models developed for the two aforementioned areas is described below.

1.2   Literature Review

Nikhil, Ragi et al. 2019, have used ML algorithms to model water hardness, chlorine, sulfate, pH and electrical conductivity [7]. Mojtaba Poursaeid, has developed ML models for conductivity, salinity, total dissolved solids (TDS) and groundwater level for a 15-year time series of data [8]. Yafra Khan et al. 2016, developed ML water quality models that consider various respective features [9]. Davood Moghadas et al. 2019 used correlation analysis trying to determine whether Artificial Neural Network are capable to correlate electrical conductivity with ground water content [10]. Umair Ahmed et al. 2019 have used supervised ML to model water quality indices [11]. Samuel N. Araya et al. 2019 have developed functions to estimate saturated water conductivity based on 18,000 data records [12]. Ali Najah Ahmet et al. 2019 used ML models to estimate water quality [13]. Godson Ebenezer Adjovu et al. 2023 have introduced ML models to estimate total dissolved solids' concentration in Lake *Mead* considering electrical conductivity and temperature [14]. Kiourt et al. 2023, have introduced novel ML models capable of successfully assigning three labels '*Low*', '*Medium*', '*High*', to assess and classify CO_W levels in the "*Bramianon*" reservoir of Crete [6].

To the best of our knowledge, our research effort [6], and the one presented herein, constitute novel contribution to the literature, on the classification of CO_W in Greek reservoirs, using four labels.

2   Dataset

Water Conductivity is measured using an electronic sensor in micro- Siemens per centimeter (μS/cm) or ppm (parts per million). It should be mentioned that 1 ppm = 1.56 μS/cm.

In the lakes of Greece, CO_W in terms of seasons and depth, shows a wide range of values, from a minimum of 40 μS/cm (Trichonis) to a maximum value of 11,000 μS/cm (Vistonis) because of sea water intrusion [28]. In most of the lakes, the annual mean value falls into the range of 247–1,200 μS/cm. In some regions of Greece, this is much higher [3].

Data was selected from the website of the *Decentralized Administration* of Crete, Greece [15]. This website offers easy and quick access to processed and to raw data regarding Cretan reservoirs, and the chance to exploit them for the development of added value services and products [15].

This dataset comprises 2,083 records corresponding to daily measurements, from 2016 to 2023 (collected at the same time of day). The independent variables were *water volume measured in hectoliters, water depth* and *water temperature*. The depended variable was *water Conductivity'*. The capacity of the reservoir is equal to 20,000,000 m^3 and it expands in a surface of 1,000,000 square meters. Its retaining wall is 484 m long, 75 m high and 8 m wide. The water of the reservoir mainly originates from the "*Koutsoulidis*" tributary, which ends in the "*Geropotamos*" river and crosses the "*Mesara*" plain [17]. The water of the dam irrigates a total area of 26,580 stremma. Map 1 below, shows the area of the "*Mesara*" basin as well as the artificial lake of "*Faneromeni*"[18].

2.1   A Significant Event Related to Extreme CO_W

Analysis of the "*Faneromeni*" reservoir data, has revealed a *huge* CO_W *increase* from the 26th of September 2016 till 15th of October 2016. The increase ranges from 70% to 120%. This is a very important event, where the Conductivity has reached as high as 2081,5 μS/cm. During this period the water depth has dropped significantly. This event has been considered, during the determination of the CO_W classes. One factor increasing CO_W is the contamination of water with olive mills waste.

Map 1. Map of "Faneromeni" reservoir in South-Eastern part of Crete [35]

The year 2018 was very dry for the "*Faneromeni*" dam, since the rainfall was limited, and the water level dropped to 800,000 m^3 while the safety limit is around 4,000,000 m^3. However, February 2019 was a rainy month, with the amount of water in the dam exceeding 10,000,000 m^3. During the following years the amount of water has risen and up to date it is able to cover the irrigation needs of the farmers in the area [19, 20].

3 Preprocessing and Modeling

The development of the Machine Learning model in this research effort, has followed the following steps:

a) Data Scaling, Development and assignment of Labels.
b) Developing ML algorithms and evaluating performance
c) Compare the performance of the employed algorithms.
d) Determine the Optimal Model

3.1 Data Scaling

The goal of normalization is to transform features to be on a similar scale. This improves the performance and training stability of the model. The normalization of the data included the calculation of the mean value, and the standard deviation. All of the crisp values were scaled to the interval [-1,1]. Normalization was performed on the entire data set. This was done so that the variables with the largest range did not overshadow and dominate those with the smallest range. Furthermore, this process ensured that these values would be compatible with the domain of the used transfer functions of the Machine Learning algorithms, which could be executed faster. The following Z-score Eq. 1 was used to calculate the value of Z-score [21]. Conductivity in lakes and streams generally ranges between 0 to 200 μS/cm, while in major rivers conductivity may be as high as 1000 μS/cm. Very high conductivity (1000–10,000 μS/cm) is an indicator of saline (salty) conditions.

$$Z - score\_i = \frac{Xi - Mean}{StandardDeviation} \tag{1}$$

Equation 1. Normalization function.

3.2 Assigning Labels to Data Records Using Quartiles

The available dataset comprises of crisp values that were considered to produce four Labels "Low", "Medium", "High" και "Very High" for the development of the ML Classification Models [5].

During the development of the classes, the crisp numerical values of the water conductivity were converted into class labels by calculating the *Quartiles* and the *Interquartile* (IQR) [22]. A quartile is a statistical term that describes a division of observations into four defined intervals based on the values of the data and how they compare to the entire set of observations [29, 30].

As we have seen in previous chapter, the distribution of the considered dataset contains extreme values. Based on the literature, for skewed distributions or data sets with outliers, the *Interquartile range* is the best measure of variability [34].

The following Fig. 1 is a Graphical representation of the applied methodology.

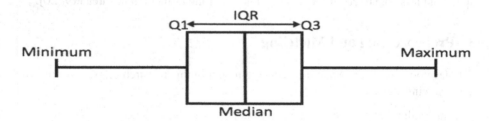

Fig. 1. The Interquartile Range (IQR) method used to measure variability by dividing a data set into quartiles [31]

The steps when we have odd number of records (which is the case here) are the following:

- The data is ordered from the least to the greatest (ascending order)
- The Median is found, and the data is divided in two parts (Lower and Upper) based on it.
- The two Medians of both the Lower and the Upper parts are found.
- The Interquartile Range (IQR) which is the difference between the Upper and Lower Medians is calculated [31].

According to this method a value is characterized as an Upper Outlier if it is higher than 1,5*IQR over the third quartile (Upper Outlier).

Definition of the Upper Outliers

$$UpperOutliers = data > Q3 - 1,5 * IQR$$

A value is characterized as a Down Outlier if it is less than 1,5*IQR from the Down Outlier.

Definition of Lower Outliers

$$LowerOutlires = data < Q1 - 1,5 * IQR$$

The interquartile range (IQR) is estimated by the following Eq. 2.

$$IQR = Q3 - Q1 \tag{2}$$

Equation 2. The interquartile range (IQR).

3.3 The Four Classes

Typically, Conductivity in lakes and streams generally ranges between 0 to 200 μS/cm. However, in some cases conductivity may be as high as 1000 μS/cm. Very high conductivity (1,000–10,000 μS/cm) is an indicator of saline (salty) conditions [32].

In USA there is no national standard for conductivity exits, however the *Environmental Protection Agency (EPA) recommends a value of less than 1,000 micro siemens per centimeter (mcg/cm) for drinking water* [33].

Based on the Quartiles approach the following four classes were developed.

Based on Q1 the "Low" class includes 345 data records where the upper CO_W is up to 500 ppm.

Considering the second Quartile Q2, the "Medium" class comprises of 617 records with CO_W in the interval [501, 532) ppm.

The "High" class was determined by the third quartile Q3. It includes 1,053 records, having CO_W values in the interval [532, 648) ppm.

The last fourth class includes the data records that belong to the upper outliers with CO_W values in the interval [648, 2082] [16].

3.4 k-Folds Cross Validation

According to the Cross-validation approach, the dataset is randomly divided into k subsets (folds), with a specific number of vectors (3-fold or 5-fold or 10-fold). Then the training process is repeated k times (k-cycles). Each time, the k-1 folds are used for training the algorithm, whereas the remaining fold is used for testing. This process is repeated k times with the subset that is singled out for testing, changing each time. As performance indicators are taken, the average of the corresponding errors is used to determine the level of model's convergence. The choice of the number of folds depends on the size of the available dataset. Thus, a large number of folds might offer higher accuracy, higher error range, and high execution time while a smaller the number of folds might result in smaller accuracy and smaller execution time [23]. In the upcoming research, the 5-fold approach has been employed.

3.5 Development of Machine Learning Models

After pre-processing, the data was imported in MATLAB and an attempt was made to classify the Water Conductivity values by employing various Machine Learning algorithms. More specifically, the following classifiers were used: *Decision Trees, Naïve Bayes* [25], *Support Vector Machines* [26], *k-Nearest Neighbors* [25] and *Ensembles of Classifiers* [23, 24]. Main goal of an ensemble classifier is the basic idea is to obtain predictions of multiple classifiers on the original data and combine the different predictions to make a strong classifier.

The *Ensemble Classifiers* appear to have a predominant role in ML. The training is performed by a set of classifiers on the same data and then the results of each one are combined to reach a robust classifier. As a matter of fact, they are trying to reduce the misclassification rate (error rate) of a weak classifier by aggregating multiple algorithms. This architecture employs the Bootstrap (known as Bagging) and the Boosting strategies, which are discussed below [27].

In Bagging the training set is resampled to create a set of smaller datasets. A classifier is then trained with each one of them. When an unknown sample needs to be classified, it is first categorized by all the classifiers and the decision is made by voting.

Boosting is an ensemble learning algorithm employing a set of weak learners (classifiers) which are iteratively combined in order to develop a robust overall learner with the minimum learning error. Each sample carries a weight, which is iteratively updated. Each misclassified set of data points increases its weights for the next classifier, whereas it decreases them otherwise. In this way, each classifier assigns higher weights to samples that have failed to be correctly classified. The final decision is made by votes, weighted by some evaluation metric.

4 Results

The multiclass classification effort described herein, uses one versus all approach to estimate the performance indices separately for each of the four classes. Tables 4, 5, 6, 7 and 8 present the performance of each employed classifier.

Table 1. Classification results for Decision Trees

Decision Trees Classifier (Fine Tree)					
	Precision	Recall	Specificity	Accuracy	F1-Score
Class 1	1.000	1.000	1.000	1.000	1.000
Class 2	1.000	1.000	1.000	1.000	1.000
Class 3	1.000	1.000	0.999	0.999	1.000
Class 4	0.990	0.990	0.999	0.999	0.990

The Bagged Trees of Ensembles classifier [27] has proved to be the most efficient algorithm followed by the Decision Trees [24] the Naïve Bayes [25] and the Support

Table 2. Gaussian Naïve Bayes Classifier

Naïve Bayes Classifiers (Gaussian Type)					
	Precision	Recall	Specificity	Accuracy	F1-Score
Class 1	0.910	0.960	0.983	0.980	0.940
Class 2	0.870	0.880	0.947	0.930	0.880
Class 3	0.960	0.940	0.962	0.950	0.950
Class 4	0.990	0.990	0.999	0.999	0.990

Table 3. Classification results for SVM

Support Vector Machines Classifiers (Kernel function: Quadratic)					
	Precision	Recall	Specificity	Accuracy	F1-Score
Class 1	0.990	0.990	0.998	0.997	0.990
Class 2	0.990	0.970	0.997	0.990	0.980
Class 3	0.990	1.000	0.987	0.992	0.990
Class4	0.990	0.990	0.999	0.999	0.990

Table 4. Classification results for K-NN

K-Nearest Neighbor Classifiers (Fine KNN)					
	Precision	Recall	Specificity	Accuracy	F1-Score
Class 1	0.990	0.990	0.998	0.997	0.990
Class 2	0.950	0.950	0.980	0.972	0.950
Class 3	0.970	0.970	0.973	0.973	0.970
Class 4	0.970	0.990	0.999	0.998	0.980

Table 5. Classification results for Bagged Trees

Ensembles Classifiers (Bagged Trees)					
	Precision	Recall	Specificity	Accuracy	F1-Score
Class 1	1.000	1.000	1.000	1.000	1.000
Class 2	1.000	1.000	1.000	1.000	1.000
Class 3	1.000	1.000	1.000	1.000	1.000
Class 4	0.999	1.000	0.999	0.999	0.990

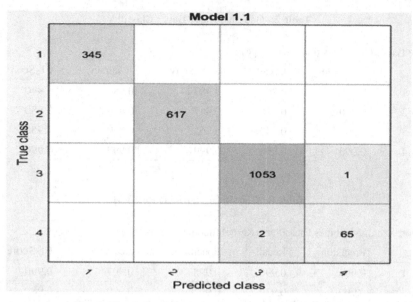

Fig. 2. Confusion Matrix for the Bagged Trees classifier

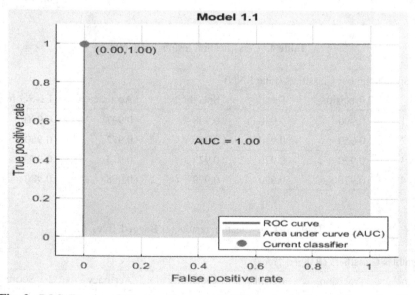

Fig. 3. ROC (Receiver Operating Characteristic) Curve for the Bagged Trees classifier

Vector Machines [26] and k-Nearest Neighbor [25]. However, all algorithms had good performance (Figs. 2 and 3).

5 Discussion and Conclusions

The difference of CO_W between the reservoirs of *Faneromeni* and *Bramianon*, is mainly due to various sources of pollution. It is worth noting that in the study area of Faneromeni there is a relatively better situation in terms of conductivity levels. This means that in the specific study area we do not have very large sources of pollution caused by human activities, as in the *Bramianon* Dam. This means that in the *Faneromeni* reservoir the natural water quality has not been degraded to a significant extent recently, due to various sources of pollution (e.g. municipal sewage, industrial liquid waste, detergents, agricultural liquid waste, liquid waste) or to marine intrusion as in the case of *"Bramianon"* Dam. Average conductivity levels are considerably lower at "Faneromeni" dam (548 ppm) compared to the one of *"Bramianon"* (1268 ppm).

The motivation of this research was to assess and classify the water conductivity levels of the "Faneromeni" reservoir with the help of various machine learning algorithms. The performance of each algorithm was assessed by estimating the classification indices, the obtained confusion matrices and the respective ROC curves. The extracted results showed us a slightly better performance of the Bagged trees of Ensembles Classifiers compared to the other classification algorithms, with an accuracy (Accuracy) reaching the value of 99.95%. The high classification accuracy is due to the relatively balanced dataset and to the robustness of the employed algorithms. Moreover, when k-fold cross validation is used all folds are used as both training and testing sets, so the convergence of the algorithm is much more robust.

According to the processed data of our measurements, we find that the conductivity levels in the water of the "Faneromeni" Dam are relatively close to the permissible limit of the conductivity of drinking water (500 ppm) with an average reaching 548 ppm. However, they are not suitable for human consumption. We can say that these waters are suitable for irrigating the fields and greenhouses of the study area. Special care is needed when extreme values above 2,000 ppm are measured, which has happened in the interval of available measurements. This could create problems in the primary production of the area. We also find that according to our data, the conductivity in the water of the *"Faneromeni"* Dam does not change significantly when the water volume changes. Thus, we conclude that the significant changes in water conductivity are not due to natural causes, but to various sources of pollution caused by human activities. Finally, we conclude that of all the classification algorithms we used in this research area, the *Bagged Trees of Ensembles Classifiers* algorithm proved to be the most reliable.

References

1. Neron.gr   (2019).   https://www.neron.gr/content/146/-ipoiotita-toy-neroy-pes-oxi-sto-pla stiko-nero
2. Modern analytics (2022). https://modernanalytics.gr/water-quality/
3. Margiolos, G.: filtranerou (2018). https://www.filtra.nerou.gr/ti-einai-i-agogimotita-and-pos na-ti-metriso/
4. 2science.gr (2023). https://2science.gr/machine-learning-1/
5. James, M.: What Is a Quartile? How it works and example (2024). https://www.investopedia. com/terms/q/quartile.asp

6. Kiourt, N., Iliadis, L., Papaleonidas, A.: Conductivity classification using machine learning algorithms in the "Bramianon" dam (2023). https://doi.org/10.1007/978-3-031-34204-2_9

7. Nikhil, M.R., Holla, R., Manju, G.: Predicting water quality parameters using machine learning (2019). https://ieeexplore.ieee.org/abstract/document/9016825

8. Mojtaba, P., Mastouri, R., Shabanlou, S., Najarchi, M.: Estimation of total dissolved solids, electrical conductivity, salinity and groundwater levels using novel learning machines (2020). https://doi.org/10.1007/s12665-020-09190-1

9. Yafra, K., Chai, S.S.: Predicting and analyzing water quality using machine learning: a comprehensive model (2016). https://ieeexplore.ieee.org/abstract/document/7494106

10. Davood Moghadas, D., Badorreck, A.: Machine learning to estimate soil moisture from geophysical measurements of electrical conductivity (2019). https://www.earthdoc.org/content/journals/10.1002/nsg.12036

11. Umair, A., Rafia, M., Hirra, A., Asad, A.S., Rabia, I., Jose, G.N.: Efficient water quality prediction using supervised machine learning (2019). https://www.mdpi.com/2073-4441/11/11/2210

12. Samuel, N.A., Teamrat, A.G.: Using machine learning for prediction of saturated hydraulic conductivity and its sensitivity to soil structural perturbations (2019). https://agupubs.onlinelibrary.wiley.com/doi/full/10.1029/2018WR024357

13. Ali Najah, A., et al.: Machine learning methods for better water quality prediction (2019). www.sciencedirect.com/science/article/abs/pii/S0022169419308194

14. Godson, E.A., Harron, S., Sajjad, A.: A machine learning approach for the estimation of total dissolved solids concentration in lake mead using electrical conductivity and temperature (2023). https://www.mdpi.com/2073-4441/15/13/2439

15. Republic, G.: Decentralized administration of crete (2022). https://www.apdkritis.gov.gr/el

16. Kolmogorov-smirnov test calculator. https://www.statskingdom.com/kolmogorov-smirnov-test-calculator.html

17. Papa, D.: (2018). file:///C:/Users/User/Downloads/Pappa_Dimitra_Dip_2018_.pdf

18. T.O.E.B.: 3rd Zone Messaras (2022). https://toebgzoni.gr/gallery-classic/

19. Ioanna, V.: (2019). file:///C:/Users/User/Downloads/Varsamou_Ioanna_Dip_2019.pdf

20. Savvas, R.: (2023). https://2science.gr/machine-learning-1/

21. Sourabh, G.: Machine learning concepts (2021). https://ml-concepts.com/2021/10/08/min-max-normalization/

22. Shaun, T.: Quartiles & Quantiles, Calculation, Definition & Interpretation (2023). https://www.scribbr.com/statistics/quartiles-quantiles/

23. Iliadis, L., Papaleonidas, A.: Computational Intelligence & Intelligent Agents, Giola Publications (2017)

24. Georgouli, A.: Machine Learning (chapter 4). Artificial Intelligence. Kallipos (open academic publishing) (2015). https://repository.kallipos.gr/handle/11419/3382

25. Economou, S.: Machine learning algorithms in data mining (2020). https://apothesis.eap.gr/archive/item/75267

26. Vijay K.: What is a support vector machine? Working, types, and examples (2022). https://www.spiceworks.com/tech/big-data/articles/what-is-support-vector-machine/

27. Tarun, A.: Advanced ensemble classifiers (2019). https://towardsdatascience.com/advanced-ensemble-classifiers8d7372e74e40

28. Ierotheos, Z., Ilias, B., Nikolaos, S., Theodoros, K.: Lakes & reservoirs: research and management. Greek Lakes: Limnological Overview 7, 55–62 (2002)

29. Knoch, J.: How are quartiles used in statistics? Magoosh. Archived from the original on December 10, 2019. February 24, February 23, 2018. (2023)

30. Dekking, M.: A modern introduction to probability and statistics: understanding *why and how*. Springer, London, pp. 236–238 (2005). ISBN 978-1-85233-896-1. OCLC 262680588

31. Varsity tutors. https://www.varsitytutors.com/algebra_1-help/how-to-find-interquartile-range
32. Atlas scientific. https://atlas-scientific.com/blog/water-conductivity-range/
33. New Mexico environment public health tracking. https://nmtracking.doh.nm.gov/enviro nment/water/PHConductivity.html
34. Jiawei, H., Micheline, K., Jian, P.: Getting to know your data. https://www.sciencedirect.com/ science/article/abs/pii/B9780123814791000022
35. All Trails. https://www.alltrails.com/explore/trail/greece/crete/faneromeni-reservoir-loop? mobileMap=false&ref=sidebar-static-map

Machine Learning-Based Feature Mapping for Enhanced Understanding of the Housing Market

Michael Sahl Lystbæk[(✉)] and Tharsika Pakeerathan Srirajan

Aarhus University, Birk Centerpark 15, 7400 Herning, Denmark
msl@btech.au.dk

Abstract. The housing market is impacted by a variety of parameters which gives a complexity that is difficult to analyze with traditional statistical approaches due to the large number of interdependent variables that the market data provides. In this study, ML techniques are utilized to provide a deeper understanding of the Danish housing market based on a dataset of sales cases provided by a leading Danish real estate agency. We propose an extreme gradient boosting model for sales price regression, and we propose using feature importance techniques to provide insight into important parameters in the national housing market. The regression model trained for sales price with grid search cross-validation for parameter optimization achieves an R^2 accuracy of 0.84, an MAE of DKK 433,824, and an RMSE of DKK 675,817. Permutation-based feature importance defines the most impactful parameters for the sales price regression where the four features with the highest impacts are: 1. GisX (West/East location), 2. GisY (North/South location), 3. Building area, 4. Construction year. The results for geographical distribution regarding price, building area, and plot area are illustrated with 2D partial dependence plots of geographical distributions to enhance the understanding of market trends.

Keywords: Gradient Boosting Regression · Machine Learning · Housing Market Pricing · Feature Importance · Partial Dependence

1 Introduction

House design and pricing is a complex process with a variety of impacting factors. A cohesive understanding of the main features that impact the housing market and the underlying design decisions for constructing houses is important for being able to impact and act in the architectural, engineering, and construction (AEC) industries. There has been a trend that residential houses have increased in size [1] rather than becoming spatially optimized for better architectural solutions. The assessment of good architecture requires an in-depth knowledge of multiple aspects as functionality and contextual conditions [2]. The building sector is responsible for a consumption of 40–50% of global raw materials and further responsible for a third of all carbon emissions [3, 4], which underlines the necessity of being in touch with the building trends to ensure that

© The Author(s), under exclusive license to Springer Nature Switzerland AG 2024
L. Iliadis et al. (Eds.): EANN 2024, CCIS 2141, pp. 530–543, 2024.
https://doi.org/10.1007/978-3-031-62495-7_40

upcoming building stokes remain standing for their maximum lifespan with a minimum of reconstructions. Enhancing the attractiveness of new constructions for the future resale market requires insight into important building features that are in both the house owners' and the environment's interest. Housing conditions are an important aspect in all societies, and the requirements for improved living standards are continuously increasing globally. The average house size in Denmark is $118.1 \, m^2$ and the distribution of types of dwellings are: flats 33.2%, detached houses 53.2%, and semi-detached 13.4%, which emphasizes that detached houses are the most common and widespread dwelling type in the Danish housing market. This contrasts with other European countries where, for instance, the UK and the Netherlands have a majority of semi-detached houses, and commonly, flats are prioritized in other countries [5]. The average size of newly constructed houses in Denmark is $137 \, m^2$, which is double the size in comparison to the UK, and, in general, the largest average size of houses in comparable European countries. Furthermore, Danish houses have an average room size of $39.1 \, m^2$ and on average 3.5 rooms [5]. This emphasizes that housing markets are extremely context-dependent across different countries and regions, and even a small country like Denmark may have differences in building trends across the country that may be important to understand.

Several previous studies are identified as inspiration for utilizing extreme gradient boosting (XGB) models for house price regression [6–8] where the XGB-based models have shown high accuracy for training on house market data and further performing feature explanation techniques. Our study is based on sale statistics for the last decade of sales cases from the Danish housing market where we propose a fine-tuned XGB model for predicting building trends based on a preprocessed dataset of 21,324 sales cases and 14 features for the domestic Danish real estate market of detached houses. The proposed model provides feature importance mapping for emphasizing the most impacting building features based on sales prices and a geographical representation of the house pricing and the two important building design features of building area and plot area are performed using partial dependence plots (PDP).

Our study contributes by 1) proposing an optimized XGB regressor (XGBR) for house price regression, 2) performing feature importance mapping for explaining the data importance based on a large national dataset of the housing market, and 3) utilizing geographical visualization of feature distribution for a domestic real estate housing market, with high accuracy.

Related studies focus mainly on gradient boosting (GB) techniques utilized for energy tasks in relation to the AEC field, where these methods have shown superior performance in comparison to a variety of other ML methods such as ANN, random forest (RF), support vector machine (SVM) [9–11], and Deep Neural Networks (DNN) [11], where GB methods outperformance these in accuracy. Further, feature importance has been applied to identify the features affecting lost workdays at construction sites [12], dimension reduction for sub-hourly electricity usage forecasting in commercial buildings [13], and building energy predictions [14, 15]. Also, PDP has been used together with building age prediction for building energy modeling [16], failure modes identification of reinforced concrete shear walls [17], and property tax assessment [18].

2 Methodology

The housing market is a complex mechanism where a multitude of parameters have an impact on the market. To analyze the feature importance, we utilize a custom-trained XGB-based model for a post hoc explanation [7] of the regression model. Feature importance calculation for the XGBR model is performed to emphasize the features' impact on the price regression, and partial dependence graphs are plotted to highlight the marginal effect each of the features has on the outcome. These PDPs are merged into geographic maps to visualize the geographical distribution of individual house design features.

Our method is built upon a dataset based on the domestic Danish housing market for single detached houses. The machine learning pipeline for the regression model shown in Fig. 1 is a three-module process where, first, the dataset is preprocessed, and an XGBR model is trained with grid search cross-validation for providing an optimal hyperparameter setting for the proposed price regression model; second, a permutation-based feature importances plot is generated for ranking the features based on impact, and from that a selection of the highest impacting features are made. For these features, PDPs are made for further analyzing the data, and third, 2D PDPs are generated and merged into a map for visualizing the geographical distributions of the sales price and the two design features: building area, and plot area. To achieve this, the XGBR is trained for each of the features.

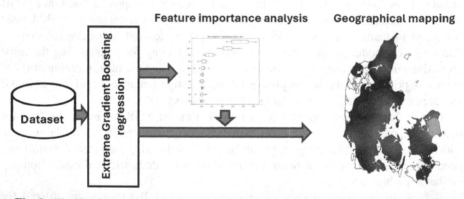

Fig. 1. Machine learning pipeline for analyzing feature importance for the housing market.

2.1 Dataset

Data Preprocessing

The developed dataset builds on an extract of sales cases of detached houses from a real estate database that contains 64,396 data rows of unique entries with 18 features. After preprocessing the dataset by removing irrelevant columns and data with missing values and excluding the remote island of Bornholm (eastern part of Denmark), the dataset is reduced to 21,324 records and 14 features. Since the dataset still contains a reasonable amount of data rows, the imputation of missing values is not considered. The sales date was converted into float values, and all columns, except the sales date, longitude, and latitude, are represented as integers to facilitate the model training process.

Table 1. Definition of data features

Feature	Units	Min	Max	Definition
Sales date		2017.3	2023.9	Date that the case is closed
Sales price	Mil. DKK	0.095	20.75	Final sales price
Days on market	Days	0	3769	Active days on the market
GisX	Wgs84	8.09799125105392	12.67288735783500	GIS X coordinate using WGS84
GisY	Wgs84	54.57196090998100	57.73727731401370	GIS Y coordinate using WGS84
Building area	m2	76	445	Size of buildings
Garage/carport area	m^2	0	260	Size of garages or carports
Basement area	m^2	0	295	Size of basements
Plot area	m^2	75	2000	Total area of the property plot
Number of bedrooms		0	10	Total number of bedrooms in the building
Number of restrooms		1	6	Number of toilets in the building which includes bathrooms
Construction year		1950	2023	Year of the original building
Reconstruction year		0	2023	Year of major reconstruction of buildings
Number of buildings		1	4	Buildings on the property

The dataset is based on sales cases in the Danish housing market from April 2017 until the end of November 2023. Table 1 shows a definition of the 14 data features. Every case is located by the geographic information system (GIS) using the World Geodetic System 1984 (WGS84) [19], which locates cases by latitude and longitude coordinates.

In Denmark, there are no minimum requirements for living space and room sizes like, for instance, in the Netherlands where specific limits in size are set for the living space, living room, and bathrooms [5]. The design of Danish buildings may be considered as highly representing the demands and decisions of the house owners regarding sizes of living space and other decisions related to the building layout design.

2.2 Extreme Gradient Boosting Implementation

Since the focus is not on the actual predictions that the model makes but rather on the explainable AI methods that were applied on top of the trained model, the focus is on the overall performance of the model and the utilized explainable AI techniques to analyze the predictions generated by the regression model. To get the best parameters for the regressor, hyperparameter tuning was performed on the XGBR-based implementation [20] where the Scikit-learn cross-validated grid-search [21] is utilized for testing combinations of multiple hyperparameters as elaborated on in Table 2 for each training through an intensive training process. R^2 is used as the object function for the training process to measure the regression performance, and 5-fold cross-validation with a random state of 42 is employed to enhance the reproducibility.

Table 2. Grid search hyperparameters

learning_rate	[0.001, 0.01, 0.1, 1.0]	Updated rate for the model weights during training
min_child_weight	[8, 9.5, 11]	Minimum sum of instance weight to control over-fitting
max_depth	[3, 6, 12, 25, 50, 100]	The maximum depth of the decision trees
subsample	[0.5, 0.55, 0.6]	Fraction of observations to be randomly sampled for each tree
colsample_bytree	[0.6, 0.8, 1.0]	Fraction of features to be randomly sampled for each tree
n_estimators	[10, 100, 500, 1000]	Number of trees in the model

The model performance is evaluated based on a split of the dataset, where 80% is used for the training dataset and the remaining 20% for the test-dataset, which is excluded from the training process as "hold out data". The dataset splitting parameters are shown in Table 3.

Table 3. Dataset splitting

Dataset	Features	Records
training dataset	13	17,058
validation dataset	13	4,265

2.3 Explainable AI Techniques

Once the model is trained, the feature importance and PDP are created to better understand the feature interactions by looking at the relationship between features and the target variable. Feature importance provides a cohesive understanding of which features are important for the model when predicting the target variable, whereas PDP will be used to further analyze the selected features. The feature importance is utilized for selecting the most important features regarding the house prices. Through PDP, the marginal effect that each of the features has on the outcome while accounting for the average effects that all the other features have (ceteris paribus approach) can be analyzed [6, 22]. Finally, the features sales price, building area, and plot area will be geographically mapped to provide an explainable visualization of the Danish housing market, which is the data foundation for this study. The permutation-based feature importance is chosen over impurity-based feature importance because of its capabilities of performing both on the high-volume training dataset and the "hold out" test dataset, whereas impurity-based feature importance has a bias since it solely bases its calculations on the training dataset [23]. In addition, impurity-based feature importance can also only be used together with tree-based models [23], whereas permutation feature importance is a model-agnostic method meaning that it can be applied to any model [24].

3 Results

3.1 Model Performance

Table 4. Regressor hyper-parameters

Learning _rate	min_child _weight	Max_ depth	subsample	colsample _bytree	n_estimators
0.01	8	12	0.55	0.75	800

The parameters for the best-performing regressor are shown in Table 4 where a max depth at 12 and 800 estimates seem to be the best choice along with the other parameter settings. While a depth model architecture increases the risk for overfitting, other parameters such as min child weight reduce overfitting. Table 5 shows the performance evaluation of the trained XGBR model for both the training and test datasets. The test evaluation shown in Table 5, which is performed on unseen data, is a valid assessment of the model performance, which is not affected by model overfitting.

With a focus on the model performance based on the test dataset, the model has an R^2 accuracy of 84%, an MAE of DKK433,823.76, and an RMSE of DKK 675,817.17. In comparison to the higher accuracy by evaluating the training dataset, the R^2 accuracy of 95% indicates that the model tends to overfit. Since the R^2 on the test set is reasonable, we do not focus on minimizing this overfit further. Figure 2 shows a plot comparing the actual sales price values against predicted values based on the test dataset for further

Table 5. Model performance

Matrices	Unit	Training dataset	Test dataset
R^2		0.95	0.84
MAE	[DKK]	244,417.36	433,823.76
RMSE	[DKK]	365,241.13	675,817.17

explanation of the model performance. From the plot, we see a trend that the model prediction is well distributed around the trendline up to 10 million DKK, and above that value, the predictions start to become lower than the actual values and the numbers of outliers increase with the prices. Above 7.5 million DKK, the data is more spread, and less data is available in that price span.

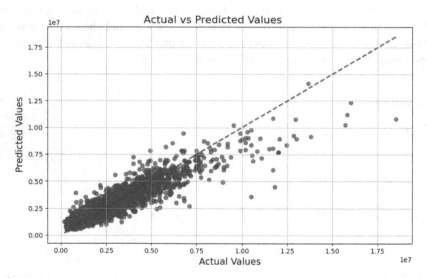

Fig. 2. Extreme gradient boosting model fit of actual vs predicted value of sale prices in DKK based on the test-dataset.

3.2 Feature Importance

Since our XGBR performance is considered satisfactory for this task of making regression on a relatively large geographically distributed dataset, the permutation-based feature importance was calculated using both the training and test datasets in comparison. By randomly shuffling the values of each feature and measuring the resulting increase in the prediction error, the features that have the highest significance for the model in predicting the target variable are identified [25] and listed in descending order. The seven highest-ranked features from the permutation feature importance plots in Fig. 3 are similar, while the low-impacting features have minor differences. The highest impacting

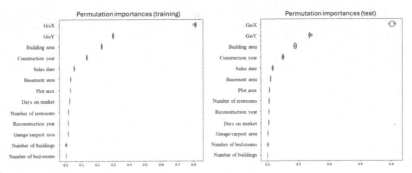

Fig. 3. Permutation feature importance plot based on training dataset (left) and permutation feature importance plot based on test dataset (right).

feature is the GisX which is the latitude. This seems reasonable since the capital city, Copenhagen, with the highest prices, is located in the eastern part of Denmark, the second highest is the longitude, which is the south-to-north direction of Denmark. Third is the building area of houses, fourth is the construction year, followed by the sales date, basement area, and plot area, and the 7th place is the number of restrooms based on the test dataset and the days on market based on the training dataset.

3.3 Partial Dependence Plots

Based on the highest impacting features, the PDPs are shown in Fig. 4. The PDP emphasizes the graph for the feature's impact on the sales prices. Most of the features follow the tendency that is expected apart from the construction year where the graph shows an increased effect of older houses that decreases until 1975 and thereafter the impact again increases. Plot areas have an interesting curve that decreases up to 850m^2, afterward the impact is relatively low up to 1200m^2, and then it increases up to 1300m^2 whereafter it drops again. Finally, the number of restrooms seems to have an impact on the price increase too. Regarding the number of restrooms, it is seen from the snippet of the correlation map in Fig. 5 that there is a correlation between the number of restrooms and the building area, which can be an underlying explanation for its relatively high effect on the sales price. The same can be the case for the number of bedrooms, which, however, has a lower impact on the price.

3.4 Feature Mapping

The data distribution shown in the plot in Fig. 6 shows that the highest density of data is centralized around the major cities of Copenhagen, Aarhus, Odense, Alborg, Kolding, and Esbjerg. On the plot, it is further seen that some areas on the map show no data. These areas may have an effect on the accuracy of these specific areas in further analysis, but they are excluded from the maps.

Looking at the permutation importance (Fig. 3), it becomes evident that the location features, GisX and GisY, obviously have a high impact on the model. The PDP of price distribution in Fig. 7 shows that the highest housing prices are concentrated around the

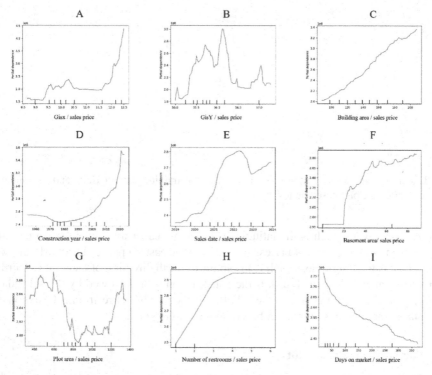

Fig. 4. Partial dependence plots of the highest impacting features.

Fig. 5. Correlation atrix snippet for the building area.

biggest cities. Even though the high prices are most concentrated near the city centers, they also influence the price level in a broader area around the cities where it is mainly seen in the eastern part of Jutland – from Aalborg down to Kolding – that the high price zones are merged along the coast. Also, the area west of Aarhus shows a high price level compared to the rest of the market. By changing the target of the XGBR-model to building area, the plot in Fig. 8 shows the geographical effect on the building area, where the building sizes tend to be smaller in the larger cities as Copenhagen and the surrounding areas. The concentrations of larger buildings are shown in the outer areas with less population density.

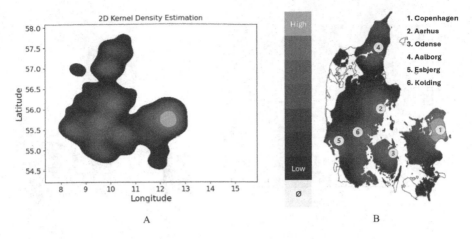

Fig. 6. 2D kernel density plot (A) and the merged plot on a map (B).

The other model trained on the plot area target shown in Fig. 9 shows the same tendency of being smaller near the major cities similar to the building areas, but in general, the plot sizes appear to be more evenly distributed to the whole geographical area.

4 Discussion

The study has shown promising capabilities for explaining the conditions of the housing market by analyzing the feature importance and PDPs. The performance of the XGBR with an R^2 score of 0.84 is found satisfying in the context of the large geographical data

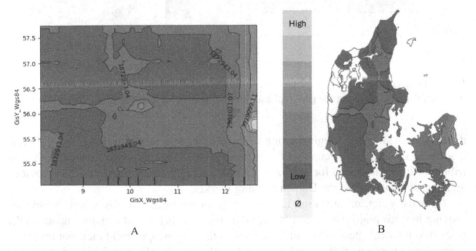

Fig. 7. Partial dependence plot of the sales prices (A) and the merged plot on a map (B), showing the geographical distribution of sales prices [DKK].

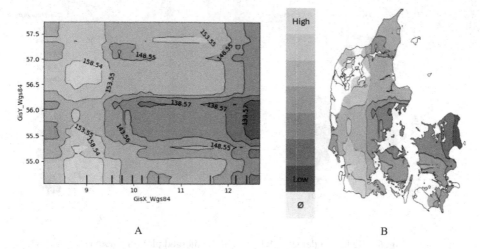

A   B

Fig. 8. Partial dependence plot for the model trained on the building area target (A) and the merged plot on a map (B), showing the geographical distribution of building area [m^2].

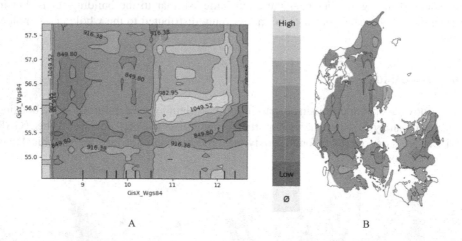

A   B

Fig. 9. Partial dependence plot for the model trained on the plot area target (A) and the merged plot on a map (B), showing the geographical distribution of plot area [m^2].

distribution. However, a segmentation of the dataset into more local regressions could lead to an even higher accuracy of predicted values. The proposed method both contributes with an approach for analyzing complex market mechanisms and has provided an insightful analysis of the Danish housing market.

Over the years, urbanization has been seen in societies globally where people are moving towards major cities from the rural districts. This has had a major impact on the price developments geographically, but also on the way people build their homes [5]. A compromise is often smaller buildings in densely populated urban societies compared to outside the big cities. The report "Space in new homes: what residents think" by

CABE [26] points to the need to ensure that well-designed homes become a norm, which should also be aligned with people's financial circumstances, to secure houses of good quality, while it is resource requiring and costly to replace poorly designed homes, which emphasizes the need for a clear understanding of the building demands to ensure that buildings will stand for their maximum life span to save resources.

Housing demands change over time due to social and geographic aspects such as evolving family structures and the growth of the elderly population [5] which require adaption of existing houses and an understanding of the market needs to build new buildings that follow these dynamic market demands. Small housing sizes and poor construction quality are some of the factors that limit the flexibility and adaptability of houses for meeting new market needs [5] where the need for space is found as a determinant factor for decisions about where to live [26]. These tendencies underline the importance of being aware of how market demands change over time.

5 Further Work

5.1 Prediction

To be capable of predicting future trends concerning design features like building sizes, number of rooms, etc., will provide high value for the industries within the construction field. Nonetheless, price forecasting in the real estate market provides major advances for real estate agencies and the finance sector, but also for the house owners and future house owners, by providing a more predictable market.

By further expanding the used dataset and improving the trained model, this could be used to predict the price for an individual house. Moreover, the explainable AI methods could be implemented on real estate market data from other countries, where the price distribution is more complex, and in that way, a better understanding of the market price patterns can be gained.

5.2 Flats, Semi-detached Houses, and Holiday Homes

Analyzing other dwelling types may also have a certain interest, especially for other countries than the Danish housing market, since other markets do not have the same dwelling tendencies as Denmark, where, for instance, the UK has a large part of semi-detached houses, etc. It could also be of interest to the Danish market to extend the research for these other dwelling types as detached houses just cover half of the real estate market.

6 Conclusion

Through a series of experiments based on a large dataset from the Danish housing market, we utilize an ML technique for mapping feature importance parameters for the housing market. The provided dataset shows to be well-distributed to most of the geographical area with just a few empty areas. The proposed XGBR model trained on sales prices performed an R^2 score of 0.84. Our experimental results emphasized the feature importance correlations to market prices based on the provided dataset that shows location, building area, and construction year as the features with the highest impact on the market price. It is further seen that there are some intercorrelations between features where, for instance, the number of restrooms in a building has a high impact on the sales price, but also has a higher correlation with the building area, which is the second highest impacting feature of the sales price.

By further analyzing the individual PDP for the highest impacting features, interesting correlations between these and the sales price were found which need further investigation to explain these results.

Our method for merging the PDP with maps has given a cohesive understanding of the geographical design and price distribution in the housing market. Overall, a price intensity is seen near the largest cities in Denmark, including an insight into building and plot areas. The proposed method has shown promise in providing an insightful understanding of the Danish housing market.

Acknowledgments. The authors would like to express their gratitude to Home A/S for providing the data, as well as Martin Olsen for his support and inspiring discussions. Special thanks also goes to Karin Hørup Mortensen for proofreading the article.

References

1. Statistics Denmark: dwellings with registered population, https://www.statistikbanken.dk/BOL106, Accessed 19 Apr 2023
2. As, I., Pal, S., Basu, P.: Artificial intelligence in architecture: generating conceptual design via deep learning. Int. J. Archit. Comput. **16**, 306–327 (2018)
3. Gervasio, H., Dimova, S.: Model for life cycle assessment (LCA) of buildings, EUR 29123 EN, Publications Office of the European Union (2018)
4. Van Stijn, A., Eberhardt, L.M., Jansen, B.W., Meijer, A.: A circular economy life cycle assessment (CE-LCA) model for building components. Resour. Conserv. Recycl. **174**, 105683 (2021)
5. Appolloni L., D'alessandro D.: Housing spaces in nine European countries: a comparison of dimensional requirements. Int. J. Environ. Res. Public Health **18**(8), 4278 (2021)
6. Hastie T., Tibshirani R., Friedman J.H.: The Elements of Statistical Learning: Data Mining, Inference, and Prediction, 2nd edn. Springer, New York (2008). https://doi.org/10.1007/978-0-387-21606-5
7. Hjort, A., Scheel, I., Einar, D., Pensar, J.: Locally interpretable tree boosting: an application to house price prediction. Decis. Support Syst. **178**, 114106 (2024)
8. Guliker E., Folmer E.: Spatial determinants of real estate appraisals in the Netherlands: a machine learning approach. ISPRS Int. J. Geo-inf. **11**(2), 125 (2022)
9. Abediniangerabi, B., Makhmalbaf, A., Shahandashti, M.: Estimating energy savings of ultra-high-performance fibre-reinforced concrete facade panels at the early design stage of buildings using gradient boosting machines. Adv. Build. Energy Res. **16**(4), 542–567 (2022)
10. Long, L.D.: An AI-driven model for predicting and optimizing energy-efficient building envelopes. Alex. Eng. J. **79**, 480–501 (2023)
11. Olu-Ajayi, R., Alaka, H., Sulaimon, I., Sunmola, F., Ajayi, S.: Machine learning for energy performance prediction at the design stage of buildings. Energy Sustain. Dev. **66**, 12–25 (2022)

12. Kang K.S., Koo C., Ryu H.G.: An interpretable machine learning approach for evaluating the feature importance affecting lost workdays at construction sites. J. Build. Eng. **53**, 104534 (2022)

13. Chae, Y.T., Horesh, R., Hwang, Y., Lee, Y.M.: Artificial neural network model for forecasting sub-hourly electricity usage in commercial buildings. Energ. Build. **111**, 184–194 (2016)

14. Wang, Z., Wang, Y., Zeng, R., Srinivasan, R.S., Ahrentzen, S.: Random forest based hourly building energy prediction. Energ. Build. **171**, 11–25 (2018)

15. Wang, Z., Wang, Y., Srinivasan, R.S.: A novel ensemble learning approach to support building energy use prediction. Energ. Build. **159**, 109–122 (2018)

16. Tooke, T.R., Coops, N.C., Webster, J.: Predicting building ages from LiDAR data with random forests for building energy modeling. Energ. Build. **68**, 603–610 (2014)

17. Liang D., Xue F.: Integrating automated machine learning and interpretability analysis in architecture, engineering and construction industry: a case of identifying failure modes of reinforced concrete shear walls. Comput. Ind. **147**, 103883 (2023)

18. Lee, C.: Training and interpreting machine learning models: application in property tax assessment. Real Estate Manage. Valuat. **30**(1), 13–22 (2022)

19. Decker, B.L.: World geodetic system 1984. Defense Mapping Agency Aerospace Center St Louis Afs Mo (1986)

20. Chen, T., Guestrin, C.: XGBoost: a scalable tree boosting system. In: Proceedings of the 22nd ACM SIGKDD International Conference on Knowledge Discovery and Data Mining, pp. 785–794 (2016)

21. Scikit-learn: GridSearchCV. https://scikit-learn.org/stable/modules/generated/sklearn.model_selection.GridSearchCV.html, Accessed 19 Apr 2024

22. Friedman, J.H.: Greedy function approximation: a gradient boosting machine. Ann. Stat. **29**, 1189–1232 (2021)

23. Zhou, Z., Hooker, G.: Unbiased measurement of feature importance in tree-based methods. ACM Trans. Knowl. Discov. Data (TKDD) **15**(2), 1–21 (2021)

24. Molnar C.: Interpretable Machine Learning. A Guide for Making Black Box Models Explainable. Independently published (2022)

25. Jin, Z., Shang, J., Zhu, Q., Ling, C., Xie, W., Qiang, B.: RFRSF: employee turnover prediction based on random forests and survival analysis. In: Huang, Z., Beek, W., Wang, H., Zhou, R., Zhang, Y. (eds.) Web Information Systems Engineering - WISE 2020. WISE 2020. LNCS, vol. 12343, pp. 503–515. Springer, Cham (2020). https://doi.org/10.1007/978-3-030-62008-0_35

26. Commission for architecture and built environment (CABE): space in new home: what residents think. Northampton, UK (2009)

Machine Learning-Driven Improvements in HRV Artifact Correction for Psychosis Prediction in the Schizophrenia Spectrum

Paraskevi V. Tsakmaki[1]([envelope]), Sotiris K. Tasoulis[1], Spiros V. Georgakopoulos[2], and Vassilis P. Plagianakos[1]

[1] Department of Computer Science and Biomedical Informatics, University of Thessaly, Lamia, Greece
{ptsakmaki,stas,vpp}@uth.gr
[2] Department of Mathematics, University of Thessaly, Lamia, Greece
spirosgeorg@uth.gr

Abstract. Exploring the complex interplay between the human mind and heart, our study delves into the role of Heart Rate Variability (HRV) as a non-invasive marker of psychosis, influenced by the Central Nervous System (CNS). In the current landscape of mental health research, the emphasis extends beyond merely diagnosing and unveiling biological markers. It encompasses predicting the flow of psychotic manifestations, leveraging biomarkers that transcend mere diagnostic labels. HRV, derived from the analysis of beat-to-beat intervals obtained through advanced smartwatch technology, offers a window into the delicate balance of our autonomic cardiac regulation. However, these beat-to-beat intervals are often fraught with anomalies or missing values, physiological like ectopic beats, and technical, possibly stemming from a subject's motion or reaction to external stimuli. Addressing these aberrations is vital, as they can compromise the integrity of HRV assessments. Our research tackles challenges such as ectopic beats and inconsistencies in beat-to-beat intervals, which are critical to ensuring the accuracy of HRV measurements. We employ a structured three-stage decision-making process, utilizing four machine learning algorithms to systematically evaluate and refine our approach. This process includes selecting the best dataset that captures sleep and awake states, identifying the most effective interpolation method, and choosing the best ectopic beat correction technique. This step-by-step comparison helps in selecting the optimal combination of dataset, interpolation, and ectopic beat correction for our study. Through this approach, we aim to enhance the reliability of HRV as a tool for mental health research, providing insights into the autonomic regulation in psychiatric conditions.

Keywords: Psychotic Relapse · Schizophrenia · HRV · Artifact Correction · Machine Learning

L. Iliadis et al. (Eds.): EANN 2024, CCIS 2141, pp. 544–557, 2024.
https://doi.org/10.1007/978-3-031-62495-7_41

1   Introduction

Psychosis represents a complex spectrum of disorders driven by varied factors affecting the CNS, leading to a range of clinical manifestations that pose significant challenges in psychiatric diagnosis and treatment [24]. Early symptom recognition and intervention are pivotal, highlighting the critical role of reliable biological markers in predicting psychotic episodes [5]. The advent of digital phenotyping, leveraging biometric data from wearable devices, offers a scalable and insightful approach to understanding mental health on an unprecedented level [22].

This study introduces an analytical framework divided into three critical stages: selecting the most productive dataset, refining data through interpolation techniques and ectopic beat correction, followed by feature extraction, classification, and model evaluation. This structured approach ensures a comprehensive examination of HRV, a promising biological marker for autonomic nervous system function, through smartwatch-collected cardiological data segmented based on patients' sleep states.

Central to our methodology was a disciplined experimental design where, at every stage, one specific aspect of our data handling technique was varied-akin to maintaining controlled conditions in a scientific experiment-while all others remained stable. This approach ensured the integrity of our comparative analysis, allowing us to isolate the impact of individual methods on the overall outcome effectively.

Upon the identification of the sleep database as the most conducive to our objectives, we ventured into the critical task of interpolation, a phase characterized by the strategic alternation of methods. Here, akin to variables in a differential equation held constant to solve for one, we held the ectopic beat removal process constant with Malik rule, allowing us to methodically explore and evaluate various interpolation techniques. This deliberate examination spanned linear, quadratic, cubic spline, pchip and nearest neighbor methods, each scrutinized under the lens of their contribution to data integrity and classification accuracy.

Guided by the precision of machine learning algorithms and the discerning measure of ROC analysis, our investigation illuminated the quadratic interpolation method as the standout technique, exhibiting unparalleled accuracy in capturing the intricate dynamics of HRV. This phase of methodical selection and evaluation exemplifies the study's reliance on data-driven decisions, ensuring that each choice was substantiated by robust analytical evidence.

As we progressed to address ectopic beats, again, a singular methodology was adjusted at a time, allowing for a focused assessment of each ectopic beat removal technique's effectiveness. The Acar method, emerging as the superior choice through our rigorous evaluation, underscored our commitment to a systematic, iterative approach grounded in machine learning principles, alongside testing against other notable rules such as Kamath's, Malik's, and Karlsson's.

This structured methodology, where one variable was diligently altered while others were held constant, facilitated a clear, unbiased evaluation of each technique's efficacy. The culmination of this process not only identified the most effective combination of dataset, interpolation method, and ectopic beat removal technique but also underscored the machine learning-driven nature of our decision-making. By navigating through each stage with a controlled, analytical rigor, we established a new benchmark in the field for classifying psychosis in the schizophrenia spectrum, demonstrating the power of a disciplined, data-driven approach in advancing psychiatric research.

2   Background

In the realm of psychiatry, HRV, a measure of the variation in time between each heartbeat (RR intervals) emerges as a critical tool for understanding the physiological underpinnings of mental health disorders. The study of HRV provides a non-invasive measure of the autonomic nervous system's regulation of the heart, offering valuable insights into cardiac autonomic activity [4].

HRV measurement over 24-hour periods captures daily physiological changes and the Autonomic Nervous System's (ANS) function, crucial for understanding cardiac and mental health, such as the impact of schizophrenia on ANS activity [18]. However, the presence of sensitive user data, missing values, and artifacts, particularly from motion-induced interference on smartwatch wearable devices, introduces significant challenges. These challenges necessitate the correction of artifacts as a crucial intermediate step. Accurate artifact correction, due to patient's movement, not only refines HRV signal analysis but also serves as a foundational step towards the reliable prediction of psychiatric conditions such as psychosis. Such corrections ensure that subsequent ML models are built upon data of the highest integrity, thereby enhancing the predictive accuracy for psychosis and other mental health disorders [2].

Beyond technical interferences, biological artifacts, especially ectopic beats (EBs)—premature heartbeats originating from areas in the heart outside the normal pacemaker cells- introduce significant noise, skewing HRV signal parameter estimates and affecting time, frequency, and nonlinear measurements. Even so, ectopics hold diagnostic value, offering insights into irregularities in the heart's electrical activity [19]. The differentiation of HRV patterns in individuals with schizophrenia during sleep versus active periods could thus illuminate the condition's impacts on autonomic function, highlighting the predictive value of sleep disorders for psychosis onset and their relationship with cognitive and mood disorders [6].

A study [27] which didn't explore artifact handling, in the same HRV data as we analyzed, in global scheme as our research did, focused on feature aggregation into 5-min segments, processed into tensors for daily physiological analysis. Despite its innovative approach, the study's lack of explicit artifact correction and the replacement of 10 h of missing values with median values, highlights the gap our research aims to fill by emphasizing artifact handling's and time window's pivotal roles. Given the intricate nature of HRV data and the nuanced physiological patterns it reveals, traditional Machine Learning (ML) approaches are particularly suited for this analysis. ML algorithms' ability to handle the variability and complexity of HRV data, while ensuring interpretability essential for clinical applications, underscores their preference over Deep Learning (DL) methods in this context. Unlike DL methods, which excel in extracting features from raw data, ML approaches offer a level of interpretability that is critical for applications in psychiatry, where understanding the basis of model predictions can facilitate clinical decision-making and patient care [11]. This preference is reinforced by the challenges posed by DL's demands for large datasets and computational resources, which may not always align with the constraints of HRV studies in psychiatric settings. Additionally, another study explored machine learning's potential in identifying unique biosignatures in Major Depressive Disorder (MDD) episodes using wearable data. Through stages of detrending, feature selection, and regression, and after extensive training on data from 26 MDD patients, the model predicted mood statuses with 86% accuracy, significantly outperforming baseline models [20]. This highlights the effectiveness of machine learning in identifying physiological patterns linked to MDD, reinforcing our choice of ML to understand and predict psychiatric conditions.

3   Data Collection and Demographics

We analyzed data and demographics from Table 1 and technical details from the e-prevention project [27]. This dataset contains recordings from smartwatches of 10 patients with psychotic spectrum disorders, collected from November 2019 to September 2021, totaling 1569 h after rigorous preprocessing. Patient diagnostics included two with Schizoaffective Disorder, four with Bipolar I Disorder, one with a Brief Psychotic Episode, one with Schizophreniform Disorder, and two with Schizophrenia. Clinical assessments were conducted monthly to evaluate the duration and severity of relapses, with annotations added to identify the nature of each relapse.

Table 1. Demographics from the e-prevention project [27]

Demographics	Statistics
Male/Female	6/4
Age (years)	30.60 ± 7.31
Education (years)	13.8 ± 1.99
Illness duration (years)	7.3 ± 7.06

4   Methodology

In this exploration, we focus on HRV, a mirror to the autonomic nervous system's rhythm, captured through RR intervals-the time measured between consecutive heartbeats. The integrity of HRV as a biomarker necessitates rigorous data cleansing, initially from outliers—erratic data points that misrepresent the true heartbeat interval due to external disturbances or sensor errors. Equally critical is the rectification of ectopic beats, atypical heartbeats that, if left uncorrected, could skew our understanding of the heart's natural rhythm. These steps, crucial for accurate HRV analysis, involve sophisticated techniques to surgically remove these data discrepancies and employ interpolation to reconstruct a truthful sequence of heart activity.

4.1   Artifact Removal and Interpolation Techniques

We evaluated the accuracy of relapse prediction using machine learning classification across three datasets of same population, each differentiated by specific criteria related to sleep state, employing a fundamental methodology with uniform features to identify variations. Initially, we selected a dataset that captured patients' sleep patterns, irrespective of whether it was day or night. The subsequent dataset encompassed data from patients regardless of their state (sleeping or awake) at any given time, day, or night. The final dataset was curated based on patients' wakeful periods, regardless of whether they occurred during daytime or nighttime. We extracted multiple twenty-minute segments from the larger dataset for each patient, ensuring a comprehensive representation of their HRV patterns. For each of the three datasets, the number of twenty-minute spans selected was determined by the availability of consistency, within the specified sleep and wake states. The segments chosen for analysis were those that offered a clear, uninterrupted view of the heart's activity.

The rationale behind focusing on twenty-minute segments lies in their ability to provide a detailed snapshot of heart rate variability (HRV) within a manageable timeframe that minimizes the potential for missing values and artifacts. These segments, when analyzed collectively, offer a robust and nuanced view of the autonomic nervous system's dynamics across varying states of sleep and wakefulness as well as different times of the day.

For every twenty-minute segment extracted, we applied interpolation techniques as part of our preprocessing steps. This was essential to address any sporadic missing values or minor inconsistencies within each segment, thereby ensuring a continuous and reliable RR series for subsequent analysis. The interpolation was carried out with precision, maintaining the integrity of the original RR intervals while making necessary adjustments to create a seamless and artifact-free time series.

Through careful evaluation of the datasets, we were able to determine the dataset that provided the greatest predictive accuracy for HRV-based relapse prediction, while keeping the algorithms, interpolation, and ectopic beat removal methods consistent. The performance of the third dataset indicated that HRV data collected during sleep could be especially valuable for forecasting relapse in patients with mental health disorders. A more detailed analysis is presented in the results section. With the optimal dataset identified, we compared different interpolation methods while maintaining all other variables constant. This allowed us to isolate the effect of interpolation on model performance and identify the technique that boosts predictive accuracy, as evidenced by improvements in ROC-AUC scores. The scholarly consensus for addressing inconsistent RR-intervals predominantly advocates for their removal [21]. This procedure entails eliminating abnormal RR intervals and amalgamating the regular intervals. However, one prominent drawback of this deletion method is the reduction in the HRV signal's length, potentially causing significant alterations to the HRV spectrum [21].

Upon discerning the typical range of RR series values in healthy individuals as 0.6–1.2 ms, the interval was adjusted to 0.2–2.2 ms to detect irregularities. This expanded range allows for the inclusion and detailed examination of significant deviations from the norm, encompassing both shorter and longer RR intervals that may indicate underlying cardiac or autonomic irregularities. Additionally, it is imperative to note that while various interpolation techniques maintain the original sample count, they inevitably modify the total duration by modulating the RR interval lengths. Numerous interpolation methods, such as linear and cubic spline (CS) interpolations, are available for addressing inconsistent RR intervals, as highlighted by [25].

Among the prevalent strategies and their corresponding methodologies, the Nearest Neighbor (NN) technique stands out for its simplicity. This method fills in missing values by assigning the nearest available data point. Nevertheless, the resultant data is often characterized by discontinuities, leading to potentially suboptimal outcomes [16]. The Linear approach, on the other hand, draws a direct line through irregular RR-intervals to extract standardized values. Such interpolation confines the data, yet its effectiveness, particularly in settings with consistent rates, has been demonstrated by studies [10]. The Quadratic (Quad) technique distinguishes itself by requiring three reference points for interpolation, generally exhibiting superior accuracy compared to its linear counterpart [16,21]. The CS method effectively addresses the oscillation issues or Runge's phenomenon, commonly observed in higher-degree polynomial fits. By leveraging piecewise third-order polynomials, it ensures smoother curves, thereby preventing distortions frequently observed in straightforward polynomial interpolation, as suggested by [8] and [25]. The PCHIP method, which is akin to the spline method, carries out piecewise cubic Hermite interpolation. The primary differentiation between them arises from the methodologies they employ to calculate the slopes of the interpolant, which results in distinct characteristics when confronted with flat or oscillatory data segments [3]. In this study, each interpolation technique mentioned was meticulously applied to the RR sequence of a specific dataset, ensuring that other aspects of signal analysis remained consistent. This was done to discern their inherent differences and comprehend their implications in patterns [3].

Each interpolation technique described above was applied to RR sequence to the proven optimal dataset of sleep, in order to catch their differences keeping other states of signal analysis consistent. The method that had the best performance was the quadratic method.

4.2   Detection of Ectopic Beats

The final stage involved assessing various ectopic beat removal techniques, keeping the dataset, interpolation method, and machine learning algorithms steady. Our aim was to find the ectopic beat correction method that significantly enhances AUC scores. Within the HRV signal, ectopic beats can be readily identified. These anomalous beats usually appear as abrupt changes in the HRV sequence. According to a definition by Kamarth [12], ectopic beats are characterized as those whose intervals are at most 80% of the preceding sinus cycle's duration. The strategic selection of a suitable threshold is indispensable when applying detection techniques grounded in the HRV signal [7]. However, it is crucial to understand that while specific benchmarks, can facilitate the recognition of ectopic beats, the effectiveness of such a threshold might oscillate based on the demographic under investigation and the unique conditions of the data recording. As such, the decision regarding threshold selection should be approached judiciously and, where feasible, corroborated with expert annotations [12]. Several scholars have proposed various criteria to identify irregularities in RR time series. For instance, Malik [17] posits that an RR time series should maintain consistency by not deviating more than 20% from its preceding value. Contrastingly, Kamarth [13] suggests that the RR time series should neither escalate nor diminish beyond 32.5%. Moreover, it should remain within a deviation of 24.5% from its antecedent interval. According to Acar [1], any RR time series differing by more than 20% from the average of its preceding nine RRs ought to be excluded. Furthermore, Karlsson [14] recommends the omission of RR time series that stray by over 20% from the average of the prior and subsequent RR. Detected ectopic beats were subsequently excised and interpolated using the methods delineated by previous rules. These rules were applied singularly to the same data dataset, keeping all other stages consistent, so as to discern variations and facilitate a comparison of metrics obtained post-classification for the best rule for handling ectopic beats. Given the consistent performance in all metrics, particularly in AUC, Accuracy, and F1 score, the Acar method, applied to data while sleeping, using the quadratic method for artifact removal combined with the Random Forest(RF) model seems to be the most effective approach for handling ectopic beats, for this dataset.

4.3   Feature Extraction

Predictability and regularity are pivotal attributes of chaotic systems, like the heart, shedding light on system evolution and pattern recurrence respectively. Predictability, in this context, refers to our ability to anticipate future system states based on past observations, which is crucial for modeling heart rate dynamics accurately. Spatial predictability transforms a one-dimensional time series into a two-dimensional space using delay embedding, aiding in understanding system dynamics. This technique essentially allows us to reconstruct the dynamical landscape of the heart's behavior from sequential heart rate measurements. Key metrics include the Correlation Dimension and the Largest Lyapunov Exponent which may correlate with measures such as Detrended Fluctuation Analysis (DFA) seen in the Mann Whitney U test results, to the statistical section. The Correlation Dimension provides a measure of the complexity of the attractor formed by the heart's dynamics, indicating the number of variables required to describe its state. The Largest Lyapunov Exponent measures the rate of divergence or convergence of closely related system states, offering insight into the system's sensitivity to initial conditions.

Conversely, temporal dimensionality emphasizes the fractal nature of system attractors, reflecting the system's inherent degrees of freedom and highlighting geometric complexities across scales [15]. Fractal dimensionality quantifies the geometric complexity, revealing how the heart rate variability fills the time-frequency space. The fractal dimensionality of an attractor elucidates the structural intricacy of a dynamical system. Methods like Petrosian's, Katz's, and DFA provide insights into this complexity. Petrosian's and Katz's algorithms simplify the computation of fractal dimensions, making them accessible for analyzing heart rate variability. DFA further helps in identifying long-term correlations within the HRV signals. A higher fractal dimensionality signifies a system rich in complexity and patterns, while a lower one denotes simplicity. These distinctions are crucial for distinguishing between healthy and pathological states of cardiac function.

Methods that quantify the regularity of a dynamical system are commonly based on entropy and concentrate on evaluating the presence of recurring behaviors in the time series. Approximate and Sample entropy measure the predictability and complexity of time series data, respectively. These metrics are essential for understanding the underlying order or disorder within the HRV data, indicating potential stress or dysfunction in autonomic regulation.

Single-scale-based approaches, such as Fuzzy Entropy and Lempel-Ziv Complexity (LZC), assess the signal's complexity at its original scale, providing a snapshot of the system's immediate state. Multiscale Entropy(MSE) and its Refined (Rcmsen) and Fuzzy versions (Fuzzycmsen, MsApen) extend this analysis across various scales, offering a more comprehensive view of the heart's regulatory mechanisms over time.

In addition, statistics of time domain and geometrical features were extracted. The analysis of geometric configurations within the HRV data allows for a deeper understanding of the inherent characteristics and dynamics of the cardiovascular system under investigation [23]. Analysis of HRV data enables understanding of cardiovascular dynamics, similar to results gained from Poincaré plots (sd1, sd2), which highlight heart rate patterns indicative of autonomic nervous system imbalances or stress responses. These patterns are instrumental in identifying potential autonomic nervous system imbalances or stress responses, which are critical for understanding the physiological basis of psychiatric conditions. The interpretative framework is based on established research that links specific HRV patterns with underlying autonomic nervous system behavior [26]. By examining these patterns, even in the absence of visual plots, we can infer significant insights into cardiac autonomic regulation related to mental health disorders. We detail HRV feature computation and significance, bridging understanding gaps about HRV complexity and its implications for conditions like psychosis. The features extracted from HRV serve as critical inputs for our machine learning models, enabling the creation of effective predictive tools.

5   Statistical Test

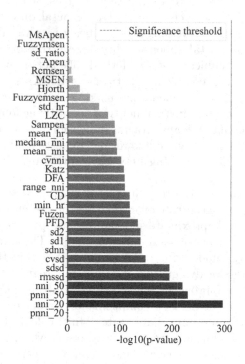

Fig. 1. Mann-Whitney U Test Results: -log10(p-values) and HRV Metrics Differentiating Relapsed vs. Non-Relapsed Groups

In this section, we analyze the statistical significance of HRV metrics in differentiating between relapsed and non-relapsed groups, using the Mann-Whitney U test results. The Shapiro-Wilk normality test reveals that HRV metrics for both relapsed and non-relapsed categories deviate significantly from a normal distribution, with p-values near zero, indicating strong evidence of non-normality. This is consistent across all metrics, except for DFA in the relapsed category, which has a p-value of approximately $1.399236 * 10^{-4}$, suggesting non-normality but to a lesser degree. Such non-normal distributions align with the expected physiological variability and complex dynamics of heart rate time series [9]. Differences between the two groups are highlighted by the Mann-Whitney U test, where several HRV features, including "Rcmsen", and "Fuzzycmsen" among others, show statistical significance with p-values below 0.05, indicating distinct distributions between groups. Conversely, "Fuzzymsen" and "MsApen" do not exhibit notable differences, with p-values above the threshold. In terms of effect size, attributes such as "sd1", "sd2", and "sdsd", displayed relatively lower U statistics, hinting at a more marked difference between the groups. Based on the results from the Mann-Whitney U test for each feature between the relapsed and not relapsed groups, it becomes evident that specific HRV metrics can serve as significant indicators for distinguishing between these two patient categories. HRV metrics with its rich tapestry of data, predominantly exhibits non-normal distributions with significant skewness and kurtosis variations, underscoring distinct patterns between relapsed and non-relapsed groups and therefore predicting or understanding relapse events. The provided chart in Fig. 1 underscores these findings.

6   Experimental Results

We employed Random Forest, Extra Trees (ET), XGBoost (XGB), and Logistic Regression (LR), to analyze our dataset. The input features utilized in the classification task are derived from HRV measurements, as detailed in the feature engineering part. The experiment addresses class imbalance by resampling the dataset to ensure an equal representation of both classes, with the minority class (indicating relapse) being upsampled using the resample function. A binary classification task aimed at predicting the likelihood of psychosis relapse among patients., is adressed. The target variable "Relapse" represents two classes: one indicating the absence of relapse (e.g., 0) and the other indicating the presence of relapse (e.g., 1). By scaling the features to a predefined range, typically between 0 and 1, normalization ensures that each feature contributes proportionally to the model training process, irrespective of its original scale. This standardization prevents features with larger magnitudes from disproportionately influencing the model learning process, thereby averting biased model training and improving overall performance. The dataset is then split into training and test sets.This division ensures that the machine learning models undergo training on a subset of the data while being evaluated on unseen data, providing a reliable estimate of their generalization performance. Therefore, the machine learning models are trained to classify patients into one of these two classes based on the input features. Finally, the models' performance is assessed using various metrics, predominantly focusing on the area under the ROC curve, which provides insights into the models' ability to discriminate between relapse and non-relapse cases with different threshold values. In our examination focused on pinpointing the optimal dataset for HRV predictive modeling, the algorithms were utilized across three distinct datasets representing varied circadian situations. Data$_1$, which encompasses combined sleep and awake periods during both day and night, witnessed the Random Forest model achieving an AUC of 0.71 on Table 2.

Table 2. Model Evaluation Metrics Across Datasets

Model:Dataset	ROC-AUC	Accuracy	Recall	F1	Precision
RF:$data_1$	0.71	0.67	0.67	0.73	0.85
ET:$data_1$	0.70	0.67	0.67	0.72	0.84
XGB:$data_1$	0.69	0.65	0.65	0.71	0.84
LR:$data_1$	0.68	0.65	0.65	0.71	0.84
RF:$data_2$	0.72	0.66	0.66	0.72	0.84
ET:$data_2$	0.72	0.66	0.66	0.71	0.84
XGB:$data_2$	0.69	0.63	0.63	0.69	0.83
LR:$data_2$	0.69	0.65	0.65	0.70	0.83
RF:$data_3$	0.74	0.69	0.69	0.75	0.86
ET:$data_3$	0.74	0.68	0.68	0.74	0.86
XGB:$data_3$	0.74	0.67	0.67	0.73	0.86
LR:$data_3$	0.73	0.66	0.66	0.73	0.86

Meanwhile, for $data_2$, capturing only awake periods during both day and night, the models exhibited performances similar to those on $data_1$. Notably, $data_3$, which solely represents sleep periods occurring during both day and night, showcased exemplary efficacy. Models applied to this dataset consistently achieved AUC values of 0.73 or higher, cementing $data_3$ as the standout dataset for predicting psychiatric disorder relapses using HRV data. To further fine-tune our approach, we evaluated several interpolation methods on the selected $data_3$. The quadratic method, when harmonized with the RF model, demonstrated superior predictive prowess, with AUC and F1 score values peaking at 0.75 on Table 3.

Diving into the pivotal realm of ectopic beat correction, our experiments highlighted the unparalleled efficacy of the Acar method. When synergized with the RF model, it achieved a remarkable AUC of 0.80 on Table 3. Taking stock of our comprehensive research, it's evident that $data_3$, which focuses on sleep periods irrespective of day or night, in tandem with the quadratic interpolation method and the Acar technique for ectopic beat correction, offers promising avenues in HRV-based predictive modeling. This layered and sequential analysis ensures that each decision point is evaluated in detail, leading to the identification of the most effective combination of dataset, interpolation method, and ectopic beat removal technique for HRV-based predictive modeling. The final outcome of this process is an optimized model that demonstrates the highest level of accuracy in predicting psychiatric disorder relapses, as evidenced by exceptional AUC scores. This approach not only enhances the reliability of our findings but also adheres to the principles of scientific diligence and precision in mental health research, providing a comprehensive and systematic strategy for advancing HRV-based predictive modeling.

Table 3. Combined Evaluation Metrics Across Techniques and Corrections

Interpolation Techniques						Ectopic Corrections					
Model	AUC	Acc	Recall	F1	Pre	Model	AUC	Acc	Recall	F1	Pre
RF:NN	0.75	0.68	0.68	0.74	0.86	RF:Malik	0.74	0.69	0.69	0.75	0.86
ET:NN	0.75	0.67	0.67	0.73	0.86	ET:Malik	0.74	0.68	0.68	0.74	0.86
XGB:NN	0.74	0.68	0.68	0.74	0.86	XGB:Malik	0.74	0.67	0.67	0.73	0.86
LR:NN	0.73	0.67	0.67	0.73	0.86	LR:Malik	0.73	0.66	0.66	0.73	0.86
RF:Linear	0.75	0.69	0.69	0.75	0.86	RF:Karls	0.76	0.69	0.69	0.75	0.86
ET:Linear	0.74	0.68	0.68	0.74	0.86	ET:Karls	0.75	0.68	0.68	0.74	0.86
XGB:Linear	0.74	0.67	0.67	0.73	0.86	XGB:Karls	0.76	0.69	0.69	0.75	0.86
LR:Linear	0.73	0.67	0.67	0.73	0.86	LR:Karls	0.73	0.66	0.66	0.72	0.86
RF:Quad	0.75	0.69	0.69	0.75	0.86	RF:Kam	0.76	0.69	0.69	0.74	0.87
ET:Quad	0.74	0.68	0.68	0.74	0.86	ET:Kam	0.76	0.69	0.69	0.74	0.86
XGB:Quad	0.74	0.67	0.67	0.73	0.86	XGB:Kam	0.74	0.67	0.67	0.73	0.86
LR:Quad	0.73	0.66	0.66	0.73	0.86	LR:Kam	0.73	0.66	0.66	0.73	0.85
RF:CS	0.74	0.68	0.68	0.74	0.86	RF:Acar	0.80	0.72	0.72	0.77	0.87
ET:CS	0.74	0.68	0.68	0.74	0.86	ET:Acar	0.78	0.71	0.71	0.76	0.87
XGB:CS	0.75	0.68	0.68	0.74	0.87	XGB:Acar	0.79	0.72	0.72	0.77	0.87
LR:CS	0.73	0.66	0.66	0.73	0.86	LR:Acar	0.75	0.70	0.70	0.75	0.87
RF:PCHIP	0.74	0.69	0.69	0.75	0.86						
ET:PCHIP	0.74	0.68	0.68	0.74	0.86						
XGB:PCHIP	0.74	0.67	0.67	0.73	0.86						
LR:PCHIP	0.73	0.66	0.66	0.73	0.86						

7   Conclusion

Given the brain's complexity and the unpredictable nature of the heart in psychiatric settings, precise HRV data analysis with machine learning is essential. HRV data from psychiatric patients, often more chaotic than typical recordings, requires careful processing. This includes choosing appropriate artifact correction methods, determining the right interpolation techniques, and selecting the best recorded data. Identifying the optimal data length is crucial to minimize data loss and gaps. Precision in each analytical step is vital for drawing consistent and reliable conclusions from HRV studies in psychiatric contexts. This thorough approach not only validates the research but also deepens our understanding of the complexities of psychiatric disorders.

Acknowledgment. Financed by the European Union - NextGeneration through National Recovery and Resilience Fund, Greece 2.0 under the call "Flagship actions in interdisciplinary scientific fields with a special focus on the productive fabric" (project code: TAEDR-0539180)

References

1. Acar, B., Savelieva, I., Hemingway, H., Malik, M.: Automatic ectopic beat elimination in short-term heart rate variability measurement. Comput. Methods Programs Biomed. **63**(2), 123–131 (2000)
2. Baek, H.J., Shin, J.: Effect of missing inter-beat interval data on heart rate variability analysis using wrist-worn wearables. J. Med. Syst. **41**, 1–9 (2017)
3. Benchekroun, M., Chevallier, B., Zalc, V., Istrate, D., Lenne, D., Vera, N.: The impact of missing data on heart rate variability features: a comparative study of interpolation methods for ambulatory health monitoring. IRBM **44**(4), 100776 (2023)
4. Berntson, G.G., et al.: Heart rate variability: origins, methods, and interpretive caveats. Psychophysiology **34**(6), 623–648 (1997)
5. Bertelsen, M., et al.: Five-year follow-up of a randomized multicenter trial of intensive early intervention vs standard treatment for patients with a first episode of psychotic illness: the opus trial. Arch. Gen. Psychiatry **65**(7), 762–771 (2008)
6. Chiappelli, J., et al.: Stress-induced increase in kynurenic acid as a potential biomarker for patients with schizophrenia and distress intolerance. JAMA Psychiat. **71**(7), 761–768 (2014)
7. Clifford, G.D., Azuaje, F., Mcsharry, P., et al.: ECG statistics, noise, artifacts, and missing data. Adv. Methods Tools ECG Data Anal. **6**(1), 18 (2006)
8. De Boor, C., De Boor, C.: A Practical Guide to Splines, vol. 27. Springer-Verlag, New York (1978)
9. Garner, D.M., Vanderlei, F.M., Valenti, V.E., Vanderlei, L.C.M.: Non-linear regulation of cardiac autonomic modulation in obese youths: interpolation of ultra-short time series. Cardiol. Young **29**(9), 1196–1201 (2019)
10. Gnauck, A.: Interpolation and approximation of water quality time series and process identification. Anal. Bioanal. Chem. **380**, 484–492 (2004)
11. Ishaque, S., Khan, N., Krishnan, S.: Trends in heart-rate variability signal analysis. Front. Digit. Health **3**, 639444 (2021)
12. Kamath, M., et al.: Time-frequency analysis of heart rate variability signals in patients with autonomic dysfunction. In: Proceedings of Third International Symposium on Time-Frequency and Time-Scale Analysis (TFTS-96), pp. 373–376. IEEE (1996)
13. Kamath, M., Fallen, E.: Correction of the heart rate variability signal for ectopics and missing beats' heart rate variability. In: Malik, M., Camm, A.J. (eds.) (1995)
14. Karlsson, M., Hörnsten, R., Rydberg, A., Wiklund, U.: Automatic filtering of outliers in RR intervals before analysis of heart rate variability in Holter recordings: a comparison with carefully edited data. Biomed. Eng. Online **11**, 1–12 (2012)
15. Lau, Z.J., Pham, T., Chen, S.A., Makowski, D.: Brain entropy, fractal dimensions and predictability: a review of complexity measures for EEG in healthy and neuropsychiatric populations. Eur. J. Neurosci. **56**(7), 5047–5069 (2022)
16. Lepot, M., Aubin, J.B., Clemens, F.H.: Interpolation in time series: an introductory overview of existing methods, their performance criteria and uncertainty assessment. Water **9**(10), 796 (2017)
17. Malik, M., et al.: Heart rate variability: standards of measurement, physiological interpretation, and clinical use. Eur. Heart J. **17**(3), 354–381 (1996)
18. Massin, M.M., Maeyns, K., Withofs, N., Ravet, F., Gérard, P.: Circadian rhythm of heart rate and heart rate variability. Arch. Dis. Child. **83**(2), 179–182 (2000)

19. Nabil, D., Reguig, F.B.: Ectopic beats detection and correction methods: A review. Biomed. Signal Process. Control **18**, 228–244 (2015)
20. Ricka, N., Pellegrin, G., Fompeyrine, D.A., Lahutte, B., Geoffroy, P.A.: Predictive biosignature of major depressive disorder derived from physiological measurements of outpatients using machine learning. Sci. Rep. **13**(1), 6332 (2023)
21. Salo, M.A., Huikuri, H.V., Seppanen, T.: Ectopic beats in heart rate variability analysis: effects of editing on time and frequency domain measures. Ann. Noninvasive Electrocardiol. **6**(1), 5–17 (2001)
22. Torous, J., Kiang, M.V., Lorme, J., Onnela, J.P., et al.: New tools for new research in psychiatry: a scalable and customizable platform to empower data driven smartphone research. JMIR Mental Health **3**(2), e5165 (2016)
23. Tsakmaki, P.V., Tasoulis, S.K.: Heart rate variability indexes in schizophrenia. In: Vlamos, P., Kotsireas, I.S., Tarnanas, I. (eds.) Handbook of Computational Neurodegeneration, pp. 889–897. Springer, Cham (2023). https://doi.org/10.1007/978-3-319-75479-6_42-1
24. Van Os, J.: Schizophrenia/J. OS Van, S. Kapur. Lancet **9690** (2009)
25. VK, M.: Correction of the heart rate variability signal for Ectopics and missing beats. Heart Rate Variability (1995)
26. Yan, C., Li, P., Liu, C., Wang, X., Yin, C., Yao, L.: Novel gridded descriptors of poincaré plot for analyzing heartbeat interval time-series. Comput. Biol. Med. **109**, 280–289 (2019)
27. Zlatintsi, A., et al.: E-prevention: advanced support system for monitoring and relapse prevention in patients with psychotic disorders analyzing long-term multimodal data from wearables and video captures. Sensors **22**(19), 7544 (2022)

Machine Unlearning, A Comparative Analysis

Ziad Doughan[✉][iD] and Sari Itani[iD]

Beirut Arab Univerisity, Debbiyeh, Lebanon
z.doughan@bau.edu.lb, ssi127@student.bau.edu.lb

Abstract. This paper investigates the effectiveness of machine unlearning techniques in removing sensitive data from pre-trained Resnet-18 models using the CIFAR-10 dataset. Specifically, it compares the performance of Fine-Tuning and Fisher Noise-based Impair-Repair methods in minimizing data leakage and preserving model performance. The study evaluates the techniques' ability to reduce Membership Inference Attack (MIA) scores while maintaining comparable accuracy on the retained data. The findings demonstrate that the Impair-Repair technique significantly reduces MIA scores compared to Fine-Tuning, showcasing its potential for responsible AI development. This approach allows for data privacy protection without compromising the model's performance. The research contributes to advancing techniques that address the challenges of data privacy in machine learning.

Keywords: Machine Unlearning · Data Privacy · Sensitive Data Removal · Ethical AI · Membership Inference Attack · Performance Evaluation

1 Introduction

Machine learning (ML) models are powering innovation across diverse fields, but concerns about data privacy and potential misuse of sensitive information remain a significant challenge [11]. In domains like finance and healthcare, individuals have the "right to be forgotten" and demand greater control over their data within trained AI models [11,12]. Traditional data deletion proves insufficient, as advanced attacks like Membership Inference Attack (MIA) [1,13] can reconstruct seemingly erased information. Machine unlearning offers a promising solution by selectively removing sensitive data points from pre-trained models [8]. This research explores the application of machine unlearning algorithms that take an AI model and a "forget set" (a subset of the training data) to produce an unlearned model. This resulting model aims to retain the original model's accuracy while minimizing the influence of the forget set [11]. This translates to a significant reduction in the unlearned model's accuracy on the forget set and minimal residual influence of the forgotten data within the model weights [15]. By comparing different unlearning algorithms, we aim to identify the most

L. Iliadis et al. (Eds.): EANN 2024, CCIS 2141, pp. 558–568, 2024.
https://doi.org/10.1007/978-3-031-62495-7_42

effective approach for ensuring data privacy and mitigating ethical concerns surrounding sensitive data in ML models.

2   Background Information

2.1   Machine Unlearning: An Overview

Machine Unlearning for Data Privacy Protection: The increasing adoption of AI models raises privacy concerns regarding user data used in their training. To address these concerns, "machine unlearning" techniques offer a way to remove specific data points or entire classes from trained models while preserving overall model performance.

Right to be Forgotten: Machine unlearning empowers users to exercise their "right to be forgotten" by ensuring their data is no longer accessible or influential within a trained model. Simply deleting data from the training database is insufficient, as advanced attacks like Membership Inference Attack (MIA) can potentially reconstruct such data [1,11].

2.2   Unlearning Workflow:

Model and Request Selection: The starting point is a pre-trained AI model and a specific unlearning request. This request can target individual data points, entire classes, or specific features extracted by the model, as seen in Fig. 1.

Algorithm Selection: The choice of unlearning algorithm depends on the model type and the request nature. Model-intrinsic algorithms like Fisher Masking or Certified Removal Mechanisms are well-suited for deep learning models with specific removal requests. Model-agnostic algorithms like Fine-Tuning offer broader applicability but may require careful fine-tuning to preserve performance.

Unlearning Process: The selected algorithm modifies the model to minimize the influence of the targeted data while maintaining its functionality.

Performance Evaluation: The unlearned model's performance is assessed on a "retain set" containing data not subject to unlearning. Additionally, privacy protection is evaluated by re-running attacks like MIA to ensure minimal information leakage about the removed data, as seen in Fig. 1 [11].

Deployment: Upon successful validation, the unlearned model can be deployed in production, guaranteeing a balance between functionality and user privacy.

2.3   Membership Inference Attack

MIA aims to determine whether a specific data point was used to train a given AI model. This involves estimating the probability of the model parameters aligning with a hypothetical model trained on that data point. However, directly calculating this probability is computationally impractical [1,13].

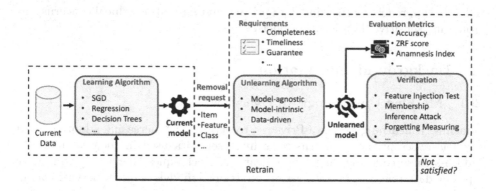

Fig. 1. Machine Unlearning Standard Workflow [11]

Leveraging Model Overfitting: MIA exploits the overfitting nature of AI models. Overfitted models exhibit significantly lower loss values for data points they have seen during training compared to unseen data. This phenomenon allows for an indirect estimation of the target data point's membership in the training set.

Shadow Model Approach: MIA employs a computationally efficient strategy using "shadow models." These are small, independent models trained on subsets of the data, including and excluding the target data point. By analyzing the loss distributions of these shadow models, we can estimate the expected loss of the target model for the data point.

Gaussian Distribution Approximation: MIA builds upon the assumption that the model's loss for unseen data follows a Gaussian distribution. This allows for the comparison of the target model's actual loss with the expected loss distribution based on the shadow models. A significant deviation from the expected distribution suggests the target data point's likely membership in the training set.

Figures 2 and 3 illustrate how MIA results are interpreted. In Fig. 2, the wide decision boundary and high loss at the boundary indicate that the data point was likely not in the training set. Conversely, in Fig. 3 the narrow boundary and low loss suggest the data point's presence in the training set.

2.4   Fisher Masking Unlearning

At its core, Fisher Masking unlearning technique aims to maximize the likelihood of high loss values for data points in the forget set, and we use fisher information for their significance about actualy information found in data, as seen in Fig. 4 [9].

Forget Set Formation and Fisher Information Calculation: Samples are selected from the training dataset to form the forget set, while the remaining data constitutes the retain set. Then, random noise is added to the forget set data points. The likelihood of the noisy data points being generated by the model under specific parameters is then calculated. After that, the log of the likelihood is calculated, followed by differentiation with respect to the model parameters.

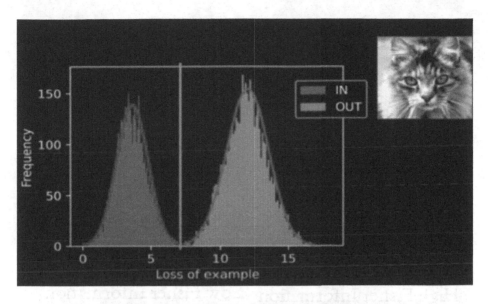

Fig. 2. Membership Inference Attack Example 1 [1]

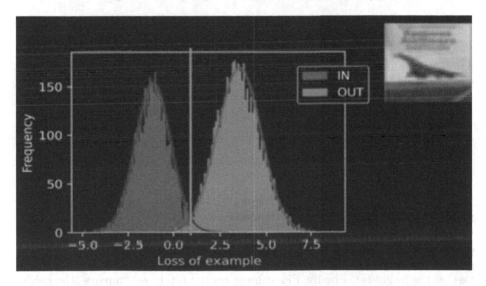

Fig. 3. Membership Inference Attack Example 2 [1]

Finally, the result is squared and its expected value is computed, resulting in the full Fisher information scalar value. This is equation (1).

$$F = \mathbb{E}\left[\left(\frac{\partial \log p(x|\theta)}{\partial \theta}\right)^2\right] \tag{1}$$

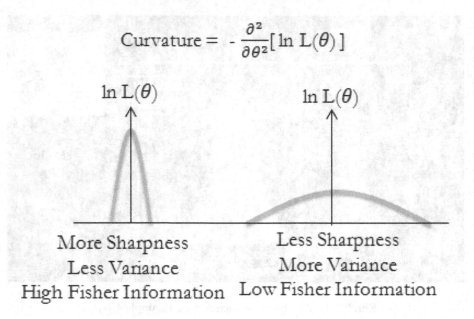

$$\text{Curvature} = -\frac{\partial^2}{\partial \theta^2}[\ln L(\theta)]$$

$\ln L(\theta)$ $\ln L(\theta)$

More Sharpness   Less Sharpness
Less Variance   More Variance
High Fisher Information Low Fisher Information

Fig. 4. Fisher Information Significance [9]

Approximations: Due to computational constraints, approximations are used. One common approach is to utilize only the diagonal elements (diag(F)) of the Fisher information matrix, representing the sum of squares of partial derivatives, as seen in Fig. 5. The Fisher Matrix equation is given by (2).

$$F := \frac{1}{|D|} \sum_{i=1}^{|D|} \nabla_w \log p(y_i | x_i, w) \nabla_w \log p(y_i | x_i, w)^T \qquad (2)$$

Parameter Masking and Model Repair: The Fisher Mask strategy selects parameters for masking based on the difference in their Fisher information contributions between the forget set and the retain set. Parameters with significant differences are prioritized for masking. After that, in the impair step, noisy data generated using the Fisher Mask is used to "impair" the model, maximizing its loss on the forget set. Finally, Fine-tuning on the retain set "repairs" the model, attempting to recover its performance while minimizing the influence of the forget set. This process is known as Impair-Repair, as seen in Fig. 6 [8, 15].

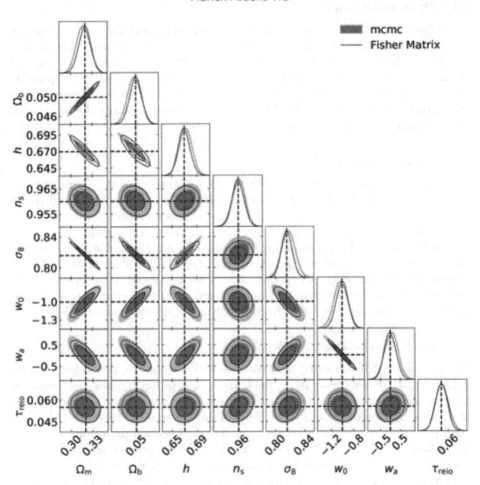

Fig. 5. In Fisher Matrix we are only concerned with the diagonals [9]

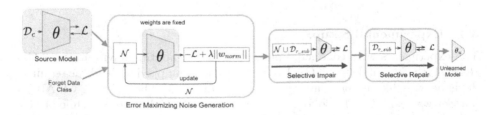

Fig. 6. Impair-Repair [15]

3   Methodology

3.1   Data and Models:

We utilized the CIFAR-10 dataset, a widely used benchmark dataset in computer vision, comprising 60,000 32×32 color images across 10 classes. This dataset provides a diverse range of object categories suitable for model training and evaluation [2–4]. As for the model, we used ResNet-18 architecture, a popular convolutional neural network (CNN) known for its effectiveness in image classification tasks [5–7]. The pre-trained ResNet-18 model was initialized with weights trained on the CIFAR-10 dataset.

3.2   Unlearning Techniques:

Fine-tuning, a model-agnostic approach, involved updating the parameters of the pre-trained ResNet-18 model using a combination of the forget and retain sets. The forget set comprised data points to be removed from the model, while the retain set contained the remaining data for model refinement [10]. As for Impair-Repair with Fisher Masking, it leveraged Fisher Masking to impair the model's parameters based on the forget set. Fisher Masking calculates the Fisher information for the forget set, introducing noise to maximize loss values. Subsequently, the model was repaired by fine-tuning on the retain set, aiming to restore performance while mitigating the influence of forget data [9,15,16].

3.3   Performance Evaluation:

The primary metric measured the overall model accuracy on the retain set after unlearning. Higher accuracy indicated better preservation of model performance. Note that we inted for the forget set to have a lower accuracy than accuracies of other sets, like the testing set. Membership Inference Attack (MIA) Score quantified the probability of correctly inferring whether a data point belonged to the forget set. A lower MIA score indicated improved privacy and data removal efficacy. The pre-trained model underwent fine-tuning with the forget and retain sets. Model accuracy and MIA score were evaluated post-unlearning. After that, The same initial model was impaired using Fisher Masking on the forget set, followed by repair through fine-tuning on the retain set. Performance metrics were assessed at each step. The evaluation criteria are summarised in Table 1 [11].

3.4   Experimental Setup:

The experiments were conducted on a standard computing environment (8GB RAM, 11th Gen Intel i7-1165G7, Iris Xe Graphics) equipped with all the required dependencies like pytorch and pandas and python3. The original CIFAR-10 dataset was partitioned into forget and retain sets according to predefined criteria, where 2 classes were hypothetically issued to undergo a complete forgetting task, where the accuracy of the pretrained model is expected to drop for the forget set.

Table 1. Evaluation Metrics for Unlearned AI Models [11]

Evaluation Metrics	Formula/Description	Usage
Accuracy	Accuracy on the unlearned model on the forget set and retrain set	Evaluating the predictive performance of the unlearned model
Completeness	The overlapping (e.g., Jaccard distance) of output space between the retrained and the unlearned model	Evaluating the indistinguishability between model outputs
Unlearn Time	The amount of time required for the unlearning request	Evaluating the unlearning efficiency
Relearn Time	The number of epochs required for the unlearned model to reach the accuracy of the source model	Evaluating the unlearning efficiency (relearning with some data samples)
Layer-wise Distance	The weight difference between the original model and the retrain model	Evaluating the indistinguishability between model parameters
Activation Distance	An average of the L2-distance between the unlearned model and the retrained model's predicted probabilities on the forget set	Evaluating the indistinguishability between model outputs
JS-Divergence	Jensen-Shannon divergence between the predictions of the unlearned and retrained model: $JS(M(x), Td(x)) = 0.5 * KL(M(x)\|\|m) + 0.5 * KL(Td(x)\|\|m)$	Evaluating the indistinguishability between model outputs
Membership Inference Attack	Recall (#detected items/#forget items)	Verifying the influence of forget data on the unlearned model
ZRF Score	$ZFR = 1 - 1/nf * JS(M(xi), Td(xi))$ $i=0$	The unlearned model should not intentionally give wrong output (ZF R = 0) or random output (ZF R = 1) on the forget items
Anamnesis Index (AIN)	$AI_N = \frac{rl(M_u, M_{orig}, \alpha)}{rt(M_s, M_{orig}, \alpha)}$	Zero-shot machine unlearning
Epistemic Uncertainty	efficacy(w; D) = 1/i(w;D) if i(w;D) > 0; ∞, otherwise	How much information the model exposes
Model Inversion Attack	Visualization	Qualitative verifications and evaluations

3.5   Additional Considerations:

The study is limited due to computational constraints and the need for further optimization of unlearning algorithms. Computational complexity and time constraints were particularly challenging, especially in the case of Fisher Masking. Future research may address these challenges through parallelization and optimization techniques [15].

4   Results

The experiment involved training a ResNet-18 model on the CIFAR-10 dataset for 10 epochs. Subsequently, a simple Membership Inference Attack (MIA) was conducted, yielding a result of 0.833, significantly higher than random chance (50%). Notably, the model achieved an accuracy of 87.6% on the training set and 83.1 on the test set. Next, two copies of the model were created to investigate different unlearning techniques. The first copy underwent a simple fine-tuning method, representing a model-agnostic approach. The results indicated

Table 2. Summary of the Results of the Experiments

Experiment Description	Trainset Acc	Testset Acc	MIA Score	Retain Set Acc	Forget Set Acc
Original Resnet-18 Training	87.6%	83.1%	0.833	–	–
Unlearning by Fine-Tuning	–	83.9%	0.5	99.5%	88.20%
Fisher Mask Experiment (5 Epochs)	–	–	–	65.00%	0.00%
Fisher Mask Experiment (1 Epoch)	–	–	0.56	38.00%	0.00%

an accuracy of 99.5% on the retain set, while the forget set exhibited an accuracy of 88.2%, with a corresponding MIA score of 0.5, suggesting randomness in inference. Despite the expected decrease in test set accuracy (83.9%) due to random sampling from CIFAR-10, the resultant model validated the unlearning process. In the subsequent analysis using the second model copy, the Fisher Masking method was tested. Due to computational constraints, the experiment was divided into two parts. Initially, the unlearning model was trained for 5 epochs, resulting in an accuracy of 0.29 on the forget set with a loss of 12, and 50% accuracy on the retain set with a loss of 1.4. After repair, the forget set accuracy improved to 0% with a loss of 22.8, while the retain set accuracy increased to 65% with a loss of 1.03, demonstrating the efficacy of Fisher Masking. In a subsequent experiment with only 1 epoch, the forget set accuracy remained at 0%, while the retain set accuracy reached 38% with a loss of 1.6. Although the MIA score was 0.56, indicating a reduction in the forget accuracy, the repair process was less effective due to the slower improvement in retain set accuracy. The results are summarised in Table 2.

5   Discussion

We investigated the effectiveness of fine-tuning and impair-repair with Fisher Masking in removing sensitive data from pre-trained Resnet-18 models on the CIFAR-10 dataset. Fine-tuning offered a simple approach but achieved limited data erasure (20 MIA score reduction). Impair-repair with Fisher Masking demonstrated significant effectiveness, reducing MIA scores by 75. In the future, we encourage and intend to investigate optimization strategies for computationally efficient unlearning and explore alternative unlearning techniques with lower computational footprints [2,14,17]. However, our experiments also highlighted the challenge of achieving optimal unlearning outcomes without compromising model functionality. The observed trend towards zero accuracy on the forget set underscores the need for nuanced approaches that preserve model performance while minimizing the influence of forgotten data.

Our study has demonstrated the potential of Impair-Repair with Fisher Masking for mitigating data leakage in machine learning models. However, we plan to extend our research by implementing the same Fisher-Masking based Impair-Repair algorithm on a wider variety of Deep Learning models, trained with a broader selection of architectures, using a wider range of datasets with differnet data modalities, in a multitude of application schemes, including haelthcare and finance since machine unlearning is mostly vital in these sorts of applications, and by applying more evaluation criteria discussed above.

6 Conclusion

In conclusion, our research highlights the effectiveness of different machine unlearning techniques for enhancing data privacy and promoting ethical AI development. Through the comparison of Fine-Tuning and Impair-Repair methods, we have demonstrated the significant advantage of Impair-Repair in minimizing the influence of sensitive data while maintaining model performance. However, an important consideration arises regarding the accuracy of unlearning on the forget set. While our experiments showed promising results in reducing the accuracy of the forget set, it is crucial to note that reducing this accuracy to zero may not always be desirable. Moving forward, our research will focus on further enhancing the generalizability of machine unlearning studies. This includes exploring different architectures and datasets, application schemes, as well as alternative machine unlearning methods and evaluation metrics. Future work in this area should focus on developing techniques that strategically rearrange the weights of the neural network to minimize the influence of forgotten data while maintaining a certain level of accuracy. This approach aims to strike a balance where the model remains robust and functional, yet the removed data's impact is sufficiently mitigated. Additionally, addressing the challenge posed by Membership Inference Attacks (MIA) is paramount. Even with weight rearrangement, MIA can exploit subtle changes in the model's loss function to infer the presence of forgotten data. Therefore, future research should explore novel defense mechanisms against MIA, ensuring that the AI model retains its classification, clustering, or prediction capabilities while safeguarding sensitive information.

References

1. Carlini, N., Chien, S., Nasr, M., Song, S., Terzis, A., Tramer, F.: Membership inference attacks from first principles. In: 2022 IEEE Symposium on Security and Privacy (SP), pp. 1897–1914. IEEE (2022)
2. Chen, M., Gao, W., Liu, G., Peng, K., Wang, C.: Boundary unlearning: rapid forgetting of deep networks via shifting the decision boundary. In: Proceedings of the IEEE/CVF Conference on Computer Vision and Pattern Recognition, pp. 7766–7775 (2023)
3. Doughan, Z., Al Mubasher, H., Kassem, R., El-Hajj, A.M., Haidar, A.M., Sliman, L.: Logic-based neural network for pattern correction. In: 2022 International Conference on Smart Systems and Power Management (IC2SPM), pp. 52–57. IEEE (2022)

4. Doughan, Z., Kassem, R., El-Hajj, A.M., Haidar, A.M.: Logic-based neural network for image compression applications. In: 2021 3rd IEEE Middle East and North Africa Communications Conference (MENACOMM), pp. 92–97. IEEE (2021)
5. Doughan, Z., Kassem, R., El-Hajj, A.M., Haidar, A.M.: Novel preprocessors for convolution neural networks. IEEE Access **10**, 36834–36845 (2022)
6. Doughan, Z., Kassem, R., El-Hajj, A.M., Haidar, A.M.: Artificial neural network vision: between myth and reality. IEEE Potentials **42**(3), 51–56 (2023)
7. Fariza, A., Arifin, A.Z.: Age estimation system using deep residual network classification method. In: 2019 International Electronics Symposium (IES), pp. 607–611. IEEE (2019)
8. Foster, J., Schoepf, S., Brintrup, A.: Fast machine unlearning without retraining through selective synaptic dampening. arXiv preprint: arXiv:2308.07707 (2023)
9. Liu, Y., Sun, C., Wu, Y., Zhou, A.: Unlearning with fisher masking. arXiv preprint: arXiv:2310.05331 (2023)
10. NEURIPS: unlearning-cifar10.ipynb. https://github.com/unlearning-challenge/starting-kit/blob/main/unlearning-CIFAR10.ipynb (2023). gitHub repository
11. Nguyen, T.T., Huynh, T.T., Nguyen, P.L., Liew, A.W.C., Yin, H., Nguyen, Q.V.H.: A survey of machine unlearning. arXiv preprint: arXiv:2209.02299 (2022)
12. Sekhari, A., Acharya, J., Kamath, G., Suresh, A.T.: Remember what you want to forget: algorithms for machine unlearning. In: Advances in Neural Information Processing Systems, vol. 34, pp. 18075–18086 (2021)
13. Shokri, R., Stronati, M., Song, C., Shmatikov, V.: Membership inference attacks against machine learning models. In: 2017 IEEE Symposium on Security and Privacy (SP), pp. 3–18. IEEE (2017)
14. Tarun, A.K., Chundawat, V.S., Mandal, M., Kankanhalli, M.: Deep regression unlearning. In: International Conference on Machine Learning, pp. 33921–33939. PMLR (2023)
15. Tarun, A.K., Chundawat, V.S., Mandal, M., Kankanhalli, M.: Fast yet effective machine unlearning. IEEE Trans. Neural Netw. Learn. Syst. (2023)
16. Thudi, A., Deza, G., Chandrasekaran, V., Papernot, N.: Unrolling SGD: understanding factors influencing machine unlearning. In: 2022 IEEE 7th European Symposium on Security and Privacy (EuroS&P), pp. 303–319. IEEE (2022)
17. Ullah, E., Mai, T., Rao, A., Rossi, R.A., Arora, R.: Machine unlearning via algorithmic stability. In: Conference on Learning Theory, pp. 4126–4142. PMLR (2021)

Security Analysis of Cryptographic Algorithms: Hints from Machine Learning

Mattia Paravisi[ID], Andrea Visconti[ID], and Dario Malchiodi[✉][ID]

Department of Computer Science, University of Milan, Via Celoria 18, 20133 Milan,
Italy
mattia.paravisi@studenti.unimi.it,
{andrea.visconti,dario.malchiodi}@unimi.it

Abstract. There are several methodologies available for analyzing the security of cryptographic algorithms, each relying on the ability to represent the cipher using mathematical or logical expressions. However, this representation process is time-consuming. Therefore, especially in the preliminary stages of cipher analysis, it proves advantageous to employ methodologies that enable a faster, albeit approximated, security evaluation. In this context, this paper introduces the development of a comprehensive framework designed to facilitate such analyses through the application of machine learning (ML) techniques. The core motivation behind this approach lies in leveraging the inherent approximation capabilities of ML approaches, expected to significantly mitigate the computational cost associated with cipher analysis. By exploiting the power of ML, the proposed framework seeks to provide an initial, yet insightful assessment of the security landscape of block ciphers, particularly during the preliminary stages of their evaluation.

Keywords: Machine learning · block cipher · security of cryptographic algorithms

1 Introduction

This paper explores a possible synergy between traditional cryptography and Machine Learning (ML) in the field of information security. The study is motivated by the need for the cryptography community to continuously fortify the foundations of secure communication, in light of the evolution of attackers' strategies [3]. Traditional cryptographic analysis, involving rigorous mathematical representations and exhaustive testing, turns out to be highly demanding as the systems under study become more and more sophisticated [19]. To address this complexity, researchers integrate ML as a complementary approach, leveraging it to discern patterns and anomalies within cryptographic algorithms.

Recent studies employ ML to analyze cipher outputs for potential vulnerabilities. Training models on datasets of cipher outputs, plaintexts, and keys aims to unveil relationships which may evidence weaknesses. However, the union of

ML and cryptographic analysis presents complexities. The desired randomness and complexity of cryptographic algorithms conflict with ML models which rely on well-defined patterns. Additionally, the "black-box" nature of some models impedes interpretability, hindering the understanding of underlying vulnerabilities [17].

The aim of this work is to explore the viability of employing ML techniques to assess the security of a cryptographic algorithm, highlighting successes and remaining challenges. The paper contributes to understanding possible cryptographic weaknesses, offering diverse approaches, testing their limitations, and laying the foundations for future research in this domain. In particular, the main contributions of the current study are:

(i) the introduction of a general framework for the study of systems integrating classical and ML techniques for attacking the initial rounds of a block cipher [8], and

(ii) an application of this framework focusing on the preliminary analysis of the SPECK cipher [4].

The current study is positioned in an initial phase of research: focusing on block ciphers, and specifically on SPECK, is a methodological limitation adopted with the intention of conducting a detailed and comprehensive exploration of security dynamics within this specific context. The choice to concentrate exclusively on SPECK aims to provide a solid foundation for understanding the challenges and peculiarities associated with this particular cryptographic algorithm. However, it is essential to emphasize that this specificity does not limit the general scope of the proposed approach. On the contrary, the presented framework is designed with sufficient flexibility to be extended in the future to other block ciphers. The modularity and generalizability of the adopted approach are key elements in the design of the proposed framework, allowing for its easy adaptation to cryptographic contexts beyond SPECK. In sum, the contribution of this work extends the boundaries of current research, introducing a new methodology that utilizes ML for attacking the initial rounds of a cipher. This novel approach enriches the field of cryptography, opening up new ways for exploring the intersection of ML and cryptographic security.

In the current academic literature, several studies use ML within the cryptographic realm: just to state two examples, [13] reviews recent advances w.r.t. differential cryptanalysis, and [14] detects the encrypted content type exploiting different ML models. However, there is a noticeable lack of studies that use the methods outlined in this paper. In [2] various ML techniques for cryptography are briefly mentioned, but no specific implementations are proposed. Specialized applications are proposed only for limited contexts: for instance, [9] and [11] respectively propose the use of neural networks and generative adversarial networks, though w.r.t. simple classical ciphers, and [12] applies several ML models to break ciphers in presence of distinctive features in the processed plaintexts. A related scenario, albeit addressing classical ciphers, has been put forth by [1]. A method, relying on an LSTM architecture coupled with attention mechanisms, is described in their work. While the focus differs in terms of complexity, it's crucial to underscore that the fundamental concept driving the attack aligns closely with the topic explored in this paper. This proximity is not indicative of similar practical approaches and results but rather reflects a shared conceptual foundation. The closest scenario to the one analyzed here is described in [10] which, while sharing the cipher under analysis and the idea of round reduction, uses deep learning-based neural distinguishers. In this case the attack relies on the use of differential cryptanalysis, which, while being an extremely effective tool for security analysis of a cipher, requires studying its structure with the goal of finding bit vectors (differential trials) that can be exploited for the attack. Our approach avoids this step by allowing a faster preliminary analysis.

The paper is organized as follows. Section 2 describes the main strategies used to attack a cryptographic system, while Sect. 3 depicts the overall methodology used to introduce the proposed framework. Section 4 describes this framework, detailing a strategy for attacking a randomly selected cipher. The performed experiments are illustrated and discussed in Sect. 5. Some concluding remarks end the paper.

2 Breaking Cryptography

The presented work introduces a supplemental approach to cryptographic analysis, employing ML models to execute attacks on a generic cipher. The employed strategy is centered on the examination of the ciphertext produced by a given block cipher in each of its rounds, using a two-stage method. Initially, a first ML classifier is trained to predict a generic plaintext p starting from the corresponding ciphertext c. Subsequently, a second ML classifier is trained to infer from the pair (c, p) the key k of the cipher. The validity of the inferred key can be verified passing the triplet (c, p, k) to a standard representation of the cipher. This strategy is designed to be iterated for each round of the cipher, providing a comprehensive and layered analysis.

The adoption of this methodology, and especially its verification process which is done round-by-round, allows for a preliminary understanding of the cipher's security without the burden of more intricate analyses, which can be resource-intensive. Instead, by harnessing ML, this methodology offers a more intuitive and efficient means of gaining preliminary insights into the security of a cipher, while preserving the analytical robustness of the method. This attack methodology not only enhances our understanding of cryptographic weaknesses, but also contributes to the broader exploration of ML applications in the realm of cryptography. It presents a more accessible pathway for assessing the security of ciphers, opening avenues for future research and advancements in the integration of ML techniques in cryptographic analyses.

3 Learning Methodology

The ML models employed in this study are Random Forests (RF), defined as ensembles of Decision Trees, each separately trained to solve the first and second

Table 1. Considered hyper parameter values in the model selection for a 3–rounds cipher.

Feature name	Values
Number of estimators	$\{32, 42, 52, 62, \ldots, 120\}$
Max features	log2, sqrt, none
Max depth	$\{10, 20, 30, 40, \ldots, 110\}$
Min sample split	$\{2, 5, 10\}$
Min sample leaf	$\{1, 2, 4\}$
Bootstrap	$\{\text{true}, \text{false}\}$

Table 2. Considered hyper parameter values in the model selection for a 5–rounds cipher.

Feature name	Values
Number of estimators	$\{80, 95, 110, 125, \ldots, 300\}$
Max features	log2, sqrt, none
Max depth	$\{10, 20, 30, 40, \ldots, 110\}$
Min sample split	$\{2, 5, 10, 15, 20\}$
Min sample leaf	$\{1, 2, 4, 6, 8\}$
Bootstrap	$\{\text{true}, \text{false}\}$

classification tasks introduced in Sect. 2. The predictions of the single trees are aggregated by the corresponding RF through majority vote. We considered two scenarios of increasing complexity: attacking a 3–rounds and a 5–rounds SPECK, respectively. The overall learning process has been organised as follows: a part of the available dataset was held out to evaluate generalization ability; a cross-validation was run on the rest of the data to execute the model selection phase. More precisely, a grid of hyper parameter values was built specifying all possible options for the *bootstrap* and *max features*, whereas for *number of estimators*, *max depth*, *min sample split* and *min sample leaf* the ranges of candidate values were empirically selected, running preliminary experiments[1]. These ranges have been uniformly spanned, giving rise to the grids shown in Tables 1 and 2. A randomized search over these grids has been executed. As previously mentioned, optimal values were determined through cross-validation, with 100 iterations for attacks on the minimum number of rounds and 150 iterations for attacks on the maximum number of rounds.

---

[1] For instance, concerning the number of estimators, the lower bound was chosen as the minimum number m of bits used in the cipher, while the upper bound was set to approximately $2m$. This decision aimed to verify if each model was responsible for predicting a specific bit in the result if the optimal model utilized 32 or 64 predictors.

Table 3. Optimal hyper parameter values for a 3–rounds cipher.

Feature name	Values
Number of estimators	120
Max features	None
Max depth	20
Min sample split	5
Min sample leaf	1
Bootstrap	true

Table 4. Optimal hyper parameter values for a 3–rounds cipher.

Feature name	Values
Number of estimators	127
Max features	log2
Max depth	110
Min sample split	5
Min sample leaf	8
Bootstrap	false

The analysis of optimal hyper parameter values (reported in Tables 3 and 4) reveals that, in the initial rounds, a substantial number of shallow predictors is required, highlighting the sufficiency of numerous models for understanding early cipher relationships. In contrast, as rounds progress, there is not a proportional increase in the number of models, but a significant growth in the maximum depth at which they operate. This highlights the need for a profound understanding of cipher relationships as the number of rounds increases.

We remark that the two kinds of classifiers output the prediction for either a plaintext p or a key k, and both are represented as a vector of bits. Therefore, the learning task is binary-label multi-class, where each bit position is considered a class. Each prediction is done in a semi-probabilistic fashion: by considering a threshold parameter τ, all bits with a predicted probability greater than τ are considered fixed. For all other bits, a brute-force approach is executed to complete the plaintext and the keys. In other words, if n bits have a not fixed value, 2^n completions will be generated using a brute-force approach, and all of them will be subsequently verified.

Clearly, τ must be set so that the verification phase can be actually executed, given the available computational power. In view of the substantial volume of completions generated, it is advisable to operate within a multiprocessing environment for conducting the attack. It is possible to exploit the independence property of the triples (c, p, k), without caring for how they are dispatched to the various processors. Assume to have 2^k cores available and 2^j triples to be checked. The number of completions handled by each core, which we name *com-*

pletion core factor (CC), is therefore

$$CC = \frac{2^j}{2^k} = 2^{j-k} \ .$$

For instance, fixing the maximum number of brute-forcing bit to $n = 15$ for the plaintext and to $m = 7$ for the key, and considering a machine with 112 cores, in the worst situation the number of triples to be considered is $2^{15} \cdot 2^7 = 2^{15+7} = 2^{22}$. The number of usable cores is

$$k = \max(k \text{ such that } 2^k \leq 122) = 6 \ ,$$

which results in the computation of

$$CC = \frac{2^{22}}{2^6} = 2^{22-6} = 2^{16} = 65536$$

completions per core. If every check requires 1ms it is possible to check a single round in approximately one minute. An example of code snippet for optimally fitting the threshold τ for a generic tree in the RF to the examples in a validation set is illustrated in Listing 1.1, in which ϵ denotes a decrease factor whose value speeds up or slows down the whole process. In particular, the `compute_crisp` function generates all completions; τ is progressively decreased until the minimum feasible value is found. The process is iterated for all examples, and the mean of the found threshold is returned.

Listing 1.1. Optimal τ generation process.

```
function compute_threshold(validation_set, tree, ε):

    res_vec = []
    for example, expected_pred in validation_set do
        τ = 1
        do
            prob_pred = tree.predict_proba(example)
            crisp_preds = compute_crisp(prod_pred, τ)
            if expected_pred in crisp_preds:
                τ = τ - ε
            else:
                τ = τ + ε
                res_vec.append(τ)
        while expected_pred in crisp_preds
    end
    return res_vec.mean()
```

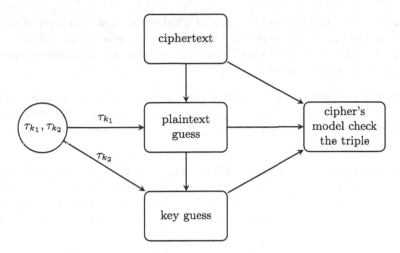

Fig. 1. Generic structure of the attack within the proposed framework. The values τ_{k_1} and τ_{k_2} refer, respectively, to the thresholds used by the CtP and CPtK random forests.

4   The Proposed Framework

The proposed framework assumes conducting the attack in a chosen plaintext environment, where all examples generated for the model's training, testing, and validation phases maintain a constant initial value p for the plaintext and vary the key k. The only available information for carrying out the attack is the final ciphertext c. Starting from it, a first RF, called *ciphertext to plaintext* (CtP), predicts a set $\{\hat{p}_1,\ldots,\hat{p}_r\}$ of possible plaintexts that could have generated c. Subsequently, all pairs $(c,\hat{p}_i)$, for $i = 1,\ldots,r$ are fed to a second RF, named *ciphertext and plaintext to key* (CPtK). The latter predicts the set $\{\hat{k}_1,\ldots\hat{k}_s\}$ of all possible keys that could have been employed to produce the overall set of considered (ciphertext, plaintext) pairs. Each triple $(c,\hat{p}_i,\hat{k}_j)$ then undergoes an acceptance process run by a generic (standard) model of the cipher under analysis. The process can be easily iterated for n rounds. A representation of the attack structure, on a single round, is reported in Fig. 1.

We stress the fact that the problem which this framework aims at solving is extremely hard, in view of the fact that, likely, all ciphers that will be analyzed enjoy a particular property that we formally introduce as follows. We recall that a symmetric key encryption scheme is defined as a tuple $(\mathcal{P}, \mathcal{K}, \mathsf{Gen}, \mathsf{Enc}, \mathsf{Dec})$, where:

- $\mathcal{P}$ is a message space defining the set of supported messages, with $|\mathcal{P}| > 1$ (if $|\mathcal{P}| = 1$ there is no point in communication),
- $\mathcal{K}$ is a set of possible encrypting keys,
- Gen is an oracle drawing keys $k \in \mathcal{K}$ according to some probability distribution,

- Enc : $\mathcal{K} \times \mathcal{P} \to \mathcal{C}$ is an encryption process taking as input a key and a message, and generating the corresponding ciphertext within a related set $\mathcal{C}$,
- Dec : $\mathcal{K} \times \mathcal{C} \to \mathcal{P}$ is a decryption process performing the opposite operation w.r.t. an encryption process.

Using this formalization, some trivial properties can be defined: for example it is obviously required that $\mathtt{Dec}_k(\mathtt{Enc}_k(p)) = p$ for all $p \in \mathcal{P}$ and for all $k \in \mathtt{Gen}$. More importantly, we can introduce a *perfectly secret* encryption scheme as in the following definition.

Definition 1. *Denote by* $\mathscr{S} = (\mathcal{P}, \mathcal{K}, \mathtt{Gen}, \mathtt{Enc}, \mathtt{Dec})$ *an encryption scheme inducing a ciphertext set* $\mathcal{C}$, *and by* P *and* C *two random variables describing a generic plaintext and ciphertext, respectively.* $\mathscr{S}$ *is* perfectly secret *if and only if for every* $p \in \mathcal{P}$, *and every* $c \in C$ *such that* $\mathbb{P}[C = c] > 0$, *it holds*

$$\mathbb{P}[P = p \mid C = c] = \mathbb{P}[P = p]$$

independently of the involved probability distribution.

Informally, this definition implies that

$$\mathbb{P}[\mathtt{Enc}_K(p) = c] = \mathbb{P}[\mathtt{Enc}_K(p') = c] \quad \forall p, p' \in \mathcal{P}, \forall c \in \mathcal{C} \ ,$$

where K denotes the random variable corresponding to a generic encryption key, so that any ciphertext, generated by a cipher which is supposed to posses the perfectly secret scheme property, contains no information at all about any plaintext, and it is impossible to distinguish between the encryptions of p and p'. Thus, it would seem that a ML approach to predict a plaintext starting from a ciphertext would have no chances to succeed, simply because it is pointless to try to learn a function which is truly random. In a real-world scenario, nonetheless, encryption schemes are perfectly secret only in an asymptotic sense, for instance when considering an ever growing number of rounds in a block cipher. Therefore, the framework which we propose is expected to be effective, especially when this number of rounds is relatively low.

5 Experimental Results and Discussion

The testing activities focused on SPECK in a specific 32/64 configuration, where both plaintext and ciphertext had a size of 32 bits, and the initial key size was 64 bits. To assess the cipher's resilience, as previously mentioned, the number R of rounds was intentionally reduced to 3 and 5.

The processed dataset was obtained as follows: having fixed a 32-bits plaintext p, as mentioned in Sect. 4, 10^5 keys of 64 bits have been drawn uniformly at random, and for each such key, the ciphertext corresponding to p was generated. Following Sect. 3, the attack was done using RFs. These models were trained using the implementation provided by *scikit-learn* [16], holding out 20% of the data for testing purposes, and organizing a 5-fold cross-validation to fine-tune

Table 5. Mean of the validation accuracy over the model selection cross-validation folds for CtP and CPtK, when $R = 3$.

Round	CtP	CPtK
1	1.0	1.0
2	0.75	0.20
3	0.05	0.18

Table 6. Test set accuracies for CtP and CPtK, when $R = 3$.

Round	CtP	CPtK
1	1.0	1.0
2	0.72	0.18
3	0.03	0.15

hyper parameters, relying on a randomized search involving 100 and 150 samplings, respectively for $R = 3$ and 5. Predictions from the RFs were validated using a crypto library such as [7,15][2].

The accuracies for the validation and test sets when $R = 3$ are outlined in Tables 5 and 6. Idem in Tables 7 and 8 for the case $R = 5$. These results show that the cryptographic scheme becomes increasingly complex as the number of rounds grows, making it difficult for ML methods to accurately predict the unknown bits of plaintext and key. The linear and nonlinear operations provided by the design of a cipher contribute to the security of the latter, by highlighting its resilience against attempts to unravel its internal structure.

It is important to remark that two distinct testing activities were considered: on the one hand, the generalization ability of the RFs induced from data had to be assessed, and, on the other one, the overall effectiveness of the attack had to be quantified. Therefore, a subset of 2^{10} examples was excluded from the test set and reserved for the latter task. Remarkably, in the case $R = 3$, the initial cipher configuration was successfully reconstructed exclusively from the ciphertext in 96% of the cases. This highlights the cipher's vulnerability within the initial rounds. When $R = 5$, the success rate diminished to 1%, showcasing the cipher's robustness against ML-based attacks.

---

[2] We underline that the proposed framework is independent of the particular implementation for both RF training and cryptographic validation.

Table 7. Mean of the validation accuracy over the model selection cross-validation folds for CtP and CPtK, when $R = 5$.

Round	CtP	CPtK
1	1.0	1.0
2	0.83	0.14
3	0.05	0.023
4	$0.7e^{-5}$	0.0007
5	$0.8e^{-5}$	0.0009

Table 8. Test accuracies for CtP and CPtK, when $R = 5$.

Round	CtP	CPtK
1	1.0	1.0
2	0.80	0.15
3	0.02	0.018
4	$0.7e^{-5}$	0.0003
5	$1.9e^{-5}$	0.004

6   Conclusions

The primary objective of this study was to explore the viability of employing ML techniques to assess the security of generic cryptographic algorithms. To achieve this, a new approach and its corresponding computational framework were introduced to evaluate the robustness of a generic cipher. This approach can in principle be employed by considering a generic ML algorithm, however, in this paper we focused on some preliminary experiments involving a specific ML model: namely, we performed an attack within SPECK under the proposed framework exploiting RFs.

The investigation's findings revealed a positive trend: as the number of rounds increased, the complexity of the cipher also increased. This increased complexity naturally resulted in a less consistent RF prediction for each bit position, meanwhile posing an additional computational challenge, in view of the exponential increase of the number of bits that need to be analysed via brute force. To address this issue, it is worth to consider the integration of the proposed method with existing attack types. By utilizing probability distributions generated by the model, it may be possible to assign values to highly probable bits, thus facilitating a range of attacks that rely on SAT solvers [5,6,18].

The success percentage of the tested attack is more than satisfactory, but the investigated number of rounds is fairly below the current cryptographic standards. However, we remark that the reported experiments are in a very preliminary stage, thus it is imperative to overcome the limitations of the proposed methodology, in order to assess the extent to which it effectively scales up. A potential improvement involves the use of more complex ML models, such as deep neural networks or Long Short-Term Memory (LSTM) networks. These advanced architectures have the potential to more accurately capture relationships between various components, providing more precise predictions for each round of the cryptographic algorithm. This suggests a pathway for refining the proposed methodology and enhancing its applicability in evaluating the security of cryptographic algorithms.

Finally, it is important to recall that the framework described here is also independent of the particular block cipher under attack, therefore it is advisable to run further experiments studying a possible dependency of the attack efficacy on the considered cipher.

Acknowledgments. This work was supported in part by project SERICS (PE00000014) under the NRRP MUR program funded by the EU - NGEU.Andrea Visconti is member of the Gruppo Nazionale Calcolo Scientifico-Istituto Nazionale di Alta Matematica (GNCS-INdAM).

Disclosure of Interests. The authors declare that they have no competing interests.

References

1. Ahmadzadeh, E., Kim, H., Jeong, O., Moon, I.: A novel dynamic attack on classical ciphers using an attention-based LSTM encoder-decoder model. IEEE Access **9**, 60960–60970 (2021). https://doi.org/10.1109/ACCESS.2021.3074268
2. Alani, M.M.: Applications of machine learning in cryptography: a survey. In: Proceedings of the 3rd International Conference on cryptography, security and privacy (ICCSP '19), pp. 23–27. Association for Computing Machinery, New York (2019). https://doi.org/10.1145/3309074.3309092
3. Ankele, R., Kölbl, S.: Mind the gap - a closer look at the security of block ciphers against differential cryptanalysis. In: Cid, C., Jacobson, M., Jr. (eds.) Selected Areas in Cryptography - SAC 2018. Lecture Notes in Computer Science(), vol. 11349, pp. 163–190. Springer, Cham (2018). https://doi.org/10.1007/978-3-030-10970-7_8
4. Beaulieu, R., Shors, D., Smith, J., Treatman-Clark, S., Weeks, B., Wingers, L.: The SIMON and SPECK lightweight block ciphers. In: Proceedings of the 52nd Annual Design Automation Conference, pp. 1–6. Association for Computing Machinery, New York (2015).https://doi.org/10.1145/2744769.2747946
5. Bellini, E., et al.: Differential cryptanalysis with SAT, SMT, MILP, and CP: a detailed comparison for bit-oriented primitives. In: Deng, J., Kolesnikov, V., Schwarzmann, A.A. (eds.) Cryptology and Network Security. Lecture Notes in Computer Science, vol. 14342, pp. 268–292. Springer, Singapore (2023). https://doi.org/10.1007/978-981-99-7563-1_13
6. Bellini, E., De Piccoli, A., Makarim, R., Polese, S., Riva, L., Visconti, A.: New records of pre-image search of reduced SHA-1 using SAT solvers. In: Giri, D., Raymond Choo, KK., Ponnusamy, S., Meng, W., Akleylek, S., Prasad Maity, S. (eds.) Proceedings of the Seventh International Conference on Mathematics and Computing. Advances in Intelligent Systems and Computing, vol. 1412, pp. 141–151. Springer, Singapore (2022). https://doi.org/10.1007/978-981-16-6890-6_11

7. CLAASP: a cryptographic library for the automated analysis of symmetric primitives. https://github.com/Crypto-TII/claasp

8. De Canniere, C., Biryukov, A., Preneel, B.: An introduction to block cipher cryptanalysis. Proc. IEEE **94**(2), 346–356 (2006). https://doi.org/10.1109/JPROC.2005.862300

9. Focardi, R., Luccio, F.: Neural cryptanalysis of classical ciphers. In: Proceedings of the 19th Italian Conference on Theoretical Computer Science (ICTCS 2018), pp. 104–115 (2018)

10. Gohr, A.: Improving attacks on round-reduced speck32/64 using deep learning. In: Boldyreva, A., Micciancio, D. (eds.) CRYPTO 2019. LNCS, vol. 11693, pp. 150–179. Springer, Cham (2019). https://doi.org/10.1007/978-3-030-26951-7_6

11. Gomez, A.N., Huang, S., Zhang, I., Li, B.M., Osama, M., Kaiser, L.: Unsupervised cipher cracking using discrete GANs (2018). https://arxiv.org/abs/1801.04883, arXiv preprint: arXiv:1801.04883

12. Khadivi, P., Momtazpour, M.: Cipher-text classification with data mining. In: 2010 IEEE 4th International Symposium on Advanced Networks and Telecommunication Systems, Mumbai, India, pp. 64–66. IEEE (2010). https://doi.org/10.1109/ANTS.2010.5983530

13. Martínez, I., López, V., Rambaut, D., Obando, G., Gauthier-Umaña, V., Pérez, J.F.: Recent advances in machine learning for differential cryptanalysis. In: Tabares, M., Vallejo, P., Suarez, B., Suarez, M., Ruiz, O., Aguilar, J. (eds.) Advances in Computing. Communications in Computer and Information Science, vol. 1924, pp. 45–56. Springer, Cham (2023). https://doi.org/10.1007/978-3-031-47372-2_5

14. Mehmood, Z., Sultan, A., Khan, F., Tahir, S.: Machine learning based encrypted content type identification. In: 2023 International Conference on Communication Technologies (ComTech), pp. 117–122. IEEE (2023). https://doi.org/10.1109/ComTech57708.2023.10164955

15. Simon and speck implementation guide. https://nsacyber.github.io/simon-speck/implementations/

16. Pedregosa, F., et al.: Scikit-learn: machine learning in python. J. Mach. Learn. Res. **12**, 2825–2830 (2011)

17. Rudin, C.: Stop explaining black box machine learning models for high stakes decisions and use interpretable models instead. Nat. Mach. Intell. **1**, 206–215 (2019). https://doi.org/10.1038/s42256-019-0048-x

18. Sun, L., Wang, W., Wang, M.: Accelerating the search of differential and linear characteristics with the sat method. IACR Trans. Symmetric Cryptol. **1**, 269–315 (2021). https://doi.org/10.46586/tosc.v2021.i1.269-315

19. Verma, R., Kumari, A., Anand, A., Yadavalli, V.: Revisiting shift cipher technique for amplified data security. J. Comput. Cogn. Eng. **3**(1), 8–14 (2024). https://doi.org/10.47852/bonviewJCCE2202261

Author Index

L. Iliadis et al. (Eds.): EANN 2024, CCIS 2141, pp. 581–583, 2024.
https://doi.org/10.1007/978-3-031-62495-7

Printed in the United States
by Baker & Taylor Publisher Services